Semper Reformandum:

Studies in Honour of Clark H. Pinnock

D1518399

Clark H. Pinnock

Photograph Courtesy of McMaster Divinity College

Semper Reformandum:

Studies in Honour of Clark H. Pinnock

Edited by

Stanley E. Porter

and

Anthony R. Cross

Paternoster:
thinking faith

First published 2003 by Paternoster

Paternoster is an imprint of Authentic Media,
9 Holdom Avenue, Bletchley, Milton Keynes, MK1 1QR, U.K.
and
P.O.Box 1047, Waynesboro, GA 30830-2047, U.S.A.

09 08 07 06 05 04 03   7 6 5 4 3 2 1

British Library Cataloguing in Publication Data
A catalogue record for this book is available from the British Library

ISBN-13: 978–1–84227–206–0
ISBN-10: 1–84227–206–3

Typeset by A.R. Cross
Printed and bound in Great Britain
for Paternoster
by Nottingham Alpha Graphics

Contents

Contributors

David Basinger Professor of Philosophy and Ethics, and Chair of the Division of Religion and Humanities, Roberts Wesleyan College, Rochester, New York, USA

Randall Basinger Dean of Curriculum and Professor of Philosophy, Messiah College, Grantham, Pennsylvania, USA

Donald G. Bloesch Emeritus Professor of Theology, University of Dubuque Theological Seminary, Dubuque, Iowa, USA

Gregory A. Boyd Senior Pastor, Woodland Hills Church, Maplewood, Minnesota, USA

Delwin Brown Vice President for Academic Affairs and Dean of the Faculty of Religion, Pacific School of Religion, Berkeley, California, USA

Barry L. Callen University Professor of Christian Studies, Anderson University, Anderson, Indiana, USA

John B. Cobb, Jr. Professor Emeritus, Claremont School of Theology, Claremont, California, USA

Robert Cook Academic Dean and Tutor in Theology, Redcliffe College, Gloucester, United Kingdom

Anthony R. Cross Fellow of the Centre for Baptist History and Heritage, Regent's Park College, Oxford, United Kingdom

Stanley J. Grenz Pioneer McDonald Professor of Theology, Carey Theological College, Vancouver, British Columbia, Canada

David Guretzki Assistant Professor of Theology, Briercrest College and Seminary, Caronport, Saskatchewan, Canada

I. Howard Marshall Honorary Research Professor of New Testament, Department of Divinity and Religious Studies, King's College, Aberdeen, United Kingdom

Roger E. Olson Professor of Theology, George W. Truett Theological Seminary, Baylor University, Waco, Texas, USA

Alan G. Padgett Professor of Systematic Theology, Luther Seminary, St Paul, Minnesota, USA

Stanley E. Porter President and Dean, and Professor of New Testament, McMaster Divinity College, McMaster University, Hamilton, Ontario, Canada

Kurt Anders Richardson Associate Professor of Systematic Theology and C. Howard and Shirley M. Bentall Chair in Evangelical Thought, McMaster Divinity College, McMaster University, Hamilton, Ontario, Canada

John Sanders Research Professor of Philosophy and Religion, Huntington College, Huntington, Indiana, USA

Archibald J. Spencer John H. Pickford Chair in Systematic Theology, Northwest Baptist Seminary, Associated Canadian Theological Schools, Trinity Western University, Langley, British Columbia, Canada

John G. Stackhouse, Jr. Sangwoo Youtong Chee Professor of Theology and Culture, Regent College, Vancouver, British Columbia, Canada

C. Mark Steinacher Adjunct Lecturer in Church History, McMaster Divinity College, Hamilton, Ontario, and Adjunct Professor of Church History, Tyndale Seminary, Toronto, Canada

Terrance L. Tiessen Professor of Systematic Theology, Providence Theological Seminary, Otterburne, Manitoba, Canada

John A. Vissers Principal of the Presbyterian College, Montreal, Faculty Lecturer in Christian Theology, McGill University, and Adjunct Professor of Systematic Theology, Tyndale Seminary, Toronto, Cananda

Amos Yong Associate Professor of Theology, Department of Biblical and Theological Studies, Bethel College, St Paul, Minnesota, USA

Introduction

Stanley E. Porter and Anthony R. Cross

One thing that becomes readily clear from the study of the church's history is that its theology—its striving to understand the triune God and his creation, and to express this understanding to other Christians and a world which is alienated from God by sin—has not remained static. It has developed through time. It has grown through encounter with God in faith and worship, but also through engagement with the world and non-Christian thought. As each generation has come to faith it has learnt from previous generations—sometimes by continuing and developing their legacies, at other times by modifying or even departing from them. But what each generation has not done, and should not do, is simply to take over previous generations' theologies and practices. Rather, it develops its own, which, in turn, become part of the legacy which succeeding generations will inherit and with which they will rightly and critically interact. As such, the church's theology and practice is *semper reformandum*, ever subject to reform. This is right, and the way theology has always been done and should continue to be done.

Tragically, however, this process of doing theology has too often been marred by controversy and mutual recrimination which have led to divisions within the church and to the impoverishment of her life and witness. This need not be so, for there is, we believe, a more excellent way—the way of love which recognizes that 'now we see in a mirror, dimly' and 'know only in part' (1 Cor. 13.12). It will not be until we all stand before the throne of God that we will know fully, as we are fully known. Till then we need to recognize the provisionality of our systems and to work together in this calling of doing theology.

Not all the contributors to this collection offered in honour of Clark H. Pinnock agree with him. He would not expect us to. Sometimes agreement will be close, at other times there will be major differences of opinion and approach, but what all the contributors do share is the wish to pay tribute to a man of God who has been willing to be led where he has thought and felt God has been leading him. The chapters of this volume are offered in this spirit by his colleagues, former students and some who have benefitted from his many writings from afar. All are in dialogue with Pinnock as an expression of respect and gratitude for his work, which has been at times controversial, at others provocative, but always offered in sincerity and with the desire to discover more of the gracious God who has drawn near to needy humanity in the person of our Lord Jesus Christ.

It would have been easy to have opted for a different arrangement of the following chapters and various arguments could have been offered to justify them. But the final order followed here has been chosen as the contributors take up various approaches and themes on which Pinnock has written. Barry Callen has followed his own theological biography of Pinnock, *Journey Toward Renewal* (Nappanee, IN: Evangel, 2000), with a sketch of Pinnock's theological biography. The use of 'journey' in the title is an appropriate one, for Pinnock's theological position is one of those which has not remained static throughout his life. Rather his thought has developed and changed, sometimes dramatically so, as he has studied, written and taught theology. This pilgrimage is then taken up by Roger Olson whose essay sets Pinnock within the contemporary evangelical context.

The following eight chapters take up various dimensions of the openness theology debate in which Pinnock is so prominent a figure. While many of these overlap, they broadly range from various aspects of the love of God (Boyd and Brown), the extent of God's knowledge (Cook and Tiessen), our knowledge of God (Sanders), the issue of election (Steinacher), the problem of evil (Basinger and Basinger), and some of the New Testament assumptions underlying open theism (Porter).

The next three studies explore the person and work of the Holy Spirit, from the great ecumenical creeds, through contemporary theology to a study of the place he is given in modern Canadian Protestantism (Guretzki, Yong and Vissers). Donald Bloesch interacts with Pinnock's apologetic theology, and John Cobb compares his apologetic approach with process theology. The place of scripture within hermeneutics and the relation of scripture to a theology of revelation are then explored by Alan Padgett and Kurt Richardson, followed by Archie Spencer's investigation of the place of general revelation in inter-religious dialogue, and Howard Marshall's study of the extent of the atonement. John Stackhouse's exploration of the nature and importance of conversion is followed by Anthony R. Cross's argument for the sacramental nature of baptism, and the volume concludes with Stanley Grenz's essay on worship as an anticipation of participation in the triune God.

Clark Pinnock has now formally retired after twenty-five years of active teaching, research and writing at McMaster Divinity College. His retirement is no less active than his working career—in many ways it is more active, as he fulfils numerous speaking engagements around the world, and even continues to teach the occasional class. McMaster Divinity College has benefitted and will continue to benefit from Pinnock's presence. Now as Professor Emeritus of Systematic Theology, he has welcomed his successor in the field of theology and continues to challenge his theological colleagues. The College counts it an honour and privilege to have been the academic home of Clark Pinnock for these many years, and we all look forward to continued discussion and debate over the issues raised in this volume.

CHAPTER 1

Clark H. Pinnock:
His Life and Work

Barry L. Callen

Clark H. Pinnock has been one of the more prominent, productive, and provocative Christian theologians in North Atlantic evangelical Christianity since the 1960s. The provocative aspect arose because he has engaged directly a series of issues sometimes sharply contested among evangelicals and he has altered some of his own views openly when he found evidence for change compelling. He has been viewed with both critical suspicion and appreciative admiration as he has championed biblical primacy while also questioning certain reigning assumptions among Christians who think of themselves as 'evangelicals'.

In a post-Christian and postmodern environment, I chose to identify Pinnock's career by titling his intellectual biography a 'journey toward renewal'. He has adapted, explored bypaths, pioneered fresh theological formulations, and sought always to remain both faithful to ancient biblical foundations and relevant to contemporary culture. While not prematurely claiming final answers, since theology is seen as an ongoing journey, 'his current faith hypotheses are well-tested and worthy'.[1]

To follow Pinnock's theological trail is to enter into the world of constructive and sometimes conflictive conversation with Christian theologians called Calvinist, Wesleyan, Pentecostal, Anabaptist, Process, Eastern Orthodox and Roman Catholic. It is to be introduced to most of the major figures and issues comprising evangelicalism since the 1940s, especially as it has functioned in Canada, England, Switzerland and the United States. It is to traverse the last half-century of evangelical Christianity, not neutrally, but through a renewing lens that has been encouraging a theological paradigm shift of significant proportions since the 1970s. Ever a loyal Baptist, Clark Pinnock has sought to belong to,

---

1   Barry L. Callen, *Clark H. Pinnock: Journey toward Renewal* (Nappanee, IN: Evangel Publishing House, 2000), p. 2.

listen to, and speak helpfully on behalf of the whole church. He has been on a pilgrimage. 'More like a pilgrim than a settler', he says of himself, 'I tread the path of discovery and do my theology en route.'[2]

Engaging the life and work of Clark Pinnock is to be introduced to the dynamics of theological change, seen either as admirable and courageous honesty or as fickle commitment and weak convictions that blow variously according to the current wind. Committed to biblical authority and the significance of genuine spiritual life in Christ, Pinnock also has been committed to church mission and the present meaningfulness of divine revelation. He often has stood in gaps, tested tensions, risked change, and weathered resulting storms.

Places of Beginning

Born in February 1937 in Ontario, Canada, Clark Pinnock was converted to new life in Christ in 1950. Soon he was a serious young Christian maturing in a 'liberal' congregation in Toronto and perceiving 'the need to be alert to defections from the true faith and to maintain a theologically sound testimony'.[3] His paternal grandparents were British Methodist missionaries to Nigeria who passed on to young Clark a keen interest in international church mission, genuine Christian piety, and an appreciation for scholarship and Christian writing. At a Canadian Keswick Bible Conference, Clark was inspired by Wycliff Bible Translators and soon entered an honors program in biblical languages at the University of Toronto. Following the BA degree from there with honors in the Ancient Near East Studies program, he received a British Commonwealth Scholarship which he took to a PhD program at the University of Manchester in England because of his English family heritage and his respect for F.F. Bruce who taught there. Under the guidance of Bruce, he centered his 1963 dissertation on the concept of the Spirit in the Epistles of Paul. Biblical rootage and the dynamics of life in the Spirit would loom large in his coming career of teaching, writing, and lecturing in Christian colleges and seminaries, and in numerous other settings of church leaders.

The PhD was completed in 1963, with Pinnock in the process having spent important summer time in Switzerland with Francis Schaeffer at the L'Abri Fellowship. Schaeffer nurtured in Pinnock the assumption of the cruciality of an 'inerrantly' inspired biblical text, an assumption that had been planted in Pinnock's early thinking by his reading of B.B. Warfield.

---

2   Clark H. Pinnock, 'A Pilgrim on the Way', *Christianity Today* (9 February 1998), p. 43.

3   Clark H. Pinnock, 'Baptists and Biblical Authority', *Journal of the Evangelical Theological Society* 17 (1974), p. 193.

Young Pinnock was a natural pietist. Warfield helped to make him more of a theological rationalist and it would not be until his 1980 book *Reason Enough* that Pinnock would express realization that Christians cannot and do not need to overwhelm liberalism and modernism with the sheer weight of superior reason. But, before his later years of critiquing the presumed cultural accommodations of 'classic' Christian evangelicalism, there would be the first stage of his teaching, lecturing and writing career. In this initial stage he was passionate and aggressive about the truth of divine revelation that he was sure was available in an inerrant Bible. He was deeply concerned about 'liberalism', resisted the invasion of neo-orthodoxy, and responded to these threats with apologetic fervor.

One day the phone rang in the Pinnocks' England apartment. It was Dr H. Leo Eddleman, president of the Southern Baptist seminary in New Orleans, Louisiana. The question posed was, would Pinnock come to lecture and candidate for a faculty position in New Testament? Carl F.H. Henry had visited Pinnock in England, was impressed, and apparently had recommended him for this pivotal post. Pinnock's answer was positive. He returned to North America with the doctorate fresh in hand and walked into the volatile circumstances of the Southern Baptist Convention in the late 1960s. He was ready and quite able to intervene on behalf of classic Christian truth. The original 1965 appointment in New Testament at New Orleans Baptist Theological Seminary shifted two years later to the field of theology in the same school, in part because Pinnock wanted to be where faith encounters today's world.

Ever a loyal Baptist, Pinnock's ecclesial identity was significantly 'catholic' and para-church in nature from his earliest years as a Christian. He once referred to the InterVarsity Christian Fellowship as 'my real ecclesial home' and later would be published by InterVarsity Press. He read with appreciation most of the mid twentieth-century evangelical greats (e.g., John Murray, Martyn Lloyd-Jones, Cornelius Van Til, Carl F.H. Henry, James I. Packer, and Paul Jewett) and began his theological life 'as a Calvinist who regarded alternate evangelical interpretations as suspect and at least mildly heretical'.[4] Early in his career he came to play a key role in the early stages of the conservative resurgence in the Southern Baptist Convention in the United States that is dominant today.

During his four years in New Orleans, Pinnock began for the first time to be noticed widely as a potential shaper of theological thought among contemporary evangelicals. He was chosen by the magazine *Christianity Today* to present its case against form criticism (July 16, 1965), delivered

4   Clark H. Pinnock, 'From Augustine to Arminius: A Pilgrimage in Theology', in Clark H. Pinnock (ed.), *The Grace of God and the Will of Man* (Grand Rapids, MI: Zondervan, 1989; rev. edn, Minneapolis: Bethany House, 1995), p. 17.

the Christian Contemporary Thought Lectures at Harvard University in 1966 (which he later called 'intellectual evangelism in my Schaefferian mode'), and published his first major theological writing titled *A Defense of Biblical Infallibility* (1967), followed the same year by *Set Forth Your Case*. These two books, along with his *Biblical Revelation* in 1971, became the foundation for the early phase of his career and established his reputation as a vigorous and sophisticated defender of biblical inerrancy and Christian faithfulness in the rapidly secularizing setting of the West. His 1969 book *Evangelism and Truth* is representative of Pinnock at this time. In it he resists relativism and skepticism, insisting that Christian evangelism and revealed biblical truth are inseparable. He loved the church and sought to cleanse it of its infection by 'liberalism'.

Geographically speaking, the Pinnock family has rich roots in England that soon led to Canada. His personal trail then leads from Canada back to England for doctoral study, to Switzerland, then to New Orleans and Trinity Evangelical Divinity School in the southern and then northern United States, and finally back to Canada for the balance of his teaching career at McMaster Divinity College, with retirement in 2002. But geography is probably not so important, although it does add much color and interest to the story. Most important intellectually is where his professional and theological trail has led within the shifting world of 'evangelicalism' and its relationships with other Christian traditions. Pinnock has traversed most of the existing territory since the 1960s, has personally planted several of today's prominent theological signposts, and has been a stimulating catalyst for evangelical reevaluation and change on various interrelated subjects over several decades.

Destabilizing the Evangelical *Status Quo*

A vigorous and very public preoccupation with the issues of biblical authority and proclamation helped lead to a professional move for Pinnock in 1969. His growing reputation had reached the expanding Trinity Evangelical Divinity School, leading to his appointment and five satisfying and eventful years as a faculty member on this key Illinois campus (1969–74). The setting reminded him of the InterVarsity ethos, just what he liked—biblical, evangelistic, interdenominational, and mildly rationalistic. During these growing and productive years at Trinity, Pinnock's theological style grew more irenic. He reported that he had become 'less threatened as an evangelical thinker in a predominantly non-evangelical world of scholarship and more open to viewpoints other than my own'.[5] He was becoming a listener as well as a defender, although always with a non-negotiable zeal for effective Christian witness and faithful Christian living based on substantive divine revelation.

Then came his three years of teaching at Regent College in Vancouver, Canada (1974–77), where he experienced more freedom to quest and be creative. He was impacted significantly by Stephen Davis' book *The Debate About the Bible: Inerrancy Versus Infallibility* (1977), which openly challenged certain assumptions about biblical inerrancy then held by Pinnock. He began to review carefully and revise cautiously his inerrancy views. Previously he had leaned on 2 Timothy 3.16-17, the only place in scripture where the term 'inspired' (*theopneustos*) occurs. But now, less a fundamentalist and more a neo-evangelical, he was looking beyond the inspiration issue to appreciate also Paul's emphasis on practical spirituality—i.e., what is inspired is 'useful for teaching, for reproof, for correction, and for training in righteousness, so that everyone who belongs to God may be proficient, equipped for every good work'. In other words, God's Spirit breathes through the biblical text to transform believers into maturing and obedient disciples. The focus should be less on textual technicalities of the past (the original text no longer fully available) and more on faithful and transformative relevance in the present.

Recalling his two early mentors, F.F. Bruce and Francis Schaeffer, Pinnock would later characterize his own shifting of perspectives in the 1970s as a move from Schaeffer's militant rationalism to Bruce's more bottom-up irenic scholarship. The fundamentalist claim to a perfect errorlessness of the non-extant autographs was an abstraction that for Pinnock had died the death of a thousand qualifications. Of key importance for him now was the dynamic authority of the present biblical text. He had grown uncomfortable with the noticeable lack of stress on the Spirit in the literature on inerrancy, and, after all, it is none other than the Spirit who causes the Bible reader to be receptive to a text's 'surplus of meaning'.[6] He realized that he had 'inflated the biblical claims for inspiration in the interests of a rationalist paradigm... I had been engaged in making the Bible say more than it wanted to in the interests of my system.'[7]

---

5   Clark H. Pinnock, in *The Scribe*, publication of Trinity Evangelical Divinity School, 1974, p. 3.

6   Clark H. Pinnock, *The Scripture Principle* (San Francisco: Harper & Row, 1984), pp. 45, 186, explains that, while the original meaning of a biblical text should always be the anchor of proper biblical interpretation, under the guidance of the Holy Spirit the present significance of the text for us 'needs to be searched out... The picture is that of a canon in which the truth unfolds gradually and dialectically.'

7   Clark H. Pinnock, as quoted in Ray C.W. Roennfeldt, *Clark H. Pinnock on Biblical Authority* (Berrien Springs, MI: Andrews University Press, 1993), p. xix.

Early in his career Pinnock had idealized absolute truths with black and white doctrinal and ethical maxims. Now the philosophical validity and theological appropriateness of this framework became questionable in his mind. An anti-establishment mood emerged in the early 1970s at Trinity and he became involved for a time in the anti-war social radicalism. For him this was not longlasting. But what was enduring came when one of the links of the Calvinistic chain of theological logic broke for Pinnock. What dawned on him had to do initially with the perseverance of the saints. Biblical study brought him to a realization that there is a 'principle of reciprocity', a profound mutuality in human dealings with God. He reports: 'I was moving away from the larger framework of Calvinism itself to more dynamic ways of thinking theologically... I was giving up the view according to which God is thought to relate primarily to us as all-determining monarch and law-giver and shifting to the paradigm in which God relates to us primarily as parent, lover, and covenant partner.'[8] Pinnock was beginning to challenge the very mindset of the reigning deterministic scholasticism characteristic of evangelicalism. He chose to champion the potential rather than be paralyzed by the possible pitfalls that admittedly exist with a more open and dialogical approach to the doing of Christian theology today.

Why the big change in Pinnock's perspective? Critics of his change have been less than charitable in their judgments. Even so, Pinnock insisted that his change was driven by biblical teaching itself. His new perspective was elaborated in the 1975 book *Grace Unlimited* that Pinnock assembled and edited. He remained Christ-centered and biblically-rooted, but now he also was a Spirit-animated risk taker prepared to hear anew the word of God on behalf of the church's mission in a postmodern world. With this new stance came another professional move of teaching location.

In 1977 Pinnock accepted an invitation to his home area of Toronto, Canada, leaving Regent for McMaster Divinity College in Hamilton, Ontario. This school had a 'mainline' mentality and was a key Baptist institution in an exciting university setting. He admits going there with something of a 'messiah' complex, prepared to help bring an evangelical revival. In fact, he was relatively successful over the years, remaining full-time until his retirement in 2002 and continuing on in a limited capacity. From this academic post at McMaster, Pinnock began in 1977 to reflect his maturing thought to ever-widening Christian publics and to apply it to an increasing range of possible implications for evangelical theology. Of particular note was his book *The Scripture Principle* (1984), in which he

---

8   Clark H. Pinnock in his Foreword to Roennfeldt, *Clark Pinnock on Biblical Authority*, pp. xx-xxi.

re-thought biblical authority in light of its witness to itself, including both its divine and human character and the spiritual dynamics of its origin and current applications. He now was in an awkward political position among evangelicals, with some saying he was dangerously watering down his earlier inerrancy conviction and others criticizing him for retaining it in any form. This 1984 book of Pinnock has been well characterized as 'as much an internal self-criticism of conservatism as it is an external critique of liberalism'.[9]

Occasionally over the years Pinnock has made formal presentations to the Evangelical Theological Society and received in return both sincere appreciation and severe criticism. His work often has been innovative and provocative—at least in this setting. A loyal man, he always has remained with his more conservative colleagues despite the occasional awkwardness. His heart is deeply rooted in the urgency of church mission in the world. By 1987 he saw the primary danger to the Southern Baptist Convention having shifted from the external assault of liberalism to a dangerous division within the Convention itself, nearly a holy war among the parties of its non-liberals (moderates to fundamentalists). A primary dividing line was between competing theories of biblical inspiration. The truly frightening prospect, as judged by Pinnock, was that in a time of unprecedented worldwide mission potential 'the possible fragmentation of believers could have disastrous consequences for world evangelization', even causing Baptists to 'snatch defeat from the jaws of victory'.[10]

As late as 1980 Clark Pinnock was still affirming clearly the existence of a rich selection of Christian evidences or indicators of truth that he judged lead to a reasonable Christian faith conclusion. By then, however, he had shifted from 'hard to soft rationality...from modernity to postmodernity',[11] from maintaining that the Christian truth can be proven by the canons of logic to the view that the truth is better represented by a cumulative argument which makes an appeal to the intuitive and ultimately to personal judgment and faith. The older religious militancy and staunch rationalism had become gentler and more self-critical; fixed opinions had opened themselves to dialogue as well as proclamation. Shifts like the one from 'hard' to 'soft' rationality would bring his prominent calls for change, his arguing for a destabilization and replacement of the evangelical 'modernist' *status quo*.

In the 1960s Pinnock had trusted C.S. Lewis as an alluringly creative and yet safely 'orthodox' Christian intellectual leader who mixed

9   Delwin Brown, 'Rethinking Authority from the Right', *Christian Scholar's Review* 19.1 (1989–90), p. 67.
10   Clark H. Pinnock, 'Parameters of Biblical Inerrancy', in *The Proceedings of the Conference on Biblical Inerrancy, 1987* (Nashville, TN: Broadman Press, 1987), p. 73.
11   Clark H. Pinnock, in Callen, *Journey Toward Renewal*, p. 229.

evangelical apologetics with 'a liberal twinge'. While Carl F.H. Henry, John Warwick Montgomery and J.I. Packer were helping to establish Pinnock in the usual rationalism characteristic of the evangelical mainstream of the time, Lewis offered a more complex model of believer-apologist that foreshadowed the mature stages of the later Pinnock himself. The later Pinnock would reflect in a major way what was already emerging in the burden of his 1963 doctoral dissertation. There he saw Paul's concept of God's Spirit rooted deeply in his rich Hebrew heritage. Therefore, Pinnock concluded, seeking a presumed relevance of the philosophies and literature of the ancient Greek world is hardly helpful since 'their relevance to the Pauline concept alters in inverse ratio as the degree of hellenization increases'.[12]

Pinnock's earliest formative contexts had been largely in the vigorous and even reactionary stream of Christian fundamentalism in the mid-twentieth century, a stream he once called 'orthodoxy in a desperate struggle with secular modernity'.[13] He appreciated this tenacious faith, but soon was to critique some aspects of its substance and spirit. For instance, he announced the following to the 1987 Conference on Biblical Inerrancy convened by the Southern Baptists: 'The reason I defended the strict view of inerrancy in my earlier years was because I desperately wanted it to be true. I wanted it to be true so badly that I passed over the obvious problems.'[14] He had found himself on a theological journey and was openly self-critical as he traveled along. Between his books *A Defense of Biblical Infallibility* in 1967 and *The Scripture Principle* in 1984, Pinnock had made some significant alterations in his own views in regard to the nature of the certainty of revealed truth and its relation to the mechanics of the biblical text and the processes of doing Christian theology.

Both early and later on this journey of change, Pinnock would care deeply and speak convictionally about the reality of divine revelation as a central principle on which the Christian faith necessarily rests. However, he would make significant adjustments to his own thought, adjustments he found warranted and important and ones that some of his conservative colleagues judged dangerous and wholly unacceptable. Speaking broadly and employing his own phrases, Pinnock's journey led him to move from a 'philosophical biblicism' to a 'simple biblicism'. By this latter phrase he means 'the delight evangelicals experience from meditating on Scripture and submitting to it... Scripture is a gift of the Spirit, and evangelicals want to be open to all that God says in this text... Not a

---

12   Clark H. Pinnock, 'The Concept of Spirit in the Epistles of Paul' (PhD thesis, University of Manchester, 1963), p. vi.
13   Clark H. Pinnock, 'Defining American Fundamentalism', in Norman Cohen (ed.), *The Fundamentalist Phenomenon* (Grand Rapids, MI: Eerdmans, 1990), pp. 40-42.
14   Pinnock, 'Parameters of Biblical Inerrancy', p. 96.

theory about the Bible, simple biblicism is the basic instinct that the Bible is supremely profitable and transforming, alive with God's breath. Without being free of every difficulty, the Bible nevertheless bears effective witness to Jesus Christ.'[15] It was the 'without being free of every difficulty' that was freeing for him and highly problematic for some others.

During the 1970s Clark Pinnock shifted his theological course and came to lead a new 'open' school of evangelical thought, one he considers biblically faithful and resistant to alien philosophical incursions, especially those of the ancient Greek world that have been so influential in the Christian theological tradition. Such openness has been prophetic, provocative, and timely, alluringly creative for many younger scholars, a fresh mix of sturdy evangelical apologetics with a 'liberal twinge'—a little like C.S. Lewis. Pinnock began a quest to help liberate the evangelical Christian community from what he came to see as its shackles of Reformed scholasticism, Hellenistic perversions, and other cultural accommodations. He has assumed that Christians are at risk of stagnating and losing the vitality of the Spirit's witness to biblical meaning for our time when they 'insist on conserving in ways reflective of past thought traditions and cultures more than of biblical thought and true Spirit life'.[16]

Pinnock's intent has been to function between the 'conservatives' who sometimes concentrate almost blindly on what they see as the unchanging biblical revelation and the 'progressives' who seek, sometimes without proper limits, to update Christian foundations by so connecting them to today's issues and experiences that they become almost unrecognizable as distinctively Christian.[17] He desired balance between 'text' and 'context', biblical identity and current intelligibility. He arrived at the view that the core tasks of Christian theology are keeping anchored, maintaining proper continuity, and engaging in effective communication, timely thinking, translating, and journeying with God's historic revelation and contemporary working. Applying divine revelation necessarily proceeds through the Spirit who is the flame of love.[18]

The contemporary maze of competing Christian theologies certainly can be destabilizing for ordinary believers. Pinnock has sought to track this maze with both intellectual integrity and practical relevance in mind.

---

15   Clark H. Pinnock, 'New Dimensions in Theological Method', in David Dockery (ed.), *New Dimensions in Evangelical Thought: Essays in Honor of Millard J. Erickson* (Downers Grove, IL: InterVarsity Press, 1998), p. 200.

16   Callen, *Journey Toward Renewal*, p. 7.

17   See Pinnock's *Tracking the Maze: Finding Our Way through Modern Theology from an Evangelical Perspective* (San Francisco: Harper & Row), 1990.

18   Clark H. Pinnock, *Flame of Love: A Theology of the Holy Spirit* (Downers Grove, IL: InterVarsity Press, 1996).

Roger Olson once asked, 'How do American evangelical Christians handle theological diversity? Have we come of age enough to avoid heresy charges and breast-beating jeremiads in response to a new doctrinal proposal that is so conscientiously based on biblical reflection rather than on rebellious accommodation to modern thought? This may be the test.'[19] Indeed, the whole theological career of Clark H. Pinnock is itself such a vital test. Olson played a key role in the formulation of the widely circulated statement 'The Word Made Fresh' in 2002. The plea of this statement for the embracing of diversity and the expression of love among evangelicals who differ at various theological points is reflective of the very heart of Clark Pinnock.

Walking with God's Spirit

From the earliest phase and throughout his long career, Clark Pinnock has focused on the meaning and significance of the Holy Spirit in the Christian life. In his 1972 book *Truth on Fire*, for instance, he argued that a Spirit-filled life is central to authentic Christianity. The only way a believer 'can find victory and bear fruit to God is to line up behind the Spirit...and be led by him'.[20] Pinnock's eventual perspective on the life and faith witness of Francis Schaeffer, one of his early mentors, illumines well his own nature and theological goals. Admitting that as a thinker Schaeffer's influence would not last long, Pinnock nonetheless concluded:

> Here was a serious disciple of Jesus Christ who paid a price for following his Lord and bore a courageous witness to the gospel. He was a godly man, a man of prayer, who wept and pleaded, intellectually and passionately, that people should heed the message of God's kingdom. He convinced me of the importance of keeping a balance of mind and heart and not backing down in the face of opposition, whether from within the church or the culture. He cared about the truth, and because he was not a prisoner to the establishment in any sense, he could speak out boldly on issues that mattered... What will last...is not the thought but the total quality of the man in whose face the glory of God shone.[21]

In this characterization of Schaeffer one can see much that Pinnock himself would come to emulate. Truth is important for Christians. The Bible is basic and to be trusted as the revealed word of God. Courage is

---

19   Roger Olson, review of *The Openness of God* by Clark Pinnock *et al.*, in *Christianity Today* (9 January 1995), pp. 30-34.

20   Clark H. Pinnock, *Truth on Fire: The Message of Galatians* (Grand Rapids, MI: Baker Book House, 1972), Preface.

21   Clark H. Pinnock, 'Schaeffer on Modern Theology', in Ronald Ruegsegger (ed.), *Reflections on Francis Schaeffer* (Grand Rapids, MI: Zondervan, 1986), p. 192.

needed to defend it in a largely unbelieving world. Challenging contemporary intellectual waywardness is a sacred duty, whether the waywardness comes from inside or outside the Christian faith community. Beyond belief that has substance and standards, being a true and wise Christian necessarily involves passion, serious discipleship, both an informed head and a warm heart open to God and not a prisoner of traditions and establishments. The well being and integrity of the church's mission in the world is paramount, larger than personal reputation and denominational particulars. Such was the legacy gladly inherited by Pinnock while he was still a young Canadian studying abroad in the 1960s.

A personal testimony yields important insight. In 1967 in New Orleans young Professor Pinnock realized that the proper mind–spirit relationship was out of balance for him. He had suffered a detached retina that left him essentially blind in one eye. He and his wife were attending Canal Street Presbyterian Church where the congregation 'oozed with piety'. Experienced by them there was an authentic 'charismatic' renewal in a mainline church. People were open to God and prayers were answered regularly. In a small group setting Pinnock asked that hands be laid on him with a prayer for healing. The result? 'I was touched by God that night. I glimpsed the dimension of the Spirit which the New Testament describes but is so often absent in churches today... Being a Christian became an exciting adventure instead of a drag. I was filled with the Spirit.'[22] Accordingly, during the 1970s Pinnock softened his negative critique of Pentecostalism without going so far as to grant spiritual experience a position of equal partnership with biblical authority in defining Christian truth.

Appearing in the *Christianity Today* issues of 8 October 1971, 14 September 1973, and 12 June 1981 were articles by Pinnock arguing that Bible-believing evangelicals should find a way to get over their rigid rationalism and inordinate fear of emotional excess in order to avoid quenching the Spirit. He was now one with charismatics, if not in their tongues speaking, at least in their 'heart dimension' of the faith. He had come to resonate with Steven Land: 'Therefore, to do theology is not to make experience the norm, but it is to recognize the epistemological priority of the Holy Spirit in prayerful receptivity.'[23] Pinnock thus found himself a prophetic voice within evangelicalism, a voice that speaks on behalf of a balanced and holistic view of Christian life and mission. He had moved in the direction of the view typical of Eastern Christianity,

---

22   Clark H. Pinnock, *The Untapped Power of Sheer Christianity* (Burlington, ON: Welch Publishing Company, 1985), p. 51. Published in the USA as *Three Keys to Spiritual Renewal* (Minneapolis: Bethany House, 1985).

23   Steven J. Land, *Pentecostal Spirituality: A Passion for the Kingdom* (Sheffield: Sheffield Academic Press, 1993), p. 38.

namely that Christian theology is essentially a *practical endeavor* instead of a *theoretical science*.

Looming large throughout Pinnock's long career have been the dynamics of passion, pietism, church mission, present faith meaning, and the significance of the person and work of God's Spirit. He has come to view a key task of Christian theology as presenting biblical truth as a living reality for the present time, not bound artificially by a rational method that claims and defends classic 'orthodoxy' while too easily silencing what the Spirit may be saying to the churches today. For him, being spiritually deaf is an intolerable faith disease. He has sought to exemplify this in his personal life of faith and certainly in his 1996 book *Flame of Love: A Theology of the Holy Spirit*, which is his attempt to put the Spirit at the center of a theological vision of all Christian believing. Pinnock once identified his central ministry concerns this way: 'To blend my writing, speaking, teaching, witnessing, relating into an effective and relevant witness to Jesus Christ. To respond to those points where the witness is under a threat, and to give some helpful direction beyond current impasses.'[24]

A current impasse in Pinnock's view involves aspects of the 'classic' doctrine of God. In 1977, when he returned to his home area of Ontario as Associate Professor of Systematic Theology at McMaster Divinity College, he was a spiritually sensitive theologian who had a relational, responsive and personally satisfying understanding of who God is and how God relates to this fallen creation. He came to believe that Augustine, influenced heavily by Greek philosophy, had long ago distorted the biblical portrait of a personal, interactive, and self-giving God, and turned it into one of a timeless, changeless, unmoved, and unmovable sovereign, a view that has had a profound, long-term, and largely adverse impact on Christian theistic 'orthodoxy'. By contrast, Pinnock began insisting on the 'openness' of God, the true biblically revealed God who is not inert or immobile, not a metaphysical iceberg, but a personal agent who desires loving relationships with fallen creatures and chooses the risks and costs of dynamic give-and-take interaction with the fallen creation. His primary statement of this 'open' theism would come in his 2001 book *Most Moved Mover*.

While not a 'process' theologian as such, Pinnock admits that 'God has used process thinkers to compel me to change certain ideas to bring them up to scriptural standards'.[25] He fears that the failure of evangelicals to embrace some process truths will drive many of them to

---

24   Quoted by Darcy Taplin, 'Clark H. Pinnock: Growing out of the Weaknesses of a Fundamentalist Past' (unpublished paper, based on a Pinnock letter to Taplin, Southern Baptist Theological Seminary, December 1980), p. 17.

25   Clark H. Pinnock, 'Between Classical and Process Theism', in Ronald Nash (ed.), *Process Theology* (Grand Rapids, MI: Baker Book House, 1987), p. 317.

accept the extremes of process thought. The cautious appreciation of Pinnock for aspects of process thought originated largely with the appearance of Delwin Brown's review of Pinnock's 1984 book *The Scripture Principle* that appeared in the *Christian Scholar's Review*. That led to some Brown–Pinnock correspondence, then an invitation for Pinnock to teach in the Aspen summer school sponsored by Iliff School of Theology where Brown was a faculty member and later dean. These two men engaged in extensive dialogue that led to their joint book *Theological Crossfire* in 1990. Beginning in 1997 Pinnock was an active participant in evangelical–process dialogue centered at Claremont School of Theology. Of particular note is the volume *Searching for an Adequate God*, co-edited in 2000 by Pinnock and John B. Cobb, Jr. For Pinnock, the key paradox is that God, always remaining truly sovereign, nonetheless allows the world to touch and affect the divine.

The implication of an 'open' approach to God that has troubled many evangelicals most is Pinnock's view that God does not have exhaustive foreknowledge. Beginning about 1986, he observed that if history is fully known by God in advance of its happening, human freedom is an illusion. In fact, counters Pinnock, God does know all that is available to be known and knows it thoroughly and rightly; but decisions of free agents not yet made are not elements of knowledge yet available to be known, even by God. Two other 'open' implications of note are Pinnock's annihilationist view of hell and his understanding of the universal working of the Holy Spirit. Both are argued by him on biblical grounds.

Regarding the universal-working implication of an 'open' view of God, Pinnock wrote extensively in his 1992 book *A Wideness in God's Mercy*. Here he insists that believing in the finality of Christ for all human salvation does not require a closure on the possibility of divine grace being at work in all people. Salvation is available only because of Christ, to be sure; but God desires to save all people, even those who never hear of Jesus Christ. He advocates a 'hermeneutic of hopefulness' on the assumption that the very nature of God argues that no person will be lost without an opportunity to choose new life by the grace of God. Rethinking the meaning of the limited biblical material on the afterlife, he adds: 'Hell is not the beginning of a new immortal life in torment but the end of a life of rebellion.'[26] The biblical language is said to be that of death and perishing. The 'eternal' of the punishment awaiting the unrepentant wicked may well mean that it will be irreversible, not an eternal punishing but a final and never-changing judgment. Such

---

26   Clark H. Pinnock, 'The Conditional View', in William Crockett (ed.), *Four Views on Hell* (Grand Rapids, MI: Zondervan, 1996), p. 137.

implications of an 'open' evangelical theism are judged by Pinnock to be 'biblically justified, pastorally crucial, and apologetically timely'.[27]

Guides for the Journey

Clark Pinnock has sought a faithful middle way between the 'text' and 'context' poles of Christian theology, the way between ancient Bible and current culture, the best way of moving beyond the extremes of a doctrinally rigid and often socially irrelevant fundamentalism and a reductionistic and compromising modernism or liberalism. According to him, we are striving 'for the dynamic equilibrium of continuity and creativity that characterizes great theology... More like a pilgrim than a settler, I tread the path of discovery and do my theology en route.'[28] While *en route*, he makes this clear: 'I am not writing theoretically or abstractly... I long for the church to come alive unto God.' Read negatively, his work presses heavily against certain of the classic evangelical boundaries of acceptable theology and threatens to endanger the stability and integrity of some sectors of conservative Christianity. Read positively, his work represents an open and generous evangelical theology that both remains true to biblical revelation and evangelical distinctives and is able to dialogue helpfully with contemporary belief systems inside and outside the Christian community—and thus is better able to carry on effective mission.

Clark Pinnock has chosen to risk the tension between biblical commitment and critical openness, trusting God as he does theology both in his books and on his knees, walking with and listening to God's Spirit as well as to Christian tradition. Once he had broken free of Protestant fundamentalism (scholasticized Calvinism) in the 1970s, he has remained Christ-centered and biblically rooted and has been a Spirit-animated risk taker prepared to hear anew the word of God on behalf of his own soul and also the church's mission in a postmodern world. He has experimented, shifted, and crossed frontiers, often moving ahead boldly and sometimes having to retreat humbly. One consistent intent has been to respect Christianity's traditional authority sources, especially the Bible, without being victimized by any classic theorizing about them that is found to be inconsistent with the whole biblical witness and the present

---

27   Callen, *Journey Toward Renewal*, p. 173.
28   Clark H. Pinnock, in Clark H. Pinnock and Roger Olson, 'A Forum: The Future of Evangelical Theology', *Christianity Today* (9 February 1998), pp. 42-43.

work of God's Spirit. To say the least, Pinnock 'has been the catalyst for much rethinking within the evangelical movement'.[29]

29   Alister E. McGrath, 'Response to Clark H. Pinnock', in Dennis Okholm and Timothy Phillips (eds), *More Than One Way? Four Views on Salvation in a Pluralistic World* (Grand Rapids, MI: Zondervan, 1995), p. 129.

CHAPTER 2

Postconservative Evangelical Theology and the Theological Pilgrimage of Clark Pinnock

Roger E. Olson

In 'Postconservative Evangelicals Greet the Postmodern Age',[1] I delineated a new mood of evangelical thought by listing and describing several common themes emerging among a disparate group of mostly younger evangelical scholars and named several names as representatives of postconservative evangelicalism. Clark Pinnock was then and still is a model of postconservative evangelical theology. However, there were and are others and I do not wish in any way to slight their contributions.[2] Here, however, my focus will be on the present state of postconservative evangelicalism (especially in theology) and on Pinnock's continuing leadership in forging this new mood.

During the seven plus years since the article was published in *Christian Century*, many people have used the postconservative label in a variety of ways. Few have actually adopted it for themselves; many have jumped to criticize not only the term but also the mood it inadequately names. A few critics have simply hijacked the label and twisted it to serve their own polemical purposes.[3] Before examining postconservative evangelicalism in some detail—updating the earlier article—I would like to clear up some of the main misconceptions about it. Some critics have treated it as

1 R.E. Olson, 'Postconservative Evangelicals Greet the Postmodern Age', *Christian Century* 112.15 (3 May 1995), pp. 480-83.

2 Other evangelical theologians I would classify as postconservative are Stanley J. Grenz, Kevin Vanhoozer, Henry (Hal) Knight, Nancey Murphy, John Sanders and Miroslav Volf.

3 Soon after my article appeared in *Christian Century* a conservative news magazine with a strongly Reformed theological editorial orientation published an article darkly implying that this new mood of evangelical theology would lead to acceptance of homosexuality in the churches. Nothing in my article even hinted at that. Other conservative critics have imputed meanings and implications to postconservative evangelicalism that have nothing whatever to do with what I wrote.

an oxymoron. How can one be both 'postconservative' and 'evangelical'? First of all, 'postconservative' does not mean 'anti-conservative'. 'Conservative' is, after all, an indexical term. It has no absolute reference point. In some senses *all evangelicals are conservative*. That is true especially vis-a-vis true liberal Protestantism and modernistic theology. To be evangelical means, among other things, to have a greater appreciation for the authority of scripture and the Great Tradition of Christian teaching than one finds among liberal theologians. So, 'postconservative evangelical' does not mean liberal or anti-orthodox. Rather, a postconservative evangelical is an *evangelical* (committed to the four historical hallmarks of evangelicalism according to David Bebbington—biblicism, conversionism, crucicentrism and activism in mission) who is uncomfortable with the status quo of evangelical theology. Jack Rogers said it well in *Confessions of a Conservative Evangelical*:

> 'Conservative' is a good word. It marks continuity with the past, preservation of enduring values, holding on to what has been proven with time. In this sense I am still a conservative. I want to 'hold fast what is good' (1 Thess. 5.21). There is another sense in which the word 'conservative' is used. The dictionary defines 'conservative' as: 'tending to favor the preservation of the existing order and to regard proposals for change with distrust.' Being conservative in that sense leads to conservat*ism*. That is the sense of being conservative which has marked much of my past. That is the sense of being conservative which I want to put behind me. That is the sense of being conservative which confuses Christianity with our culture. Salvation is not found in the *status quo*. From apostolic times Christians have challenged the existing order.[4]

What I wanted to say with Jack Rogers in my 1995 article is that there are many truly evangelical Christians in the late twentieth and early twenty-first centuries who believe that 'It's okay—you can become less conservative and more evangelical'.[5] How? Not by becoming 'post-evangelical' or departing from basic Christian orthodoxy. Rather, by becoming postconservative while retaining and even strengthening evangelical distinctives; by being open to revision in belief and practice that is required by fresh understanding of God's word. Unfortunately, 'conservative' in theology designates something much more than merely commitment to the authority of God and his word or even great respect for orthodox teaching. It has come to mean strict adherence to a particular tradition such that it becomes inseparably united with the word of God itself. Within evangelicalism, 'conservatism' often signals holding fast to 'the received evangelical tradition' (which always means

---

4   J. Rogers, *Confessions of a Conservative Evangelical* (Philadelphia: Westminster Press, 1974), p. 11.
5   Rogers, *Confessions*, p. 12.

someone's interpretation of the historical evangelical consensus) and refusing to consider seriously the possibility that it may have been mistaken and stands in need of some revision at certain crucial points. A 'conservative evangelical', then, is not just someone who is *not liberal*; it is someone who emphatically rejects reform of evangelical belief and practice *even when such reform is consistent with scripture.* A conservative evangelical places such value on the *status quo* that he or she is closed-minded with regard to theological creativity and innovation even when they are fueled by faithful exegesis and believing reflection on God's word. Of course not everyone who calls himself or herself a 'conservative evangelical' is like that! I am dealing with ideal types and not individual persons or institutions. I am convinced, as are many evangelicals and commentators on evangelicalism, that 'fundamentalism' is being replaced with the label 'conservative evangelicalism' while retaining fundamentalistic habits of heart and mind. When a person proclaims himself or herself a 'conservative evangelical', more often than not it indicates commitment to strict biblical inerrancy, a fairly literalistic hermeneutic, a passionate commitment to a perceived 'golden age' of Protestant orthodoxy to be rediscovered and preserved, and a suspicion of all new proposals in theology, biblical interpretation, spirituality, mission and worship. Once again—lest anyone misunderstand or misuse this label or my description of it here—I emphatically reiterate that *all evangelicals are conservative in the sense of adhering to the authority of God's word as the norming norm of theology and to the value of basic Christian orthodoxy.*[6] That is part of the very definition of 'evangelical' in the contemporary world. (I happen to believe it is not a sufficient definition, but I believe it is a necessary aspect of evangelicalism's definition.)

First and foremost, then, postconservative evangelical theology is *a form of evangelical Christian reflection.* All postconservatives are committed to the supreme authority of God the Father, his Son Jesus Christ (who is God the Son as well as the Son of God) and the Holy Spirit mediated through the gospel that is expressed normatively in the supernaturally inspired written word of God, the Bible, which is the norming norm of all Christian belief and practice. All are also committed to basic Christian orthodoxy which affirms the deity and humanity of Jesus Christ and the triunity of God. All are Protestants who confess that there is no salvation without Christ and his cross and that we are saved only by grace through faith. All believe that authentic Christian life necessarily involves a conversion experience of repentance and trust in

---

6   By 'basic Christian orthodoxy' here I mean the Great Tradition of Christian belief that includes God's triunity and Jesus Christ's full humanity and deity. I do not mean a detailed system of theology such as one finds in the tomes of medieval or Protestant scholasticism.

God through Jesus Christ that results in justification and regeneration, and that such authentic Christian life evolves through a personal relationship with Jesus Christ (conversional piety). All also engage in witness through evangelism and mission to a lost and dying world. All affirm a supernatural worldview (even though they may have qualms about the term 'supernatural') that avoids reducing reality to matter, energy and natural laws. Some are monergists (God is the sole active agent in history and especially in salvation) while some are synergists (much of history and especially salvation involves cooperation between divine and human agencies). Some are amillennialists and some are premillennialists; some baptize infants and some insist on baptizing only believers. There is tremendous diversity within evangelicalism and its theology. One can find postconservatives throughout that diversity; they are not tied to any particular confessional tradition within the evangelical movement. *But they are evangelicals* and *they are not fundamentalists.* They believe that in secondary matters of belief that do not touch directly on the gospel itself theological pluralism should be allowed—even among evangelicals—and that doctrinal revision is valuable insofar as it is faithful to scripture and required by logic, culture, experience.[7] The word (gospel) must always be made fresh; God always has more light to break forth from his word.[8]

What, then, is postconservative evangelical theology beyond being evangelical? I would like to make clear at the beginning that it is *not a bounded set category.* Like evangelicalism itself 'postconservative evangelicalism' is somewhat fluid and dynamic. It has no definite boundaries. There is no magisterium that decides who's 'in' and who's 'out'. Rather, it is a *centered set category* defined by its core rather than by boundaries.[9] Its core consists of a set of common characteristics or family resemblances, but an individual is usually *more or less* postconservative

---

7   One critic of Clark Pinnock complained bitterly that he confessed that he gave up his early Augustinianism for open theism 'because logic required it and Scripture allowed it'. The critic argued that this is a dangerous hermeneutical move. However, that critic (like so many) is a five-point Calvinist who affirms limited atonement. What possible justification can there be for that doctrine other than 'logic (i.e., the Calvinist system) requires it and Scripture allows it?'

8   One critic of postconservative evangelicals sniped that 'God always has more light to break forth from his Word' (preached by Separatist minister John Robinson to half his congregation as they sailed for the New World) is used by liberal mainline Protestants to justify 'welcoming and affirming' gay persons into church membership and even ministry. Of course, any good maxim can be misused and eventually will be. 'The received evangelical tradition' has been used by aggressive fundamentalists to elevate premillennialism to the status of dogma.

9   For more on 'centered set' versus 'bounded set' categories, see P.G. Hiebert, 'Conversion, Culture and Cognitive Categories', *Gospel in Context* 1.4 (October, 1978), pp. 24-29.

among evangelicals. I would liken postconservative evangelicalism and its theology to progressive (not liberal or modernistic!) Roman Catholic theology after Vatican II.[10] The Second Vatican Council threw open the windows of the church to let the fresh breezes of the Spirit blow through. Some Catholics flowed with the Spirit's fresh breezes and some did not. (Admittedly some have used Vatican II as license to fly off into rank heresy, but that is not the fault of Vatican II or its movers and shakers and faithful followers within the church.) Some Catholics called integralists have resisted those fresh breezes and tried to move the church back to its pre-Vatican II status. Vatican II did not add to or take away anything from the doctrinal deposit of the church; it engaged in *aggiornamento*—renewal of church order and practices. It opened the door of the church to genuinely fresh thinking without liberating it for unfettered theological experimentation. Because of Vatican II Roman Catholics may now consider Protestants Christians ('separated brethren') and may enter their churches and even worship with them (but not take communion with them). Some Roman Catholics still will not regard Protestants as saved persons let alone Christians. Postconservative evangelicalism is a movement[11] for renewal and reform of evangelicalism much as post-Vatican II Catholic theology continues the renewing and reforming work of the council. But there is no list of post-Vatican II theologians; it is not a closed or bounded set. So postconservative evangelicalism is not a closed or bounded set either.

The first characteristic of postconservative evangelical theology—including Clark Pinnock's theology—is that it is *thoroughly and authentically evangelical*. It is not 'postevangelical'. Postconservative evangelical theology passionately embraces and works out of commitment to the basic principles and hallmarks of evangelical Protestant faith: biblicism (the supreme authority of the Bible as God's supernaturally inspired, written word), conversionism (true salvation always includes a supernatural work of God's grace that includes the

---

10   Like all analogies, this one is open to misunderstanding. Unlike the Roman Catholic Church, evangelicalism is a movement and not a hierarchical organization. It is not an organization at all. That is why it does not have to have and indeed cannot have 'boundaries'. Evangelicalism is not a church or even an ecclesial community. It is a coalition or network of ecclesial and parachurch organizations including denominations, congregations, universities, Bible colleges, publishers, etc. The analogy I draw here between post-Vatican II Catholic thought and evangelical theology does not depend on any direct comparison between the Catholic Church and evangelicalism structurally or doctrinally.

11   I sometimes use the term 'movement' for postconservative evangelicalism without wishing to imply that it is a cohesive movement with a structure, headquarters, hierarchy, etc. It is certainly not that! It is a movement of mood; a paradigm shift without organization.

human response of repentance and faith and the divine gifts of regeneration and justification), crucicentrism (focus on the atoning death of Jesus Christ as the only source and basis of reconciliation between humanity and God), and activism in evangelism and social witness (transformation of the world through proclamation of the gospel and meeting the physical, spiritual and emotional needs of humanity).[12] Postconservative evangelicals are conservative in those senses. They are God-fearing, Bible-believing, Jesus-loving Christians. Anyone who knows Clark Pinnock personally knows this is a true portrayal of his Christianity.[13] It is true of all postconservative evangelicals. Their detractors cannot accuse them of denying any of this; the accusation is often that they undermine these evangelical hallmarks by their willingness to reform and revise their traditional interpretations and by their emphasis on *experience* over or at least alongside of *doctrine* as the enduring essence of evangelical Christianity. That brings us to the second and third characteristics of postconservative evangelicalism.

Postconservative evangelicalism embraces a vision of *critical and generous orthodoxy*. Postconservative evangelicals like Clark Pinnock believe that appeal to tradition can never be the final word in theological debate. Reconstruction of time-honored interpretations of scripture and revision of doctrinal formulations in the light of scripture, using reason as a guide and culture as a conversation partner, are absolutely necessary tasks of evangelical theology. Why? Because scripture itself demands it. To say otherwise is to elevate tradition to an authority above scripture. Constructive theology based on faithful reflection on the Bible and in conversation with contemporary culture (including scholarship) is necessary for Christian theology to escape obscurantism and be both fully faithful and relevant. Clark Pinnock expressed this well in his 1979 programmatic essay 'An Evangelical Theology: Conservative and Contemporary'.[14] There he outlined a method of evangelical theology that would be bi-polar (in the positive sense). It would discover truth in the conversation and tension between scripture and contemporary

---

12   See D.W. Bebbington, *Evangelicalism in Modern Britain: A History from the 1730s to the 1980s* (London: Unwin Hyman, 1989), pp. 2-17.

13   For glowing testimonials regarding Pinnock as an evangelical scholar, mentor, and person of profound spiritual devotion see *Christian Week* ('Clark Pinnock Special') 16.16 (Autumn, 2002).

14   C.H. Pinnock, 'An Evangelical Theology: Conservative and Contemporary', *Christianity Today* (5 January 1979), pp. 23-29. See also the secondary essay by R.M. Price, 'Clark H. Pinnock: Conservative and Contemporary', *Evangelical Quarterly* 88.2 (1988), pp. 157-83. In both articles 'conservative' does not mean 'defending the *status quo*' but rather 'biblically faithful' as well as 'respectful of tradition'. In his 1979 article Pinnock began moving away from traditionalism toward what is here being called postconservative evangelicalism.

culture. Pinnock made clear then and has made clear ever since that for him scripture is the superior partner in that conversation and if conflict between scripture and culture appears scripture trumps culture. This commitment to the scripture principle is the source of fundamental disagreement between Pinnock and his liberal dialogue partner Delwin Brown in their book *Theological Crossfire: An Evangelical/Liberal Dialogue*.[15] All postconservative evangelicals affirm the scripture principle in a twofold sense. First, scripture is the supreme authoritative source and norm for Christian theology.[16] Second, scripture is the critical criterion of tradition and even the 'received evangelical tradition' must be held somewhat lightly and revised when necessary as required by fresh insights into the meaning of scripture. Conservative evangelicals may pay lip service to this critical principle, but they are extremely reluctant to revise the received evangelical tradition. Functionally that tradition serves as a norm equal with scripture for many conservatives. For them it functions as the (to Catholics) 'missing magisterium' in Protestant theology. For example, for some conservative evangelical theologians the 'stout and persistent theology of Charles Hodge' serves as a norm for judging later theological proposals; whatever is inconsistent with Hodge's theology is treated as suspect at best and heterodox at worst. Postconservative evangelicals eschew any such magisterium outside of scripture. Theological language, for them, is secondary language; it never carries the weight that scripture carries and is always at best reflected glory. Does this mean, then, that postconservatives discard dogmas and ignore heresy? Of course not. It only means that for them orthodoxy is always a human and not a divine construct[17] and that charges of heresy must be made with all humility and sorrow in full knowledge that no one 'thinks God's thoughts after him'. Orthodoxy, then, must be as generous and flexible as possible—given the level of clarity found in scripture and given the diversity of interpretation of scripture found among equally God-fearing, Bible-believing, Jesus-loving Christians.

---

15   C.H. Pinnock and D. Brown, *Theological Crossfire: An Evangelical/Liberal Dialogue* (Grand Rapids, MI: Zondervan, 1990).

16   Of course, all Christians would agree that in some sense scripture is secondary to God. Many—including many evangelicals—would claim that Jesus Christ stands over scripture and that scripture must be interpreted christologically. Postconservatives agree. The point here, however, is that for postconservative evangelicals, as for all evangelicals, scripture is the highest court of appeal in theological debates because it carries the (delegated) authority of God and is our only source of knowledge about the mind of Christ.

17   A conservative letter writer to a major Baptist state newspaper condemned open theism as 'man-made theology'. Postconservatives regard all theology as 'man-made' and are concerned that many conservative theologians regard some theology as divinely revealed or on the same level with divine revelation itself.

Pinnock has expressed these features of postconservative evangelical theology well in several volumes including especially *The Scripture Principle* (1984), *Tracking the Maze* (1990) and *Flame of Love* (1996). In all three of these books, as elsewhere, he affirmed the importance of basic Christian orthodoxy and the Great Tradition of Christian teaching as hermeneutical guides while upholding the biblical message itself—the gospel of Jesus Christ—as superior to tradition in authority: 'Protestantism stands for the freedom of the Word of God to critique church traditions and to bring them back into line with the gospel. It means abandoning traditions, if necessary, to get back on track.'[18] For Pinnock, as for most (if not all) postconservative evangelicals, doctrinal language is second-order language and not to be equated with revelation itself: 'Theology is a secondary language that lives off the power of the story [of God's self-disclosure in history] and explicates its meaning to God's people on the move. It uses the biblical story in the context of the community to make sense of life and put people into touch with the divine mystery.'[19] Throughout all of his writings (at least since the mid-1970s) he has celebrated the pilgrim spirit of theology that is ever moving forward guided but not bound by tradition and the diversity of Christian witnesses to the one truth. In *Flame of Love* especially, Pinnock draws on a rich variety of Christian sources and traditions including Eastern Orthodoxy, Catholic mysticism, Pentecostalism and the Charismatic movement, and contemporary theologians of hope such as Jürgen Moltmann. His appreciation for John Wesley does not push aside the positive contributions of Luther and Calvin. But he does not feel obligated to pay homage to any one theologian or school of theology and seeks restlessly to break out of evangelical bondage to Protestant scholasticism with its obsessions with discovering systematic coherence among divinely revealed propositions and constructing rational systems of apologetics and theology.

The third common characteristic of postconservative evangelicalism is *belief in experience rather than doctrine as the enduring essence of evangelical Christianity.* Conservative evangelical theologians tend to identify doctrine (right belief) as the enduring essence of authentic Christianity and that which supremely identifies authentic evangelical faith. Postconservative evangelical theologians such as Stanley J. Grenz elevate 'conversional piety'—the spirituality of mediated immediacy of relationship between the person and God through Jesus Christ—as their

---

18   C.H. Pinnock, *The Scripture Principle* (San Francisco: Harper & Row, 1990), p. 81.

19   C.H. Pinnock, *Flame of Love: A Theology of the Holy Spirit* (Downers Grove, IL: InterVarsity Press, 1996), p. 227.

essence and touchstone of evangelical identity.[20] Scripture is God's instrument of enabling and guiding conversional piety (not only of individuals but also of communities) and doctrine is devout reflection on scripture in the light of the experience of conversion to God through Jesus Christ. People were being transformed by the power of God and living in reconciled relationship with him through Jesus Christ before there was either a formal canon of scripture or a formal system of doctrines. People are often converted to Christ before they are fully aware of the authority of scripture or know anything of doctrine. Evangelicals' main concern is to bring people into saving relationship with God through Jesus Christ; teaching them scripture and doctrine often (if not usually) comes later. The emphasis of evangelical Christianity has always been on spirituality—transformational relationship between God and persons. This spirituality has since the Great Awakening revolved around conversion and a 'personal relationship with Jesus Christ'. Postconservative evangelicals point back to evangelicalism's revivalistic roots and its enduring identity as a spiritual renewal movement. What has unified evangelicalism as a movement has been proclamation of the gospel through preaching, singing and testifying. Woven in and through all of that has always been a strong interest in doctrinal correctness, but that has not been the unifying force of the movement. Post-WWII evangelicalism has been unified largely by the evangelistic ministry of Billy Graham and his appeal to 'make a personal decision for Christ'. A tremendous doctrinal latitude has been allowed within it; people have been invited to come 'just as you are' including doctrinal beliefs that may seem strange to other evangelicals.[21] This means that for postconservative evangelicals, in contrast to conservatives, evangelicalism is a centered-set category rather than a bounded-set category. What all evangelicals have in common is the experience of being transformed by a relationship with Jesus Christ that centers around conversion; they all experience it and are passionately committed to promoting it among others. This experiential center of the evangelical movement has cognitive implications; it is not subjective or intellectually vacuous. The most important cognitive commitment it carries is immediate conviction of the Lordship of Jesus Christ and the authority of scripture. Other beliefs are intimately connected with these convictions, but they are secondary to them and often remain relatively unknown for a while after conversion. Some of the most effective evangelical workers have been relatively untutored in doctrine. Evangelicalism includes all God-fearing, Bible-believing, Jesus-loving Christians who have ex-

20   S.J. Grenz, *Revisioning Evangelical Theology: A Fresh Agenda for the 21st Century* (Downers Grove, IL: InterVarsity Press, 1993).

21   See D.W. Dayton and R.K. Johnston (eds), *The Variety of American Evangelicalism* (Downers Grove, IL: InterVarsity Press, 1991).

perienced conversion to Christ through the power of the Holy Spirit and who are embarked on a life of being transformed into Christ-like disciples through the indwelling and empowering Holy Spirit. Part of becoming Christ's disciples includes growing in grace and knowledge, so doctrinal understanding is not unimportant. But the movement as a whole, while possessing an identifying and unifying gravitationally forceful center, does not have clear and distinct boundaries. Organizations (including denominations) have boundaries; movements do not. Postconservative evangelicals are interested in preserving this relatively open and flexible nature of evangelicalism with all of its diversity and dynamic quality.

Although Pinnock has nowhere expressly identified experience as the core or enduring essence of evangelical Christianity, one can reasonably infer that from books such as *Flame of Love* and from his several autobiographical reflections and interviews. *Flame of Love* brings the experience of being forgiven and transformed by the Spirit of God into the image of God and into Christ-likeness to the foreground of evangelical and even Christian identity: 'To be a real Christian is to be alive in the Spirit in a life-transforming manner.'[22] Clearly, for Pinnock, as for Grenz and other postconservative evangelicals, doctrine is important in the service of the experience of Jesus Christ as Lord through the indwelling presence and power of the Holy Spirit. But it is the latter that actually forms evangelical Christianity's permanent and pervasive essence. Some critics have darkly suggested that in this Grenz, Pinnock and other postconservative evangelicals are flirting with the liberalism of Friedrich Schleiermacher and his liberal heirs. Schleiermacher elevated experience over doctrine, but the experience he placed at the center of Christianity was not conversion or the 'personal relationship with Jesus Christ' promoted as the *sine qua non* of evangelicalism by post-conservatives; it was rather universal human God-consciousness or *Gefühl*—a religious *a priori* that takes precedence over the personal encounter with Jesus Christ and the resulting indwelling of the Holy Spirit that supernaturally transforms one's existence into discipleship to Jesus Christ. There is a qualitative difference between the experience Pinnock writes about so eloquently in *Flame of Love* and Schleiermacher's cosmic piety that forms the essence of religion including Christianity. Conservative critics of postconservative theology—including Pinnock's reflections—are fearful of subjectivism; to avoid it they place objective doctrine at the heart of authentic evangelical Christian identity. But in doing so they flirt with the danger of dead orthodoxy that substitutes propositional belief for the living presence of God in people's lives. This is a danger Pinnock is aware of and while affirming the importance of

---

22   Pinnock, *Flame of Love*, p. 164.

doctrine he makes absolutely clear that it cannot take the place of or hold primacy over the experience of new life in the Holy Spirit that comes with faith and repentance and the continuous infilling of the Holy Spirit.

A fourth common feature of postconservative evangelical theology is *discomfort with foundationalism and embrace of critical realism*. This is where postconservative evangelical theology and postmodernism meet. But the meeting is far from total agreement or accommodation. Some postconservative evangelicals find much of value in postmodernity—especially in its emphasis on communal knowing as opposed to individually determined knowledge. Postmodernity is non-foundationalist; so is postconservative evangelical theology. Postmodernists tend to reject epistemological and metaphysical realism; postconservative evangelicals work from a modified, critical realism in epistemology and metaphysics. Postconservative evangelicals fear that conservative evangelicalism is captive to what some scholars refer to as the 'evangelical enlightenment'. That is, just as enlightenment philosophy sought to base all knowledge on indubitable foundations in order to secure absolute certainty and just as it sought to identify truth with demonstrably true propositions, so conservative evangelical apologetics and theology has tended to identify theological truth with a system of coherent propositions based on *a priori* foundations. The foundations may be data derived from a common sense reception of empirical and historical reality or they may be presupposed data that yield a more comprehensive and coherent account of reality than others. In either and any case, the methodology is rationalistic employing evidence and logic to realize a rationally certain grasp of reality as it 'really is'. The epistemic distance between theological propositions and divine reality is thereby downplayed; the overall impression given is of 'thinking God's thoughts after him'. Ambiguity and uncertainty are enemies to be expunged from theology if not evidences of irrationality and possibly spiritual weakness. Postconservative evangelicals eschew foundationalism of that sort in preference for a web, matrix, or mosaic of beliefs and truth communicated not only through propositions but also through narratives. Revelation is viewed less as a set of timeless truths to be mined from scripture and constructed into a timeless, rationally coherent system of propositions than as a theodrama (Pinnock prefers the terms 'eucatastrophe' and 'epic story of redemption') that discloses the inner meaning of histories—universal and personal. Interpretation of the theodrama inevitably yields propositions, but they are not timeless truths dropped from heaven; they are culturally conditioned attempts to bring the meaning of the divine drama of revelation to speech.

Postconservatives recognize and acknowledge that there are 'revealed propositions'; they are not interested in reducing revelation to a noncognitive *Heilsgeschichte* or existential encounter. But the revealed propositions are clues to the inner meaning of the theodrama given within it and they stand in need of interpretation. Thus, there is always some distance between our contemporary, culturally conditioned interpretations of the revealed divine drama (including its supernaturally inspired interpretations in scripture itself) and that reality itself. This is one of the hallmarks of postconservative evangelical thought: distinction between human interpretation of revelation and revelation itself. That is where critical realism enters the picture. Postconservatives do not deny the objective reality of revealed truth; revelation exists and that to which it points exists. Revelation is not merely experience of divine–human encounter or universal God-consciousness. God speaks and shows. But God often speaks and shows in narrative form; stories also reveal God. For postconservative evangelicals God is the master storyteller. Fortunately, he has also provided some interpretations of the narratives within the overall theodrama that constitutes scripture. Nevertheless, scripture is not a system of theological propositions waiting to be systematized. Postconservative evangelicals worry that conservative evangelicals look upon scripture as just that—a pre-systematized system of timeless truths just waiting to be organized into a coherent system which could then replace scripture (except for devotional use).

Postconservative evangelicals view scripture in a variety of ways; there is no universal agreement about the Bible among them. But by and large they reject the conservative evangelical insistence on treating scripture as a textbook of univocally true propositions just waiting to be properly exegeted and organized. Instead, for all their diversity, they tend to view it as realistic narrative that contains clues to its own meaning in culturally-conditioned didactic explanations. Biblical narrative communicates truth just as effectively as do the didactic portions and the two must never be torn apart or pitted against each other. For scripture to be understood correctly (a never ending process) every part must be interpreted in the light of the whole and then placed in the contemporary context for reciprocal interrogation. The whole identifies God; that is scripture's purpose. Who God is may be understood from the narratives of scripture just as effectively as from the epistles, and that understanding remains incomplete apart from some attempt to relate it to the contemporary cultural context. Furthermore, that interpretive task is never the sole task of an individual scholar; it is a communal process involving the people of God. Finally, it is a never-ending task that evolves through trial and error that takes place within the community of God's people. It takes into account traditional interpretations without enshrining them as absolute and unrevisable; for postconservative evangelical thinkers tradition gets a vote but never a veto in the ongoing interpretive conversation. The ultimate authority is the biblical narrative, the theodrama of God's relationship with humanity unfolding through history. Reason is a tool of interpretation; tradition is a secondary norm to be respected and heard. Experience focuses attention on aspects of revelation that many a purely rational reading may miss; contemporary culture raises questions that the theodrama answers. Theology's communal task is faithfully to inhabit the biblical narrative—allowing the text to absorb the world (Hans Frei)— and interpret for the church how it identifies God for us and relate the world to that. Theology's task is also to examine Christian beliefs in the light of the biblical narrative and its identification of God and reconstruct them so that they more faithfully reflect the God–world relationship communicated there. Doctrine emerges through that process; it is always under construction which is not to relativize it but to acknowledge its humanness. For postconservatives, doctrine is not identical with revelation; it is the human endeavor faithfully to interpret and communicate for the whole church what revelation says and implies. The purpose is not to exclude people (although that may happen) but to purify and regulate the proclamation, teaching and worship of God's people. Doctrine does not have a constitutive function; its purpose is regulative. It also expresses the common faith of the church.

All of the above—postconservative evangelical theology's fourth family resemblance—correlates with Pinnock's views on revelation, scripture and doctrine. For him, revelation is not so much experiential or propositional as dramatic. That is, the gospel expressed in and through the 'epic story of redemption' contained in scripture (which Pinnock affirms as inspired and in some sense inerrant) is primary revelation; it is God's self-disclosure in history and story more than it is a set of timeless truths dropped out of heaven. In *The Scripture Principle* Pinnock emphasized the christological nature of revelation and referred to scripture as witness to revelation that participates in revelation.[23] This was a postconservative move in that conservative evangelical thought usually equates the Bible with revelation refusing to regard even Jesus Christ as a higher locus of revelation. Postconservatives consider this conservative equation of the words of the Bible with divine revelation without the christological primacy a move that borders on bibliolatry; it tends to make the Bible another incarnation. In *Tracking the Maze* Pinnock moved further away from bibliolatry and at the same time back toward identifying the Bible with revelation. He did this by means of narrative theology. According to the Pinnock of *Tracking the Maze* revelation is an epic story of redemption that is grounded in history and narrated in scripture: '[t]he Bible exists to tell a grand story, and therein lies its central purpose as storybook'.[24] Pinnock makes absolutely clear that he

---

23   Pinnock, *The Scripture Principle*, p. 16.

24   C.H. Pinnock, *Tracking the Maze: Finding our Way Through Modern Theology from an Evangelical Perspective* (San Francisco: Harper & Row, 1990), p. 171.

does not regard the story told in scripture—divine revelation—as unhistorical even though it does contain cultural conditioning including some elements that are history-like without likely being strictly factual. Nevertheless, the epic drama of redemption told in the Bible is historical; it happened in space and time and is not existential myth about human self-understanding alone. Pinnock expresses well the postconservative view of revelation and the Bible near the end of *Tracking the Maze*:

> It used to be that theology could assume that it possessed in its Bible propositional divine revelation, untouched by human factors and conditions. But now everyone realizes that the Bible is more of a historically conditioned witness than we used to acknowledge. It is not just the pure Word of God dictated by God and dropped from heaven. Even conservative theologians admit that the text is more human in texture than premodern Christians used to admit. Does this mean that theology is on the brink of collapse as some on both sides of the great theological divide suggest? I do not think so, because theology rests, not on a scripture principle as such, but upon Jesus Christ and the Christian story, mediated to us by means of a rich complex of norms. These norms may not yield the kind of absolute certainty we used to think we needed and possessed, but it does yield the kind of Christian certainty we actually need and may have. We must stop regarding the fact that we have this treasure in earthen vessels as if it were a negative fact, as if our only knowing in part and our prophecy being imperfect were unfortunate facts, when in reality they are God's own way of dealing with humankind.[25]

Clearly, then, Pinnock has moved away from foundationalism in theology and toward critical realism. Revelation is not a foundation so much as it is a catalyst; doctrine is not so much rational description of reality-in-itself as it is faithful witness to the grand story of Jesus Christ that changes lives. The aim and criterion of truth in theology is not so much rational certainty as it is proper confidence of the reality and loving kindness of the God who tells us his story and ours in the mediation of the biblical narrative.

A fifth family resemblance among postconservative evangelicals is *a strong interest in dialogue between diverse groups of theologians*. Conservative evangelicals tend to be suspicious of dialogue and their attempts at it often devolve into apologetics, polemics or efforts at evangelism. Postconservative evangelicals do not believe in religious pluralism and are not relativists, but neither do they think that evangelicals hold a monopoly on truth. They often go out of their way to engage in genuine, respectful conversation with adherents of alternative Christian theological perspectives. So far they have not shown the same level of interest in dialogue with non-Christian religions. Unlike many conservative evangelicals postconservatives do not feel threatened by alternative Christian points of view and they readily admit that they may

---

25   Pinnock, *Tracking the Maze*, p. 171.

have much to learn from them. They have engaged in sustained, structured dialogue with Roman Catholics, Eastern Orthodox, liberal Protestants (e.g., process theologians) and liberation theologians. Clark Pinnock has been a pioneer in this postconservative project of evangelical dialogue with non-evangelical thinkers. In the 1980s he held talks about the inspiration of scripture with Paul Achtemeier of Union Theological Seminary of Richmond, Virginia. They clearly did not agree about the nature of scripture, but they came to understand one another's perspectives better and challenged each other to think more deeply about their respective positions. In *Theological Crossfire* Pinnock engaged in rigorous dialogue and debate with liberal Protestant theologian Delwin Brown of Iliff School of Theology and again, although the dialogue partners disagreed more than they agreed, they came to understand each other better through the hard work of respectful listening and responding. In 1994 postconservative evangelicals hosted an event of theological dialogue at evangelical Messiah College in Grantham, Pennsylvania, entitled 'Re-Forming the Center: Beyond the Two-Party System of American Protestantism'. Representatives of various Protestant traditions including liberalism came together for three days of discussion about the past, present and future of the American churches. An evangelical theology professor at Bethel Seminary in St Paul, Minnesota, taught a course on evangelical–liberal dialogue in the 1990s. His co-professor was a noted liberal Protestant theologian from nearby United Theological Seminary of the Twin Cities. These are just some of the moves toward dialogue with non-evangelicals sponsored by post-conservative evangelicals in recent years. In general it is safe to say that postconservatives are more comfortable with the risk of theological dialogue across theological 'party lines' than are conservative evangelicals who generally keep their distance from non-evangelical thinkers.

A sixth distinguishing characteristic of postconservative evangelical theology is *a broad and relatively inclusive vision of evangelicalism*. Postconservatives talk about evangelicalism as a 'broad tent' phenomenon that has room for many different perspectives both theologically and socio-politically. They are painfully aware of evangelicalism's captivity to white, middle class, male leadership and seek to draw into their theological circles persons of color and women. They also seek to include within the evangelical 'tent' (a metaphor for community derived from the evangelical history of revivalism) as much theological diversity as possible. Postconservatives tend to trust people's claims to being evangelical whereas many conservative evangelicals take a more cautious and suspicious approach, seeking evidence of authentic evangelical belief in those who wish to be included in the evangelical community. Postconservatives regard all God-fearing, Bible-believing, Jesus-loving Christians as evangelicals unless they prove they are not (e.g., by affirming belief in baptismal regeneration without necessity of personal repentance and faith at some later point). They are willing to acknowledge as fully and authentically evangelical premillennialists, amillennialists and postmillennialists, annihilationists and believers in eternal suffering of the wicked, young earth creationists and theistic evolutionists, five point Calvinists and Wesleyan Arminians, Pentecostals and dispensational cessationists, political conservatives and economic socialists, egalitarians and complementarians. They take as their motto the old Pietist saying 'In essentials unity, in non-essentials liberty, in all things charity', and unlike many conservative evangelicals who espouse the same irenic principle they do not empty it by moving all but a few items of belief into the 'essentials' category. For postconservative evangelicals the 'essentials' category contains only those few beliefs that are central to the gospel and the experience of the transforming grace of God in Jesus Christ. Most would place some understanding of the Trinity in that category while acknowledging that many well-meaning but confused evangelicals hold to modalistic views of God's triunity. No postconservative evangelical would regard subordinationism or unitarianism as authentically evangelical. They allow many different interpretations of the Trinity and the incarnation to coexist on an equal plane within the evangelical tent. Neither the psychological nor the social analogy is normative for true evangelical faith nor is either belief in divine kenosis in the incarnation or affirmation of two minds in Christ. Conservative evangelicals tend to be critical of kenotic christology that teaches the self-emptying of the eternal, divine Son of God in the event of incarnation. Some even go so far as to call it heresy. Postconservatives pay attention to the fact that kenosis does not mean that the Son of God gave up his deity but only that he restricted the divine attributes of glory in order to go through a normal human development. Conservatives worry that this christology may detract from Christ's full and true deity without noticing that the more classical christology does not take with full seriousness his humanity. Postconservative evangelicals are comfortable with limited doctrinal diversity within the evangelical camp and they are reluctant to declare any truly God-fearing, Bible-believing, Jesus-loving Christian to be not truly evangelical unless that person blatantly denies one of evangelical Christianity's four hallmarks. They tend to see separatism and exclusion as a greater threat within the evangelical community than pluralism or latitudinarianism.

Pinnock's agreement with the fifth and sixth features of postconservative evangelical theology is obvious from his later writings, even though he does not explicitly address them as directly as some of postconservative theology's other characteristics. His own theological journey from place to place within evangelical thought testifies to the broadness of his vision of authentic evangelicalism. In *Flame of Love* he encourages evangelicals to include within their scope of legitimate belief a broader range of ideas about Christ and salvation. For example, he endorses a version of the Eastern Orthodox concept of salvation as *theosis*—divinization—without discarding more traditional evangelical ideas of justification and regeneration. He also affirms kenosis while upholding classical incarnational christology and he suggests that evangelicals rediscover Spirit-christology (from the second century church fathers) without rejecting Logos-christology. Pinnock's commitment to dialogue between evangelicals and non-evangelicals is manifest; he has gone out of his way to engage in it at some risk to his own reputation. The very idea of engaging in civil, respectful dialogue (as opposed to debate) with liberal theologians is anathema to many conservative evangelicals. In true postconservative spirit Pinnock believes that evangelicals have much to learn from other Christian traditions and communities and much to offer to them. Only the risk of true dialogue can reveal common ground, illuminate genuine differences (as opposed to only apparent differences), and stimulate unity and reform.

A seventh hallmark of postconservative evangelical theology is *a relational view of reality including a relational vision of God's being.* Many, if not most, postconservative evangelicals are uncomfortable with so-called 'classical Christian theism' because of its emphasis on God's present absolute self-sufficiency apart from the world. The God of classical theism, they believe, is largely defined by Greek philosophical categories of perfection. According to this way of thinking that crept into Christian thought very early (e.g., with the second-century apologists) perfection is incompatible with change and therefore God cannot change in any way. God, according to classical theism, is pure actuality without potentiality; God is incapable of changing or suffering in any way. Of course, conservative evangelical theologians who defend classical theism argue that its God is not static because he makes decisions and acts. They often mistakenly describe '*actus purus*' as 'pure activity' when in reality it means pure actuality without potentiality. God is already always what he will be and cannot 'become' in any sense. Postconservative evangelicals regard this as incompatible with the God portrayed in the biblical narrative as intimately involved with creatures in history. The God of the Bible, they argue, is relational and not self-enclosed; this God allows himself to be affected by humanity. They point to the incarnation as the most important clue to what God is capable of and reject scholastic arguments about Jesus Christ only suffering in his humanity and not in his divinity. According to postconservatives, then, the very fabric of reality as it is described in the revelational theodrama recorded in scripture is dynamic and relational. Creatures exist in relation to each other and to God; God exists in relation to creatures and in inner-trinitarian relatedness. Reality is relational because God its creator is relational as an eternal community of three persons.

This turn toward a more dynamic concept of God as relational is an example of postconservative evangelicals' willingness to alter traditional doctrine in the light of fresh readings of scripture. They believe that the traditional Christian understanding of God has been under the spell of philosophical theism for almost two thousand years. Even Luther, who rejected philosophy, could not escape the influence of nominalism as he developed his own concept of the *deus absconditus*—the 'hidden God'. Postconservatives like Clark Pinnock (and other open theists but not only open theists) wish to reconsider philosophical Christian theism in the light of biblical narrative that places God in situations of grieving and changing his mind in relation to human rebellion and repentance. These are not merely anthropomorphisms, but must be understood as revealing something about God's personal nature. Postconservative evangelicals have been influenced in this by the biblical theology movement as well as by the anti-speculative and anti-metaphysical theologies of Karl Barth and Emil Brunner both of whom exalted the transcendence of God while at the same time revelling in God's free relationality with creatures. Many of them have also been influenced by Dietrich Bonhoeffer, Thomas F. Torrance, Eberhard Jüngel and Jürgen Moltmann, all of whom rejected classical philosophical theism in favor of a more dynamic view of God as taking risks and allowing the world to play a role in his own life and experience. Divine temporality is not a frightening thought to postconservatives even though they all reject process theology's panentheism. God and the world do not coexist in eternal reciprocal interdependence; God possesses 'prior actuality' (Austin Farrer) to the world even though he freely condescends to make space within his own triune life for the life of humanity.

Thus, for postconservatives, God enters into a history with the world while remaining the superior covenant partner (Hendrikus Berkhof) who determines the ultimate outcomes of history. This is the basic postconservative theistic vision of God laid out by Clark Pinnock in his 1979 essay 'The Need for a Scriptural, and Therefore a Neo-Classical Theism'.[26] Later he developed it further as open theism (that God does not know the future infallibly and exhaustively) in 'God Limits His Knowledge',[27] *The Openness of God* (written with four other open

---

26   C.H. Pinnock, 'The Need for a Scriptural, and Therefore a Neo-Classical Theism', in K.S. Kantzer and S. Gundry (eds), *Perspectives on Evangelical Theology* (Grand Rapids, MI: Baker Book House, 1979), pp. 37-42.
27   C.H. Pinnock, 'God Limits His Knowledge', in D. Basinger and R. Basinger (eds), *Predestination and Free Will: Four Views of Divine Sovereignty and Human Freedom* (Downers Grove, IL: InterVarsity Press, 1986), pp. 143-62.

theists)[28] and *Most Moved Mover.*[29] In *Flame of Love* Pinnock advocated a relational ontology not explicitly tied to open theism but rather correlated with the doctrine of the Trinity: 'Loving mutuality and relationship belong to the essence of God. In recognizing this, theology makes explicit what the heart has always known. Let God not be defined so much by holiness and sovereignty in which loving relatedness is incidental, but by the dance of trinitarian life.'[30]

Many of Pinnock's critics have equated his view of God—especially his open theism—with process theology or have argued that it is at the top of (or halfway down) a slippery slope to process theism. Pinnock has made abundantly clear that this is not the case. Like all evangelicals (including all postconservative evangelicals) he affirms God's prior actuality to the world and God's superior power over the world; like all evangelicals Pinnock (and all postconservative evangelicals) believes in God's supernatural power to work miracles and in God's creation of the world *ex nihilo.* This puts him (and them) on an entirely different plane from process theology as becomes clear in the volume of dialogue with process theologians that Pinnock co-edited with John B. Cobb entitled *Searching for an Adequate God.*[31] Not all postconservative evangelical thinkers are open theists and some may not even be particularly interested in reforming the classical Christian doctrine of God away from philosophical theism toward a more relational, dynamic concept of God. Overall and in general, however, postconservatives feel the need to reconsider at least some aspects of traditional theistic teaching (e.g., impassibility and strict immutability) in order to make the Christian account of God's being more biblical, reasonable and consistent with Christian experience of a personal relationship with the living God.

The eighth and final tendency among postconservative evangelicals is *an inclusivist attitude toward salvation.* Conservative evangelicals tend to restrict the possibility of salvation to persons who actually receive (by hearing or reading) the gospel of Jesus Christ and explicitly respond to it by expressing faith in him. Thus, for most conservative evangelicals, there is no hope of salvation for the unevangelized.[32] Postconservative

---

28   Clark Pinnock, Richard Rice, John Sanders, William Hasker and David Basinger, *The Openness of God: A Biblical Challenge to the Traditional Understanding of God* (Downers Grove, IL: InterVarsity Press, 1994).

29   Clark H. Pinnock, *Most Moved Mover: A Theology of God's Openness* (Grand Rapids, MI: Baker Academic, 2001).

30   Pinnock, *Flame of Love*, p. 47.

31   J.B. Cobb and C.H. Pinnock (eds), *Searching for an Adequate God: A Dialogue between Process and Free Will Theists* (Grand Rapids, MI: Eerdmans, 2000).

32   See Ronald Nash's 'Restrictivism' in J. Sanders (ed.), *What About Those Who Have Never Heard? Three Views on the Destiny of the Unevangelized* (Downers Grove, IL: InterVarsity Press, 1995), pp. 107-39. There Nash, a conservative evangelical, argues

evangelicals fear that conservatives have turned the gospel into bad news by implying that Christ's coming and crucifixion 'unsaved' all those who lived in right relationship with God by 'Abrahamic faith' during Jesus' own lifetime on earth but who were never reached by Christian apostles and witnesses. Presumably, according to the restrictivist account, they could not die and enter into the kingdom of heaven without explicit knowledge of and and clear response to the proclamation of the gospel including the name of Jesus Christ. What if, like Anna and Simeon, some of the people alive at the moment Jesus died on the cross were 'righteous' through their faith in the promises of God (like Abraham) but died before they could hear of Jesus? Did the cross 'unsave them'? Conservative restrictivists may brush aside such questions as hypothetical and speculative, but inquiring minds want to know how their restrictivism would deal with that problem and with the comparable situation of persons who die unreached by Christian missionaries. Is there any hope of their salvation? When conservative restrictivists say there is not they immediately raise the question of Christ and his cross unsaving many people in the Roman Empire (if not throughout the world) who (like Anna and Simeon) had a right relationship with the God of Abraham, Isaac and Jacob by faith. They also raise the question of the goodness of God in relation to all of the unevangelized; would not a God of love make some provision for them? Postconservative evangelicals refuse to take the universalistic route because it is incompatible with the biblical narrative that includes judgment and damnation; the reality of hell (whether it is understood as eternal torment or annihilation) is inescapable in the biblical theodrama. However, many postconservatives do opt for inclusivism that regards the gospel as unconditional good news (God's universal will for the salvation of all people) and believes in the wideness of God's mercy that extends beyond the boundaries of human evangelism. In other words, God is the supreme evangelist and postconservatives do not limit his gracious work for the salvation of people to the extent of human missions and evangelism. By his prevenient grace God attempts to draw all people to himself. He is not willing that any should perish but that all should come to repentance. Postconservatives hope for the salvation of many who follow the light of God's truth flickering however dimly in their own cultures and religions and are met by the God of Jesus Christ on their journey toward ultimate truth.

---

that evangelical belief is that there is no possibility of salvation apart from explicit knowledge and acceptance of Jesus Christ. This stands in stark contrast with Billy Graham's statement in an interview with *McCall's* magazine in January, 1978 ('I Can't Play God Any More', pp. 156-58).

Clark Pinnock presented such a postconservative vision of salvation in his 1992 volume *A Wideness in God's Mercy*.[33] There he argued for an 'optimism of salvation' based on the biblical identification of God as loving kindness (not niceness!). Without ignoring the wrath of God postconservative evangelicals tend to view love as the primary attribute of God whereas many conservatives elevate God's holiness, majesty or power to primacy (even to the neglect of God's love for all people). According to Pinnock and other postconservatives, God desires to be an equal opportunity savior; that not everyone has an equal opportunity for salvation is against God's will and God works to equalize opportunity for salvation by leaving clues to his grace and mercy and humans' need for repentance and faith throughout human cultures and in human subjectivity itself (e.g., conscience and transcendental experiences). Some conservative evangelical critics have charged Pinnock (and other postconservatives) with flirting with universalism. That is no more true than the accusation (charitably never made) that many conservatives (especially Calvinists) hope for the damnation of all people except themselves! Nowhere has Pinnock or any other postconservative evangelical seriously flirted with universalism. The irony is that many conservative evangelicals express strong admiration for Pope John Paul II because of his strong stands against abortion and ordination of women, but they overlook the fact that he has endorsed hope for universal salvation (without endorsing universalism which is affirmation that all will be saved). Postconservatives are universalists *only* in the sense of believing that God desires and works for the salvation of all people because of his universal love.

Is there one major unifying motif of postconservative evangelicalism that distinguishes it from other types of evangelical thought and especially from conservatism? What is the 'one thing' that identifies it as a mood within evangelical theology? Conservative critics are simply wrong to label it 'left'. Postconservatives are not interested in accommodation to modernity or postmodernity; they are actively disinterested in being 'liberal'. I would argue that their one universal interest that makes them *postconservative* is *commitment to ongoing reform of evangelical life, worship and belief in the light of God's word.* Conservative evangelicals may claim interest in reform, but by that they mean retrieval of tradition—especially the 'received evangelical tradition'. More often than not this amounts to a repristination of Protestant scholasticism and a neo-fundamentalist hardening of categories against fresh thinking about the contemporary meaning of God's word. Postconservative evangelicals like Clark Pinnock believe that

---

33   C.H. Pinnock, *A Wideness in God's Mercy: The Finality of Jesus Christ in a World of Religions* (Grand Rapids, MI: Zondervan, 1992).

theology's task includes critical examination and reconstruction of traditions—including the 'received evangelical tradition'—insofar as they fall short of bringing faithfully to expression for contemporary men and women the whole gospel of the whole Bible. Postconservative evangelicals are suspicious of claims to closure of theological examination, reflection and construction. They believe that many, if not all, conservative evangelicals restrict the task of theology to criticism of anything and everything that is perceived as lying outside the boundaries of the 'received evangelical tradition' and that this inevitably leads to a Catholic-like elevation of tradition to a status of authority alongside of or higher than scripture itself. Conservatives, of course, view postconservative interest in continuing reform as liberal doctrinal drift and 'worshiping at the feet of the goddess of novelty' (as one particularly harsh critic of postconservative evangelical theology expressed it). Nothing could be further from the truth. Anyone who knows Clark Pinnock and other postconservative evangelical theologians (many of whom are involved in the Evangelical Theology Group of the American Academy of Religion) must recognize that they are not interested in change for change's sake or in accommodation to the shifting winds of culture. Their expressions of interest in postmodernity have nothing to do with denying the truth of the biblical metanarrative (theodrama) but everything to do with denying the totalizing imposition of theological interpretations on everyone. Postconservatives are only interested in continuing the reforming work begun by Luther who refused to recant his 'novel' beliefs unless he could be convinced by scripture and reason because his mind was held captive to the word of God.

CHAPTER 3

Unbounded Love and the Openness of the Future: An Exploration and Critique of Pinnock's Theological Pilgrimage

Gregory A. Boyd

From 'Unmoved Mover' to 'Most Moved Mover'

Clark Pinnock is a theological pilgrim if ever there was one. Rarely has a theologian changed their views as radically and as publicly as Clark Pinnock has over the last thirty years. While some may judge this as evidence of a 'weakness of intelligence or character', others such as myself view it as evidence of an open mind, humble heart and courageous spirit.[1] Indeed, the inability or unwillingness to seriously consider new perspectives and change when reason calls for it may be evidence that one has an idolatrous relationship to their own belief system. If one gets their worth, well-being and/or security from their presupposed theological or ethical correctness, they can't openly, humbly, and courageously consider the possibility that they are mistaken.

Whatever else one might say about Clark Pinnock, he has consistently demonstrated the humility and self-security of a man who knows he's finite, fallen and thus likely to be wrong at points.

---

1   Pinnock, 'From Augustine to Arminius: A Pilgrimage in Theology', in C.H. Pinnock (ed.), *The Grace of God, the Will of Man* (Grand Rapids, MI: Zondervan, 1989), p. 16, writes: 'I do not apologize for admitting to being on a pilgrimage in theology, as if it were in itself some kind of weakness of intelligence or character'. See also his *Most Moved Mover: A Theology of Openness* (Grand Rapids, MI: Baker Academic, 2001), p. ix. For a thorough and sympathetic analysis of Pinnock's pilgrimage, see B.L. Callen, *Clark H. Pinnock: Journey toward Renewal* (Nappanee, IN: Evangel Publishing House, 2000).

A Pilgrimage Toward Unbounded Love

It must also be said, however, that Pinnock's various changes of opinion have not been in any sense random. To the contrary, I submit that all the particular modifications of Pinnock's theology over the years have been aspects of a single unfolding paradigm shift. More specifically, every step of Pinnock's pilgrimage from a five-point conservative Calvinist to a progressive evangelical and inclusivistic open theist can be understood as part of a singularly focused, courageous, sustained effort to ruthlessly work out the implications of one thing: namely, the meaning of confessing that God is a God of unbounded love.[2]

This is perhaps most evident in Pinnock's re-working of the classical attributes of God. In 1970 Pinnock became convinced that a God of love could not be exclusively unilateral in his dealings with humans. Love, he came to believe, requires 'reciprocity'.[3] The relationship between humans and God must be a two way street. Humans must have the capacity to choose for or against love, and their choices must genuinely affect God.

This insight further entails that God must to some extent limit the exercise of his power so as to allow humans space to exercise power through free choice. Omnipotence thus does not mean that God exercises all control, but that he has the power to create any kind of world he desires—including a world in which he doesn't control everything, namely, a world in which he enters into reciprocal relationships with others.[4]

---

2   See C.H. Pinnock and R. Brow, *Unbounded Love: A Good News Theology for the 21st Century* (Downers Grove, IL: InterVarsity Press, 1994). The core of Pinnock's mature thought is that 'Love is more than an attribute; it is God's very nature', *Most Moved Mover*, p. 81. This pilgrimage could also be described as a journey toward a truly trinitarian conception of God, for in Pinnock's view, the meaning of the doctrine of the Trinity is that God is eternally and essentially a tri-personal relationship of unsurpassable love. See C.H. Pinnock, *Flame of Love: A Theology of the Holy Spirit* (Downers Grove, IL: InterVarsity Press, 1996), pp. 21-48; 'Systematic Theology', in C. Pinnock, R. Rice, J. Sanders, W. Hasker and D. Basinger, *The Openness of God: A Biblical Challenge to the Traditional Understanding of God* (Downers Grove, IL: InterVarsity Press, 1994), pp. 107-09; *Most Moved Mover*, pp. 28, 83-84.

3   Pinnock, 'Augustine to Arminius', p. 19, refers to the 'insight of reciprocity' as a driving force in his theological metamorphosis. For succinct illustrations of the logic that led Pinnock from this initial insight of reciprocity to a reworking of the traditional attributes of God and into a full-fledged open view of the future, see *Most Moved Mover*, chs 2–3, and 'Systematic Theology'.

4   Pinnock, *Most Moved Mover*, p. 92, writes: 'We must not forget that God is "sovereign over his sovereignty" and can make the kind of world he likes—in this case, a world with free creatures in it.' Again, '[God] could create a race of automata if he wanted to. Or he could create beings capable of engaging in free actions. His decision to do the

This perspective also entails that God cannot be in every respect 'immutable'. To be sure, God's essence, character, faithfulness and purposes are beyond change. But God's experience of us must be open to change if he is genuinely affected by us. In other words, '*who* God *is* does not change, but *what* God *experiences* changes'.[5]

So too, if God is a God of love who invites us into a reciprocal relationship with himself, God cannot be 'impassable', as the tradition taught. To the contrary, a God who genuinely loves us must be open to experiencing delight as well as anguish over us. God of course doesn't experience fickle emotions and suffer inappropriately as we do. But this doesn't imply that God doesn't experience any emotions or any suffering. God's love implies that he does. Indeed, in Pinnock's view, '[d]ivine suffering lies at the heart of the Christian faith'.[6]

The love of God also implies that God is not timeless. How could we possibly affect God unless God moves with us in time? We act and God responds: God acts and we respond. Such interaction presupposes that God's experience is sequentially related to ours. To be sure, we have no reason to suppose that God *measures* the duration of sequences as we do—God is not 'in time' as we are. The whole of world history is undoubtedly but the blinking of the eye to God, but this doesn't undermine the truth God's experience is sequenced with ours.

As a result of working out the implications that God is love, Pinnock arrived at a view of God that is quite obviously significantly at odds with the classical view of God. Whereas the God of classical theology is logically similar to the 'unmoved mover' of Aristotle, the view of God that has been unfolding in Pinnock's theology since the early 1970s is best characterized as 'the most moved mover'.[7]

---

latter is a revelation, not a denial, of his omnipotence.' So C.H. Pinnock, 'God Limits His Knowledge', in D. Basinger and R. Basinger (eds), *Predestination and Free Will: Four Views of Divine Sovereignty and Free Will* (Downers Grove, IL: InterVarsity Press, 1986), p. 153. According to Pinnock, 'Systematic Theology,' p. 113, God 'does not cling to his right to dominate and control', but rather 'voluntarily gives creatures room to flourish. By inviting them to have dominion over the world (for example), God willingly surrenders power and makes possible a partnership with the creature'. Cf. *Most Moved Mover*, pp. 92-96.

5   Pinnock, *Most Moved Mover*, p. 85.
6   Pinnock, *Most Moved Mover*, p. 89, cf. pp. 56-59.
7   For Pinnock's critique of classical theology as overly influenced by Hellenistic philosophy, see *Most Moved Mover*, ch. 2.

A Biblical and Christocentric Foundation

It would be a mistake, however, to think that Pinnock's revised picture of God is primarily the result of logical deductions from a self-evident premise. To the contrary, Pinnock has always been first and foremost a *biblical* theologian. It would thus be more correct to see the unfolding logic that moved Pinnock from the 'unmoved mover' to the 'most moved mover' as gradually opening his eyes to discover truths in scripture that he and the classical tradition had previously minimized.

The God of scripture, Pinnock argues, is a God who is affected by us, changes in response to us, experiences delight and anguish over us, and moves with us in time. The primary problem with classical theology, in Pinnock's view, is not that it was not logical enough (though he certainly believes this too), but that it wasn't biblical enough.

Detractors of course argue that the 'most moved mover' conception of God is less glorious and praiseworthy than the God of classical theism. Consequently, they interpret many passages Pinnock cites to biblically ground his view of God as phenomenological or anthropomorphic expressions which cannot be taken at face value.[8] Here, I believe, is where the significance of Pinnock's paradigm shift is most evident.

It is obvious that one's paradigm of God and his relationship to the world strongly influences what one allows scripture to say about God. Pinnock does not interpret passages that speak of God being affected by others, changing, experiencing grief and frustration and moving with us in time as anthropomorphic figures of speech because his paradigm of God's relationship with the world doesn't require him to.

Indeed, in Pinnock's model, God is most glorious *precisely because* he is *not* immutable, impassible and timeless in the classical definitions of these attributes. In his view, a God who is open to being significantly impacted by others, open to suffering at the hands of others, and open to moving with his creation from the past into the future is more beautiful and praiseworthy than a God who is supposedly 'above' being affected, experiencing emotions and moving in temporal sequence. Hence, passages that depict God in these terms do not need to be reinterpreted to preserve God's glory. To the contrary, for Pinnock and other open theists, they are highlighted as most emphatically displaying God's glory.

Even more importantly, for Pinnock as well as many others, only this 'most moved mover' paradigm of God is consistent with the central Christian conviction that God is decisively revealed in the person of Jesus

---

8   On the common criticism that the passages Pinnock and other openness theologians rely on are anthropomorphic or phenomenological figures of speech, see *Most Moved Mover*, pp. 60-64.

Christ.[9] How can we resist ascribing significant change to God if God became a man and died on a cross on our behalf? How can we not say that we affect God and that God suffers when Christ suffered a hellish death at our hands, and on our behalf? And how can we deny that God moves with us in time when God lived among us, died among us, and rose among us two thousand years ago?

The Openness of the Future

In the mid 1980s Pinnock landed upon what was to become perhaps the most controversial of all his theological modifications as he endeavored to unpack the implications of confessing that God is a God of unbounded love. Pinnock concluded that the future is partly composed of possibilities.[10] Since God knows things as they are and not otherwise, God knows the future to be partly composed of possibilities. According to Pinnock, therefore, God sees the future partly in terms of what *may* or *may not* be instead of exhaustively in terms of what *will* be. God is thus open to the future, and the future is thus open to God. Consequently, this view has come to be labeled 'the Openness of God'.[11] At least six considerations led Pinnock to this conclusion.

1) *The Logic of Divine Love.* As said above, the beginning of Pinnock's paradigm shift was the conviction that a God of unbounded love is not a unilaterally acting God. God desires loving reciprocity, which involves choice on our part. Not only this, but Pinnock became convinced that a God of perfect love would not predestine people to be involved in sin, to experience horrifying pain, and especially to suffer eternal punishment (for the sin he predestined them to carry out!).

---

9   Pinnock, *Most Moved Mover*, pp. 58-59.

10   In personal correspondence Pinnock has told me that the concept of a partly open future first became plausible to him while reading Richard Swinburne's book *The Coherence of Theism* (Oxford: Clarendon Press, 1977). His first publication espousing what has come to be called 'open theism' was 'God Limits His Knowledge' published in 1986. Interestingly enough, a number of other theologians who have become advocates of open theism, including John Sanders, Richard Rice, David and Richard Basinger and myself, were independently arriving at similar conclusions in the mid 1980s.

11   The label is primarily the result of the title of the book, *The Openness of God*, that constituted the first collaborative effort by openness theologians and essentially launched the contemporary openness debate. I personally believe the label is somewhat unfortunate, for it suggests that the distinctness of this openness view lies primarily in its view of God rather than its understanding of creation—more specifically, its understanding of the nature of the future. For reasons to be given shortly, I believe that this has led to many misunderstandings and misguided criticisms of the view.

By the late 80s this conviction came to encompass God's foreknowledge. Why, Pinnock wondered, would God strive with people to get them to enter into a saving relationship with him if he knows from all eternity that they will not respond positively to his efforts?[12] In Pinnock's view, God's universal love for all people, and God's on-going efforts to redeem all people, entail a genuine hope on God's part for all people. And this further entails that their future includes the possibility, though not the certainty, that they will be saved.[13]

2) *The Logic of Freedom.* The openness of the future is implied in the affirmation of human freedom. If the future were exhaustively foreknown, Pinnock argues,

> the future would be fixed and determined, much as is the past. Total knowledge of the future would imply a fixity of events. Nothing in the future would need to be decided.[14]

For Pinnock, morally responsible freedom *means* that agents transition possibilities into actualities, non-definite realities into definite realities.[15] But if the future is exhaustively settled in God's mind, then there are no genuine possibilities left to be resolved. From all eternity, reality is a settled matter. It is definitely one way and definitely not any other way.[16]

---

12   Pinnock, 'Systematic Theology', p. 115.

13   On Pinnock's understanding of God's universal hope for humans and his inclusivist understanding of salvation, see C.H. Pinnock, *A Wideness in God's Mercy: The Finality of Jesus Christ in a World of Religions* (Grand Rapids, MI: Zondervan, 1992); *Flame of Love*, pp. 185-214; and 'An Inclusivist View', in D. Okholm and T. Phillips (eds), *More Than One Way? Four Views on Salvation in a Pluralistic World* (Grand Rapids, MI: Zondervan, 1995), pp. 95-123.

14   Pinnock, 'Systematic Theology', p. 121.

15   Determinists often defend 'compatiblistic freedom'—freedom that is compatible with determinism. In their view, an agent is free if nothing hinders them from doing what they want, though what an agent wants is determined and itself determines how the agent acts. Pinnock, along with all other Arminians and open theists, does not think compatiblistic freedom is consistent with our sense of moral responsibility. Nor is it adequate in accounting for the biblical data on human freedom. See Pinnock, *Most Moved Mover*, pp. 127-28, and 'Systematic Theology', pp. 114-15.

16   If God eternally knows the future as occurring one way rather than any alternative way, the future is eternally 'definite'. The facticity or 'thatness' of each occurrence eternally precedes its actual occurrence. Whether God unilaterally gave the world its exhaustive definiteness or facticity, as Calvinism claims, or whether he simply knows it from eternity as exhaustively definite and factual, is inconsequential to the problem being raised here. If the definiteness of all our future acts eternally precedes our free decisions, we don't in our actual histories *create* the definiteness with our free decisions. We don't transition indefinite possibilities into definite actualities. Conversely, if we affirm that we *do* transition indefinite possibilities into definite actualities, then we must affirm that the world is to this degree indefinite. Hence God,

Hence, our phenomenological experience of resolving indefinite realities (possibilities) into definite realities (actualities) by our choices is misleading. Indeed, if the future is exhaustively definite in God's mind from all eternity, there are no genuine possibilities for us to resolve.[17]

3) *The Experience of Freedom.* The openness of the future is suggested by our experience of freedom, according to Pinnock. Early on in his theological pilgrimage out of Calvinism, Pinnock wrote:

> Universal man...talks and feels *as if* he were free. He perceives himself to be a person capable of rising above his situation, of shaping his life and destiny, and of making a significant impact upon history. This fundamental self-perception is, I believe, an important clue as to the nature of reality.[18]

We act on the conviction that the future is, to some extent at least, *up to us* to decide. 'When faced with a decision', Pinnock writes, 'we *know* with a subjective certainty that we can take one of the two or more alternatives before us'.[19] The very act of deliberating between alternatives manifests our core existential conviction that we believe it is *up to us* to decide between them. Determinism thus cannot be illustrated in our decision making, while the open view of the future cannot help but be illustrated.[20] And for Pinnock, myself and others, this is a very strong argument in favor of the open view of the future.

What is more, our sense of moral responsibility is grounded in this fundamental datum of human experience. '[H]uman freedom is the precondition of moral and intellectual responsibility.'[21] Calvinists may argue that humans and the devil himself are morally responsible for their evil actions even though they are exhaustively predestined to do what they do, but there is simply no way to form a coherent conception of this supposed moral responsibility. All talk about 'concurrent causality' and

---

who knows all reality just as it is and not otherwise, must know it as to this degree indefinite.

17   Of course, in the classical view, all we shall freely do is *logically* possible before we do it. And there are *logical* possibilities we *theoretically* could actualize that we shall never actualize. But if the definiteness or facticity of world history is exhaustively and eternally present for God to know, there can be no *historical* possibilities for us to resolve—that is, possible alternative courses of action that we in our historical situation are able to choose between. For agents to be free, it is not enough to affirm that their choices are not logically necessary, for this can be said of any contingent reality. Freedom is the power of an agent to choose among viable (not just logical) possibilities and thereby transition possibilities into actualities.

18   C.H. Pinnock, 'Responsible Freedom and the Flow of Biblical History', in C.H. Pinnock (ed.), *Grace Unlimited* (Minneapolis, MN: Bethany Fellowship, 1975), p. 95.

19   Pinnock, 'Responsible Freedom', p. 96.

20   See Pinnock, *Most Moved Mover*, pp. 154-57.

21   Pinnock, 'Responsible Freedom', pp. 95-96.

'primary and secondary causes', etc., only re-labels the incoherence: it does not explain it. Our core convictions about moral responsibility are inextricably rooted in the sense that one is responsible for a deed only if they could have done otherwise. And it can only be true that they could have done otherwise if what they did wasn't settled in eternity before they ever existed.[22]

If, as Pinnock holds, one of the central tasks of any theological program is to make sense of our experience, the unavoidable conviction that we are free and morally responsible takes on enormous significance. Indeed, since the only slice of reality we know directly is our own experience, the experience of freedom should be taken as 'an important clue as to the nature of reality'.

In time, Pinnock realized that this 'important clue' entailed that reality is itself partly open. We experience ourselves, the future and even God in an open-ended way—as though some things were up to us to resolve. The open view of the future and of God is in fact nothing more than an affirmation that this fundamental experience in principle *reflects the way reality actually is*. Every other perspective to some degree has to deny that this is the case. And they then have to explain away, rather than utilize, this primary datum of human experience.

4) *Apologetic Advantages*. Pinnock has always had a passion for communicating the gospel intelligently and persuasively to contemporary non-Christians. On this account, Pinnock argues, the open view of God and of the future has significant advantages over classical theism.

For one thing, Pinnock is convinced that the open view is the evangelical option that is most consistent with the ever-increasing dynamic categories of modern and post-modern thought. In contrast to the general tendency of Hellenistic philosophy, modern and post-modern thought doesn't see change, flexibility, relationality, spontaneity and open-ended processes as defective. To the contrary, such concepts are becoming centrally important in almost all fields of thought, including physics, biology, cosmology and even economics. This gives the open view an apologetic advantage over views that are more tied to classical, static, substantival categories.[23]

---

22   Pinnock, *Most Moved Mover*, pp. 127-29. Here again, it is not enough to say that an agent *logically* could have done otherwise. An agent is morally responsible only if they *historically* could have done otherwise. That is, it must have been possible in the *actual history of an agent* for them to have acted differently than they in fact acted if they are to be praised or blamed for their action.

23   Pinnock, 'Systematic Theology', p. 107, writes: 'Modern culture can actually assist us in this task because the contemporary horizon is more congenial to dynamic thinking about God than is the Greek portrait.' And again, 'From Augustine to Arminius', p. 27: 'we are making peace with the culture of modernity... We are experiencing reality

Along the same lines, Pinnock is convinced that the open view of God and the future is more plausible to modern people because it avoids many of the unresolvable and, in his view, unnecessary puzzles the classical view required people to accept. Why does God create people he is certain will commit unspeakable evil and damn themselves? How can we be morally responsible for what God predestines us to do? Why does God strive to save people he eternally knows will never be saved? How can God be genuinely interactive with us if his experience of the world is timeless? How can we be free if our future choices are eternally settled in the mind of God? The open view is the only view that altogether avoids these conundrums. And as such, it is the view that is most plausible to modern, thoughtful seekers.[24]

5) *Practical Consequences.* The open view also offers advantages to Christians on a practical level. It has an 'as if' benefit, Pinnock argues, meaning that it is beneficial to live 'as if the model is true'.[25] According to Pinnock, one of the most unfortunate implications of believing that everything happens according to God's will is that it encourages people to invest their energy in trying to accept things as the way they are rather than in changing them to the way God would want them to be.

In terms I have used elsewhere, it encourages a 'theology of resignation' rather than a 'theology of revolt'.[26] It produces a people who, despite their Christian faith, act and sound much more like ancient Stoics than the way the Jesus of the Gospels acted. And the reason is because it's difficult for people to urgently pray and work to bring God's will 'on earth as it is in heaven' (Mt. 6.10) when they believe that God's will is *already* being done on earth as it is in heaven.

By contrast, when one believes that the future is partly open-ended and thus that one's prayers and decisions *really* make a difference in influencing what comes to pass, one is motivated to become an activist. They are more inclined to own up to the morally responsible 'say-so' God has invested in them and, following the example of Jesus, to revolt

---

as something dynamic and historical and are consequently seeing things in the Bible we never saw before.' See also *Most Moved Mover*, pp. 117-22, 150-51.

24   Pinnock, 'Systematic Theology', p. 104, asks: 'How can we expect Christians to delight in God or outsiders to seek God if we portray God in biblically flawed, rationally suspect and existentially repugnant ways? We cannot expect it.' See also 'God Limits His Knowledge', pp. 143-44, and *Most Moved Mover*, pp. 1-3, 117-18.

25   Pinnock, *Most Moved Mover*, p. 155. The whole of ch. 4 of this work, entitled 'The Existential Fit', is relevant to this section.

26   See G. Boyd, *God at War: The Bible and Spiritual Conflict* (Downers Grove, IL: InterVarsity Press, 1997), pp. 21-22, 201, 214, 217.

against all aspects of creation that do not align with God's will rather than accept them as part of God's will.[27]

6) *Biblical Foundation*. But we have not yet addressed the central reason why Pinnock has come to conclude that the future is partly open. As forceful as considerations of logic, experience, apologetics and practicality may be, it is unlikely Pinnock would have come to the conclusion he came to if the view was not firmly grounded in scripture.

As Pinnock worked through his paradigm shift, he came to see that the God of the Bible frequently strives to accomplish things that do not come to pass and is frustrated and grieved when they don't come to pass (e.g. Ps. 78.10; Ezek. 22.30-31; Isa. 54.6; 63.10; Mt. 23.37; Rom. 10.21).[28] How are we to make sense of this unless we suppose that the outcome God strove for was genuinely possible to accomplish? Would an all wise God strive to achieve a goal that he eternally knew was not attainable? Would he then get frustrated and be grieved when the goal he knew could not be attained was not attained by his striving?

Pinnock also came to see that the God of scripture frequently changes his mind in response to changing circumstances (e.g., Ex. 32.10-14; Dt. 9.13-29; 2 Kgs 20.1-7; 1 Chron. 21.15; Jer. 18.6-10; 26.2-3, 13, 19; Jon. 3.10). Indeed, the Bible depicts God's flexibility as one of his praiseworthy attributes (Jon. 4.2; Joel 2.12-13). If the future is exhaustively settled in God's mind from all eternity, it is difficult to take seriously the Bible's repeated declarations that God *intended* to do one thing and then *decided* to do another. How can we speak of an agent genuinely intending to do something they are certain they won't do?

Along similar lines, sometimes the Bible depicts God as expecting people to do one thing when in fact they do another (e.g., Jer. 3.6-7, 19-20; Isa. 5.1-5). This is understandable if God perfectly knows the probabilities of human behavior, but not if he eternally knows future decisions as definite realities. Relatedly, the Bible frequently depicts God as 'testing' people 'to know' how they will respond (e.g. Gen. 22.12; Ex. 16.4; Dt. 8.2; 13.1-3; Judg. 2.22; 3.4; 2 Chron. 32.31). How can the Bible say that these testings are *for God* to know if God eternally knows how people will respond?

Pinnock also came to realize that the Bible frequently depicts God as thinking and speaking about the future in terms of what may or may not occur (e.g., Ex. 3.18–4.9; 13.17; Jer. 26.3). This is difficult to understand if the future in fact contains no 'maybes' to God. For example, God motivated Ezekiel to enact a prophecy by telling him, '*Perhaps* [the people] will understand and listen' (Ezek. 12.3). As it

---

27   On prayer and moral responsibility in the open view, see Pinnock, *Most Moved Mover*, p. 46, and 'God Limits His Knowledge', p. 152.

28   For Pinnock's most thorough exposition of the biblical foundation for his view, see *Most Moved Mover*, ch. 1.

turns out, the people did not understand or listen. If God was *certain* all along the people *wouldn't* understand, what are we to think of him encouraging Ezekiel with the promise that they *might* understand? Would God not be guilty of lying to Ezekiel?

When combined with the earlier mentioned considerations, these biblical data led Pinnock to the conclusion that God is open to a partly open future.

While opponents operating out of a classical paradigm view the God of openness theology as weak, Pinnock and others view the God of openness theology as more beautifully sovereign and wise than the God of classical theology.[29] This is a view of God who is so sovereign he doesn't need to micro-control his creation to achieve his purposes.[30] He is a God who is so confident he is willing to take risks. He is a God who is so wise he doesn't need to foreknow all that will happen in order to perfectly anticipate and prepare a response to whatever happens.[31] He is a God who is so committed to love he is willing to use persuasion rather than coercion as a means of attaining his goals, even if this requires that he die on a cross to do it. He is a God who is immutable in every way it is praiseworthy to be immutable, but flexible in every way it is praiseworthy to be flexible. He is a God who patiently and passionately strives to bring his creation into the everlasting dance of his triune love. And he does so by displaying his beauty, not his biceps.

A Critique

Pinnock's defense of the 'most moved mover' view of God in general and of the open view of God and the future in particular has been increasingly strong throughout his career. He would be the first to admit, however, that it has not been without its shortcomings. I would like to conclude this essay by offering a critique of what I believe are the two greatest shortcomings of Pinnock's defense of the open view. The first concerns Pinnock's inadequate view of omniscience and addresses what is perhaps the major academic objection to the open view. The second concerns Pinnock's understanding of God's anticipation of possible

---

29   See especially Pinnock, *Most Moved Mover*, pp. 79-104.

30   Pinnock, 'Systematic Theology', p. 116: 'Divine Sovereignty involves a flexible out-working of God's purposes in history. It refers to his ability, as the only wise God, to manage things, despite resistance to his will. Owing to the emphasis in theology on almightiness, we have tended to neglect the form of power called persuasion.'

31   Pinnock, 'God Limits His Knowledge', p. 146: 'Nothing can happen which God has not anticipated or cannot handle.' I shall shortly argue that this motif is not consistently expressed or sufficiently developed in Pinnock's published theology.

future events and addresses what is perhaps the most prevalent emotive objection to the open view on a popular level.

Qualifying Omniscience

Pinnock has repeatedly defined omniscience as 'knowing all that can be known'.[32] As a number of critics have pointed out, this seems to be an inadequate definition of omniscience. It leaves open the possibility that there are things that exist (including propositions) that cannot be known, even by God. While I'm sympathetic to Pinnock's concern to reconcile omniscience with an open future, I'm also convinced that this is not the way to do it.

Among other difficulties, the suggestion that there are things that cannot be known seems to directly contradict the meaning of omniscience. To say that God is all knowing (*om*niscient) says something not only about the scope of God's knowledge but also about the nature of reality: namely, it is knowable by God. If an omniscient being exists, therefore, there simply can't be things that are intrinsically unknowable or propositions the truth values of which are unknowable.

To make matters worse, Pinnock has sometimes spoken of God limiting his omniscience—as though God *could* know all things if he wanted, including future free acts.[33] Among other problems, it is not clear how God could know where to limit his omniscience unless he first exercised *unlimited* omniscience. He would have to first know what it is he doesn't want to know in order to shield himself from knowing it! Moreover, even if this could be rendered intelligible, it's not at all clear what it would accomplish. How would God choosing not to know something he could in principle know ensure freedom? If the definiteness of future acts eternally exists, there are no indefinite possibilities for agents to transition from possibilities into definite actualities—whether this eternal definiteness is known by God or not.

On a related note, Pinnock has at times contrasted the open view with the view that God possesses 'limitless foreknowledge' or 'exhaustive foreknowledge' thereby conceding that his view entails that God has limited and non-exhaustive foreknowledge.[34] This too suggests that the

---

32   Pinnock, 'Systematic Theology', p. 121, affirms that 'God must know all things that can be known and know them truly'. See also 'God Limits His Knowledge', p. 157, and 'From Augustine to Arminius', p. 25.

33   Note, for example, the title of his 1986 essay 'God Limits His Knowledge',

34   E.g. 'Systematic Theology', p. 122; *Most Moved Mover*, pp. 52, 77. The open view does not require denying that God possesses exhaustive foreknowledge so long as it is understood that this foreknowledge includes events that may or may not take place as well as events that will and will not take place. What the open view denies is that God's

future would be knowable if only God was not limited in what he knows. Other times Pinnock has referred to the classical view of omniscience that he opposes as advocating 'strong omniscience'—as though he and other openness theologians advocated 'weak omniscience'.[35] Such ill-advised and unnecessary ways of speaking play into the hands of openness detractors who are already inclined to believe that the God of openness theology is a weak and limited deity made in humanity's own image.[36]

Still other times Pinnock has referred to the classical view as embracing 'total omniscience' and contrasted his view with 'exhaustive omniscience'—as though he was advocating a limited omniscience.[37] But again, an 'all' that is limited is no longer an 'all', so an omniscience that is limited is no longer *omni*science. And finally, Pinnock has sometimes spoken of God as a 'learner' in the sense that he 'enjoys continuing to get to know [the creation] in a love that never changes'.[38] This way of speaking could be interpreted as suggesting that God doesn't know all things from the start, but has to slowly acquire his knowledge as he gets to know his creation through a learning process.

Now, people should in fairness cut Pinnock and other open theists a certain amount of slack in their phraseology. While defenders of the classical view have had centuries of discussion to hammer out and fine tune their positions, open theists are at the very beginning of this process. The modern day openness movement is not yet two decades old, so it would be unreasonable to expect from us a fully developed, perfectly nuanced, position. I am quite convinced that my disagreement with Pinnock is more with his phraseology than with the substance of his position. Still, it is only by critiquing the way we open theists express our views that we will be able to fully develop and nuance our position.

---

foreknowledge is eternally and exhaustively *definite* (that is, characterized by facts that are definite in one direction as opposed to every other possible direction they could be). I shall argue that, as a matter of fact, it is those who deny that foreknowledge can include 'maybes' who unwittingly deny omniscience, not open theists who affirm that 'maybes' are part of God's foreknowledge.

35   Pinnock, 'God Limits His Knowledge', p. 156: 'I agree with the traditional Calvinists that strong omniscience entails strong predestination.'

36   See, e.g., N. Geisler, *Creating God in the Image of Man? The New Open View of God—Neotheism's Dangerous Drift* (Minneapolis, MN: Bethany, 1997); N. Geisler and H.W. House, *The Battle for God: Responding to the Challenge of Neotheism* (Grand Rapids, MI: Kregel, 2001); A.B. Caneday, 'God in the Image and Likeness of Adam—Clark Pinnock's Use of Scripture in His Argument "God Limits His Knowledge"', *Journal of Biblical Apologetics* 1 (2001), pp. 20-27; D. Wilson (ed.), *Bound Only Once: The Failure of Open Theism* (Moscow, ID: Canon, 2001).

37   Pinnock, 'Systematic Theology', p. 122; *Most Moved Mover*, p. 49; 'From Augustine to Arminius', p. 25.

38   Pinnock, 'Systematic Theology', pp. 123, 124.

In this light, it has to be said that the above cited ways Pinnock espouses his position are unfortunate, if not incoherent. It has made his otherwise strong position an easy target for opponents of the openness position.

OMNISCIENCE AND MIGHT-COUNTERFACTUALS

Even more importantly, the attempt to preserve omniscience while affirming the openness of the future by speaking of it as 'limited' or 'weak' is altogether unnecessary. For, as I shall now show, there is absolutely no incompatibility between affirming that God is all knowing in the strongest sense of the term, on the one hand, and affirming that God knows some of the future as what 'might' happen rather than what 'will' happen, on the other. Indeed, I shall argue that affirming omniscience logically requires us to affirm that he knows the truth value of all propositions expressing what may and may not take place.

The problem Pinnock wants to resolve can be most succinctly stated as follows:

P1: If God is omniscient, he must know the truth value of all propositions.
P2: Propositions about future free acts are either true or false.
P3: God knows the truth value of propositions about future free acts.
Conclusion: God possesses exhaustive definite foreknowledge of all future free acts.

As we have seen, Pinnock attempts to avoid this conclusion by qualifying God's omniscience, thus rejecting P1. A better approach, I submit, is to accept the formal validity of this argument but show how it doesn't entail that God possesses exhaustively definite foreknowledge of all that shall come to pass. The reason it is usually assumed that the argument demonstrates exhaustive definite foreknowledge, I shall argue, is that we have neglected a set of propositions that should be included in P2.

To begin, it is usually assumed that propositions of the form 'x will do y' or 'x will not do y' cover the whole of the future. But this is the case only if we assume the classical view that the whole of the future is eternally and exhaustively definite. In this case future events either will (definitely) or will not (definitely) happen. Hence, propositions are either true or false in relation to these eternally definite realities. And the omniscient God of course knows them as such.

But if we don't make this metaphysical assumption—an assumption, note, which is strictly about the nature of the world God created, not about the scope of God's knowledge—then we immediately see that there's no reason to assume that everything about the future can be expressed in this 'will' or 'will not' form. The future could include things that that 'may' or 'may not' happen. And propositions that express these 'maybes' must be included as among the propositions in P2 that an omniscient God would know.

In my estimation, one of the most significant omissions in the classical tradition's reflections on the nature of omniscience was that it never considered the distinctive set of what we might call 'might-counterfactual' propositions. To be sure, Molinists considered the set of 'would-counterfactual' propositions and thus held that God not only knows what will and will not happen, but also what would and would not happen in every alternative possible world (God's 'middle knowledge'). Would-counterfactuals in this schema are essentially 'will' and 'will-not' propositions applied to counterfactual worlds. What classical Molinists failed to see, however, was that the set of would-counterfactual propositions logically requires the logically distinct category of might-counterfactual propositions. For on the square of oppositions, the negation of a would-counterfactual is not a would-not counterfactual, but a *might*-not counterfactual.

To illustrate, if God knows that it is false that 'George would eat a cookie if offered', God knows that 'George *might not* eat a cookie if offered', not that 'George *would not* eat a cookie if offered'. God may of course also know that, as a matter of fact, George would not eat a cookie if offered. But this piece of information is distinct from his simply knowing the falsity of the proposition 'George would eat a cookie if offered'. The only thing God knows *by virtue of his knowing this proposition as false* is that 'George *might* not eat a cookie if offered'.

The ramifications of this insight are significant. For it means that there is a set of counterfactual propositions the truth value of which an omniscient God must know but which have not been given serious consideration in the church's theological tradition. If God knows the truth value of would-counterfactuals, he *must* by logical necessity know the truth value of might-counterfactuals.[39]

Now, one might argue that God knows the true value of all might-counterfactuals simply by knowing the truth value of all would-counterfactuals. The argument fails, however, for one cannot reduce might-counterfactuals to a logical subset of would-counterfactuals any more than one can reduce would-counterfactuals to a subset of might-counterfactuals.

---

39   Strictly speaking, referring to true propositions of the form 'x might and might not occur' as 'might-counterfactuals' is inaccurate, for true 'might-propositions' are *factual*, not *counter*factual. The assumption that all might-propositions express might-counterfactuals assumes that the future, as a matter of fact, is exhaustively settled. Hence all statements other than 'will-propositions' are *counter*factual. Still, to keep this essay from becoming overly idiosyncratic with new jargon I decided to use the standard logical semantics of referring to might-propositions as 'might-counterfactuals'.

To illustrate, if God knows George would eat a cookie if offered, God by logical necessity knows George might eat a cookie if offered. But merely by virtue of knowing George might eat a cookie if offered, God does not thereby know that George *would* eat a cookie if offered. The might-counterfactual can be true while the corresponding would-counterfactual is false. This demonstrates that might-counterfactuals constitute a distinct class of propositions the truth value of which an omniscient God must know.

The distinctness of might-counterfactuals is also demonstrated by noting that while the sub-contraries of would-counterfactuals cannot both be true—namely, it cannot be the case that 'George would *and* would not eat a cookie if offered'—the sub-contraries of might-counterfactuals *can* both be true—'George might and *might not* eat a cookie if offered'. If all might-counterfactuals were logically entailed by would-counter-factuals, by logical necessity it could never be the case that an agent might and might not do something, which seems patently absurd. If we grant that it is not a logical contradiction to affirm the truth of the proposition 'George might and might not eat a cookie', then we must grant that might-counterfactuals form a distinct class of propositions the truth value of which an omniscient God must know.

This demonstrates that there is no logical incompatibility between affirming that God is omniscient, on the one hand, while affirming that he knows some of the future as what might and might not happen, on the other. Indeed, it demonstrates that there *is* an incompatibility between affirming that God is omniscient, on the one hand, while *denying* that he could know some of the future as what might and might not happen, on the other.

It was, I believe, a metaphysical assumption about the eternally and exhaustively definite nature of reality on the part of classical theologians that led them to assume that 'will' and 'will not' (and, by extension to possible worlds, 'would' and 'would-not') propositions exhaust the set of propositions in P2 that an omniscient God would know. Jettison this assumption—which again, is an assumption about the nature of the world God created, not an assumption about the scope of omniscience—and one sees that P2 must include propositions about what 'might' and 'might not' happen.

WHAT 'WILL' AND 'MIGHT' BE TRUE

In the alternative framework I am proposing, God is omniscient in the strongest (and really only) sense of the term. God knows all truths and believes no falsehoods.

Propositions of the form 'x will occur' or 'x will not occur' are true if and only if the occurrence or non-occurrence of x is a definite feature of reality.[40] If in reality x may and may not occur, it is, strictly speaking, false to say 'x will occur' or 'x will not occur', or even that 'x would occur' or 'x would not occur', *even if x ends up occurring*. For at the time the proposition was uttered, the occurrence of x was not a definite aspect of the future—something that will or will not happen—but merely a *possible* occurrence (or possible non-occurrence) of the future. The propositions 'x will occur' or 'x will not occur' thus did not correspond to reality at the time the proposition was considered. If and when the occurrence of x becomes a definite aspect of the future, *then* it will be true to say 'x will occur' or that 'x would occur' in such and such a situation.

This proposal will undoubtedly strike some as paradoxical, for we are not accustomed to distinguishing between 'will' and 'will not' propositions and 'might' and 'might not' propositions in this fashion. Conventional language rarely requires us to, on the one hand, and we in the Western tradition are accustomed to assuming an exhaustively definite view of reality and speaking about it in this fashion, on the other. We thus tend to assume that something either will or will not take place and that our talk of 'maybe's' is merely due to our ignorance of whether something will or will not take place. I suspect it was this assumption that explains why Pinnock inadvertently slipped into speaking about future free acts as unknowable realities—as though the facticity of these future acts in some sense already existed, but was unknowable.

Yet, if we grant that philosophy often has to make distinctions that conventional language isn't accustomed to making, and if we see that the assumption that reality is exhaustively and eternally definite is simply an assumption, not entailed by the omniscience of God, we will see that the distinction between events that 'will' or 'will not' happen and events that 'might' and 'might not' happen is valid and that it addresses ontology, not just epistemology. God is not bound by logical or metaphysical necessity to create a world the facticity of which is tenselessly given. The omniscient God could create a world in which some of the future is a 'maybe' if he so chose.[41] The uniqueness of the openness position lies in

---

40   The same applies to propositions of the form 'x would occur' or 'x would not occur'. They are true if and only if the occurrence or non-occurrence of x is a definite feature of the counterfactual possible world the propositions are indexed to.

41   Pinnock, 'Systematic Theology', p. 123, insightfully challenges classical theologians to 'ask themselves if they think God could create a world where he would not be in total control of everything, where he would experience risk and where he would not foreknow all decisions of his creatures in advance'. And he adds: 'Surely this must be possible if God is all-powerful.' One could more forcefully rephrase this as follows: Unless it is logically contradictory to affirm that an agent 'might and might not' make a choice, then denying that God could create a world in which some of the future is a

its claim that we have compelling grounds for believing that God created just such a world.

One may reject the openness position Pinnock has come to defend in his on-going endeavor to work out the implications of affirming a God of unbounded love. But despite his own occasional ill-advised expressions to the contrary, they cannot do so on the grounds that this view is incompatible with omniscience.

God's Infallible Anticipation

The second shortcoming of Pinnock's defense of the open view I wish to address may be considered more briefly. Pinnock has at times spoken of God in ways that give the impression that God can be caught off guard. For example, he refers to God as 'an "ad hoc" God...who responds and adapts to surprises and to the unexpected'.[42] He argues that since the 'future does not yet exist' it 'cannot be infallibly anticipated, even by God'.[43] Hence, for example, Pinnock maintains that 'God had not anticipated' Israel's rebellion.[44]

Now, I am again convinced my disagreement with Pinnock is more over phraseology than substance.[45] But it must be said that such ways of speaking only reinforce the impression expressed by Pinnock's critics that he does not really believe in the omniscience of God. They also play into the hands of the opponents such as Bruce Ware, who argues that the God of open theism is an anthropomorphic deity who 'can only guess what much of the future will bring' and who thus wrings his hands while he passively hopes for the best.[46] Such caricatures of the open view hit a

---

'maybe' constitutes a denial of God's omnipotence. For in this case one would be denying God the ability to do something that is logically possible to do.

It should also be noted that even if God chose to create a world that was eternally and exhaustively definite, as the classical view holds, he would *still* have to know the truth value of all might-counterfactuals. He would by divine fiat simply have rendered them all false. An omniscient God cannot avoid knowing the true value of propositions that are logically possible, whether they correspond to the reality he created or not. And might-counterfactual propositions are logically possible.

42   Pinnock, 'Systematic Theology', p. 113.
43   Pinnock, 'Systematic Theology', p. 123.
44   Pinnock, 'Systematic Theology', p. 122.
45   At other times Pinnock rightly emphasizes God's wise providential control over the world. See *Most Moved Mover*, pp. 102-104. In 'God Limits His Knowledge', p. 146, he even goes so far as to say: 'Nothing can happen which God has not anticipated or cannot handle.' I am convinced that Pinnock is simply not consistent in working out and expressing this theme.
46   B. Ware, *God's Lesser Glory: The Diminished God of Open Theism* (Wheaton, IL: Crossways Books, 2000), pp. 20-21, 216.

strong cord with the masses whose belief systems are significantly fueled by a need for security.

This way of construing God's relationship to the open future is unnecessary and misleading. For if we grant that God possesses unlimited intelligence, as scripture and the Christian tradition maintain, it becomes apparent that God can anticipate and prepare for possibilities as perfectly as he can future definite facts.

Consider that humans anticipate future definite facts we are certain of better than we do possibilities we are uncertain of only because *our intelligence is limited.* Having only so much intelligence to go around, we have to spread it thin in proportion to the number of possibilities we have to anticipate. The more possibilities we have to simultaneously consider, the less adept we are at anticipating them. This is why playing chess is much more stressful for us than (say) working on a perfectly predictable assembly line.

If we are not careful to avoid limiting God by making him in our own image, we end up ascribing the same difficulty to God. If God faces a multitude of possibilities as he moves into the future, some worry, he must only be capable of guessing at the future while anxiously wringing his hands! But this conclusion is premised on a complete denial of the infinite intelligence of God.

If God is truly unlimited in his intelligence, he doesn't have to divide it up, as it were, to cover any number of possibilities he might face. Indeed, a God of unlimited intelligence can consider each and every possibility within a virtually infinite set of possibilities as though each one were the *only* possibility he had to consider. We might say that for God to play any opponent in chess would be no more intellectually stressful than working on a perfectly predictable assembly line. Whatever possible game of chess his opponent might play, it would be from God's perspective as though it were the only possible game his opponent could play. Though there are millions of possible moves his opponent might make, whatever combination of moves he ends up making was perfectly anticipated by God before the game ever started!

This means that even if God faces a future partly composed of possibilities, he can never be caught off guard and is never fallible in his anticipation. True, when improbable events occur, a God who knows all probabilities with perfect accuracy and who wisely correlates his expectations with these probabilities would be in a limited sense surprised. He would be unwise if he *expected* the *improbable.* But being infinitely intelligent, he would be no less prepared for the unlikely than he is for the very likely or even the absolutely certain. Whatever transpires, however unlikely, God has been anticipating it *as though it was certain* from the foundation of the world.[47]

This demonstrates that the open view of God can ascribe to God at least the same level of providential control over the world as any view that ascribes exhaustive definite foreknowledge to God while ascribing libertarian freedom to agents.[48] This also demonstrates that the main emotive objection to open theism—namely, that it presents an anthropomorphic God who cannot be trusted—is altogether unfounded. Though the criticism accuses the open view of being anthropomorphic, in truth the criticism itself presupposes an anthropomorphic God. Only a God limited in intelligence as we are would be reduced to guessing at the future, hoping for the best and wringing his hands in worry simply because he created a world in which he plays chess with free agents rather than works on a perfectly predictable assembly line.

Whatever transpires, the open theist can affirm along with the classical theists that 'God had anticipated this and was preparing a response to this from the foundation of the world'. The uniqueness of the open view lies in its additional belief that God is so smart he didn't need to be certain the event was going to take place in order for this to be true. If something else had taken place instead, *we'd be saying the exact same thing*!

In conclusion, I believe Pinnock has all the right intuitions regarding the nature of God and the nature of his providential control over the world. I find many of his arguments supporting his 'most moved mover' perspective to be brilliant and powerful. But his case would be strengthened even further if he was a bit more careful with the way he expressed himself and if he incorporated the above arguments regarding

---

47   Some have criticized the open view on the grounds that it attributes false beliefs to God. But if God is infinitely intelligent and thus correlates his beliefs perfectly with the probabilities he perfectly knows, there is no reason to ascribe to God mistaken beliefs. For example, God may infallibly believe that there is (say) a 90% likelihood that Israel would turn to him in response to his love and discipline and thus wisely believes that they will turn to him. Hence God is forthright in telling us he *thought* Israel would turn to him even though it turned out they did not (Jer. 3.6-9, 19-20). Yet their failure to turn didn't falsify God's belief, for God *also* believed there was a 10% chance that Israel *would not* turn to him. On the other hand, if we follow the classical tradition and ascribe to God *only* beliefs that are 100% certain, *now* we have to ascribe to God false beliefs when he tells us he *thought* or *expected* one outcome when in fact a different outcome came to pass (cf. Isa. 5.1-5).

48   In point of fact the open view ascribes *more* providential control to God than the common Arminian view that holds that God simply foreknows what will come to pass ('Simple Foreknowledge'). For if God simply knows what *will* come to pass, he can't do anything about it. It *will* come to pass. God's view of the future only benefits his providential control if God can foreknow what *may* come to pass in order to *respond* to it, thereby affecting what *does* come to pass.

God's knowledge of might-counterfactuals and God's unlimited intelligence.

CHAPTER 4

The Love of an Open God

Delwin Brown

The open view of God, or 'openness theism', opens a number of avenues in theology today. Its most significant contribution is its idea of God, but openness theism is also important in other ways. It reintroduces into North American theological conservatism a dynamism and intellectual courage that characterized it only rarely during the past century. To find a comparable conservative creativity one must go back to the genuine debates and willingness to change that characterized the Princeton School at its high point in the late 1800s. Openness theism also opens up North American evangelicalism as a religious movement in hopeful ways. The siege mentality of evangelicalism, its isolationism and indifference to modern thought, and the too frequent arrogance of its most visible spokespersons are absent among the openness thinkers, who rightly claim the evangelical heritage as their own. Finally, openness theology furthers in quite remarkable ways the break up of the labels and stereotypes that characterized North American Christian theology at least since the mid-twentieth century. Liberal or conservative, ecclesiastical or academic, and even modern or postmodern are increasingly fuzzy distinctions, and this is illustrated by the openness theologies which stand within the tradition that has in much of its past depended on sharp distinctions as a vehicle of its self-identity.

The openness of openness theism—and, I think, the openness of any theological perspective at its best—is nowhere better exemplified than in the writings of Clark Pinnock. Among the works by Pinnock on my shelves I keep two side by side, *A Defense of Biblical Infallibility*[1] and *The Scripture Principle*.[2] Together they demonstrate that theologians can be guided by abiding convictions without being imprisoned by dog-

---

1   C.H. Pinnock, *A Defense of Biblical Infallibility* (Philadelphia: Presbyterian and Reformed Publishing Company, 1967).
2   C.H. Pinnock, *The Scripture Principle* (San Francisco: Harper & Row, 1984).

matism. Pinnock's work has always been characterized by intellectual honesty, analytical care, and moral intensity, and driven by an unswerving confidence in the providential worth of scripture. These have been changeless. But together in him they have somehow generated an openness to criticism, alternatives and change that deserves nothing but the highest admiration and appreciation, even from those of us who disagree with him.[3]

God is Love

Classical Christian theology developed within the context of a Hellenistic worldview. Understandably, it was both enriched and limited by the resources of this worldview. Chief among these limitations for Christian theology was the idea of perfection inherited from the Greeks.[4] According to this idea a perfect being is fully self-contained, meaning for the Greeks a being that is unchanging and therefore unrelated to and unaffected by anything beyond itself. Since the Christian God is perfect, the ancient theologians reasoned, it must follow that God is unchanging, unrelated, and unaffected. But these are strange claims to make about the God of the Bible, who appears to be intimately related to the world, interacting with it, and to whom this world seems to make a difference. How can a God who lovingly created a changing world be unrelated to it and unaffected by it? Much of the energy of classical theology was directed toward trying to square the biblical portrayal of God with Greek philosophical assumptions and cultural values because these were at the time the prerequisites of credible thinking. The results were impressive and often ingenious but, in the end, manifestly inadequate.

Openness theologians, among many others, have noted that the contemporary Western worldview, including that of science, is in important ways more hospitable to Christian claims about the biblical God.[5] Change, relatedness and sensitivity are now deemed to be values in

---

3   The intent of this essay, however, is not to promote another point of view. The intent is to offer an 'internal criticism' of openness theology, that is, to adopt its general standpoint for the purpose of collegial exploration and to suggest how the viewpoint might be differently, and perhaps better, developed in order to achieve its own ends.

4   C.H. Pinnock, *Most Moved Mover: A Theology of God's Openness* (Grand Rapids, MI: Baker Books, 2001), pp. 116-19. See also W. Hasker, 'A Philosophical Perspective', in C. Pinnock, R. Rice, J. Sanders, W. Hasker and D. Basinger, *The Openness of God: A Biblical Challenge to the Traditional Understanding of God* (Downers Grove, IL: InterVarsity Press, 1994), pp. 127-34.

5   Pinnock, *Most Moved Mover*, pp. 119-22. See also Hasker, 'Philosophical Perspective', pp. 127-34.

human relations and held to have analogues in the natural sphere. Perfection, then, is hardly their absence; rather, in some respect or other perfection is likely to be their chief exemplification. And what more fully encompasses an openness to healthy change, sensitivity, and relatedness than love? So what concept could better express the meaning of perfection than the idea of a God of love?

Openness theologians, however, do not make love the central attribute of God because the modern worldview seems more amenable to it. While welcoming this more hospitable intellectual and cultural environment, they assert that God is love because that is the Christian claim. Richard Rice writes, '[T]he statement *God is love* embodies an essential biblical truth. It indicates that love is central, not incidental, to the nature of God... [I]t is the one divine activity that most fully and vividly discloses God's inner reality. Love, therefore, is the very essence of the divine nature.'[6] And two pages later he adds: 'Love...is the basic source from which *all* of God's attributes arise.'[7] Others, too, make love the essence of the divine. According to Clark Pinnock, 'The open view of God emphasizes that he is a loving person; love is the very essence of his being... Love is more than an attribute; it is God's very nature. How strange then that love appears so far down on the list of God's attributes in conventional theism—it comes after discussions of the metaphysical and under the category of ethical attributes. This arrangement itself shows the influence of Greek thought. Where is the fundamental insight that God is essentially self-communicating love?'[8]

The insight that God is 'self-communicating love' finds its fullest and most systematic expression, according to openness theists, in the doctrine of the Trinity. 'The doctrine of the Trinity is the centerpiece of Christian theism', Pinnock says. 'It does not portray God as a solitary, domineering individual but as the essence of loving community... The Trinity points to a relational ontology in which God is...essentially relational, ecstatic and alive. God exists as diverse persons united in a communion of love and freedom.'[9] John Sanders makes the same point: 'The Father, Son and Holy Spirit love one another. They are involved in a tripersonal community in which each member of the triune being gives and receives love from the others. Relationality is an *essential* aspect of God. The

---

6   R. Rice, 'Biblical Support for a New Perspective', in Pinnock, Rice, Sanders, Hasker and Basinger, *Openness of God*, pp. 18-19.

7   Rice, 'Biblical Support', p. 21.

8   Pinnock, *Most Moved Mover*, pp. 81-82.

9   C.H. Pinnock, 'Systematic Theology', in Pinnock, Rice, Sanders, Hasker and Basinger, *Openness of God*, pp. 107-108. Cf., too, Pinnock, *Most Moved Mover*, pp. 83-84.

tripersonal God is the perfection of love and communion'.[10] Sanders adds: 'the Trinity experiences and manifests the fullness of love. The members of the Trinity experience the agape love of one another: an unselfish, nonmanipulative love.'[11]

The importance of the doctrine of the Trinity, for openness theology as for classical theology, is not simply quantitative, i.e., its delineation of the 'tripartite' nature of deity. It is even more important qualitatively because it defines the nature of the godhead. God is communal, relational, interactive, open, dynamic, etc., and God is these, moreover, in a manner that must be understood in the context of divine love. Even this, however, is insufficient to capture the distinctiveness of the Christian view of deity. The love of God, according to the historic Christian witness, is agape. Self-communicating agape is the central and defining feature of the divine nature. Speaking about agape, Richard Rice makes the point quite effectively: 'From a Christian perspective, *love* is the first and last word in the biblical portrait of God. According to 1 John 4:8: "Whoever does not love does not know God, because God is love [agape]." The immediate context of these familiar words is instructive. "This is how God showed his love among us: He sent his one and only Son into the world that we might live through him. This is love…that [God] loved us and sent his Son as an atoning sacrifice for our sins."… As these verses show, God's love was completed in sending his Son.'[12] The love that is manifest 'in sending his Son' is agape.

Love is Agape

Twentieth-century discussions of the meaning and place of agape in Christian thought were decisively influenced by Anders Nygren's work, *Agape and Eros*.[13] Nygren argued that agape love is the fundamental motif of Christianity and that by which Christianity is set apart from all other religions. More than that, Nygren insisted that agape is incommensurate with other forms of love, in particular with the Greek notion of eros which is the human longing for and ascent to the divine. Agape, as we see in the quotation from Richard Rice, is that love that gives of itself wholly and without restriction for another. And the 'other' as Rice and 1 John 4.8 depict it has a special meaning, a meaning best understood in the contrast of agape and eros. If eros is to be viewed as the love of the lesser for an other that is greater and thus deserving, agape

---

10   J. Sanders, *The God Who Risks: A Theology of Providence* (Downers Grove, IL: InterVarsity Press, 1998), p. 175.

11   Sanders, *God Who Risks*, p. 176.

12   Rice, 'Biblical Support', p. 18.

13   A. Nygren, *Agape and Eros* (Philadelphia: Westminster Press, 4th edn, 1953).

is to be viewed as the love of the greater for an other that is lesser and thus undeserving—God 'sent his Son...for our sins'.

The criticisms of Nygren have been many and frequently justified. Nygren's assumption that each religion has a single, fundamental motif is hard to demonstrate. His contention that other religions contain no hint of a self-giving love for the lesser is too strong. His claim that agape is the only love espoused in Christianity is odd; it makes puzzling, for example, the biblical injunction that humans should love God. His insistence that agape is incompatible with other forms of love—such as the love of the higher (eros) and the love of the equal (mutuality)—is untenable. At the base of Nygren's error lies his failure to take into account the relational character of all things, including humans and God. As Daniel Day Williams observed soon after the publication of *Agape and Eros*, 'Nygren overlooks the fact that the relationship between a man and his neighbor and between man and God is fundamentally a social relationship in which the good of one actually does become the good of the other'.[14] It follows that giving to the other, other-love, can also be giving to oneself, i.e., self-love, and vice versa. Love of the other is compatible with love of the self; love of the self is compatible with love of the other. Therefore it also follows that no object of love can be wholly unworthy of love, for even if we were to bracket claims of the intrinsic worth of every creature it remains the case that any love of the other can in principle also be a love that contributes to the self.

These criticisms aside, Nygren's insistence that God's love includes a love of the lesser remains central, I think, to the Christian claim about God. This is the import of the insight that God's love is agapic. We need not say that it is the love of the undeserving, though there is an important sense in which that is the case with respect to humans, and certainly we need not say that agape is the love of that which is, or those who are, without merit, without worth. Nor must we say that God's love is only agapic. But Nygren highlights a persistent Christian insight when he insists that divine love is a love of that which is less than God and therefore a love that is graciously given, a love emergent from the character of the lover independent of the quality of the loved. That is why agape is deemed to be of the essence of God; God's love of the lesser is not simply a fortunate turn of events but an irrepressible expression of the very being of God and therefore of the nature of things. It is of God's essence, and thus an essential fact of reality. Even that which is of qualified value is loved by God without qualification.

---

14   D.D. Williams, *God's Grace and Man's Hope* (New York: Harper & Brothers, 1949), p. 72. See, too, D.D. Williams, *The Spirit and the Forms of Love* (New York: Harper & Row, 1968).

This is a claim of enormous pastoral importance. To affirm that God is agape is to affirm that creatures of all gradations of worth are cherished, and, moreover, that their being so valued is not some fortunate evolutionary accident or a human construction; it is a fact grounded in the very nature of things. All things, whatever the measure of their worth, are loved. This is so crucial because obviously there are gradations of value, whether within the human community or in the larger creation. As for humans, the musical talents of some individuals are superior to those of others, certain forms of art are in some cultural traditions more advanced than in others, some political systems are better for certain purposes than others, and these examples ignore the moral gradations that are of such overriding existential import in human life. The examples are endless, even if many are also quite properly debated, and even if our judgments in these matters are relative to circumstance and always fallible. We live and decide based on the assumption that gradations of real value or worth relative to certain purposes do exist. But if there is a God who transcends all other values and yet cherishes each, then no gradations are absolute because all differentiations of worth are trumped by a universal love that loves all that is, inexhaustibly and without reservation. The agape of God for the world grounds the worth of each and every creature in the nature of deity and thus in the fundamental truth about all things.

Those who believe in the agapic God, then, enjoy a sense of worth beyond the relative and variable worths that are of human making. But further, those who love the agapic God love what this God loves. The difference that divine agape makes is not only the grounding of all value, including one's own, in a loving deity; it is also the experience of one's own obligation to cherish what God cherishes. To love the God of agape is to strive to live a life that manifests agape. The one who loves God strives for a love of others that is not bound to calibrations of worth. God's love is given defiant of gradations; so, too, should ours be given. If the social character of existence is kept in mind, the health of agape is apparent. To enrich the other with a love not bound by calculations is to enrich one's self as well as the other. To be the recipient of that love even when we are unworthy relative to others is to be given a transforming treasure. The notion that God is agape gives a sense of personal worth, and a vision for living in the world.

The persistent claim of Christians has been that God is essentially agape. This is revolutionary in the human sphere because it overturns the utilitarian way in which humans are prone to assess and value others and the world. The Christian claim about God means that this revolutionary vision is grounded in the nature of things. To understand reality is to understand that this is the way things are essentially and therefore fundamentally, because this is the way God is essentially and fundamentally.

Agape is Creator

Many theologians today locate what appears to be distinctive in, and certainly what they deem to be decisive about, the Christian understanding of God in the doctrine of the Trinity. The principal point of trinitarian doctrine, many add, is its insight that God is relational, interactive, dynamic and loving.[15] To make this point, of course, the doctrine of the Trinity must be rescued from its more liberal construal which is the view that the Father, Son and Holy Spirit are 'persons' only in the sense of being different manifestations or roles of the divine, much as one woman can be mother, wife, and musician. Historically, the doctrine of the Trinity has been the much more difficult claim that God is three subjects of experience in some perfect unity.[16] As perplexing as it is, this concept of Trinity conveys in quite an astonishing way the sense of a deity whose very being is communal love. So even before the creation of the world, God was, and is eternally, a social reality whose being is constituted by the interactive life of Father, Son and Spirit. The persons of the Godhead exist in social relationships—they are related, they interact, they are a relational community of shared love.[17]

What this construal of the Trinity conveys about God is insightful, and powerful—God is essentially social, God is essentially relational, God is essentially dynamic, God is essentially loving. It does not, however, convey everything of importance that one might wish to say about God. To illustrate, Sanders observes that the doctrine of the Trinity does not communicate the vulnerability and even precariousness that might be said to characterize God's love.[18] The love of the members of the Trinity for each other is not subject to refusal or the risk of rejection. Trinitarian love is fully shared, fully assured. One may or may not, then, want to say that God's love is essentially and thus eternally vulnerable, but if one does wish to say that then Sanders is correct in observing that the trinitarian character of God is an insufficient basis for the claim.

Sanders' observation points to a larger issue: neither is the trinitarian character of God sufficient to ground the claim that God is agape.

---

15 See, e.g., the quite interesting Calvinist interpretation of the Trinity in D.L. Migliore, *Faith Seeking Understanding: An Introduction to Christian Theology* (Grand Rapids, MI: Eerdmans, 1991).

16 J. Moltmann, *The Trinity and the Kingdom of God* (San Francisco: Harper & Row, 1981).

17 Sanders, *God Who Risks*, p. 175

18 Sanders, *God Who Risks*, p. 178.

Indeed, if God can exist solely within the trinitarian community, if the essence of God is conveyed in the Trinity, then God is not essentially agape. Why? Because there is no lesser in the Trinity; trinitarian love is shared among equals. Therefore the love that characterizes the trinitarian community is not an agapic love any more than it is a vulnerable love or a precarious love. It is mutual, egalitarian love. Divine agape can only be expressed in relation to a world. Only if there is a world of lesser value than God—indeed, only *when* there is such a world—can God be agape. Further, if there is not always a world, God cannot always be agape, and if God cannot always be agape then it can hardly be said that agape is in any sense the 'essence' of the divine.

Christian theology has consistently maintained that God is love. More than that, Christian theology has consistently claimed that the love of God is agapic love. In addition, Christian theology has frequently stated and commonly implied that agape is not simply one among the many characteristics of God; it is the definitive characteristic. In other words, it is impossible to think of the God of the Christian witness of faith without thinking of this God as agape. But that is precisely what we are able to do if we can think of the Christian God as existing independently of some world. And if it is possible for God to exist apart from the world, then God is not essentially agape.

This conclusion could perhaps be avoided in a couple of different ways. One is to say that there was a time in God's life before which the divine essence was realized. That is odd language, at the very least, and in any case it seems to imply that there was a time before which God reached the perfection of agape. Another is to distinguish between what we are able to think about God and God's reality—not simply to say that God exceeds our thoughts, which no one denies, but rather to say that God in reality contradicts what is true about God in human thought. The former, even if coherent, is tantamount to saying that God is characterized by moral development. The latter embraces a kind of anti-rationalism. Neither option, I assume, would be attractive to openness theologians.

The choice, at least for openness theology, appears to be this: either God is essentially agape in which case God and world—some world outside of God—co-exist everlastingly, or God as Trinity preexisted the world and so the essence of God is love, but not agapic love. In sum, the doctrine that God is essentially agape seems to force us to deny creation *ex nihilo*; the doctrine of creation *ex nihilo* seems to force us to deny that God is essentially agape. Should agape be abandoned?

Earlier I noted the pastoral importance of saying that the essence of God is agape. It means that there is no truth more fundamental than the claim that the highest good reaches down in love to us and to all that is less than God. It means that divine compassion is the ultimate and ineradicable truth of things. And this intuition is so contrary to conventional thought, and in such tension with ordinary evidence, that it has, of seeming necessity, been grounded in some special evidentiary locus. It has been grounded in christology. Indeed, one might say quite plausibly that here, precisely, is the point of christology: 'This is love...that [God]...sent his Son as an atoning sacrifice for our sins.' Christology would certainly seem to be the claim that God is agape, and if Christ is properly said to reveal the essence of God then the essence of God is agape. So the pastoral point is tightly connected to a systematic christological point.

Another way to contemplate the cost of abandoning the claim that the essence of God is agape is to review the following statements, all *adapted* from the openness theologians quoted above in order to make explicit what I assume to be their evangelical (in the root sense of the term) meaning:

> The statement 'God is agape' embodies an essential biblical truth. It indicates that agape is central, not incidental, to the nature of God. It is the one divine activity that most fully and vividly discloses God's inner reality. Agape, therefore, is the very essence of the divine nature.

> Agape is the basic source from which *all* of God's attributes arise.

> The open view of God emphasizes that agape is the very essence of God's being.

> Agape is more than an attribute; it is God's very nature.

> How strange that agape appears so far down on the list of God's attributes in conventional theism—it comes after discussions of the metaphysical and under the category of ethical attributes. This arrangement itself shows the influence of Greek thought. Where is the fundamental insight that God is essentially self-communicating agape?

The point of reviewing these adapted statements is this: they are impossible if agape is not essential to the nature of God. It is true that these openness theologians did not specifically use the term 'agape' in the statements cited, but surely that is the intent of their claims, and correctly so, precisely because their claims are so consistently based in christology. To abandon the claim that agape is essential to the divine nature is to abandon the claim that Christ discloses the fundamental truth about God and thus the fundamental truth about the world: 'This is love...that God sent his Son.'

Divine Agape and Divine Freedom

In order to preserve the claim that God is essentially agape, should we abandon the doctrine of creation *ex nihilo*? Should we accept the other alternative identified above, namely that there is always some world beyond God that is the object of God's agape?

Openness theologians consistently and vigorously maintain the doctrine of creation *ex nihilo*. Significantly, they do not place heavy emphasis on the biblical texts in support of their viewpoint. This is in part the case, one assumes, because they are adverse to proof-texting, but in this instance it would probably be futile because the drift of the scant evidence of a biblical view is not clearly in the direction of creation *ex nihilo*. Genesis 1.1-3 speaks of God as creator of heaven and earth, but immediately goes on to say that this creation was 'out of' something else, something without form and void. Isaiah 43.1, 7 and 45.8 equate divine creation—whether of a person, of Israel, or of the heavens and earth— with the potter's activity of forming a pot out of pre-existing clay. Pinnock cites Hebrews 11.3 and Romans 4.17 as, apparently, precursors of the idea of creation *ex nihilo*.[19] The Hebrews passage says that the world was created by the word of God out of things that do not appear, and Romans refers to God calling into existence things that do not exist. Either verse could perhaps be construed in rough support of Pinnock, but neither passage presupposes creatio *ex nihilo* as its only interpretive framework. In fact, it would probably be impossible to discern any clear view on this topic in the Bible because the biblical writers were not likely given to thinking about this matter, at least in any fine detail.

The more important basis for the doctrine of creation *ex nihilo* among openness theologians is theological. The theological rationale appears to be two-fold. First, there is the desire to protect God's self-sufficiency.[20] Partly this seems to mean that God is self-sufficient in being, needing 'nothing else in order to be',[21] and partly that God is self-sufficient in value, complete 'in himself' so that nothing, not even the world, could make God greater. Pinnock effectively puts both points together: 'Putting it bluntly, God's nature would be complete and his love fulfilled even without a world to love.'[22] The other theological reason for defending creation *ex nihilo* is the desire to affirm creation as an act of grace, an act of divine freedom not required by God's nature, not even

---

19   Pinnock, *Most Moved Mover*, p. 146.
20   Pinnock, *Most Moved Mover*, pp. 125, 145; and 'Systematic Theology', p. 110.
21   Pinnock, 'Systematic Theology', p. 113.
22   Pinnock, *Most Moved Mover*, p. 145, cf. p. 125.

by God's love.[23] 'Creation', Pinnock says, 'is an act of free grace and generosity, the work of a God whose disposition is to be generous'.[24]

With respect to God's self-sufficiency in value, Pinnock writes: 'Creation is a more than necessary fact and God is no greater for having done it. God is unsurpassable, whether or not there is a world.'[25] In a certain sense this point is well-taken. Left unelaborated, however, it seems to trade on the substance metaphysics of the classical worldview which openness theists have taken pains to reject. In the classical worldview, stemming from the Greeks, the most self-sufficient things are the least related, so an absolutely self-sufficient entity would be wholly unrelated to anything beyond itself. From this perspective, divine self-sufficiency means that relationships beyond the Godhead (that is, beyond God's trinitarian self-relatedness) are extraneous to the divine nature. Read from this perspective, Pinnock's statement seems to reiterate the classical dismissal of needed relationships as signs of weakness. In the modern worldview, on the contrary, to be at all is to be related; relationships are 'needed' simply in order to be. They are a condition of being at all. In this worldview, God's perfect self-sufficiency is God's unsurpassable capacity to be, not unrelated, but perfectly related—related to all things, without restriction or impediment. This very capacity, however, issues into full and unencumbered relationships with the world, and necessarily so if this value in God, the value of relatedness, is real. After all, a God who is able to be related but is not related is deficient. The imperfect value of that to which God might be related would not threaten or compromise the divine 'self-sufficiency'. God's self-sufficiency refers to the comprehensiveness and completeness of God's relationships to all that is, and to God's unlimited capacity to assimilate these relationships into the divine experience for the furtherance of the divine purposes.

On this view, an agapic God is no greater for having created a world precisely because the idea of such a God not creating a world is a contradictory idea. In other words, 'God's not creating' is not a conceivable condition or state to which a greater or lesser comparison can be made. Pinnock is therefore correct to say that 'God does not need a world in the sense of having a deficiency in his nature'.[26] But that, of course, is because in a relational world relationships are not deficiencies, especially not for God, and being related to a world is not a deficiency, especially not for the God of agapic love.

With respect to whether creation can be a gift of grace if it is compelled by God's love, we can perhaps clarify this issue by noting that we do not

---

23   Pinnock, *Most Moved Mover*, pp. 125, 144-45; Pinnock, 'Systematic Theology', pp. 110-11.

24   Pinnock, *Most Moved Mover*, p. 145.

25   Pinnock, *Most Moved Mover*, p. 125.

26   Pinnock, 'Systematic Theology', p. 110.

ordinarily say of a gift given in love that it is not free. Actions compelled by love or kindness are still regarded as gracious actions, if, that is, they are caused by such inner qualities and not forced by external circumstance. Why, then, is saying that God, being agape, could not refrain from creating a good world, tantamount to saying that the creation is not free and therefore not a gracious act? For openness theologians the nub of the matter seems to be divine freedom. That is a reasonable concern. In human relationships if we were to discover that the love that issued in gift-giving was produced by a secretly administered drug, or that the issuance of the gift was itself produced by hypnosis, we would not think of the gift as freely and graciously given. It therefore makes sense for Pinnock to want to say, on the one hand, that the creation is 'a product of God's overflowing love', and yet, on the other, that the 'creation is a more than necessary fact', meaning that God's creation of a world is an act of divine freedom.[27] But is there a way to affirm the freedom of divine creation and, at the same time, to affirm that the essence of God is agape?

A debate in theology since at least the high Middle Ages may be of some assistance here. The alternatives are represented (whether or not accurately is a separate question) by Thomas Aquinas and John Duns Scotus. Aquinas made the intellect primary in the divine nature, whereas Scotus insisted that God's will is primary. The debates among their followers led into some rather arcane discussions, but the primary insistence of Duns Scotus was simply that God is free, that the essence of God is the divine freedom. The issue was primarily one of God's self-sufficiency, particularly with respect to the being of God.

The freedom of God was conceived so radically as to say that the very being of God emerges out of God's own freedom. This is the medieval doctrine of the divine aseity—God is *a se*, God comes from Godself. Neither the being of God nor the character of God depends on circumstances beyond God, from which it follows that God's reality and God's nature can be absolutely dependable. And the Christian belief is that this possibility is realized, that in fact God is dependable—God is faithful.

The divine faithfulness under discussion here, of course, is analogous to its imperfect representation in humans, not to the 'mechanical' regularity of things in non-human nature. The sun rises regularly but not faithfully. We can say that humans are faithful to a cause, however, because we assume that their consistent support arises out of their freedom, i.e., they are free to do something other than what they regularly do on behalf of the cause. Their faithful actions come from themselves, their own relative freedom. The 'Scotist' contention, similarly, is that God's

---

27   Pinnock, *Most Moved Mover*, p. 125.

actions are faithful precisely because they arise out of God's freedom. From this claim there arose in the medieval discussion the question whether it is therefore possible for God to choose to sin. The answer to that presumably depends on what one means by sin, but certainly it would have to be said that a free God is able to choose to be something other than agape love. If God is agape, that love stems from divine choice, not from divine necessity. God is faithfully loving because God's love for us emerges from and continuously depends on God's choosing to be loving. Christians believe that God is essentially agape. The 'Scotist' argument is, in effect, that for agape to be a gift of divine faithfulness it must arise out of God's freedom. Hence, the essence of God is freedom.

Now the question arises whether there is any substantive sense in which both claims can be true—that God is essentially free, and that God is essentially agape.

If above all else the openness theologians wish to protect the freedom of God (for a number of perfectly good reasons), then they are bound to say that God's essence, in a metaphysical sense, is freedom. Freedom is God's essence. But freedom in itself is formless, the capacity to do something. Of necessity, freedom actualized must be expressed in this way or that. The Christian claim is that in God freedom takes the form of agape; in freedom God consistently constitutes the divine self as agape. One way to put this is to say that freedom is God's metaphysical essence, but agape is God's volitional essence.[28] To be sure, agape, on this view, is not the divine essence in the sense of strict necessity. The Christian claim that God is agape, however, is probably not best understood as a metaphysical claim; it is a religious claim about God's character. It is the claim that everywhere and in all circumstances God is the one who reaches down in love even to the least ones. Agape is not one divine quality among others; it *is* the divine character constituted in divine freedom.

The conviction that God, being agape, everlastingly loves a world, however, presupposes another: that God everlastingly gives being to the world that is always the object of divine love. Thomas Aquinas pointed out that from a Christian standpoint God would be the explanation of the world if the world always existed or if it came into being 'in time'. Whatever its duration, Thomas insisted, we still must give an account of the fact that the world is at all. The explanation of the world, whether finite or infinite, is God.

If the world always is, the explanation of the world is always God. Affirming that the world always is, that there is always some world created

---

28   I developed this view at greater length in *To Set At Liberty: Christian Faith and Human Freedom* (Maryknoll, NY: Orbis, 1981).

by God, enables the openness theologian to protect the insight that God is agape. On this view, there is always a world, not as a given presented to God,[29] but as that to which God gives being. God does need the world, but this is a need that God, in choosing love, has chosen for himself. God is always agape because God in freedom is always the creator of a world which is the object of God's love.[30]

---

29   The typical view of process theology is that the world (some world) is an everlasting given for God, like God without beginning or end. God does not account for the existence of the world; the divine role lies in continuously interacting with and thus lovingly shaping the world that co-exists with God.

30   I am grateful to Mr Demian Wheeler for his research assistance in the preparation of this essay.

CHAPTER 5

Knowing and Supposing:
The Prescience of God

Robert Cook

We dance round in a ring and suppose,
But the Secret sits in the middle and knows.
Robert Frost

I feel genuinely honoured to have a part in this *Festschrift*. It seems that Pinnock's work has funded my thinking ever since I started my theological journey in the 1970s. Indeed, my early teaching was pretentiously peppered with references to my 'ektheses', a term I had culled from *Biblical Revelation*[1] and even now only half understand (when exactly does a thesis become an ekthesis?). My most endearing memory of him, however, was at the 1991 London Tyndale conference on religious pluralism. He sat laconically before a pretty straight-laced audience of British evangelical academics and stretching out his rangy legs he congratulated the participants on a typical British conference of highly technical and erudite papers about nothing of any central interest. He then proceeded to look at all the important issues regarding the salvation of the unevangelized, eloquently propounding his bold version of inclusivism. I recall some were scandalized and he certainly faced a hostile discussion session afterwards (is it significant that his paper did not appear in the book of the conference?[2]). But I was enthralled and within me his fan-base grew.

My chapter will examine some elements of a more recent controversy, however, that of openness theism and the problem of divine fore-knowledge. Pinnock has been stirring it up again and I have been

---

1   C.H. Pinnock, *Biblical Revelation* (Chicago, IL: Moody Press, 1971).

2   A.D. Clarke and B.W. Winter (eds), *One God, One Lord in a World of Religious Pluralism* (Cambridge: Tyndale House, 1991).

scalding my hands reading some of the articles and correspondence in *Christianity Today*.[3] Recently re-reading Plato's *Apology* I found myself thanking God for healthy controversialists like Pinnock. Here is Socrates defending himself in a trial for his life and it has a surprisingly current ring about it:

> It is literally true, even if it sounds rather comical, that God has specially appointed me to this city, as though it were a large thoroughbred horse which because of its great size is inclined to be lazy and needs the stimulation of some stinging fly. It seems to me that God has attached me to this city to perform the office of such a fly, and all day long I never cease to settle here, there, and everywhere, rousing, persuading, reproving every one of you. You will not easily find another like me, gentlemen, and if you take my advice you will spare my life.[4]

So I write this out of great respect for a contemporary gadfly who is no stranger to trials by his peers.[5] But Pinnock, please keep off the hemlock!

So, to the issue of divine prescience. I have long admired the Frost couplet that forms the epigraph to this chapter. In our context it has a neat ambiguity. Certainly too often we theologians claim an unwarranted certainty and in the current foreknowledge debate it would be refreshing to find more sentences in the literature beginning, 'I suppose...' But also Frost reminds us that, uniquely, 'the Secret' has supreme knowledge. The point at issue, however, is what constitutes supreme knowledge? God knows all that is logically knowable but does this include the contingent future?

There is a maxim of Goethe: 'Everything has been thought of before, but the problem is to think of it again.' This is not least true of the foreknowledge controversy and it is my purpose to remind both sides of some insights which can be, and often have been, overlooked in the current evangelical discussion. After some preliminary thoughts on the hermeneutics and epistemology employed, I will present some challenges first to Pinnock and then to his opponents before finally focusing on the practical issues of guidance and providence.

---

3   Particularly from February 2000 to August 2001.
4   Plato, *The Collected Dialogues* (New York: Bollingen Foundation, 1963), pp. 16-17.
5   In response to Pinnock's view, the prestigious American Evangelical Theological Society passed a resolution in 2001 affirming God's foreknowledge (253 to 66 with 41 members abstaining).

Hermeneutics and Epistemology

While his opponents have criticized Pinnock for squeezing scripture through the sieve of process theism with his teaching on the immanence and temporality of God, he has retorted by accusing them of Hellenistic presuppositions with their tendency towards a static divine ontology.[6] Both sides object, protesting that they are governed by the testimony of scripture, the role of philosophy being to enable them to elucidate this testimony. This view is, in fact, commonly emphasized by evangelical scholars when engaged in this debate, for instance G.A. Boyd writes, 'exegesis should always drive our philosophy, instead of the other way around'.[7]

In contrast, I want to suggest that while one might want to make the strong ontological affirmation that one's ultimate religious authority is scripture[8] and that scripture is true in all that it affirms, in fact the hermeneutical task of understanding scripture involves a very complex and dialectical epistemology where a variety of knowledge sources are employed. Indeed, it is just not possible, or desirable, to place all one's culture, tradition, philosophy and experience in abeyance so as to hear the pure strains of biblical revelation. Nor is it possible, even, to place these sources into a hierarchy, for inevitably it is as true to say as a Christian that I understand scripture in the light of my culture and experience as it is that I understand my experience in the light of scripture and culture. There is a non-foundational, interlocking epistemological chain-mail here.

Neither is it possible to find a manifestly literal and univocal biblical ascription of God by which to judge other claims, philosophical, experiential or otherwise. As Nicholas Wolterstorff has pointed out, even in puzzling over such basics as whether God is self-consistent it would not be enough to find a verse which records 'I, God, do not contradict myself', because the proposition could have been uttered ironically.[9] There is just no way round developing a Perfect Being natural theology which one will expect to be consistent with divine biblical disclosure. This is not reducing scripture to a 'nose of wax' because, as has been said, the process is dialectical. One's notion of Perfect Being will be affected, for instance, by the challenging teaching and example of Jesus Christ as

---

6   T. Gray and C. Sinkinson (eds), *Reconstructing Theology: A Critical Assessment of the Theology of Clark Pinnock* (Carlisle: Paternoster Press, 2000), p. 147.

7   G.A. Boyd, 'The Open-Theism View', in J. Belby and P. Eddy (eds), *Divine Foreknowledge: Four Views* (Carlisle: Paternoster Press, 2001), p. 14.

8   Isn't it preferable to say that God is the ultimate authority and observe that scripture itself points to the concomitant revelation of God in the world, e.g. Ps. 19.1-4?

9   N. Wolterstorff, *Divine Discourse: Philosophical Reflections on the Claim that God Speaks* (Cambridge: Cambridge University Press, 1995), p. 206.

recorded in scripture. There is the dual danger then of, on the one hand, failing to hear what God is actually saying in scripture because of presuppositional prejudice of what it is thought God must be like, and, on the other hand, of reading scripture and concluding that God must be a certain kind of being who actually falls short of reasonable canons of ethics and perfection. As in so many areas of the Christian life, certainty is not humanly available and we must proceed with humility and fear and trembling in the realm of 'supposing'. Let us not naively assume, therefore, that it is a straightforward matter to critique one's experience or culture or philosophy by subjecting it to the clear teaching of scripture.

Background to the Recent Discussion of Foreknowledge

It is astonishing that openness theism has outraged so many. Arminianism with its rejection of God's total monergistic control of the future has been around since the seventeenth century and has been accepted within the evangelical mainstream. I would argue that this is the real Rubicon. Calvinism and Arminianism do have profoundly different conceptions of God and his ways. Kenneth Cracknell has been heard to quip that he worships with people of other faiths every Sunday in church.[10] And yet the two schools have learned to peacefully coexist, for example, the Reformed Baptist can lie down beside the Methodist. But now the relatively small step of Arminians querying foreknowledge has caused an evangelical outcry at the end of the last century. This is most surprising. For one thing it is not a new position or an idiosyncratic one of Pinnock and a few friends. One could, of course, go back to the Socinians in the sixteenth century, but moving to the twentieth, scholars have been arguing the case throughout most of the century. The American personalist philosopher, E.S. Brightman, for example, was writing in 1930, 'a God whose purpose is to develop a society of free persons must forgo some knowledge and some power if he is to attain his purpose'.[11] Since the 1970s, western theology has been dominated by the major schools of process theism in North America and the theology of hope in Europe. Following A.N. Whitehead, process theology rejected foreknowledge but it is perhaps not so well known that both Pannenberg and Moltmann reject exhaustive divine foreknowledge as well. Pannenberg, for example, has written, 'An almighty and omniscient

---

10   M. Forward, *A Short Introduction: Inter-Religious Dialogue* (Oxford: One World Publications, 2001), p. 120.

11   Quoted in C. Hartshorne and W.L. Reese (eds), *Philosophers Speak of God* (Chicago: University of Chicago Press, 1953), p. 362.

being thought of as existing at the beginning of all temporal process excludes freedom within the realm of his creation'.[12]

Today the river has become a flood. Major Christian writers across the theological spectrum have been convinced by the arguments for limited foreknowledge. To give an eminent sample from Britain: theologians like Keith Ward,[13] philosophers like Richard Swinburne,[14] and scientist-theologians like John Polkinghorne.[15] Pinnock is not an eccentric maverick, therefore, and it is clear that he has been convinced by the same kind of arguments as they have. Let us briefly rehearse some of them.

First, the notion of God as completely outside time has proved more and more problematic since the time of Hegel. Suggested examples of timeless entities have included numbers and universals but these are lifeless and inert, pointing to a God who is at best *ton Theon* rather than *ho Theos*. Significantly, these entities can be thought about but they themselves cannot think. What is more, an atemporal being lacks the qualities that the biblical God exhibits. Stewart Sutherland enumerates some of these:

> A timeless being cannot utter, but neither can he represent to himself. He cannot physically make or create, but neither can he deliberate, reflect, anticipate or intend, for these are all essential temporal notions... He cannot, of course, remember or predict, suspect or confirm; nor is it easy to grasp what timeless love really can be.[16]

It is true to say that just as our medieval ancestors expended immense intellectual effort attempting to understand Being, since the Renaissance the focus has shifted to the study of Time. History became an important focus of enquiry and then the process of evolution and finally, with Einstein, the interconnectedness of space and time. With quantum mechanics has come the realization that flux and activity are integral to reality. Thus has come the realization that 'Time is not something that thought must escape, for it is at the heart of the way things are'.[17] It is realized that God must honour time and dignify it with his presence. He must be our companion through history and he must be the God not of *apatheia* but of empathy for, in Paul Fiddes' words, 'the designer of a

---

12   W. Pannenberg, *The Idea of God and Human Freedom* (Philadelphia: Westminster Press, 1973), p. 108.
13   K. Ward, *Holding Fast to God* (London: SPCK, 1982), p. 36.
14   R. Swinburne, *The Coherence of Theism* (Oxford: Clarendon Press, 1977), p. 176.
15   J. Polkinghorne, *Science and Providence* (London: SPCK, 1989), p. 79.
16   S. Sutherland, *God, Jesus and Belief* (Oxford: Blackwell, 1984), p. 56.
17   C. Gunton, *Becoming and Being* (Oxford: Oxford University Press, 1978), p. 6.

community has to work *inside* it, suffering its growing pains and leading it to the aim he has for it'.[18]

Secondly, an omni-controlling God has proved more and more repellent. Again the movement gained momentum with the Renaissance and it reached its historic outworking in the English Civil War when the old concept of the divine right of kings gave way to a new vision which was later articulated by philosophers like John Locke as the social contract theory. Despotic rule, no matter how enlightened, could be the ideal no longer. Gradually a new paradigm emerged: the ideal ruler became the one who provided parameters in which his subjects could develop their potential to flourish as human beings. As Don Cupitt has written, healthy people today 'insist that it is better to live one's own life, even if unsuccessfully, than to live a life which is merely the acting of a part written for us by somebody else, and the principle holds even if that "somebody else" is a god'.[19] Feminist theologians have challenged the elevation of 'masculine' virtues like power, control and independence over more 'feminine' ones, such as nurturance, emotional sensitivity and interdependence. As Ian Barbour explains, they insist the latter qualities do not weaken God's power but highlight:

> a different form of power—not power as control over another person, but power as empowerment of another person. Creative empowerment is not a 'zero-sum' game (in which one person loses something when the other person gains it) but rather a 'positive-sum' game (in which both parties can gain).[20]

Many Calvinists[21] argue that this picture is too simplistic for there is a middle-way between determinism and the libertarian notion of freewill that openness theists trade in; this is the time honoured notion of soft-determinism or compatibilism espoused by philosophers like Hobbes and Hume. The view holds that I am free when I am not coerced to do something against my will and the Calvinist will argue that this is compatible with the sovereign God causing the state of my will. But this will not do. For on a soft-determinist model a sinful action can no longer be said to stem from my will, even though it may be mediated through it, and therefore, that action is not really mine, it is God's. As Norman Geisler bluntly states, 'moral determinism makes God immoral and

---

18   P.S. Fiddes, *The Creative Suffering of God* (Oxford: Clarendon Press, 1988), p. 39.

19   D. Cupitt, *Taking Leave of God* (London: SCM Press, 1980), p. 4.

20   I.G. Barbour, 'God's Power: A Process View', in J. Polkinghorne (ed.), *The Work of Love: Creation as Kenosis* (London: SPCK, 2001), p. 10.

21   For example, D.A. Carson, *Divine Sovereignty and Human Responsibility* (London: Marshall, Morgan and Scott, 1981).

makes humans amoral';[22] immoral because God is the ultimate cause of everything, including, presumably, evil human acts, and amoral because humans have too inadequate a mode of freedom to entail true responsibility. To be significantly free we need to possess not only freedom *from* external constraint, but also freedom *to* act in different ways with the same internal factors operating. It is difficult to avoid John Hick's verdict: 'If all our thoughts and actions are divinely predestined, however free and morally responsible we may seem to be to ourselves, we cannot be free and morally responsible in the sight of God, but instead be his helpless puppets.'[23] Kant was right when he described soft-determinism as 'a miserable subterfuge' as was William James who dismissed it as 'a quagmire of evasion'.[24]

Realizing this, some Calvinists[25] have admitted that libertarian freedom is required along with absolute divine sovereignty and have argued that although these are logically incompatible, they are both biblical and therefore we must believe in both as an antinomy. The trouble with antinomies, however, is that they are conceptually empty; what is given with one hand is taken away by the other ('God causes a person...' negated by '...to choose him freely'). As J.L. Mackie has written: 'A logical contradiction is not a state of affairs which it is supremely difficult to produce, but only a form of words which fails to describe any state of affairs'.[26] Another problem is where to put the theological brake on. Why not proliferate these antinomies to include every area upon which Bible-believing evangelicals disagree? For example, why not welcome the antinomy of annihilationism and eternal conscious suffering and promulgate the profound doctrine of Hell as the everlasting conscious torment of non-existent beings? Clearly that way madness lies. And yet through the habit of custom we have been lulled into thinking that the freewill/predestination antinomy is the deepest of mysteries rather than literal non-sense.

Now once it is conceded both that God is a co-temporal traveller with us and that, since God creates and sustains a free universe, the future is open and therefore unpredictable by a perfect cognisance of present

---

22   N. Geisler, 'God Knows All Things', in D. Basinger and R. Basinger (eds), *Predestination and Freewill: Four Views of Divine Sovereignty and Human Freedom* (Downers Grove, IL: InterVarsity Press, 1986), p. 75.

23   J. Hick, *Philosophy of Religion* (Englewood Cliffs, NJ: Prentice Hall, 1963), p. 39.

24   Quoted in J. Trusted, *Freewill and Responsibility* (Oxford: Oxford University Press, 1984), p. 47.

25   E.g., P.K. Jewett, *Election and Predestination* (Grand Rapids, MI: Eerdmans, 1985).

26   Quoted in R.H. Nash, *The Concept of God* (Grand Rapids, MI: Zondervan, 1983), p. 40.

causes, foreknowledge becomes seriously problematic. So problematic, in fact, that Pinnock and many others have concluded that it is both philosophically impossible and, they contend, also unscriptural.

What I propose to do now is to demonstrate that both of these conclusions are corrigible. We are in the realm not of knowing but of supposing. I do this to help some evangelical readers who may be convinced that God is everlasting rather than timeless and who reject an omni-controlling notion of divine sovereignty and yet are unconvinced by Pinnock's biblical case for limited foreknowledge.

Biblical Prophecy

Pinnock argues that predictive prophecies can be explained by the fact that (a) some merely state what God shall do and are therefore more about omnipotence than omniscience; (b) some are explicitly or implicitly conditional on human choices; (c) some are imprecise forecasts based on present trends; and (d) some are fulfilled in ways other than what the prophet had in mind.[27] There are some stubborn exceptions to this, however, that cause some fellow travellers to draw back from his limited omniscience conclusion. Let us look at one example. In 1 Kings 13.2-3, king Josiah is mentioned by name and his sacrifice of the priests is forecast apparently some three hundred and thirty years before the event which is recorded in 2 Kings 23. The particularity of this forecast of a contingent state of affairs cannot be explained by any of Pinnock's four points above. Non-evangelical scholars like Wellhausen have been quick to explain the apparent remarkable prediction as a case of *vaticinium ex eventu* with an actual literary dependence of the 1 Kings passage on the 2 Kings record. But for there to be clear evidence of this there would have to be either independent checks such as the existence of early manuscripts omitting the story, or the presence of an introductory formula such as 'the interpretation concerns' which one finds in the Qumran commentaries when midrashic interpolations occur.[28] Such evidence is completely lacking with regard to 1 Kings 13 as it is, indeed, regarding all of the material of the Old Testament. I believe that Pinnock needs to wrestle more with such passages and recognize that his passing over them opens himself to the criticism that philosophical presuppositions are wagging the tail of biblical theology.

---

27   C.H. Pinnock, *Most Moved Mover: A Theology of God's Openness* (Carlisle: Paternoster Press, 2001), pp. 50-51.

28   P.E. Copeland, 'A Guide to the Study of the Prophets', *Themelios* 10 (1984), p. 5.

Theological Fatalism

The main philosophical problem Pinnock seems to have with exhaustive foreknowledge is that it apparently entails fatalism. He states that if God possesses complete foreknowledge

> the future would be fixed and determined, much as is the past. Total knowledge of the future would imply a fixity of events. Nothing in the future would need to be decided. It also would imply that human freedom is an illusion, that we make no difference and are not responsible.[29]

But Pinnock's conclusion is too quick. There is a massive body of philosophical argumentation challenging the view that foreknowledge entails fatalism. Pinnock's open theist colleague, William Hasker, is clearly well aware of this and in the same volume he writes, 'There is a minor cottage industry among philosophers of religion seeking to devise an escape from this argument... [N]one of these evasions are successful.'[30] Hasker's dismissive tone is unfortunate. In the same vein many a Muslim would reject the strenuous, complex efforts of Christian theologians to present a coherent doctrine of the Trinity. If, as many biblical scholars believe, foreknowledge is a biblical datum, Christian philosophers must be encouraged to articulate how this may be possible.

Let us explore, then, how Pinnock's fatalist fears might be answered. The subject is indeed complicated and has engaged some of the best minds from William of Ockham[31] to the present day. In fact the fatalist case is found presented as early as Boethius who averred, 'If God foresees all things and cannot be mistaken in any way, what Providence has foreseen as a future event must happen'.[32] Using a medieval distinction between two kinds of necessity, *de re* and *de dicto*, Alvin Plantinga has shown, however, that while such a sentence (*de dicto*) as Boethius' must be true of necessity since it is a tautology, nevertheless it does not entail that the future event (*de re*) must also happen of necessity. From his knowledge of the future it follows that what God knows will in fact happen, but it does not follow that it must happen fatalistically; it could happen otherwise but it simply will not. If it hypothetically were to

29   C.H. Pinnock, 'Systematic Theology', in C. Pinnock, R. Rice, J. Sanders, W. Hasker and D. Basinger, *The Openness of God: A Biblical Challenge to the Traditional Understanding of God* (Downers Grove, IL: InterVarsity Press, 1994), p. 121.

30   W. Hasker, 'A Philosophical Perspective', in Pinnock *et al.*, *Openness of God*, pp. 148-49.

31   W. Ockham, *Predestination, God's Foreknowledge and Future Contingents* (trans. M.M. Adams and N. Kretzmann; Indianapolis: Hackett Press, 1983).

32   Boethius, *The Consolation of Philosophy*, Book 5 (trans. V.E. Watts; Harmondsworth: Penguin, 1969), p. 150.

happen otherwise, God's foreknowledge would have been different. Plantinga applied his rediscovered insight to N. Pike's argument for theological fatalism which contended that if I were truly free I could falsify God's infallible foreknowledge (a logical absurdity) and I could alter the contents of God's essentially omniscient knowledge (another logical nonsense); therefore since God is omniscient, I cannot be free. Plantinga responded by pointing out that it is not a matter of alteration but, using Pike's example of a fictional Jones,

> it was within Jones' power to do something such that if he had done it, then God would not have held a belief that in fact (in the actual world) He did not. But by no stretch of the imagination does it follow that if Jones had done it, then it would have been true that God did *hold* a belief He didn't hold... It is not essential to Him to hold the beliefs He does hold; what is essential to Him is the quite different property of holding only true beliefs.[33]

In the words of William Lane Craig, this response to fatalism which employs contrary-to-fact or subjunctive conditional statements 'does not express the ability to change or undo the past, but the ability to act such that the past *would* have been different than it is'.[34] God's knowledge guarantees that I will choose a specific act but not that I must of necessity so choose. My choice is, in fact, logically prior but temporally posterior to God's foreknowledge.

The Ontological Basis of Divine Foreknowledge

Pinnock is also at a loss to see how omniscience could know that which is contingent and is not in existence to be observed. He writes: 'The future does not yet exist and therefore cannot be infallibly anticipated, even by God.'[35] This contention is reminiscent of that of his colleague Richard Rice who states that 'to say that God is ignorant of future creaturely decisions is like saying that God is deaf to silence. It makes no sense, because before they exist such decisions are nothing for God to be ignorant *of*.'[36]

Perhaps the best kind of reply is to view foreknowledge as analogous to memory. The connection between memory of an undetermined past

---

33   A. Plantinga, *God, Freedom and Evil* (Grand Rapids, MI: Eerdmans, 1974), pp. 71-72.

34   W.L. Craig in his review of R. Sorabji, *Time, Creation and the Continuum*, in *International Philosophical Quarterly* 25 (1985), p. 321.

35   Pinnock, 'Systematic Theology', p. 123.

36   R. Rice, 'Divine Foreknowledge and Free-Will Theism', in C.H. Pinnock (ed.), *The Grace of God, the Will of Man* (Grand Rapids, MI: Zondervan, 1989), p. 129.

and foreknowledge of an open future goes back at least to Augustine who wrote: 'Just as you do not compel past events to happen by your memory of them, so God does not compel events of the future to take place by his knowledge of them.'[37] Now an accurate memory of an event requires neither that the knowledge is inferred from present causes, nor that it is currently perceived with the senses. Just as memory is cognition of what no longer exists, so precognition is knowledge of what does not yet exist. To be true foreknowledge, the cognition does not require that the known future event exists now, it merely requires that it will one day exist. Some primitive creatures only live in the now, we humans enjoy this awareness as well as memory, God then would enjoy present awareness and both memory and what might be termed 'pre-memory'.

This divine faculty in an everlasting being would require reverse causation whereby a future event brings about the contents of God's pre-memory or, if this is deemed untenable, one would have to argue that God's knowledge is innate. This latter position has been the majority one amongst classical Christian theists. For instance, Carl Henry writes: 'It is a direct spiritual comprehension, a single act of cognition, independent of insight conditioned on space-time realities.'[38] This view is straightforward for a determinist like Henry whereby God's knowledge of his plans and the actualization of these plans are coterminous (as Aquinas taught, *scientia dei causa rerum*). An open universe makes the view problematic however. But there are advocates. For example, William Lane Craig has argued that the relationship between the future event and divine foreknowledge is not one of cause and effect but ground and consequent; the event being not causally but logically prior. A useful analogy might be how my dead grandfather can become a great-grandfather through my having a child. Craig contends that the attribute of omniscience ensures that God knows all true propositions, and since future tense propositions have a truth value, God knows them. 'God never learned or acquired his knowledge, but has eternally known an innate store of only and all true statements.'[39] Craig offers basic human intuitions like moral judgement and the knowledge of other minds as analogies of what God's innate knowledge might be like, and one might add the sometimes detailed instincts of animals such as the intricate nest of the weaver bird.

My purpose behind this section has been on the one hand to challenge Pinnock to listen harder to the biblical and philosophical arguments in favour of divine foreknowledge and, on the other, to encourage those

---

37 Augustine, *De Libero Arbitrio* 3.411 (trans. R.P. Russel; The Fathers of the Church, 59; Washington, DC: Catholic University of America Press, 1968), p. 175,

38 C.F.H. Henry, *God, Revelation and Authority*, Volume 5 (Waco, TX: Word, 1982), p. 270.

39 W.L. Craig, *The Only Wise God* (Grand Rapids, MI: Baker Book House, 1987), p. 123.

evangelicals who are no longer convinced by the hard-sovereignty position of Calvinism but believe quite literally that Yahweh is able to 'make known the end from the beginning' (Isa. 46.10) by showing them some strategies for cohering the two contentions. But it is now time to join forces with Pinnock and face his critics.

The Need of Exhaustive Foreknowledge for Sound Planning

In his book length attack on openness theism, Bruce Ware writes:

> But what is especially poignant in the openness view is the notion that God plans and works without the advantage of knowing the future. Hence, the whole venture is, quite literally, an enormous risk for God, not to mention for the entire world that he has made.[40]

Although this line of argument can be traced back to such early church fathers as Justin Martyr and Tertullian,[41] careful consideration reveals the simple and surprising truth that exhaustive knowledge of an open future can avail nothing; practically it is otiose. This fact was skilfully uncovered in an influential article by David Basinger in which he presents the key insight that 'Knowledge of the actual results of a decision *cannot* be presupposed in making the decision'.[42] In other words, God's fore-knowledge must be posterior (logically not temporally) to his decision to create a certain kind of universe or his decision to intervene in specific ways within that universe. He cannot, therefore, act *on the basis* of his foreknowledge. Since the future can no more be altered than the past, God cannot foresee the future and then decide to change it through various modes of intervention. Hasker makes the same point in a slightly different way:

> what God foreknows is *not* certain antecedents which, unless interfered with in some way, *lead* to the occurrence of the event; rather, it is *the event itself* that is foreknown as occurring, and it is contradictory to suppose that an event is *known* to occur but then also is *prevented* from occurring. In the logical order of dependence of events, one might say, by the 'time' God knows something will

---

40   B.A. Ware, *God's Lesser Glory* (Leicester: Apollos, 2000), p. 146.

41   See B.W. Farley, *The Providence of God* (Grand Rapids, MI: Baker Book House, 1988), pp. 79, 86.

42   D. Basinger, 'Middle Knowledge and Classical Christian Thought', *Religious Studies* 22 (1986), p. 418.

happen, it is 'too late' either to *bring about* its happening or to *prevent* it from happening.[43]

Hasker believes that this crucial insight has been largely overlooked by theologians owing to their muddling of divine foreknowledge with the kind of fallible foresight that we humans sometimes experience as we engage in informed contemplation of the future in order that we might influence and change events such as the impending ecological disaster. Such intervention involves no vicious paradox. 'But if we could foresee *everything*, then for us, as for God, it would be too late to do anything about it.'[44] Foreknowledge would neither be useful to God in an unpredictable free universe nor in a determined Calvinist one since foreknowledge would then be contingent upon predetermination.

The only useful foreknowledge, in fact, would be in the context of middle-knowledge whereby God would know the truth-value of counter-factual subjunctive propositions such as 'If the Second World War had not occurred, there would have been no unification of Western Europe, nor liberation of the British Empire, nor the foundation of the Jewish state'. On the basis of such foreknowledge God could usefully plan his future influence and intervention, and choose which possible universe to actualize. However, most philosophers feel that middle knowledge is rather like the perpetual motion machine: if it worked it would answer intractable problems but unfortunately it logically cannot. They conclude either that counter-factual propositions cannot have a truth value or that the truth value is that they are necessarily false because the specific outcome they describe is in fact indeterminate. Critics sense an illicit reification of abstract states of affairs—possible worlds do not exist to be the objects of omniscient knowledge. Nevertheless, there are powerful advocates of middle-knowledge such as Plantinga,[45] but this is not the place to pursue the argument.[46]

Without Foreknowledge Might God's Purposes Fail?

This seems to worry many of Pinnock's opponents. For instance, again Ware writes:

---

43   W. Hasker, *God, Time and Knowledge* (Ithaca, NY: Cornell University Press, 1989), pp. 57-58.

44   Hasker, *God, Time and Knowledge*, p. 62.

45   Plantinga, *God, Freedom and Evil*.

46   As I do elsewhere, see R.R. Cook, 'God, Middle Knowledge and Alternative Worlds', *Evangelical Quarterly* 62.4 (1990), pp. 293-310.

Deficient knowledge and wisdom surely mean that neither we nor God can be certain about just what will happen in the end. Will God succeed in fulfilling his goals? Will history move in the direction he hopes it will? Are God's predictions and promises sure? The only answer open theists can give to these questions is that they are hopeful that somehow God will pull it off.[47]

Tony Gray seems equally concerned and considers some specific problems. He wonders, for example, what would have happened if Mary had refused to bear the Messiah and, what is worse, if all the other possible 'Marys' followed suit.[48]

Now the first thing to note again is that, in fact, simple exhaustive foreknowledge is not the issue here since it would not help God in the providential outworking of his plans. The problem actually arises in any non-deterministic notion of the future. I suppose, in answer to Gray, one may surmise that Mary could have found herself pregnant anyway; mothers do not usually have the luxury of veto and is it indeed statistically possible that all Mary's contemporaries would have declined the offer? Here it is important to note that many systems which are in principle unpredictable in detail are predictable at the aggregate level. Examples would include sub-atomic events which follow stochastic laws as do large groups of people, for instance the number of suicides remains fairly constant year on year. Actuaries and racing bookies grow rich by successfully mastering the odds.

Freedom *is* consistent with determinate outcomes. David Bartholomew has given some interesting examples.[49] He shows how free processes can follow unpredictable pathways and yet have outcomes which are certain. Take the case of travellers at the North Pole who are told that they may travel in a straight-line in any direction. They have a considerable choice of routes but will certainly arrive at a specific destination—the South Pole. Or take the sowing of a rumour in an office. The exact path the rumour will take is unknowable but the outcome is certain: eventually everyone will hear of it. With the inclusion of the notion of non-coercive interaction, Keith Ward offers an example with relation to God's providence:

God can leave it open to many individual physicists to take a route which will lead to the discovery of the laws of mechanics, but might make it certain that some physicist, within some finite period of time, will discover them. Even if all physicists turn out to be so lazy and selfish that none of them discover the laws, God can inspire the mind of one of them to make the discovery. Just because God

47   Ware, *God's Lesser Glory*, p. 20.
48   T. Gray, 'Pinnock's Doctrine of God and the Evangelical Tradition', in Gray and Sinkinson (eds), *Reconstructing Theology*, p. 145.
49   D.J. Bartholomew, *God of Chance* (London: SCM Press, 1984), pp. 73-82.

does not determine everything, it does not follow that God cannot determine anything.[50]

The only kind of freedom that judgement requires is that everyone has the genuine libertarian choice of whether to seek happiness in God or through self-aggrandisement, and there is no biblical prediction regarding the percentage of humans that will enter the kingdom. Nothing in the Bible approximates the specificity of the lyric, 'The odds for getting to heaven are six to one'.

Actually there is a real problem getting the critic of openness theism to specify what these concrete eschatological plans of God are. Patrick Richmond at least has a shot: the gates of Hades will never prevail against the church (Mt. 16.18).[51] To this there are several answers I suppose. The stochastic laws might come into play[52] or one could argue that, even if the church militant were to vanish from the earth, the church triumphant would defy Hades (death) and survive forever in God's kingdom. It is important to balance Richmond's reference with Luke 18.8 where Jesus pensively wonders, 'when the Son of Man comes, will he find faith on the earth?'.

In my judgement, theologically there is only one cardinal eschatological requirement and this is that in order to maintain an adequate theodicy there has to be a guarantee that every ensouled creature has the genuine opportunity of eternal flourishing with God. Pinnock has rightly seen that this requires that one postulate post-mortem opportunity.[53]

Foreknowledge and Divine Freedom

Much has been written about how divine foreknowledge is thought to curtail human freedom, but Pinnock is on to something when he considers divine freedom. He writes, 'Think of what it would mean for God's freedom if everything were settled. God himself would not be free to act except in predestined ways. He would have to consult his own

---

50   K. Ward, *Religion and Creation* (Oxford: Clarendon Press, 1996), p. 260.

51   P. Richmond, 'Openness to the Bible? A Traditional Challenge to Clark Pinnock's Understanding of God', in Gray and Sinkinson (eds), *Reconstructing Theology*, p. 118.

52   E.g., J. Hick follows Augustine in contending that with regard to God we are created *ad te* and remain restless until we find our rest in God. Thus our path to God will remain unpredictable but like a moth we will surely find the flame. J. Hick, *Death and Eternal Life* (London: Macmillan, 1976), p. 254.

53   C.H. Pinnock, *A Wideness in God's Mercy: The Finality of Jesus Christ in a World of Religions* (Grand Rapids, MI: Zondervan, 1992), pp. 168-72.

foreknowledge to know what to do next.'[54] Pinnock is not alone in this concern. R. La Croix concludes: 'So, it is a consequence of the doctrine of divine omniprescience that God could neither decide to refrain nor actually refrain from performing any of the acts he does perform nor decide to perform or actually perform any of the acts he does *not* perform.'[55]

Now, the first observation to make is that La Croix is slipping again into the ancient model error of confusing *de dicto* and *de re* necessity. In fact, foreknowledge entails only that God *will* do what he knows he will do, but not that he *must* so do. P. Quinn is thus correct when he insists that:

> a theist can consistently maintain both that God has foreknowledge of every action he will, in fact, perform and that some or all of the actions which God will, in fact, perform are such that he might refrain from performing them, though, to be sure, he will not so refrain.[56]

Were he to refrain, his foreknowledge would, of course, have been different.

Granting the inadequacy of the fatalist case, the sceptic can mount another major attack on the advocate of divine foreknowledge and freedom: if God foresees he will choose x, has he not, in effect, already chosen x? Rice states the argument well:

> To know exactly what you are going to decide is to have made the decision already. There is nothing left to be decided. Consequently, it makes no sense to speak of divine decisions if we attribute absolute foreknowledge to God, for he must know everything he is going to decide. It is equally impossible to imagine a time before which God had decided to do something—to create, for example. For if he had absolute foreknowledge of his future actions, he had already made the decision. So, it seems, there is no coherent way to think of God as changing, if we hold to the notion of absolute foreknowledge.[57]

However, it is by no means self-evident that foreknowledge of one's own act is tantamount to the decision to perform it. For example, yesterday my daughter decided to bake a cake and, despite realizing that she ought to watch her calorie intake, she knows on the basis of past performance that, when it comes down to it, she will succumb to licking the icing around the bowl. Now tomorrow she will light the oven without

---

54   Pinnock, *Most Moved Mover*, p. 51.

55   R. La Croix, 'Omniprescience and Divine Determinism', *Religious Studies* 12 (1976), p. 374.

56   P. Quinn, 'Divine Foreknowledge and Divine Freedom', *International Journal for Philosophy of Religion* 9 (1978), p. 228.

57   Rice, 'Divine Foreknowledge and Free-Will Theism', pp. 126-27.

deliberation because she had already decided to bake at that time, but when she is again faced with the sugary bowl, she will not lick it without much prior conscious consultation and struggle of will. Foreknowledge is not equivalent to decision making. As Bruce Reichenbach neatly expresses it: 'Deliberation relates to the reasons for doing an action for the purpose of deciding to act; it does not relate to my knowledge of the outcome of my decision.'[58] Cogitation is distinct from cognition. Volition and cognition must not be confused or conflated. Thus it is not incoherent to envisage God knowing what he will decide, and yet, when the time comes, he makes that decision not because he knows he will (not 'must' as we have already seen when examining the fatalist argument) but because he concludes that it is the best decision to make in the circumstances. It must not be forgotten that the decision is logically prior although the knowledge is temporally prior; the knowledge is based on the decision, not *vice versa*.

But Rice has a subsidiary argument: 'If [God] knows exactly not only what will happen but also how he will respond to every situation, then, in effect, he already has the experience... It is, therefore, impossible to attribute both absolute foreknowledge and momentary sensitivity to God.'[59] Here Rice seems to claim that life would be very tedious for such a deity, but why should it be? Anticipation can enhance an experience as the lover knows who has already planned every step of his impending night-out with his woman. Familiarity can intensify pleasure as any concert-goer knows on her way to hear a favourite symphony. And if omniscience should entail boredom, why not omnipotence as well? For it could be argued that an all-powerful being must surely lack a sense of challenge. In reply to Rice's charge that a deity with foreknowledge could not change or experience present sensitivity, it should be acknowledged that he could not grow in factual knowledge but he would develop in terms of existential awareness and emotional enrichment as the knowledge of anticipation gives way to the knowledge of experience. The scriptures themselves intimate that divine sympathy became divine empathy as God experienced incarnation (Heb. 2.18).

D. Pailin offers a final powerful objection to the notion of an everlasting God with foreknowledge. He seems to be trading off the insight that God's foreknowledge must be contingent upon his acting in a certain way; he cannot foreknow an event and then act to prevent it happening for the precognized future is as logically unchangeable as the remembered past. 'What will be will be' is an analytic proposition (it is, of course, a tautology). Consequently, as God makes his decision he

---

58 B. Reichenbach, 'Omniscience and Deliberation', *International Journal for Philosophy of Religion* 16 (1984), p. 230.

59 R. Rice, *God's Foreknowledge and Man's Free Will* (Minneapolis: Bethany Press, 1980), p. 23.

already knows its outcome which may be less than optimum, yet he cannot but make that decision. Pailin deserves to be quoted at length:

> If God knows not only what has happened and what is happening but also what will happen, God must thereby know what will be the effectiveness or ineffectiveness of whatever is the divine (or any other) response to any present event. Divine involvement in the passage of events would thus be like the frustrated state of people in some science-fiction scenario reliving their past while being conscious that they are reliving it. Faced with the present problem, they not only make a decision about what to do but as they make it they know what will happen, whether or not it is what they intend... Although it is arguable that it does not entail preordination, it leaves God with the nightmare of knowing what is going to occur and knowing that no one, not even God, can prevent it because what each agent will do and how others will respond is already completely known and hence unalterable.[60]

The tempting response is to affirm that, unlike creatures, God would never be disappointed or frustrated by his perfect decisions, but this assertion is far from incontrovertible. David Basinger has cogently argued that, since God's knowledge of the future must be logically subsequent to his decision to act, 'knowledge of the actual results of a decision cannot be presupposed in making the decision'.[61] Further, he maintains, God would need to know such results, and indeed he would need to know what the results would have been had he made a different choice, in order to be able to make the wisest possible decision. Lacking such knowledge God could make an error of judgement which would be regrettable. In practical terms, therefore, a deity with this kind of foreknowledge would have no advantage over a God lacking exhaustive knowledge of the future as far as the decision-making process is concerned. In fact, according to Pailin he would be disadvantaged because he would always throughout eternity know of his mistake. The only kind of foreknowledge that would provide an escape from this nightmare situation is middle-knowledge.

Guidance

The issue of personal guidance seems particularly to concern traditionalists. It is perceived that a God with limited power who could be frustrated by free agents and who only enjoys limited foreknowledge would be an inadequate adviser. Ware is incredulous:

---

60   D.A. Pailin, *God and the Process of Reality* (London: Routledge, 1989), p. 86.
61   Basinger, 'Middle Knowledge and Classical Christian Thought', p. 418.

> Why would one ever think that it is a *benefit* to us that God takes into account what we think as he decides what is best? How can it be *better* that God and I decide my future *together*, rather than leaving this altogether in God's infinitely wise and perfect hands?[62]

In contrast, Ware continues, 'The God of the Bible is the God of greater glory, the One upon whom we trust every moment of every day, knowing that his ways are absolutely perfect'.[63]

The answer to Ware's question is to ponder the nature of healthy human development and optimum parental relationship and we must never forget that the heart of our faith is a life-long (eternal) relationship with our heavenly Father. His desire is for intimacy with us which is not being achieved if we perceive him primarily as an on-line almanac. Now a young child may need to be fairly passive in the planning and decision-making of the family but as she grows older the parent will want to involve her more and more to encourage her into maturity. After some time with his disciples Jesus called them no more servants but friends (Jn 15.15).

The influential British psychoanalyst, D.W. Winnicott, has presented some helpful insights concerning what he calls 'good enough' parenting. Paradoxically, the 'perfect' parent who is completely in tune with the child and provides his every need and is in total control of every situation will inhibit that child's development. The parent will be perceived to be oppressive and stifling. In contrast, the 'good enough' mother, who is in fact the ideal mother, is neither omniscient nor omnipotent. Her limitations result in the healthy outcome of the child developing a sense of self and also a sense of the mother's separate identity so that love can become a genuine possibility. Speaking to a conference on Family Evangelism in 1968, Winnicott said:

> The sort of thing I have been talking about could not be done by a computer—it must be human reliability (that is, unreliability, really). In the development of adaptation, the mother's great adaptation to the baby gradually becomes less; accordingly the baby begins to be frustrated and to be angry and needs to identify with the mother. I remember a baby of three months who, when feeding at the mother's breast, would put his hand to her mouth to feed her before he took her breast. He was able to get an idea of what the mother was feeling like.[64]

Thus, we can conclude that the God whom Ware craves would be an infantilizing presence. Like a 'good enough' earthly parent, Yahweh

---

62   Ware, *God's Lesser Glory*, pp. 188-89.

63   Ware, *God's Lesser Glory*, p. 185.

64   D.W. Winnicott, 'Children Learning', in *Home is Where we Start From* (Harmondsworth: Penguin, 1986), p. 146.

both admits and permits frustration leading to the possibility of mutual support and cooperation.

Providence

I have long felt that it is possible to fear the Calvinist God who predetermines everything and predestines only some to eternal life, but I cannot love him. I am much more drawn to that element of God which attracted the early T.S. Eliot:

> The notion of some infinitely gentle
> Infinitely suffering thing[65]

and which is glimpsed in the vulnerable God of Hosea. A deity who humbly limited himself at creation to allow an emergent universe to make mistakes and have the opportunity to learn from them—from the level of genetics where experimental variation can sometimes lead to a leap in evolution but at others to the development of cancer cells, on to the choices inherent in the maturation of a human life. This God can be grieved and disappointed. This God can commission a king Saul with high hopes which would, in fact, be dashed. Yes, in guidance he may be frustrated but his motives are always for the best and his plans are always made in love and the important thing is that, as we travel through time together, he is there for me in intimate fellowship. This fellowship *is* eternal life.

Conclusion

Perhaps I could conclude with a brief testimony since it is often stated that openness theism offers an existentially inadequate God. During the course of planning and writing this chapter my wife of twenty-six years died of cancer at the age of fifty-one. While pensively and painfully considering the enormity of this event, the title of a book by Boethius popped into my mind, *The Consolation of Philosophy*, and I realized that, indeed, my hard-won Arminian philosophy coloured by process insights of a free and loose jointed universe afforded me deep solace. Clark, you have been a significant mentor in the development of this Christian worldview and I would like publicly to thank you now.

---

65   T.S. Eliot, 'Preludes', in *Collected Poems 1909–1962* (London: Faber & Faber, 1963), p. 25.

The divine passion began even before creation, as Moltmann suggests: '"The Lamb slain from the foundation of the world" (Rev. 18.8) is a symbol to show that there was already a cross in the heart of God...before Christ was crucified on Golgotha.'[66] The Secret who holds us is gracious. The Alpha and Omega of the universe is Love and, as W.H. Vanstone has eloquently written, in the progress of love 'each step is a precarious step into the unknown, in which each triumph contains new potential for tragedy, and each tragedy can be redeemed into a wider triumph'.[67]

Kenosis began at creation and we live in a universe sustained and inspired by a persuasive seraphic love that desires the flourishing and fulfilment of all emergent things. Even the great American religious sceptic, Wallace Stevens, began to sense this and in a late poem he adumbrates the vision tentatively but compellingly. I close with some extracts:

> The afternoon is visibly a source,
> Too wide, too irised, to be more than calm,
>
> Too much like thinking to be less than thought,
> Obscurest parent, obscurest patriarch,
> A daily majesty of meditation,
>
> That comes and goes in silences of its own.
>
> The spirit comes from the body of the world,
> Whose blunt laws make an affectation of mind,
>
> The mannerism of nature caught in a glass
> And there become a spirit's mannerism,
> A glass aswarm with things going as far as they can.[68]

---

66   J. Moltmann, 'God's Kenosis in the Creation and Consummation of the World', in Polkinghorne (ed.), *Work of Love*, pp. 146-47.

67   W.H. Vanstone, *Love's Endeavour, Love's Expense* (London: Darton, Longman & Todd, 1977), p. 63.

68   W. Stevens, 'Looking Across the Fields and Watching the Birds Fly', in *Collected Poems of Wallace Stevens* (London: Faber and Faber, 1955), pp. 518-19.

CHAPTER 6

Can God be Responsive if the Future is Not Open?

Terrance L. Tiessen

Introduction

'[T]hose who affirm the open model believe the status of petitionary prayer within this model to be one of its most attractive features... [T]he open model of God is one of the few in which petitionary prayer is efficacious in the manner still presupposed by most Christians: as an activity that can initiate unilateral divine activity that would not have taken place if we had not utilized our God-given power of choice to request his assistance.'[1] So wrote David Basinger in the work which rapidly brought open theism to the attention of many evangelicals. Having been identified with the open theist project from the appearance of that first volume, Clark Pinnock has continued to be an enthusiastic supporter of this way of conceptualizing God's work in the world.

Concern to give full weight to indications in the biblical narrative that God *responds* to his creatures is not limited to open theism. It has characterized other theological proposals which might be grouped under the general category of 'risk models' of divine providence.[2] They all believe that one major deficiency of risk-free models of divine providence is the fact that God cannot genuinely be said to respond if he has already decided ahead of time (as viewed from the human standpoint)

---

1   David Basinger, 'Practical Implications', in Clark Pinnock, Richard Rice, John Sanders, William Hasker and David Basinger, *The Openness of God: A Biblical Challenge to the Traditional Understanding of God* (Downers Grove, IL: InterVarsity Press, 1994), p. 162.

2   Of the eleven models that I have expounded in my book on divine providence and human prayer, six might be designated 'risk' models and five of them posit 'no risk' on God's part. See Terrance Tiessen, *Providence and Prayer: How Does God Work in the World?* (Downers Grove, IL: InterVarsity Press, 2000). Some of the material in this essay is adapted from that work.

what he will do in every situation throughout the history of the world. But, open theists are convinced that their proposal best accounts for the biblical portrayal of God as responding to human petitions. Thus Pinnock sees the model as 'a more coherent alternative to Calvinism than Arminians have presented before'.[3] I do not question the inner coherence of open theism, nor even that it surpasses classical Arminianism in this regard, but I am not convinced that it gives a more biblical account of God than does Calvinism. Nevertheless, I take seriously the concerns of Pinnock and other open theists that classical theism does not offer a plausible account of genuine divine responsiveness. In this essay, therefore, I plan not to critique open theism but to propose a means of understanding God as genuinely responsive to our prayers, even though he knows the future comprehensively because he has chosen what that future will be, as part of his eternal purpose. If no such account is plausible, on biblical grounds, then space would seem to have been made for open theists to offer one that is.

Pinnock on the Superiority of Open Theism as an Account of God's Responsiveness to Us

Clark Pinnock believes that genuine responsiveness on God's part requires a world in which God has made significant space for humans to determine the future, by leaving it open, even to the extent that he himself does not know its details. To Pinnock's eye, the God of classical theism is 'an aloof monarch, removed from the contingencies of the world, unchangeable in every aspect of being', his is 'an all determining and irresistible power, aware of everything that will ever happen and never taking risks'.[4] Pinnock opines that 'it is hard for conventional theism to deal with a relational and personal God, with a God really involved in the world, in short, with the God of the Bible'.[5] Over against such a God, Pinnock puts forward one who is 'a caring parent with qualities of love and responsiveness, generosity and sensitivity, openness and vulnerability, a person (rather than a metaphysical principle) who experiences the world, responds to what happens, relates to us and interacts dynamically with humans'.[6]

Pinnock is surprised by the strength of negative reaction to open theism because it appears to him that all biblical Christians 'live as if the

---

3   Clark H. Pinnock, *Most Moved Mover: A Theology of God's Openness* (Grand Rapids, MI: Baker Academic, 2001), p. xii; cf. p. 13.

4   Clark H. Pinnock, 'Systematic Theology', in Pinnock, Rice, Sanders, Hasker and Basinger, *Openness of God*, p. 103.

5   Pinnock, *Most Moved Mover*, p. 6.

6   Pinnock, *Most Moved Mover*, p. 6.

open view were true' because 'we have real relations whatever theory we hold'.[7] The superiority of open theism lies, Pinnock suggests, in the fact that 'personhood, relationality and community are more central to our understanding of God than independence and control'.[8] As a result of God's fundamental relationality, he has voluntarily 'made himself dependent on [the world] in some important respects' and allows himself to be 'affected by the world'.[9] Thus, the biblical language concerning God's repenting, grieving, interacting, weeping, crying out and responding to prayer is all taken quite literally as indicating that 'God is free to alter his course of action where appropriate and follow a plan different from the one previously announced'.[10] A God who cannot change would be unable to hear and respond to prayers, but the God of scripture 'makes himself dependent on the prayers of his people' and 'loves to move in response to our prayers'.[11] He responds 'to the changing needs of his people' and alters 'direction where necessary'.[12]

If the future were not open, Pinnock argues, neither God nor humanity could contribute to it so, 'why pray, if prayer changes nothing?'[13] He posits, therefore, that 'in prayer the practicality of the open view of God shines', for 'God treats us as subjects not objects and real dialogue takes place'.[14] God allows prayer to influence him 'so that it becomes an effective contributor to the flow of events'.[15] Pinnock confidently asserts: 'If you believe that prayer changes things, my whole position is established. If you do not believe it does, you are far from biblical religion.'[16]

The Biblical Indication that God Responds

Unquestionably, the biblical narrative portrays God as responding to people. Thus, in the days of Noah, the Lord 'saw how great the wickedness of the human race had become on the earth', he 'was grieved...and his heart was filled with pain' and *so* he decided to destroy

---

7   Pinnock, *Most Moved Mover*, p. 18.
8   Pinnock, *Most Moved Mover*, p. 29.
9   Pinnock, *Most Moved Mover*, p. 31; cf. p. 33.
10   Pinnock, *Most Moved Mover*, p. 63.
11   Pinnock, *Most Moved Mover*, p. 135.
12   Pinnock, *Most Moved Mover*, p. 87.
13   Pinnock, *Most Moved Mover*, p. 137; cf. p. 155.
14   Pinnock, *Most Moved Mover*, p. 171.
15   Pinnock, *Most Moved Mover*, p. 172.
16   Clark H. Pinnock, 'God Limits His Knowledge', in David Basinger and Randall Basinger (eds), *Predestination and Free Will: Four Views of Divine Sovereignty and Human Freedom* (Downers Grove, IL: InterVarsity Press, 1986), p. 152.

everyone but Noah and his family by flood, because 'Noah found favour in the eyes of the Lord' (Gen. 6.5-8).[17] To Moses, God said 'I have indeed seen the misery of my people in Egypt. I have heard them crying out because of their slave drivers, and I am concerned about their suffering. *So* I have come down to rescue them' (Ex. 3.7-8, emphasis supplied). But later, when the people sinned grievously by worshipping a golden calf, God announced to Moses his intention to destroy them and start a new nation with Moses. In response to Moses' intercession, however, we read that 'the Lord relented and did not bring on his people the disaster he had threatened' (Ex. 32.14).

When Hezekiah was deathly ill, Isaiah gave him a message from the Lord that he was going to die and would not recover but Hezekiah wept bitterly and prayed for recovery and the Lord sent Isaiah back to tell him that 'I have heard your prayer and seen your tears; I will heal you' and 'add fifteen years to your life' (2 Kgs 20.5-6). (Pinnock takes this as evidence that 'the king's death was shifted to a date more remote in time', which 'shows that the exact time of death was not forever settled in God's mind but was something flexible, depending on the circumstances'.[18]) Such instances could be multiplied from both Testaments and we could add the encouragement of our Lord that we should ask God for what we need *because* he will hear and *answer* the prayers of his people (Mt. 7.7). The frequent biblical injunctions to prayer all leave the impression that it is worthwhile because God responds to our prayers.

The Simple Foreknowledge Calvinist Attempt to Preserve Divine Responsiveness without Positing an Open Future

Among the no-risk models of providence, I consider the classic Calvinist proposal to be very close to the best that we can do, though I will later propose how I think it can be improved. John Calvin felt no conflict between a firm trust in God's sovereign providence over the details of life and an earnest practice of petitionary prayer which assumes God's responsiveness. The one who 'knows and feels that men and their counsels, and the issues of all things, are ruled and overruled by the Providence of God' will commit herself 'wholly unto God, and depend entirely upon Him'. Where there is this state of mind, 'prayers will ever follow, that God will begin and perfect every work which we undertake, while we thus rest on Him in all quietness, and on Him alone'.[19] Those

17 Scripture quotations are from the *New International Version Inclusive Language Edition* (London: Hodder & Stoughton, 1996).

18 Pinnock, *Most Moved Mover*, p. 48.

19 John Calvin, *A Defence of the Secret Providence of God: By Which He Executes His Eternal Decrees: Being a Reply to the 'Slanderous Reports' (Rom. iii. 8) of a Certain*

who are aware of God's 'all-ruling hand' will never hesitate to 'cast all their cares upon him', and they 'will all the while rest assured that the devil and all wicked men, whatever tumults they may cause, are not only held of God by their feet in chains, but are compelled to do His pleasure, under which assurance they will pass their lives in security and peace'.[20] It is precisely because we know that 'the dispensation of all those things which he [God] has made is in his own hand and power and that we are indeed his children, whom he has received into his faithful protection to nourish and educate', that we are 'to petition him for whatever we desire; and we are to recognize as a blessing from him, and thankfully to acknowledge, every benefit that falls to our share'.[21] Clearly, such gratitude would be inappropriate if the blessing we receive were not a gift from God *in response to* our request.

Donald MacKay argues that there is 'logical indeterminacy in the situation that confronts us moment by moment. This implies that we have a genuine share in determining what the future shall be, and that if our Creator is willing to meet us as God-in-time, then our dialogue with him in prayer may also affect the future in ways beyond the causal reach of our physical powers'.[22] Calvin asserts that just as God has ordained labour as a means by which to provide our physical needs, so he has established prayer as a means by which to obtain from God those things which we need him to provide.[23] Consequently, God's providence does not relieve us from responsibility, as was argued by Calvin's objectors who said that prayer is superfluous since everything is fixed in the decree.[24] On the contrary, since we know that God is 'the master and bestower of all things, who invites us to request them of him', were we not to do so we would be like people who neglect a treasure buried in the earth, after it has been pointed out to them.[25] Prayer is the means by which 'we reach those riches which are laid up for us with the Heavenly Father', for there is nothing which is 'promised to be expected from the Lord, which we are not also bidden to ask of him in prayers'.[26]

Worthless Calumniator Directed Against the Secret Providence of God [Calvin's Calvinism. Part II.] (trans. Henry Cole; London: Sovereign Grace Union, 1927 [1558]), pp. 229-30.

20   Calvin, *Secret Providence*, p. 230.

21   John Calvin, *Institutes of the Christian Religion* (ed. John T. McNeill; trans. Ford Lewis Battles; Library of Christian Classics, 20–21; London: SCM Press, 1960), I.14.22.

22   Donald M. MacKay, *The Open Mind and Other Essays* (Leicester: Inter-Varsity Press, 1988), p. 196.

23   Calvin, *Secret Providence*, p. 236.

24   Calvin, *Institutes*, I.17.3.

25   Calvin, *Institutes*, III.20.1.

26   Calvin, *Institutes*, III.20.2.

Moreover, the knowledge that God wishes to give us something is not a disincentive to prayer. Elijah was 'sure of God's purpose, after he has deliberately promised rain to King Ahab', yet he 'still anxiously prays with his head between his knees, and sends his servant seven times to look (1 Kings 18.42), not because he would discredit prophecy, but because he knew it was his duty, lest his faith be sleepy or sluggish, to lay his desires before God'.[27]

Even when we are confident of God's meticulous providence, prayer must not be separated from 'the total matrix of events and actions of which it forms a part'. Paul Helm illustrates this from the case of a student who studies hard for an exam, prays for success and then passes. On such an occasion, it should not be assumed that the success was caused by hard work alone, as though prayer only served to strengthen that will because, if that were true, prayer would be merely talking to oneself.[28] Because of this, we cannot ask what would have happened if a person had not prayed. To do so would be to remove the prayer from the matrix and thereby to change the total matrix. In some cases, the efficacy of a prayer is established by prior promise regarding the item of request, as in the promise 'if you seek me you will find me'. There may indeed be cases where God indicates that certain events will take place *only if* people pray.[29]

Donald MacKay describes things in a slightly different manner, but the substance of his understanding is similar to Helm's. He claims that 'it becomes luminously evident that in general "had we not prayed", things *could* have turned out otherwise; for from this standpoint "had we not..." means "had the Creator conceived the drama differently"—and once we say this, we can use no firm inferences to prescribe or proscribe the outcome, for our only firm ground of inference is our drama as the Creator *has* conceived it, together with his promise to be faithful to that conception (e.g. to Noah in Genesis 8:22)'.[30]

Prayer is 'not one physical factor—like a chemical or mechanical force—among many other such forces in a set of physical equations'.[31] In the unrepeatable history of the universe, the particular matrix of divine and human actions that is focused on for consideration is unique and unrepeatable. It is consequently not subject to scientific investigation, and it is impossible to say what would have happened if the unique matrix had been different, through the addition or omission of a petitioner's prayer. Given that God ordained both the ends and the means to them,

---

27   Calvin, *Institutes*, III.20.3.
28   Paul Helm, *The Providence of God* (Contours of Christian Theology; Downers Grove, IL: InterVarsity Press, 1993), pp. 154-55.
29   Helm, *Providence of God*, pp. 155-56.
30   MacKay, *Open Mind*, p. 195.
31   Helm, *Providence of God*, p. 157.

there are some cases in which people's prayer is part of the total matrix, and God acts *because* people asked him to do so. If they had not asked, the conditions in the whole matrix would have been insufficient for production of what is asked for. This was Augustine's point when he averred that 'prayers are useful in obtaining those favours which He [God] foresaw He would bestow on those who should pray for them'.[32] However, Helm suggests that Christians are also invited to pray for things which are unconditional, an example of which would be the coming of the kingdom of God. In these instances, the prayer is not so much a petition as an expression of desire, 'an affirmation of solidarity with the unfolding will of God'.[33] Doubtless, such prayers also foster our personal relationship with God.

I find the Calvinist reading of the biblical narrative generally persuasive. It affirms God's total control but asserts that human agents are nevertheless morally responsible when they act voluntarily or spontaneously, without external coercion. It believes that prayer has an effect on the way things come to be in the future and that it does so because God chooses to act in particular ways in response to the requests of his people. Calvinists frequently agree with Thomists in regard to the timelessness or 'time-freeness'[34] of God's own being but, because they believe human freedom to be spontaneous rather than contracausal, this does not have the same importance in their explanation of the responsiveness of a risk-free God as it does in the Thomist model.

Like the Thomists, Calvinists believe that God knows all future occurrences. In the Thomist view, however, God's foreordination and his foreknowledge were neither temporally nor logically prior to one another because God is simple. From John Feinberg's perspective this is a 'mistake of the first order', to treat God's thoughts as part of his essence.[35] It should also be noted, however, that Calvinist scholars are not necessarily committed to divine timelessness.[36] Thus, John Frame is able to assert that God 'can feel with human beings the flow of time from one moment to the next', so that 'he can react to events in a significant sense (events which, to be sure, he has foreordained)', and 'can hear and

---

32   Augustine, *City of God*, V.10, cited by Helm, *Providence of God*, p. 157.

33   Helm, *Providence of God*, p. 158.

34   The term preferred by Paul Helm, *Eternal God: A Study of God Without Time* (Oxford: Clarendon Press, 1988), pp. 36-37.

35   John Feinberg, 'God Ordains All Things', in Basinger and Basinger (eds), *Predestination and Free Will*, p. 86.

36   See for instance, John Feinberg, *No One Like Him: The Doctrine of God* (Foundations of Evangelical Theology; Wheaton, IL: Crossway Books, 2001), pp. 427-33; John M. Frame, *No Other God: A Response to Open Theism* (Philippsburg, NJ: P&R Publishing, 2001), pp. 157-59; and John M. Frame, *The Doctrine of God: A Theology of Lordship* (Philippsburg, NJ: Puritan & Reformed Publishing, 2002), pp. 557-59.

respond to prayer in time'. Because God dwells in time, 'there is give-and-take between him and human beings'.[37] God is genuinely responsive to prayer precisely because 'he ordains that many of his purposes will be achieved through the means of human prayers and actions'.[38]

Clark Pinnock's contention that prayer is a demonstration that the future is open[39] would only be true if he were correct in his rejection of comprehensive divine foreknowledge. Paul Helm suggests that we distinguish between two kinds of foreknowledge, O and A. O-foreknowledge is to know ahead of time without bringing the event about. A-foreknowledge is to know the future event as a result of 'ordaining or effectively willing or otherwise ensuring that p is true'. O-foreknowledge, also described as 'simple foreknowledge', is commonly asserted by Arminian theologians. A-foreknowledge was affirmed by Augustine,[40] Anselm,[41] Aquinas[42] and Calvin.[43] However, Helm considers unclear the extent to which A-foreknowledge is causative, since even Augustine distinguishes between foreknowledge and predestination, and conceptualizes states which God knows without learning but which he does not cause.[44] Helm proposes that, so long as God's A-foreknowledge of the actual world is not necessitated by the laws of logic alone, logical determinism or fatalism is not entailed by it.[45] However, it would not be compatible with indeterministic human freedom and so neither the classical Arminian nor the Thomist model is feasible. This point has been acknowledged by open theists and it is here that they pose a serious challenge to classical Arminianism.

Pinnock's contention that evidence of divine response to prayer is proof of open theism might well be echoed by classical Arminians but they would cite libertarian human freedom as the point that is proved, rather than the entire open theist package, which includes limited divine foreknowledge. To the contrary, I argue, as John Feinberg does, that 'libertarian free will creates tremendous problems', in regard to

---

37   Frame, *No Other God*, p. 159.
38   Frame, *No Other God*, p. 167.
39   Clark Pinnock, 'God Limits', in Basinger and Basinger (eds), *Predestination and Free Will*, p. 152.
40   Augustine, *On the Trinity*, XV.13.
41   Anselm, *On Foreknowledge, Predestination and the Grace of God*, in Jasper Hopkins and Herbert W. Richardson (eds), *Trinity, Incarnation and Redemption* (Lewiston, NY: Edwin Mellen Press, 1989), p. 166.
42   Aquinas, *Summa Theologica*, Ia, q.14, a.8.
43   Calvin, *Institutes*, III.23.6.
44   Augustine, *On the Predestination of the Saints*, XIX, cited by Helm, *Eternal God*, p. 131.
45   Helm, *Eternal God*, p. 149.

petitionary prayer.[46] As Feinberg points out, there is no problem if we 'ask God to do something that in no way involves human free will', but if we make a petition about ourselves or others that involves free will, 'these are to a large degree absurd requests' unless we really want God to override our freedom or that of others.[47] 'If I am not asking God to override someone else's freedom, then I'm asking him to do something which I believe he cannot do (make it the case that someone else does something freely).'[48] Since 'at the moment of free decision making nothing decisively inclines their will, regardless of what God or anyone else does or says', making petitions to God 'may be hopeless'.[49] Feinberg concludes that 'there is good reason for anyone committed to libertarian free will who understands the implications of the position to 'think twice before offering intercessory prayers' which involve the change of either our or others' actions.[50] At the very least, this compatibilist argument makes it clear that the practice of petitionary prayer is not so evidently a proof of either the libertarian nature of human freedom or of the concomitant openness of the future as Pinnock has proposed.

As to the proposed benefit in regard to divine responsiveness to our prayer which would be gained from God's not knowing the future acts of libertarianly free creatures, Bruce Ware correctly discerns that the perceived gain is illusory because open theists believe that God does know the past and present comprehensively. As a result, we are unable to give God information concerning our desires which he does not already have, when we pray. Ware correctly identifies a desire in the work of proponents of open theism to make God's interaction with us as dynamic and mutual as our relationship with other humans is. But, this can only be achieved if we 'deny of God not only his exhaustive knowledge of the future but also of the past and present'.[51]

Thus far the general framework of Calvinism's portrayal of God's responsiveness looks to me to be very plausible. A problem arises, however, in regard to the biblical language of divine response if God only has foreknowledge of the actual future, even (or especially) if that is the knowledge of his own will. Calvinists believe that God knows from eternity all that will occur in the future because it is all part of his eternal purpose, whether he has decided to bring it about through his own action or to permit it to be brought about by free creatures. This appears to

46   Feinberg, *No One Like Him*, pp. 704-706.
47   Feinberg, *No One Like Him*, pp. 704-705.
48   Feinberg, *No One Like Him*, p. 705.
49   Feinberg, *No One Like Him*, p. 705.
50   Feinberg, *No One Like Him*, p. 705.
51   Bruce Ware, *God's Lesser Glory: The Diminished God of Open Theism* (Wheaton, IL: Crossway Books, 2000), p. 167.

allow no moment (logically or temporally) within the divine purposing for God to know counterfactually the action of a creature and then to decide his response. That is, it leaves no room for God to know what a creature *would* do in a particular situation and then for God to act in ways that will bring about the situation in which creatures will freely act in a manner that will contribute to the accomplishment of God's general purpose for his creation. It is my thesis that only a soft determinist account of the world will enable such knowledge of future counterfactuals of free creatures and that a soft determinist account (such as is put forward by many Calvinist theologians) actually *requires* God to have this kind of knowledge. *God's knowledge of what* would *happen in all possible situations, even though such situations never actually occur, is essential to our understanding of the biblical language of divine responsiveness within a model of providence in which the future is fixed within God's eternal plan.*

A Middle Knowledge Calvinist Proposal in Defence of Divine Responsiveness

Vincent Brümmer has argued that 'to say that God brings about events *by means of* our prayers is not the same as to say that he brings about events *because of* our prayers'.[52] I contend, however, that we can overcome this disjunction through the acknowledgement that God knows not only all future possibilities but also future counterfactuals (i.e., events which *would* occur *if* particular circumstances existed). Since God has chosen to respond to our prayers, we can speak of his acting *because of* them but, since he has chosen to include those very prayers within his eternal purpose, we can also say that he accomplishes his will *by means of* them.[53] The fact that our petition has itself become a part of God's decree does not detract either from its genuine agency or from the personal relationship that exists between God and us.[54] As Paul Helm puts

---

52   Vincent Brümmer, *What Are We Doing When We Pray? A Philosophical Enquiry* (London: SCM Press, 1984), p. 51.

53   As B.M. Palmer, *The Theology of Prayer* (Harrisonburg, VA: Sprinkle Publications, 1980 reprint), p. 134, put it, prayer 'is not the cause which procures through its own efficiency, but merely the antecedent condition upon which a predetermined benefit is suspended. The purpose to give is, on Jehovah's part, sovereign and free; it is the spontaneous movement of His own gracious and loving will. Yet, in the exercise of the same sovereignty and goodness, He interposes the prayer of the creature as the channel through which His favor shall descend.'

54   Paul Helm responds helpfully to this concern of Brümmer's, effectively defending the genuinely interpersonal nature of the relationship that exists between God the King and his praying subjects ('Prayer and Providence', in Gijsbert van den Brink,

it, there are cases in which people's prayer is part of the total matrix and God acts *because* people asked him to. Had they not done so, the conditions in the whole matrix would have been insufficient for production of what is asked for.[55] Similarly, Augustine states that 'prayers are useful in obtaining those favours which He foresaw He would bestow on those who should pray for them'.[56]

The objection that there is no place for impetratory prayer if the future is not open is disturbing precisely because James 4.2 and other passages of scripture teach us that prayer *is* efficacious in obtaining certain blessings from God, and that we sometimes fail to get things *because* we do not ask for them. James explicitly connects our asking and our receiving. This is common in scripture. Clearly, in the model of divine providence presented by Calvin, God does not do things *because* we request them, in the sense that he had intended to do something else but changed his mind on account of our prayer. That is precisely the position taken within the openness model and it is not surprising that they wish to reserve the language of causal dependence for the sense which it carries within their model. But, I would argue, it is legitimate to use this language in a sense which coheres with a model of meticulous providence and to interpret James in a manner equally consistent with it.

James teaches us that there are occasions upon which the whole complex of factors contributing to the outcome includes prayer as one of its *necessary* ingredients. It really makes no difference whether this is by God's predetermination or not. For example, God could have predetermined that he would act to deliver Israel from Egypt and that he would do so even though no one prayed about it. On the other hand, God could have determined that this particular act of deliverance should be an event which his people would rightly discern as God's response to their prayers and which would properly elicit praise to God for his greatness and kindness.

What troubles theologians of the openness model, as they contemplate no-risk models, is that the prayers themselves are as much part of God's eternal purpose as are the answers. It gives them the impression that God is, in fact, the only one who is at work and the people who pray are simply manipulated by him to produce the whole 'puppet show'. It is at this point that the inclusion of God's knowledge of counterfactuals (in a

---

Luco J. van den Brom and Marcel Sarot [eds], *Christian Faith and Philosophical Theology: Essays in Honour of Vincent Brümmer Presented on the Occasion of the Twenty-fifth Anniversary of His Professorship in the Philosophy of Religion in the University of Utrecht* [Kampen: Kok Pharos Publishing House, 1992], pp. 103-15). See also Helm, *Providence of God*, pp. 147-53. I appreciate his line of argument even though I do not share his commitment to divine eternity as absolute timelessness.

55   Helm, *Providence of God*, p. 157.
56   Augustine, *City of God*, V.10, cited by Helm, *The Providence of God*, p. 157.

moment of 'middle knowledge') within a compatibilist model is helpful. In fact, I believe that the Calvinist model implicitly assumes it and will not work without it.

Furthermore, only such a no-risk model *could* include divine middle knowledge. I agree with critics of the Molinist appeal to middle knowledge who argue that it is impossible to know a future counter-factual of libertarian freedom. Contrary to open theists and even to many of my fellow Calvinists,[57] I am prepared to grant the possibility that *actual* libertarianly free future actions can be known by God because they have truth value and God knows all true propositions. (*How* he knows this, if creatures are libertarianly free, is admittedly much more mysterious than is his knowledge of such future actions when they are part of the future God has sovereignly chosen.) The same is not true, however, of libertarianly free counterfactuals, that is, of events which would have happened if important factors had been different than they were. By definition of the terms, it is impossible to know what a person *would* decide to do in a given situation if the person's decision is conceived to be indeterministically free. Surely, as Molinists have argued, there are many future counterfactuals that do have truth value. This is correct particularly in regard to negative statements concerning the future. One who has God's comprehensive knowledge of the past and present can identify with certainty many things which will not happen in the future. Unfortunately, this is not enough to satisfy the requirements of Molinist middle knowledge. For the proposal to work, God must know what a person would do in every possible situation and one cannot know that if the person's decision is ultimately indeterminate.[58]

In other words, I believe that a knowledge of future, contingent, purely hypothetical events is only available to God in a situation where free selves determine their actions in ways that implement all the facets of their selfhood. If one knows all those facets of the person and all the factors of the situation in which the person would make a decision, one can predict what that decision would be. Therefore, I agree that Molinist middle knowledge of future contingent possibilities that are never actualized is incoherent. However, I do not agree with Reformed

---

57   E.g., Helm, *Eternal God*, p. 98; Feinberg, *No One Like Him*, pp. 741, 747; Frame, *Doctrine of God*, p. 143. On the other hand, that God knows the future comprehensively appears very clear to me in scripture. Consequently, I must agree with John Frame, *Doctrine of God*, p. 143, who states that if, as open theists aver, it is impossible for God to foreknow the future acts of libertarianly free creatures, open theists 'would have been wiser to reject libertarianism, rather than drastically reconstruct their theology to make it consistent with libertarianism'.

58   John Feinberg, 'God Ordains All Things', p. 34, rightly asks: 'how can God *know*, even counterfactually, what *would* follow from anything else unless some form of determinism is correct?'

theologians like Karl Barth that we must reject the concept of middle knowledge because of the use for which the theory was formulated by Molina, namely the harmonizing of absolute divine sovereignty with libertarian human freedom.[59] In fact, I am convinced that the critique of simple foreknowledge both by Molinists and open God theologians is correct. If God only has simple foreknowledge, that is, knowledge of the actual future, his knowledge is useless to his providential care. By the time God knows what is actually going to happen, it is 'too late' for him to do anything about it and this is true whether or not creatures have libertarian free will,[60] and whether or not God is atemporal.

By introducing the logical (or even, in some sense, chronological) moment of middle knowledge, we allow for God's eternal purpose to be established with the creaturely desires 'in mind'. God knows what his children would do freely or spontaneously, being the people they have become through an amazingly complex array of factors physical, psychological, relational and divinely gracious. Certainly God has played a part in bringing them to that point in their human and spiritual maturity but he has not done so coercively. He has graciously worked by his Spirit, along with the 'natural' and circumstantial factors of their lives, to bring them to this point in the conformity to the image of Christ which is his goal for them. So, in one sense it is true that they are what God has 'made' them. But, in another very significant sense, the people they have become through a multitude of choices made during their lives are the people that God has taken into account when forming his eternal purpose. No one determines who will be the objects of God's special grace; that is God's free prerogative or it would be earned, a proposal that Christian theology has regularly rejected, though not always with equal consistency. At the moment that these people pray, however, it is they who do so, not God. And it is to *their* petitions, and not to himself, that God responds when he acts in the way that they have requested. They then have *because* they asked, just as, in some situations, they would *not* have had *because* they did *not* ask.

I cannot deny that the human action is *less* determinative of the outcome in my model than it is in the openness model. But, I do insist that, within God's overall control, he has given us genuinely effective agency so that our actions, including our prayer, are real (though

---

59   Karl Barth, *Church Dogmatics: Volume II Part 1. The Doctrine of God* (ed. G.W. Bromiley and T.F. Torrance; trans. T.H.L. Parker, W.B. Johnston, Harold Knight and J.L.M. Haire; Edinburgh: T. & T. Clark, 1957 [1950]), p. 575. Among Reformed scholars who affirmed Molinism, Barth cites F. Gomarus and A. Walaeus, and he cites J. Gerhard and J. Quensted as Lutherans who adopted the view.

60   This point is made forcefully in William Hasker, *God, Time and Knowledge* (Ithaca, NY: Cornell University Press, 1989), pp. 51-63.

secondary) 'causes' of the way things turn out, and hence may legitimately be spoken of in the language of 'because'.

In his helpful critique of the pre-published manuscript of my *Providence and Prayer*, John Sanders made the statement that proponents of a non-risk model of providence and prayer 'should use the same careful word selection they use when discussing the doctrine of election so as not to mislead people into believing that God is actually affected by our prayers'. This is a very important analogy and it does form a significant warning to those of us who believe and teach no-risk models. Since the Arminian controversy within Calvinism, Reformed theologians have clearly asserted that God's electing grace is unconditional. God does not elect people because of anything about them, including their faith which he merely foresees; he chooses them in free and sovereign grace and the faith he foresees is the faith he has chosen to give, from before the creation of the world. Calvinist or Reformed theologians affirm the instrumentality of faith in salvation but they insist that we are saved *by* faith but only *because* of the work of Christ. We are not saved *because* of faith and God's choice of us was not *because* of our faith, our faith is *because* of his choice.

By analogy, using the terms in the same way, a Calvinist would have to say that prayer is instrumental but not causal. Subsequent to our petition, God acts in response to our request, which was part of the complex of factors included in his plan to act as he does, but his *choice* to act in this way was not *caused* by our prayers. In other words, God's *act* of extending Hezekiah's life may have been caused by Hezekiah's petition but his *decision* to heal Hezekiah was not. On the other hand, the openness model can assert that even God's decision to heal Hezekiah was caused by Hezekiah's petition. So, there is a difference and that difference needs to be clearly explained to those with whom we converse, but it is not a difference between one legitimate use of the language of cause and another illegitimate use, nor between the presence and absence of divine response.

If someone asks a Calvinist why God justified her, she may legitimately answer: 'Because I believed in Jesus'. But, if asked further: 'Why did you believe in Jesus?', she might answer: 'Because my pastor preached the gospel and the Spirit of God drew me to Christ, opened my heart and gave me faith.' If God had not chosen her to salvation, the gospel preaching of her pastor would have been ineffective. On the other hand, since gospel proclamation was the instrument God chose to bring her to faith, it would not be incorrect for her to say to her pastor: 'Thank you for explaining the good news of salvation so clearly. I was saved *because* you preached the gospel.'

In the same way, when Hezekiah was healed, if someone asked him: 'Why did God heal you after Isaiah had predicted your death?', he might properly answer: '*Because* I wept and prayed'. In saying so, however, Hezekiah ought not to think that God's *decision* within his eternal purpose was *caused* by his prayer. God freely and graciously decided that he would extend Hezekiah's life, just as he decided that he would deliver the apostle Peter but not deacon Stephen. He decided, however, that he would do this in response to the prayers of Hezekiah and possibly of others in his family. Yet, the grace that put Hezekiah into a relationship with God that gave him the right to pray to Yahweh, and the work of God's Spirit that urged him to pray, were all the work of God's kindness and hence not conditioned on any action of Hezekiah. Thus, there is a sense in which the very prayer of Hezekiah was God's work and Hezekiah could give God praise not only for delivering him but for so graciously bringing him into a relationship in which his own prayer could be a causal factor in that deliverance. In such an understanding, all the glory must unmistakably go to God![61]

Speaking of the efficacy of prayer, Donald M. MacKay aptly suggests that there is no guarantee 'that if God had created a drama in which you had not prayed, he would still have made it one in which help was sent off in time to rescue you'.[62] We have God's promise that he hears prayer and that he cooperates for our good and so we pray, 'confident that if the Creator sees that good would be served by a positive response, he will have ordered accordingly events that may otherwise have no "causal

---

61   Gregory Boyd, *God of the Possible: A Biblical Introduction to the Open View of God* (Grand Rapids, MI: Baker, 2000), p. 82, has asked an appropriate question: 'If we accept the classical view of foreknowledge and suppose that the Lord was certain that he would *not* let Hezekiah die, wasn't he being duplicitous when he initially told Hezekiah that he would not recover? And if we suppose that the Lord was certain all along that Hezekiah would, in fact, live fifteen years after this episode, wasn't it misleading for God to tell him that he was *adding* fifteen years to his life? Wouldn't Jeremiah also be mistaken in announcing that God *changed his mind* when he reversed his stated intentions to Hezekiah—if, in fact, God's mind never really changes?'

It *would* be duplicitous for God to deal with us this way *if* he had not specifically told us, through that same prophet, that this is how God works (Jer. 18.5-10). He always acts appropriately and this means that when circumstances and people change, God's action changes so that he can remain consistent with his moral nature. In the instances of intercession by Moses, the petition of Hezekiah and the repentance of Nineveh in response to Jonah's announcement of God's intended judgment, we see this principle at work. We are prepared for the fact that God might warn us of a coming disaster precisely to stir us to prayer so that we can participate in the averting of that otherwise certain trouble. It is not at all surprising that Jeremiah should speak of such an occurrence as a *change of God's mind* even though he knew the principle at work as it was so clearly revealed to and through him.

62   Donald M. MacKay, *Science, Chance and Providence* (Oxford: Oxford University Press, 1978), p. 55.

connection" (in the scientific sense) with the action of praying'.[63] Consequently, 'there is no inconsistency between recognizing an event as an answer to prayer and recognizing that it was predictable by others— even if the prediction could have been validly made by them (though not by you) before the prayer was offered'.[64]

The objective of prayer is not to change God's mind but to discern it and to ask God to do what he wills to do. As we were taught by our Lord, all of our prayers should be part of our overall desire that God's will, in particular his moral will, should be done on earth as it is in heaven (Mt. 5.10). The apostle John gave us a fundamental principle regarding prayer when he assured us that our prayers will be heard and that God will *respond* to them and give us what we ask for 'if we ask anything according to his will' (1 Jn 5.14-15). Here, I take the will of God to be the will of his eternal purpose. The effectiveness of the Holy Spirit's intercession for us is not his ability to change the mind of the Father but the fact that 'the Spirit intercedes for the saints in accordance with God's will' (Rom. 8.27). Once again, this must be the will of God's eternal purpose because it is ludicrous to think that the Spirit might pray for something immoral. God will be *responsive* to our prayers and we will be effective in prayer to the degree that we are led by the Spirit of God, discern the mind of God and ask him to do what he wills to do in the situation. Such discerning and effective prayer is a fruit of the Spirit's work in our own minds so that we increasingly have the mind of Christ.

Conclusion

Just as 'freedom' does not mean the same thing to proponents of risk models of providence, including open theists, or even to non-risk Thomists, as it does to believers in God's meticulous and risk-free governing of the world, so 'response' has a slightly different meaning. With the aid of God's middle knowledge, however, we are able to conceptualize how God is able to include both our prayers and his own responses to those prayers in his eternal plan. In times of need, we can pray earnestly that God will act and if he does as we have asked, we can rightly be grateful that he acted *in response* to our prayer. Our prayers have an important part in the establishment of the ultimate outcome, even if their role is not to change God's mind about his own action. Fervent petition and joyful thanksgiving are all part of the life of the Christian who believes that God is totally in control but that God has chosen to include us in the accomplishment of his plan and to do so in a way that

---

63   MacKay, *Science, Chance and Providence*, p. 55.
64   MacKay, *Science, Chance and Providence*, p. 60.

respects the freedom and dignity which he has given to us as creatures in his image.

CHAPTER 7

Reducing God to Human Proportions

John Sanders

Introduction

Norman Geisler claims that open theists, such as Clark Pinnock, are 'creating God in the image of man'; Bruce Ware argues that open theists seriously 'diminish God'; and Ronald Nash claims that open theists worship a 'finite God'.[1] Basically, these all boil down to the claim that open theists bring God down to the level of creatures—reducing God to an exalted human being.

In order to see whether this criticism is appropriate I will first survey some of the intellectual history, both Eastern and Western, regarding what people have thought it means to reduce God. Then I will focus on the issues surrounding the interpretation of biblical texts regarding immutability and omniscience detailing the criticisms of reducing God. It will be shown that in order for the accusations of reducing God to stick, a certain vantage point must be assumed, and if one does not affirm this vantage point, then the charge falls like water off a duck's back.

What does it Mean to 'Reduce' God?

Generally, to reduce God has been defined as one of the following: (1) the absolute cannot be relativised; (2) the finite cannot contain the infinite; (3) the infinite cannot be described by finite terms; or (4) God is completely unlike anything in creation. Though there is disagreement

---

1   N.H. Geisler, *Creating God in the Image of Man?* (Minneapolis: Bethany House, 1997); B.A. Ware, *God's Lesser Glory: The Diminished God of Open Theism* (Wheaton, IL: Crossway, 2000); R.H. Nash, *Life's Ultimate Questions* (Grand Rapids, MI: Zondervan, 1999).

regarding the details, there is an amazing similarity between a variety
Eastern and Western thinkers on these points.

The Denial of Predication

The great Hindu theologian, Shankara, wrestled with applying human
language to Brahman (ultimate reality). 'Brahman is eternal, all-knowing,
absolutely self-sufficient, ever pure, intelligent and free, pure knowledge,
absolute bliss.'[2] However, a being that has bliss and intelligence seems to
have characteristics in common with humans—that is, finite characteristics. Shankara realized the problem and so made his famous distinction
between *saguna* Brahman (God with characteristics) and *nirguna*
Brahman (God without characteristics). The common interpretation of
Shankara is that he believed that *saguna* Brahman was for purely
propaedutic reasons to help us towards enlightenment while *nirguna*
Brahman corresponds to reality.[3] Consequently, Brahman is not related to
the world, cannot receive anything, and is beyond all finite characteristics.
The categories of time and change do not apply to Brahman.[4] To think
of Brahman as possessing qualities is to place Brahman under limiting
conditions—to reduce God to human proportions. Though some Hindu
theologians (e.g. Ramanuja) rejected Shankara's *nirguna–saguna*
distinction, the notion that Brahman is simple and therefore beyond
characteristics has become a central tenet of advaita (non dualism).

A similar claim is made by many Buddhists. According to Asvaghosa
all of our present thought and interpretation of our experience is
conditioned by the realm of impermanence. Everything fades away—our
health, our friendships—nothing lasts. Time and change mark our
existence. There is, however, another realm that is absolutely unconditioned, unaffected by change, beyond the limitations of our existence.
This unconditioned realm is ineffable for we cannot use human language
to speak of it or rationality to understand it because all language and

---

2   S. Radhakrishnan and C.A. Moore (eds), *A Sourcebook of Indian Philosophy*
(Prrinceton, NJ: Princeton University Press, 1957), p. 512.

3   Recent interpreters of Shankara make a good case that he believed that Brahman
really is personal and, hence, not beyond limiting categories. See B.J. Malkovsky, 'The
Personhood of Samkara's *Para Brahman*', *Journal of Religion* 77 (1997), pp. 541-62;
B.J. Malkovsky, 'Samkara on Divine Grace', in B.J. Malkovsky (ed.), *New Perspectives
on Advaita Vedanta* (Leiden: Brill, 2000), pp. 70-83; Richard DeSmet, 'Forward Steps in
Sankara Research', *Darshana International* 26 (1987), pp. 33-46. Even if the standard
reading of Shankara is overturned, the view that predicating attributes of Brahman reduces
Brahman remains true of post-Shankara advaita.

4   Radhakrishnan and Moore (eds), *Sourcebook of Indian Philosophy*, pp. 515,
522, 529-31.

rationality occur within the realm of the conditioned—the limited. That which is truly unlimited cannot be spoken.[5] The ultimate reality is wholly beyond our words and concepts—we must not reduce it to human proportions.[6] If we do speak of it then the doctrine of the 'double truth' must be kept in mind. According to this doctrine (which functions like the *saguna–nirguna* distinction), lower truth is conveyed in language but higher truth surpasses predication.

Western thinkers have faced the same issue.[7] For instance, in Plato's system a personal God is not the highest form of reality. Rather, his ultimate reality is the forms. Though he does not work out his views in a fully consistent manner, Plato places the Good beyond all finite categories such as time, space, change, personhood, intelligence and will. That is, his ultimate metaphysical principle is timeless, immutable, incorporeal and impersonal. It is not aware of anything and cannot be affected by anything (impassible). To believe otherwise is to reduce ultimate reality to human proportions. Below the Good is the demiurge (God). God is timeless, completely immutable, impassible and incapable of love. He argues that God is perfect and that a perfect being would never change as any change could only be a change for the worse. God 'cannot be supposed to have either joy or sorrow. Certainly not! There would be great impropriety in the assumption of either alternative.'[8] God cannot love because love implies a deficiency—a need or lack of some kind. The only reason one loves is because one wants something that you do not have. Since God is self-sufficient, God does not love. Plato's God is highly exalted but does have the finite characteristics of omniscience and omnipotence. Yet, overall, he tries very hard not to reduce God to human proportions since that involves 'great impropriety'.

Aristotle's ultimate deity is his unmoved-mover. God is a timeless, self-sufficient, immutable, impassible and simple (no differentiation) being of pure consciousness. God has no potentiality and so never changes in any

---

5   C. Hartshorne and W.L. Reese (eds), *Philosophers Speak of God* (Chicago: University of Chicago Press, 1953), p. 168.

6   Not all Buddhists agree with this way of thinking. On the debates between Buddhists, see K. Ward, *Concepts of God in Five Religious Traditions* (Oxford: One World, 1987), pp. 59-80.

7   For further discussion on these and other Western thinkers, see J. Sanders, 'Historical Considerations', in Clark Pinnock, Richard Rice, John Sanders, William Hasker and David Basinger, *The Openness of God: A Biblical Challenge to the Traditional View of God* (Downers Grove, IL: InterVarsity Press, 1994), pp. 59-100. For comparisons of Eastern and Western theologians on the nature of God, see J.B. Carman, *Majesty and Meekness: A Comparative Study of Contrast and Harmony in the Concept of God* (Grand Rapids, MI: Eerdmans, 1994).

8   Plato, *Philebus* 33, in *The Dialogues of Plato* (trans. B. Jowett; 2 vols; New York: Random House, 1937), II, p. 366.

respect. God has no relations with any being external to himself. If God had relations with others then God would be dependent upon the others in order to have the relationship. God cannot have any friends. In fact, God is not even aware that we exist as that would make him less than perfect and would mean that God was conditioned by finite beings thus reducing the magnificence of God. To think of God in relationship with us is to render God finite!

The Greek skeptic, Carneades, argued that if one attributes to God properties such as life, intelligence and bliss, then one has rendered the infinite finite. 'It is impossible to ascribe the characteristics of personal existence to deity without limiting its infinity.'[9]

According to the influential writer, Plotinus, the best name for the ultimate reality is the 'One'. However, even this name does not really apply since the One is so utterly transcendent as to be beyond being, essence and life. The One is not a soul or mind for if one ascribed personal characteristics to it then it would be limited. Truly, nothing can be predicated of it—it is wholly ineffable—completely beyond all finite categories. If we were to assert that the One has life, intelligence, or will or any attribute, then we would be placing limits on the divine.

Skipping ahead to the contemporary scene, the same sentiments continue to be expressed. Paul Tillich, following in this distinguished tradition, argued that the only non-symbolic statement we could make about God is that God is 'Being-Itself'. God is not *a being* existing alongside other beings as that would make God finite. All existing beings are a mix of being and nonbeing but God is infinite containing no potentiality or mutability. God, as Being-Itself, does not even exist, since to exist is to possess nonbeing which is obviously inapplicable to God. Also, to think of creatures having interpersonal relations with God is impossible since to have a relationship is to posit two beings existing alongside each other. 'It is an insult to the divine holiness to treat God as a partner with whom one collaborates or as a superior power whom one influences by rites and prayers.'[10] Why is it an insult? Because to think of God as personal and relating to us reduces God to a great being existing alongside lesser beings—clearly reducing God to human proportions.

According to Harvard theologian Gordon Kaufman, the word 'God' is the symbol for the ultimate mystery behind human existence.[11] He speaks of the 'real God' (God-in-himself) which is completely ineffable and the 'available God' (God in relation to us) which is a human

---

9   Hartshorne and Reese (eds), *Philosophers Speak of God*, p. 416.

10   P. Tillich, *Systematic Theology* (3 vols; Chicago: University of Chicago Press, 1951–63), I, pp. 271-72.

11   See G. Kaufman, *In the Face of Mystery: A Constructive Theology* (Cambridge, MA: Harvard University Press, 1993), and *God the Problem* (Cambridge, MA: Harvard University Press, 1972).

construct of our theological imagination. Although we are cut off from knowing anything about this mystery we are forced to construct models of God in order to give meaning to our lives. Kaufman believes God is totally infinite and so all human language is inappropriate for speaking of God. Consequently, he heaps ridicule on any anthropomorphic conception of God—especially the personalistic conceptions of ordinary Christians (he calls such a God a 'spook').

According to John Hick, 'God', or what he prefers to call the 'Real', is outside all human experience and language so we cannot make predications about the Real for to do so implies that the Real is an object within human experience.[12] The finite cannot contain the infinite so no human thought or words are able to grasp the being of God. There is simply no way of knowing what God really is, whether personal or impersonal, good or bad, intelligent or ignorant.

A common thread running through all these thinkers is the belief that there is an *infinite* qualitative difference separating divinity from humanity. We must not reduce the infinite deity to our finite human understandings. The appeal to God's absolute infinity argues that thinking of God as personal in a straightforward (reality depicting) way overlooks the fact that the concept 'personal' when used for God is actually a finite category. Depicting God in personal symbols, as biblical writers do, limits God. J.N. Findlay charges that it is 'wholly anomalous to worship anything *limited* in any thinkable manner'.[13] Consequently, to speak of God utilizing any human concepts is to affirm a 'finite' God and thus commit idolatry.[14]

The Reduced God of Scripture

In light of these remarks consider how grossly anthropomorphic the following biblical descriptions are because they apply finite character-

---

12   J. Hick, *An Interpretation of Religion: Human Responses to the Transcendent* (New Haven, CT: Yale University Press, 1989). Curiously, for Hick the various deities of the religions (Yahweh, Allah, heavenly Father, etc.) are 'finite' manifestations of the infinite Real. If so, then those who actually participate in worship of these deities are worshipping finite beings. That is, the only beings 'available' for worship are finite beings, according to Hick.

13   Cited in F.G. Kirkpatrick, *Together Bound: God, History, and the Religious Community* (New York: Oxford University Press, 1994), p. 46.

14   Paul Knitter accuses anyone who worships Jesus as the unsurpassable revelation of God of being an idolater since Jesus is 'finite'. Given his definition of idolatry I concede that I commit idolatry. See J. Sanders, 'Idolater Indeed!', in L. Swidler and P. Mojzes (eds), *The Uniqueness of Jesus: A Dialogue with Paul F. Knitter* (Maryknoll, NY: Orbis, 1997), pp. 121-25.

istics to God. 'Yahweh your God is the God of gods and the Lord of lords, the great the mighty, and the awesome God who does not show partiality, nor take a bribe. He executes justice for the orphan and the widow, and shows his love for the alien by giving him food and clothing' (Dt. 10.17-18).[15] God is 'gracious and compassionate, slow to anger, abounding in loving kindness, and relenting of evil' (Joel 2.13). A God who cares about orphans, widows and aliens? A God who is slow to anger? How anthropomorphic can you get? According to the authors cited above, the biblical writers are guilty of reducing God to human proportions.

Classical Theism

There is a long tradition in Jewish and Christian theology, known as Classical Theism, that also shies away from these biblical descriptions. The problem is that the scriptures are simply too anthropomorphic. A deity who gets angry is a deity that experiences change. A deity that experiences change, experiences time. Such a being cannot be immutable, impassible, simple or timeless. Consequently, asserting that God can get angry or change his mind is to reduce God to human proportions. However, these theologians, unlike those above, are willing to attribute some finite characteristics to God. For instance, in the Judeo-Christian tradition it has commonly been non-negotiable that God is a personal being.

According to the Jewish theologian, Philo of Alexandria, we cannot know what God is like (God's essence), we can only know that he exists. The Septuagint rendered the divine name in Exodus 3.14 as 'He who is'. Philo took this to mean 'My nature is to be, not to be described by name'.[16] God is anonymous or nameless, for to name is to define and to define is to apply finite categories and so to limit.[17] Philo's God is absolutely transcendent and so is ineffable. God is so transcendent that he has no contact with human reason let alone with matter.

God is perfect, timeless, omnipotent, omniscient (including fore-knowledge), simple, incorporeal, alone, self-sufficient, immutable and impassible. Philo claims that though God's self-sufficiency cannot allow

---

15   Scripture quotations are from the New American Standard Bible (Carol Stream, IL: Creation House, 1960).

16   Philo, *On the Change of Names* 11, in *The Works of Philo* (trans. C.D. Yonge; Peabody, MA: Hendrickson, 1993), p. 342.

17   In ascribing anonymity to God, Philo was following the Septuagint which never uses a name for God: *Yahweh* is always translated *kyrios*. See T.E. Pollard, 'The Impassibility of God', *Scottish Journal of Theology* 8 (1955), pp. 355-56, and A. Konig, *Here Am I* (Grand Rapids, MI: Eerdmans, 1982), p. 67.

reciprocal relations, God's activities produce effects upon the world that are not true relations but 'quasi-relations'. Regarding God's immutability and impassibility, he holds that God cannot be acted upon and that 'God is not susceptible to any passion at all'.[18] Philo is well aware of the many biblical texts that say God repents (changes his mind) or feels anger. In Philo's mind such texts do not tell us what God is really like. Rather, they are anthropomorphisms for the benefit of the 'duller folk' who cannot understand the true nature of God. 'For what can be a greater act of wickedness than to think that the unchangeable God can be changed?'[19] That would certainly be reducing God to human proportions.

The Western church is heavily indebted to Philo for he furnished Christian thinkers with the basic methodology concerning the 'correct' way of reading the scriptures so as not to diminish the divine glory. However, Christians did not agree with Philo on everything due to their understanding that God had come to us in Jesus.

For this survey, Augustine is the most important Western theologian due to his unparalleled influence. Augustine sees God as self-sufficient, impassible, immutable, omniscient, omnipotent, timeless, ineffable and simple.[20] For him immutability is a key attribute. He writes: 'Whatever is changeable is not the most high God.'[21] He claims that God cannot even be capable of change in any respect or he would suffer a loss of being. 'Only what does not only not change but also cannot change at all falls most truly...under the category of being.'[22] Like Philo, Augustine is well aware of the numerous biblical texts which speak of God being angry or joyful but such texts are written for 'babes' and do not properly refer to God.[23] The Bible, when speaking of divine wrath, anger, love and mercy, does not describe God as he is. All change is to be explained as a change in us and not God. To believe otherwise on these matters is to turn God into a finite God.

In the Middle Ages the Jewish theologian Maimonides affirmed the God of classical theism when he asserted that God is simple, perfect and

18 Philo, *On the Immutability of God* 52, in *Works*, p. 162.
19 Philo, *On the Immutability of God* 22, in *Works*, p. 160.
20 See Augustine's *Confessions* 7.11; 11.18; 12.15; 13.16; *The Trinity* 1.1.3; 5.2.3; 4.5-6; 7.5.10; and *City of God* 8.6; 11.10; 22.2. See also J.K. Mozley, *The Impassibility of God* (New York: Cambridge University Press, 1926), pp. 104-109; J. Hallman, *The Descent of God* (Minneapolis: Fortress Press, 1991), pp. 105-23; B.W. Farley, *The Providence of God* (Grand Rapids, MI: Baker Book House, 1988), pp. 101-106; and C.B. Kaiser, *The Doctrine of God* (Westchester, IL: Crossway, 1982), pp. 75-81.
21 Augustine, *City of God* 8.6. See also *Confessions* 7.11.
22 Augustine, *The Trinity* 5.2.3.
23 Augustine, *Trinity* 1.1.2.

'has nothing in common with creatures' for God is free from all limitation.[24] He writes: 'The negative attributes of God are the true attributes.'[25] We are not to even come close to taking the biblical portrayals of God as reality depicting. They do not represent God as he is. If we took them to affirm that God is a person in some fairly recognizable sense, we would be reducing God to human proportions.

Similarly, the Medieval Muslim theologian Al-Ghazzali, asserted that no confusion of human and divine is allowed. Following Aristotle, he writes: 'To bear relationship to what is imperfect carries with it imperfection.'[26] He acknowledges that we 'worship a deity that hears, sees, and has knowledge, power, will, (and) life', but he relegates these attributes to a lower level of understanding much like the *saguna* Brahman of Shankara. If we are not to reduce the glory of God then we should 'avoid denoting him by attributers altogether'.[27] As with Philo, Al-Ghazzali says we can know that God exists but not what God is like (God's essence). All care must be taken not to reduce the magnificence of God by attribution of limiting qualities.

Moral to the Story

We could continue this survey but enough has been said to highlight that one of the central facets of classical theism, whether in its Jewish, Christian or Muslim forms is that God cannot change in any respect. There can be no changing relations or emotions for God has no potentiality for any such changes. For Augustine, anyone who says that God is even capable of change is reducing God. What then are we to make of those contemporary evangelical Calvinists such as Bruce Ware and Ronald Nash who claim to be classical theists but assert that God is capable of changing in some respects?[28] If Ware and Nash were brought before Augustine's tribunal with the charge of reducing God to human proportions, Saint Augustine would render a guilty verdict.

There is a moral to this story: one should be extremely careful when casting stones about reducing God for the windows in your theological house may be smashed, in turn, by those who believe you have reduced God. That is, 'reducing God' is a relative concept depending upon your vantage point. Some evangelical critics of open theism believe it reduces God to human proportions while the classical theists just cited would

---

24   Ward, *Concepts of God*, p. 103.
25   Ward, *Concepts of God*, p. 102.
26   Ward, *Concepts of God*, p. 122.
27   Ward, *Concepts of God*, p. 123.
28   Ware, *God's Lesser Glory*, p. 164; and R. Nash, *The Concept of God* (Grand Rapids, MI: Zondervan, 1983), pp. 105, 114.

claim that all evangelicals (including the critics of open theism) are guilty of reducing God to human proportions. Finally, many Hindu, Buddhist and Western thinkers would assert that even the classical theists are guilty of reducing God. Consequently, those going around accusing open theism of diminishing God's glory had better beware for they are also guilty of this according to the great classical theists and others.

How are we to move forward from this impasse? I suggest two points. First, that we make a distinction between saying God is not completely like anything in creation and saying God is completely unlike anything in creation. Certainly, a great many of the theologians and philosophers from various religions have affirmed the latter (God's total difference). But this ends up in agnosticism. If we hold that God is not completely like anything in creation then we can allow that some attributes can justifiably be predicated of God. Moreover, if humans are created in the image of God then there is some sort of correspondence between God and humanity and hence it is legitimate to apply human language and conceptions to God. The issue will be which ones.[29]

My second suggestion is that the God who comes to us in Jesus is the real God. Not that Jesus discloses everything about God but that what he reveals is the way God is. This is similar to Rahner's rule: the economic Trinity is the immanent Trinity. The God with us (*quoad nos*) is who God is (*in se*). God is always more than we can understand, but if we are to accept Immanuel (Jn 1; Heb. 1.3; Col. 2.9), then we must take the divine disclosure in Jesus as the way God is unless we have good reasons for doing otherwise. What would be such reasons? Typically, they have been the arguments given above involving perfections, immutability and infinity. The question will be whether those arguments are substantial enough to legitimize challenging the scriptural portrayals of God. Natural theology is permissible but we will have to debate the role of hermeneutical and theological presuppositions as criteriological for the interpretation of scripture.[30] At a minimum this approach means that at least in some respects it is legitimate to speak of God using finite/creaturely categories. The dispute will be over which ones are best in light of scripture, tradition, reason and the Christian life.

---

29   See J. Sanders, *The God Who Risks: A Theology of Providence* (Downers Grove, IL: InterVarsity Press, 1998), p. 29.

30   See Amos Yong, 'Divine Omniscience and Future Contingents: Weighing the Presuppositional Issues in the Contemporary Debate', *Evangelical Review of Theology* 26.3 (2002), pp. 240-64.

Does Open Theism Reduce God?

Having observed the range of views in history among various traditions on what it means to reduce God, I now want to focus on the charge against open theism. In this section I will concentrate on the work of Reformed philosopher Paul Helm for he believes open theism reduces God in two areas in particular: immutability and omniscience.

Immutability

There are passages in scripture that say that God does not change. 'I the LORD do not change therefore you [Israel] are not destroyed' (Mal. 3.6). God is 'not human that he should change his mind' (Num. 23.19; 1 Sam. 15.29). On the other hand, there are passages that say that God does change. The Lord was grieved that he made humans because they continually sinned (Gen. 6.6). God changed his mind about what he said he would do (Ex. 32.14; 1 Sam. 15.11, 35).

What are we to do with these seemingly contrary teachings? In his book, *The Providence of God*, Paul Helm says that scripture does not contradict itself so we must do something with these apparent contradictions.[31] According to Helm we have two options. (1) We can hold that the texts that say that God changes are the clear, strong and correct texts and subordinate the passages about God not changing to them. Or, (2) we can reverse this and claim that the passages about God not changing are the clear, strong and correct texts and subordinate the changing God texts to them. That is, we must resolve the problem by establishing one set of texts as the clear passages and interpret the other set of texts (the unclear) by them. One set gives us the proper teaching about the divine nature while the other set is comprised of 'anthropomorphisms'. But how are we to decide which set is the 'clear' teaching?

If we place set (2), God can change in some respects, over set (1), God cannot change in any respect, then, according to Helm, we can say that God can change his mind, that he can be affected by our prayers, and that some of his intentions can be thwarted. Moreover, he says we could attribute a 'rich, ever-changing emotional life' to God. Many will find this appealing, but not Helm. The choice, he says, 'seems obvious'. We must subordinate set (2) to set (1). The texts about God not changing are the clear and correct teachings about God. If we did not say this, then we will allow the 'weaker' statements in scripture to control the stronger, resulting in 'theological reductionism in which God is distilled to human

---

31   P. Helm, *The Providence of God* (Contours of Christian Theology; Downers Grove, IL: InterVarsity Press, 1994), pp. 51-54.

proportions' as it is in open theism according to Helm. That is, we must use the clear, strong texts of scripture that teach complete immutability and meticulous providence to interpret the unclear, weak texts that seem to teach that God changes and that some of God's intentions can be resisted.[32] Otherwise, we make God into a very large human—creating God in the image of humans. Who wants to do that?

Helm's method for handling the problem follows in the line of Philo, Augustine, Calvin and other classical theists. But there are a number of problems with it. First, we should notice that Helm has used a philosophical criterion to determine the correct interpretation of these biblical texts. This is legitimate but we should be up front about what is going on—subordinating biblical texts to philosophical argument. Helm claims it is improper to think of God having human characteristics such as changes of mind and emotions. Why so? Because we don't want to reduce God! Reduce God from what? From an exalted conception of divine transcendence and sovereignty. After all, any God worth his salt is strongly immutable, impassible, timeless, exercises total control over creation and never, ever, takes any risks that humans would do things God does not want done. But if we are going to use such philosophical arguments to tell us which texts of scripture teach the truth about God and which texts do not, then we need to put those arguments on the table for debate. Simply asserting that open theists are 'reducing God' or that they are being impious may be effective rhetorical devices, but they are not arguments.

A second problem is that Helm begs the question. He says we must take the clear/strong texts and read the weaker ones in light of them. But that is precisely what is being debated. On what grounds does he decide which texts are the strong ones? Those texts that agree with his view of God! The passages about God not changing and exercising meticulous providence are the clear teaching of scripture because they agree with his understanding of the divine nature. Otherwise, we don't really have a God at all. In other words, for Helm, only the strong Calvinist view affirms a 'real' God. However, this begs the question by assuming that

---

32 Several critics of open theism have argued that attributing libertarian freedom to humans reduces God because it implies that God's will can, for some things, be thwarted. B. Ware makes this claim in his *God's Lesser Glory*, p. 226. R. Highfield argues that the very notions of divine self-limitation and human libertarian freedom lead to a 'monstrous scene', for they imply a 'little god' which 'diminishes the unique deity of God'. See his 'The Function of Divine Self-Limitation in Open Theism: Great Wall or Picket Fence?', *Journal of the Evangelical Theological Society* 45.2 (2002), pp. 279-99. What such critics fail to realize is that anyone who affirms libertarian freedom, such as Arminians and Molinists, are guilty of a 'monstrous scene' and not just open theists. In fact, anyone who utilizes the freewill defense for the problem of evil would be found guilty of reducing God according to this criterion.

his view of God is the correct one. Moreover, it can be argued that Helm's understanding of God is a reduction of God to human proportions. After all, for many the image of the ideal Western male is a go it alone individual, not relying on anyone's cooperation, who is never affected by what others do and whose will is always done.[33] Such characters are the mainstay of American movies and fiction.

Helm's methodology here is replicated by most of the critics of open theism to characterize the open view as a diminished deity. For Helm and others, any deity that does not exercise total control is deficient and diminished. Any God that takes risks is a lesser God than one that takes no risks. What many fail to notice is that this claim means that Arminians worship a lesser God, not the real God. This attack on open theists is also an attack on all Arminian theology as well as that of many of the early church fathers.[34]

I want to propose a different solution. Helm claims that it is obvious that we must subordinate the scriptural texts about God responding to humans to the texts about God not changing. But do we have to subordinate either set to the other? We need to ask whether the two sets of texts actually conflict. In order to have a conflict between these different texts we have to interpret, as Helm does, Malachi 3.6 to mean God cannot change in any respect. If God cannot change in any way then clearly God does not grieve over human sin or respond to our prayers. But do the verses about God not changing say that God does not change in any way? No, they do not. What Malachi says is that God is faithful to his covenant people and he refuses to sever his relationship with them. Malachi is not stating an abstract philosophical principle about divine immutability! He is speaking of God's covenant faithfulness to his people. The same is true of Numbers 23.19 and 1 Samuel 15.29 (which is a quotation of Num. 23.19). God refuses in these two situations to change his mind. These texts do not say that it is impossible for God to change, only that in these specific situations God will not change his mind no matter what the human response is.

In my view, we can affirm both sets of biblical texts rather than subordinating one to the other. Whereas Helm holds that only one type of text speaks the truth about God, open theists maintain that both types

---

33   Millard J. Erickson accuses open theists of 'feminizing' God (introducing feminine characteristics into the divine attributes). Even if this charge is true, so what? Is it inherently better to affirm a deity full of testosterone? See his *God the Father Almighty: A Contemporary Exploration of the Divine Attributes* (Grand Rapids, MI: Baker Book House, 1998), p. 161.

34   Roger Olson makes this observation in his *The Mosaic of Christian Belief: Twenty Centuries of Unity and Diversity* (Downers Grove, IL: InterVarsity Press, 2002), p. 196. Ware, *God's Lesser Glory*, pp. 42, 208, 226, also acknowledges that his main criticisms of open theism are also criticisms of Arminianism.

of texts speak the truth about God. There is no conflict between the texts if we hold that God's nature does not change but God can change in some respects. For open theists, God is not wishy-washy but neither is God a stone. God is steadfast to his covenant but the exact way in which he carries out its fulfillment is not set in concrete. God's unconditional promises are unwavering but God can and does change in his thoughts, decisions and emotions. Moreover, God can be affected by the prayers of his people.[35] Christianity does not require an absolutely immutable God—one who cannot change in any respect—it only requires a faithful God. Because open theism can coherently hold both types of texts regarding divine mutability and immutability together rather than subordinating one to the other, it provides a superior theological model than does Helm's.

Omniscience

Now I want to apply this same line of reasoning to the issue of divine omniscience and the status of the future. There seem to be two types of texts in scripture important for a discussion of divine omniscience. Set A contains those where God is portrayed as learning by testing people (Gen. 22.12), changing his mind (Ex. 32.14) and switching to alternative courses of action in response to human actions (Ex. 4.14-16). Set B contains texts where God is portrayed as declaring that a specific event will occur (Isa. 42.9 and 44.28). If God knows all that will happen in our future, then God does not actually test people to learn how they will respond and certainly cannot change his mind. However, things are not so simple. There are biblical texts in which God says something specific will happen and it does come to pass but there are other texts where God says something specific will happen and it does not come about (Ezek. 26.17-21; 29.12-20; Jonah 3.4). In order to resolve the tension between such texts Helm and others say that we must subordinate one set of scriptures to the other. To say that God changes his mind, switches to Plan B or comes to know something that God did not know previously, is to diminish God. Consequently, the 'clear' teaching of scripture is that God knows every detail of what will happen in the future—the future is completely definite for God.

---

35 Classical theists believe it is a reduction of God to think that God may be affected by our prayers. Dallas Willard, who affirms a form of open theism, replies: to assert that 'because of the interchange God does what he had not previously intended, or refrains from something he previously had intended to do, is nothing against God's dignity if it is *an arrangement that he himself has chosen*'. See his *The Divine Conspiracy* (New York: Harper Collins, 1998), p. 253.

There are significant arguments to support this view of God. For instance, it is claimed that if God's knowledge of what creatures will do in the future is *dependent* upon the creatures, then God is dependent and no longer self-sufficient. If some of the content of divine omniscience depends upon anything other than the divine being, then God is reduced. This is one reason why, for instance, traditional Thomists and Calvinists have rejected both Molinism and simple foreknowledge. In Molinism the counterfactuals of human freedom are not under God's control for what the creatures do in any possible world is determined by them, not God. In simple foreknowledge (the traditional Arminian view), God's knowledge of what the creatures will do is dependent upon the creatures. Both Molinism and Arminianism render some of the content of divine omniscience, not to mention the divine will, dependent upon humans—a clear reduction of God to human proportions.[36]

However, open theists find these arguments problematic. Is God not freely sovereign to decide what type of freedom (libertarian or compatibilist) God shall grant humans? Cannot God decide to create humans with libertarian freedom and thus sovereignly decide that some of his knowledge and will are to be dependent upon creatures? That is, cannot God decide to restrain the use of his power (be self-limiting)? I will return to this issue shortly, but first I want to address the issue of the biblical texts.

Proponents of openness theology think there is a better way of handling the types of scriptural texts mentioned above. They claim that we do not have to place either set of texts, A or B, 'over' the other.[37] Set 'A' may be called the 'motif of the open future' while set 'B' is the 'motif of closed future'. That is, some aspects of the future are definite or settled while others are indefinite or not determined. Helm and others believe that the motif of the closed future is the way God really is (*in se*) while the motif of the open future is the way God only 'seems' to be in relation to us (*quoad nos*). Hence, one set of scriptures is true while the other set represents God's 'accommodation' to us (i.e. they do not depict God as he truly is).

But what if both sets of texts are true? Helm and Ware believe that set B teaches that God has exhaustive definite foreknowledge such that the

---

36   In soteriology, Louis Berkhof argued that only supralapsarians retained the full glory of God. Infralapsarians reduced God by making God's decision to redeem dependent upon the human decision to sin. The problem, he says, is that saying that God *responded* to human sin means that God is then conditioned or affected by creatures—God is reacting to them! This flies in the face of strong impassibility and immutability—diminishing the divine glory. See his *Systematic Theology* (Grand Rapids, MI: Eerdmans, 3rd edn, 1946), pp. 118-25.

37   G. Boyd, *God of the Possible: A Biblical Introduction to the Open View of God* (Grand Rapids, MI: Baker Book House, 2000), pp. 13-15, discusses this.

future is completely definite or determined. Consequently, they believe that only one set of scriptures teaches the real truth. Proponents of openness theology reject this. For them, set B is about that *part* of the future that is definite or determined.[38] Some aspects of the future are definite and God knows them as such and so God can utter predictions about what will happen. Set A then is about that *part* of the future that is indefinite or open—yet to be determined—and God knows it as such. Hence, both sets of texts teach the real truth about God and neither has to be subordinated to the other for they are not contradictory. God can declare the future regarding those events that are definite and be grieved, change his mind, or opt for Plan B about those future events that are indefinite. God knows reality as it is so divine omniscience contains both definite and indefinite beliefs because reality is both definite and indefinite. The future is partly open and partly closed because God decided reality would be that way. If God had wanted a completely closed future so that God would possess exhaustive definite foreknowledge, God could have made that sort of world. However, open theists believe God decided not to create that sort of world. Hence, open theists are not reducing God because it is what *God* freely decided to bring about.[39]

The openness approach allows us to maintain that God is open to our prayers—allows himself to sometimes be persuaded by them—that God has a rich emotional life, that God enters into reciprocal relations of love with us, and responds to us. It also allows us to maintain that God is faithful, steadfast and that the divine nature does not change. This model provides a more coherent account of the biblical portrayal of divine omniscience and the status of the future as partly definite and partly indefinite. This model better handles the scriptural data that Helm wants to explain and it does not sacrifice notions of God that many of us find important such as divine relationality and divine faithfulness. Also, it does not subordinate one set of texts to the other but allows both to speak to us since there is no contradiction at all. Hence, in terms of theory formation, openness is a more coherent and comprehensive theological model of divine omniscience.

---

38   Though some biblical predictions that might seem to be part of B are not for they are conditional pronouncements (e.g. Jonah 3.4). Predictions that are conditional (even if they came to pass) were not about a definite future.

39   If one maintains, as Helm apparently does, that *God cannot* create a world over which God does not exercise meticulous control, then that is certainly a limitation for God.

Conclusion

As we have seen, the history of thought is filled with examples of people seeking to define what it means to reduce God to human proportions. This has resulted in a range of views on the subject. The evangelicals accusing open theists of reducing God are themselves accused of reducing God by genuine classical theists. What we have is Bob claiming that Susan reduces God while Anthony claims that both Bob and Susan reduce God. Finally, Reba claims that only her view does full justice to God's transcendence for all the other views end up reducing God. In my opinion, only those who say that we can know nothing of the nature of God are innocent of reducing God to human proportions in the strictest sense. However, if we are in the divine image then perhaps we are not reducing God. Rather, God has created beings that have some degree of correspondence to himself. Also, given the incarnation, God himself has come to us. So, instead of reducing God to anthropomorphism perhaps God has made it possible for us to have theomorphism. Following Abraham Joshua Heschel we could say that the concern for love and justice attributed to God in Deuteronomy 10.17-18 is not an anthropomorphism. Instead, the human concern for love and justice is a theomorphism.

We all negotiate various doctrines utilizing axiological criteria and this is certainly the case when it comes to the divine attributes.[40] What is most important to one group of believers may not be as important to another group. Hence, one faith community may be willing to give up something that another faith community is unwilling to sacrifice. The result is that one group may consider that the other group has reduced God while the other group believes it has not. It is doubtful that from this side of the eschaton we will be able to definitively settle this issue. What then are we to do? One option is to wage war against those we believe are diminishing God and establish a hegemonic rule to ensure that our side is the only voice that gets heard. We can 'battle for God' and seek to destroy the other.[41]   Another option is to admit our finitude and learn to dialogue about our differences in love (Eph. 4.15).[42]

---

40   See Yong, 'Divine Omniscience', pp. 255-56.

41   As do N.H. Geisler and H.W. House, *The Battle for God: Responding to the Challenge of Neotheism* (Grand Rapids, MI: Kregel, 2001).

42   See M. Volf, *Exclusion and Embrace: A Theological Exploration of Identity, Otherness, and Reconciliation* (Nashville: Abingdon, 1996).

CHAPTER 8

Election and Openness: New Insights from Chaos/Complexity Theory

C. Mark Steinacher

Pioneers are much easier to deal with once they are dead. Alive, they challenge the *status quo*, pushing outward not only the physical parameters of human activity but also the psychological parameters of human society. Their work is, of necessity, unstable and unpredictable; they are bent on discovery, on expanding horizons. All that changes, of course, once they are dead. No longer can they go about their disruptive work. Safely out of reach, and no longer able to speak in their own defense, they become the raw material for revisionism. The generations which follow groom (sometimes sanitize) the pioneers' actions, often obscuring their motivations, or deliberately co-opt them, recasting their ideals in order to rationalize current trends. Pioneers are tamed after death, their images often reduced to providing colorful characters to populate floats in centenary parades. Clark Pinnock is very much alive, not only physically, but also spiritually and intellectually. He is a rough-and-tumble pioneer. Therein lies the problem.

In many ways, this fixture at McMaster Divinity College for over a quarter of a century is an unlikely pioneer. Scion of a mission-oriented Baptist family, Pinnock earned his spurs as a defender of a conservative Calvinism. Apologetics have been central to his work; indeed, this avenue of theological endeavor appears to have led Pinnock on a spiritual pilgrimage that has taken him through unfamiliar territory into fields of open theism. Sensitive to changes around him, Pinnock not only recognizes the reality of an emerging philosophical paradigm shift in broader society, but also has devised a project to keep evangelical theology current and relevant. Awakened to the need to state afresh the truths arising from the events of the life, death and resurrection of Jesus Christ, he became acutely aware of the distorting influence of pagan concepts, accretions from earlier attempts to enculturate the gospel, and of the need for a picture of God more faithful to scriptural data than pagan philosophy. As necessary and helpful as the work of Augustine and Aquinas was in each of their days, the net effect for contemporary evangelicalism has been a 'Calvinist package' which Pinnock believes must either be embraced or rejected as a whole.[1] A key to his pioneering thought is open process, the belief that the future is 'partly settled and partly not settled',[2] and that believers are thus in a real and powerful collaboration with their creator.

Criticism can be ludicrous; charging him with rank paganism.[3] Less outlandish is the suggestion that he is a retreaded process theologian. Pinnock admits some resemblance between open theism and process thought, but also highlights key contrasts, including process theologians' desire to distance their work from his.[4] Some are concerned that Pinnock so over-emphasizes relevance and downplays continuity with tradition that the result is a novel, 'user-friendly' substitute for the 'faith once delivered'.[5] To my mind, Pinnock does not go far enough, either negatively or positively. Negatively, if the whole Calvinist package is on the table, then the whole package must be open for discussion, including areas like the Trinity and the possibility of God's failing. Not willing to go down that road, I seek a less extensive recasting of theology. Positively, he is not sufficiently radical in his application of the new, post-Newtonian constellation of philosophical ideas he has encountered. Rather than a digital 'stark alternative' between the entire Calvinist package and open theism, one is faced by a range of possibilities that defies a single normative solution.

As Clark Pinnock celebrates the anniversary of his retirement from full-time educational ministry, I mark the twentieth anniversary of my ordination. I share his concern for the integration of theology and practice.[6] Dissonance between elements of theology I had assimilated in seminary, including some from Pinnock, and what I encountered in a northern Alberta pastorate started me on a quest. Along the way, my musings have been enhanced by concepts gleaned from a new set of ideas introduced to me while I was Alan Hayes' teaching assistant: 'Chaos/Complexity theory'. ('Chaos theory' and 'Complexity theory' are often used almost interchangeably. Complexity theory is apparently the broader of the two terms. Chaos theory refers to a more limited range

---

1   C.H. Pinnock, *Most Moved Mover: A Theology of God's Openness* (Carlisle: Paternoster Press, and Grand Rapids, MI: Eerdmans, 2001), pp. 49, 77, 106, 180, 184. As *Most Moved Mover* is Pinnock's most recent work and his volume most suited to my discussion, it is the sole work of his cited in this chapter.

2   Pinnock, *Most Moved Mover*, pp. 13, 47-52, 180.

3   Pinnock, *Most Moved Mover*, p. 16.

4   Pinnock, *Most Moved Mover*, pp. 10, 16, 25, 29, 107, 140-50.

5   Pinnock, *Most Moved Mover*, pp. 10, 104, 140.

6   Pinnock, *Most Moved Mover*, p. 153.

of phenomena, which are predictably unpredictable. Together the two refer to the unusual behavior of systems at 'the edge of chaos'. Although somewhat cumbersome, the term 'Chaos/Complexity theory' will be used to denote this array of concepts.)[7] The overall results of my venture are not wholly unlike Pinnock's, although some of my tentative findings concerning election are at odds with his thrust. From my first introduction to Chaos/Complexity, I saw neo-Augustinian possibilities. Chaos/Complexity theory also provided a solution to an otherwise intractable problem in my doctoral dissertation. Therein lies its promise here.

The promise of Chaos/Complexity theory for this discussion is not merely as a pragmatic means to resolve a problem. It also isolates a core issue underpinning the often rabid reaction to Pinnock's innovations: the concepts of paradigm and paradigm change. The remainder of this chapter will develop the idea of paradigm change, specifically arguing that the appropriate level of paradigm realignment is mesoparadigm, rather than macroparadigm. After arguing that the current state of the question actually distorts discussion, the paper will turn to consider the doctrine of 'election' as a suitable and helpful mesoparadigm in which to apply insights from Chaos/Complexity theory. The concept will be developed in terms of its bases both in scripture (general stories and particular words) and in pastoral practice, the notion of God's having 'landmarks' around which human actions on various paths contribute to the coalescing of particular possibilities. This process rejects as a false dichotomy the notion that God's standing above time entails God's being an abstraction. It also assumes that God issues 'mission-type orders' which allow for partial human compliance with his will, as well as human defiance of that will. The article closes with a consideration of pitfalls with this approach, as well as a suggested direction out of moral and spiritual paralysis.

Otherwise unimpeachably 'orthodox' evangelical biblical commentators, such as Joyce Baldwin and Kyle M. Yates Sr., wrote unambiguously of God's changing God's plans, without being pilloried,[8] so one wonders

---

7   Cf. R. Beaumont, *War, Chaos and History* (Westport, CT: Praeger Publishers, 1994), p. xiv; J. Horgan, 'From Complexity to Perplexity', *Scientific American* 272.6 (June, 1995), pp. 105-106; R. Lewin, *Complexity: Life at the Edge of Chaos* (New York: Macmillan, 1992), p. 12. For a more thorough discussion of the application of Chaos/ Complexity theory in the humanities, cf. C.M. Steinacher, 'An Aleatory Folk: An Historical-Theological Approach to the Transition of the Christian Church in Canada from Fringe to Maintsream 1792–1898' (ThD thesis, Wycliffe College, University of Toronto, 1999), ch. 1. A. James Reimer, my *Doktorvater*, forced me to think carefully about the appropriate application of these concepts to historiography.

8   J. Baldwin, 'Ruth', in D. Guthrie and J.A. Motyer (eds), *The New Bible Commentary* (Grand Rapids, MI: Eerdmans, 3rd edn, 1970), p. 283, col. 2: 'The writer

why Pinnock's work elicits visceral responses. The answer lies, to a large extent, in paradigm change. While their comments may or may not be consistent with the wider implications of the broad traditions in which they place themselves, neither earlier scholar intentionally challenged the regnant paradigm. Pinnock, on the other hand, not only challenges the Calvinist mindset to which he once adhered, but positively revels in doing so. Innovators on such a grand scale are often labeled 'heresiarchs', targets worthy of eradication.[9]

A 'paradigm', as Thomas Kuhn so elegantly stated, is 'an entire constellation of beliefs, values, techniques and so on shared by a given community'; paradigms, as Hans Küng argues in his application of the concept to theology, come in different sizes.[10] On the smallest scale (microparadigms), one is dealing with isolated elements of a problem (e.g. the nature of the hypostatic union in Christ); in the mid-range (mesoparadigms), one is dealing with significant sets of related problems (e.g. the definition, nature and function of sacraments as a whole); on the broadest scale (macroparadigms), one is recasting overall interpretive systems (e.g. the Aristotelean synthesis). Paradigms, at whatever level, often alter or shift when the explanatory power of the regnant paradigm is perceived to be failing or has failed already.[11] Emergent paradigms impact their ailing predecessors in different ways. Some challenges will be readily suppressed (e.g. Joachimite spiritualism), while others will effectively displace much of the existing paradigm (e.g. Augustine's Neoplatonism). Still other emerging contenders will be absorbed by the regnant view, even as the latter is altered by the very process of assimilating its erstwhile competitor.[12]

Pinnock's project entails the construction of a new macroparadigm. His motivation appears not only to be apologetic, but pastoral. How best may one interpret the profound evil encountered in life without placing the blame squarely on God's shoulders?[13] Great pain has been endured

---

wanted us to know that future destinies were in the balance when Ruth made her apparently private decision to stand by Naomi and worship the God of Israel.' K.M. Yates Sr., 'Genesis', in C.F. Pfeiffer and E.F. Harrison (eds), *Wycliffe Bible Commentary* (Chicago: Moody Press, 1962), p. 12, col. 2, comments on 'repented' in Gen. 6.6: 'God's purposes and plans had failed to produce the precious fruit that he had anticipated, because sinful man had prevented their full fruition.' These are but two examples discovered serendipitously while preparing sermons.

9   H. Küng, 'Paradigm Change in Theology: A Proposal for Discussion', in H. Küng and D. Tracy (eds), *Paradigm Change in Theology: A Symposium for the Future* (trans M. Kohl; New York: Crossroad Publishing, 1991), pp. 3-4.

10   Küng, 'Paradigm Change', pp. 9-10.

11   Küng, 'Paradigm Change', pp. 20-27.

12   Küng, 'Paradigm Change', pp. 13, 27-28.

13   Pinnock, *Most Moved Mover*, pp. 16-17, 46, 155, 176.

within Fundamentalist circles as the implications of an Augustine-inspired determinism are worked out in real-life situations.[14] Pinnock is to be lauded not merely for his courage, but for his thoughtful attempt to disentangle the concept of God from the pagan philosophical accretions which have, at least by our day, often served more to distort God's relationship with creation than to foster clearer understanding. He calls for a critical interface with current philosophical thought, in order to describe a God who more closely reflects the biblical portrayal than the Augustinian or Thomist vision of God.[15]

Given the immensity of the project, it is inevitable that mistakes will be made, as Pinnock himself humbly acknowledges.[16] Moved at the unfairness of critiques which slam his work as a spiritually-lethal equivalent of traversing the Donner Pass, yet concerned that the current version of open theism may lead less reflective or spiritually sensitive souls into unhealthy territory, I suggest a different route through the mountains, a synthesis which attempts to incorporate the arguably more salient of Pinnock's grievances into the existing model. What is required is a new 'mesoparadigm', a rethinking of the problem which amounts to more than tinkering with, yet is less than a total reconstruction of, what passes for the current evangelical consensus. While Pinnock is correct about the negative influence of Newtonian[17] (perhaps more accurately LaPlacian)[18] ontology, I believe that the force of his critique of classical theism can be absorbed in a way that leaves the latter permanently enriched. Indeed, a more intense discussion than is possible in this context may reveal that the burden of Pinnock's concern lies more with the expressions of Calvinism that developed in the early Enlightenment era than with the Genevan reformer himself. My desire to circumscribe the catchment area of open theism is, perhaps, an extension of my belief that Chaos/ Complexity theory yields its greatest intellectual fruit when treated as a mesoparadigm, correcting and expanding Newtonian insights without

---

14   Myriad are the books on the topic; the latest to cross my desk is S. Ulstein, *Growing Up Fundamentalist: Journeys in Legalism and Grace* (Downers Grove, IL: InterVarsity Press, 1995). Many pastors have encountered similar circumstances in their own lives as well as in their ministries.

15   Pinnock, *Most Moved Mover*, pp. 19-20.

16   Pinnock, *Most Moved Mover*, pp. 64, 110, 179. One of the most unsettling aspects of the collective feeling-forward of evangelicalism towards a valid postmodern expression of the faith is the apparent insouciance of some theological students concerning potential pitfalls. Many who would not be caught dead being 'Thoroughly Modern Millies' gleefully line up to become 'Thoroughly Postmodern Pollies'. The sobering truth is that not all postmodern forms of the faith will be orthodox.

17   Pinnock, *Most Moved Mover*, p. 120.

18   J. Polkinghorne, *Science and Providence: God's Interaction with the World* (Boston: Shambhala New Science Library, 1989), p. 72.

displacing them absolutely. As Ali Bulent Çambel cogently observes: 'the challenge of reconciling the coexistence of determinism and chance in the same open structure' is facilitated by the realization that while our computers process information according to modern physics, they still sit on our desks according to classical physics.[19]

The very terms in which the open theism question is currently framed distort the course of discussion. Underlying the vast pool of ink spilt to date is the assumption that one faces a digital choice, an 'either/or' logical gate. This is a consequence of demanding that issues be addressed on the macroparadigm level. To restrict options to taking the entire Calvinist package or open theism actually ignores some of the flexibility inherent to the latter position. Pinnock justifiably criticizes any who would stop short, by arbitrary decision, from plucking all of the petals from the Calvinist 'TULIP',[20] yet if one takes seriously his claim that all of the elements of the Calvinist package are indeed tightly bound, then he is open to the same criticism. There are no tenets that are free from examination. Even God's 'risk' is not privileged. To aver that 'God may well be doing all that he can do in every situation given the variables',[21] or to question God's wisdom,[22] certainly raises the specter of God's miscalculating. Why is it not possible for a voluntarily self-limiting God to miscalculate and set up conditions for his own defeat? This is not a loaded rhetorical question. An *ad hominem* quip that those who doubt lack faith[23] is not sufficient counter-argument. While Pinnock disavows process theology's indeterminate view of God' victory,[24] he faces a greater burden of proof than he acknowledges.

It is not necessary, however, to cut such a maverick path. The logical interconnection of the various components of the Calvinist synthesis is not as strong as Pinnock avows. Despite his objections to the contrary, it will be argued that meaningful interaction of God and creation within time and God's standing over time are not mutually exclusive. Attempting to confront Pinnock's concerns on a mesoparadigm level allows the use of a 'both/and' logical operator (although one could throw in 'fuzzy logic' as a kind of analytical *deus ex machina*, the temptation will be resisted[25]). Open theism envisions a 'partly settled/partly unsettled'

---

19   A.B. Çambel, *Applied Chaos Theory: A Paradigm for Complexity* (San Diego: Academic Press, 1993), p. 21.

20   Pinnock, *Most Moved Mover*, p. 170.

21   Pinnock, *Most Moved Mover*, p. 148.

22   Pinnock, *Most Moved Mover*, p. 137.

23   Pinnock, *Most Moved Mover*, pp. 108, 135.

24   Pinnock, *Most Moved Mover*, p. 144.

25   This is not to suggest that there is not a place for 'fuzzy logic' in theology, particularly as the critique of Aristotlean-based theology expands. Discussion 'merely' of

future; Chaos/Complexity theory allows one to envision how God may truly interact with creation temporally while standing over time as its creator. The particular territory to be explored is the concept of 'election', approaching the topic in terms of highly contingent, emergent possibilities interspersed with 'landmarks' of God's will.

'Election', the notion of God's choosing absolutely and irrevocably some individuals to be saved, not only runs entirely counter to Pinnock's agenda, but also possibly does not sit well with some who would otherwise identify themselves as Calvinists. The idea flies in the face of the tenor of our time. Election, however, is not simply a Calvinist or an Augustinian category. Its relative unpopularity, however, cannot function as arbiter of its ultimate usefulness. The idea is woven through both the Old and New Testaments. While 'chaos' is not a biblical word (even in the Septuagint), verbs such as 'choose', 'determine' or 'set apart' (ὁρίζω, ἀφορίζω or προορίζω), 'foreknow' (προγινώσκω) and 'foresee' (προοράω) or the noun 'foreknowledge' (πρόγνωσις) cannot easily be swept under the interpretive carpet. Granted, these are words the use of which pales in comparison to more majestic themes such as 'love' or 'hope', yet they constitute part of the biblical legacy with which we must struggle in order faithfully to interpret to our generation God's truth. It is safest to say that while more exhaustive study of these word groups is not likely to deliver a knockdown blow against Pinnock's position, they present a far more serious challenge to open theism than he has appeared willing to admit to date.

On the one hand, the Newtonian mind wants to resolve the issue into a digital solution: either God chooses or humans do. On the other hand, it is possible to employ the language of election without affirming its substance, in effect allowing that God merely 'chooses those who choose themselves'. The absolute breadth of God's choice, as postulated in *Most Moved Mover*,[26] that it includes all but not all will ratify God's choice, essentially guts the concept. Yet even Pinnock's affirmation that human behavior is 'partially self-determining'[27] implies that human behavior is thus also partially not self-determining, that God has some definitive input. It is essential at this point to contend that belief in 'predestination to salvation' does not inexorably require 'double predestination' (that is 'predestination to damnation') as its matching bookend.[28] It is possible to conceive of some being 'elect', irrevocably so, without determining the fate of others, whose salvation is contingent. There would be no way

the implications of the overthrow of the concept of 'excluded mean' could fill a monograph.

26   Pinnock, *Most Moved Mover*, pp. 164-65.
27   Pinnock, *Most Moved Mover*, p. 160.
28   There is no third class, those unalterably damned, as the Sethian Gnostics taught.

to know absolutely whether or not one is a member of the elect, as opposed to 'the rest' of the population, for whom salvation is contingent. In practice, there would be no difference, as one would still need to seek God and to trust.

It was pastoral practice that forced me to wrestle with 'election'. Deeply impressed by what Pinnock taught as a 'bi-polar' methodology,[29] I sought a meaningful 'fit' of theology and experience. Two vignettes from my first pastorate stand out in particular: the 'death-bed' conversion of an old woman and a heart-rending cry for spiritual help from a priest. In the first instance, I had been out of town for several days and had a mere quarter of an hour at home before I had to leave for another meeting out of town. In those few minutes, I received a call from the local hospital, informing me that a member of the congregation had been admitted just after I had first left and had not been expected to live through the night, let alone the several days which had passed since. Unable to excuse myself from the meeting, I left town, promising to visit the hospital later that night. When I arrived shortly before midnight, I expected to be called upon to comfort the family. Instead, I was ushered into the old woman's room. Reduced to monosyllabic responses, she nonetheless conveyed a profound sense of anxiety over her spiritual unpreparedness for death. I explained my understanding of salvation to her, prayed a line at a time to allow her to voice assent, and was amazed by the instant change in her countenance after the prayer. She died four or five hours later. In the second instance, I found myself alone one evening with the local Roman Catholic priest. After supper, he bared his soul concerning his absence of personal faith. Unprepared for such unabashed honesty, I fumbled my words and said nothing of any significance. Devastated by my failure, I thought up wonderful ideas to share with him, but the next time we met he rebuffed any spiritual discussion. A few months later he suffered a total mental collapse and entered an institution for long-term care. In one case, I was the instrument by which someone found peace literally in the last minutes of her life, in the other, I failed to provide solace. What insights might Chaos/Complexity theory provide regarding God's choice of these two people, particularly as mediated through the ministry of human agents?

It is possible, in the course of theological rumination, to range so far and wide in search of ideas that make sense of our experience that the connection of those ideas to scripture becomes tenuous. Without resorting to combing the Bible for cracks in stories which will allow one

---

29   Pinnock, *Most Moved Mover*, p. 19. The description there matches my recollection of Pinnock's method in the 'Twentieth Century Comparative Theology' course I took from him during the Winter of 1980. Clark traveled once a week from Hamilton to Knox College, Toronto School of Theology, to deliver it. John Vissers was also in that class.

to squeeze in one's existing prejudices eisegetically, it is possible to find scriptural examples of what might be described as an open Augustinianism, that is, God's working by means of fixed landmarks with open paths between them. A story that comes quickly to mind is that of Samson (Judg. 13–16). There were many paths by which Samson could have gotten to the destruction of the temple of Dagon. As it turns out, he made decisions at various bifurcation points which locked in certain options, barring the miraculous, and made others more likely. Those decisions proved to be costly for him, ones that created greater pain and evil, both for Samson and for others, than was necessary. God did not force Samson, nor does he force us, to make good and healthful decisions, even if God has a broad brush-stroke plan for our lives that will ultimately be achieved.

Exercise of faith is required to take the optimum path through any given situation. It is not simply a matter that the faithful get noticed, or that one would never have heard of them had they not proved faithful, as Pinnock remarks concerning Jeremiah's having been chosen by God.[30] Consider a second pericope, that of the Israelite midwives who attended Moses' mother (Ex. 1–2). If God's landmark were the deliverance of the Israelite people from bondage, then the failure of some to respond simply requires God's call to others to reach a similar end. As it happens, the good decisions of Shiphrah and Puah showcase their bravery, making them examples of women of faith, but had they fallen short, others could easily have taken their place. Indeed, they may represent the fruit of God's 'Plan B', his first choices for initiating the Hebrews' deliverance having declined to cooperate.

Turning to finer exegetical details, one may discern a similar process by which God allows humans true risk as they exercise choices concerning the future. The use of 'determine' in Hebrews 4.7 seems to demand some flexibility of process. It suggests that God has the end of 'today' in mind, but that humans cannot know when that will be. In the interim, there is limited room to decide or to put off decision. In Ephesians 1.4-5, the 'choosing' of some 'in him' before creation might refer to the generic idea of folk being chosen without any fixity as to who will respond, but 'predestined' does seem to be far more specific. Taken together, these words bespeak God's fixed foreknowledge of the salvation of some, even if it is not 'exhaustive' foreknowledge of the time and date upon a decision might be made. The landmark is an individual's coming to faith, without the precise route to conversion being fixed. Likewise, Luke 22.22 allows that God had a landmark, Jesus' betrayal, but that human action will still lead to the precise unfolding of that 'decreed' event. The movie *Sliding Doors* worked on

---

30 Pinnock, *Most Moved Mover*, p. 49.

this nonlinear premise. It opens with a young woman running to catch a London 'tube'. The action then splits in two: in one version, she catches the train, in another, she misses it. The dual plots unfold in parallel, with other points of contact between the independent strains. In each instance, her lover is cheating on her, although in one story-line she is aware of the betrayal, in the other she is not. In each she meets another man, the same man on each track, but with different bells and whistles as to the maturing of their relationship. There are dozens of possibilities along the way, but the outcome is ultimately the same, a fixed landmark in the midst of raging potentialities. Without spoiling the movie, it is safe to say that the bifurcated plot-lines are eventually recombined (with a wild twist!), allowing viewers to discuss which of the two courses was actually 'best' for the protagonist.

Another way to talk of this is coalescing possibilities. There exists a great swirl of potential outcomes between God's grand landmarks. Human decisions make certain potentialities evaporate and others begin to emerge as realities. Ultimately, only one set of events will become concrete, all other potentialities receding to extinction. This helps explain the all-too-common experience of having a goal 'so close you can taste it', only to have the project fail. As one reflects upon the experience of dating, the same phenomenon underlies the ebb and flow of selecting a partner. Even more to the point, the very act of writing displays the characteristics of emergent possibility. Key ideas scribbled on the backs of table napkins become nodes around which fully-developed and properly formed paragraphs coalesce. The final wording is not the only way that it might work, but it is the way it happens to be. Indeed, while I wrote this article, the word processor crashed. Only a few minutes' work were lost, but a fairly significant sentence disappeared in the gap between uses of the 'save' command. Essentially the same sentence re-emerged, including one particular turn of phrase which was the result of some devoted effort, although there were also minor differences in sentence structure. The meaning is identical, even if the grammatical construction is not. Life under God's providence unfolds in much the same way.

As events unfold, some actions will permanently disappear from the realm of potential. As people die, as artifacts are destroyed or modified, certain possibilities are precluded. Otherwise, there are manifold possibilities. This lends a greater sense of reality to a variety of events in Jesus' life, such as his almost being trapped by questions. If there were no possibility of Jesus' giving a less effective answer, no negative potentialities to emerge had he spoken less wisely, then one could caricature his human life as a video-taped monolog.[31] Similarly, the precise date of his substitutionary death need not be viewed as fixed

---

31   Pinnock, *Most Moved Mover*, pp. 41, 52, 102.

absolutely. Would the world have ended if, instead of dying at the end of roughly three years of public ministry, Jesus had been trapped by one of the trick questions posed by the Pharisees, and then been put to death months earlier? Granted, the absence of a triumphal entry into Jerusalem would impoverish the faith, by removing powerful symbolic allusions to Christ's kingship that enrich both evangelism and spiritual growth, but it would not alter the substance of the faith, the essence of the process by which salvation was made possible would remain intact. The cross is the ultimate landmark, yet the path to the cross need not have been fixed. Such examples embody both the authenticity of Jesus' choices and the actuality of how our choices bear consequences for others, for better or for worse. We live in an interconnected reality, where our decisions inescapably impact others. Our choices influence others both directly (if I fail a marginal student, that may have a profound impact on his/her career track) and indirectly (another person does not receive a blessing because that failed student was not in the right place to provide it, or else was there, but, being inadequately prepared, was not able to impart a word or an action which provided tangible aid).

Both Pinnock and John Polkinghorne utilize the metaphor of God as Grand Chess master.[32] If such an analogy is valid, and it is extended to a global scale, the implications are staggering. God is indeed 'playing' (not 'toying', but 'interacting') with every single human. The point is not just that God is utilizing contingent means by which a desired purpose or end for an individual may be reached, but that there is interconnection between each of the 'games'. God does play one on one, vitally interacting with individuals, but the games are not insulated from each other. Every game is dynamically interrelated, so that the outcome of game 238,521 has real and meaningful impact on the development of game 5,293,877, which changes the way that the player of game 2,766,492,338 reacts to God's moves. There is the added complication that some of the players are 'cooperating' with God, while others are not. God is able to adjust for the malevolence of the non-Christian player of game 27, the complacency and unfaithfulness of the mature Christian player of game 121,777,906, as well as the 'zeal without knowledge' of the newly-converted player of game 11,600,000,173. If estimates of the cumulative prior world population are added to the current world population, then to date God monitors at least twelve billion 'games'. Any computer attempting merely to track, let alone influence, the activities of so many variables would soon be overwhelmed by intract-

---

32 Pinnock, *Most Moved Mover*, pp. 10, 52, 139; Polkinghorne, *Science and Providence*, p. 98; also Polkinghorne's 3 October 2002 seminar at McMaster Divinity College, 'Science and Faith in the New Millennium'.

ability,[33] yet God's ability to track hairs on a head is an element of what
sets God's essence apart from his creatures. Without falling into Aquinas'
error[34] of conflating the results of philosophical speculation with the very
being of God, that is, without reducing the Christian God to *Men in
Black*'s 'Great Attractor', it is possible to speak meaningfully of this trait
of transcending intractability as one of God's relationally-revealed
attributes. Therein lie many possibilities.

This is also where Pinnock and I most profoundly disagree. For open
process to work, I see a necessity of God's standing above and outside
time, in order to redirect the myriad details necessary to guarantee
attainment of his eternal goals. That Aquinas taught that God's standing
outside of time means the simultaneity of all human events in God's eyes
does not make this the only option;[35] it was Thomas' option, but not a
necessary option. Pinnock seems particularly concerned that simul-
taneous perception by God negates sequence, so that one could speak of
God's knowing one's death before one's great-grandmothers had been
born.[36] A net effect of sequential confusion would be to empty human
action of meaningfulness. One suspects that the criticism that Pinnock
presents a 'user-friendly' stand-in for the gospel results in part from a
fear that he merely baptizes the vacuous narcissism of an age whose
members cannot conceive of their actions not holding earth-shaking
potential. To be fair to Pinnock, his central concern is to circumvent
existential despair. Only God's total engagement in the temporal process,
to his mind, assures humans that their actions are not preprogrammed
fare forced upon them by an abstract or deistic God.[37] Yet God's
standing above created time does not necessarily imply lack of sequence,
and certainly is not synonymous with his being 'abstract' or uninvolved.
To reject God's standing above time as mutually exclusive with
interaction within time is to limit God unnecessarily, by insisting upon a
false dichotomy. Just as a parent is not necessarily less solicitous of a
child's needs because s/he does not get into the crib with the child, so
God is not necessarily less engaged vitally with his creatures if he is not
totally immersed in time. God's total submergence in time, on the other

---

33   For a brief and useful overview of this topic, see J.F. Traub and H.
Wozniakowski, 'Breaking Intractability', *Scientific American* 270.1 (January, 1994),
pp. 102-107.

34   Pinnock, *Most Moved Mover*, p. 70.

35   Pinnock, *Most Moved Mover*, pp. 70-71.

36   The 'death before birth' scenario cropped up during a personal conversation at
coffee-break sometime in the summer of 2001 or 2002. Cf. Pinnock, *Most Moved
Mover*, pp. 117, 156; and Polkinghorne, *Science and Providence*, pp. 72, 79.

37   Pinnock, *Most Moved Mover*, pp. 6, 53, 88. Pinnock is aware of criticism that
he so stresses immanence as to dispense with transcendence, but, p. 10, rejects it as
misguided and invalid.

hand, does not guarantee that interaction will be purposeful, loving or meaningful, as the gods' cavorting in many Greek and Hindu myths abundantly illustrates.

A truly open historical process need not deny the reality of some fixed points along the way. Pinnock himself allows that some elements of the future may be settled in God's mind.[38] For this to be more than verbal sleight of hand, there must be some absolute permanence to at least some elements of God's plan. A God able at once to be intimate with his timely creatures and yet also master over the process of time logically integrates the 'settled/unsettled' nature of unfolding time. It is the very fixity of God's landmarks that allows for the paths between those points not to be fixed in the slightest. There is room for both true and significant human participation in the process and God's direction from outside of time, reaching into it in a sequential fashion. For a century and a half, military planners have experimented with 'mission-type orders'.[39] In this approach, field commanders are not issued detailed action plans, but given broadly defined objectives which they are to seek to attain using prescribed resources. If New Testament faith is based upon precept rather than law, then those precepts may be envisioned as functioning as 'mission-type orders' to guide believers into wise and healthy choices for the paths between fixed points. To switch similes, loose parameter order is not unlike the guiding of children as they learn to bake. Imprecise measurement may result in a bit more flour and a little less baking soda than called for in the recipe, but the amounts are close enough to make it work. Intervention is necessary only when parameters are seriously exceeded. In this view, there is no grand 'risk' on God's part, but there are a series of lesser risks, the risks lying in the gaps between the landmarks. God's intervention could be as limited as the wooing of hearts and minds to obedience.

Even Calvin accepted the idea underpinning 'mission-type orders'! Professional interviewers employ a technique to overcome the tendency of overly self-conscious subjects to defend tenaciously a set position. When the camera is moved behind the subject (so the view is of the interviewer over the subject's shoulder), the subject tends to relax and says things that s/he would not otherwise say. Calvin's deterministic view of God's action was rooted in soteriological concern. Determined to defend that central concern, he reaffirmed the absence of independent human action in any context in which it could conceivably be threatened. If one 'puts the camera behind him', looking for instances where he does not perceive such a threat, Calvin can become more garrulous. In the *Institutes* 4.20 on 'Civil Government', for example, he affirmed that

---

38 Pinnock, *Most Moved Mover*, pp. 13, 47.
39 Beaumont, *War, Chaos, and History*, pp. 8, 79.

there are many peculiar forms into which legislation may emerge, as long as the end product conforms to God's general design: 'surely every nation is left free to make such laws as it foresees to be profitable for itself'.[40] That is, there is a freedom, a dynamism, in Calvin's conception of the creation of civil law. In particular, he repudiated as nonsense the idea of aligning any particular system of government with Christ's kingdom, as it presumes a degree of perfection which humans are not free to attain.[41] With that eschatological concern safeguarded, he relaxed, allowing that particular pieces of legislation can and will differ, as long as they all aim for the same end, aligning with God's eternal law. What is the test of conformity that any legislation must pass? It is to the 'perpetual rule of love' that Calvin looks to ensure that varied legal forms meet the same purpose.[42] Put another way, Calvin allowed that there is more than one uniform means for human action to fulfill God's eternal purpose, and that fulfillment of God's purpose is verified in the resulting enactments by the presence of a particular aspect of God's personal nature, love.

God's planning and sovereignty, in this scenario, are not displayed in his having an iron-clad plan from which he never deviates, but rather that God has landmarks which he shall achieve, even if there are many possible ways to get to a particular goal. If a Christian operates at fifty percent of God's will, less blessing will be unleashed than if that person operates at sixty percent of God's will. A pastor, for example, may commit some serious sin outside of the public spotlight, yet still function reasonably well. By only partially completing one's calling, partially arriving at God's will, that person impacts not merely him or herself, but also a spreading activation of persons who come within range of his/her ministry. One might attempt to graph this spreading impact, but there would be so many graph-lines to represent all the individuals that the general picture would defy comprehension. Statisticians use the construct of a line of 'best fit' to summarize the tendency of a series of numbers. It provides a description of the corporate character of the data-set. In this case, one could conceive of a line representing the general tendency of a group of believers, a collective reflection of the individuals' states. Many small changes in tendency among individuals will profoundly affect the general tendency.

This representation of tendency is a potentially powerful tool, both for speculative reflection and for practical exhortation. No individual can tell at the moment at which s/he makes a personal moral decision what the

---

40   J. Calvin, *Institutes of the Christian Religion* (2 vols; ed. John T. McNeill; trans. Ford Lewis Battles; Library of Christian Classics, 20–21; Philadelphia: Westminster Press, 1960), p. 1503.

41   Calvin, *Institutes*, p. 1486.

42   Calvin, *Institutes*, pp. 1503, 1505, 1509.

overall picture is. In some instances, the overall picture will be good, so that their individual sin may have no particular or discernible impact on the whole. At other times, that very same action may have a horrendous, nonlinear impact, one out of all proportion with its own setting, if the overall picture is bleak and that individual's sin concatenates with other individuals' sins to damage or even destroy an overall tendency of obedience to God. That is, if an individual's sin works in harmony with a tendency of the folk to evil, then the entire group, denomination, culture or other collectivity may be plunged into difficulty. The flip side is that if there is a general tendency toward obedience to God among the group, then the individual's good choice 'works in harmony with' (συνεργέω), or concatenates with, the good choices by other individuals which create that general tendency, producing a good result out of proportion with the original action. It raises the term 'fellow worker' from a mere convention to a vital expression of the capability of Christian community in liaison with their creator. Therein lies the power.

The view of election informed by Chaos/Complexity theory is not just *It's A Wonderful Life* with an evangelical and biblical veneer. One may argue that this is a very 'Free Church' approach to ethical action. Newtonian thought, and that of LaPlace subsequently, formerly was used to bolster hierarchical power relationships in society.[43] The Free Church movement embodied a rejection of such hierarchical society. Indeed, some nineteenth-century North American restorationist movements intuited the need to be rid of all hierarchical elements, in medicine, law and politics, as well as in religion.[44] The open theism view of God is a Free Church view, one which has shaken off many of the Newtonian shackles. Modified by insights from Chaos/Complexity theory, an open Augustinian mesoparadigm is a highly Free Church proposition. It provides freedom for real interaction between individual believers, as well as between God and believers, holding in tension both determinism and unpredictable process. This view also makes 'election' an issue of practical spirituality, answering John Wesley's concern that any form of the doctrine of predestination necessarily undermines the quest for holiness.[45]

There are two small clouds on the horizon, threatening to grow into serious obstacles to the Chaos/Complexity-informed view of election. On the one hand, critics may object that this view amounts to nothing more than a particularly subtle way for God to manipulate the world system, to bully through his agenda at the expense of true human initiative. Pinnock

---

43   P.L. Baker, *Centring the Periphery: Chaos, Order, and the Ethnohistory of Dominica* (Montreal and Kingston: McGill-Queen's University Press, 1994), pp. 6, 9, 82.

44   Cf. Steinacher, 'An Aleatory Folk', chs 1 and 2, *passim*.

45   Pinnock, *Most Moved Mover*, p. 168.

speaks of God as a 'chess-master', working to achieve his ends. Does this Chaos/Complexity view essentially portray a God not much above the level of the programmer of a computerized backgammon game I once owned, who designed the game to cheat if it were in danger of losing? If a human player outplayed the algorithm, the computer began to roll itself almost endless strings of 'double sixes' (a great tactical advantage)[46] while allowing the human small, unhelpful numbers. When the computer managed to win, it displayed a gloating message about the human's having succumbed to a superior mind. If God does in fact elect some, and massage process to achieve his landmarks, might not it appear that God gives a similar message to the world? First, this critique would apply to any and every view which allows God some degree of sovereign choice, whether one speaks of God's wooing adherence to his plan, or taking more forcible steps to ensure compliance. Second, this critique misses a key element of God's nature and character. If one takes Pinnock's lead of putting 'love' front and center, the whole issue of God's motivation comes into clear focus. There is not a gram of self-aggrandizement in God. Everything which proceeds from God arises from pure, untainted, selfless love. There will be no undeserved 'Aha!' at the end. That perfect selflessness then becomes the model for our lesser emulation of love.

The other small cloud arises from a negative appreciation of the realization that 'election' is significant not merely for eternity, but for the present. One might validly object that acceptance of the view of election put forward in this article could undermine a full appreciation of God's grace, instead leading folk to 'obsess' about performance. If every little action counts, then one must fastidiously control all aspects of life. Luther's obsessive confession to von Staupitz comes to mind. Initially one may respond that this view is not necessarily any worse than the existing problem of believers of Calvinistic outlook obsessing over finding the one true critical path through life which God already exhaustively foreknows but leaves us to find by trial and error. Further, one may argue that the Chaos/Complexity approach underscores grace. A biblical theological anthropology reminds us that one can never follow God absolutely. One will, always, at some point, fall short. A Chaos/Complexity view also allows one better to grasp how God's will may also be restorative. As a young Christian, I was assured of the importance of obedience, because one failure could result in my missing God's plan for my entire life. That one failure would render the entirety of my remaining years futile. If one grasps the significance of a

---

46   For the terminally curious: careful observation revealed the trigger for the game's cheating. Anytime the human had one or more of the computer's stones 'on the bar' while beginning to 'bear off' his/her own stones, the computer opted to cheat.

landmark-studded open process, then if one fails God, there is still hope. There is hope for one's own life, as well as for those who will be affected by one's failure.

The crucial motivation for all of life must be to look beyond one's own needs and desires, to emulate Christ's love while attempting to find and follow God's highest will for oneself. What might the implications for 'fullness of life' here and now have been for the old woman in the anecdote, had she come to faith younger? How much richer might her life, and the lives of those whom she encountered, have been had she had vital contact with God years before? Whose lives might have been changed had she had the opportunity to share her faith directly? What of the priest who was crushed by the weight of his own inadequacy apart from God? How much deeper and effective counsel might he have been able to give as a result of finding the love he admitted lacking? I draw comfort from the idea that his eternal destiny does not hinge upon my single failed opportunity to 'speak the truth in love'. I also draw great inspiration to serve faithfully, whether in great or small matters, because 'all things work together for the good of those who love God, who have been called according to his purpose' (Rom. 8.28). Therein lies our privilege.

CHAPTER 9

Theodicy: A Comparative Analysis

David Basinger and Randall Basinger

The topic of this paper is the age-old 'problem of evil'. However, what we propose is neither a new theodicy nor a criticism of any specific existing theodicy. What we plan can perhaps best be described as an exercise in 'comparative theology'. Specifically, we intend to compare how three theistic perspectives—theological determinism, freewill theism and process theism—do (in fact, must) approach the reality of evil in this world, reflect on whether any of these approaches can be judged superior to the others, and then draw some general conclusions about the nature and value of intra-theistic debates on this issue.

What drives this project are two related assumptions. First, it is inaccurate, we believe, to portray the debate over the problem of evil as only, or even primarily, a debate between 'theism' and 'non-theism'. Many of the most heated, interesting and controversial discussions take place among theists. In fact, the perceived ability or inability to explain evil is often one of the most important parts of any debate over the superiority of rival theistic systems. Second, the nature of any actual 'problem of evil' is determined by the specific concept of God in question. Since the theistic perspectives we are considering conceive of God in significantly different ways, it is appropriate to talk about distinct and, in fact, rival theistic responses to the challenge evil poses.

What is Evil?

As we begin our comparative analysis, we must first reflect on the meaning of 'evil', and this is no easy task. Philosophers freely talk about the problem of evil but have often been hard-pressed to come up with a clear definition. We do not claim to have a privileged position, but we will stipulate how we will be using this term. Evil, in its most general sense, will be defined as any inherently undesirable state of affairs. More specifically, it is a state of affairs that not only lacks inherent value; it has 'negative value'. That is, when considered in isolation, it actually detracts from or diminishes the value of our world. Some obvious examples of evil would be physical and psychological pain and suffering, disrupted social relations, unfulfilled potential, and natural catastrophes.

Evil, understood in this way, can in turn be divided into two basic categories: justified and unjustified. Justified evil is any evil that is necessary for (unavoidably connected to) the occurrence of a morally acceptable goal (given the evil in question). Sometimes evil is justified because its *actual occurrence* is necessarily connected to a goal that is morally acceptable. For example, some actual pain and suffering (an evil) might be necessary to acquire a certain quality of patience or compassion (a desirable goal). Or, in some contexts, a shot of Novocain may be necessary to avoid the pain of a live nerve being touched by the drill bit.

At other times, it is the *possible occurrence* of the evil that is necessary for the occurrence of a morally acceptable goal (given the evil in question). Let us assume, for instance, that a teen learning to drive hits a tree and is injured. The actual occurrence of the injury was not necessary for the goal (learning to drive). The goal could have occurred without the actual occurrence of the evil, and the evil adds nothing positive to the situation. But allowing a teenager to learn to drive a car (a good goal) necessitates the possibility of such an injury.

Unjustified evil is that evil that is either (1) not necessarily connected to an envisioned goal or (2) is necessarily connected to a goal that is not morally acceptable. For example, spanking a child might be connected to a morally acceptable end (correcting behavior), but there might be ways to bring about the same end without as much pain and suffering. Here the evil would be connected to a goal but not necessarily connected. In contrast, the risk of injury might be necessary (unavoidably required) when allowing a teenager to drive to a store to rent a movie during an ice storm. But an accident in this instance would clearly be an unjustified evil because, while the risk of such evil is necessarily connected to a goal, the goal (seeing a movie) is clearly not morally acceptable, given the evil in question.

In What Sense is Evil a Problem for God?

The occurrence of an evil event is often not a problem for finite moral agents because they are in no way causally involved in (causally responsible for) its occurrence. On the other hand, finite humans are at times responsible for the occurrence of evil. Sometimes this involvement is justified, and sometimes it is not. As long as the evil is justified—as long as its actuality or at least its possibility was necessarily connected to a morally acceptable goal—the person is morally justified in doing or allowing the evil. Humans are only morally blameworthy if the evils they perform or allow are unjustified—not necessarily connected to an envisioned goal or necessarily connected to an envisioned goal that is not morally acceptable.

The same holds true for God. Justified evils in no way count against the goodness of God. God's involvement in the evil events is only blameworthy if such evil is unjustified. Given this fact, it should not be surprising that the generic form of all challenges to God's existence or nature based on evil is the same. The critic of a given view of God must argue that at least some evil is unjustified—is either (1) not necessarily connected to an envisioned goal or (2) necessarily connected to an envisioned goal that is not morally acceptable.

Likewise, the general form of all theistic responses (all theodicies) is the same. All theists attempt to defend the claim that the actuality and/or possibility of every evil that occurs is justified—is necessarily connected to a morally acceptable goal. However, the specific manner in which this general theodicy is developed within a given theism is determined by the perceived relationship between God and the world. All three of the theistic perspectives under consideration are similar in that each stakes out a view of the God–world relationship somewhere between deism on the one hand and pantheism on the other. Unlike deism, each affirms that God is personally and immanently involved in the world. Unlike pantheism, each affirms a personal God who transcends the world. Beyond this agreement, however, they differ over the extent to which God is able to providentially influence and control the world process. And these differences are, of course, crucial for theodicy.

Process Theism

In the context of the problem of evil, the key assumption of process theists is that all actual entities (all individuals who exist in the world) possess some power of creative self-determination (freedom). Hence, God cannot unilaterally bring about any state of affairs in the world. While the God of process theism is at every moment attempting to persuade each entity to actualize its best option, what actually occurs in the world is ultimately the result in part of how each relevant actual entity responds to its past and God's lure. In brief, God does not unilaterally create or cause anything to occur. The actual world is in a quite literal and straightforward sense a 'co-creation' of God and all other entities.

Given this view of divine power and providence, the basic theodicy of process theism can be summarized as follows. Since God cannot unilaterally bring about any specific state of affairs, God cannot unilaterally bring about or prohibit any actual evil. Thus, God is not directly responsible for any actual instance of evil. God could, it is true, have chosen not to lure (by noncoercive persuasion) the world to greater complexity—could have rejected this creative goal—and thereby avoided some (much) of the worst evils. Consequently, there is a sense in which God is responsible for the possibility of the kinds of evil that actually occur in our world. But a world with greater complexity, even with the possibility for greater evil, is a better world than one with less evil but more triviality (and thus less possibility for good). Accordingly, since all the possible occurrences of evil are necessarily connected to this morally acceptable creative goal, such evil is justified, and God, therefore, is not morally blameworthy for bringing it about.

Critics, however, have questioned whether process theists can justifiably claim that the possibility of all the evil we experience is necessary, given the process metaphysic. Specifically, critics have questioned whether the fact that all entities always possess some measure of self-determination necessitates the possibility of such evil.

The key process assumption is that God cannot unilaterally intervene in earthly affairs. But the well-documented ability of advertisers to manipulate our consumer activities and the media to manipulate our social and political perspectives bears witness to the fact that our attitudes and desires, and thus our behavior, can on the whole quite consistently and effectively be controlled by persuasive power alone.

Accordingly, it has been argued, since the God of process theism knows exactly what will motivate us to act in certain ways better than even the best psychologist, advertising executive, parent, friend or spouse, there exists no reason to believe that the God of process theism could not more effectively reduce the amount evil produced by human decision-making, and do so without the use of coercion.[1]

Process theists, however, are not without a reply. While it may appear to some that the God of process theism could better control human behavior by the judicious use of perfect persuasive power, there is no way to demonstrate objectively, argue process theists, that this is so. Specifically, contends process theist David Griffin, there is no way to demonstrate objectively that God could persuasively control our behavior to a greater degree than has been done.[2]

---

1   See, for instance, D. Basinger, 'Divine Persuasion: Could the Process God do More?', *Journal of Religion* 64.3 (1984), pp. 332-47. A revised version appears in D. Basinger, *Divine Power in Process Theism: A Philosophical Critique* (Albany: SUNY Press, 1988), ch. 1.

2   D. Griffin, *Evil Revisited: Responses and Reconsiderations* (Albany: SUNY Press, 1991), pp. 108-109.

But even if the possibility of all evil is necessary within the process system, concern about the goal that makes evil a necessary possibility remains.

Process theists acknowledge that, although God did not unilaterally bring about anything, God did successfully lure reality into its present general form. And God did so, they maintain, because God values intense novelty (which allows for both greater good and evil) over triviality (which minimizes both good and evil). But to create on the basis of this divine goal, it can be argued, was surely unjustified, given the horrendous evils that have come about as a result of this divine choice.[3]

In response, process theists grant that God's desire to lure the world to greater complexity has resulted in many horrendous evils: physical and psychological suffering, individuals like Hitler. But they also point to the value that has also been produced: our conscious ability to engage in meaningful relationships, individuals like Ghandi and Martin Luther King. And, they argue, there is no way to demonstrate objectively that a world with the amount of complexity (and the accompanying goods) ours contains cannot reasonably be considered a morally justifiable goal in spite of the unavoidable evil accompanying this world.[4]

Freewill Theism

The key assumption for the freewill theist is that God can and does unilaterally intervene in earthly affairs. Unlike the God of process theism, the providential power of the God of freewill theism is not limited to persuasion. However, the freewill theist's God cannot unilaterally ensure that any creature exercising free choice will make the decisions God would have it make (and thus act as God would have it act). And since humans, as a matter of fact, do sometimes exercise free will, to the extent that God does allow freedom, God is not always able to guarantee that what God wants to occur in the actual world will occur.

Given this view of God's power and providence, the basic theodicy of freewill theism is not difficult to state. To the extent that God does unilaterally bring about evil, its actual occurrence is necessarily connected to a morally acceptable divine goal and thus justified. However, since God cannot both grant us meaningful freedom and unilaterally control its use, to the extent that God grants us freedom, the

3   David Griffin notes this as a possibility in *God, Power and Evil: A Process Theodicy* (Philadelphia: Westminster Press, 1976), p. 309; J.B. Cobb and Griffin identify this as a possible problem in *Process Theology: An Introductory Exposition* (Philadelphia: Westminster Press, 1976), p. 75.

4   Implicit in Griffin, *Evil Revisited*, pp. 108-109, and *God, Power and Evil*, p. 309.

possibility of evil is necessitated (cannot be avoided). And since allowing us to exercise meaningful freedom is a morally acceptable goal, God is justified in not prohibiting the evil such freedom generates.

Critics again challenge both the claim that all evil is necessarily connected to an envisioned goal and that, if so, the goal is morally acceptable.

The freewill theodicy is based primarily on the assumption that God cannot both grant us meaningful freedom and prohibit the negative consequences such freedom can produce. But it is implausible, argue other theists, to believe that God could not have accomplished the stated goals without causing or allowing all actual evils—implausible to believe all evils are necessarily connected to the divine goals in question. For instance, process theist David Griffin argues, surely God could have removed some of Hitler's freedom without negatively affecting the ability of people in general to exercise meaningful freedom.[5]

Freewill theists acknowledge that it may seem implausible to some that the God of freewill theism could not have granted us significant freedom and yet prohibited or eliminated more evil. But there exists no way to demonstrate objectively, they argue, that God could unilaterally intervene more often without negatively affecting human freedom.[6] Specifically, freewill theists such as Bruce Reichenbach and William Hasker grant that it may appear easy to identify specific 'free choices' that God could have vetoed without harming the moral integrity of our universe. They deny, however, that there exists any way to demonstrate objectively that God could unilaterally intervene more often without negatively affecting human freedom.[7]

But even if all of the evil we experience is necessarily connected to meaningful human freedom, process theists contend, it seems unlikely that a perfectly good being would ever consider this or any other creative goal a morally justifiable basis for allowing the existence of a world containing as much of this type of evil as we experience.[8]

---

5   Griffin, *God, Power and Evil*, p. 271, and *Evil Revisited*, pp. 87-89.

6   See J. Feinberg, *The Many Faces of Evil* (Grand Rapids, MI: Zondervan, 1994), ch. 9; B. Reichenbach, 'Natural Evils and Natural Laws: A Theodicy for Natural Evils', *International Philosophical Quarterly* 16 (1976), pp. 179-88; D. Basinger and R. Basinger, 'Divine Omnipotence: Plantinga vs. Griffin', *Process Studies* 11 (1981), pp. 11-24; A. Plantinga, 'Epistemic Probability and Evil', *Archivio di Filosophia* 56 (1988), p. 561.

7   See Reichenbach, 'Natural Evils and Natural Laws', pp. 179-88; W. Hasker, 'The Necessity of Gratuitous Evil', *Faith and Philosophy* 9 (1992), pp. 23-44.

8   Griffin, *Evil Revisited*, pp. 17-19, 91-92; W.L. Rowe, 'Ruminations About Evil', *Philosophical Perspectives* 5 (1991), p. 72. See also D. Basinger, 'Divine Omniscience and the Soteriological Problem of Evil: Is the Type of Knowledge God Possesses Relevant?', *Religious Studies* 28 (1992), pp. 1-18.

In response, freewill theists contend that there is no way to demonstrate objectively that God's desire to create a world containing such freedom (even given the evil it has caused) cannot reasonably be considered a morally justifiable goal.[9]

Theological Determinism

In contrast to both process theists and freewill theists, the theological determinist assumes that divine control is compatible with human freedom. That is, it is assumed God can both grant an individual significant freedom and also control its use (in direct contradiction to what freewill theists affirm). Therefore, all that occurs in the actual world is a necessary component in God's plan. All and only that which God has decided should occur does occur.

Given this view of divine power and providence, we have the following basic theodicy. Since no other source of power (including human decision-making) limits God's ability to bring about the divine goals, it is never the case that only the possibility of evil is required for the actualization of any such goal. Rather, every instance of evil we experience is allowed because its actual occurrence is necessarily connected to a morally justifiable goal and is thus justified.[10]

Theological determinists face the same two basic challenges faced by our other theisms and offer similar responses.

While process theists can claim that there are many evils God would remove if God had the power to intervene unilaterally, and freewill theists can claim that there are many evils God would remove if God could control free choice, such responses are not available to theological determinists. Since God can unilaterally control even human choice, theological determinists must hold that all evil is actually (and not just possibly) necessary to God's preordained plan. For instance, theological determinists must acknowledge that all of the evils we experience—the Holocaust, mass starvation, pervasive sexual abuse of children—are actually required in the world God has deemed best to bring into existence. And in the minds of many theists, this seems inconceivable since we can imagine a world without such evils, and it is hard to see how these evils are necessary for the goods we seek or how a world without

---

9   This line of reasoning is implicit in W. Hasker, *God, Time and Knowledge* (Ithaca, NY: Cornell University Press, 1989), ch. 10; T. Christlieb, 'Which Theisms Face an Evidential Problem of Evil?', *Faith and Philosophy* 9 (1992), pp. 45-64.

10   See, for instance, G.H. Clark, *Religion, Reason and Revelation* (Philadelphia: Presbyterian & Reformed Publishing, 1961), and P. Helm, *The Providence of God* (Downers Grove, IL: InterVarsity Press, 1994), p. 198.

these evils could be considered in a normal sense less desirable than the actual world.

Theological determinists readily admit that they cannot demonstrate how every actual evil is necessarily connected to a divine goal. However, they point out, for the critic to claim simply that a better world can be imagined is very misleading. What a critic must do is describe a world— in all its interconnected details—which contains all the goods without all the evils. But since this is a task that only an omniscient mind could meaningfully undertake, we as humans, maintain theological determinists such as Gordon Clark, are certainly in no position to argue objectively that any of the evil we experience is not required to meet some divine goal.[11]

And both freewill theists and process theists argue that, even if all evil is, as theological determinists maintain, in some unfathomable way actually (and not just possibly) necessary in God's perfect, preordained plan, then the goals necessitating such evils cannot reasonably be considered morally justifiable.[12]

Theological determinists maintain, though, that since we are not even in a position to know with certainty all of God's goals related to any evil, we are certainly not in a position to argue objectively that the goals that require any evil cannot reasonably be considered morally acceptable.[13]

Comments on the Debate Thus Far

As we now see, proponents of each of our theisms have argued that the competing theodicies are implausible for one of two reasons: either (1) some evil is not necessarily connected to envisioned divine goals or (2) the envisioned goals are not morally acceptable.

In assessing these challenges, we must be careful because there are at least two relevant ways in which we can interpret the contention that a given theodicy is implausible. One interpretation is person-relative: that although everyone need not agree, it is justifiable for a person, herself, to maintain that a given theodicy is implausible. The other interpretation is nonperson-relative: that even though personal opinion on the issue may

---

11   This line of reasoning is implicit in Clark, *Religion, Reason and Revelation*, ch. 5.

12   A version of this challenge leveled against theological determinists can be found in C.H. Pinnock, 'Clark Pinnock's Response [to John Feinberg]', in D. Basinger and R. Basinger (eds), *Predestination and Free Will* (Downers Grove, IL: InterVarsity Press, 1986), pp. 57-60.

13   Such reasoning is implicit in both Clark, *Religion, Reason and Revelation*, ch. 5, and J. Feinberg, 'God Ordains All Things', in Basinger and Basinger (eds), *Predestination and Free Will*, pp. 19-43.

differ, it can be successfully argued in an objective manner that a given theodicy actually is implausible.

It seems to us that the two challenges to our three theodicies—that the evil is not necessarily connected to envisioned divine goals and that not all such goals are morally acceptable—are best interpreted in this latter sense of implausibility. For instance, when David Griffin claims that, since there is no reason to believe that the God of freewill theism couldn't unilaterally prohibit more evil without negatively affecting human freedom in general, the freewill theodicy is implausible, or when the freewill theist argues that the primary goal guiding the lure of the God of process theism—intense novelty—is not acceptable given the horrendous evil such novelty has produced, what is being argued, it appears, is not simply that a person can, himself or herself, justifiably make such a claim. What is being argued, it seems, is that no reasonable person can justifiably disagree.

Understood in this way, has either of the two challenges in question been successful? That is, do either of these challenges show any of our three theodicies (and thus the related theisms) to be implausible in an objective sense? It is important to acknowledge that the two challenges are each related to a key concept under consideration in any discussion of the relationship between God and evil: the nature of God's providential control and the nature of God's moral character.

The first challenge each of our three theisms faces centers on God's providential control.

Providential Control Challenge

God could have done more to eliminate evil without negatively affecting the relevant divine goals. Thus, to believe that all the evil we experience is necessarily connected to envisioned divine goals is implausible.

Is this challenge decisive for any of our three theisms? It might appear initially that the process theist is least vulnerable at this point. As providential power decreases, the ability to eliminate evil in our world also clearly decreases. The less providential control a God possesses the more this God will be forced to allow evil. Thus, since the God of process theism has the least providential power, the amount and types of evil we experience might seem to be less of a problem for this theistic perspective in comparison to the others.

There are, however, understandings of God in which God has even less providential power than the God of process theism—for instance, robust finite understandings of God or metaphysical dualisms in which God faces a rival reality/power. Accordingly, if the process theist wants to argue that she has an advantage over freewill theists or theological determinists because her God has the least providential power of the three theisms, she must then acknowledge that proponents of those perspectives postulating a God with even less providential power than the God of process theism have an advantage over process theists.

In response, the process theist might argue that when the whole evidential situation is considered—when all of the evidential factors that determine whether a theistic perspective is a plausible option are considered—those theistic perspectives that postulate a God with less providential power do not survive as serious contenders. But then, of course, the freewill theist and theological determinist can (and in fact do) use this same line of reasoning to counter any intrinsic advantage process theists might want to claim in this context.

So we see that if the assumption on which this challenge is based holds—that is, if we are, in principle, in a position to determine whether God could have done more to eliminate evil without negatively affecting the relevant divine goals—then none of our three theisms emerges victorious. In fact, the winner would be either a theism more finite than process theism or atheism.

But does the assumption in question hold? Are individuals actually in a position to determine what evils would reasonably be required (actually or possibly), given any set of divine goals? We don't see how proponents of any of our three theisms could be in a position to make this determination in a nonperson-relative sense as we don't see how anyone could be in a position to know what would be required to actualize given divine goals. Accordingly, the Providential Control Challenge, as we see it, fails to eliminate, or even seriously harm, any of our three theisms.

The second challenge centers on the nature of God's moral character.

Moral Character Challenge

Even if all of the evil we experience is necessarily connected to envisioned divine goals, not all of these goals are, or could be, morally acceptable. Thus, it is implausible to believe that all the envisioned goals necessary to justify evil are acceptable.

It might seem that both process and freewill theists have an advantage here. Within both of these theisms, the key divine goal is a desire for a world in which individuals have the power to make meaningful moral decisions that shape their lives and the lives of others. And this is a concept gaining increasing acceptance today. Conversely, while theological determinists give some hints as to the types of goals that guide God's activity, many admit that we as humans do not know (and perhaps would not understand) the purpose of actual evil that exists.

However, this seeming advantage is in a very important sense question-begging. It is true that process and freewill theists can cite goals that seem reasonable to many. But it does not follow from the fact that theological determinists cannot always cite reasonable goals that such goals do not exist.

Furthermore, it is not clear to us how this challenge could produce a winner. At the human level, we differ significantly not only with respect to which goals are inherently worthy but also on what can be allowed to accomplish such goals and which are most significant when conflicts between inherently worthy goals arise. For example, we differ significantly on the degree to which the greatest good for the greatest number or universalizability or self-interest ought be viewed as morally acceptable general goals. Likewise, we differ on whether bombing buildings containing innocent children or cities containing innocent individuals is justifiable even if it is intended to save more lives or protect freedom for many. And although most of us believe that protecting innocent individuals from harm and protecting individual rights are both morally acceptable goals, we differ significantly on which ought to take precedence when the two come into conflict—for example, when we weigh the harmful effects of allowing the mothers of young children to chain-smoke in their own homes against the significant intrusion of personal liberty that would be entailed by laws prohibiting such smoking.

The situation becomes even more complex when we begin to discuss the moral acceptability of divine goals that allegedly necessitate the evils we experience. Not only is there no agreement on the moral value of those divine goals clearly acknowledged by proponents of our theistic perspectives—for example, the inherent value of freedom or novelty or maximal good—but neither freewill theists nor theological determinists claim to have exhaustive knowledge of the divine goals themselves. Accordingly, we doubt that it can be argued in an objective manner that all must consider the acceptability of any such goal highly implausible.

Or, stated differently, it is clear that moral intuitions significantly differ at this point. Proponents of each perspective do clearly believe that the goals guiding the activity of the God of their perspective are morally acceptable, while claiming that at least some of the acknowledged goals of the other perspectives cannot reasonably be considered to be so. But we are aware of no set of objective, non-question-begging criteria for determining which goals can actually be reasonably considered morally acceptable and which cannot. Hence, we conclude that the Moral Character Challenge does not render any of our three theisms implausible, or even less plausible than the others.

Moving the Debate to a New Level

The debate does not stop here. Even if it is acknowledged that all three theisms can meet the two challenges above, the discussion often shifts to another level. Specifically, even if we grant that the theodicies of each of our three theisms can plausibly reconcile God and evil, some will argue that this can be accomplished only by forfeiting an adequate view of 'God' or an adequate view of 'evil'.

Let us first consider what we shall call the worship-worthiness challenge.

Worship-Worthiness Challenge

Even if all the evil we experience is necessarily connected to morally acceptable goals, the God postulated does not remain worthy of worship since this being does not possess the power required to retain the label of 'God'.

Process theism appears to be the *prima facie* loser here. Even if we assume, maintain freewill theists, that harmonious complexity is a morally acceptable goal and that, given this goal, the God of process theism cannot more effectively reduce the amount evil we experience, a being who cannot unilaterally intervene in earthly affairs is surely too weak to be worthy of worship. For instance, claims freewill theist Clark Pinnock, 'a godling of this small proportion is not big enough to satisfy [our] religious needs. [We] would naturally feel that a God who is neither creator or [sic] redeemer of the world in any strong sense does not deserve to be called God, and is vastly inferior to the God of the Bible.'[14]

However, the God of freewill theism, argue theological determinists, is in no better position. Why would anyone, they ask, want to worship a being who has voluntarily given up control of earthly affairs and who is thus so absolutely dependent on the whims of human decision-making?[15]

This might appear to make the theological determinist the victor here. Specifically, it might seem that since only the God of theological determinism can bring about any logically possible state of affairs, and thus unilaterally control what occurs, clearly only this God retains enough power to be considered worthy of our worship.

However, this line of reasoning again backfires. Some theistic perspectives posit Gods with even more power than the God of theological determinism—for example, Gods who are not limited even by

---

14   C.H. Pinnock, 'Between Classical and Process Theism', in R. Nash (ed.), *Process Theology* (Grand Rapids, MI: Baker Book House, 1987), p. 318.

15   See, for example, Clark, *Religion, Reason and Revelation*, pp. 220-41.

logical consistency. Thus, if it really is true that the greater a being's power, the more worthy it is of praise, the God of theological determinism is not most worthy of worship.[16]

If theological determinists argue in response that sheer power is not a sufficient gauge of worship worthiness, then this argument can be used against theological determinists by freewill theists, and in turn against freewill theists by process theists.

Moreover, we don't see how this challenge could be used as an objective way to comparatively assess our three theodicies. Proponents of each of our theisms respond to this type of criticism in the same basic fashion: while the critic is entitled to her or his own concept of 'worship worthiness', there exists no objective basis for the claim that the God in question cannot plausibly be considered worthy of worship. And this seems to us to be an appropriate response in each case. It is certainly true that many individuals do have strongly held opinions on what a being must (or would have to) possess to be worthy of worship. In fact, it may be that a majority of individuals in any specific theistic context (denomination, cultural community) agree on the necessary and sufficient characteristics of such a being. But there clearly continues to be widespread disagreement on such characteristics, and there appears at present to be no set of neutral criteria for worship worthiness that would allow this issue to be decided in an objective manner. In fact, we cannot conceive of how any such criteria could be produced in a non-question-begging manner. So we conclude that the Worship-Worthiness Challenge is also not a decisive, or even a distinguishing, criticism with respect to the plausibility of our theisms.

This leaves yet the challenge related to the nature of evil.

'Evilness' Challenge

Even if all of the evil we experience is necessarily connected to divine goals that are morally justifiable, the theism in question trivializes (minimizes the negative value of) evil. In fact, the 'evilness' of evil is so trivialized that the relevant theism cannot be considered plausible.

All three theisms are susceptible to this charge to some degree. All of them strive to show that every evil—in either its actuality or possibility—is justified. But is justified evil really evil? While at one level it clearly is—it is still inherently undesirable—justified evil is at another level desirable. Its presence, or at least its possible presence, is necessary for some good

16   Descartes appears to fit into this category. M.Y. Stewart offers a useful discussion of Descartes' position in *The Greater Good Defense* (New York: St Martin's Press, 1993), pp. 21-25. See also P.T. Geach, *Providence and Evil* (Cambridge: Cambridge University Press, 1977), pp. 3-12.

end. Without the evil or at least the possibility of the evil, the world as a whole would be less desirable. But does this understanding of the evil we encounter in this world fit with our experience of evil? Doesn't this redemptive evil fly in the face of our experience of the utter gratuity or meaninglessness of evil?

This is the precise challenge that process theists and freewill theists fervently marshal against theological determinists.[17] Within theological determinism, every actual evil is necessarily connected to God's purposes. In this sense, every actual evil contributes to making this a worthwhile world. Without any one of the actual evils that have occurred, this world becomes less than it could or should be. But how does this fit with our moral experience? We fight evil on the assumption that there are some things this world would be better without—on the assumption that the actual occurrence of some evil is not necessarily connected to a greater good. And since God commands us and works with us at preventing such evils, we can only assume that God also experiences the actual evils in the same way.

In contrast to theological determinists, process theists and freewill theists can argue that, while the possibility of all evil is justified, there are actual evils in this would that are not justified. There are evils—which from both the human and divine perspective—this world would have been better without.

The main problem with this line of argument is that it backfires on both freewill and process theists. If the negative value of evil increases in inverse proportion to the amount of providential power possessed by God, then the very reason that freewill theism can claim to take evil more seriously than theological determinism is a reason why process theism can claim to be superior to freewill theism in this respect. But the same holds true for process theism. If the 'evilness' of evil increases in inverse proportion to the amount of providential power possessed by God, then those theological perspectives that postulate Gods with less providential power than the God of process theism enjoy an advantage over process theism at this point.[18]

Moreover, we don't see how a victor could appear, given this challenge. All three theisms acknowledge that evil really exists in the sense that events lacking an inherent value occur. In other words, all three see evil as real and genuine. Of course, how they ultimately view evil differs in relation to how they see evil connected instrumentally to God's envisioned goals. But the question of just how little instrumental value evil must possess to be true to our moral intuitions and how we respond

---

17   Griffin, *Evil Revisited*, pp. 81-83; M. Peterson, *Evil and the Christian God* (Grand Rapids, MI: Baker Book House, 1982).

18   K. Chrzan, 'When is Gratuitous Evil Really Gratuitous Evil?', *International Journal for the Philosophy of Religion* 24 (1988), pp. 90-91.

to the evil we experience comes down to some sort of basic intuition. And we can conceive of no objective, non-question-begging way to resolve that issue—we can conceive of no approach that does not reduce simply to special pleading by its advocates. Accordingly, we conclude that the 'Evilness' Challenge is also not a decisive criticism of the plausibility of any of the three theisms.

Furthermore, we can conceive of no other way to objectively compare the plausibility of our three theodicies (and thus theisms). Hence, it is our overall judgment that there is no objective winner in this respect. That is, as we see it, it cannot be shown objectively that any of our three theodicies is superior.[19]

Conclusion

It is important in closing to emphasize what we have and have not been arguing. We have not denied that a person can justifiably maintain for himself or herself that one or more of the theodicies in question is implausible. That is, we grant that a person can justifiably maintain that, as he or she assesses the evidence, one or more of these theodicies (and thus the related theism) should be rejected as an implausible explanation for the evil we experience. And we traced the sorts of arguments that have been used to make such a claim. In fact, we are not even claiming that there could be no compelling nonperson-relative arguments demonstrating the superiority of one of the theodicies. We are saying only that none to date seems to us to succeed in this respect. That is, our claim is only that we are aware of no objective basis for claiming justifiably that any one of our three theodicies (and thus theisms) is in fact more plausible than the others.

If we are right—if there is no objective winner—then why, someone might argue, should we even bother comparing theodicies? In other words, if the debate between our rival theisms actually does come down to differing intuitions about God and the world—about how much power a God must possess, how 'evil' the evil in this world must be, what divine

---

19 Some have sought to answer this question by an appeal to probability theory. They have wanted to claim that the probability that process theism or freewill theism or theological determinism is true, given their response to evil, is greater than the other options. However, as Alvin Plantinga has convincingly argued in great detail, the probability that any theistic perspective is true, given any set of evidential factors and using any model of probability, will ultimately be a function of the *a priori* (inherent) probability accorded the theism in question. And we see no non-question-begging way of arguing in this context that the inherent probability of any of these theisms is higher than any other. See A. Plantinga, 'The Probabilistic Argument from Evil', *Philosophical Studies* 35 (1979), pp. 1-53.

goals are worth pursuing, to what extent human freedom limits God—
then why engage in such an exercise at all?

In response, while the type of comparative discussion in which we have
engaged may not be able to identify a winner, such discussions can
clarify crucial issues. For instance, they can help proponents of the
various perspectives (or those seeking a view of their own) become more
aware of the assumptions inherent in the various options and the tradeoffs
that must be made in the adoption of any position. Such discussions can
also help proponents of a given theodicy develop objective—albeit
person-relative—arguments defending their position. And this, we
believe, is reason enough to continue the debate.[20]

---

20   An earlier version of this paper appeared in *The Journal for Christian
Theological Research* [http://apu.edu/~CTRF/articles/1998_articles/basinger.html] 3.3
(1998).

CHAPTER 10

An Assessment of Some New Testament-Related Assumptions for Open Theism in the Writings of Clark Pinnock

Stanley E. Porter

Open theism, as it is usually described, has only emerged on the theological scene relatively recently. In 1976, the book *Tensions in Contemporary Theology*, in its expanded edition, highlighted the fact that it was only then including liberation theologies within its ambit,[1] an inclusion that seems rather quaint in the light of recent controversies. In the chapter on the 'Conservative Option', the only reference to Pinnock, who was about a year from beginning his career at McMaster Divinity College, is in terms of his sharing a position with J. Warwick Montgomery in taking a historical and rationalistic rather than a presuppositionalist approach to apologetics.[2] The only publication by Pinnock cited in the book, also cited at the end of Brown's article, is his well-known *Biblical Revelation*.[3] Yet at the heart of the recent and continuing dispute over

---

1   S.N. Gundry and A.F. Johnson (eds), *Tensions in Contemporary Theology* (Chicago: Moody, expanded edn, 1976). It is ironic to note that the foreword of this book is written by Roger Nicole, who has become one of Pinnock's major adversaries over the openness of God.

2   H.O.J. Brown, 'Conservative Option', in Gundry and Johnson (eds), *Tensions*, pp. 452-53, and 455 (not 442-43 and 445 as in the index). This is of course understandable, since to that point a good portion of what Pinnock had written was in the area of apologetics (see the bibliography in this volume). Several of those writing on Pinnock's life and career have noted this linkage. One cannot help but note that even the more recent S.J. Grenz and R.E. Olson, *20th-Century Theology: God and the World in a Transitional Age* (Downers Grove, IL: InterVarsity Press, 1992), does not apparently discuss open theism or its advocates.

3   C.H. Pinnock, *Biblical Revelation—The Foundation of Christian Theology* (Chicago: Moody, 1971). This volume was my introduction to Clark Pinnock, since it was a required textbook in my first term of systematic theology at Trinity Evangelical Divinity School (fall 1980).

openness theology squarely stands Clark Pinnock, the worthy recipient of this *Festschrift* from his colleagues and peers—of whom I am a recent addition. Since the mid-1970s much has happened in the area of evangelical theology, so much so that the Evangelical Theological Society stands poised on the brink of another crisis, similar to that surrounding the work of Robert Gundry. The crisis, to my mind, is less about theology, or even about what it means to be evangelical, than it is a crisis of integrity for an academic society that has come to be dominated by a conservatism that stifles and opposes 'believing criticism'[4] in a direction other than that accepted by many of its members. As much as has happened and is happening to evangelical theology, more has apparently happened in the life and beliefs of Clark Pinnock, so that he stands today a much different theologian than he was thirty years ago.[5] His current theological reflection focuses upon the broad notion of open theism, and how it relates to Arminianism, process theology and Pente-costalism, among other things.

In the course of reading in Pinnock's work, and in the light of my focus upon the New Testament, it came to my attention that there were some still neglected areas of discussion in Pinnock's work on open theism—especially in relation to the New Testament—that needed to be subjected to scrutiny. I am not going to focus upon the New Testament evidence per se, since in the course of my study I came to realize that Pinnock offers very little sustained discussion of New Testament texts (apart from Romans 9–11, which I note below). Instead, I wish to single out three assumptions that seem to underlie his biblical view, and that are especially relevant to New Testament studies. I do not pretend to have read everything on open theism by its various advocates, or even all that has been written by Pinnock,[6] but I have tried to examine his major writings that address the issues in New Testament study and out of that examination has emerged a concern for some of the fundamental

---

4   A phrase used by M.A. Noll, *Between Faith and Criticism: Evangelicals, Scholarship and the Bible* (Leicester: Apollos, 2nd edn, 1991), p. 173, but see his discussion, pp. 167-73, of the 'controversy' which surrounded the publication of R.H. Gundry's *Matthew: A Commentary on His Literary and Theological Art* (Grand Rapids, MI: Eerdmans, 1981), and the similar one surrounding the publication of J.R. Michaels' *Servant and Son: Jesus in Parable and Gospel* (Atlanta: John Knox, 1981).

5   B.L. Callen, *Clark H. Pinnock: Journey toward Renewal. An Intellectual Biography* (Nappanee, IN: Evangel Publishing, 2000), provides a fine introduction to the life and work of Pinnock.

6   I must commend Pinnock for the tone that he maintains in his recent writings, even though some of those who write in opposition to him are less generous and restrained.

assumptions that seem to underlie discussion of the New Testament.[7] Although some of the conclusions of my analysis are negative, they are offered in the spirit of helping us all to see how theology building is sometimes less about the clear sense of texts than it is about some fundamental assumptions that are brought to bear on these texts, and how important it is to be able to articulate and defend these assumptions. I will bring to bear a couple of New Testament passages that recur in Pinnock's discussion, but will focus more specifically on a number of critical assumptions that are related to his handling of New Testament passages.[8]

Critical Assumptions by Pinnock Related to New Testament Studies

In the light of work in the realm of philosophy of science, it has become clear to many that every intellectual discipline—including science, but also theology—is subject to presuppositions and the need for model building based upon critical assumptions.[9] Much of the discussion regarding open theism revolves around a number of major theological

---

7   The article by Simon Gathercole should be noted: 'The New Testament and Openness Theism', in T. Gray and C. Sinkinson (eds), *Reconstructing Theology: A Critical Assessment of the Theology of Clark Pinnock* (Carlisle: Paternoster Press, 2000), pp. 49-80. This is the most sustained critique of how the New Testament evidence is used by advocates of open theism, in particular Pinnock. I am indebted to this article, but have developed my ideas in different ways, concentrating less on systematic theology itself, or even on particular New Testament texts, and more on fundamental theoretical assumptions.

8   Other open theists have addressed issues regarding the New Testament, but I wish to focus upon the work of Pinnock for two reasons—first, because this is his *Festschrift* and not that of the others (they will have to wait for theirs), and secondly, because he remains to my mind the most significant of the open theists, having distinguished himself in a number of areas of systematic theology and in a number of major institutions. One serious shortcoming of many of the books involved in the discussion of open theism, and one that has inevitably hindered my treatment I am sure, is that they are inadequately indexed, certainly in failing to provide scripture indexes (and sometimes any indexes at all!).

9   Some important works in this area (that I have found helpful) are M. Polanyi, *Science, Faith and Society* (Chicago: University of Chicago Press, 1964 [1946]); T. Kuhn, *The Structure of Scientific Revolutions* (Chicago: University of Chicago Press, 2nd edn, 1970 [1962]); K.R. Popper, *Conjectures and Refutations: The Growth of Scientific Knowledge* (London: Routledge & Kegan Paul, 4th edn, 1972 [1963]); and I. Lakatos and A. Musgrave (eds), *Criticism and the Growth of Knowledge* (Cambridge: Cambridge University Press, 1970). An attempt from an evangelical perspective to discuss some of the issues raised is found in V.S. Poythress, *Science and Hermeneutics: Implications of Scientific Method for Biblical Interpretation* (Grand Rapids, MI: Zondervan, 1988).

and philosophical assumptions. In the study of the New Testament, as most who have engaged in it realize, not only are there particular texts that come to the fore with regard to a given issue, but there are critical assumptions that also must, and inevitably do, come into play with regard to how the evidence is presented and viewed. My reading of Pinnock's recent work in terms of major assumptions related to New Testament study reveals that there are three that stand at the centre of his theological agenda. These are related to his relational view of God, his view of corporate election, and his belief that Greek philosophical thought has permeated biblical views of God. I will take these in order, and present briefly how Pinnock uses them and then subject the assumption itself to scrutiny in the light of recent scholarly research.

Relational View of God

Although there is much more that he probably wishes to appeal to in terms of establishing the relational view of God, one of Pinnock's significant foci is the New Testament, in particular some relational language and incidents in the New Testament. In recapitulating the major tenets of his open view of God in the introduction to his *Most Moved Mover*—to date his most complete statement of his recent open theological position—Pinnock states the following regarding that position and a relational view of God:

> This was the perspective I saw reflected in Jesus' intimate address to God. His use of *Abba*, an Aramaic word suggesting 'daddy' (Mk. 14:36), expressed the heart of his relationship to God—the God of boundless grace and mercy.[10]

Later in the same book, he returns to the use of *abba* in terms of the loving nature of a triune God. This revelation

> is a revelation of unheard of relatedness and intimacy. It leads us into knowledge of God as threefold in nature and as a triune community of love. This is the picture revealed in Jesus Christ, the Father's Son and bearer of the Spirit. We see the Son in relation to his, *Abba*, Father and ministering in the power of the Spirit.[11]

---

10   C.H. Pinnock, *Most Moved Mover: A Theology of God's Openness* (Grand Rapids, MI: Baker, 2001), p. 3. He cites one of the standard works for such a position, J. Jeremias, *New Testament Theology: The Proclamation of Jesus* (trans. J. Bowden; London: SCM Press/New York: Scribners, 1971 [1971]), pp. 61-68. See also J. Jeremias, 'Abba', in *The Prayers of Jesus* (trans. J. Bowden; London: SCM Press, 1967 [1966]), pp. 11-65; *idem*, 'Abba', in *The Central Message of the New Testament* (London: SCM Press, 1965), pp. 9-30.
11   Pinnock, *Most Moved Mover*, p. 28.

Pinnock clearly uses his conception of *abba* as a means of establishing the relational and loving nature of God, with the first quotation showing the basis and the second the extension of his thought on this topic.

Scholars since at least Gustav Dalman have recognized the possible linkage between the use of Aramaic *abba* and the Greek πατήρ in the New Testament. Dalman renders the usage, however, simply as 'father' or 'my father'.[12] It was not until this linkage became caught up in the web of theological lexicography that its full theological potential began to be exploited, especially in the work of such scholars as Gerhard Kittel[13] and Joachim Jeremias,[14] the latter of whom Pinnock relies upon in his formulation and with whom this notion is now identified. In many circles it is now a commonplace to accept that *abba* means 'Daddy', as reflected in Pinnock's comments. This is one of the bases of Pinnock's view of God as relational.

This linkage in terms of *abba* meaning 'Daddy' can be questioned along two lines, however. The first is in terms of the linguistic evidence itself, and the second is in terms of the theological lexicography of which it has become a part. In what is now the classic debunking of an enduring myth of scholarship, James Barr published an article in 1988 that called Jeremias's philology regarding *abba* into serious question.[15] Jeremias had argued that the Aramaic form was in the vocative and probably went back to childish babble. He contended that the same word was used by both children and adults, and that by the time of Jesus it had become a word used by adults. On the basis of its origins in child-language (so Jeremias thought based upon phonological similarities), however, it thus was best rendered by the affectionate term 'Daddy'. Barr's article attacks Jeremias on virtually every point. The major plank of Jeremias's case rests on the child-language origins of the usage. The origins of the sound *abba* in childish babble have been called into serious question,[16] as has the relevance of this (even if it were true) for the later developed usage. Without the link between the childish-language and the sound, Jeremias's

---

12   See G. Dalman, *The Words of Jesus Considered in the Light of Post-Biblical Jewish Writings and the Aramaic Language* (trans. D.M. Kay; Edinburgh: T. & T. Clark, 1909 [1898]), pp. 190-94; *idem, Jesus–Jeshua: Studies in the Gospels* (trans. P.P. Levertoff; London: SPCK, 1929 [1922]), pp. 20, 210.

13   G. Kittel, 'ἀββᾶ', *Theological Dictionary of the New Testament* (trans. G.W. Bromiley; Grand Rapids, MI: Eerdmans, 1964 [1933]), I, pp. 5-6; *idem, Lexicographia Sacra* (London: SPCK, 1938), pp. 14-16.

14   See n. 10 for references to Jeremias.

15   J. Barr, 'Abba isn't Daddy', *Journal of Theological Studies* 39 (1988), pp. 28-47. See also S.E. Porter, *Studies in the Greek New Testament: Theory and Practice* (Studies in Biblical Greek 6; New York: Lang, 1996), pp. 49-74, esp. p. 61.

16   Similarly, the origins of English *pa* and *ma* in child-language to refer to parents have also been called into question.

case collapses, however. The fact that both children and adults are recorded as using *abba* does not necessarily imply that the term is being used intimately. In fact, to the contrary, one can argue that it is an honorific form of address. This conclusion is especially evident when, as Barr points out, many of the instances of usage do not appear to have such an intimate or childish context of usage. In the New Testament, when *abba* is used (Mk 14.36, as Pinnock notes, but also Rom. 8.15 and Gal. 4.6), it is always glossed by ὁ πατήρ ('father'), which is entirely appropriate for use as a term of respect. Other instances where πατήρ is used—whether or not they have *abba* behind their usage, as Jeremias and others have speculated—rarely if ever have the intimate context that Jeremias posits either. In none of the instances in the New Testament is the diminutive form of πατήρ used, which was available in Greek and would have indicated the more intimate context and form of address. There is the final difficulty with Jeremias's view that much of the Aramaic evidence that he cites is too late to have relevance for discussion of the New Testament.

The second difficulty regarding use of this example is that the entire biblical lexicography movement has come under severe attack. Theological lexicography was one of the elements of the larger Biblical Theology movement of the early- to mid-twentieth century,[17] and was explicitly defined in Kittel's two lectures, delivered in Cambridge in 1937, on sacred lexicography (*Lexicographia Sacra*).[18] I have questioned it elsewhere:

> Theological lexicography is essentially an attempt to describe words and their histories, especially those words with theological significance. The significance lies in the use of words that can be tied to definite historical events to which they bear witness. In other words, words are thought to bear witness to facts, with the facts behind these events, or the fundamental events, being even more significant than the words themselves. Language then exists not as a self-referring system but as a crystal through which to make concepts visible. For Kittel, genuine lexicography is the study of this relationship. For this purpose, the language that is analysed is the language of the New Testament treated as a distinct language heavily influenced by Semitic thought. Its development is seen to be completely distinct from that of other Greek and not to follow the kinds of patterns seen in the development of other languages.[19]

Numerous examples of such treatments of words could be given, including not only *abba* but numerous words discussed in especially the pre-1961 volumes of Kittel's *Theological Dictionary of the New Testa-*

---

17   A thorough critique of this movement is provided in B.S. Childs, *Biblical Theology in Crisis* (Philadelphia: Westminster Press, 1970).
18   See n. 13.
19   Porter, *Studies in the Greek New Testament*, pp. 60-61.

ment.[20] This theological lexicographic program, and with it the ety-
mologizing that accompanied it, invoked a number of questionable
assumptions. These included such factors as a disjunction between
Hebrew and Greek thought on the basis of and as reflected in language,
the linguistic determinism that resulted (that is, people thought certain
ways on the basis of their differences in language), an almost mystical
view of language, the positing of distinctly Christian words, and the
equation of word and concept. This entire program was soundly attacked
by James Barr and, since then, a host of others within biblical studies and
outside it,[21] so that it as a whole—and the individual parts that make it
up—can no longer simply be invoked to provide support for the kind of
theologizing on the basis of language that once took place. Each point
must be argued anew, without a facile appeal to numerous unproved (or
worse yet, disproved) assumptions.

    Thus, this is not to say that a relational view of God is wrong, or that it
cannot be substantiated through other means. What it does indicate, I
believe, is that a relational view of the New Testament notion of God that
relies upon theological lexicography, and more particularly the supposed
use of *abba*, cannot be sustained as it is and must be substantiated along

---

    20   This project was published over the course of 1933–73 in German (Stuttgart:
Kohlhammer) and in English translation from 1964–76 (trans. G.W. Bromiley; Grand
Rapids, MI: Eerdmans). Other seminal figures who relied upon language in their
theological formulation were T. Boman, *Hebrew Thought Compared with Greek* (trans.
J.L. Moreau; London: SCM Press, 1960 [1954]); O. Cullmann, *Christ and Time: The
Primitive Christian Conception of Time and History* (trans. F.V. Filson; London: SCM
Press, 1951 [1946]); and N. Turner, *Christian Words* (Edinburgh: T. & T. Clark, 1980),
among many others. Unfortunately, Pinnock, *Most Moved Mover*, p. 33, cites
Cullmann, *Christ and Time*, p. 63, with approval for his statement that 'Primitive
Christianity knows nothing of a timeless God'. Cullmann's assertion grows out of his
radical disjunction between Hebraic and Greek thought, in which Hebraic is linear and
Greek is cyclical. This formulation has been clearly shown to be nonsense by, among
others, James Barr in his *Biblical Words for Time* (London: SCM Press, 1962), pp. 143-
49, 181-82, and *passim*.
    21   See J. Barr, *The Semantics of Biblical Language* (Oxford: Oxford University
Press, 1961), esp. pp. 206-62; *idem, Biblical Words for Time*, where he mortally wounds
the assertions of Cullmann and others; M. Silva, *Biblical Words and their Meaning: An
Introduction to Lexical Semantics* (Grand Rapids, MI: Zondervan, 1983), pp. 22-28; P.
Cotterell and M. Turner, *Linguistics and Biblical Interpretation* (London: SPCK, 1989),
pp. 106-28; S.E. Porter, 'Two Myths: Corporate Personality and Language/Mentality
Determinism', *Scottish Journal of Theology* 43 (1990), pp. 289-307, esp. pp. 299-306;
idem, Studies in the Greek New Testament, pp. 58-63; *idem*, 'Is *dipsuchos* (James 1,8;
4,8) a "Christian" Word?', *Biblica* 71 (1990), pp. 469-98. For an updating of my
position on linguistic determinism, see S.E. Porter, 'The Greek Language of the New
Testament', in S.E. Porter (ed.), *Handbook to Exegesis of the New Testament* (New
Testament Tools and Studies, 25; Leiden: Brill, 1997), pp. 99-130, esp. pp. 124-29.

other lines. An important distinction here is that the theological notion may be correct (I have no comment to make at this point, since I am not analyzing the theological notion per se), but that the philological and textual evidence that has been invoked on the basis of an assumption regarding such usage does not provide the support for such a notion. The relational view of God in terms of this philologically based argument thus remains unproved.

Corporate Identity

The discussion of the misunderstanding of *abba* leads to the second major assumption that I wish to discuss. This assumption in Pinnock's work is that the notion of election in the New Testament is not individual but corporate. As he states, 'The Old Testament makes it clear that the election of Israel is a corporate election (not an election of individuals) and a call to service (not to privilege)'. He goes on to say that 'God chose Israel because he had a special task for the Jews to perform, not because he loved them as opposed to loving others, or because they were better than the rest'. He thinks that 'Few would deny that this corporate emphasis is the orientation of the Old Testament's doctrine of election. Election in the Hebrew Bible refers to God's calling of Israel as a corporate entity to service.' Regarding the New Testament, Pinnock thinks that the New Testament reflects a similar view: 'It is hard to exaggerate the importance of this point. Election has nothing to do with the eternal salvation of individuals but refers instead to God's way of saving the nations.'[22] This revised notion of election, developed first in terms of his shift to Arminianism, is important for his open theistic view as well.[23]

There are several considerations worth noting with regard to his position on corporate election. One is that a large number of scholars have joined their theological or exegetical programs to the notion that biblical thought is corporate. The notion of corporate election as Pinnock defines it, and in terms of the secondary sources that he refers to, is

---

22   C.H. Pinnock, *A Wideness in God's Mercy: The Finality of Jesus Christ in a World of Religions* (Grand Rapids, MI: Zondervan, 1992), pp. 24-25. Pinnock establishes his position regarding the Old Testament with reference to the work of H.H. Rowley, *The Biblical Doctrine of Election* (London: Lutterworth, 1950), and the New Testament, W.W. Klein, *The New Chosen People: A Corporate View of Election* (Grand Rapids, MI: Zondervan, 1990).

23   See C.H. Pinnock, 'From Augustine to Arminius: A Pilgrimage in Theology', in C.H. Pinnock (ed.), *The Grace of God, the Will of Man* (Grand Rapids, MI: Zondervan, 1989), pp. 15-30, esp. pp. 19-20. Pinnock here cites R. Shank, *Elect in the Son* (Springfield, MO: Westcott, 1970).

clearly derived from the notion of corporate identity as formulated originally by H. Wheeler Robinson.[24] This notion of corporate identity became a part of the Biblical Theology movement as a part of its attempt to distinguish between a Semitic and Greek view of the person. The focal point of much discussion in New Testament studies has been Romans 5.12, and its treatment of how it is that all of humanity could sin in relation to Adam.[25] This is also often linked to discussion of the meaning of the phrase 'in Christ'. New Testament and related scholars who have responded at least somewhat sympathetically to this corporate line of thought include, among others, C.H. Dodd,[26] A. Nygren,[27] H.H.

---

24   This theme appears in many of Robinson's works. See, for example, *Deuteronomy and Joshua* (New Century Bible; Edinburgh: T.C. & E.C. Jack, 1907), p. 300; 'Hebrew Psychology in Relation to Pauline Anthropology', in *Mansfield College Essays* (Festschrift A.M. Fairbairn; London: Hodder & Stoughton, 1909), pp. 265-86; *The Religious Ideas of the Old Testament* (London: Duckworth, 1913), *passim*; *The Christian Doctrine of Man* (Edinburgh: T. & T. Clark, 3rd edn, 1926 [1911]), *passim*; 'Hebrew Psychology', in A.S. Peake (ed.), *The People and the Book: Essays on the Old Testament* (Oxford: Clarendon Press, 1925), pp. 353-82; *The Cross of the Servant: A Study in Deutero-Isaiah* (London: SCM Press, 1926), *passim*; 'The Hebrew Conception of Corporate Personality', in P. Volz, F. Stummer and J. Hempel (eds), *Werden und Wesen des Alten Testaments* (Beihefte zur Zeitschrift für die alttestamentliche Wissenschaft, 66; Berlin: Töpelmann, 1936), pp. 49-62; 'The Group and the Individual in Israel', in E.R. Hughes (ed.), *The Individual in East and West* (London: Oxford University Press, 1937), pp. 153-70 (the last two essays are conveniently reprinted in H.W. Robinson, *Corporate Personality in Ancient Israel* [ed. C. Rodd; Edinburgh: T. & T. Clark, 2nd edn, 1981], pp. 25-44 and pp. 45-60 respectively); *The Old Testament: Its Making and Meaning* (London: University of London Press, Hodder & Stoughton, 1937), *passim*. A complete bibliography of Robinson's works is provided in M.E. Polley, 'Bibliography of H. Wheeler Robinson's Writings', *Baptist Quarterly* 24.6 (1972), pp. 296-322. See also A.R. Johnson, *The One and the Many in the Israelite Conception of God* (Cardiff: University of Wales Press, 1942); *The Cultic Prophet in Ancient Israel* (Cardiff: University of Wales Press, 1962 [1944]); *The Vitality of the Individual in the Thought of Ancient Israel* (Cardiff: University of Wales Press, 1949).

25   I render this phrasing intentionally ambiguously, since the discussion of how to render the phrase ἐφ' ᾧ is at the heart of the matter.

26   *Epistle of Paul to the Romans* (Moffatt New Testament Commentary; London: Hodder & Stoughton, 1932), pp. 79-80, 86.

27   *Commentary on Romans* (trans. C.C. Rasmussen; London: SCM Press, 1952 [1944]), p. 213.

Rowley,[28] W.D. Davies,[29] J.A.T. Robinson,[30] E. Best,[31] E.E. Ellis,[32] F.J. Leenhardt,[33] R.P. Shedd,[34] M.D. Hooker,[35] J. Knox,[36] F.F. Bruce,[37] D.S. Russell,[38] D.E.H. Whiteley,[39] H. Ridderbos,[40] C.F.D. Moule,[41] P.T.

---

28 *The Relevance of Apocalyptic: A Study of Jewish and Christian Apocalypses from Daniel to the Revelation* (London: Lutterworth, 2nd edn, 1947 [1944]), pp. 120-21, 160; *Biblical Doctrine of Election, passim.*

29 *Paul and Rabbinic Judaism: Some Rabbinic Elements in Pauline Theology* (Philadelphia: Fortress Press, 4th edn, 1980 [1948]), pp. 31-32, 109, 272.

30 *The Body: A Study in Pauline Theology* (Studies in Biblical Theology; London: SCM Press, 1952), pp. 13-14.

31 *One Body in Christ* (London: SPCK, 1955), *passim.*

32 *Paul's Use of the Old Testament* (repr. Grand Rapids, MI: Baker, 1981 [1957]), pp. 58-60; 'How the New Testament Uses the Old', in I.H. Marshall (ed.), *New Testament Interpretation: Essays on Principles and Methods* (Grand Rapids, MI: Eerdmans, 1977), pp. 199-219, esp. pp. 212-13 and n. 89, where he fails to note that if the foundation has collapsed, the arguments based upon it do as well.

33 *The Epistle to the Romans* (trans. H. Knight; London: Lutterworth, 1961 [1957]), pp. 140-44.

34 *Man in Community: A Study of St Paul's Application of Old Testament and Early Jewish Conceptions of Human Solidarity* (London: Epworth Press, 1958), *passim.*

35 *Jesus and the Servant: The Influence of the Servant Concept of Deutero-Isaiah in the New Testament* (London: SPCK, 1959), *passim.*

36 *Life in Christ Jesus: Reflections on Romans 5–8* (Greenwich, CT: Seabury, 1961), pp. 41-42.

37 *Romans* (Tyndale New Testament Commentaries; Grand Rapids, MI: Eerdmans, 2nd edn, 1984 [1963]), p. 120, where he acknowledges but apparently does not accept criticism of the concept; *Paul: Apostle of the Heart Set Free* (Grand Rapids, MI: Eerdmans, 1977), pp. 329, 420-21. Cf. S.-H. Quek, 'Adam and Christ According to Paul', in D.A. Hagner and M.J. Harris (eds), *Pauline Studies* (Festschrift F.F. Bruce; Exeter: Paternoster, 1980), pp. 67-79, esp. pp. 72-73 and nn. 43-45, who is completely befuddled by the concept.

38 *The Method and Message of Jewish Apocalyptic* (London: SCM Press, 1964); *Apocalyptic: Ancient and Modern* (London: SCM Press, 1978), esp. pp. 37-38.

39 *The Theology of St Paul* (Oxford: Blackwell, 2nd edn, 1974 [1964]), pp. 45-46, 292, in an appendix added for the 1974 edition in which he shows himself unrepentant, despite criticism of the concept.

40 *Paul: An Outline of his Theology* (trans. J.R. de Witt; Grand Rapids, MI: Eerdmans, 1975 [1966]), pp. 38-39, 61-62.

41 *The Phenomenon of the New Testament* (London: SCM Press, 1967), esp. pp. 20-42; *The Origin of Christology* (Cambridge: Cambridge University Press, 1977), pp. 51-53.

O'Brien,[42] A.J.M. Wedderburn,[43] W.W. Klein,[44] D.J. Moo,[45] T.R. Schreiner,[46] D.G. Powers,[47] and many others. Thus, it is very understandable that Pinnock, who studied with Bruce for his doctorate in Pauline theology, would readily adopt such a framework from his trusted mentor. The framework is based upon a notion of a Hebrew 'primitive psychology', in which there was thought to be a quasi-physical soul, the personality was accessed by external extra-sensory influences, and there was a lack of a sense of individuality but instead a psychical unity. This was called by Robinson 'corporate personality': 'We find men dealt with, in primitive legislation and religion, not on the basis of the single life which consciousness binds together for each of us, but as members of a tribe, a clan, or a family.'[48] This is clearly the notion that stands behind Pinnock's use of the notion of corporate election. This has been further developed by Rowley, Klein and now Pinnock into the distinction between election being corporate and related to nations, but selection of individuals being for service.[49]

There are two major responses that can be made to this framework. The first is that the notion of corporate election in the Old and New Testaments has been greatly misunderstood, and in fact is probably wrong, despite its facile acceptance by many scholars. The second is that recent research in New Testament studies has moved away from this position in decisive ways.

---

42   *Colossians, Philemon* (Word Biblical Commentary, 44; Waco, TX: Word, 1982), *passim.*

43   *Baptism and Resurrection: Studies in Pauline Theology against Its Graeco–Roman Background* (Wissenschaftliche Untersuchungen zum Neuen Testament, 44; Tübingen: Mohr Siebeck, 1987), esp. pp. 351-56.

44   *New Chosen People,* esp. pp. 35-44, but who effectively ignores the recent criticism noted below.

45   *The Epistle to the Romans* (New International Commentary on the New Testament; Grand Rapids, MI: Eerdmans, 1996), pp. 327-28 and nn. 59-62, who endorses corporate solidarity, while rejecting the excessive notion of corporate personality.

46   *Romans* (Baker Exegetical Commentary on the New Testament; Grand Rapids, MI: Baker, 1998), p. 289 and n. 14, but who appears to be confused on the point, invoking language of corporate representation and solidarity in the main text, and then toying with the idea of corporate responsibility or corporate personality in the note.

47   *Salvation through Participation: An Examination of the Notion of the Believers' Corporate Unity with Christ in Early Christian Soteriology* (Leuven: Peeters, 2001), esp. pp. 16-17.

48   Robinson, *Christian Doctrine of Man,* p. 8.

49   I cannot resist noting also how this notion of corporate personality is so closely associated with Baptist scholars—though certainly not exclusively. Nevertheless, many of its major proponents through the ages—Wheeler Robinson, Johnson, Rowley, Ellis, Shedd, Russell, and Klein, besides Pinnock, possibly among others—have Baptist ties.

Serious questions have been raised about the notion of corporate personality since around 1965,[50] when J.R. Porter wrote a significant article that called into question the legal dimensions of 'corporate personality' in the Old Testament and whether Israelite law even envisaged the kind of 'psychic community' or 'psychic unity' that Robinson conceived of. Instead, he saw the Israelite legal system dealing with individual guilt and punishment.[51] Porter confined his criticism to one area of Old Testament thought, its legal system. It was left to John Rogerson effectively to render the notion unviable when he called into question the entire theoretical basis of Robinson's and similar work and disputed its application to the Old Testament.[52] Rather than actually going back to the Old Testament as he supposed, Robinson's framework was clearly dependent almost entirely upon nineteenth-century anthropology and psychology, which posited the notion of primitive mentality. Since then, the notion of a primitive mentality has been called into question. Nevertheless, even if one were to think that it existed, the question of whether ancient Israel should have been thought to possess it must also be asked. Rogerson thinks not. In fact, the analysis of the Hebrew scriptures that has ensued would clearly indicate not. Rogerson also calls into question Robinson's anachronistic acceptance of socio-logical work that wished to equate modern Bedouin and ancient Israelite society. Rogerson points out that there is little basis for drawing the two together for the sake of analysis, to say nothing of using the former to understand the latter.

Rogerson notes further that Robinson, as well as those who followed his work, used the concept of 'corporate personality' in at least two ways. One was in terms of corporate representation, and the other was in terms of psychical unity. It was the latter notion that became dominant in Robinson's writings and for most of those who followed him. This conceptual ambiguity not only indicates terminological and definitional difficulties with the notions involved, but provides the seeds of what

---

50   I rely here upon my 'Two Myths', pp. 289-99. Klein, *New Chosen People*, p. 40, notes that in 1960 G.E. Mendenhall, 'The Relation of the Individual to Political Society in Ancient Israel', in J.M. Myers *et al.* (eds), *Biblical Studies in Memory of C.C. Allemann* (Locust Valley, NY: Augustin, 1960), pp. 89-108, esp. p. 91, called the notion a cliché and a myth.

51   J.R. Porter, 'The Legal Aspects of the Concept of "Corporate Personality" in the Old Testament', *Vetus Testamentum* 15 (1965), pp. 361-80; and 'Corporate Personality', *Anchor Bible Dictionary* (1992), I, pp. 1156-57. See now J.S. Kaminsky, *Corporate Responsibility in the Hebrew Bible* (Journal for the Study of the Old Testament Supplement Series, 196; Sheffield: Sheffield Academic Press, 1995).

52   J.W. Rogerson, 'The Hebrew Conception of Corporate Personality: A Re-Examination', *Journal of Theological Studies* ns 21 (1970), pp. 1-16; *Anthropology and the Old Testament* (Biblical Seminar; Sheffield: JSOT Press, 1984 [1978]), pp. 46-65.

Rogerson sees as the solution to the conceptual difficulties. Rogerson accepts the notion of corporate representation in the Old Testament, in much the same was the modern person does. For example, one can identify with one's favorite sports team even if one does not play on it or even play the sport at all, and the Prime Minister or President is seen to speak and act on behalf of a given nation, such that the decisions of this leader often have direct consequences for the citizens of that state. No sense of the loss of an individual is involved in either case. In fact, one can go further than Rogerson and note that even in Greek thinking of the ancient world there was a similar sense of corporate representation.[53] In Sophocles's *Oedipus the King*, for example, at the outset a priest treats Oedipus as the city's representative to determine the source of its afflictions. Creon, Oedipus's brother-in-law, also brings an oracle that states that the entire city is suffering from the pollution of one who must be punished.[54] The course of the drama is the discovery that the single man, Oedipus, is the cause of the city's distress. In this context, when Oedipus says to Teiresis the prophet, 'for we are in you' (ἐν σοὶ γάρ ἐσμεν) (line 314), he is not simply saying that 'we are in your hands',[55] but that one group is being represented by an individual such that its fortunes are dependent upon that person. To my knowledge, the arguments made above, especially by Rogerson, have not been refuted. In fact, in most places where Rogerson is cited, they are acknowledged as being valid, even when scholars refuse to accept the full force of their implications. However, to my mind, the arguments above call into serious question the entire notion of corporate solidarity, leaving only a sense of corporate representation that is not unique to Semitic thought but clearly found in both ancient (Greek included) and modern worlds.[56]

53   See Porter, 'Two Myths', pp. 296-98.
54   See H.D.F. Kitto, *Greek Tragedy: A Literary Study* (London: Methuen, 1961), pp. 140-42, who seems to have this understanding.
55   Moule, *Phenomenon*, p. 39, dismisses this example with the translation 'we are in your hands', but misses a true conceptual parallel established by the entire play. See also C.H. Dodd, *The Interpretation of the Fourth Gospel* (Cambridge: Cambridge University Press, 1953), pp. 187-88, who notes further potential parallels: Sophocles, *Oedipus at Colonus* 247: 'we lie dependent upon you as upon God'; Pindar, *Olynthics* 13.104: 'now I have hope, but the end is in God'. Dodd describes this usage with the preposition ἐν: 'The preposition indicates complete dependence on a person, whether human or divine. It may be that originally a man's fate was thought of, with naive realism, as an invisible something lying within the hands of the person, God or man, who had power over him...' (p. 188). One need not go so far as Dodd to see that the example is germane.
56   Those unrepentant include some of those noted above, but also M.R. Wilson, *Our Father Abraham: Jewish Roots of the Christian Faith* (Grand Rapids, MI: Eerdmans, 1988), esp. pp. 187-88; and R. Mason, 'H. Wheeler Robinson Revisited', *Baptist Quarterly* 37.5 (1998), pp. 213-26. Mason appears to be working so hard to defend

In terms of the New Testament itself, Simon Gathercole has raised two objections to the way that corporate election is used by Pinnock—although he seems to accept the corporate notion in theory. One is that there are logical difficulties with Pinnock's formulation, since there is such an emphasis upon the communal or corporate dimension that the fact that corporate entities are made up of individuals has been overlooked. As Gathercole says, 'In Pinnock's scheme, "the elect" is an empty set, with no actual members when God designs his purpose for them'.[57] The second objection that he raises is that there are instances in the New Testament where people are elected, such as Rufus in Romans 16.13 (and examples in Acts).[58] The latter point is no doubt true, and its implications are larger than even Gathercole appreciates, since by implication all individuals who are specifically elect could well be seen to constitute the elect (who else might there be?), rendering the notion of corporate election both unnecessary and even non-sensical.

This tacit recognition, combined with the conceptual problems noted above regarding corporate solidarity, perhaps helps to understand why a number of recent New Testament scholars, especially those writing on the book of Romans, have come to outright reject the corporate solidarity/ personality idea. For example, in discussing Romans 5.12, Ernst Käsemann says 'we are hardly carried further by the greatly overworked Semitic idea of "corporate personality", although in many circles this is regarded as a pat solution', at which point he cites a number who have invoked the idea. He continues: 'In the Judaism of the age it was probably much less vital than among contemporary expositors, who have

---

Robinson that he gets a few details wrong. Of my 1990 article, 'Two Myths', he contends that my linkage of Robinson with the Biblical Theology movement was a 'distortion' of Robinson's thinking (p. 222). However, Mason himself cites elsewhere in the article (p. 225 n. 4) R.A. Coughenor, who in a 1987 paper did similarly. More to the point, Childs in his *Biblical Theology in Crisis* sees Robinson as one of those who laid the foundation for the Biblical Theology movement (see p. 24, where the link between Robinson and Rowley is noted; p. 40, where Robinson's foundational role is noted; and p. 46, where Robinson's enormous influence on the distinction between Greek and Hebrew thought is noted). Further, Mason contends in n. 29 (p. 226) that I have misunderstood Robinson's ideas on linguistic determinism. Actually, I do not bring Robinson into my discussion of that topic in my paper—but Childs clearly does as noted above (on p. 46). Lastly, Mason says in n. 29 (p. 226) that 'Porter merely repeats the criticisms others have made about the concept of "corporate personality"'. Of course, this says nothing about the validity of the criticisms (and certainly repeating them does not diminish them). Since so many of the criticisms have not been fully appreciated, perhaps they bear repeating again. However, the use of the example from Sophocles that brings ancient Greek thought clearly to bear is, so far as I know, my contribution to the discussion. I do not believe it is an insignificant one.

57　Gathercole, 'New Testament and Openness Theism', p. 72.
58　Gathercole, 'New Testament and Openness Theism', p. 72.

discovered in it what seems to be a way out of a much too crude mythology'.[59] Charles Cranfield in his commentary says

> we may register our agreement with Käsemann's impatience with the excessive confidence which in recent years has often been placed in the appeal to 'the Hebrew conception of corporate personality' as a key to the understanding of Paul's thought. In our view,...the truth of the solidarity of all men in their sinfulness is readily understandable without our needing to have recourse to allegedly special semitic ways of thinking... The one solidarity is an altogether natural solidarity, the evidence of which is to be observed on all sides...[60]

Similarly, James Dunn says that 'the concept of "corporate personality"...is more of a hindrance than a help here...'[61] Lastly, Joseph Fitzmyer says that the corporate personality or solidarity view in Romans 5.12 would have required the sense of 'in whom', which would have been written as ἐν ᾧ ('in whom'), not ἐφ' ᾧ (usually, though not always, 'because').[62]

As Cyril Rodd so aptly and concisely concludes his introduction to Robinson's collected essays,

> It is indeed surprising that corporate personality should ever have been taken up by New Testament scholars. It required little reflection to realize that it is completely inappropriate. For what was being proposed was to adopt a way of thought that had been put forward as pertaining to primitive peoples (the ancient Israelites being identified as such) and then to claim that Paul, who came from a hellenistic city within the Roman empire many centuries later, continued to think in this way. This is plain nonsense. However Paul's teaching about the significance of Adam's sin, the concept of Christians being 'in Christ', and the designation of the church as the body of Christ are to be understood, corporate personality cannot provide an explanation.[63]

Thus, any theory, whether exegetical or theological, that relies on such a corporate framework, including interpreting the New Testament in terms of corporate national election but individual selection for service, must be

---

59   E. Käsemann, *Commentary on Romans* (trans. G.W. Bromiley; Grand Rapids, MI: Eerdmans, 1980), p. 142.

60   C.E.B. Cranfield, *A Critical and Exegetical Commentary on the Epistle to the Romans* (International Critical Commentary; 2 vols; Edinburgh: T. & T. Clark, 1975–79), II, pp. 837-38. His quotation is the title of one of Robinson's essays.

61   J.D.G. Dunn, *Romans* (Word Biblical Commentary, 38A, B; Dallas: Word, 1988), I, p. 272.

62   J.A. Fitzmyer, *Romans* (Anchor Bible, 33; New York: Doubleday, 1993), p. 414.

63   C.S. Rodd, 'Introduction', in Robinson, *Corporate Personality*, pp. 7-14, here p. 13.

seriously rethought and re-established, and cannot simply invoke ideas that perhaps were not well formulated or conceptualized from the start.

Greek Philosophical Thought Regarding God

The third and final assumption to examine is one that pervades much of Pinnock's recent work. This is the notion that Greek philosophical thought regarding God's nature has permeated biblical views of God. This notion is one that is found in some form in most of the work that Pinnock has done, especially of late. Although elusive in its particulars, the argument seems to be that Greek philosophical thought as found in Plato, Aristotle and the like has permeated the biblical conception of God, so that later Christian thinkers have been unduly influenced and affected by it. So, in his article in the volume on predestination and free will, in which he defends the idea that God limits his knowledge, Pinnock addresses the issue of the nature of God. He says that, first, 'we must reject the Greek model of immutability', and, secondly, 'we must be very skeptical of the claim that God is impassible—another axiom of Platonic theology'.[64] He draws the discussion to a conclusion by asserting that it is important, if 'we are going to preach the Bible', to 'diminish our commitment to the changeless divinity implied in Greek philosophy'.[65] In his article on his pilgrimage towards Arminianism, Pinnock points out that a major problem was 'the fact that the classical model of Christian theism' was 'shaped so decisively by Augustine under the influence of Greek philosophy'.[66] He says that he realized that he needed to 'clarify what we meant by the divine immutability. I saw that we have been far too influenced by Plato's idea that a perfect being would not change... The effect of this piece of Greek natural theology on Christian thinking had been to picture God as virtually incapable of responsiveness.'[67] In his discussion of systematic theology in *The Openness of God*, Pinnock contends that 'Traditional theology has been biased in the direction of transcendence as the result of undue philosophical influences. Greek thinking located the ultimate and the perfect in the realm of the

---

64   C.H. Pinnock, 'God Limits his Knowledge', in D. Basinger and R. Basinger (eds), *Predestination and Free Will: Four Views of Divine Sovereignty and Human Freedom* (Downers Grove, IL: InterVarsity Press, 1986), pp. 141-62, here p. 155.

65   Pinnock, 'God Limits his Knowledge', p. 158. However, the only biblical verses that he cites in this section are Genesis 22.12 and Jonah 3.10 (p. 157).

66   Pinnock, 'From Augustine to Arminius', p. 23.

67   Pinnock, 'From Augustine to Arminius', p. 24. However, the only biblical verses that he cites in this section are Jeremiah 3.7, Ezekiel 12.3, Jeremiah 7.5-7, and Hosea 6.4 (p. 26).

immutable and absolutely transcendent.'[68] He then cites what he calls the transmutation of the 'I am' statement of Exodus 3.14 into the notion of the 'being who is' in the Septuagint.[69] In an article on divine relationality, Pinnock includes a section on the perfections of God. There he warns that 'We must pay heed to what God says he is and not privilege Plato and Aristotle over the apostles and prophets as sources of our knowledge of God. Classical theism is a synthesis of the Bible and Greek philosophy, and that should be a warning to us.'[70] The fullest exposition of his ideas on this topic that I know of is a chapter in his most recent book, *Most Moved Mover*, on 'Overcoming a Pagan Inheritance'.[71] In discussing the pagan legacy, Pinnock begins by boldly stating 'Jesus spoke Aramaic, not Greek, and the Bible was written in Jerusalem, not Athens'.[72] He goes on to say that 'the Christian doctrine of God was,

---

68   C.H. Pinnock, 'Systematic Theology', in C. Pinnock *et al.*, *The Openness of God: A Biblical Challenge to the Traditional Understanding of God* (Downers Grove, IL: InterVarsity Press, 1994), pp. 101-25, here p. 106.

69   Apart from Exodus 3.14, the only other biblical verse cited in this section is Isaiah 57.15.

70   C.H. Pinnock, 'Divine Relationality: A Pentecostal Contribution to the Doctrine of God', *Journal of Pentecostal Theology* 16 (2000), pp. 3-26, here p. 18. There is no biblical text cited in this section of the essay. Cf. C.H. Pinnock, 'Response to Daniel Strange and Amos Yong', *Evangelical Quarterly* 71.4 (1999), pp. 349-57, where even in an article on another topic he states: 'I find it sad when I think of the freedom shown by Augustine in his liberal use of neo-Platonic insights, by Aquinas in his liberal appropriations of the philosophy of Aristotle, and by Calvin in his liberal use of the humanist resources of the Renaissance that evangelicals today fall under suspicion if they dare to name truths known to pagans' (p. 356). In this section of the essay he cites Hebrews 11.6, Acts 10.35, Acts 14.17 and Philippians 4.8, but none of them with direct relevance to this topic.

71   Pinnock, *Most Moved Mover*, pp. 65-111. Cf. C.H. Pinnock, 'Clark Pinnock's Response to Part 2', in Gray and Sinkinson (eds), *Reconstructing Theology*, pp. 147-52, esp. p.147.

72   Pinnock, *Most Moved Mover*, p. 68. Is Pinnock being hyperbolic? Although Jesus no doubt spoke Aramaic, he almost assuredly also spoke Greek, as many scholars have recognized for well over one-hundred years (see S.E. Porter, *The Criteria for Authenticity in Historical-Jesus Research: Previous Discussion and New Proposals* [Journal for the Study of the New Testament Supplement Series, 191; Sheffield: Sheffield Academic Press, 2000], esp. pp. 127-41, 164-80). Most scholars believe that only a few books if any of the New Testament were written in Jerusalem. Probably none of the Gospels were, nor Acts, nor any of the Pauline epistles, nor the Johannine epistles, nor Revelation. The only books that may have been were Hebrews, James, the Petrine epistles and Jude, and that probably requires that the disputed of these books were authentic—a conclusion many scholars do not hold to (although I have no inherent problem with that notion). The New Testament was probably not even written entirely by Jews (Luke being a case in point).

however, shaped in an atmosphere influenced by Greek thought'.[73] He then cites Plato's argument for the unchangeableness of God and Aristotle's belief in an unmoved mover.[74] At this point Pinnock, engages in a brief discussion of the influence of Greek thinking on Philo of Alexandria, Augustine, and Thomas Aquinas.[75]

In the light of this significant massing of comments, one would have thought that this point was firmly made. However, I believe that there are at least three potential difficulties that need to be brought to the fore. The first is that this formulation of the issue seems to have fallen unfortunate victim to a form of unhelpful disjunctive thinking. The disjunction is between the biblical and non-biblical or Greek/Hellenistic thought. This is akin to the Biblical Theology notion mentioned above of suggesting a fundamental disjunction between Hebrew and Greek mindsets. In the disjunction noted above, it is the Hebrew mindset (or biblical one, as Pinnock characterizes it; see below) that is the one to be endorsed, while the Greek one is to be shunned.[76] This overlooks the clear fact that the New Testament was written during the Hellenistic period, and in many ways reflects Greek ways of thinking. Pinnock seems also to overlook the fact that Plato and Aristotle, as well as a number of other Greek thinkers such as Philo, wrote before or were contemporary with the writers of the

---

The latter part of Pinnock's statement seems to be an allusion to Tertullian's 'What indeed has Athens to do with Jerusalem? What has the Academy to do with the Church?' (*De Praescriptione Haereticorum* 7), and, therefore, a claim that Christian theology ought to be based on the Judeo-Christian tradition, not Greek philosophical concepts. However, when put as starkly as this it is impossible to agree with such a view as from the fourth century BC Judaism was increasingly influence by Hellenism. It should also be noted that Tertullian himself, while repudiating the influence of philosophy on Christian thought, was never able to escape from it, as his use particularly of Stoic concepts shows.

73 Pinnock, *Most Moved Mover*, p. 68.

74 Pinnock, *Most Moved Mover*, p. 68. However, he gives a reference to Plato, *Physics* 8.5, after discussing Aristotle, not including a reference to Aristotle.

75 Pinnock, *Most Moved Mover*, pp. 69-74. No biblical verses are cited in this section. The entire chapter only cites a few passages, most of them from the Old Testament. The New Testament passages cited in the chapter are 1 John 4.7 (p. 83), Matthew 17.2 and Luke 22.44 in a quotation from Henri Nouwen (p. 90), 1 Corinthians 1.18 (p. 93), Revelation 1.4 (p. 96), and Romans 9–11 (p. 103).

76 Cf. Pinnock, *Most Moved Mover*, p. 7, where he states: 'These two ideals, the Hellenic and the biblical, cannot really be fused successfully. A decision needs to be made whether to go with one or the other, with the philosophers or with God's self-disclosure in Jesus Christ.' A further question is how seriously the ancients themselves took their ideas. See P. Veyne, *Did the Greeks Believe in their Myths? An Essay on The Constitutive Imagination* (trans. P. Wissing; Chicago: University of Chicago Press, 1988 [1983]); A.B. Drachmann, *Atheism in Pagan Antiquity* (Chicago: Ares, 1977 [1922]).

New Testament, and that the two major writers of the New Testament—
Paul and Luke (who are responsible for writing over half of the New
Testament)—were clearly Hellenists. Luke was almost assuredly a Gentile,
and Paul was born in the Diaspora in Tarsus, knew Greek as his first
language, and was thoroughly at home in the Greco–Roman world. This
was the world of the New Testament, and to contend—since there is no
real evidence mustered from the New Testament that otherwise is the
case—that the New Testament was or should be thought to be ostracized
from its own context gives a mistaken notion of its thought world.

A second possible problem—and one that helps to explain the
disjunctive thinking noted above—is that Pinnock's conception of the
biblical view of God seems to be confined to the Old Testament view of
God. The relative lack of references to the New Testament throughout his
discussion (as noted in the notes above), and the emphasis upon Old
Testament passages, illustrate this.[77] Here is not the place to raise the
question of whether in fact Old Testament thinking itself had at any time
come under the influence of Greek thinking,[78] but it is recognized by
many scholars that Judaism had long been under the influence of
Hellenism,[79] so it is hard to imagine how the writers of the New
Testament, such as Paul, who was raised at least partly in Tarsus before
coming to Jerusalem, traveled widely in the Greco–Roman world and
visited many of its leading cities, could have avoided such influence. In
fact, he did not.

Evidence of the influence of Greek thought upon that of the New
Testament can indeed be found in abundance. This is not to say that the
New Testament writers simply adopted the thinking of the world around
them—far from it. What it does say, however, is that the kind of

---

77   One of the reasons that I have not concentrated more fully upon explicit New
Testament passages in this paper is that there are few recurring New Testament passages
that provide any type of extended exegetical discussion. A possible exception is Romans
9–11, cited in Pinnock, *Most Moved Mover*, pp. 54, 103 and *idem*, 'From Augustine to
Arminius', p. 29 n. 10. See Gathercole, 'New Testament and Open Theism', pp. 62-64,
on Romans 9. The entire chapter on 'The Scriptural Foundations' in *Most Moved Mover*
(pp. 25-64) only cites thirteen New Testament passages in all.

78   Such has been discussed, however. See, for example, C.H. Gordon, *Before the
Bible: The Common Background of Greek and Hebrew Civilizations* (New York: Harper,
1962).

79   See, for example, T.F. Glasson, *Greek Influence in Jewish Eschatology*
(London: SPCK, 1961); M. Hengel, *Judaism and Hellenism: Studies in their Encounter in
Palestine during the Early Hellenistic Period* (2 vols; trans. J. Bowden; Philadelphia:
Fortress Press, 1974 [1973]); *idem* with C. Markschies, *The 'Hellenization' of Judaea in
the First Century after Christ* (trans. J. Bowden; London: SCM Press, 1989); J.J. Collins,
Between Athens and Jerusalem: Jewish Identity in the Hellenistic Diaspora (Grand
Rapids, MI: Eerdmans, 2nd edn, 2000 [1984]); L.I. Levine, *Judaism and Hellenism in
Antiquity: Conflict or Confluence?* (Peabody, MA: Hendrickson, 1998), pp. 3-95.

dichotomy depicted above is an unfair characterization of what one might expect for the New Testament—whatever opinion one might have for the Old Testament. The famous Stoic 'Hymn to Zeus' by Cleanthes offers in short compass the very kind of perspective on the divine that Pinnock seeks in the Bible. In his discussion with Delwin Brown, Pinnock asks the question, 'what about the relation between divine sovereignty and human freedom? Classical theism has been committed to a strong doctrine of God's sovereignty that does not leave much room for genuine human freedom.'[80] In this hymn to Zeus, notions of both divine sovereignty and human freedom are presented. It begins with praise of 'ever omnipotent Zeus, prime mover of nature, who with your law steers all things'.[81] Regarding the universe, the hymn says: 'All this cosmos, as it spins around the earth, obeys you whichever way you lead, and willingly submits to your sway.' By Zeus's thunderbolts, 'all the works of nature are accomplished. With it you direct the universal reason which runs through all things and intermingles with the lights of heaven both great and small.' The second part of the poem, however, introduces the human element. As far as human action, it is true, 'No deed is done on earth...without your offices'—but note, 'save what bad men do in their folly'. The poem then notes that the 'everlasting reason' is 'shunned and neglected by the bad among mortal men'. These people do not respond to 'god's universal law, by obeying which they could lead a good life in partnership with intelligence'. The poem concludes with a call to joint human and divine action: 'Let us achieve the power of judgement by trusting in which you steer all things with justice'. I believe that this important and substantial third-century BC poem by one of the most important Stoic thinkers clearly illustrates that the stereotype of Greek thought so often invoked is in many ways wrong, and that in fact much Greek thought of the time reflected debate over the issues of divine sovereignty and human freedom.[82] It is true that these are biblical issues,

---

80   C.H. Pinnock and D. Brown, *Theological Crossfire: An Evangelical/Liberal Dialogue* (Grand Rapids, MI: Zondervan, 1990), p. 70.

81   I slightly adapt the translation from A.A. Long and D. Sedley, *Hellenistic Philosophy* (2 vols; Cambridge: Cambridge University Press, 1987), II, pp. 326-27.

82   See R.D. Hicks, *Stoic and Epicurean* (London: Longmans Green, 1910), pp. 14-18, who characterizes the thrust of the poem in this way: 'while all the universe is ruled by Zeus and all things everywhere are wrought by His purpose, yet it is evident that man holds a privileged position' (p. 16). He recognizes the dilemma this creates (he calls it a 'permissible oxymoron', p. 17), but perhaps it is not only modern theologians but ancient ones who faced such dilemmas. See also A.A. Long, 'Freedom and Determinism in the Stoic Theory of Human Action', in A.A. Long (ed.), *Problems in Stoicism* (London: Athlone Press, 1971), pp. 173-99, esp. p. 179.

but they are also larger theological issues struggled with by other thinkers of the time.[83]

It is readily observed that there was a widespread interplay between Hellenism and Christian thought at the time of the events and writing of the New Testament.[84] Fairweather summarizes the situation well when he says,

> It is not uncommon to regard the Christian faith as purely the product of Christ's teaching on Palestinian soil, and as wholly unaffected by contact with forces from without... This opinion, however, is untenable in the light of the history of Palestine during the two or three centuries immediately preceding the Christian era. That history shows the existence of an active pagan propaganda, which had important results for Judaism, and afterwards for Christianity as well.[85]

Not as well known but worth mentioning here, however, is the influence of classical Greek thought on the New Testament, especially Paul. In an important work, E.B. Howell shows that Paul is clearly indebted to Plato—though not only Plato—for both language and concepts that he uses, and that he quotes or alludes to classical authors and the various arenas of language usage of the day, such as the theatre, court or stadium.[86] Illustrative examples include similarities between the view of the universe as made in God's image that Paul has in Colossians 1.15-16 and 26 and that depicted by Plato in his *Timaeus* (28c and 92e), or the view of God as creator found in 1 Corinthians 12.6 and Plato's *Republic* (596bc).[87] Further, as in the hymn to Zeus, Paul on several occasions in

---

83   The Stoics were concerned with a number of these issues. See, for example, A.A. Long, *Hellenistic Philosophy: Stoics, Epicureans, Sceptics* (London: Duckworth, 2nd edn, 1986).

84   See, for example, T.R. Glover, *The Conflict of Religions in the Early Roman Empire* (London: Methuen, 1909); F. Cumont, *Oriental Religions in Roman Paganism* (New York: Dover, 1956 [1911]); W. Fairweather, *Jesus and the Greeks, or Early Christianity in the Tideway of Hellenism* (Edinburgh: T. & T. Clark, 1924), esp. pp. 219-327; G.H. Gilbert, *Greek Thought in the New Testament* (New York: Macmillan, 1928); S. Angus, *The Religious Quests of the Graeco–Roman World: A Study in the Historical Background of Early Christianity* (London: John Murray, 1929), esp. pp. 93-106, but *passim*; G.H.C. MacGregor and A.C. Purdy, *Jew and Greek: Tutors unto Christ. The Jewish and Hellenistic Background of the New Testament* (London: Ivor Nicholson and Watson, 1936); J. Ferguson, *The Religions of the Roman Empire* (Ithaca: Cornell University Press, 1970), esp. pp. 211-43; R.M. Grant, *Gods and the One God: Christian Theology in the Graeco–Roman World* (Philadelphia: Westminster Press, 1986).

85   Fairweather, *Jesus and the Greeks*, pp. 219-20.

86   E.B. Howell, 'St Paul and the Greek World', *Greece & Rome* 11 (1964), pp. 7-29, esp. p. 8. See the appendix for specific citations, pp. 21-29.

87   Howell, 'St Paul', pp. 26-27, 28-29. For further examples, see A. Fox, *Plato and the Christians* (London: SCM Press, 1957). Cf. D.A. deSilva, *Introducing the*

Acts (at Lystra, 14.15-17, and Athens, 17.22-31) invokes a natural
theology argument that is very similar to the one that he uses in Romans
1.18-32, where he includes reference to God as creator that would have
been familiar from Stoic thought.[88]

A last example to cite is one that clearly illustrates the need to move
beyond simple disjunctions and stereotypes in discussion. This example
illustrates that it is not demeaning to the New Testament to recognize that
it was theologically understandable to other Greek thinkers of the time.
Pinnock invokes Revelation 1.4 as illustrating that God experiences time
sequentially.[89] However, what he fails to notice is that the language used
by the author of Revelation here is at home in a Greek-speaking world.
In his recent commentary, David Aune notes that this phrase, 'the one
who is and who was and who is coming' (ὁ ὢν καὶ ὁ ἦν καὶ ὁ
ἐρχόμενος), found also in Revelation 1.8 and in a slightly altered form in
4.8, is tripartite in nature. The first part of the phrase, 'the one who is',
was probably derived from the Septuagint translation of Exodus 3.14, 'I
am the one who is'.[90] Philo, according to Aune, uses this phrase, 'the one
who is', of God as a divine name. He also notes that this phrase was
familiar to Jews in Asia Minor (for whom Greek would have been their
first language), on the basis of an inscription found at Pergamon. It
reads: 'God Lord who is forever'.[91]

Apocrypha: Message, Context, and Significance (Grand Rapids, MI: Baker, 2002), pp.
140-42, who notes the influence of Platonic and Stoic thought on Wisdom of Solomon.

88   See S.E. Porter, *The Paul of Acts: Essays in Literary Criticism, Theology, and
Rhetoric* (Wissenschaftliche Untersuchungen zum Neuen Testament, 115; Tübingen:
Mohr Siebeck, 1999), pp. 136-49. The argument from natural theology is endorsed by,
among others, M. Black, *Romans* (New Century Bible; Grand Rapids, MI: Eerdmans,
1973), p. 49; Dunn, *Romans*, I, pp. 56-57; Fitzmyer, *Romans*, p. 273; Moo, *Romans*, p.
97.

89   As noted above, it is not a distinctively Hebraic or Jewish idea to have a linear
view of time. Greek thought was similar, as recent research has indicated. See n. 20.

90   Pinnock, *Most Moved Mover*, p. 80 on Exodus 3.14 cites with sympathy
Northrop Frye, *The Great Code: The Bible and Literature* (London: Routledge and Kegan
Paul, 1982), pp. 17-18, who argues for a return to 'a conception of language in which
words were words of power, conveying primarily the sense of forces and energies rather
than analogues of physical bodies'. Frye's romantic hermeneutics of words having power
has been soundly refuted by A.C. Thiselton, 'The Supposed Power of Words in the
Biblical Writings', *Journal of Theological Studies* 25 (1974), pp. 283-99.

91   D.E. Aune, *Revelation* (Word Biblical Commentary, 52A, B, C; Dallas: Word,
1997–98), I, p. 30.

Conclusion

My conclusion is that all three of the major assumptions related to the New Testament that seem to underlie several significant concepts in open theism are to be questioned, and are in need of further support. The assumptions that are invoked seem to have originated with the Biblical Theology movement and no doubt reflect the kinds of critical assumptions that may well have been more commonly accepted in the middle of last century. Since then, each of them has been subject to severe scrutiny, so much so that I would contend that they can no longer be relied upon in the form in which they are often presented to provide foundational assumptions for establishing the kind of framework needed for open theism, if it is to withstand the onslaught of criticism.

Upon further reflection, one might well wonder at the relative lack of substantive and explicit New Testament evidence for the open theism position. I too have noticed this lack. In fact, after a recent lecture at McMaster Divinity College by Clark Pinnock outlining his position, in which the entirety of his biblical defense consisted of Old Testament passages, I asked him whether he realized this. He expressed surprise at this revelation, but, in his typical gracious manner, acknowledged that my account of the limited range of evidence was accurate. My survey of the published material confirms that the amount of specific appeal to the New Testament is highly limited, especially in comparison with the Old Testament evidence. This in itself raises questions, to my mind, when one considers the role that the New Testament should play in establishing the basis for a Christian theological position. However, the primary purpose of this paper has been to examine the assumptions that lie behind discussion of the New Testament in Pinnock's open theism. From that standpoint, the methodological framework reflects a set of unworkable assumptions in their present form and, from that standpoint, perhaps renders the attempt to erect a structure on such a foundation precarious. Therefore, the most that one can conclude with regard to the New Testament basis of the open theism position is that it remains unproven and unsubstantiated, and it requires much further work in terms of its assumptions and its exegetical basis before it can prove convincing.

CHAPTER 11

The *Filioque*:
Assessing Evangelical Approaches to
a Knotty Problem

David Guretzki

[The *filioque* question] is an excellent specimen of the race of 'extinct controversies'. *Dean Stanley* (1861)

The question of the *filioque*...becomes an opportunity to develop together the meaning of the Trinity. And could any undertaking be more important than this for the development of common theological, spiritual and liturgical perspectives? *Lukas Vischer* (1981)

Few theological issues bear greater symbolic weight than the long-standing dispute concerning the *filioque*. Briefly summarized, historians agree that it was in sixth-century Spain that the Latin word *filioque* first appeared as an interpolation to the third article of the Niceno-Constantinopolitan Creed. Whereas the original Greek text of the Creed (AD 381) confessed belief 'in the Holy Spirit...who proceeds from the Father',[1] the addition of *filioque* (Latin 'and from the Son') altered the

---

1   Εἰς τὸ πνεῦμα τὸ ἅγιον...ἐκ τοῦ πατρὸς ἐκπορευόμενον πιστεύομεν...εἰς τὸ ἅγιον πνεῦμα. Credal texts are taken from Philip Schaff (ed.), *The Creeds of Christendom: Volume 2. The Greek and Latin Creeds* (rev. edn David S. Schaff; Grand Rapids, MI: Baker Books, 1993), pp. 57-59. The text of the Nicene Creed adopted in AD 325 had no more to say than πιστεύομεν...εἰς τὸ ἅγιον πνεῦμα ('We believe...in the Holy Spirit'). Zizioulas identifies constitutive issues that emerged between the Nicene (325) and Constantinopolitan (381) councils which led to a more substantive third article. They were: 1) the developing dialectic arising between notions of 'created' and 'uncreated'; 2) the questioning of substantialist language and the subsequent emergence of *hypostasis* ('person') as an ontological category; and 3) the rise of a 'doxological' theology and the contrast between *theologia* and *oikonomia*. See John D. Zizioulas, 'The Teaching of the Second Ecumenical Council on the Holy Spirit in Historical and Ecumenical Perspective', *Credo in Spiritum Sanctum* (Vatican City: Libreria Editrice Vaticana, 1983), I, pp. 29-45.

Creed to confess belief 'in the Holy Spirit...who proceeds from the Father and the Son (*filioque*)'.[2] Thus, the *filioque* symbolically encapsulates the Western pneumatological tradition that teaches a 'double procession' of the Holy Spirit from the Father and the Son.[3]

The use of the interpolated Creed was generally restricted to the Latin Western churches, but eventually became a point of contention by theologians from the Greek speaking churches of the East, mainly on grounds that the *filioque* did not enjoy ecumenical approval.[4] The dispute was exponentially intensified in 867 when Patriarch Photius produced a polemical treatise against the *filioque*.[5] It was Photius' so-called 'monopatrist' teaching (that the Holy Spirit proceeds from the Father alone[6]) that eventually became associated with the standard Orthodox theological position. Coupled with the unstable political relationship between Eastern and Western parts of the empire, the controversy over the *filioque* eventually became the theological grounds for the Great Schism that took place in 1054—a schism that resulted in the separation of Christendom into the Holy Orthodox Church and the Roman Catholic Church. Unfortunately, the schism formally remains to this day.[7]

---

2   Et in SPIRITUM SANCTUM...qui ex Patre [Filioque] procedit. See Schaff, *Creeds*, II, p. 59.

3   It is commonly asserted by Eastern and Western theologians alike that the doctrine of the Spirit's 'double procession' was an 'Augustinian doctrine'. See Emilianos Timiadis, 'Problems Behind the *Filioque* Clause', in *The Nicene Creed: Our Common Faith* (Philadelphia, PA: Fortress Press, 1983), p. 81; and Wolfhart Pannenberg, *Systematic Theology* (3 vols; Grand Rapids, MI: Eerdmans, 1991–98), I, p. 318. However, closer attention to pre-Augustinian Latin thinkers such as Hilary of Poitiers, Ambrose and Epiphanius indicates that the concept of a 'double procession' of the Holy Spirit was not foreign to them. Though Augustine may have been the clearest proponent and ablest defender of the double procession in the post-Nicene milieu, it is historically inaccurate to say that he was the originator of the doctrine. On some of the problems associated with the history of the Western addition to the Creed, see J.N.D. Kelly, *Early Christian Creeds* (London: Longman, 3rd edn, 1972), pp. 358-67.

4   Gerald Bray has rightly argued that at this stage the problem of the *filioque* was finally beginning to be understood (i.e., unlike the situation from the sixth to the early ninth centuries), but was nevertheless still thought to be fundamentally unimportant. Gerald Bray, 'The *Filioque* Clause in History and Theology,' *Tyndale Bulletin* 34 (1983), pp. 118-21.

5   Photius I, *Mystagogia Spiritus Sanctus [On the Mystagogy of the Holy Spirit]* (trans. Holy Transfiguration Monastery; Astoria, NY: Studion Publishers, 1983).

6   So, ἐκ μόνου τοῦ πατρός. It is noteworthy that Photius' treatise was largely responsible for a hardening of the Eastern position by insisting that the simple Nicene confession that the Spirit proceeds from the Father *means* that the Spirit proceeds from the Father *alone*—even though the Creed does not include the term μόνου per se.

7   Walter F. Adeney, *The Greek and Eastern Churches* (New York: Charles Scribner's Sons, 1939), p. 229. Methodius Fouyas (Greek Orthodox Archbishop of Aksum) has suggested that the three main doctrinal obstacles to the reunification of the

The separation of the church into Eastern and Western factions has had far reaching historical, political and theological effects. From a theological perspective, none has stated this as forcefully as Orthodox theologian Vladimir Lossky. Even if he is judged to have inflated the ultimate significance of the issue, it is difficult to ignore him when he asserts:

> Whether we like it or not, the question of the procession of the Holy Spirit has been the sole dogmatic grounds for the separation of East and West. All other divergences which, historically, accompanied or followed the first dogmatic controversy about the *Filioque*, in the measure in which they too had some dogmatic importance, are more or less dependent upon that original issue... Thus the polemical battle between the Greeks and the Latins was fought principally about the question of the Holy Spirit.[8]

Orthodox and Catholic Churches revolve around a) the procession of the Holy Spirit; b) the Roman papacy; and c) Mary. See Methodius Fouyas, *Orthodoxy, Roman Catholicism and Anglicanism* (London: Oxford University Press, 1972), pp. 206-209. On the political and ecclesiastical situation in the tenth and eleventh centuries, see Steven Runciman, *The Eastern Schism: A Study of the Papacy and the Eastern Churches During the Eleventh and Twelfth Centuries* (Oxford: Clarendon Press, 1955). More recently, Pope John Paul II requested that the Pontifical Council for Promoting Christian Unity would produce a document in which clarification of the Catholic doctrine of the *filioque* would be provided in light of ecumenical discussions with the Orthodox Church. The resultant document is entitled, 'The Greek and Latin Traditions regarding the Procession of the Holy Spirit' and was published in *L'Obsservatore Romano*, N. 38 (1408) (20 September 1995), pp. 3, 6. For a critical analysis of the document by a Roman Catholic theologian, see David Coffey, 'The Roman "Clarification" of the Doctrine of the Filioque', *International Journal of Systematic Theology* 5.1 (March, 2003), pp. 3-21. Dialogue has also been carried on between Reformed and Orthodox Churches who have shown promising signs of progress toward a solution to the *filioque* problem and has been published as 'A Joint Statement of the Official Dialogue Between the Orthodox Church and the World Alliance of Reformed Churches' in March 1991. See Thomas F. Torrance (ed.), *Theological Dialogue Between Orthodox and Reformed Churches*, volume 2 (Edinburgh: Scottish Academic Press, 1985).

8   Vladimir Lossky, *In the Image and Likeness of God* (trans. John H. Erickson and Thomas E. Bird; Paris: Aubier-Montaigne, 1967; reprint, Crestwood, NY: St Vladimir's Seminary Press, 1985), p. 71. The focus of this chapter necessarily prohibits an examination of the history of the *filioque* debate. However, two monographs deserve mention as 'bookends' of modern historical research on the *filioque* doctrine and controversy. H.B. Swete's 1876 study stands as a classic work on the history of the 'double procession' doctrine up to and including the time of Emperor Charlemagne. See H.B. Swete, *On the History of the Doctrine of the Procession of the Holy Spirit From the Apostolic Age to the Death of Charlemange* (Cambridge: Cambridge University Press, 1876). More recently, B. Oberdorfer has surveyed the history and theology of the *filioque* through to the modern ecumenical discussions. See Bernd Oberdorfer, *Filioque: Geschichte und Theologie eines ökumenischen Problems* (Göttingen: Vandenhoeck &

Despite the attention given to the question of the *filioque* by Roman Catholic, Orthodox and some Anglican theologians, relatively few Protestants have given sustained attention to the problem and even fewer evangelicals have bothered to deal with it at all. Even so, when evangelical theologians have discussed the *filioque*, it has generally been only briefly and with significantly divergent results. Thus, the first task at hand will be to identify evangelical approaches to the problem of the *filioque*. However, in so doing, less attention will be given to what evangelicals have actually concluded about the *filioque* as much as discerning how they have approached the problem in the first place. In other words, no attempt is being made here to accomplish what certainly would be the presumptuous task of proposing a new theological argument either for or against the *filioque*.[9] Rather, the more modest goal will be to assess the

---

Ruprecht, 2001). For an Orthodox perspective on the history of the controversy, see Ioannes Metaxas-Mariatos, 'The Filioque Controversy: Chapters From the Eastern Orthodox Reaction' (MA thesis, University of Durham, 1988); Boris Bobrinskoy, *The Mystery of the Trinity: Trinitarian Experience and Vision in the Biblical and Patristic Tradition* (trans. Anthony P. Gythiel; Crestwood, NY: St Vladimir's Seminary Press, 1999), pp. 279-303; and Boris Bobrinskoy, 'The Filioque Yesterday and Today', in *La Signification et L'Actualite du IIe Concile Oecumenique Pour Le Monde Chretien D'Aujourd'hui* (Chambesy: Du Centre Orthodoxe du Patriarcat Oecumenique, 1982), pp. 275-87. Other noteworthy historical surveys of the *filioque* deserving attention (and not cited elsewhere in this chapter) include (in chronological order): Martino Jugie, 'Origine De La Controverse Sur L'addition Du Filioque Au Symbole', *Revue des sciences philosophiques et theologiques* 28 (1939), pp. 369-85; George S. Hendry, 'From the Father and the Son: The *Filioque* After Nine Hundred Years', *Theology Today* 11 (January, 1955), pp. 449-59; André de Halleux, 'Pour Un Accord Oecuménique Sur La Procession De L'Esprit Saint Et L'addition Du "Filioque" Au Symbole', *Irénikon* 51.4 (1978), pp. 451-69; Dietrich Ritschl, 'The History of the Filioque Controversy', in Hans Küng and Jürgen Moltmann (eds), *Conflicts About the Holy Spirit* (New York: Seabury Press, 1979), pp. 3-14; Dietrich Ritschl, 'Historical Development and Implications of the Filioque Controversy', in Lukas Vischer (ed.), *Spirit of God, Spirit of Christ: Ecumenical Reflections on the Filioque Controversy* (London: SPCK, 1981), pp. 46-65; Bertrand de Margerie, *The Christian Trinity in History* (trans. Edmund J. Fortman; Still River, MA: St Bede's Publications, 1982), pp. 147-98; Mary Corinne Winter, 'Ecclesiological Implications of the Current *Filioque* Discussion' (PhD thesis, University of Notre Dame, 1995), pp. 10-60; Nick Needham, 'The *Filioque* Clause: East or West?', *Scottish Bulletin of Evangelical Theology* 15.2 (1997), pp. 142-62; Yves Congar, *I Believe in the Holy Spirit* (trans. David Smith; 3 vols; Geoffrey Chapman, 1983; reprint, New York: Crossroad, 2001), III, pp. 49-78; Brian E. Daley, 'Revisiting the "Filioque": Roots and Branches of an Old Debate, Part One', *Pro Ecclesia* 10.1 (2001), pp. 31-62. Unfortunately, no monograph length work in English devoted to a history of the *filioque* has appeared in the last century. This is an area that sorely needs attention.

9   Without question, the most important programmatic efforts to date to work toward an ecumenical solution to the *filioque* can be found in the proceedings of the Faith

methodological moves that evangelicals have made concerning the *filioque* and thereby to suggest a possible agenda for further discussion of this important issue from an evangelical perspective.

Evangelical Approaches to the *Filioque* Question

For better or for worse, the *filioque* has been almost entirely outside the theological horizon of many, if not most, evangelical theologians. That this is the case is actually rather unremarkable, especially in light of the hermeneutical habit of most evangelicals to start with scripture rather than creed.[10] Because the *filioque* controversy arose first as a dispute over the wording of a creed rather than a dispute over what scripture says, evangelicals have, in many cases, remained either intentionally or unintentionally distant to the question altogether. Or, when they have been introduced to the problem, they have often viewed it as little more than a 'theological fossil' uncovered in medieval church history. Consequently, the debate itself is viewed as that which may be of interest to Roman Catholic or Orthodox theologians who work with a heightened view of the authority of ecclesiastical tradition, but certainly not to evangelicals who affirm scripture as their primary, if not sole, theological authority. Furthermore, that evangelicals have tended to ignore the *filioque* question is unsurprising, at least in part, because of the reticence toward studying any theological issue, whether patristic or medieval, that antedates the Reformation period to which so many evangelicals trace their roots.[11] Though other reasons might be given for lack of attention to the *filioque*, these reasons at least, suggest a general evangelical mood toward the question: ambivalence, if not outright suspicion.

The general evangelical ambivalence to the *filioque* question, however, does not mean evangelicals have completely ignored it. When it comes specifically to the *filioque* question, a representative survey of evangelical

---

and Order Commission of the World Council of Churches that convened in 1978 and 1979. See Vischer (ed.), *Spirit of God, Spirit of Christ*.

10   Indeed, for some evangelical denominations (such as the Christian Church [Disciples of Christ]), slogans such as 'No Creed but Christ' or 'No Book but the Bible' have at times functioned as theological distinctives. But for a fascinating study of how these slogans may have actually misrepresented the thought of the founders of the Christian Church (Disciples of Christ) denomination, see William Tabbernee, 'Alexander Campbell and the Apostolic Tradition', in D.H. Williams (ed.), *The Free Church and the Early Church* (Grand Rapids, MI: Eerdmans, 2002), pp. 163-80.

11   Beginning with the influential work of Thomas Oden, there are promising signs of renewal of interest in the patristic period, however. See, e.g., Daniel H. Williams, *Retrieving the Tradition and Renewing Evangelicalism: Primer for Suspicious Protestants* (Grand Rapids, MI: Eerdmans, 1999).

theologians writing in the last quarter of the twentieth century reveals at least five distinct approaches toward the *filioque* question.[12]

The Filioque *is a Metaphysical Speculation*

First, some evangelical theologians have been extremely cautious, or even suspicious, of the *filioque* debate. For these, the *filioque* controversy is a wholly speculative debate that cannot be settled either positively or negatively without transgressing the canonical boundaries of scripture. This is the position, for example, of Reformed theologian Robert L. Reymond who argues that propositions concerning the eternal generation of the Son or the eternal procession of the Spirit are 'beyond the deliverances of Scripture and [therefore] should not be made elements of Trinitarian orthodoxy'.[13] Indeed, such an attempt to go beyond scripture (as read from the perspective of a 'covenant of redemption') is in danger of becoming 'pretentious metaphysical speculation'.[14] Though not speaking explicitly of the *filioque* per se, John G. Stackhouse, Jr., might express a similar sentiment toward the *filioque* when he cautions evangelicals against 'repeating the scholastic mistake of presuming to venture much beyond the scriptural text into the abyss of Godself'.[15] According to Stackhouse,

> we evangelicals ought to maintain our Christological approach and Christocentric emphasis in all doctrine, including the doctrine of God. This tradition will keep us from presuming to know more about, and emphasizing more than we should about, the Holy Spirit, or God the Father, or the Triune God in Godself. God the Holy Spirit points us to Christ, and Christ is the one who shows us God the Father.[16]

---

12   It is clearly impossible to claim comprehensiveness in the survey to follow. However, theologians have been chosen who are better known representatives of the evangelical household.

13   Robert L. Reymond, *A New Systematic Theology of the Christian Faith* (Nashville, TN: Thomas Nelson Publishers, 1998), p. 341.

14   Reymond, *New Systematic Theology*, p. 337.

15   John G. Stackhouse, Jr., *Evangelical Landscapes: Facing Critical Issues of the Day* (Grand Rapids, MI: Brazos Press, 2002), p. 173.

16   Stackhouse, *Evangelical Landscapes*, p. 169. Ironically, it is precisely Stackhouse's last sentence which functioned as the rationale for Karl Barth in arguing for the necessity of a doctrine of the *filioque* for a christocentric theology, i.e., that the Holy Spirit points to Christ must arise from the theological fact that the Spirit proceeds from Christ. For Barth's rigorous defence of the *filioque*, see Karl Barth, *Church Dogmatics* (Edinburgh: T. & T. Clark, 1975), I.1, pp. 473-87.

The Filioque *is Biblical, but Theologically Insignificant*

Second, there are those evangelical theologians who accept the *filioque* as a doctrine supported by scripture, but who nevertheless deem it to be an issue of relative unimportance. In his widely received *Christian Theology*, Baptist theologian Millard Erickson explicitly mentions the *filioque* once, and then only for the purpose of downplaying its theological significance in the separation of Eastern and Western churches.[17] However, he does go on to say that '[t]here is a close relationship between Christ and the Spirit, closer than is often realized'. For Erickson, this close relationship is expressed in terms of the Spirit being the bond of union between the believer and Christ.[18] Notably, these expressions are evidence of Erickson's reception of Western filioquism, but the absence of any further discussion of the *filioque* in his systematic theology suggests Erickson's ambivalence toward it. Similarly, Wesleyan theologian J. Kenneth Grider argues that 'the Reformers never made the *filioque* an issue'[19] and he clearly follows suit in his systematic theology since he never mentions it again!

Still others go further to support the *filioque* and do provide some attempt to show its scriptural support. Lewis and Demarest suggest that the *filioque* has scriptural precedent on the basis that the Holy Spirit is presented in scripture both as the Spirit of Jesus Christ and the Spirit of God.[20] Wayne Grudem also argues that the Western position is to be supported because scripture testifies both to the procession of the Spirit from the Father (Jn 15.26) and to the Spirit being sent by the Son (Jn 16.7). Therefore, he concludes, 'by analogy it would seem appropriate to say that this reflects eternal ordering of their relationships'. Yet despite his attempt to support the doctrine scripturally, Grudem admits, 'this is not something that we can clearly insist on based on any specific verse, but much of our understanding of the *eternal* relationships among the Father, Son, and Holy Spirit comes by analogy from what the Scripture tells us about the way they related to the creation *in time*'.[21] Though relative importance of the *filioque* could be plotted on a spectrum even within this group, suffice it to say that both the minimal attention given to the *filioque* and the minimal efforts to support it from scripture suggest

17   Millard J. Erickson, *Christian Theology* (Grand Rapids, MI: Baker, 1985), p. 852.

18   Erickson, *Christian Theology*, pp. 952-53.

19   J. Kenneth Grider, *A Wesleyan-Holiness Theology* (Kansas City: Beacon Hill Press of Kansas City, 1994), p. 148.

20   Gordon R. Lewis and Bruce A. Demarest, *Integrative Theology* (3 vols; Grand Rapids, MI: Zondervan, 1987–94), I, pp. 278-79.

21   Wayne Grudem, *Systematic Theology: An Introduction to Biblical Doctrine* (Grand Rapids, MI: Zondervan, 1994), p. 247.

that for these evangelicals, at least, the *filioque* is of minor significance, even if it is received and defended.

The Filioque *is Theologically Necessary*

A third group of evangelical theologians shares with the second group a common acceptance of the *filioque* as part of the Western theological heritage, but these thinkers are more vocally adamant about its theological significance. Consequently, they extend greater efforts to argue the case in favour of the *filioque* as a theologically crucial, even necessary, part of the confession of an evangelical pneumatology. No evangelical writer better represents this position than Anglican theologian Gerald Bray who has studied and written extensively on the *filioque*.[22] For Bray, the doctrine of the 'double procession' of the Spirit is something more than just the regrettable addition of a word to an ancient creed. Accordingly, Bray insists that those who call the Western churches to drop the word altogether fail to understand the theological import of the debate. As he puts it,

> even if the reasons given for th[e] deletion [of the *filioque*] are ones of propriety, most people will assume that a question of truth is involved... The truth issue will not go away: Does the Holy Spirit proceed from the Son as well as from the Father—and, if he does, does this matter?[23]

Thus, according to Bray, 'this is the nub of the issue—and, unless it is decided one way or the other, tinkering with the words of the Nicene Creed will make very little difference either way'.[24] Indeed, Bray has expressed serious doubts that the Anglican–Orthodox dialogues resulting in the so-called 'Moscow Agreement' whereby Anglicans agreed to remove the *filioque* from the Creed for use in worship have made any real progress on the question at all.[25]

Donald Bloesch also perceives that 'the doctrine of the *filioque*... is under attack, even in evangelical circles'.[26] For Bloesch, 'the *filioque* is not only based on a solid biblical witness but is also congruous with a

---

22   See especially Gerald Bray, 'The Double Procession of the Holy Spirit in Evangelical Theology Today: Do We Still Need It?', *Journal of the Evangelical Theological Society* 41.3 (1998), pp. 415-26.

23   Bray, 'Double Procession', p. 420.

24   Bray, 'Double Procession', p. 420.

25   Gerald Bray, '*Filioque* and Anglican Orthodox Dialogue', *Churchman* 93.2 (1979), p. 133.

26   Donald G. Bloesch, *The Holy Spirit* (Downers Grove, IL: InterVarsity Press, 2000), p. 271.

broad line of patristic interpretation'.[27] However, despite his conviction of the important truth to which the *filioque* points, Bloesch concedes that the *filioque* cannot be viewed as all that can be said about the Holy Spirit. Rather,

> the key to orthodoxy is to confess that the mystery of the Trinity can only be dimly apprehended, that our attempts to elucidate and expound will always fall short of a rational resolution. The mystery of the Trinity is best described in terms of paradox, and this perception is in full accord not only with the biblical witness but also with church tradition.[28]

Even if the *filioque* cannot be expected to carry the full weight of what is needed for an evangelical pneumatology, for Bloesch it is nevertheless a significant part of that same pneumatology.[29]

There is a Mediating or Synthetic Position between Filioque *and Non-*Filioque *Positions*

A fourth approach toward the *filioque* question is represented by Baptist theologian Stanley Grenz. Unlike the previous three groups who see the *filioque* either as unimportant or as a crucial component of the evangelical confession on the Holy Spirit, Grenz seeks rather to forge a middle path of understanding between Eastern and Western positions. Grenz argues that it is important to try to understand the theological rationale on both sides of the debate and to incorporate positive aspects from either side into an evangelical pneumatology. On the one hand, Grenz observes that the non-filioquist position of the East does not necessitate developing a strict connection between the work of the Spirit and Christ as might be demanded by a filioquist theology. Consequently, 'Eastern thinkers are in a better theological position to develop a Christian conception of creation which links God's work in making the world with his activity in saving it'.[30] On the other hand, Grenz also sees the merits of a Western position, both from a scriptural and theological perspective. Scripturally, the *filioque* is implied because the Bible consistently speaks both of the Spirit of God and the Spirit of the Son.

---

27   Bloesch, *Holy Spirit*, p. 271.
28   Bloesch, *Holy Spirit*, p. 274.
29   It is undoubtedly less than coincidental that both Bray and Bloesch have been significantly open to the work of Karl Barth on this issue, particularly Barth's adamant defence of the *filioque* in his *Church Dogmatics*. Barth himself would definitely fall into this third category as an ardent supporter of the *filioque* as theologically significant.
30   Stanley J. Grenz, *Theology for the Community of God* (Nashville, TN: Broadman & Holman, 1994), p. 89.

Theologically, the *filioque* guarantees 'the continuity of the present work of the Spirit with the completed work of the Son'.[31] Therefore, Grenz concludes,

> the *filioque* controversy allows us to understand more fully the relational dynamic of the triune God. Two movements logically inhere within the one God. From the West, we learn that the second movement, the procession of the Spirit, is connected with both the Father and the Son. But the position of the East reminds us that ultimately both movements find their source in the priority of the Father.[32]

Though Grenz attempts to balance the benefits of Eastern and Western positions, in the end it is evident that he still comes out with the scales tipped in favour of the *filioque*. Indeed, he contends that 'viewed salvation-historically, the Western church was correct in adding the *filioque* clause to the ancient creed'. This is because the 'clause emphasizes the normative significance of the work of Christ for the Christian understanding of the Spirit's activity'.[33] Grenz thus stands as an example of an evangelical who perceives the theological significance of the *filioque* but who nevertheless desires evangelicals to see both sides of the debate and thereby to learn from it.

The Filioque *is to be Rejected for Ecumenical and Theological Reasons*

The fifth evangelical approach toward the *filioque* stands in greater contrast to the previous four. Following the criticisms of the *filioque* from the Orthodox tradition, these evangelicals sense that the *filioque* was a negative development in the Christian tradition and, as such, Western appropriation of the *filioque* ought be reversed in favour of the original wording of the Creed. Clark Pinnock, in whose honour this chapter is written, is one such influential evangelical theologian who takes this position.

Though no single work of Pinnock's is easily identified as his *magnum opus*, his book on the Holy Spirit, *Flame of Love*, comes closest to this designation. There Pinnock admits that he has tried harder than ever to be genuinely 'catholic' in the sense of 'respect[ing] the beliefs and practices of the historic churches'. In order to accomplish this, Pinnock says, 'I have dipped in to the treasure of Catholic and Orthodox traditions in ways I had not done before'.[34] Given his admission to be

---

31   Grenz, *Theology for the Community*, p. 90.
32   Grenz, *Theology for the Community*, p. 90.
33   Grenz, *Theology for the Community*, p. 484.
34   Clark H. Pinnock, *Flame of Love: A Theology of the Holy Spirit* (Downers Grove, IL: InterVarsity Press, 1996), p. 18.

open to the broader Christian traditions, it is certainly interesting to observe how Pinnock handles the *filioque* question.

Given Pinnock's desire to be broadly 'catholic' (as opposed to strictly 'Catholic') in drawing upon the resources of tradition in constructing his pneumatology, it is not surprising that Pinnock is opposed to the *filioque* primarily on ecumenical grounds. As he puts it, 'The Western church acted unilaterally by inserting this term without heeding protests from the East, and this resulted in the first great division of the church. Making this insertion represented a misuse of power.'[35] Pinnock thereby privileges the Orthodox position, at least in part, by the recognition of the importance of ecclesiastical authority in theological debate. This move of Pinnock's, largely against the mainstream evangelical theologians mentioned above, should also come as no surprise, given how often Pinnock finds himself swimming against such theological streams.

That Pinnock can freely appeal to ecclesiastical tradition is consistent with his methodological adoption of a quadrilateral of sources (scripture, tradition, reason and experience),[36] though many evangelicals might question the extent to which an appeal to ecclesiastical tradition violates the evangelical 'scripture principle'. Nevertheless, Pinnock does go on to assert that his rejection of the *filioque* is not based solely on such ecclesiastical issues, nor even because he views the *filioque* as perverse theologically, but because he perceives that the addition of the phrase into the Nicene Creed by Western theologians 'adversely affects our understanding of salvation'.[37] According to Pinnock, the *filioque* could discount the fact 'that the Spirit is universally present, implementing the universal salvific will of Father and Son'.[38]

Pinnock's approach to the *filioque* is representative of an increasing number of evangelical and mainline Protestant thinkers alike. Ironically, Pinnock, who is usually regarded as a theological innovator, thus stands in the mainstream of the current *filioque* debate with theological luminaries such as Jürgen Moltmann,[39] Wolfhart Pannenberg[40] and

---

35   Pinnock, *Flame of Love*, p. 196.

36   For assessment of Pinnock's theological methodology, see David Guretzki, 'The Theological Methodology of Clark H. Pinnock' (MA thesis, Briercrest Biblical Seminary, 1995).

37   Pinnock, *Flame of Love*, p. 197.

38   Pinnock, *Flame of Love*, p. 196.

39   Jürgen Moltmann, *The Trinity and the Kingdom* (Minneapolis: Fortress Press, 1993), pp. 178-87, and Jürgen Moltmann, 'Theological Proposals Towards the Resolution of the Filioque Controversy', in Vischer (ed.), *Spirit of God, Spirit of Christ*, pp. 164-73.

40   Pannenberg, *Systematic Theology*, I, pp. 317-19.

Robert Jenson,[41] to name but three theologians who argue along similar lines. In addition, the recommendation of the highly influential Klingenthal Memorandum (which brought together theologians from Orthodox, Catholic, Anglican and Reformed wings of Christianity in order to consult on the *filioque* question) reads:

> We therefore recommend: ...that the original form of the third article of the Creed, without the *filioque*, should everywhere be recognized as the normative one and restored, so that the whole Christian people may be able, in this formula, to confess their common faith in the Holy Spirit.[42]

Given this formidable assemblage of voices from such diverse theological traditions, it immediately becomes evident how powerful the argument is that the *filioque* should be abandoned, and stands, in some senses, as the 'majority position'. Thus, of all the current attitudes toward the *filioque*, it is this last one, of which Pinnock is representative, that provides considerable influence toward encouraging evangelicals, especially those with ecumenical sensitivities, to leave the *filioque* behind.

Assessing Evangelical Approaches to the *Filioque*

If it is granted that the above survey of evangelical thinkers at least roughly represents the evangelical horizon of approaches to the *filioque* question, we are left asking how these approaches ought to be assessed. In other words, which, if any, of these approaches to the knotty *filioque* problem should be adopted? Though it is possible that there is something to be learned from each evangelical approach to the *filioque*, the argument here will be that none is adequate to the theological task at hand. Indeed, limited progress on this question may well point to the reality that current evangelical approaches to the *filioque* question have reached their limits, especially in light of the broader advances in scholarship on the *filioque* question outside the evangelical community of scholarship.

On the one hand, the problem of the *filioque* might ultimately be judged to be a 'pseudo-problem' if, according to the first approach, the question presumes to answer something that is beyond answering with the resources available. In other words, if the *filioque* question is one that can only be answered by speculation 'beyond the deliverances of

---

41   Robert W. Jenson, 'You Wonder Where the Spirit Went', *Pro Ecclesia* 2.3 (1993), pp. 296-304.

42   'The Filioque Clause in Ecumenical Perspective', in Vischer (ed.), *Spirit of God, Spirit of Christ*, p. 18.

Scripture',[43] then the *filioque* debate can be conveniently ignored and relegated to the category of 'Questions-I-will-ask-God-in-heaven'. For, it might by argued, scripture simply does not give a clear indication of how the Son and the Spirit are eternally or ontologically related, nor should we seek to give an answer to such a question.

On the other hand, the question arises as to what constitutes, in the words of Reymond, 'pretentious metaphysical speculation'[44] in regard to the doctrine of the Trinity. From Reymond's perspective, statements such as that the Holy Spirit eternally and essentially proceeds from the Father and the Son 'should not be made elements of Trinitarian orthodoxy'.[45] Conversely, Reymond is quite confident in his discernment of the limits of what scripture reveals about God, namely that: 1) there is but one living and true God who is eternally and immutably indivisible; 2) the Father, Son and Holy Spirit are each fully and equally God; and 3) the Father, Son and Holy Spirit are distinct persons.[46] Presumably, Reymond feels that these three assertions *should* be made elements of Trinitarian orthodoxy. However, this immediately raises the question of why *these* three statements are assumed to be non-speculative (and indeed, non-pretentious) assertions in regard to the doctrine of the Trinity. Could one not easily ask why the affirmation (or more accurately, the negation) that God is 'immutably indivisible' is not itself a metaphysical speculation that extends beyond the borders of scripture? Where are these terms present in scripture? Are these terms not themselves imported from the Hellenistic metaphysical tradition? Or why is the assertion that the three members of the Godhead are 'distinct persons' not also a 'metaphysical speculation' about God in Godself? Is this not a way of speaking about the Trinity (traditional as it is) that is plainly a theological speculation beyond the deliverance of scripture? Indeed, where in scripture is 'person' (*hypostasis*) applied equally to the three members of the Godhead as precise distinctions between them? [47]

I raise these questions not in an attempt to refute Reymond on his three assertions (though, technically, I believe the way in which he has stated his assertions are open to criticism and clarification), but to demonstrate the slippery and rather unhelpful way in which charges about 'metaphysical speculation' are used to stave off what is considered *a priori* to be illegitimate theological investigation. In contrast, would it not

---

43   Reymond, *New Systematic Theology*, p. 341.
44   Reymond, *New Systematic Theology*, p. 337.
45   Reymond, *New Systematic Theology*, p. 341.
46   Reymond, *New Systematic Theology*, p. 205.
47   Indeed, G.W.H. Lampe stands as at least one scholar who affirms that 'the Trinitarian model is in the end less satisfactory for the articulation of our basic Christian experience than the unifying concept [in scripture] of God as Spirit'. See G.W.H. Lampe, *God as Spirit* (Oxford: Clarendon Press, 1977), p. 228.

be better humbly to admit that all doctrinal conclusions regarding the nature of God are human exercises in 'metaphysical speculation'? Unless we are content to read scripture without translation, commentary or attempts at doctrinal synthesis, every doctrinal conclusion becomes suspect of the charge of 'metaphysical speculation'. Even the somewhat innocent attempt to explain the meaning of biblical terms like 'eternal' or 'almighty' in reference to God leads the theologian to 'speculate' and to extrapolate beyond the deliverances of scripture in terms and language that claim to say what scripture says in words other than scripture.[48] Ironically, it is not immediately clear, at least in the above cited instance, why affirming that God is 'immutably indivisible' or constituted by 'three distinct persons' is *not* a metaphysical speculation while the affirmation that 'the Spirit proceeds from the Father' (or, 'the Spirit proceeds from the Father and the Son') *is* a metaphysical speculation, even though the latter statement(s) are nearly a direct citation of John 15.26![49]

This leads me to suggest not that Reymond's caution against 'speculation' should be ignored as much as to state that it needs to be carefully qualified. Reymond is right to caution evangelicals against making assertions concerning a doctrine of God that cannot be supported by scripture. This is, after all, the evangelical way. But the caution would be better stated by making a distinction between 'grounded' and 'groundless' speculation. Whether evangelicals eventually buy into a 'foundationalist' or 'non-foundationalist' theory of scripture, they should be able to at least agree that all doctrinal conclusions must in some way return to scripture as the primary source. Surely a qualitative difference must be drawn between theological assertions that have no connection or appeal whatsoever to scripture (for example, Einstein's desire 'to know the thoughts of God' through the exploration of physics)[50] and those assertions that arise out of an examination of

---

48   Even Reymond cites with approval Warfield's dictum that 'it is better to preserve the truth of Scripture than the words of Scripture'. As cited in Reymond, *New Systematic Theology*, p. 206.

49   That it was assumed that there were severe limits to the depth of knowledge possible concerning the Triune nature of God can be traced back to the nominalist leanings of Luther and Melanchthon. This suspicion of metaphysical knowledge of God was sharpened even further with Kant's split between the noumenal and phenomenal (and his own suspicions of the 'practical value' of the doctrine of the Trinity) and came to full fruition in the complete absence of the doctrine of the Trinity in the thought of Rudolf Bultmann. For an insightful tracing of this theme, see Samuel Powell, *The Trinity in German Thought* (Cambridge: Cambridge University Press, 2001).

50   Cited by Rami M. Shapiro, 'Science and Religion: A Marriage Made in Heaven?', in Robert L. Hermann (ed.), *Expanding Humanity's Vision of God* (Philadelphia: Templeton Foundation Press, 2001), p. 291.

scripture and the historical interpretation of scripture, including the great christological and trinitarian developments of the first five centuries. But to suggest that investigation into the procession of the Spirit is an exercise in 'pretentious metaphysical speculation' is presumptuous in itself because it claims to know, in advance, what scripture does and does not teach.

It may well be the case that no *biblical* solution to the *filioque* will be found; but this should in no way prevent the theologian from continuing to try. I, for one, believe that the depth of the riches of scripture have not yet been exhausted and it may well be that evangelicals, in their characteristic attention to the text of scripture, could yet offer something of value to this question, but only if the question is not ruled out of theological court before the investigation begins.

If it can be accepted that the *filioque* question cannot be ruled out in advance as a legitimate topic of theological inquiry, then evangelicals who are called upon to wrestle with this problem will rightly turn to scripture and ask, 'What does the Bible teach concerning the relationship of the Holy Spirit to the Father and the Son?' Lewis and Demarest conclude that because the Bible speaks of the Spirit as both the Spirit of God and the Spirit of Christ that the scriptural inference is that the Spirit proceeds from both. Grudem follows a slightly different tack in seeking scriptural support for the *filioque* by appealing to how the Bible speaks both of the 'procession' of the Spirit from the Father and the 'sending' of the Spirit from the Son. Taken together, Grudem understands these two terms to be virtually synonymous and thus that scripture implies a double procession of the Spirit from Father and Son.[51]

While it is laudable that Lewis and Demarest and Grudem attempt to discern from scripture the answer to the question of the Spirit's procession, the problem is that the 'scriptural' conclusions in support of the *filioque* by both Lewis and Demarest and Grudem could equally be accepted by Orthodox thinkers if important qualifiers were included. Indeed, many Orthodox theologians affirm, without hesitation, that the Spirit is the Spirit of both Father and Son. This is the necessary conclusion by attention to the hypostatic relations of the Triune economy as attested to in scripture. Further, it is doubtful that any Orthodox theologian would reject the assertion that the Spirit is sent by the Son because again, the scriptural evidence for such an assertion is indisputably clear from the scriptural text (e.g., Jn 15.26). But despite these scriptural inferences in favour of the *filioque*, Orthodox thinkers

---

51 Interestingly, D.A. Carson agrees with Grudem's assessment that the terms 'procession' and 'sent' are an example of 'synonymous parallelism', but in contrast concludes that the terms 'refer not to some ontological "procession" but to the mission of the Spirit'. D.A. Carson, *The Gospel According to John* (Grand Rapids, MI: Eerdmans, 1991), pp. 528-29.

continue flatly to deny that the *filioque* is true. Even Lossky, who admits of the possibility of an Orthodox interpretation of the *filioque*, feels compelled to reject the *filioque* because 'by the dogma of the *Filioque*, the God of the philosophers and savants is introduced into the heart of the Living God'.[52] Though Western theologians might view this as a stubborn refusal to 'face up to the facts' of scripture on the part of Eastern theologians, things are not as simple as they might appear. This is because two fundamentally different theological presuppositions are governing how scripture itself is being read.

A fundamental Western theological presupposition is made manifest when Grudem admits that his argument from scripture in favour of the *filioque* is successful only because he assumes 'much of our understanding of the *eternal* relationships among the Father, Son, and Holy Spirit comes by analogy from what the Scripture tells us about the way they related to the creation *in time*'.[53] However, Orthodox thinkers clearly do not share that optimism. As Lossky puts it, theological contemplation upon the Holy Spirit (or any member of the Trinity) leads the Orthodox theologian to 'reach a paradoxical conclusion: all that we know of the Holy Spirit refers to his economy; all that we do not know makes us venerate his Person, as we venerate the ineffable diversity of the consubstantial Three'.[54] Later, Lossky explains: 'Precisely because God is unknowable in that which He is, Orthodox theology distinguishes between the essence of God and His energies, between the inaccessible nature of the Holy Trinity and its "natural processions".'[55]

In light of these radically differing perspectives as to how scripture reveals God, the question of the *filioque* does less to test the exegetical abilities of those involved in its investigation and does more to identify fundamental theological presuppositions that are themselves difficult, if not impossible, to substantiate from scripture itself. For the theologian investigating the question, the methodological first order of business is to decide what it is scripture is *doing* when it uses the language of God the Father, Son and Holy Spirit. For the Orthodox theologian, 'The Bible, in its concrete language, speaks of nothing other than "energies" when it tells us of the "glory of the God"—a glory with innumerable names which surrounds the inaccessible Being of God, making himself known outside Himself, while concealing what He is in Himself'.[56] But in contrast, when the Western theologian investigating the question of the *filioque* goes to the Bible, he or she expects that God is in his essence as he presents himself to us in the economy (cf. Grudem). Many

52   Lossky, *Image of God*, p. 88.
53   Grudem, *Systematic Theology*, p. 247.
54   Lossky, *Image of God*, p. 75.
55   Lossky, *Image of God*, p. 89.
56   Lossky, *Image of God*, p. 90.

evangelicals, whatever their general assessment of Barth, would concur with his assertion that 'statements about the divine modes of being [*Seinsweisen*, i.e., 'persons'] antecedently in themselves cannot be different in content from those that are to be made about their reality in revelation' and 'the reality of God which encounters us in His revelation is His reality in all the depths of eternity'.[57] Rahner, too, upholds this identification of the economic and immanent Trinity by his famous axiom in which '*the "economic" Trinity is the "immanent" Trinity and the "immanent" Trinity is the "economic" Trinity*'.[58]

In reference to the matter at hand, then, evangelicals (and indeed, all Christians) are faced not simply with *two* possible conclusions (either for or against the doctrine of double procession)[59] but with *four*. This is because there are also two fundamental theological stances to take on the relationship between God as he has revealed himself economically and God as he is immanently in eternity. Either the economy reflects fully God in his immanence, or else the economy (or, in Orthodox terms, 'energies') of God reveal God only in his ineffable hiddenness. In theory, then, one might conclude that the Spirit 1) does or 2) does not proceed from the Son in the economic Trinity as in the immanent Trinity *or* the Spirit 3) does or 4) does not proceed from the Son in the economic Trinity alone. By now it should be evident that no appeal to scripture will be able to solve this problem without first deciding upon the extent to which the economic Trinity parallels or hides the immanent Trinity. I, for one, cannot at this time conceive of how or where one might turn to settle this dispute and this is an area that needs extensive theological reflection. Unfortunately, sharper exegesis and increased appeals to scripture seem unlikely to succeed in bringing about a solution to this massive theological problem.[60]

An excellent and extremely helpful study of the theological implications of the two fundamentally different presuppositions of Western and Orthodox theologians is found in Duncan Reid's

---

57   Barth, *Church Dogmatics*, I.1, p. 479.

58   Karl Rahner, *The Trinity* (New York: Herder and Herder, 1970), p. 22, italics original.

59   This appears to be the stance of Gerald Bray who quite rightly wants to ask the question of the truth of the *filioque* even apart from its ecumenical legitimacy. Nevertheless, Bray asserts, 'unless [the *filioque* question] is decided one way or another, tinkering with the words of the Nicene Creed will make very little difference'. Bray, 'Double Procession', p. 420.

60   This is not to say the problem is *a priori* insoluble, but simply to say the axiomatic nature of these presuppositions precisely as *axioms* are theological givens not subject to regular 'rules' or 'practices' of scriptural exegesis.

monograph *Energies of the Spirit*.[61] Reid's study compares the Western doctrines of the Trinity of Barth and Rahner with the Eastern doctrines of the Trinity of Lossky and Florovsky.[62] Typical comparisons of Western and Eastern positions on the *filioque* assume that East and West had a *common concern* (i.e., trying to discern whether the Spirit proceeds from the Father and the Son) but a *different intention* (i.e., with the West safeguarding the divinity of the Spirit and the East safeguarding the monarchy of the Father).[63] However, Reid helpfully inverts the comparison and notes a *common intention* between East and West (i.e., 'to take seriously and give expression to the biblical experience of God'[64]) but *different concerns*. Whereas the Western 'principle of identity' between the economic and immanent Trinity was concerned with safeguarding the 'reliability or faithfulness of God',[65] the Eastern Palamite[66] 'doctrine of energies emphasizes the inaccessibility of God in Godself' while simultaneously allowing for the 'possibility of an "unmediated" mystical experience of the divine glory'.[67] This inversion of the typical comparisons between East and West calls into question the viability of incorporating insights from both models into a synthetic theological solution, despite a certain quantity of common theological grammar, without denigrating one or the other's primary theological concern. This may partially explain why, in the end, Grenz, for example, takes his stance in favour of the Western position, even though he apparently wants to garner insights from both sides. He is forced to make this choice, I contend, because the Eastern and Western positions are mutually exclusive in their concerns and thus resist synthetic resolution.[68]

---

61   Duncan Reid, *Energies of the Spirit: Trinitarian Models in Eastern Orthodox and Western Theology* (Atlanta, GA: Scholars Press, 1997).

62   For a more general comparative study between the Trinitarian theologies of West and East, including Barth and Lossky, see Alar Laats, *Doctrines of the Trinity in Eastern and Western Theologies: A Study with Special Reference to K. Barth and V. Lossky* (Frankfurt: Peter Lang, 1999).

63   This is essentially how Grenz outlines the differences between the Eastern and Western models. See pp. 191-92 above.

64   Reid, *Energies*, p. 121.

65   Reid, *Energies*, p. 123.

66   An important issue not discussed here is the reliance of much of Orthodox theology on the fourteenth-century theologian Gregory Palamas and the development of his doctrine of the 'energies'.

67   Reid, *Energies*, p. 123.

68   That Eastern and Western models cannot be synthesized is the main thesis of Mary Ann Fatula, a Roman Catholic theologian, who calls Eastern and Western doctrines of the Spirit two 'irreducible traditions'. Fatula calls for the gracious allowance, in ecumenical debate, of the possibility of 'dogmatic pluralism' in reference to the *filioque*. See Mary Ann Fatula, 'The Eternal Relation Between Son and Spirit in Eastern and Western Trinitarian Theology' (PhD thesis, The Catholic University of America, 1983);

This finally leads to the question of how we are to assess those evangelicals who, quite unlike the previous ones mentioned, are ready to accede to the Eastern position and recommend dropping the *filioque* entirely from Western theologizing. At the outset, it is clear that ecumenically this approach has much to commend to it. Though there are and will remain a number of evangelicals who are dubious, if not suspicious, of ecumenical dialogue with Roman Catholic, Orthodox and mainline Protestant denominations, the approach taken by Pinnock, for example, is indicative of an increasing awareness of the theological and missiological implications of the longstanding ecclesiological division that has been a reality for the body of Christ from the eleventh century on.[69] This is something that evangelicals must, in my opinion, take ever more seriously.

However, I want to suggest that many of the reasons given for simply rejecting the *filioque* are problematic both generally speaking from the perspective of the Western tradition and more specifically from an evangelical stance. In order to deal with these issues, I will seek to dialogue more fully with Clark Pinnock's pneumatological reflections on the *filioque*.

Pinnock wisely concedes that the Western addition of the *filioque* was not in itself perverse theologically.[70] However, he does go on to suggest that the *filioque* can lead to a possible misunderstanding, mainly that it could threaten the universality of the Spirit. As Pinnock puts it,

> [The *filioque*] might suggest to the worshiper that Spirit is not the gift of the Father to creation universally but a gift confined to the sphere of the Son and even the sphere of the Church. It could give the impression that the Spirit is not present in the whole world but limited to Christian territories. Though it need not, the *filioque* might threaten the principle of universality—the truth that the Spirit is universally present, implementing the universal salvific will of Father and Son.[71]

One can sense Pinnock's cautious wording here. He is rightly cautious not to assert that the *filioque* phrase *is* the reason for pneumatological limitation, but instead uses phrases such as 'it could give the impression'

Mary Ann Fatula, 'The Holy Spirit in East and West: Two Irreducible Traditions', *One in Christ* 19.4 (1983), pp. 379-86; and Mary Ann Fatula, 'The Council of Florence and Pluralism in Dogma', *One in Christ* 19.1 (1983), pp. 14-27.

69   Though dealing specifically with the ecclesiological division in the West between Roman Catholics and Protestants, Ephraim Radner's study of pneumatology in the divided church has profound implications both for the narrower divisions among Protestants and evangelicals, but also for the broader ecumenical divisions between East and West. See Ephraim Radner, *The End of the Church: A Pneumatology of Christian Division in the West* (Grand Rapids, MI: Eerdmans, 1998).

70   Pinnock, *Flame of Love*, p. 196.

71   Pinnock, *Flame of Love*, p. 196.

or 'it might' and even the qualifier 'though it need not'. But it is precisely these qualifiers that need careful assessment.

In the first place, Pinnock's cautionary stance indicates his awareness that the systematic implications of either adopting or rejecting the *filioque* are extremely difficult to pinpoint. Indeed, if there is one theological practice that needs to be challenged, it is the practice of accepting or rejecting a theological position on the basis of what *might* result in a theology, rather than through careful attention to how the adoption of a position *actually* works itself out in a systematic theology.[72] While Pinnock's cautions should not be ignored, the dangers will only be identified through critical assessment of actual Western theologies and their consequent pneumatology, ecclesiology, christology, etc.[73] Consequently, acceptance or rejection of the *filioque* is itself a task done *a posteriori* upon consideration of its actual, rather than potential, theological and systemic implications. This is where the role of careful historical theologians can be of great service, particularly as they seek to trace the effects of either a filioquist or non-filioquist theology through a particular theologian's thought. In other words, it is not immediately clear nor necessary that the adoption of the *filioque* leads to the dangers that Pinnock identifies.

Second, if Pinnock is right in his last qualifier, that the *filioque* 'need not' result in the limitations upon the Spirit's universality that he fears, then it is also a legitimate question to ask what 'might' or 'could' happen if the *filioque* is ignored, as it is so meticulously in the Orthodox tradition. If it is granted, for the sake of argument, that the introduction of the *filioque* into the Western theological tradition did lead to the pneumatological limitations that Pinnock suggests, then it is also equally appropriate to ask what the introduction of the Photian monopatristic emphasis has meant for the consequent development of Orthodox pneumatology. This is a question that none that I am aware of have bothered to explore in any great depth, being as it is that the Western tradition itself tends to be more often on the defensive when it comes to the *filioque*,[74] not to mention the fact that so few evangelicals are

---

72   It is exactly upon this premise that my own research that is leading me to do a careful analysis of the ecclesiological implications of the *filioque* in Karl Barth's *Church Dogmatics*.

73   It is important to note in this connection that Yves Congar, for example, has argued that the ecclesiological implications of the *filioque* are ambiguous—and this despite the protests to the contrary by ardent anti-filioquists such as Lossky. See Yves Congar, 'Did the *Filioque* have an Ecclesiastical Impact?, in his *I Believe in the Holy Spirit*, III, pp. 208-12.

74   In this regard, see Bruce D. Marshall, 'The Defense of the *Filioque* in Classical Lutheran Theology: An Ecumenical Appreciation', *Neue Zeitschrift für Systematische Theologie und Religionsphilosophie* 44.2 (2002), pp. 154-73.

equipped to investigate Orthodox theology from within its own ecclesiological and systemic logic. Even though it is true that many modern Orthodox theologians have distanced themselves from the Photian tradition that argued that the Holy Spirit proceeds from the Father *alone*, it is nevertheless the case that the monopatrist tradition is still alive and well in certain sectors of modern Orthodox theology, Vladimir Lossky being the best twentieth-century example.[75] For it cannot be denied that the monopatrist tradition is a historical develop- ment beyond the Creed itself, the protests of certain Orthodox theologians such as Lossky notwithstanding.

In this regard, proposals by evangelicals to adopt an Eastern position fail to consider the intrasystemic developments of both Eastern and Western traditions and tend to focus upon a very narrow slice of the problem. The problem itself is constructed in a rather static, ahistorical form that does not consider the massive difficulty of making such a paradigmatic shift 'mid-stream' nor the role that theological reception of the *filioque* has played in the rise of evangelical theology itself.[76]

Third, given the fundamental differences between the axiomatic presuppositions of Eastern and Western positions, it is a legitimate question to ask how it is possible to adopt, out of theological context, as it were, a portion of the Eastern tradition while simultaneously neglecting (or refusing) to adopt some of the less familiar aspects of that same tradition, e.g., the doctrine of the energies. It is difficult not to be slightly suspicious that adoption of an Eastern position against the *filioque* is more the result of its apparent compatibility with previously held pneumatological convictions of a Western flavour. Thus, Pinnock, for example, is concerned about the universality of the Spirit, particularly in the context of a discussion of world religions, and he sees the Eastern position as commensurate with such universality. But how does one go about reconciling the actual historical theological isolationism and the common Orthodox attitude of its superior ecclesiology to the exclusion of Western ecclesiologies, not to mention the longstanding difficulty in convincing Orthodox theologians to enter into ecumenical debate on this very issue? Are these not signs of pneumatological restrictiveness? These factors, while again not refutations, should also be considered when looking for ways to safeguard the Spirit's universality.

All this is not to say that we ought not consider the possible negative theological implications of the *filioque* that Pinnock raises. On the

75 The monopatristic emphasis was also confirmed to me in a recent conversation I had concerning this very issue with a practicing Orthodox priest, Fr Stacey Richter of Holy Trinity Orthodox Church of Moose Jaw, Saskatchewan.

76 For a thorough consideration of the role of theological reception or acquisition in theology, see Reinhard Hütter, *Suffering Divine Things: Theology as Church Practice* (Grand Rapids, MI: Eerdmans, 2000).

contrary, a defender of the *filioque* must face these criticisms head on. Thus, briefly, how might one respond to Pinnock's concern that the *filioque* fosters pneumatological restrictiveness?

Pinnock suggests the original wording of the Creed upheld the freedom of the Spirit to operate everywhere and did not suggest his confinement. On the one hand, Pinnock cites Greek Orthodox bishop Kallistos Ware as support for the common Orthodox view that 'as a result of the *filioque*, the Spirit in Western thought has become subordinated to the Son—if not in theory, then in practice'. Ware goes on to suggest that 'the West pays insufficient attention to the work of the Spirit in the world, in the church, in the daily life of each man [*sic*]'.[77] On the other hand, Pinnock infers that the Western inclusion of the *filioque* confines the Spirit christologically. But since Pinnock appeals to the original wording of the Creed, this objection to the *filioque* must be dealt with from an historical perspective. Was this really the issue at stake, both in the original construction of the Creed and in the subsequent *filioque* debates that ensued in the ninth century? If nothing else, the historical accounts of the *filioque* controversy have made it clear that neither account was of pressing concern. That is to say, it is clear that the Eastern churches were *not* attempting to define the Spirit in universal terms by a deliberate omission of the *filioque*, nor were the Western churches attempting to restrict the Spirit ecclesiologically or christologically. On the contrary, the original wording of the Creed can be explained by the patristic habit of sticking as close to the biblical phraseology as possible. Thus, since John 15.26 explicitly states that the Spirit proceeds from the Father, this best explains the subsequent phrasing of the original Nicene statement. But it is not clear that the Greek-speaking theologians of the day were deliberately avoiding confessing the procession of the Spirit from the Father and the Son for no other reason than it did not occur to them that it would be an issue at a later point in theological history. Furthermore, it is clear that the eventual Western addition of the *filioque* phrase was originally included as a defence of the Spirit's divinity against Arian or Pneumatomachian factions.[78] The confession of the Spirit's procession from the Son who was 'consubstantial' with the Father was a failsafe way to safeguard the Spirit's divine status and it was clearly not assumed to be

---

77   K. Ware, *The Orthodox Church* (London: Penguin, 1963), p. 222, cited in Pinnock, *Flame of Love*, p. 197. Of course, one wonders what is meant by Ware's accusation, especially considering the fact that large portions of Western Christianity have been influenced by the 'charismatic' and 'Pentecostal' movements where the Spirit is not only acknowledged, but supposedly experienced 'in the daily life of each man [*sic*]' in very meaningful ways.

78   See J.N.D. Kelly, *Early Christian Doctrines* (San Francisco: Harper & Row, 2nd edn, 1960), pp. 259-63. In this regard, see also Barth, *Church Dogmatics*, I.1, pp. 477-79.

a means of subordination of the Spirit to the Son any more than the Eastern belief that the Spirit proceeds from the Father made the Spirit ontologically subordinated to the Father in an Origenistic way. Thus, appeals to the 'original wording' of the Creed can hardly be called upon to settle later (and legitimate) theological concerns that Pinnock raises.

One last item to be raised concerns what, in my opinion, runs contrary to Pinnock's stated intention of seeking fresh ways of speaking about the Holy Spirit from an evangelical perspective. Here I view Pinnock's (and other evangelicals who follow suit) attempt to suppress the *filioque* as a valid theological presupposition as inherently counter-productive to the development of a progressive, yet biblical, doctrine of the Spirit. I do not see why evangelicals need to be restricted in this way. Could not a thorough rethinking of a filioquist theology, even potentially, succeed in maintaining a christological centre without a pneumatological want? Is it possible to predict the results even before it is tried? Indeed, given the fact that evangelical theology itself traces its historical roots back to the Protestant Reformers, most of whom sought to uphold the *filioque*, could not this living tradition itself be reconsidered and reapplied to the current questions of ecumenical concern? Is not the Reformation movement a movement that is always seeking to reform itself (*Semper Reformandum*)? And more specifically, is the evangelical heritage so seriously misguided, so ironically unaware of the role of the Holy Spirit in its development, that we are forced to turn to a tradition whose fundamental theological and cultural concerns have been so different from ours in order to find pneumatological answers? In the good Pinnockian fashion that I have come so much to appreciate, I say, 'Let the debate go on!' lest we prematurely close a pneumatological discussion that could be, historically speaking, only at the earliest formative stage!

Implications and Conclusion

This chapter has clearly not attempted to provide a new (or old!) solution to the knotty problem of whether the Holy Spirit proceeds from the Father or from the Father and the Son. However, it is my hope that the preceding examination and assessment of evangelical approaches to the *filioque* question has indicated, quite strongly, that much remains to be done on this problem. Unfortunately, it is also the case that current approaches will not likely be sufficient to bring about any potential solution—or even progress towards a solution—to this problem. Nevertheless, I also hope that the preceding examination has outlined the contours of why the question matters and why it should be on the evangelical theological agenda. In what follows, I propose five reasons why the *filioque* question should matter to evangelicals.

First, the question of the *filioque* plays an important role in identifying fundamental and axiomatic presuppositions regarding how we view the relationship of God's revelation in and through scripture to the nature of God himself. As a question that probes the heart of Trinitarian doctrine, the *filioque* points to the rather uncomfortable, but necessary, conclusion that certain theological axioms cannot be proven by either reason or direct appeal to scripture, but must arise out of the practice of theologizing itself. Theological practice does not proceed without these assumptions, but theological practice can in no way shore up the axiomatic nature of these assumptions. Rather, it is imperative that theologians take into account and become self-critically aware of these axiomatic stances.

Second, the *filioque* question matters because it raises the question of evangelical involvement in ecumenical dialogue, including the question of whether ecumenical involvement can, in good conscience, be avoided by evangelicals at this stage of theological history. The *filioque* question, after all, concerns *all* branches of Christian theology and the extent to which one engages this question also indicates the narrowness or broadness of our evangelical willingness to learn from other traditions. But conversely, the *filioque* raises the question of whether evangelicals may be in the unique position of putting theological proposals regarding the doctrine of the procession of the Spirit on the ecumenical table in unhindered ways that traditional Orthodox and Roman Catholic traditions are prevented from doing because of their strict adherence to tradition. The representatives presented above, however, show that evangelicals have greater freedoms to engage the question from either side of the debate, provided they recognize that in taking a stance they also necessarily adopt a larger systematic and theological tradition that cannot simply be ignored.

Third, the *filioque* question matters from the perspective of evangelical theological identity. Rising as it has out of the Western tradition in which the *filioque* was usually assumed, evangelical thought must ask the question of how a filioquist (or a non-filioquist) stance has *actually* (and not merely *potentially*) influenced evangelical pneumatology. This requires careful attention to the history of evangelical theology with an eye to its pneumatological theory and practice rather than speculation on how a filioquist theology may or may not affect pneumatological concerns. We must do our historical theology well before concluding whether the *filioque* is really as dangerous or superfluous as we might think.

Fourth, the *filioque* question matters because of its theological heuristic value. Rather than closing off the question of the *filioque* prematurely by pegging it as a metaphysical speculation or by prematurely adopting and defending without hesitation either a Western or Eastern position, evangelical theologians might benefit greatly by studying the multi-faceted aspects of this perennial problem. By considering possible connections in other areas of systematic theology to the question of the *filioque*, it may open up new ways of dealing with questions of the role of world religions, the relationship of the church to the world (i.e., political theology), the question of sanctification and of cosmic eschatology, for example. Evangelicals might do well to work through these questions with the *filioque* at the foreground of the investigation. There are no guarantees that this will yield great theological fruit, but neither is it clear that ignoring the discussion or ending the discussion in favour of one or the other sides is a guarantee of a great theological crop either. My point is that the *filioque* question is too fundamentally associated with central concerns of Christian faith—God as Father, Son and Holy Spirit—to allow it, as Stanley thought in 1861, to be categorized as specimen of the race of 'extinct controversies'.

Finally, the fact that many will likely disagree with my assessment of evangelical approaches to the *filioque* question does not negate my contention that the *filioque* is a topic worthy of ongoing evangelical attention. In fact, it is precisely because I anticipate disagreement that the call for further research on this issue is so aptly located in a book in honour of Clark Pinnock, who has become famously (or notoriously, depending on one's perspective!) known for spurring evangelicals on to consider questions not previously considered. If I spur at least some evangelicals on to consider the *filioque* more seriously than they have done before, I will be gratified to know that at least some part of my purposes for writing has been accomplished.

CHAPTER 12

A Theology of the Third Article? Hegel and the Contemporary Enterprise in First Philosophy and First Theology

Amos Yong

The appearance of Clark Pinnock's *Flame of Love* in 1996 signaled an important landmark in the renaissance of pneumatology in Christian theology underway since the middle of the twentieth century.[1] One of the unique accomplishments of *Flame of Love* is that it presents not only a theology of the *Holy Spirit* considered as an object of reflection, but also a *theology* of the Holy Spirit—viz., a pneumatological theology wherein pneumatology functions hermeneutically, giving shape and structure (as a subject) to the theological enterprise. In this way, while traditional theology has categorized only certain loci under the rubric of pneumatology—e.g., ecclesiology, soteriology, and eschatology—*Flame of Love* revisits and reconceptualizes the entire theological spectrum, including the doctrines of the Trinity, creation and christology, from a pneumatological perspective.[2] Its guiding motifs are deeply informed by a pneumatological imagination and consciousness, so much so that whereas the doctrine of the Holy Spirit has traditionally been ignored, forgotten, or just rendered at the end of the theological system, in this case, pneumatology is given theological priority. *Flame of Love* thus signals not the end but the potential of a project we might call a 'first theology of the Third Article', referencing here the doctrine of the Spirit as the

---

1   C.H. Pinnock, *Flame of Love: A Theology of the Holy Spirit* (Downers Grove, IL: InterVarsity Press, 1996). An important work at the beginning of this renaissance is H.P. van Dusen, *Spirit, Son and Father: Christian Faith in the Light of the Holy Spirit* (New York: Charles Scribner's Sons, 1958).

2   For an overview of *Flame of Love* in dialogue with Pinnock's project of developing a pneumatological theology of religions, see A. Yong, 'Whither Theological Inclusivism: The Development and Critique of an Evangelical Theology of Religions', *Evangelical Quarterly* 71.4 (1999), pp. 327-48.

Third Article of the Christian (Nicene) creed functioning method-ologically as a starting point. Such a theology would, potentially, complement and complete patrological and christological projects which have preceded it. And, there is evidence of a massive rethinking of traditional theological topics from pneumatological perspectives taking place across the contemporary theological scene.[3]

Yet the question that immediately arises in our post-Enlightenment, post-foundationalist and post-theological world is whether or not such a project in pneumatological theology is just another parochial option amidst the dizzying plurality of contemporary approaches to theology. Why privilege the pneumatological framework and why take up a theology of the Third Article, rather than liberationist, feminist, revisionist, etc., options? Of course, the usual response is the quaint, 'Oh, that's interesting...'—reflecting precisely the sense that our postmodern orientation not only opens up space for and legitimates a diversity of methods, disciplines and perspectives in the theological task, but also in some sense requires such a pluralism. The unsaid assumption in all of this is that there is no normative standard to which theological method is held accountable, and this least of all in approaches informed by pneuma-tology—historically associated with enthusiasm, emotionalism and experientialism, hallmarks of the subjectivistic dimension of religion and theology.

Is this, however, necessarily the case for a pneumatological approach to theology in general and for a theology of the Third Article more specifically? In order to get at the various issues involved in these questions, I want to return to the philosophical theology of Hegel in order to explore the hypothesis that the roots of the contemporary turn to pneumatology can be located, at least in part, in his project. In what follows, I will suggest the plausibility of re-reading Hegel's philosophical theology in a pneumatological key (§I). Next, I will trace out the fruits of such a pneumatological reading in contemporary first philosophy (§II). Finally, I will locate at least some of the main trajectories and themes of Hegel's project read pneumatologically in contemporary first theology (§III). If it can be demonstrated that the turn to pneumatology in Hegel successfully advances the quests for first philosophy and first theology in our time, then at least provisional answers can be given to the questions concerning 'Why and how a first theology of the Third Article in a

---

3   See, e.g., A. Yong, *Spirit–Word–Community: Theological Hermeneutics in Trinitarian Perspective* (Aldershot and Burlington, VT: Ashgate, 2002), esp. pp. 7-14, and my editor's introduction, 'Toward a Theology of the Third Article', in V.-M. Kärkkäinen, *Toward a Pneumatological Theology: Pentecostal and Ecumenical Perspectives on Ecclesiology, Soteriology, and Theology of Mission* (ed. A. Yong; Lanham, MD: University Press of America, 2002), pp. xiii-xx.

postmodern world?'[4] But, perhaps just as, if not more, important, the entire question of the meaning of 'our time'—allegedly as postmodern, post-Enlightenment, post-foundationalist, post-theological, post-philosophical, and even post-Christian—might need to be revisited, depending on the evidence for or against my hypothesis relating the turn to pneumatology to and in Hegel, typically considered the arch-rationalist of modernity itself.

Before we proceed, however, three caveats need to be registered. First, what follows should not be mistaken for Hegel scholarship. I am neither a Hegel expert, nor am I trained in the complexities in text-criticism and exegesis which pertain to the broad spectrum of the Hegelian corpus. Second, only in a very loose sense can this essay be considered as a work in intellectual history. I do not attempt to prove the Hegelian lineage of contemporary first philosophy or first theology. Finally, the selective nature of the reading of Hegel in this essay should caution us against an uncritical embracing of the entirety of his project. There have been and always will be problematic aspects of Hegel's thought for posterity, both philosophically and theologically, not to mention the many other disciplines with which Hegel engaged, and any retrieval of Hegel should proceed cautiously. What follows is no exception. It represents only a preliminary attempt to re-read Hegel against himself, to uncover some of the roots of contemporary movements in pneumatological philosophy and theology, and to locate the contemporary renaissance in pneumatological thinking within and against the larger discourses of modernity and postmodernity. What emerges will, hopefully, illuminate the distinctive features of our time 'on the boundaries', and clarify the 'roots and fruits' of the Enlightenment experiment and of our post-Enlightenment situation.

I. Hegel and the Turn to Pneumatology

Not coincidentally, at the center of the revival of Hegel scholarship in the decades after the second World War has been the recognition of his concern with things of the spirit. From his early essay 'On the Spirit of Christianity and Its Fate' (1797–98), through his massive *Phenomenology of Spirit* (1807), and culminating with the 'Philosophy of Spirit' in part three of his *Encyclopedia of the Philosophical Sciences* (3rd edn,

---

4   When I first began doing work in pneumatological theology, I already intuited then that at some point, I would need to come to terms with the influence of Hegel—for better or for worse—for this project (see A. Yong, 'On Divine Presence and Divine Agency: Toward a Foundational Pneumatology', *Asian Journal of Pentecostal Studies* 3.2 [2000], p. 187 n. 35). This essay is the first fruits of an anticipated book-length effort to confront the specter of Hegel in contemporary first philosophy and first theology.

1830), it is no secret that spirit is Hegel's grand philosophical category. Hegel has thus been called a 'theologian of the spirit' and his philosophy identified as 'speculative pneumatology'.[5] Alan Olson's thesis that Hegel's philosophy should be understood first and foremost as pneumatology connects directly with the concerns of this essay. Olson suggests that the dialectical pneumatology of Luther's *Small Catechism* mediated to Hegel through the Württemberg Pietism of his youth informs the mature philosopher's encounter with the age of Enlightenment, including its Christian manifestations. The result is that what Luther understands to be the source of revelation (against the impotencies of reason) and salvation (against the bondage of the will) is given speculative content by Hegel's reconception of spirit as dialectical *ordo salutus*, revealing the life of the Absolute and reconciling what is otherwise estranged in thought and in reality. In this way, Hegel accomplishes what Olson calls the 'pneumatological transformation of dialectic'[6] so that philosophy now becomes soteriology. Spirit is understood to be the key which overcomes the oppositions between reason and revelation; between intellect and feeling; between rationalism and pietism; between Enlightenment and Romanticism; between necessity and freedom; and between nature and history.

Olson's conclusions are the starting point of this project. As a Hegel scholar and a comparative philosopher of religion, Olson explicates the pneumatological *leitmotif* of the Hegelian philosophy biographically and exegetically. My own interests, however, are primarily theological, and that defined by the horizons of the contemporary discussion. As such, my historical and exegetical questions to Hegel are not for their own sake, but for how they might illuminate our own theological situation. In what follows, then, I propose a pneumatological reading of Hegel motivated by post-foundationalist concerns. Put in terms of what is traditionally known as 'first philosophy', our query focuses on how pneumatology might be defended as a starting point for thought in general, and for theological thinking more specifically, in a post-Enlightenment and postmodern world. As we shall see, however, such concerns may have been Hegel's as well.

Objections are immediately raised, however, on both sides of the inquiry. On the one side are philosophers (and first philosophers) who resist the encroachment of a theological category into their domain. On the other side are theologians who reject the idea that Hegel, arch-rationalist and non-orthodox (at best) theist, could contribute to the

---

5   See, e.g., P.C. Hodgson (ed.), *G.W.F. Hegel: Theologian of the Spirit* (Minneapolis: Fortress Press, 1997), and, on Hegel as a speculative pneumatologist, A.M. Olson, *Hegel and the Spirit: Philosophy as Pneumatology* (Princeton: Princeton University Press, 1992).
6   Olson, *Hegel and the Spirit*, p. 13.

theological task. These objections, however, derive from the ambiguity and polyvalency of *Geist* within, not to mention without, the Hegelian system of thought.[7] Since my goal is to resolve neither this ambiguity nor the related controversy between left- and right-wing interpretations of Hegel,[8] my strategy is to follow Hegel into the thicket of history—in this case, into the life and texts of Hegel himself—and see what emerges. Yet as a Christian theologian, my own biases cannot be checked completely at the door. In that light, my question to Hegel can be much more pointed: is it possible that a *Christian* pneumatology might be defended as a starting point for thought in general and for theology in particular in a post-Enlightenment and postmodern world?

But what else might a *Christian* pneumatology be other than that which identifies spirit not ambiguously or in any terms, but specifically as the Spirit of Jesus the Christ? And, if so, does not this result in a forced reading of Hegel who says little about Jesus except in his early theological writings where the carpenter from Nazareth is presented as a moral exemplar?[9] Perhaps; but perhaps not. What about Hegel's numer-

---

7   Michael Inwood identifies nine ways in which *Geist* is used in the Hegelian corpus: (1) spirit denoting the human mind; (2) 'subjective spirit' referring to the psychological life of the individual; (3) spirit as the more specific intellectual aspects of the psyche, especially its consciousness of objects; (4) 'objective spirit' as the customs, laws, and institutions of a social group; (5) 'absolute spirit' as the self-consciousness of God, manifest in art, religion and philosophy; (6) *Weltgeist* or 'world spirit' analogous to the world-soul, the cosmic spirit of nature, of the spirit of human history; (7) *Volkgeist*, or manifestation of (6) in a particular people group (4); (8) *Geist der Zeit* or 'spirit of the age', a phase of *Weltgeist* in general and *Volkgeist* more particularly; and (9) the Holy Spirit of Christian faith and theology, immanent in the Christian community; see M. Inwood, *A Hegel Dictionary* (Oxford: Blackwell, 1992), pp. 275-76. To be clear, because of the specifically theological agenda pursued here, capitalized Spirit in this essay refers to the Holy Spirit (except when quoting, in which case the context will need to be discerned).

8   Leftist readings of Hegel as an atheist (at worst) or humanist (at best) have a long tradition from Bauer, Strauss, Feuerbach and Marx in the nineteenth century to Walter Kaufman, Alexandre Kojéve, Eric Voegelin and Robert Solomon in the twentieth. R. Solomon's *In the Spirit of Hegel: A Study of G.W.F. Hegel's Phenomenology of Spirit* (New York: Oxford University Press, 1983) is the most recent and articulate statement. For what it is worth, my own sense is that this question of whether or not Hegel was a Christian is being increasingly marginalized, and being replaced by the question of Hegel's Lutheran identity; on this point, see M.C. Mattes, 'Hegel's Lutheran Claim', *Lutheran Quarterly* 14.3 (2000), pp. 249-79.

9   See, e.g., Hegel's 'The Positivity of the Christian Religion' and 'The Spirit of Christianity and Its Fate', both in G.W.F. Hegel, *On Christianity: Early Theological Writings* (trans. T.M. Knox; 1948; reprint, New York: Harper Torchbooks, 1961), and 'The Life of Jesus', in G.W.F. Hegel, *Three Essays, 1793–1795: The Tübingen Essay, Berne Fragments, The Life of Jesus* (ed. P. Fuss and J. Dobbins; Notre Dame: University of Notre Dame Press, 1984).

ous allusions to the prime symbol of Christian faith: the cross? It is here, perhaps, that an important key to Hegel's turn to pneumatology is signaled. In fact, Hegel himself links pneumatology and the cross in the famous closing sentences to the *Phenomenology of Spirit* when he makes reference to the 'Calvary of absolute Spirit'.[10] The cryptic nature of this reference is only further obscured by its context wherein Hegel is describing the 'Absolute Knowing' of 'Spirit that knows itself as Spirit' which 'has for its path the recollection of the Spirits as they are in themselves and as they accomplish the organization of their realm'. Hegel seems to be identifying, at the conclusion of the *Phenomenology*, the course of Spirit's recollection of creaturely spirits with Spirit's self-diremption and self-alienation in nature and history. Hence the 'Calvary of absolute Spirit' refers implicitly to the natural and historical processes of spirit's life, and explicitly to the death of spirit as experienced on the cross, a death which spirit (necessarily?) endures in order to accomplish its recollecting or reconciling work.

This understanding of the 'Calvary of absolute Spirit' is anticipated in a key passage at the end of Hegel's second major publication, his essay *Faith and Knowledge* (1802), where it comes to initial expression. I reproduce the passage in full in order to comment on it:

> But the pure concept or infinity as the abyss of nothingness in which all being is engulfed, must signify the infinite grief [of the finite] purely as a moment of the supreme Idea, and no more than a moment. Formerly, the infinite grief only existed historically in the formative process of culture. It existed as the feeling that 'God Himself is dead', upon which the religion of more recent times rests; the same feeling that Pascal expressed in so to speak sheerly empirical form:... [Nature is such that it *signifies* everywhere a *lost* God both within and outside man.] By marking this feeling as a moment of the supreme Idea, the pure concept must give philosophical existence to what used to be either the moral precept that we must sacrifice the empirical being (*Wesen*), or the concept of formal abstraction [e.g., the categorical imperative]. Thereby it must re-establish for philosophy the Idea of absolute freedom and along with it the absolute Passion, the speculative Good Friday in place of the historic Good Friday. Good Friday must be speculatively re-established in the whole truth and harshness of its Godforsakenness. Since the [more] serene, less well grounded, and more individual style of the dogmatic philosophies and of the natural religions must vanish, the highest totality can and must achieve its resurrection solely from this harsh consciousness of loss, encompassing everything, and ascending in all its earnestness and out of its deepest ground to the most serene freedom of its shape.[11]

---

10   G.W.F. Hegel, *Phenomenology of Spirit* (trans. A.V. Miller; Oxford: Oxford University Press, 1978), §808, p. 493.

11   G.W.F. Hegel, *Faith and Knowledge* (trans. H.S. Harris and W. Cerf; Albany: SUNY Press, 1977), pp. 190-91; all brackets and parentheses original to the translation.

While there is no space here for an extended commentary, let me highlight three aspects directed toward clarifying Hegel's pneumatological philosophy of the cross. First, the importance of the 'death of God' for Hegel's philosophy is here pronounced.[12] This idea has an ancient history going back to the debate regarding patripassianism in the early church, retrieved in Luther's theology of the cross, and mediated to Hegel through Pascal's existentialist and Württemberg's Romanticist pietism.[13] For Hegel, however, the historical crucifixion and death of God is significant only insofar as it points toward the possibility of the resurrection. If a grain of wheat bears much fruit only after it falls to the ground and dies (cf. Jn 12.24), then the resurrection of Easter Sunday is possible only in, through, and after the God-forsakenness of Good Friday. It is in the symbol of the cross where the opposites of 'infinite grief' and the 'supreme Idea' come together. In Hegel's hands, then, the historic Good Friday must give way to the speculative Good Friday in order for the resurrection of thought to occur. And of course, while Hegel mentions the resurrection in this text apart from any specific reference to the Spirit, this connection is made explicit in the 'Calvary of absolute Spirit' passage in the *Phenomenology*, and in his later lectures in the philosophy of religion. It is, after all, only through the Spirit that Christ was raised from the dead (cf. Rom. 1.4 and 8.11).

This leads, second, to the cross as the symbolic site of the regeneration of culture and religion. Here it is important to point out that Hegel was a

---

12   Others have commented at length on the centrality of this idea in Hegel's philosophy; see, e.g., S. Crites, 'The Golgotha of Absolute Spirit', in M. Westphal (ed.), *Method and Speculation in Hegel's Phenomenology* (Atlantic Highlands, NJ: Humanities Press International, 1982), pp. 47-56; idem, *Dialectic and Gospel in the Development of Hegel's Thinking* (University Park, PA: Pennsylvania State University Press, 1998), pp. 190-96, and Part IV; E. Wyschogrod, *Spirit in Ashes: Hegel, Heidegger, and Man-Made Mass Death* (New Haven and London: Yale University Press, 1985), pp. 140-47; D.S. Anderson, *Hegel's Speculative Good Friday: The Death of God in Philosophical Perspective* (American Academy of Religion Reflection and Theory in the Study of Religion, 4; Atlanta: Scholars Press, 1996); and T.A. Carlson, *Indiscretion: Finitude and the Naming of God* (Chicago and London: University of Chicago Press, 1999), ch. 3.

13   Widely known in Romanticist and Pietist circles was the Lutheran hymn 'O Traurigkeit, O Herzeleid', by Johannes Rist (1641); its second stanza reads:

O grosse Not!	O great woe!
Gott selbst liegt tot.	God himself lies dead.
Am Kreuz ist er gestorben;	On the cross he has died;
hat dadurch das Himmelreich	And thus he has gained for us
uns aus Lieb' erworben	By love the kingdom of heaven

From G.W.F. Hegel, *Lectures on the Philosophy of Religion*. Volume III: *The Consummate Religion* (ed. P.C. Hodgson; trans. R.F. Brown *et al.*; Berkeley: University of California Press, 1985), p. 125, n. 163.

seminarian at Tübingen (from 1788–91, taking his final theological exams in 1793) when the French Revolution broke out. Needless to say, the Revolution caused reverberations across Europe and Hegel was swept up by movements anticipating the dawn of a new historical era of freedom and responsibility. Expectedly, the young Hegel committed himself as a *Volkerzieher* to a program of cultural renewal and socio-political reintegration for Germany, at that time still no more than a collection of almost 300 independent states united only theoretically under what was left of the Holy Roman Empire. These circumstances illuminate Hegel's references to the 'formative process of culture' and the 'Idea of absolute freedom' at the end of *Faith and Knowledge*. To achieve this renewal, Romanticist thinkers returned to the model of the ancients, especially the Greeks. Yet such retrieval brought its own questions. How can Germany overcome the fatalism of the Greeks and of the Hellenized form of Christian thought that she has inherited? How is the Enlightenment ideal of freedom attainable? The answer, in part, was that freedom was possible only as emergent from the 'absolute Passion' seen on Good Friday, when its subject freely chose to lay down his life (cf. Jn 10.18) rather than have it taken from him.[14] From this abyss of infinite grief is resurrected the 'most serene freedom'.

Inextricably related to the *Volkerzieher*'s goal of moral and cultural renewal is the religion of the people. This explains, at least in part, why Hegel devotes almost one-half of *Faith and Knowledge* to an engagement with the philosophy of Friedrich Jacobi (1743–1819). In Hegel's reading of Jacobi, the latter's advocacy both of knowledge emergent from an immediate intuition of being and of the principle of religious faith as providing for certainty signaled the apex of the subjectivism of Kant's critical philosophy. Not only was such wrongheaded philosophical thinking, but it also, in Hegel's estimation, reflected the Romanticist and Pietist religion of feeling given eloquent rhetorical but empty theological expression both by Kant and by Schleiermacher (whose *Speeches on Religion* appeared, it should be recalled, in 1799, shortly before *Faith and Knowledge*). In this way, Jacobi himself falls finally into a Kantian kind of agnosticism regarding the objective truth and reality of divinity: 'The sphere common to both philosophies is the absoluteness of the antithesis between, on one side, finitude, the natural, knowledge—which in this antithesis is bound to be merely formal knowledge—and, on the other, the supernatural, supersensuousness and infinity. For both of them what is truly Absolute

---

14   On this point, see H.S. Harris, *Hegel's Development.* Volume 1: *Toward the Sunlight, 1770–1801* (Oxford and New York: Clarendon Press and Oxford University Press, 1972), p. xxvii.

is an absolute Beyond in faith and in feeling; for cognitive Reason it is nothing.'[15] The problem here is that Enlightenment Christianity had reacted to the authoritarianism and dogmatism of the medieval church with its own dogmatism of subjectivity. Thus the pietist Protestantism of Hegel's day is described as dominated by the subjectivist principle 'for which beauty and truth present themselves in feelings and persuasions, in love and intellect. Religion builds its temples and altars in the heart of the individual.'[16] Here, Hegel's insistence at the end of *Faith and Knowledge* that 'natural religions must vanish' is illuminated. The end of natural religions is Jacobi's dilemma: '*Either* God exists and exists *outside* me, a living being subsisting apart; or *else* I am God. There is no third way.'[17] Hegel, however, refuses Jacobi's dictum. There has to be a third way between or beyond either transcendentalism or pantheism; beyond either Catholic objectivism or Protestant subjectivism; beyond either ecclesial authoritarianism or Romanticist intuitionism; or beyond either medieval communalism or Enlightenment individualism. Natural religiosity must give way toward the religion of the spirit. And this takes place only

---

15   Hegel, *Faith and Knowledge*, p. 147. Of Schleiermacher, Hegel writes: 'Jacobi's principle has in fact attained this highest level in [Schleiermacher's 1799] *Speeches on Religion*. In Jacobi's philosophy Reason is conceived only as instinct and feeling; ethical conduct occurs only in a context of empirical contingency, and as dependence on things given by experience and inclination and the way of the heart; and knowledge is nothing but an awareness of particularities and peculiarities, whether external or internal. In [Schleiermacher's] *Speeches*, by contrast, nature, as a collection of finite facts, is extinguished and acknowledged as the Universe. Because of this, the yearning is brought back from its escape out of actuality into an eternal beyond, the partition between the cognitive subject and the absolutely unattainable object is torn down, grief is assuaged in joy, and the endless striving is satisfied in intuition' (*Faith and Knowledge*, p. 150; brackets original to translation).

16   Hegel, *Faith and Knowledge*, p. 57. Thus, in Protestant Christianity, the pastor/priest becomes a virtuoso or religious artist, even while the congregation 'takes the role of immaturity on itself and is supposed to have the aim and intent of letting the priest, as a virtuoso of edification and enthusiasm, produce in it the inwardness of intuition. Instead of extinguishing or at least not acknowledging a subjective privacy of intuition—a man is called an *idiot* insofar as his life is private—one is to give in to it so far that this particularity forms the principle of a private congregation. So it is that the little congregations and peculiarities assert themselves and multiply *ad infinitum*; they float apart and gather together by happenstance; every moment the groupings alter like the patterns in a sea of sand given over to the play of the winds. Yet at the same time—as is only fair—every group regards the private and distinctive peculiarity of its view as something so otiose and even unremarkable that it does not mind whether it is acknowledged or not, and gives up all claims to objectivity' (*Faith and Knowledge*, p. 151; italics original).

17   Hegel, *Faith and Knowledge*, p. 169, italics original.

through the death and burial of natural religions, thereby releasing their resurrection to true life.

Correlatively, the third and final (for our purposes) comment is that the cross signifies the turning point and renewal of philosophy itself. By this time (1803), Hegel had come to realize that his own contribution to the *Volkerzieher* program was going to be as a philosopher.[18] *Faith and Knowledge* thus takes up Kant's gauntlet by engaging the philosopher himself, as well as Jacobi and Fichte, the latter at that time the recognized successor to Kant. Yet the problem, as already hinted at, is that the Kantian philosophy represented simply the culmination of the Cartesian turn to the subject, and as such, remained within the realm of finitude:

> Reason, having in this way become mere intellect, acknowledges its own nothingness by placing that which is better than it in a *faith outside and above* itself, as a beyond [to be believed in]. This is what has happened in the *philosophies of Kant, Jacobi, and Fichte*. Philosophy has made itself the handmaid of a faith once more... All of them agree that, as the old distinction put it, the Absolute is no more against Reason than it is for it; it is beyond Reason. The Enlightenment, in its positive aspect, was a hubbub of vanity without a firm core. It obtained a core in its negative procedure by grasping its own negativity. Through the purity and infinity of the negative it freed itself from its insipidity but precisely for this reason it could admit positive knowledge only of the finite and empirical.[19]

For this reason, Hegel's conclusion in *Faith and Knowledge* (quoted above) is that the future of philosophy rests on its ability to move beyond both the 'dogmatism of being' (the medieval, pre-Reformation paradigm) and the 'dogmatism of thinking' (the subjective paradigm of the critical philosophies), beyond both the earlier philosophy of the infinite (Descartes) and the philosophy of the finite (Kant).[20] He does not specify here how this is to be accomplished except in hinting that resurrection occurs 'solely from this harsh consciousness of loss'. The loss that is to be confronted is both the Enlightenment exaltation of reason and the Romanticist subjectivization of reason. Is Hegel suggesting that recognition and acceptance of this loss is a prelude to the experience of the resurrection of true reason? Is this a prelude to Hegel's notion of spirit's achievement arising out of dialectical negation?

From this, it should be clear that part of the task of philosophy that Hegel wrestled with leading up to his writing the *Phenomenology of Spirit* is the question of how it is possible for thought and rationality to engage

---

18   This is argued at length by H.S. Harris, *Hegel's Development, Volume 2: Night Thoughts (Jena 1801–1806)* (Oxford and New York: Clarendon Press and Oxford University Press, 1983).

19   Hegel, *Faith and Knowledge*, p. 56; brackets original to translation.

20   Hegel, *Faith and Knowledge*, pp. 189-90.

transcendence in a post-Kantian world. The symbolic watershed of the cross and resurrection is intimated in *Faith and Knowledge*. This consists in the identification of the problem and an inkling of the solution. Clarification of the how of the solution is not fully achieved until later when, at the end of the *Phenomenology*, it is recognized that the speculative Good Friday yearned for is the 'Calvary of Absolute Spirit'. Briefly put, the Hegelian strategy is to overcome the chasm between divinity and humanity through and from Golgotha by the power of the Spirit whose reconciling work is accomplished precisely through the preservation of opposites or negations. Just as natural religion cannot overcome its own liabilities or redeem itself apart from Spirit's mediation, so also are objectivism and subjectivism, reason and feeling, knowledge and faith, etc., all overcome and preserved (*Aufhebung*) not through a reconstructed and indubitable foundation for thought, but rather through the absolute idea of spirit unfolding itself as a dynamic and historical intersubjectivity.[21] The result is the proper re-establishment of reason (*Vernunft*) and knowledge as the science of consciousness, as spirit experiencing itself and coming to self-consciousness, through all of its negations, in the community of the redeemed.[22] Spirit thus makes way for the liberation, harmonization and reconciliation of faith and knowledge. At this point, then, Hegel's turn to pneumatology is complete.

II. Pneumatology and Contemporary First Philosophy

Much more can and should be said about Hegel and the Spirit which needs to be postponed. My immediate goal is to explore the Hegelian roots of the recent renaissance in pneumatological theology and to ascertain, at least initially, the plausibility of the hypothesis that there are Hegelian impulses that anticipate and inform the development of a contemporary first theology of the Third Article. In order to continue this line of thinking, we need to take an unfortunately quick detour through recent discussions in first philosophy.

---

21   Argued at length by T. Rockmore, *Hegel's Circular Epistemology* (Bloomington: Indiana University Press, 1986), and *Cognition: An Introduction to Hegel's Phenomenology of Spirit* (Berkeley: University of California Press, 1997).

22   See especially the discussion in G.W.F. Hegel, *Lectures on the Philosophy of Religion: One-Volume Edition, The Lectures of 1827* (ed. P.C. Hodgson; Berkeley: University of California Press, 1988), pp. 464-70, on 'The Death of Christ and the Transition to Spiritual Presence'. Because my focus in this essay is on Hegel's turn to pneumatology, I will leave the rich discussion of the pneumatology developed by Hegel in his lectures on the philosophy of religion for another occasion.

The question of first philosophy is as old as Aristotle. Never univocally defined in the *Metaphysics*, the subsequent discussion has proceeded along Aristotelian lines, at one point engaging the discussion of first philosophy as aetiology or theory of causes, at another as ontology or theory of being, at a third as ousiology or theory of substance, and, finally, even as theology or theory of the supersensible.[23] The turn from this set of questions to epistemology, arguably, began with Augustine's own turn toward interiority and introspection. From this, a path was further opened by the medieval schoolmen for Descartes' quest for clear and distinct ideas through the natural light of introspection, albeit undergirded by the medieval axiom of faith seeking understanding.[24] The Cartesian quest for the indubitable foundations of knowledge was taken in empiricistic and rationalistic directions by Enlightenment thinkers. Put in an oversimplified sense, then, two dominant paradigms in first philosophy have come down to us: the classical/medieval ontological-theological and the modern humanistic-epistemological paradigms.

Interestingly, the twentieth century has seen both a strong reaction to and indeed rejection of first philosophy as traditionally conceived (and, indeed, of philosophy itself), and, at the same time, the revitalization of the quest for first philosophy. Both responses, ironically, appeal to Hegel for legitimation. The rejection of first philosophy comes in large measure from the turn toward history first given extensive consideration in Hegel's corpus. The end of the road here is Nietzsche, whose legacy continues to sustain postmodern notions of the end of philosophy and of metanarratives.[25] The revitalization movement itself features two trajectories, both of which are informed by Hegel's attempt to overcome the Kantian dilemma via the notion of intersubjectivity, albeit taken in slightly different directions. The first, receiving only honorable mention

---

23   See the discussion in G. Reale, *The Concept of First Philosophy and the Unity of the Metaphysics of Aristotle* (ed. J.R. Catan; Albany: SUNY Press, 3rd edn, 1980), pp. 1-8; cf. also R.S. Brumbaugh, 'Aristotle's Outline of the Problems of First Philosophy', *Review of Metaphysics* 7.3 (1954), pp. 510-21.

24   See J.F. Wippel, 'The Title First Philosophy According to Thomas Aquinas and His Different Justifications for the Same', *Review of Metaphysics* 27.3 (1974), pp. 585-600; K. Dorter, 'First Philosophy: Metaphysics or Epistemology', *Dialogue* 11 (1972), pp. 1-22; and R. Descartes, *Discourse on the Method and Meditations on First Philosophy* (ed. D. Weissman; New Haven and London: Yale University Press, 1996). That Descartes' doubt was never severed from Christian faith has too often been overlooked in contemporary assessments of Descartes as the 'whipping boy of modernity'.

25   Commenting further on this Hegelian genealogy will take us too far afield. For analysis and criticism, see C. Page, *Philosophical Historicism and the Betrayal of First Philosophy* (University Park, PA: Pennsylvania State University Press, 1995).

here, is the transcendental pragmatist or transcendental semiotic strategy emergent from Peirce's reading of Kant and Hegel.[26] Its focus is on the linguistic nature of consciousness or experience, especially as socially and communally embodied, which takes off from Hegel's notion of spirit as intersubjectivity. In this case, the *via media* between the focus on the real object of traditional metaphysics (the Aristotelian paradigm) and that on the real subject of modern epistemology (the Cartesian/Kantian paradigm) is the course charted by the language or sign-system of intersubjective and pragmatic semiotics.[27]

The other constructive response, building on Hegel's phenomenological approach, was launched by Edmund Husserl at the beginning of the twentieth century. Reacting still to the Kantian bifurcation between the phenomena and the thing in itself, Husserl's phenomenology sought to establish knowledge once-for-all on a pure scientific base. If Kant is right that all we have access to are the categorically perceived phenomena, then the phenomenological turn would engage those categorical representations seriously. Thus Husserl affirmed Hegel's turn toward consciousness, except that Husserl emphasized that all consciousness is consciousness of something—specifically, of phenomena— including, thereby, the notion of consciousness as intentionality. In this way, through what Husserl called the 'transcendental reduction'— whereby the world of phenomena is truly is as it appears to be and is immediately intuited in consciousness by the intending transcendental ego—the Kantian distance is overcome and the foundations of scientific knowledge secured.[28]

---

26   The most ardent contemporary advocate is the Peircean philosopher, K.-O. Apel, 'Transcendental Semiotics and the Paradigms of First Philosophy', *Philosophic Exchange* 2 (1978), pp. 3-22, and 'The Cartesian Paradigm of First Philosophy: A Critical Appreciation from the Perspective of Another (the Next?) Paradigm', *International Journal of Philosophical Studies* 6.1 (1998), pp. 1-16; see also J. Dealy, 'Semiotics and First Philosophy', *Proceedings of the American Catholic Philosophical Association* 62 (1988), pp. 136-46. For my own reading of Peirce vis-à-vis first philosophy, see A. Yong, 'The Demise of Foundationalism and the Retention of Truth: What Evangelicals Can Learn from C.S. Peirce', *Christian Scholar's Review* 29.3 (2000), pp. 563-89.

27   This line extends from Peirce through Royce and Mead to Robert Neville, Robert Corrington and Donald Gelpi in our time. Not coincidentally, I suggest, is the centrality of 'foundational pneumatology' in Gelpi's reconstruction of Peirce's metaphysics; for an overview of Gelpi's project, see A. Yong, 'In Search of Foundations: The *Oeuvre* of Donald L. Gelpi, SJ, and Its Significance for Pentecostal Theology and Philosophy', *Journal of Pentecostal Theology* 11.1 (2002), pp. 3-26.

28   Husserl's epistemological pursuit via phenomenology led to his offering a course on first philosophy during the winter semester of 1923–24 at the University of Freibourg-im-Breisgau, and available in E. Husserl, *Erste Philosophie (1923/24)* (2 vols; ed. R. Boehm; Husserliana, 7–8; The Hague: Martinus Nijhoff, 1956–59). For more on

Later phenomenologists beginning with Heidegger, however, have questioned whether or not Husserl's program results in the kind of Kantian idealism that phenomenology itself was initially designed to overcome. In their responses to Husserl, the post-Husserlian phenomenologists have taken a further step and rejected completely the bifurcation between things as they appear to the transcendental ego and as they are in themselves. Thus, our phenomenological investigations engage things not only as intuited, but as they give themselves fully to our intuitions.[29] Yet while such phenomenological givenness confronts us with the full force of the other, the other is no longer simply an object of ownership or under my control. Rather, the other remains radically other in its (and especially his or her) alterity, infinitely transcending my understanding either because of the overflowing surplus or saturatedness of what is given to me (Marion) or because of the finite capacities of my consciousness (Levinas). Further, and more importantly, in a post-Holocaust world, the other becomes a subject who places me under infinite responsibility and obligation. The phenomenological turn has, in this sense, retrieved the Hegelian *leitmotif* of intersubjectivity. In this case, however, this motif addresses not only epistemological and ontological questions but, more importantly, ethical ones. Thus Emmanuel Levinas has insisted, 'Morality is not a branch of philosophy, but first philosophy'.[30] In Levinas' hands, in fact, ethics as first philosophy means that the onto-theological questions of the philosophical tradition, including those mediated by the transcendental phenomenology of Husserl and Heidegger, are now subordinated (at best) or misguided and irrelevant (at worst). The ontological question of the meaning of being is therefore necessarily reconfigured: 'not the ontology of the understanding of that extraordinary verb, but the ethics of its justice. The question *par excellence* or the question of philosophy. Not "Why being rather than nothing?", but how being justifies itself.'[31]

Husserl's quest for first philosophy, see J. Allen, 'What is Husserl's First Philosophy?', *Philosophy and Phenomenological Research* 42.4 (1982), pp. 610-20, and G. Funke, 'Husserl's Kant Reception and the Foundations of His Transcendental Phenomenological "First Philosophy"', in T.J. Stapleton (ed.), *The Question of Hermeneutics: Essays in Honor of Joseph J. Kockelmans* (trans. Michael Heim; Dordrecht: Kluwer Academic Publishers, 1994), pp. 91-112.

29   See J.-L. Marion, 'The Other First Philosophy and the Question of Givenness', *Critical Inquiry* 25.4 (1999), pp. 784-800.

30   E. Levinas, *Totality and Infinity: An Essay on Exteriority* (trans. A. Lingis; Duquesne Studies Philosophical Series, 24; The Hague: Martinus Nijhoff/Pittsburgh: Duquesne University Press, 1969), p. 304.

31   E. Levinas, 'Ethics as First Philosophy', in S. Hand (ed.), *The Levinas Reader* (Oxford: Blackwell, 1999), pp. 75-87, quotation from p. 86. For more on Levinas' first philosophy, see R.J.S. Manning, *Interpreting Otherwise than Heidegger: Emmanuel*

The suggestiveness of these insights stretching from Hegel through Husserlian phenomenology to Levinas' ethics comes together in Steven G. Smith's project in first philosophy. Smith begins, actually, with Levinas' philosophy of alterity.[32] Recognizing the validity of Levinas' critique of Heidegger and the onto-theological tradition, he argues that the claims of the other upon us means that we do not first and foremost argue against the other, nor negotiate truth claims purely on logical or evidentiary terms. Rather, the other puts us under obligation, and truth claims are significant of the many (oftentimes conflicting) responsibilities our relationship with others assumes and presents. We meet the other not as subject confronts and then proceeds to manipulate object, but as constitutive aspects of an encounter better understood as a dynamic event. Hegel's doctrine of intersubjectivity and Buber's philosophy of I–Thou–We, among other resources, inform Smith's argument throughout. (Smith makes explicit and extensive connections between Levinas' notion of the other's transcendence, and Karl Barth's theological notion of divine transcendence, but exploring this further at present would take us too far afield.)

These insights break through to a creative argument in pneumatological first philosophy in Smith's *The Concept of the Spiritual*.[33] In setting the stage for his own argument, Smith follows in large part the outline adopted here regarding the fortunes of the quest for first philosophy. The three positive approaches include that which begins from the nature of being (what I have identified as the Aristotelian paradigm), that which emphasizes the question of knowing (the Cartesian/Kantian paradigm), and the approach from the saying (that of the philosophy of language, of which Peirce's semiotics was a forerunner). In Smith's retelling of the story, however, this last attempt at resolving the great questions of first philosophy presuppose and require a

---

Levinas's Ethics as First Philosophy (Pittsburgh: Duquesne University Press, 1993); J. Bloechl, 'Ethics as First Philosophy and Religion', in J. Bloechl (ed.), *The Face of the Other and the Trace of God* (Perspectives in Continental Philosophy, 10; New York: Fordham University Press, 2000), pp. 130-51; M.D. Dahnke, 'Ethics as First Philosophy', *Auslegung* 24.2 (2001), pp. 199-213; and the essays in Part Two of A.T. Peperzak (ed.), *Ethics as First Philosophy: The Significance of Emmanuel Levinas for Philosophy, Literature and Religion* (New York and London: Routledge, 1995).

32   S.G. Smith, *The Argument to the Other: Reason beyond Reason in the Thought of Karl Barth and Emmanuel Levinas* (American Academy of Religion Academy Series, 42; Chico, CA: Scholars Press, 1983).

33   S.G. Smith, *The Concept of the Spiritual: An Essay in First Philosophy* (Philadelphia: Temple University Press, 1988).

community of interpersonal and intentional beings.[34] This leads Smith to retrieve the concept of spirit for first philosophy:

> I claim...that the term 'spiritual' remains uniquely suited to bear an adequate conception of the original situation where the order of priority in questions begins. To say that we are spiritual beings is to attain the correct orientation for addressing the question that imposes itself as a condition on all others—How will we live?— remaining aware that this first consideration is indeed a *question* (How—) concerning not simply you or me but all of *us* as *intenders* (—will we—) and in every respect of our existence (—live?).[35]

Now Smith recognizes the polynomony of the term 'spirit' in the Western tradition. Thus, ancient Greek notions of *psyche* or *nous*, Hebraic understandings of *ruach*, Pauline and Philonic renditions of *pneuma*, Augustinian and Cartesian readings of *Spiritus* and *Esprit*, the Kantian and Hegelian *Geist* and the variations it has spawned in later German philosophy, Marcel, Ebner, Buber, and Levinas—each of these contribute vital elements to Smith's proposed definition of 'spirit' as relationship, as the 'intentional togetherness of beings who are for themselves "I" and for others "You," that is, other to each other'.[36] This move enables Smith to take up the questions of being and of knowing, yet transfigure both within the framework of relationship in general and intersubjective relationship more specifically. Further, it underwrites talk about rationality in a post-Enlightenment world, and legitimates notions of meaning and causality in a postmodern context. Finally, and most importantly, the turn to the spiritual provides additional conceptual resources by which to engage Levinas' ethical first philosophy. And in so doing, Smith gives a specifically spiritual interpretation to Levinas' notions not only of the mutuality of the relationship between self and other, but also of the indebtedness and obligatedness of the self in the face of the other. At this point, the connection with Hegel comes full circle since it is precisely the 'Calvary of absolute Spirit' which brings about the death of the self as a controlling, set-apart being over-and-against others—in Paul's terms, 'I die every day' (1 Cor. 15.31a)—and which precipitates resurrection and enables the constitution of authentic selves-in-community.

---

34   I would suggest that the Peircean solution as developed by Royce and Mead in the American pragmatist tradition addresses Smith's concerns on this point. More, Peircean semiotics enables and invigorates a phenomenology and philosophy of nature so urgently needed in our time alongside the communal notion of interpretation which Smith advocates. For further details of my own reading of Peirce and Levinas alongside each other, see Part Two of my *Spirit–Word–Community*, esp. chs 4 and 6.

35   Smith, *Concept of the Spiritual*, pp. 4-5; emphases Smith's.

36   Smith, *Concept of the Spiritual*, pp. 63-64.

Understood in this way, Smith's retrieval of the concept of the spiritual lends credence to the hypothesis regarding the continued reverberation of Hegelian ideas in contemporary philosophical discourse. Besides Smith's own acknowledged reliance upon specific features of Hegel's concept of *Geist* at significant points in his argument—for example, drawing on Hegel's philosophy of right with regard to the problem of rectifying relationships, and retrieving aspects of Hegel's relating spirit to history—Smith's overall argument accomplishes an updating of Hegel's grand philosophical category. More importantly, Smith demonstrates the possibility of an ongoing dialogue between philosophical and theological notions of spirit. For Christian theology, specifically, Smith suggests:

> A spirit is a program of inquiry, and any strong program of inquiry represents a spirit... Christian thinking about the Holy Spirit that is focused on the Kingdom of God is focused also on the true center of first philosophy's concern with spirits, namely, the question of right-enough relationship among beings, preeminently of intentional beings with each other, and not abstractly but in the mode of proposing and exercising unreservedly serious handlings of that question. Christianity is best-warranted, ultimately reasonable, just insofar as it is led by its pneumatology, that is, insofar as its doctrines are aimed and aerated by the Christian community's wrestling with the question of the Kingdom of God.[37]

The foregoing discussion remains horribly over-generalized. My purposes in this section, however, are simply to call attention to certain trajectories in first philosophy and to make initial links with Hegel's turn to pneumatology. Much more work needs to be done on this 'genealogy' in order to provide full argumentation. But enough has been said, I think, to be suggestive regarding the plausibility of the connections. And this plausibility only increases as we turn to work being done in first theology.

III. Pneumatology and Contemporary First Theology

By 'first theology', I intend nothing more than the quest in the theological disciplines to provide an indubitable or foundational starting point for theological knowledge. In this case, then, a first theology of the Third Article would be a theology that is thoroughly structured and shaped by the doctrine (or doctrines) of the Spirit, and therefore, in that sense, set within a pneumatological framework and 'grounded by' or

---

37   S.G. Smith, 'Topics in Philosophical Pneumatology: Inspiration, Wonder, Heart', in B.E. Hinze and D.L. Dabney (eds), *Advents of the Spirit: An Introduction to the Current Study of Pneumatology* (Marquette Studies in Theology, 30; Milwaukee: Marquette University Press, 2001), pp. 208-32; quotations from pp. 218 and 226.

'founded on' a pneumatological starting point. The question being explored in this paper concerns some of the roots of just such a pneumatological theology, especially as mediated through and given impetus by the Hegelian project.

As we have now seen, Hegel himself sought to respond to the Cartesian and Kantian turns-to-the-subject and the resulting empiricist, rationalist, Romanticist, and pietist trajectories set afoot by these developments. I have suggested in the foregoing that Hegel's own resolution to the dualisms generated by the Enlightenment paradigms was to draw from and build on the notion of spirit as sublating (*Aufhebung*)—canceling out on the one hand, and preserving on the other—both subject and object, both self and others, both history and nature, etc. And, the post-Kantian quest in first philosophy has also resulted in a retrieval and reappropriation of the Hegelian *Geist*, especially in Smith's concept of the spiritual.

Now what about the post-Hegelian fortunes of first theology?[38] In an oversimplified sense, whereas theology in the Scholastic and medieval paradigm was dominated methodologically by the reception of accepted authorities, the Lutheran Reformation served up a turn-to-the subject in theology parallel to what Cartesian and Kantian events accomplished for philosophy. This subjectivism in Protestant theology was exactly what Hegel was reacting to in his polemics against Jacobi and Schleiermacher. Later nineteenth-century developments took Hegel's lead and sought to combat theological subjectivism through a rigorous application of historical and scientific methods of inquiry. The Fundamentalist reaction at the turn of the twentieth century re-established the foundational and normative self-revelation of God as preserved in the Bible for the theological task. Attempting to mediate between Fundamentalism and liberalism, dialectical theology, taking off from the Kierkegaardian legacy, gave rise to two distinct but related approaches. On the one hand, the Barthian trajectory acknowledged the gains made through historical and scientific research, but secured faith via a christocentric hermeneutic at the cost of continuing the bifurcation between immanence and transcendence. The Tillichian trajectory, on the other hand, sought truth as an existentially felt correlation between the human condition and divine revelation. Most recently, Kevin Vanhoozer's *First Theology* suggests that the entire project of grounding theology is misguided since theological method cannot be simplistically separated from theological content as the latter always informs the former both presuppositionally and conscientiously (and vice versa). Vanhoozer's response as an evangelical is to insist on the interconnectedness of hermeneutical

---

38   Various aspects of the following overview are fleshed out in Francis Schüssler Fiorenza, *Foundational Theology* (New York: Crossroad, 1984), esp. chs 9–10.

theology and theological hermeneutics, of God/theology and scripture, and yet emphasize the normativity of the latter (the biblical revelation) through a theory of divine communication.[39] The result is that in the two hundred years since Hegel, first theology has traversed what appears to be the entire spectrum and seemed unable to surmount the chasms between transcendence and immanence; between scripture and experience; between revelation and the situation; between theology and method; etc.

It is against this backdrop that the recent project in first theology of the Third Article by D. Lyle Dabney takes on significance. In a series of essays and articles, Dabney has sketched out a proposal regarding the need of a pneumatological first theology for our time.[40] Dabney situates his project in ways similar to Hegel (albeit without explicit reference to Hegel) by correlating foundational theological projects and historical periods. In the scheme he provides, the history of Christian theology has seen the emergence of a first theology of the First Article, the paradigm of medieval and Scholastic theology predicated upon God as creator and nature as distinct from but not opposed to grace,[41] and a first theology of the Second Article, the paradigm of Reformation theology predicated upon a christological hermeneutic emphasizing the fallenness and depravity of human beings, our need for redemption, and provision of that redemption by Christ who is the sole bridge between divine transcendence and the human condition. In each case, Dabney suggests, theological grounding is provided by divine self-revelation, whether it be in nature or in scripture, correlating with the emphases of First Article and Second Article paradigms.

The problem today is that we live neither in the hierarchically ordered or unified world of medieval Christendom, nor in the oppositional or confrontative environment of the Protestant Reformation. Further, we no longer have the confidence in Reason which the Scholastics and the

---

39   Kevin Vanhoozer, 'First Theology: Meditations in a Postmodern Toolshed', in K. Vanhoozer, *First Theology: God, Scripture and Hermeneutics* (Downers Grove, IL: InterVarsity Press, 2002), pp. 15-41.

40   D.L. Dabney, 'Otherwise Engaged in the Spirit: A First Theology for the Twenty-first Century', in M. Volf, C. Krieg and T. Kucharz (eds), *The Future of Theology: Essays in Honor of Jürgen Moltmann* (Grand Rapids, MI: Eerdmans, 1996), pp. 154-63; 'Starting with the Spirit: Why the Last Should Now be First', in G. Preece and S. Pickard (eds), *Starting with the Spirit: The Task of Theology Today II* (Hindmarsh: Australian Theological Forum/Adelaide: Openbook Publishers, 2001), pp. 3-27; and 'Why Should the Last Be First? The Priority of Pneumatology in Recent Theological Discussion', in Hinze and Dabney (eds), *Advents of the Spirit*, pp. 240-61.

41   For more on Dabney's reading of the medieval paradigm, see his 'Nature Dis-Graced and Grace De-Natured: The Problematic of the Augustinian Doctrine of Grace for Contemporary Theology', *Journal for Christian Theological Research* [http://home.apu.edu/~CTRF/articles/2000_articles/dabney.html] 5.3 (2000).

Enlightenment philosophés possessed. Rather, our 'postmodern' situation can be characterized by a sort of oxymoronic image: that of a shrinking global village yet continually deconstructed by radical plurality and diversity. How can Christians give a theological account of themselves in this new situation? How can theological method be reconceived if the older approaches—either a medieval theology of ascent or a Reformation theology of descent—are no longer viable? What if the older categories—either the medieval notion of *fulfilment* or the Reformation idea of *contradiction*—no longer speak to us? When theological categories—such as the medieval *common* grace or the Reformation common *grace*—no longer engage us, what then?

It is here that Dabney's proposal for a first theology of the Third Article comes into focus. He notes that in light of the creation account, 'in the order of questions to be asked in theology, we must *first* ask about the Spirit of God if we would speak of the self-revealing Word of God'.[42] This leads to a pneumatological reconception of theology 'with a prolegomena giving an account of "interpersonal relationship in the Spirit" instead of "identity in the continuity of God-consciousness" or "otherness in the discontinuity of the Word"'.[43] The resulting theology—directed toward the *transjectivity* of the Spirit beyond objectivism and subjectivism—is truly a first theology: *first* because it points to our always already being engaged with God, and *theology* because it is always already a soteriology of God's encounter with and saving of us.

On this note, Dabney's retrieval of the thought of John Wesley is significant for developing a pneumatological theology in our time.[44] Wesley himself, it may be recalled, sought a third way through a number of theological conundrums: between Calvinism and Arminianism; between Anglicanism and Puritanism; between rationalism and enthusiasm; between doctrine and mysticism; etc. The beginnings of his solution were to be found in his heart-warming experience of the Spirit. It is this pneumatic event that lies at the heart of Wesley's doctrine of perfection and entire sanctification. Wesley's third way therefore brought head and heart together in Christian praxis and ethical living. The posthumously designated 'Wesleyan quadrilateral' further captures Wesley's conviction that theology arises out of the life of the Spirit that includes and brings together scripture, tradition, reason and experience.

---

42 Dabney, 'Otherwise Engaged in the Spirit', p. 160.
43 Dabney, 'Otherwise Engaged in the Spirit', p. 159.
44 See D.L. Dabney, 'Jürgen Moltmann and John Wesley's Third Article Theology', *Wesleyan Theological Journal* 29.1–2 (1994), pp. 140-48, and 'Unfinished Business: John Wesley and Friedrich Schleiermacher on the Doctrine of the Holy Spirit', unpublished MS [formerly available on the *Wesleyan Studies Online Journal* 1 (2001), a now defunct website].

The result is that Wesleyan perfectionism provides a teleological orientation for theology in as much as it seeks the transformative consummation of creation and redemption in and through the working of the Holy Spirit.

The significance of Wesley for pneumatological theology in a postmodern world is (at least) three-fold. First, Wesley foreshadows, at least theologically, Hegel's turn to pneumatology. In Wesley's case, of course, the pneumatological strands of Luther's and Calvin's theology are pressed into more explicit service for theology and Christian praxis. For Wesley, the solution to the theological controversies of his day was to be found finally in holy living. That theology emerges from a life in, of and by the Spirit could be said to anticipate Hegel's philosophical claim that speculative pneumatology emerges from the unfolding of the life of the Spirit in history. Second, Christian perfection involved not only a pure heart before God, but right relationships with one's neighbors. To that extent, then, Wesleyan theology contains, at least implicitly, an intersubjectivist orientation. What it lacks theoretically regarding the horizontal nature of communal intersubjectivity, it makes up with a robust theological account of the vertical human interpersonal relationship with God. Finally, the eschatological bearings of Wesley's perfectionism connect with Steven Smith's notion of a pneumatological theology directed to the kingdom of God. The mutual thread in both visions is the turn to pneumatology.

Dabney suggests, however, that there is a flaw in Wesley's own thinking which needs to be redressed in contemporary pneumatological theology. Insofar as sanctification and pneumatology are still afterthoughts to christology in Wesley, this reflects the domination of Reformation categories in Wesleyanism. If the work of the Holy Spirit is limited to applying salvation to the lives of believers, then pneumatology risks being defined 'materially in terms of an activity in the human soul that shapes human conscience'; conversely, discernment of the Spirit is not given a christological or theological identification, but is relegated to what might be called the 'sanctificationist' criteria of the fruits of the Spirit in the believer's life. The result is the possibility of Holiness and Pentecostal excesses so often realized in the history of these two traditions on the one hand, and a filioquist subordinationism discernible in Wesleyan and Pentecostal pneumatology on the other.[45]

Correcting these imbalances is part and parcel of formulating a pneumatological theology suitable to the demands of Christian faith in a postmodern world. Along the way, Dabney's primary dialogue partner has been Jürgen Moltmann, under whom he completed his doctoral

---

45   Dabney, 'Unfinished Business', pp. 23-25 of printed MS.

studies.[46] Moltmann's theology extends the Wesleyan doctrine of sanctification from that of persons to that of the cosmos as a whole. More important for our purposes, however, is that it is Moltmann who leads Dabney to ask the key question of pneumatological theology: who or what is the identity of the spirit we are theologizing about? The answer can only be discerned by following, in a Hegelian sense, the life of the Spirit from creation through redemption to reconciliation. Here is Moltmann's own theological journey, proceeding from his early *Theology of Hope* (the 1960s), through his trinitarian *theologia crucis* (culminating in *The Crucified God* in 1972), toward the recognition of the pneumatological lacuna at the heart of his theology of the cross and remedied in more recent work (from *Church in the Power of the Spirit* in the mid-70s to *The Spirit of Life: A Universal Affirmation* in the early 1990s). And central to this Moltmannian trek is the gradual realization that the spirit is no other than the Spirit of the crucified God!

While Moltmann does make explicit connections on this point with the theology of Hegel,[47] it is Dabney—in dialogue explicitly with Moltmann, and therefore at least implicitly, also with Hegel—who has further developed the theological implications of the Spirit's relationship to the cross.[48] Here, he has done important work in insisting that any attempt at

---

46   Besides the previously mentioned 'Jürgen Moltmann and John Wesley's Third Article Theology', see also D.L. Dabney, 'The Advent of the Spirit: The Turn to Pneumatology in the Theology of Jürgen Moltmann', *Asbury Theological Journal* 48.1 (1993), pp. 81-107.
47   See J. Moltmann, *Theology of Hope: On the Ground and Implications of a Christian Eschatology* (trans. J.W. Leitch; New York: Harper & Row, 1975), pp. 165-72. Other theological commentaries on Hegel, *theologia crucis* and the death of God include H. Thielicke, *The Evangelical Faith*. Volume 1: *Prolegomena: The Relation of Theology to Modern Thought Forms* (trans. G.W. Bromiley; Grand Rapids, MI: Eerdmans, 1974), ch. XIV, esp. pp. 259-64; E. Jüngel, *God as the Mystery of the World: On the Foundations of the Theology of the Crucified One in the Dispute between Theism and Atheism* (trans. D.L. Guder; Grand Rapids, MI: Eerdmans, 1983), ch. II, esp. pp. 63-100; H. Küng, *The Incarnation of God: An Introduction to Hegel's Theological Thought as Prolegomena to a Future Christology* (trans. J.R. Stephenson; New York: Crossroad, 1987), pp. 162-74; and H. Schöndorf, SJ, 'The Othering (Becoming Other) and Reconciliation of God in Hegel's *Phenomenology of Spirit*' (trans. J. Stewart), in J. Stewart (ed.), *The Phenomenology of Spirit Reader: Critical and Interpretive Essays* (Albany: SUNY Press, 1998), pp. 375-400. I will need to return to this conversation at a later date, as my focus here is on the work of Dabney.
48   See esp. D.L. Dabney, *'Pneumatologia Crucis*: Reclaiming *Theologia Crucis* for a Theology of the Spirit Today', *Scottish Journal of Theology* 53.4 (2000), pp. 511-24; cf. 'Naming the Spirit: Towards a Pneumatology of the Cross', in Preece and Pickard (eds), *Starting with the Spirit*, pp. 28-58. The book-length argument is provided in Dabney's published dissertation: *Die Kenosis des Geistes: Kontinuität zwischen*

a pneumatological theology must be centered on the Spirit's foundational work in the life, death and resurrection of Christ, and therefore begin with the interpersonal particularity of Jesus Christ and his redemptive community. A theology of the Third Article should therefore present a pneumatological vision deeply informed by the cross of Christ—a *pneumatologia crucis*, as it were—as the starting-point for theology. So when Dabney writes, 'the Spirit of the Cross is the presence of God with the Son in the eschatological absence of the Father',[49] he is calling attention to the mystery of the divine absence and yet presence at the cross, the mystery of Jesus' abandonment by the Father and yet resurrection by the Spirit. In this way, a theological, christological and trinitarian account of the identity of the Spirit is given which serves as a normative standard for the featured components of a pneumatological theology—e.g., a pneumatological ecclesiology, a pneumatological soteriology, a pneumatological eschatology, and so on[50]—thus enabling the complex task of discernment of spirits.

Have we come full circle in traversing developments from Hegel's speculative Good Friday and 'Calvary of absolute Spirit' to Dabney's pneumatology of the cross? In some senses, apparently so. However, the circle can be understood in terms of the hermeneutical spiral. And, depending on which image is utilized, the spiral continues to take us either inward toward the heart of the divine mystery, or outward toward the mystery of the divine creation—or both at the same time, thereby confirming the suggestiveness of a theology of the Third Article for our time. In either case, a 'pneumatological engine' is needed to continue propelling the theological quest. Does this justify reconceiving a theology of the Third Article in terms of first theology? If so, can it be that this 'engine' was articulated explicitly by Hegel some two hundred years ago, but signaled historically at the cross of Christ by the presence

---

Schöpfung und Erlösung in Werk des Heiligen Geist (Neukirchen-Vluyn: Neukirchener Verlag, 1997).

49   Dabney, '*Pneumatologia Crucis*', p. 524.

50   See D.L. Dabney, 'The Church as a Community of (Un)Common Grace: Toward a Postmodern Ecclesiology', unpublished paper presented to the annual meeting of the Christian Theological Research Fellowship of the American Academy of Religion, 1997 [http://home.apu.edu/~CTRF/papers/1997_papers/dabney.html]; 'The Justification of the Spirit: Soteriological Reflections on the Resurrection', in Preece and Pickard (eds), *Starting with the Spirit*, pp. 59-82; reprinted in 'Justified by the Spirit: Soteriological Reflections on the Resurrection', *International Journal of Systematic Theology* 3.1 (2001), pp. 46-68; and 'The Nature of the Spirit: Creation as a Premonition of God', in Preece and Pickard (eds), *Starting with the Spirit*, pp. 83-110. Dabney is at the beginning stages of a four volume pneumatologically-structured systematic theology beginning with (what else?) pneumatology, proceeding through christology and patrology, and culminating with the Trinity.

of the Spirit in the absence of the Father almost two thousand years ago?[51]

---

51   I am grateful to Joseph Bracken, SJ, and Alan Padgett for their comments on an earlier draft of this essay. Of course, the faults remain my own.

CHAPTER 13

The Holy Spirit and the Church in Modern Canadian Protestantism

John A. Vissers

The average church member would not be a little upset were one of his fellow-worshippers to insist on speaking to him in regard to the 'joy' to be had in the Holy Spirit.[1]

The unlikely source of this friendly provocation is a Canadian Presbyterian theologian whose own Reformed tradition has often been charged with ignoring the work and reality of the Holy Spirit.[2] Walter W. Bryden, Professor and Principal at Knox College, Toronto, in the years following church union in Canada, took that charge seriously and redirected it against modern Protestant theology and church life in general. As a theologian of the Spirit Bryden was a rather rare person, 'an original Canadian theologian who sought to address the peculiarities of the Canadian scene in the light of the insights of Biblical theology' while refusing to shrink from the prophetic critique that inevitably set him at odds with the dominant ecclesiastical ethos of his time.[3] If, as Joseph C. McLelland has argued, the natural theology of Canada is natural theology, 'the study of religious truths through reason rather than divine revelation', then Walter Bryden's conception of the Holy Spirit

---

1   W.W. Bryden, 'The Holy Spirit and the Church', in D.V. Wade (ed.), *Separated Unto the Gospel* (Toronto: Burns and MacEachern, 1956), p. 38.

2   The American Presbyterian theologian Lewis Mudge has summarized this critique by saying that Reformed creeds and confessions do not do justice to the biblical emphasis on the work of the Holy Spirit with the result that 'in reading what the Bible says about the Spirit we are blind and deaf'. See Lewis Mudge, *One Church: Catholic and Reformed* (Philadelphia: Westminster Press, 1963), p. 63, cited in I. John Hesselink, *On Being Reformed: Distinctive Characteristics and Common Misunderstandings* (Ann Arbor, MI: Servant Books, 1983), p. 73.

3   J. Charles Hay, 'Allan L. Farris', in John Moir (ed.), *The Tide of Time* (Toronto: Knox College, 1978), p. 16.

and the church sounded a note of protest against the natural theology of establishment Protestantism in Canada.[4] As a theologian of the Spirit, Bryden was a theologian of the cross, a stern prophet whose terse observations in the classroom shaped an entire generation of Presbyterian leaders.

In this essay I use Bryden's theological protest as a lens through which to view the church's understanding of the Holy Spirit in modern Protestantism. Bryden's theology, not widely known outside Canada, provides an interesting case study in pneumatology which is of limited but enduring value. It is limited because it is bound to a particular expression of the Reformed tradition in the twentieth century, namely Canadian Presbyterianism, and because Bryden often painted the views of his theological adversaries with a broad brush. But it is also enduring because it is rooted in a theology of the cross that contains the seeds of ongoing theological protest and renewal for the church. Bryden's theology was truly *semper Reformandum*, a theology in the service of a church reformed and reforming according to the Word of God, a theology worked out under the continual illumination of the Holy Spirit. After briefly describing his theology and ministry, I proceed by (1) setting forth Bryden's critique of the church's domestication of the Spirit; (2) describing the theology of Word and Spirit out of which this critique emerges; (3) outlining the vision Bryden casts for a confessing church; and (4) evaluating the theological significance of Bryden's protest as a theology of the cross.

The pneumatology of Walter Bryden was forged in the midst of a career as a pastor and theological educator within the Presbyterian Church in Canada in the first half of the twentieth century. Born in 1883, Bryden served congregations in Alberta, Ontario and Saskatchewan before assuming the chairs of church history and the history and philosophy of religion at Knox College, Toronto, in 1925, serving as principal of the college from 1945 until his death in 1952. His influence upon the so-called continuing Presbyterian Church following the formation of the United Church of Canada was immense. As a professor and a principal, Bryden taught theological students for the pastoral ministry of a church that had gone through a major crisis. Noted as one of the earliest interpreters of Karl Barth's theology in Canada, Bryden's theology reflected the theological movement known as neo-orthodoxy. His particular emphasis on a confessional theology of Word and Spirit, shaped by the neo-orthodox impulse, provided a post-union

---

4   Joseph C. McLelland, 'The Natural Theology of Canada: Philosophy of Religion in Canadian Theological Education', in Graham Brown (ed.), *Theological Education in Canada* (Toronto: United Church Publishing House, 1998), p. 1.

ecclesiological rationale for continuing Presbyterians.[5] Among his more important books are *The Spirit of Jesus in St Paul* (1925), *Why I Am A Presbyterian* (1934), *The Presbyterian Conception of the Word of God* (1935), *The Christian's Knowledge of God* (1940), *The Significance of the Westminster Confession of Faith* (1943), and an unpublished manuscript titled *After Modernism, What?*

The Domestication of the Spirit

Bryden's pneumatology was motivated by what he understood to be three reductionist conceptions of the Holy Spirit at work in the churches of his day: rationalism, enthusiasm, and idealism. In the first instance, Bryden looked at his own Reformed tradition and identified those who treated the Holy Spirit in a merely scholastic fashion, as nothing more than a Christian doctrine to be fitted into an accepted system of Christian theology. Mere academic interest, however sincere, Bryden contended, could yield no genuine knowledge of God's Spirit. Rationalistic conceptions of the Spirit, however necessary, could not create spiritual life and community within the church.[6] While Bryden's critique of rationalism was directed at a church which, in his mind, had allowed reason to replace revelation, his particular concern was the view of the fundamentalists of his day, those whom he described as rationally orthodox. This view was one in which 'the Word of God is to be identified simply with the written Holy Scripture, in its wholeness; this Scripture to be literally interpreted because it is verbally inerrant and plenarily inspired'.[7] Emphasizing the Spirit's role in inspiration, the rationally orthodox ignored the Spirit's role in authenticating the Bible as the Word of God (the internal testimony of the Holy Spirit) which was central to Calvin's theology of Word and Spirit. This identification of the Spirit with the Word, Bryden argued, originated in the scholastic aftermath of the Reformation.

    In the second instance, Bryden noted that the history of the church is filled with a whole series of what might be called 'spiritual' reactions representing various understandable protests against ecclesiastical formal-

    5   John A. Vissers, 'W.W. Bryden and the Reformed Protestant Tradition in Canada', *The Toronto Journal of Theology* 6.1 (1990), pp. 70-85; James D. Smart, 'The Evangelist as Theologian', in Wade (ed.), *Separated Unto the Gospel*, pp. vii-xi; Joseph C. McLelland, 'Walter Bryden: "By Circumstance and God"', in W. Stanford Reid (ed.), *Called to Witness*. Volume 2 (Hamilton, ON: The Presbyterian Church in Canada, Committee on History, 1980), pp. 119-26.

    6   Bryden, 'The Holy Spirit and the Church', p. 31.

    7   Bryden, 'The Presbyterian Conception of the Word of God', in Wade (ed.), *Separated Unto the Gospel*, p. 181.

isms, spiritual apathies and orthodox rationalizations of the faith.[8] Such movements of enthusiasm pointed to the spontaneous life of the Spirit as providing the one mark of a true and living church. Citing a range of movements from the New Testament era to the twentieth century, including the radical Anabaptists, the Pietists, and numerous Protestant sects of his own day, Bryden contended that all could be explained as reactionary movements inspired by an apparent spiritual vacuum in the church.[9] As one might expect from a Reformed analysis of such movements, Bryden concluded that this 'particular emphasis on the Spirit has too often been at the expense of any intelligent understanding of Jesus Christ and His true work, and has therefore, resulted in sheer individualisms, immoral excesses on the one hand, meticulous moralisms on the other, or has degenerated into mere enthusiasms of a purely subjective nature, devoid of any reliable means of evaluating Christian life at all'.[10] Bryden's point is clear: mere reactions to rationalism, formalism, and nominalism in the church which emphasized experience and enthusiasm were driven by reductionist conceptions of the Holy Spirit, views in which the Spirit becomes identified almost exclusively with religious feelings or extraordinary experiences. Indeed, Bryden saw '(as few besides Karl Barth have) the inner connection between mysticism and rationalism'.[11]

As significant as the challenges of rationalism and enthusiasm were to the church, they did not constitute, separately or together, the most serious threat to the spiritual life of modern Protestantism. That threat consisted in idealism. As a teacher in a theological college, Bryden had the impression that many students, 'though assuming a knowledge of, and belief in God and Jesus Christ, acknowledge at the same time that the Holy Spirit conveys little, if any, meaning to them'.[12] This perplexity among students, he argued, reflected a condition prevalent in the church as a whole, due at least in part to the theological vagaries of the modern church. More precisely, it was due to the dominance of idealism in modern Christian thought and practice, a religious atmosphere in which people have been encouraged to think of their Christian responsibility merely as accepting Christ's life and teachings as so many ideals to be achieved, or as representing approved principles to be applied by good men and women to the existing conditions of life and society.[13] Idealism, accompanied by a new legalism, reduced the Holy Spirit to a general principle of life. Devoid of spiritual life, the church turns to elaborate

8   Bryden, 'The Holy Spirit and the Church', p. 39.
9   Bryden, 'The Holy Spirit and the Church', pp. 39-40.
10 Bryden, 'The Holy Spirit and the Church', pp. 39-40.
11 McLelland, '"By Circumstance and God"', p. 125.
12 Bryden, 'The Holy Spirit and the Church', p. 32.
13 Bryden, 'The Holy Spirit and the Church', pp. 32-33.

organizations, splendid efficiencies of one kind or another, programs for unity and renewal, but somehow it lacks power to do those things for which God called the church into existence, i.e. actually to change people's lives, to humble the world, to embarrass the world's selfishness, its self-conceits, self deceptions and misguided intrigues. With few exceptions the churches of the early twentieth century in Canada were not persecuted, Bryden argued, because they posed no threat, real or imagined, no danger, clear or present, to the state or to society, in whole or in part. In fact, the idealism of the church, Bryden averred, muted the voice of the Spirit speaking to the churches, and allowed the churches to prop up a society that was the very antithesis of life in the Spirit. The rich and powerful patronize the church, political leaders praise the church for its loyalty to the state, but they never fear the church. The Spirit has been 'secularized' and 'civilized' to the point that the church has become an expression of the *Zeitgeist*. The spirit of the churches, Bryden protests, has become the spirit of culture Protestantism. The church serves to help society advance material welfare, pursue intellectual and cultural ideals, and promote national interests.[14]

Bryden's judgment of the modern church was rooted in his understanding of Enlightenment idealism, especially the philosophy of Hegel. Idealism in this form, Bryden argued, is actually the resurgence of the Greek concept of the *logos*, that so-called higher rational principle immanent in human beings and in the world, presumed to be the sole creative agency of all that is of worth in civilization, culture and religion. Modern Protestants have been taught to think of the Spirit in this way, creating an antithesis between the inner, moral, rational and disciplined life and the more external sensual, unregulated, passionate life. The Spirit is that which orders life and creates a culture within which men and women may flourish as civilized beings. Bryden did not quarrel with this insight, but contended that when this is the only way in which the Holy Spirit is understood, the practical consequence is disastrous for Christianity. The Holy Spirit is used to engender self-sufficiency and independence at the personal and national levels. The 'fruits of the Holy Spirit' are transformed into civic and political virtues and cultural appreciations, reducing the term 'Christian' to the status of the good citizen. More seriously, it promotes among Anglo-Saxons a sense of racial, ethnic and cultural superiority. Rather than calling men and women to repentance and confession before God, the Spirit is identified as that which precludes the need for dependence upon God. In short, the idealization of the Spirit transforms Christianity into the very antithesis of what it was intended to be by marrying the language of the Christian message to the aspirations and ideals of western culture. While in

---

14   Bryden, 'The Holy Spirit and the Church', pp. 37-41.

American Christianity the philosophical tool that had facilitated this marriage was pragmatism, the modern Protestant churches in Canada had been shaped by idealism.[15]

The Spirit of God's Judging–Saving Word

By now it is clear that when it came to modern church life Bryden operated with a hermeneutic of suspicion. But what was the basis of this suspicion? Was it simply the protest of a disgruntled church leader or a disillusioned theological teacher? To be sure, we'll never know all that motivated Bryden's critique. However, we do know something about the theology out of which it emerged. His concern about the understandings of the Spirit operative in the church arose from a theology of the Word in which revelation is conceived as an act of God. As such, revelation is the act of a free and divine subject, the self-giving of a God who shares self-knowledge with human subjects. In love and freedom God elects to share this divine self-knowledge in the person of Jesus Christ by the power and presence of the Holy Spirit. The reality of this revelation is marked by its dialectical and paradoxical character (i.e. it contains both an affirmation—salvation, and a negation—judgment) and by the crisis it creates for human existence. As such, the Word and the Spirit are bound together in the event of revelation, an event which is created again and again by a sovereign God, an event for which there is no prior basis in the creature. God is God, wholly other, God's freedom is not bound by the human correspondent in divine revelation, and any claim by Christians to identify the Holy Spirit with a particular aspect of the church's faith and life was to be resisted.

Bryden's journey of discovery beyond the bounds of a modern understanding of the Holy Spirit and the church began in his study of the Corinthian correspondence, published in 1925 as *The Spirit of Jesus in St Paul*. Bryden examined Paul's religious experience arguing that there was a continuity and spiritual unity between Jesus and Paul based upon Paul's identification of the Holy Spirit with the Lord. Over against the tendency in modern scholarship to drive a wedge between Paul and Jesus Bryden argued that the Holy Spirit is the Spirit of Jesus operative in the life of the apostle as a power and presence which creates ethical and spiritual realities. Paul knew that his heart and mind were not inclined to a knowledge of God in and of themselves, only by the power of the Spirit could his life be united with Christ. Paul's faith could not be reduced to mere assent to facts about the history of Jesus or to the ethical imitation of the ideals embodied by Jesus. The knowledge of God that molded and

---

15 Bryden, 'The Holy Spirit and the Church', pp. 40-44.

motivated Paul was a knowledge of Jesus mediated by the Spirit of Jesus as an existential reality. There is no other adequate explanation, Bryden believed, for Paul's ministry. In short, in Paul Bryden 'finds a Christ-mysticism, a case of Christ's being formed in man by the energy of the Holy Spirit, and he reckons that this is authentic mysticism and the proper mystery'.[16]

In Bryden's judgment this traditional witness to the relation existing between the Holy Spirit and the church had been set aside by modern Protestantism. The early Reformers, he argued, contended that there could be no knowledge of God except through God's own Word and Spirit. Human beings have a truly saving knowledge of God only in a knowledge sealed by the Holy Spirit in the heart. The confession of having been apprehended by the Holy Spirit therefore becomes the decisive mark of true membership in the church. Only the Holy Spirit enables men and women to cry, 'Abba, Father'; by the Holy Spirit alone can men and women discern the true meaning of scripture and acknowledge Christ as indeed Lord.[17] To sum up: 'God is never known except as Triune God, and in such knowledge the third Person of this Trinity is the final and ultimate factor. Those, moreover, who acknowledge God in this manner, constitute the true Church.'[18] But the church is not constituted by their confession. The church is created by the Holy Spirit poured out on a community gathered around the Word in whom this confession is made. Only by the work of the Holy Spirit can men and women believe the faith confessed by the creeds because no one can 'say that the Church actually exists, that the "communion of Saints" is a reality, that there is "remission of sins, resurrection of the flesh and life everlasting", apart from the Holy Spirit's work'.[19]

The church exists, therefore, where men and women have been apprehended by a knowledge of God through the power and presence of the Holy Spirit. Such a knowledge of God, Bryden argues, is not to be identified with general human religious experience, human reasoning about it, or human ethical and cultural projects that might emerge from such experience. The church exists because in grace God mediates a genuine knowledge of the divine by faith through the Holy Spirit. God is both the object of such knowledge for the human soul and the means by which such knowledge is apprehended. God is mediated only by God and the church exists because God shares divine self-knowledge by the Spirit with a people created for fellowship and witness.

Bryden's argument thus far appears to be a rather straight-forward restatement of traditional theology over against the idealism of modern

16   McLelland, '"By Circumstance and God"', p. 125.
17   Bryden, 'The Holy Spirit and the Church', pp. 33-34.
18   Bryden, 'The Holy Spirit and the Church', p. 34.
19   Bryden, 'The Holy Spirit and the Church', p. 36.

Protestantism. As such it might simply stand as one dogmatic and absolute position beside another, in danger of itself being domesticated by the church. That is, until one understands that the Spirit about whom Bryden speaks is the Spirit of the judging–saving Word of God. The Word of God from whom the Spirit proceeds and to whom the Spirit witnesses is 'Jesus Christ, and Him crucified, with nothing to be added or subtracted from simply that'.[20] Bryden operates with a dialectical, christocentric conception of the Word of God centered in the cross of Christ. The Spirit is identified with the self-emptying of God's crucified Messiah, the Spirit of the One who became nothing for the sake of the other. The Word of God in Jesus Christ encounters human beings by the power of this Spirit as that which completely disillusions them, calling into question the independence of human existence and all attempts to domesticate the divine reality. This is the judgment of the Word of God. In the first instance, the Holy Spirit does not come as a presence and power to confirm the life of the church and the civilization within which the church finds itself. The Spirit comes as One who radically questions whether men and women have experienced the new life inaugurated by the resurrection of Jesus from the dead and his reign over all things in heaven and earth. The experience of faith generated by the Holy Spirit, therefore, is an experience of utter negation, an experience of being judged, questioned, and even destroyed. 'In some essential sense an Absolute must negate, if it is to prove itself such, i.e. if it is to authenticate itself. The truth is, man in his entire life's experience, is never encountered by that which truly negates him except in that event when God comes personally and establishes a relationship with him.'[21] God negates before God affirms, God excludes before God embraces. The paradox of Christian faith is that the Absolute known to faith is a personal-Absolute who proves himself to be such by the power of the Holy Spirit to challenge human existence in its alienation from the Absolute. This experience of negation is what the Bible describes as death to self, that which occurs before resurrection to new life in the reign of God. The Holy Spirit makes men and women see their lives in terms of God's crucified Messiah, confirming that God is God and human beings are human beings, making them know that as frail and fallen creatures they are 'sinners', enemies of God and alienated from God's reign. The judgment of the Spirit reminds us that nothing on the human side makes possible the reality and reception of God's grace.

Bryden was one of the few theologians to see the significance of Luther's *theologia crucis* for the experience of faith. Luther emphasized

20   W.W. Bryden, *The Christian's Knowledge of God* (Toronto: Thorn Press, 1940), p. 173.
21   Bryden, *Christian's Knowledge of God*, pp. 132-33.

that 'the humiliation and suffering of Christ, in which God hides his revelation, correspond to the humiliation and suffering of the sinner, for whom God conceals his real work (*opus proprium*) of salvation behind his strange work (*opus alienum*) of alienation, which furthers it. Only the humbled sinner, struck down by the experience of what Luther called *Anfechtung* ("spiritual conflict") can know the God who for his/her justification underwent the humiliation and condemnation of the cross.'[22] Following Luther, Bryden insisted on an experiential basis for a theology of the cross and could affirm Luther's experience: 'Living, or rather dying and being damned make a theologian, not understanding, reading or speculating.'[23] Bryden applied this insight to the church by insisting that living, dying, and being damned make the church the church by the work of the Spirit.

But there is more. The Word of God is also a Word which encounters us in grace and therefore affirms human existence in Jesus Christ. This is the salvation of the Word of God. The same Spirit who stands over us is also at work in us, affirming human existence, creating new life in union with Jesus Christ. The Word of God affirms life precisely because it negates it. In the midst of utter negation a human being cries out to God for deliverance, for salvation, since then and only then does a human being know that God is truly concerned about his/her life. The paradox of the Christian faith is that it is at one and the same time world-denying and world-affirming. It denies a world which imagines itself as a place of human flourishing apart from God, and it affirms the reality and significance of human life in a world where the Word became flesh, and where men and women live in union with that Word under God's reign. Such an affirmation of the world is more profound, Bryden contends, than any ancient or modern idealism. The Spirit condemns the whole person in order to create a new person. When a person becomes a Christian there cannot be a preparation for this experience cobbled together from that which already exists. In redemption, God creates out of nothing, God brings existence out of non-existence, life out of death. God judges the non-existence and death of the old person, and brings existence and life. This is the experience of God's electing grace, an experience of freedom which 'arises out of the most radical of all self-negating human experiences, namely repentance and confession'.[24]

---

22   Richard J. Bauckham, 'Cross, Theology of the', in Sinclair B. Ferguson, David F. Wright and James I. Packer (eds), *New Dictionary of Theology* (Downers Grove, IL: InterVarsity Press, 1988), pp. 181-83.

23   Martin Luther, *Weimarer Ausgabe 5*, p. 163, cited in Bauckham, 'Cross, Theology of the', p. 182.

24   Bryden, *Christian's Knowledge of God*, p. 31.

The Spirit of a Confessing Church

Walter Bryden's conception of the Holy Spirit as the Spirit of the judging–saving Word explains why he resisted any and all attempts to identify the Word of God and the work of the Spirit with cultural ideals and ecclesial programs. Every understanding of faith that assumes a human horizon or describes humankind's 'openness' to revelation without taking seriously the constitutive nature of that revelation must be radically questioned.[25] The church is not created against such a human horizon; the people of God are created by the Spirit against the horizon of the reign of God's crucified Messiah. Such a people, visited and redeemed by God's Word and Spirit, are called to witness to the judging–saving Word and constrained to reflect on the church's faith and life in a disciplined way beneath the cross. If the church is to be the church it must come to terms with the fact that it has no life of its own. The church is a creature of the Word and Spirit of God—that Word and Spirit which gave rise to holy scripture, and apart from which the church cannot stand.[26] The Holy Spirit gathers a fellowship of people in union with the Word in whom and through whom the identity of the church resides.

The vocation of the church gathered by the Spirit of God is confession. Confession is a witness to the Word of God empowered by the same Spirit who gathers the church around the Word. Such confession, Bryden argues, emanates from a church living under the constraint of God's Word. 'It is easy to make statements of our faith', Bryden notes, 'but confessions are wrung from men who have been on their knees'.[27] As the church is continually confronted by the Word of God in the power of the Spirit of God the community of faith undergoes a process of continuous conversion which empowers its continuous confession. The church can never declare that it has obtained the goal and possesses the prize; rather, the church must press on to makes it its own, because Christ Jesus has made the people of God his own (Phil. 3.12). The church lives between the already and the not yet; the church is reformed and reforming according to the Word of God under the illumination of the Spirit of God; and the church lives and moves and has its being under both the judgment and the salvation of the Word of God.

Such a church, Bryden believed, was to be *in* the world but not *of* the world. However, too often the church forgets that it lives under the judging–saving Word of a God who judges the self-righteousness and injustice of the world. 'There is a righteousness of God which brings into

---

25   McLelland, '"By Circumstance and God"', p. 123.
26   Bryden, *Christian's Knowledge of God*, p. x.
27   W.W. Bryden, 'Continental Movements and the Theological Thought of Tomorrow', *United Church Observer* 5 June 1941, pp. 11, 28.

judgment all the varied righteousnesses of men, yea, all their loyalties, their patriotisms, their nationalisms, and even their exclusive brotherhoods and boasted classisms.'[28] 'Only the judging–saving Word which judges man as such, rich and poor, civilized and uncivilized alike, ever succeeds in truly mellowing the hearts of men in such wise that they will truly be concerned about one another.'[29] The Holy Spirit at work in the church bears witness to God's judging–saving Word, questions the political, social, and economic realm within which the church lives, and points to the inauguration of the new humanity in Jesus Christ. The church that is in step with the Spirit lives in a state of constant crisis, tempted by the values of the world, and called by the virtues of God's reign breaking into the world. Whenever and wherever the church yields to the temptation, it grieves the Spirit of God and allows itself to be domesticated by the ideals, enthusiasms, and rationalisms of its time.

So in conclusion, Bryden argues, the

> Church of God in Christ is that sphere alone where God's Spirit dwells, where, through His operation, a new eternal life makes its presence felt in this world of sin. The Church, therefore, is no human or historic achievement, but a Gift of God, the consequence of God's descent into the world for its redemption. What distinguishes the Church from everything else in the world is that, however humanly imperfect, when faithful at all to its vocation, it possesses a life *empowered from on high*. Its need today as ever is not in the many things so freely suggested, but simply one thing, namely, that it be given Grace to become more Church.[30]

The Spirit, the Cross and the Church

A number of observations and critical reflections may be offered on the basis of this summary exposition of Walter Bryden's pneumatology and ecclesiology. First, Bryden operates within the Reformed tradition, most notably in his emphasis on a theology of the Word. His critique of modern theology presupposes that a recovery of the sixteenth-century Reformation conception of revelation is both possible and necessary. 'It is not too much to hold', he argues, that it was 'a completely fresh and living apprehension of the Word of God which constituted the primal inspiration of the Reformation movement as a whole', and for Calvin in particular.[31] On the one hand, Bryden's emphasis on the Word raises

---

28   'The Presbyterian Conception of the Word of God' (unpublished portion of manuscript, 1935), p. 49.
29   Bryden, *Christian's Knowledge of God*, p. 259.
30   Bryden, 'The Holy Spirit and the Church', p. 45.
31   Bryden, 'Presbyterian Conception of the Word of God', p. 179.

questions about the way in which the Spirit is subordinated to the Word in Reformed theology. Is Bryden's theology simply another example of the Reformed appropriation of the *filioque* clause? Perhaps. On the other hand, Bryden emphasizes the need to recover 'the completely fresh and living apprehension of the Word of God' which created the Reformation movement, i.e. he is concerned about the conception of the Word in the life of the Christian believer and the church. Bryden's choice of the word 'conception' is deliberate and is to be distinguished from the idea of a concept or a doctrine. The Word of God, in Bryden's theology, is not to be rationalized or objectified. It belongs to the realm of faith, that is, 'A relationship or an experience which may exist between the soul of a human being and God, through Christ, and without any other necessary form of mediation'.[32] There is a relational, experiential, or existential dimension to the reality of the Word of God that is incomprehensible apart from the reality and work of the Holy Spirit. At the same time, in truly Reformed fashion, Bryden cannot conceive of the reality and work of the Spirit apart from the Word.

Secondly, Bryden's pneumatology and ecclesiology represent an early Canadian reception of Karl Barth's early theology. By the late 1920s Bryden was sounding the themes that were to signal his lifelong engagement with Barth whom he referred to as 'the stern new prophet of Europe' and 'the modern scion of the Reformation spirit', and whose theology he described as 'real Calvinism in a modern dress'.[33] Like the early Barth and many of the neo-orthodox theologians, Bryden emphasized the negative pole of the 'the judging–saving Word'. As noted above, he rejected any possibility of a natural relationship between God and human beings prior to and apart from faith in Jesus Christ in order to emphasize the radical character of grace as gift. He pointed again and again to the sovereign Spirit whose ministry alone gave structure and content to the encounter of the human with the divine, creating a human being of authentic Christian faith. However, unlike Barth, he failed to move beyond the resounding *No!* to the positive *Yes!* of the gospel without which the *No!* cannot stand. Because Bryden could not discern the signs of the Spirit's presence clearly, he continued to sound the *No!* like a prophet with a single burden whose harping on a single note becomes tiresome.[34] The irony of the neo-orthodox movement (and Walter Bryden's theology is a good example of this) was that the prophetic word-centered pneumatology it set over against the Protestant establishment of the first half of the twentieth century became in some quarters the theological basis for that very Protestant

32   Bryden, 'Presbyterian Conception of the Word of God', p. 175.
33   Bryden, 'The Triumph of Reality', in Wade (ed.), *Separated Unto the Gospel*, p. 135; see also 'The Presbyterian Conception of the Word of God', p. 49.
34   McLelland, '"By Circumstance and God"', p. 125.

establishment following the Second World War. The theology of neo-orthodoxy, with its emphasis on the dialectics of Word and Spirit, was itself domesticated. Daring paradoxes became stale platitudes and by the 1960s the neo-orthodox consensus in North American theology had begun to disintegrate.

Thirdly, the Holy Spirit and the church, as Bryden conceived of these theological themes, became a post-union apologetic for the continuing Presbyterian Church in Canada after 1925. Although Bryden was not widely known outside Canada, his theology of the Spirit functioned in a powerful manner within his own ecclesial context. In his book *Why I Am a Presbyterian* he harnessed his criticisms of modern Protestantism in general and directed them against the theological rationale for the creation of The United Church of Canada. The kind of church unity created by the Holy Spirit, he argued, did not consist in institutional and programmatic uniformity. Rather than being grounded in the desire for a deep spiritual unity centered in Jesus Christ, Bryden believed that the establishment of a larger Protestant church in Canada arose primarily from the accommodation of the church to the culture which he had already so roundly criticized.

As a neo-reformation theologian in Canada Bryden's theological protest stands in the classic Protestant tradition, 'making one point over and over, taking it as the crucial and decisive point and hedging it on all sides against every attempt to qualify it'.[35] He sometimes painted with a broad brush in order to make that point. His highly charged polemic against the view of reason emanating from the Enlightenment also made him vulnerable to the accusation of being a fideist, or as F.H. Anderson suggested in a critical review of *The Christian's Knowledge of God* in a 1941 issue of *The University of Toronto Quarterly*, an 'irrational enthusiast'.[36] At the same time, he rejected what he described as rational orthodoxy by drawing a sharp distinction between the Reformation and Protestant scholasticism, without engaging the latter with the same seriousness that he took the liberal Protestant tradition. Writing as a church historian, it is clear that Bryden understood the significance of movements of enthusiasm for the church in general. But what was Bryden concerned about in Canadian Protestantism on this point? Who and where were the enthusiasts in his own day? While he may have had a passing acquaintance with evangelical pietist groups, the Anabaptist traditions, and the newer Pentecostal churches, as a so-called mainline Protestant theologian Bryden does not appear to be concerned about their

---

35   McLelland, '"By Circumstance and God"', p. 123.

36   F.H. Anderson, 'On a Certain Revival of Enthusiasm', *The University of Toronto Quarterly* 10.2 (January, 1941), pp. 182-96.

enthusiasms. Rather, he seems concerned about a form of mysticism that found its way into Canadian Protestantism.

Given the limitations of Bryden's theological critique, what then, if anything, is the legacy of his understanding of the Holy Spirit and the church? Simply this: *no church without the Spirit of God.* The church must learn to let the Spirit of God be the Spirit of God. He reminded the church that the people of God live and move and have their being by the sheer grace of God through the power and presence of the Holy Spirit and that they must therefore turn away from any and all worldly pretense. His theology calls the church to forsake, in Luther's terms, a theology of glory (*theologiae gloriae*) in which the church perceives the glory of God—God's power, wisdom and goodness, manifest in the works of creation; and turn to a theology of the cross (*theologiae crucis*) in which the church places its faith in the God hidden in the suffering and humiliation of the cross. Like Luther, Bryden believed that the natural knowledge of God to be gained from the created order, when left in the hands of sinners, even sinners redeemed by grace and called to be the church, resulted in attempts at self-justification by moral, intellectual, cultural, social, political and economic achievement. A theology of glory creates a church that domesticates the Spirit of God. A church that looks at the invisible things of God as they are seen in the visible things does not deserve to be called a church. But the church that looks on the visible rearward parts of God (*visiblia et posteriora Dei*) as seen in suffering and the cross does deserve to be called a church. A theology of the cross creates a church in which all human preconceptions of deity and human perceptions about how God may be known and how God may act in the world are shattered. In the cross of God's crucified Messiah, the judging–saving Word, God is revealed not in the power and glory which we usually associate with the Absolute, but in human disgrace, poverty, suffering and death. The church created by the Spirit of God, therefore, is a paradox, hidden in the world, marked by weakness and foolishness. Evidence of the Spirit's presence and power is to be found precisely at those moments in the life of the church when the church doubts that the Spirit is present because it is precisely at such moments that the people of God are thrown in utter and absolute dependence upon God. In the midst of uncertainty and doubt the church is vulnerable enough to be led by the Spirit. Whenever and wherever the church believes that it has identified the presence of the Spirit clearly, one can be sure that a theology of glory is at work. The mystery of the gospel is that in the midst of the God-forsakenness of the cross the Spirit is at work. In the midst of the God-forsakenness of the world the Spirit is present, hovering, transforming weakness into power, foolishness into wisdom, and death into life. Within this horizon of the Spirit's work we discover the reality of a people called to be and become church.

As a theologian of the cross Bryden's 'single-minded articulation of this theme marks him as one who conveys a spirit, a way of doing theology, rather than a content, a system of doctrine'.[37] And as a theologian of the cross in the twentieth century Bryden shares many of the same concerns as Karl Barth, Jürgen Moltmann, Eberhard Jüngel and Douglas John Hall, all of whom point to the humiliation of the cross as the basis for understanding the church in the power and presence of the Holy Spirit. Bryden's theology, therefore, stands as a constant reminder to Canadian Protestantism that the church is always in danger of co-opting the Holy Spirit to justify its own existence and advance its own agenda. Bryden identified the ways in which he believed the church of his own day had domesticated the Spirit. The question posed by his theology is simply this: in what ways are the Canadian churches of the twenty-first century in danger of domesticating the Spirit?

---

37   McLelland, '"By Circumstance and God"', p. 125.

CHAPTER 14

Clark Pinnock's Apologetic Theology

Donald G. Bloesch

Just as Augustine came to terms with ancient Greek thinking, so we are making peace with the culture of modernity. *Clark Pinnock*

I am delighted to have been invited to participate in this colloquy on Clark Pinnock's theology. Brenda and I have fond memories of the warm hospitality shown us by Clark and Dorothy during our visit to their home some years ago. Clark has lectured at Dubuque Theological Seminary and was well received by students and faculty alike.

Through the years I have found Clark Pinnock to be supportive and encouraging with regard to my theological writing. We converge much more than diverge, but in the area of apologetics it seems that we have palpably different approaches. Even here, however, we share many of the same concerns. Both of us affirm the centrality of the evangelical proclamation in the church's witness. Pinnock wishes to undergird and supplement this proclamation by apologetic argument; yet he is adamant that evangelism takes precedence over apologetics. Apologetics indeed is in the service of evangelism. He writes: 'A sound grasp of Christian apologetics is an indispensable tool for evangelism... If our apologetic prevents us from explaining the gospel to any person, it is an inadequate apologetic.'[1]

Where I have appreciated Pinnock is in his unremitting passion to reach the spiritually destitute for Jesus Christ. He counsels not withdrawal from the culture wars but instead participation in these conflicts so that the kingdom of God might be advanced. Apologetics understood as a defense of the faith in the public forum is viewed as integral to the church's mission.

---

1   Clark H. Pinnock, *Set Forth Your Case: Studies in Christian Apologetics* (Nutley, NJ: Craig Press, 1968), p. 7.

Even when I have to take exception to some of his assertions I admire him for his honesty and basic fidelity to the gospel. But I have difficulty with his determined efforts to support the gospel with arguments and evidences rather than allowing the gospel to defend itself as we meet attacks upon it from the world outside the church.

Pinnock is not a theologian who stands still. He is forever on the move—always willing to change or refurbish his positions in the light that continues to break forth from God's holy Word. Whereas his earlier stance was basically an evangelical rationalism belonging to the tradition of John Locke and Thomas Reid, he began to change as he interacted with new voices in both conservative and liberal theology that deem the search for evidences of the faith suspect. In his later years a shift can be detected from apologetic theology to narrative theology, where the emphasis is on sharing the story of personal experience rather than showing the credibility of the ontological claims of the faith. Yet even in his more mature thought the apologetic cast of his theology remains. His championing of open theism is rooted in the apologetic concern to reach the outsider for the gospel. The goal in this kind of narrative theology is to expose the inconsistencies in the stories of our hearers so that they might become more open to the metastory in the Bible.

It is interesting to note the mentors who have contributed to Pinnock's theological pilgrimage. In the early years he voiced his appreciation for such well-known defenders of the faith as Francis Schaeffer, C.S. Lewis, Benjamin Warfield and John Warwick Montgomery. Later he turned to John Cobb, Teilhard de Chardin, Paul Tillich, Wolfhart Pannenberg and Gregory Boyd, among others. He has always maintained a certain distance from Søren Kierkegaard and Karl Barth. While acknowledging their immense contributions to the shaping of modern theology, he finds in them a retreat to the upper story of theology—the realm of faith that is somehow separated from the quest of reason. Pinnock as a *bona fide* apologetic theologian posits a basic congruity between faith and reason rather than a disjunction. The question is whether this position leads him to ignore or underplay those aspects of the biblical witness that portray the helplessness and impotence of sinful humanity to come to a right knowledge of God.

A New Venture in Apologetics

Clark Pinnock offers a new venture in apologetics, but it is not wholly new, for it draws on a long apologetic tradition. Just as many of the church fathers, including Augustine, sought to come to terms with the classical worldview so Pinnock seeks to build bridges to the modern worldview.[2] His appeal is not to the law of noncontradiction but to the signs and wonders that form a part of the sacred history mirrored in the Bible.[3] He generally does not try to support the claims of faith by arguing for their logical coherence; rather he bases his case on the credibility of the historical testimony to the faith.[4] Apologetics is valuable in his eyes because it prepares the way for faith and also because it validates the claims of faith. It does not compel people by the rigor of logic to assent to the affirmations of faith, but it makes these affirmations convincing so that they might lead to a meaningful commitment. As he phrases it: 'The intent of Christian apologetics and evidences is not to coerce people to accept the Christian faith, but to make it possible for them to do so intelligently.'[5] Whereas the task of dogmatics is 'to define the content of revealed truth', the task of apologetics 'is to defend its validity'.[6]

Apologetics always seeks for common ground with the adversary of faith, and Pinnock finds this in a respect for evidences. Here one can see his affinity with the Enlightenment, which stressed the empirical and the practical over the abstractions of logic. According to Pinnock apologetics can present 'reasonable probabilities for faith' but not logical proofs. He sides with evidentialism over coherentism, though not discarding the latter completely. He can say that God's existence 'is necessary *logically* because our assumption of order, design, and rationality rests upon it'.[7] He is uncomfortable with the presuppositionalism of Cornelius Van Til and Carl Henry in which we begin with untested metaphysical pre-suppositions and then try to relate these to the testimony of history.[8]

Pinnock is much more at home in correlationism than in existentialism. We do not find God beyond culture and history in a leap of faith, but we

---

2   Clark H. Pinnock, 'From Augustine to Arminius: A Pilgrimage in Theology', in Clark H. Pinnock (ed.), *The Grace of God, the Will of Man: A Case for Arminianism* (Minneapolis: Bethany House Publishers, 1989), p. 27.

3   Pinnock still holds to the law of noncontradiction, but it is not pivotal in his apologetics. Signs, evidences and miracles weigh more heavily in his argument. He regards the resurrection of Christ as the greatest miracle. 'The credibility of that miracle, based upon the historical testimony of eyewitnesses, is very high', Clark H. Pinnock, *Biblical Revelation: The Foundation of Christian Theology* (Chicago: Moody Press, 1971), p. 202.

4   See Clark H. Pinnock, 'Toward a Rational Apologetic Based upon History', *Journal of the Evangelical Theological Society* 11.3 (1968), pp. 147-51. Also see his *Set Forth Your Case*, pp. 44-45.

5   Pinnock, *Set Forth Your Case*, p. 44.

6   Pinnock, *Set Forth Your Case*, p. 3.

7   Pinnock, *Set Forth Your Case*, p. 77.

8   Clark H. Pinnock, *Tracking the Maze: Finding Our Way through Modern Theology from an Evangelical Perspective* (San Francisco: Harper & Row, 1990), pp. 43-48.

discover questions and insights in culture that lead to faith and that corroborate faith. The universe raises the questions of God's existence, and faith provides the answer. The role of the Spirit is to help us 'correlate God's Word with the challenges of our day'.[9]

In his early years he contended that there must be an 'accommodation to the intellectual and spiritual currents of our day'.[10] At the same time he voiced the need for confronting the hybris of the age by revealing the inconsistency and absurdity in non-Christian positions.

Pinnock also acknowledges the pivotal role of the ethical validation of Christian truth claims. He astutely discerns that outsiders will become more open to Christian faith when they see faith in action in works of mercy and charity.[11] This approach remains a minor one for Pinnock and is never developed satisfactorily. Rationalism seems more dominant in his thought than pietism.[12] He is an avowed opponent of fideism.[13]

While firm in his commitment to apologetics, he also recognizes its limitations. We can present cogent arguments for faith, but we cannot create or induce faith. We can 'establish the credible atmosphere in which faith can be born and can grow'.[14] Apologetics at its best is not coercive but provocative. It raises questions that only faith can answer, though faith itself is a gift of God.

Pinnock's embracing of open theism powerfully attests the apologetic motivation that is at work even in his later theology. He believes that a faulty conceptualization of God can be a barrier to faith. 'We cannot believe if we have conceptualized God in existentially repugnant ways. It makes a difference whether God is portrayed as genuinely related to human life or as standing aloof from it and indifferent to human needs.'[15] In the open view Christian theism can become intellectually

---

9 Clark H. Pinnock, *Flame of Love: A Theology of the Holy Spirit* (Downers Grove, IL: InterVarsity Press, 1996), p. 230.

10 Pinnock, *Set Forth Your Case*, p. 90.

11 Pinnock, *Reason Enough: A Case for the Christian Faith* (Downers Grove, IL: InterVarsity Press, 1980), p. 93.

12 Pietism is more conspicuous in his book on the Holy Spirit where he claims that the final authority for faith is charismatic. Pinnock, *Flame of Love*, pp. 232-33.

13 Pinnock regards Karl Barth as the foremost exponent of fideism in the twentieth century, *Biblical Revelation*, p. 42. See also Pinnock, 'Toward a Rational Apologetic Based upon History', pp. 147-51; and his *A Wideness in God's Mercy: The Finality of Jesus Christ in a World of Religions* (Eugene, OR: Wipf and Stock, 1997 [1992]), pp. 136-37, 108.

14 Pinnock, *Reason Enough*, p. 18.

15 Clark H. Pinnock, 'Systematic Theology', in Clark Pinnock, Richard Rice, John Sanders, William Hasker and David Basinger, *The Openness of God: A Biblical Challenge to the Traditional Understanding of God* (Downers Grove, IL: InterVarsity Press, 1994), p. 102.

viable again, deserving of serious consideration.[16] 'The openness model will help us communicate belief in God more intelligibly to people at large and liberate believers to love God more passionately.'[17] The question remains, of course, whether a deity of the limited cognizance and power of open theism will be of interest and appeal to potential believers.

The Fissure in Theology

Paul Tillich pointed to the fissure that has existed in the church almost from the very beginning when he made the helpful distinction between two types of theology—the apologetic and the kerygmatic.[18] It is well to note that Pinnock freely acknowledges a kinship with Tillich in the area of methodology.[19]

I should here like to amplify on this typology, sharing my reflections on what it might imply for the church's witness. Apologetic theology engages in the task of finding a point of contact with the culture so that the claims of faith can be supported by the highest insights of the culture. Kerygmatic theology on the other hand insists that only the Holy Spirit is the point of contact with the unregenerate person and that the Spirit has chosen to act through the preaching of the word of God, though this is not preaching in isolation but related to the life of prayer and service. Apologetic theology seeks to make the tenets of faith palatable to the cultured despisers of religion.[20] Kerygmatic theology by contrast is content to present the claims of faith in the hope that the Spirit will be at work through this presentation convicting of sin and assuring God's mercy to those who repent and believe. Apologetic theology is a mediating theology: its aim is to mediate between Christ and culture, faith and reason, theology and philosophy. Kerygmatic theology is a fortress theology: it remains in the fortress of biblical faith and invites the outsider to come in. Apologetic theology strives to forge links between Christ and culture. It is a bridge-building rather than a bridge-burning theology. For kerygmatic theology the way to combat unbelief is to

---

16   Clark H. Pinnock, *Most Moved Mover: A Theology of God's Openness* (Grand Rapids, MI: Baker, 2001), p. 151.

17   Pinnock, *Most Moved Mover*, p. 9.

18   Paul Tillich, *Systematic Theology* (2 vols; Chicago: University of Chicago Press, 1951), I, pp. 6-8.

19   Pinnock, *Most Moved Mover*, p. 19; *Tracking the Maze,* p. 6; *Biblical Revelation*, p. 123.

20   Friedrich Schleiermacher, *On Religion: Speeches to its Cultured Despisers* (trans. John Oman; New York: Harper & Row, 1958).

preach to unbelief. For apologetic theology we counter unbelief by arguments that reveal the absurdity of unbelief.

Tillich did not develop this typology to any significant extent, but the way he used it clearly had reference to his conflict with Karl Barth, who in the modern age is the pre-eminent exemplar of kerygmatic theology.[21] Barth held that the gospel alone can penetrate the wall of unbelief that prevents the unregenerate person from assenting to the claims of Christian faith. Tillich was convinced that the gospel must be reinforced by a concerted attempt to show how the creative questions of the culture find their answer in the story of salvation in Jesus Christ. Barth's position is that we cannot begin to ask the right questions until our inner eyes have been opened to the right answer.

Both types of theology have noteworthy proponents in the history of the church. Apologetic theology is conspicuous in Justin Martyr, Clement of Alexandria, Augustine, Thomas Aquinas, Joseph Butler, Friedrich Schleiermacher, Ernst Troeltsch, Paul Tillich, Wolfhart Pannenberg and Reinhold Niebuhr.[22] Kerygmatic theology numbers among its protagonists Paul the Apostle, Irenaeus, Luther, Calvin, John Wesley, George Whitefield, Charles H. Spurgeon, P.T. Forsyth, Arthur Cochrane, Karl Barth and Donald Bloesch. Thinkers like Tertullian, Augustine, Pascal, Kierkegaard and Emil Brunner include elements of both types of theology.

Pinnock sometimes appeals to Helmut Thielicke, whose basic thrust is kerygmatic, yet who considers dialogue with the culture necessary in order to delineate the social and intellectual implications of the gospel. In contrast to Pinnock, at least in his earlier phase, Thielicke does not set forth an apologetics in the sense of demonstrating the superiority of the Christian worldview over that of the secularist or humanist. In fact he sternly opposes such a strategy.[23]

In perusing Clark Pinnock's writings I find the apologetic approach much more pervasive than the kerygmatic, though the latter is not absent. It seems that for Pinnock the purpose of the sermon is to persuade rather than to impart information. In our preaching we defend the gospel rather than simply bear witness to it. I see Pinnock close to Augustine who wrote that we must understand in order to believe. Yet Augustine also said: 'We

21   See Donald G. Bloesch, 'Penetrating the World with the Gospel', in Todd E. Johnson (ed.), *The Conviction of Things Not Seen* (Grand Rapids, MI: Brazos Press, 2002), pp. 183-97.

22   See Donald G. Bloesch, *Reinhold Niebuhr's Apologetics* (Eugene, OR: Wipf & Stock Publishers, 2002).

23   See Helmut Thielicke, *Encounter with Spurgeon* (trans. John W. Doberstein; Philadelphia: Fortress Press, 1963); and Ray S. Anderson, 'Evangelical Theology', in David F. Ford (ed.), *The Modern Theologians* (Oxford: Blackwell, 2nd edn, 1997), pp. 487-89.

must believe in order to understand.' He perceived that although we by ourselves can understand the words of the preacher, to hear in these words the transcendent word of God is truly a matter of faith.[24]

Barth has been accused by Emil Brunner of denying all points of contact between faith and culture.[25] Yet Barth would encourage Christians to seek for sociological or purely cultural points of contact with our hearers, since we must learn to speak in their language and relate to their problems. On the other hand, we must avoid trying to find in non-Christian thought a viable basis for building a Christian view of reality. We should be careful not to appeal to a criterion held in common with secular thought; instead we should submit criteria drawn from the culture and human experience to the judgment of the transcendent criterion of the gospel.

Speaking as an open theist Pinnock tells us that he is attracted to such authors as 'Hegel, Pierre Teilhard de Chardin and Whitehead', for 'they make room in their thinking for ideas like change, incarnation and divine suffering'.[26] In the Barthian perspective we may make use of the language and skills of secular philosophy, but we must not try to combine Christian and secular wisdom lest we empty the gospel of its power to convict and persuade (cf. 1 Cor. 1.17). Barth freely drew upon the insights of such eminent thinkers as Plato, Anselm, Kant, Hegel and Kierkegaard, but he never remained with these thinkers in explicating the truth of Christian faith. For Barth the primary goal of theology is not to construct a Christian view of reality (as in philosophical theology) but to herald a definitive message of God's redeeming work in a particular history—that presented in holy Scripture. The danger in the Barthian approach is to give up reaching the lost on the grounds that only Jesus Christ can convert, only his word convicts. The danger in the Tillichian approach is trusting in the strength of our arguments. Furthermore, by following Tillich and his spiritual father Schleiermacher we may lose sight of the fact that sinners are converted not by an apologetic strategy but only by the message of the cross illumined by the Holy Spirit.

---

24   Augustine phrased it this way: 'Understand, in order that thou mayest believe my words; believe, in order that thou mayest understand the word of God', *Sermons* xliii, iii, 4; vii, 9, in Erich Przywara (ed.), *An Augustine Synthesis* (London: Sheed & Ward, 1936), p. 54.

25   See Emil Brunner, 'Nature and Grace', and Karl Barth 'No!', in John Baillie (ed.), *Natural Theology* (trans. Peter Fraenkel; London: Centenary Press, 1946), pp. 15-64 and 65-128.

26   Pinnock, *Most Moved Mover*, p. 142.

The Scripture Principle

As an evangelical theologian Pinnock strongly adheres to the Scripture principle—treating Scripture as the unfailing resource for faith and practice.[27] The question immediately arises whether Scripture is supportive of the apologetic effort. A close reading of relevant Scripture texts suggests that this may not be so. From the biblical perspective faith is not so much the outcome of reason as the catalyst that renews and reshapes reason. Pinnock claims that 'faith is based upon credible evidence which people can recognize as trustworthy in accord with proper criteria for truth'.[28] I contend that this claim is foreign to the biblical ethos. In the scriptural understanding faith rests not on a rational quest for truth but on a divine intervention into history that reveals our quest as a flight from God. We begin not with human experience and then try to reason ourselves to faith, but with a divine revelation that contradicts the claims of autonomous reason. The Psalmist declares:

> Oh send out thy light and thy truth;
>   let them lead me,
> Let them bring me to thy holy hill
>   and to thy dwelling! (Ps. 43.3)

To be sure, reason is not extinguished by faith, but instead converted. In Isaiah 1.18 we read: 'Come now, let us reason together, says the Lord.' Apart from God our reason is in the service of our sinful will. But once we receive the gift of the Holy Spirit we are then enabled to reason rightly concerning the things of God. To enter into a dialogue with God requires that we be 'willing and obedient' (Isa. 1.19). Reason on its own can only lead the unregenerate person deeper into sin. But reason can be a wholesome instrument of the Spirit of God when it is exercised by the regenerate person—the person of faith.

Kierkegaard rediscovered the biblical dictum that there is an infinite qualitative difference between God and humanity (cf. Eccles. 5.2).[29] This difference can be bridged only from the side of God who condescends to our level in Jesus Christ. The discontinuity between God and the human self is made clear in Second Isaiah:

---

27   See Clark H. Pinnock, *The Scripture Principle* (San Francisco: Harper & Row, 1984).

28   Pinnock, *Set Forth Your Case*, p. 3.

29   See Søren Kierkegaard, *The Sickness unto Death* (ed. & trans. Howard V. Hong and Edna H. Hong; Princeton: Princeton University Press, 1980), p. 126. Also see H.V. Martin, *The Wings of Faith* (New York: Philosophical Library, 1951), pp. 64-68; and Pinnock, 'Toward a Rational Apologetic Based upon History', p. 149.

> For my thoughts are not your thoughts,
>   neither are your ways my ways, says the Lord.
> For as the heavens are higher than the earth,
>   so are my ways higher than your ways
>   and my thoughts than your thoughts. (Isa. 55.8-9)

The utter transcendence of God's word over human reason is reaffirmed by Paul: 'O the depth of the riches and wisdom and knowledge of God! How unsearchable are his judgments and how inscrutable his ways!' (Rom. 11.33; cf. Eph. 3.8).

Apologists often point to Paul's ministry in Athens (Acts 17) as a biblical example of how apologetics might reach the unbelieving world. Yet it should be noted that Paul embarked on a different strategy in Corinth, possibly due to the paucity of converts at Athens. In Athens Paul sought to penetrate the world of philosophy; in Corinth he questioned all claims to worldly wisdom, having concluded it is 'through the folly of what we preach' that God acts 'to save those who believe' (1 Cor. 1.21). It is not by the wisdom of the world but through the foolishness of preaching that we bring people into the kingdom (1 Cor. 1.20-21; Rom. 10.17).

We must be careful, however, not to misinterpret Paul's approach in Athens. It could be argued that Paul did preach the gospel in Athens, though he began with the witness of creation, not the word of redemption. Moreover, when he preached about the resurrection of Christ people turned away in disgust. Paul did try to connect with his hearers by pointing to their altar to an unknown God (Acts 17.23). Yet this was surely a sociological, not a theological, point of contact. In all his addresses Paul speaks only of the living God in history, not the solitary god of Greek philosophy. At Athens Paul sought to connect with the culture, not to accommodate to it. His intention was not to set a rational foundation for faith nor build a bridge between faith and unbelief, but to confront unbelief with the claims of faith.

Paul acknowledged in his Athenian address that God created all people so that they might search for him and in searching find him (Acts 17.27). Yet the apostle painfully recognized that because of human sin our searchings become misdirected and actually lead away from the true knowledge of God. In Romans he quotes from Isaiah: 'I have been found by those who did not seek me; I have shown myself to those who did not ask for me' (Rom. 10.20; Isa. 65.1). In the same epistle he cites the Psalmist: 'None is righteous, no, not one; no one understands, no one seeks for God' (Rom. 3.10-11; Ps. 14.1-3; cf. Eccles. 8.17).

Christian thinkers who embrace apologetics often appeal to 1 Peter 3.15: 'Always be prepared to make a defense to any one who calls you to account for the hope that is in you, yet do it with gentleness and reverence.' Yet when we examine this passage in its context it seems that the emphasis is on reaching the natural person with love rather than with reason. What is efficacious is our 'good behavior in Christ', which puts to shame those who oppose us (v. 16). The New Living Translation phrases it this way: 'And if you are asked about your Christian hope, always be ready to explain it. But you must do this in a gentle and respectful way' (vv. 15-16). This text might lend support to an *ad hoc* apologetics, in which we simply give an answer when a challenge to the faith is directed to us. But this is a far cry from an apologetic strategy in which we prepare beforehand how to penetrate the bastions of unbelief. We should be ready to give reasons for our faith, but we cannot reason either ourselves or others into faith.

Apologetic theology, including that of Clark Pinnock, underplays the note of mystery and paradox in faith, which runs through the Bible. Mystery is often reduced to logic in an apologetic theology. Pinnock, for example, argues on the basis of logic that it is impossible to affirm both divine determination and human free will.[30] For Pinnock salvation is worked by the human person cooperating with God (synergism), not by God alone (monergism). The biblical or prophetic view is much closer to the dynamism of Christian faith: it might be described as the mystery of double agency in which God does all but in and through human striving.[31]

Like Francis Schaeffer, Pinnock is staunchly opposed to the Kirke-gaardian view that the object of faith is a paradox to human under-standing. He writes: 'Faith is not believing what you know to be absurd. It is trusting what on excellent testimony appears to be true.'[32] With Edward J. Carnell he describes faith as the 'resting of the heart in the sufficiency of the evidences'.[33] A more solidly scriptural definition would be the following: faith is holding fast to the promises of the living Lord and Savior, Jesus Christ.

Apologetic theology is almost always natural theology, since it begins with human reason and experience and then proceeds to make contact with the divine revelation in the Bible. Pinnock claims that natural theology is 'a preparatory step' toward taking seriously the message of faith.[34] 'Starting where man is, it is our duty to inform him of his

---

30   Pinnock, 'Systematic Theology', pp. 114-15.

31   See my discussion in Donald G. Bloesch, *The Holy Spirit* (Downers Grove, IL: InterVarsity Press, 2000) p. 362; and *The Church* (Downers Grove, IL: InterVarsity Press, 2002) p. 62.

32   Pinnock, *Set Forth Your Case*, p. 49.

33   Pinnock, *Set Forth Your Case*, p. 48.

34   Pinnock, *Reason Enough*, p. 70.

inconsistency, and at the same time both nudge him to the logic of his own position and urge him to the logic of ours.'[35]

It seems that in the biblical perspective arguments for the faith can be helpful to those who already believe, but they are suspect in the eyes of those whose vision is dimmed by unbelief. Thomas Aquinas is often cited by proponents of apologetic theology in support of the apologetic enterprise.[36] Yet it can be shown that Aquinas did not identify the God of rational argument with the God of revelation. One interpreter concludes: 'Aquinas does not regard natural theology as offering proofs for faith, but as offering support for faith from within the context of an existing faith.'[37] Aquinas cautioned against the effort to prove articles of faith by necessary reasons. 'This would belittle the sublimity of the Faith, whose truth exceeds not only human minds but also those of angels; we believe in them only because they are revealed by God.'[38] Thomas did believe that we can prepare the way for faith by arguments that lend support to the existence of a higher power, but he did not confound this higher power with the God of Christian faith.[39] Pinnock complains that Thomas leans too heavily on Greek philosophy in his defense of the impassibility and unchangeability of God.[40] Pinnock's approach is oriented much more toward empirical evidences for the faith than toward human logic (as in Thomas).

Creative Reinterpretation

Pinnock rightly sees that theology consists of more than a mere reaffirmation of old truths. It entails a creative reinterpretation of these truths—one that speaks to contemporary times. Pinnock is a pioneering theologian, and for this I pay tribute to him. What I would want from him is a confession that we do not find the gospel in the contemporary age. We find the gospel in the Bible and then endeavor to relate this discovery to the cultural and religious situation in which we find ourselves.

---

35   Pinnock, *Set Forth Your Case*, pp. 32-33.

36   Evangelicals who confess their indebtedness to Thomas Aquinas include Norman Geisler and R.C. Sproul. Interestingly Pinnock maintains his distance from Aquinas.

37   Alister E. McGrath, *A Scientific Theology* (Grand Rapids, MI: Eerdmans, 2001), I, p. 266.

38   See David B. Burrell, 'From Interfaith Dialogue to Apologetics', *Christian History* 73 (vol. 21.1, 2002), p. 38.

39   Pinnock does not seem to have grasped this dimension of Aquinas—that revelation radically transcends even as it does not negate human reason.

40   Pinnock, *Set Forth Your Case*, p. 75; *Most Moved Mover*, pp. 70-71.

Another place where I stand with Pinnock is in his unswerving commitment to Christian unity. In his book on the Holy Spirit he freely draws upon the Catholic and Orthodox traditions of the church as well as the Protestant.[41] He also treats Pentecostalism seriously and seeks to build bridges to that tradition. Like Gabriel Fackre and me he would willingly call himself an ecumenical evangelical.[42]

Pinnock's principal weakness is that he stands too heavily in the legacy of evangelical rationalism. His theology is anchored more in the Enlightenment with its trust in reason than in the Reformation, which emphasized the limitations of reason. Pinnock adheres not only to a theology of revelation but also to a natural theology in which we begin with human culture and experience and then proceed to the great affirmations of faith. He is sharply critical of what I have called the biblical–classical synthesis, so pervasive in the patristic and medieval traditions; yet he substitutes for this a biblical–modern synthesis where Hegel, Schleiermacher, Tillich, Whitehead and Teilhard de Chardin play a major role.

Pinnock contends that we must undergo a 'radical unmasking' before we are ready to receive the gospel.[43] Here we see an existentialist and perhaps also a pietist component in his theology. The Pietists taught that outsiders must first be brought to the point of despair before they can make the leap of faith. Pinnock endeavors to show unbelievers that their position is a house of cards that speedily collapses under the impact of critical scrutiny. When we realize that what we have pinned our hopes on cannot withstand critical analysis we are then supposedly ready to place our hopes elsewhere. With Karl Barth I believe that we must first hear the gospel before we are ready to follow the law.[44] The conviction of sin does not precede the commitment of faith but forms a part of this commitment.

There are two sides in Pinnock. On the one hand, he is firmly committed to the apologetic task and believes that our witness is truncated unless we give serious attention to the attacks upon the faith from the culture. On the other hand, he perspicaciously discerns the pitfalls in apologetics. He realizes 'how easy it is, in the pursuit of relevance, to lose Christian identity'[45] and admits that 'even the soundest apologetic has no power to make a man a Christian, or coerce a sinner to repent'.[46] He

---

41   See Pinnock, *The Flame of Love*.

42   Interestingly Pinnock dedicated his book *The Scripture Principle* to Gabriel Fackre and me.

43   Pinnock, *Set Forth Your Case*, p. 84.

44   For my position on the law and the gospel, see Donald G. Bloesch, *Jesus Christ: Savior and Lord* (Downers Grove, IL: InterVarsity Press, 1997), pp. 198-209.

45   Pinnock, *Tracking the Maze*, p. 30.

46   Pinnock, *Set Forth Your Case*, p. 7.

draws back from Christian rationalism in his perception that 'it is quite possible that we are dealing, not so much with a failure of intellect, as with a failure of experience, an alienation from the experiential roots of Christianity'.[47]

Pinnock tries to take seriously the Pauline dictum that we must become all things to all people that we might by all means save some (1 Cor. 9.22). As ambassadors of Christ we should not preach at people, but we should try to enter into their situation with a gospel that transcends human reason and culture. Our mandate is to incarnate our message in the cultural context in which we live, but we must not allow the culture to dictate the content of this message.

Part of my problem with Pinnock is that he too often envisions the gospel as a worldview that can be set over against cultural and philosophical worldviews. It would then appear permissible for the Christian to seek to validate this worldview with the tools of cultural wisdom and to invalidate worldviews that conflict with the Christian one. But what if the gospel is not simply a worldview but a new reality that bursts into the human horizon of meaning from the beyond? Our task is then not primarily to remove impediments to human understanding but to bring a message that liberates the human will. There is still a place for reasoning that illumines faith, but the creation of faith rests upon conversion through the power of the Holy Spirit. Pinnock acknowledges that what is required to convert the unregenerate person to Jesus Christ is 'the miracle of regeneration coincident with the presentation of the gospel'.[48] We are here not far apart, but Pinnock's position would be stronger if it were more solidly anchored in a theology of Word and Spirit in which the Spirit speaks not independently of the Word but in and through the Word.[49]

Against popular evangelicalism I contend that the gospel is not a call to decision that brings about salvation, but the gift of salvation that makes human decision inevitable. We are called to believe and accept what has already been done for us in Christ, but our believing does not in and of itself save us. We are saved not by faith as an act of obedience, but by grace working through faith, which itself is a gift of God (Eph. 2.8). From this perspective apologetics follows dogmatics rather than sets the stage for dogmatics.

Pinnock would probably have difficulty with this way of viewing the problem. My position is more Reformed and Pinnock's more

---

47   Pinnock, *Reason Enough*, pp. 48-49.

48   Pinnock, *Set Forth Your Case*, p. 85.

49   I have tried to construct a Word and Spirit theology in Donald G. Bloesch, *A Theology of Word and Spirit* (Downers Grove, IL: InterVarsity Press, 1992). For my approach to apologetics see pp. 212-49.

Arminian.[50] I find the basis for hope in the freedom of God to break down the defenses of sinful humanity. Pinnock trusts in the freedom of humanity to cooperate with the Spirit of God in bringing in the kingdom. From my perspective apologetics has to be radically reconceived if it is to find a place in the theological enterprise. Pinnock might agree that apologetics needs a new role, but not in the way I would propose.

---

50   Pinnock has in recent years become more critical of Arminius, but he still prefers Arminianism over classical Calvinism. Timothy George suggests that of all Reformation figures Pinnock can best be compared with Faustus Socinus, an earnest seeker after truth who united evangelical and rationalist themes. Yet there are wide differences between these two thinkers. Pinnock's forthright affirmation of the Trinity as well as his empathy with the creedal consensus of the early church, particularly in the area of christology, would preclude him from being classified as a Socinian (George would agree). See Timothy George, 'Foreword', in Tony Gray and Christopher Sinkinson (eds), *Reconstructing Theology: A Critical Assessment of the Theology of Clark Pinnock* (Waynesboro, GA: Paternoster Press, 2000), pp. x-xi. I see Pinnock as being closer to Erasmus, who was more eclectic and inclusive than either the mainline Reformers or Arminius. Not surprisingly Pinnock tells us that he prefers Erasmus over Luther and Calvin (*A Wideness in God's Mercy*, pp. 42, 177, 183). In my opinion Pinnock is best understood as a postmodern theist who seeks biblical support for a position that approaches but does not embrace process theology. Pinnock's theology signifies a rapprochement between evangelical Christianity and the philosophy of life, with its roots in the nineteenth century.

CHAPTER 15

Clark Pinnock and Process Theology

John B. Cobb, Jr.

It is a pleasure and an honor to have this opportunity to interact with Clark Pinnock. It is not the case that all theologians, in their relations with one another, display the virtues of which they write in their theology. Pinnock does. On important points he disagrees with process theology. But he does not demean, caricature, or distort the positions with which he disagrees. He expresses appreciation for much of what process theologians say and carefully indicates where and why he disagrees. In other words, he deals with us with the love that he affirms to be central to Christian faith and life. He works with the honesty, respect, and accuracy that love requires. It is my hope that my response as a process theologian will be similarly, and equally, loving.

Actually, I am happy, in this instance, that we can agree to disagree. I believe that we are both called to be apologists for the gospel. I believe we are called to do so in different contexts and that this requires different strategies. I believe that this difference in calling and in audience determines our theological differences rather than any deep disagreement in our understanding of the gospel or of the practical implications of the positions we take.

In what follows I will explain what I mean by the foregoing statements. First, I will rehearse, one more time, our doctrinal differences and the differences in theological methodology that lead to them. Second, I will make my own effort to describe what I take to be the difference in our calling.

Our Theological Differences

I focus on differences in this essay, not because I think they are of primary importance, but, quite the contrary, because I think they are not. However, to say of theological differences that they are not important itself requires justification. Indeed, I suspect that Pinnock and I disagree on this point. It may well be that the differences seem more important to him than they do to me.

Perhaps the central theological difference between us is that Pinnock holds that God has, or could have, all-controlling power. He makes clear, however, that God does not, in fact, exercise that kind of power in relation to the world. Pinnock describes the actual relation of God and the world, especially human beings, in ways that are almost identical with process theology.

Process theologians rejoice in this support. But Pinnock's contribution to the cause goes far beyond this. Process theologians have claimed congruence with scripture for our views. Pinnock has gone much further than any process theologian in amassing the evidence in the Bible for the interactive view of God and human beings that is asserted by both openness theology and process theology.

Nevertheless, for Pinnock it is important to affirm that God has freely chosen to relate to the world in this way. The relation is not inherent in the nature of things. For process theologians, on the other hand, to be actual at all involves possessing power. Hence it is an inescapable part of creation that God share power with creatures. For us, 'omnipotence' is a self-destructive notion.

Now we may ask why Pinnock insists on asserting divine omnipotence. Probably a major reason is the strong support for this doctrine in the tradition. However, on other topics, Pinnock criticizes the tradition and seeks to ground his theology in the scripture. Does Pinnock believe that the doctrine of omnipotence is biblical?

What evidence can we find for that? Some biblical writers seem to have read God's will directly from historical events in a way that implies God's total control, but Pinnock does not appeal to that. On the contrary, he emphasizes the far more numerous passages that indicate that what happens is a result of the divine–human interaction. The idea of omnipotence has certainly been read back into the Bible. This occurred most dramatically when the Septuagint translators substituted 'God Almighty' for the Hebrew *el Shaddai*. This gives the reader of English translations, most of which have followed the Septuagint in this practice, the false impression that biblical writers frequently spoke of God as almighty, especially in Genesis and Job. Pinnock certainly does not trade on this error. Traditionally, a major argument for the view of God's omnipotent freedom in relation to creation has been the reading into the Bible of the idea of creation out of nothing, chiefly in Genesis 1.1. Pinnock knows that this is not what the verse says.

The idea that God has a power God does not ordinarily exercise can be used to explain miracles. For example, in the later tradition many thought that most events can be explained in terms of cause–effect sequences in nature and history, but that there have been occasional events that do not fit this pattern. These show God's omnipotence, that is, God's ability unilaterally to make whatever God chooses happen.

But such a use of the doctrine of God's self-limitation is closed to Pinnock. His theodicy depends on treating the self-limitation of God as irrevocable. If he agreed that God sometimes unilaterally causes events to occur that are contrary to what natural causality would bring about, then he would have to explain why God did not intervene in this way to prevent the Holocaust and other great historical horrors as well as more intimate personal ones.

The idea of God as self-limiting is a recent theory, not clearly taught in either the Bible or the older tradition. So far as I can see, in Pinnock's theology nothing follows from the adoption of this idea. On the other hand, it helps to distinguish openness theology from process theology, thereby making openness theology less offensive to conservative evangelicals. If it is reassuring to them, that may be reason enough for Pinnock to adopt it. In any case, Pinnock likes it, or, perhaps more accurately, he does not like what he takes to be the alternative. 'I cannot accept that God is metaphysically limited.'[1] So far as I am concerned, these are good practical reasons for him to adopt the doctrine of divine self-limitation, since I regard the doctrine as almost harmless.

Nevertheless, I will explain why, as a process theologian, I do not accept this doctrine even though doing so would reduce the opposition to our position. To do so I will describe our methodological differences somewhat differently from the way Pinnock sometimes presents them. One way that Pinnock distinguishes openness theology from process theology is that openness theology turns to the Bible as authority whereas process theology is based on A.N. Whitehead's philosophy. There is a difference between us to which such statements point, but this formulation misrepresents that difference.

The formulation would apply to some process *philosophers*. But to the best of my knowledge all those who identify themselves as Christian process theologians are Christians first, and Whiteheadians, secondarily. We have found Whitehead helpful for our theological work. But we became Whiteheadians because Whitehead helped us to articulate our faith. We did not become Christians because we believed Whitehead's philosophy to be true, although studying his philosophy may have enabled some of us to remain Christian believers when we were troubled by certain traditional doctrines and by the implications of modern thought.

On the other side, it is true that openness theology is not obligated to any pre-given philosophical scheme. Yet Pinnock does not minimize the

---

1   Clark H. Pinnock, *Most Moved Mover: A Theology of God's Openness* (Grand Rapids, MI: Baker Academic, 2001), p. 149.

need to discuss the philosophical issues that the biblical vision raises. He understands that to discuss them philosophically involves some commitment to conceptual clarity and coherence of thought. He is free to develop his own philosophy for this purpose or to borrow from others as long as the results are clear and coherent. Apparently he thinks that he can do this better than philosophers such as Whitehead and Charles Hartshorne have done it or else that the Bible provides clues the development of which conflicts with their schemes.

The question before us now is the relation of divine power and creaturely freedom. But does the Bible provide clues on this relation that are best articulated in a doctrine of divine, voluntary self-limitation? This needs to be shown. Can Pinnock produce a scheme of thought that includes both self-limitation and the other ideas he has found in the Bible and holds up under critical inquiry? If the Bible does not provide reasons for affirming self-limitation, and if, as I believe, this doctrine weakens Pinnock's coherence in other respects, then, as I believe, the pragmatic reasons for its adoption must outweigh the philosophical problems. The disagreement between us on this point, one that Pinnock regards as central to our differences, is not a matter of his being biblical and my being philosophical. The question is, which formulation is better? On rational grounds, quite apart from any appeal to the authority of process philosophers, I believe the choice of process theologians is better. The reason for the other choice is its greater acceptability in the Christian community.

I said that I regard Pinnock's doctrine here as 'almost harmless', but it is not entirely so. It creates problems in two areas. First, there is the old question about what God was doing before the creation of the world. If God is love, then loving relations must have existed always. Pinnock recognizes this logic. A popular answer in recent years has been the appeal to the Trinity. Before there was anything else to love, the members of the Trinity loved one another. Here the appeal is not to the Bible but to later doctrinal formulations. But let us suppose it can be argued that these are indirectly based on the Bible. What, then, is the problem?

The problem is the interpretation of the Trinity required in order that the theory make sense. What we understand by love in this context, whether human or divine, requires an otherness of the lover and the one loved. Otherwise we call it self-love, and, though this is also important, it is not the love Pinnock believes to be revealed as the essential character of God. This means that we must understand the love among the members of the Trinity as analogous to the love between distinct creatures or God and creatures. For this doctrine to work, God must be understood as everlastingly three persons in the modern sense of 'person'. That way lies tri-theism. If the theologian then warns against a tri-theistic interpretation, insisting that there is only one God and that the relations are within that one God, then the kind of love that is revealed as the essential nature of God is not the sort of love that we believe God has for us.

The solution can be to tell us this is a paradox and mystery. Well and good. But if one is trying to make the Christian faith plausible and convincing, the appeal to paradox and mystery at this crucial point is a disadvantage. That there is such a disadvantage does not entail that the doctrine is wrong. It simply cuts against the pragmatic reasons for affirming it.

The second disadvantage is one Pinnock recognizes. It has to do with the problem of evil. Pinnock's understanding, shared with process thought, that what happens in the world is a product of the interaction of God and creatures provides him a way of greatly easing the problem of evil. To the question 'Why did God do that?', the answer is that it happened more because of natural causes or human decisions than because of God's direct agency. The problem arises in answer to the second question. Why did not God prevent this evil from occurring? Here Pinnock's answer is that God is everlastingly committed to God's self-limitation, which prevents God from exercising the power involved in such prevention of evil. Again, well and good.

But there is a third question. Why did God commit Godself so totally to this self-limitation? The self-limitation was out of love and for the sake of human freedom. But when the human freedom of a few is employed to destroy the freedom and lives of myriads of others, why does not God intervene to stop this? Is the answer for Pinnock that such an intervention would do more harm than good? Is that convincing to him? It is not to me, and I think Pinnock is himself not entirely comfortable with this answer. He writes: 'I am forced to say that God has made a commitment to the creation project that constrains His actions.'[2]

My point is that the doctrine of God's self-limitation, employed to show that the limitation is voluntary rather than metaphysical, does lead to consequences that can be harmful. It drives in one direction to the appeal to mystery to answer a fairly straightforward question. That does not help to make Christian truth accessible. In the other direction, it attributes to God at least one act that does not conform to the love that is said to be God's essence.

Pinnock rightly points out that the reasons many Calvinist evangelicals reject his position is not that it is unbiblical but that it does not conform to well-established features of the tradition. Is it possible that this is also Pinnock's reason for not accepting process theology? Of course, that does not make the rejection invalid in either case. Commitment to tradition is an understandable position. But when one picks and chooses

---

2   Pinnock, *Most Moved Mover*, p. 149.

which parts of the tradition to cling to, it may be well to give some explanation of one's choices.

I suspect that one reason for Pinnock's personal inability to accept the process view lies in the way he has formulated it. He thinks that process theology affirms that God is metaphysically limited. The connotation is that God might have been greater in some way than in actuality God is. In short, it implies that God is less than perfect.

This is not the way the process doctrine is normally formulated by its proponents. For Hartshorne, for example, God's very existence follows from God's perfection. That is, the argument for the existence of God is the argument that perfection exists. But the formulation is common among the opponents of process theology. It derives from that Calvinist ethos from which the severest critics of Pinnock also come.

Behind this formulation, that God is metaphysically limited, lies the assumption that power is the ability to control and determine what happens. If that is the understanding, then if anything other than God has any independent effect on what happens, God's power is thereby limited. To avoid saying that God's power is inherently and necessarily limited by creatures, one must say either that there could be creatures that had no independent power at all or there was once a situation in which there were no creatures. In the former case, we are using the word 'creature' in a very questionable way. What would a creature be that had no power at all? Plato tells us that being is power. These 'creatures' would have no being! What is gained theologically by such speculations?

The other choice is to say that there was when nothing besides God existed. Then God had all the power there was. But what sort of power is that? If the power we are considering is the ability to control and determine what happens, then God is exercising power over nothing, that is, exercising no power at all. God may then have all the power there is, but this remains zero power. We are only saying that God could control and determine what happens if there were anything to happen. But for something to happen requires that there be temporal creatures, and for them to exist requires that they have some power. Creation then can be said to 'limit' God's power by its very nature. But it is only through creation that God's power becomes actual.

Is this 'metaphysical limitation' in any way demeaning of God? Process theologians do not see it that way. The greater the power of creatures, the greater is the power of God exercised in and through them.

But this is not the main point of the process doctrine of God's power. The main point is that the revelation of God's love is also a revelation of the nature of God's power. Divine power is not the power to control and destroy, a power that reduces the power of that on which it is exercised. It is the power to empower, to enliven, and to liberate. The more effectively God's power is exercised, the more powerful, alive, and free are the creatures affected by it. The idea of God having all the power makes no sense when power is understood relationally. The more God empowers creatures, the more powerful is God.

This is the kind of power primarily exercised by Jesus. It is the kind of power we are called to exercise as well. We process theologians believe this is the teaching of the Bible, particularly in the New Testament. We do not think we are appealing to the authority of a philosopher instead of the Bible, although we are grateful to the philosophers who have helped us to grasp what so many theologians have neglected or ignored. Too often the church has attributed to God the power revealed in Caesar instead of the power revealed in Jesus.

Some process theologians, notably Schubert Ogden, have chosen to redefine 'omnipotence' instead of opposing it. Since the idea of omnipotence as having all the power there is leads to absurdities, we may rethink the term as meaning having all the power that any one entity can have. If we combine that with a rethinking of the very nature of power, then process theologians can assert that we do in fact affirm God's 'omnipotence'.

This is analogous to the way most of us deal with omniscience. God, we assert, knows all that is to be known. But with respect to future human actions, this is knowledge of the probability that events of particular sorts will occur, not knowledge that one or another such event will in fact occur. In other words, God knows what is fact as fact, what may be as what may be. To 'know' as fact what is not fact but only possibility would not be true knowledge.

The choice between rejecting divine 'omnipotence' and redefining it is a practical one. If we want to retain the language of the church while helping people to find meanings in it that make sense, we should redefine. If, on the other hand, we judge that the harmful connotations of the word are too deep to be uprooted in this way and that direct confrontation is needed, we allow its present meanings to stand and reject the concept. God has, then, 'ideal' or 'perfect' power but not 'all' power as the term 'omnipotence' implies.

Now it may be that Pinnock cannot accept this, and if he cannot, he cannot. But I continue to believe that it is good Christian teaching all the same. To me it seems far more central to the gospel than any speculation about what God could do, but has chosen not to do.

The Difference of our Calling

I have made it clear by my arguments that I am not indifferent to the theological issues between us. But I have also emphasized that, in the wider scheme of things, I do not consider them very important. When

Pinnock sums up 'The Existential Fit' nothing that he says differentiates the effects of openness theology from those of process theology. In other words, 'where the rubber hits the road' only our commonality matters.

Why then do we both direct so much attention to our differences? Partly it is that theologians want to be as careful as possible in their formulations, and this care seems most important where something is controversial. We do not need to give so much attention to our agreements. Partly it is because, even if the differences do not affect the main impact of our theologies, they do have some importance to us personally and potentially for our hearers. Partly it is because in the communities to which we are called to work, there are needs and boundaries that must be respected. It is this feature of our differences to which I want to turn attention.

Both Pinnock and I are apologists. That does not mean that either of us really expects to reach many of those who are fully outside the faith and to draw them into it. We would be very pleased if that happened, and perhaps it does occasionally. But that is not the main audience for either of us.

In both cases, I suspect, an important part of the audience is ourselves. We want to formulate the faith in a way that makes sense to us. If we cannot do that, we are unlikely to be of much help to others. But we have in mind those others also. At different times we have addressed somewhat different audiences, but I will make a stab at identifying what is probably primary in the two cases.

My apologetic is addressed primarily to persons in the old-line churches who do not feel comfortable simply repeating traditional formulations and who have been made unsure of the truth of the faith by their encounter with modernity. I address also those who have moved to the fringes of the church or have given up on the church altogether. These people have reacted in various ways against what they take to be the Christian tradition. Often they have caricatured that tradition, perhaps because it has been presented to them in distorted form. They have not given up on Christianity altogether, but they are quite sure that they will not believe anything simply because it is said to be traditional or biblical. They are determined to be free from that kind of fideism or authoritarianism. The ideas presented as Christian must be convincing on their own terms.

Furthermore, although they think Christianity teaches that those who are not Christian are damned or unsaved or at least inferior in some way, they refuse to believe that. They have engaged with persons of other faiths and are sure that these people deserve respect. They want to know whether one can be a Christian without any of this exclusivism.

Similarly, they are inclined to think that Christianity is incompatible with our best scientific knowledge. They have no intention of being drawn into a battle against science. They can be Christian only if that allows them to treat science as authoritative in its own domain.

They also are likely to identify Christianity with moralistic teachings, especially about sexuality. They have outgrown that moralism. They are repelled by anything that seems to try to re-impose it on them. They are sensitive to any teaching that demeans human beings by emphasizing their sinfulness. They associate this emphasis with self-rejection and the guilt trips that they know to be damaging.

Some of these people are pillars of their local congregations. Some have long since stopped attending. Both, in my view, need help. Their honesty and unwillingness to be drawn back into authoritarian, exclusivist, and moralistic teaching are admirable. Often they are alienated from traditional language, even very basic traditional language, such as 'God', 'Christ' and 'sin'. Their tendency is to solve the problem, if at all, by emphasizing what one does not believe and having very little left. Sometimes it seems that their struggling with their inherited faith takes the form of peeling the onion. Sometimes they stop short, somewhat arbitrarily, of the final steps. I am convinced there is a better way and I have hoped to show that in my writings.

At the same time that I try to write for people like this, I have in mind also a situation in the church where some, observing what happens among those who progressively simplify their belief system, call for renewal of the full range of traditional affirmations. I know that those who are committed to this strategy cannot hear me. But there are also many who are attracted to it out of distress at what they see to be the alternative. I am deeply concerned that these people recognize that there are other options. Otherwise, they are forced to participate in the further deepening of the division within the church between traditionalists and radicals.

I have personally found in process theology an effective alternative. It neither peels the onion nor reaffirms the tradition. It provides a way of understanding the gospel that is rich in meaning for our individual and collective lives without asking us to surrender the intellect, accept things on pure authority, return to moralism or exclusivism, or minimize the value and truth of the sciences. It also provides a clear Christian perspective from which to appraise what is going on in the world and propose alternatives. In my judgment, this is good news.

For this good news to be heard and trusted by those who have reacted against their earlier understanding of the faith, the difference must be made clear. Making this clear requires emphasizing that the scriptures are human, fallible documents, that there is much that is confused, erroneous, and harmful in the church's historic teaching; that there is no possibility of arriving at final truth, that the depths of feeling against much of what they reject in the tradition, and often in their upbringing in the church, are justified. As long as what one says sounds as though it is calling people back into the system they have rejected, it cannot be heard. But I also feel the need to show that peeling the onion will not bring us closer to the truth.

In contemporary language, I find it important to assure my hearers that I share their necessary deconstruction of what they have received. Only so can I communicate that there is a quite different way of approaching matters that is not preoccupied with deconstruction but focuses on reconstruction. Of course, I am not always successful, but I think a few have benefited from this kind of wholesale setting aside and beginning again. I hope so.

For me and for many, the primary issue is God. Christianity without God does not make much sense, but many people have come to find what the word 'God' connotes to them both repressive and incredible. It is repressive because it is so closely associated with 'thou shalt' and 'thou shalt not'. This is a matter both of belief and practice. Many have felt guilty about their doubts as well as about their sexuality. Talk of God is bound up with that.

Talk of God is incredible to them because, as they understand God, it leads to expectations about prayer and about justice that are not fulfilled. If they were fulfilled, belief in God would be in conflict with scientific thought. In any case, it assumes a sphere or dimension for whose reality experience and science appear to give no evidence.

Many are quite sure, therefore, that what the word 'God' earlier meant to them has no reality outside the realm of language and imagery. But they are not sure that they can get along altogether without some way of referring to what is other than and more than themselves. Some prefer more neutral language such as 'Ultimate Reality' or 'Being'. The language of 'Spirit' attracts some. Others like the mystical language of 'Nothingness' or the Buddhist talk of 'Emptiness'. Some are prepared to talk about the Goddess. And, of course, many still speak of 'God'. There is no consensus in the spiritual quest of hungry, open-minded people who find traditional Christian ways of speaking of God unconvincing or worse.

To gain a hearing in this context, it is important to emphasize the novelty of the way of speaking of God that one offers. This novelty need not be affirmed in a radical sense. It is novel in relation to the views that have been rejected and are now under discussion. I usually claim that it harks back to the way Jesus revealed God. I point out that if we think of God this way, then God is an actual factor in our lives. But what is at work is a persuasive and empowering influence that has little to do with the controlling and moralistic God my audience has rejected. The language of Spirit is realistic. Prayer makes sense. We can then consider what God or the Spirit is doing in other cultures and traditions.

To the question of biblical authority and the uses of the tradition I would come only later. Once people see that the message of the Bible makes sense and is the source of rich insights, they can consider again the issues of inspiration and revelation. If I begin with them, then it sounds to people of this sort that one wants to make them accept something on the basis of an arbitrary authority.

This is more than enough. I am simply trying to indicate that apologetics in this context requires initially separating what one has to offer from what the hearers have experienced as the tradition, including the scriptures. Subsequently, one can re-think the connections. The lack of emphasis on scriptural authority and revelation, which so disturbs many evangelicals when they encounter process theology, has its apologetic purpose.

Now let me hazard my impression of the community to which Pinnock addresses himself. It is composed of evangelicals many of whom identify themselves as conservative. Their churches have not felt the impact of liberal theology in their interior life. They are to be understood more as heirs of the earlier evangelical theology that fell out of favor in the seminaries of the mainline churches in the latter part of the nineteenth century. Indeed, they come from denominations, or segments of denominations, that watched the development of liberal theologies and their impact on the churches with some horror. They emphasize faithfulness to scripture as the antidote to this decline.

Despite the great emphasis on scripture, in fact they were deeply influenced by the tradition in their interpretation of scripture and in the theologies they developed from it. Some stood in the Wesleyan tradition; more, in the Calvinist. To some degree they engaged the liberals, but they did so from assumptions the liberals did not share. Their own evangelical teaching was little affected by critical historical biblical scholarship, the study of the history of religions, the incorporation of scientific thought, and in more recent times, repentance for anti-Judaism and patriarchy. They have not yet been much involved in efforts to rethink Christianity so as to make Christians more sensitive to the Earth. The standard evangelical teaching retained the idea of the exclusivity of salvation and the need to convert others to the faith.

Nevertheless, the questions that had been introduced by various forms of liberal and liberationist theology were not wholly silenced. Some rigidified the inherited doctrines in order to avoid any slippage into liberalism. Others became uncomfortable with these rigid formulations. They appreciated the vitality and fervor of evangelical communities, but did not want to be committed to teachings that seemed harsh and rejecting of others. When they heard liberal criticism of traditional doctrines and their current adherents, they felt some resonance of truth but also an element of unfairness. The critics missed the authentic faith and deep personal commitment that characterized the evangelical communities.

Pinnock, I think, addresses evangelicals who have felt uncomfortable with some of the doctrines to which they suppose they should be committed. They have feared that rejecting those doctrines will lead them away from the true biblical faith. Pinnock shows that often those unattractive doctrines are in fact not found in the Bible, that the teachings of the Bible itself have a quite different character and can be affirmed enthusiastically.

Showing this sometimes involves rejecting elements of the tradition that are in opposition to scripture. Evangelical culture allows for that. But evangelicals prefer not to jettison tradition. The more traditional they can remain, in faithfulness to scripture and to their own current sensibility, the better. Pinnock responds to this preference and need.

The conservative evangelicals addressed by Pinnock are not committed to strict doctrines of biblical inerrancy, but they are committed to the authority of the Bible. It is biblical teaching that will guide them, and the conviction that ideas are biblical gives them authority. Pinnock speaks from that context to those who share it. His concern is to free his evangelical hearers from those aspects of the message they have heard that have in fact become bad news for them. In their place he sets the good news that is truly the gospel.

I believe that each of us is called to bring the gospel to troubled people. But the people we address are at very different places. My way of performing my task may have limited success with anyone, but it certainly is not effective among those for whom Pinnock writes. It does not reassure its readers that what is being said is the true meaning of scripture. It is cavalier with regard to authority in general. It initially presents ideas on their own merits rather than as responsibly Christian. All this can only confirm the worst fears of evangelicals about 'liberals'. It cannot get a hearing for the message.

But similarly Pinnock's approach will not speak well to those who have moved so far away from traditional doctrine. They will hear it as calling them back part way into the bondage from which they have extricated themselves. They will appreciate the fresh and more positive reading of the scriptures, but they will wonder whether Pinnock has wrestled with the intellectual problems involved in speaking of God as something more than a term in religious language. They will note that he still uses masculine language about God and says little about the church's need to repent for its massive historical sins. He is unlikely to get through to them.

In the context in which I am speaking, I sometimes tell people that I do not like the doctrine of creation out of nothing and prefer to speak of continuing creation instead. That expresses the freedom from authority that is important to gain a hearing. I then say that it seems that physics is returning us to something more like creation out of nothing. If so we must adjust our Christian teaching to take account of it. This emphasizes the importance of taking science seriously and being open to change theology, including that influenced by Whitehead's philosophy, if the evidence warrants. I indicate that the Bible can be read either way. I then express doubts about how much difference that makes with respect to our understanding of the gospel. This would be very poor strategy among evangelicals. On the other hand, clinging to a doctrine of divine omnipotence through positing the voluntary self-limitation of God would seem, to many I address, to express bondage to out-dated and harmful doctrines.

So, is one of us correct and the other wrong? Perhaps in some ultimate metaphysical sense the answer is Yes. Or, more probably, in any such ultimate sense, we are both wrong. We are grappling with questions beyond our ability truly to answer. I will continue to think that my answer is more coherent and adequate to what facts we know. Pinnock will find that it does not speak to him and, in any case, would not help him to communicate to his audience. The real answer is that only God knows!

But the kind of 'correctness' that really matters here is whether the gospel is made real to people. I have no doubt that Pinnock communicates the gospel to many in the evangelical community. I feel quite sure that he is more successful in reaching his audience than I am in reaching the one for which I write. But that is also an audience that needs the gospel and for which some of us are called to write. I hope that, for some, what I have written has been 'good news'. I am sustained by that hope.

At this juncture we do best to go our separate ways. Process theology will not help Pinnock in his task beyond what he has already appropriated from it. Indeed, I suspect that he pays a high price in the evangelical community for his honesty in recognizing his debt to process thinkers and his friendship with process theologians. I appreciate his willingness to pay that price rather than to deny our commonalities.

I am deeply grateful for the refreshing biblical study that is done by openness theologians. On the other hand, I cannot appropriate for my task what is different in their doctrines. If I identified too closely with 'evangelicals' in the current ecclesiastic situation, I would lose what credibility I have in some other circles. The most I can do is to assure people, whose image of evangelicals is formed by extremist and unattractive representatives, that among evangelicals there are many open persons who are seeking to understand God just as honestly as any in the liberal tradition. I can testify to the wonderful spirit and dedication of many of these people.

Friendship and appreciation may be what is primarily called for now. But there is more. The awareness of the theoretical convergence of two schools, coming out of very different contexts, can be confirmatory for both of us as we seek to change the way the Bible is read and the tradition is understood. Further, there may, in the longer run, be possibilities for new alignments in the church cutting across the worn out distinction between conservatives and liberals. Perhaps new distinctions will supersede the old, distinctions that deal with how we understand God and God's relation to us. On one side, then, may be those who seriously believe in the living God known as love in Jesus Christ, interacting with creatures in individual lives and in historical processes. On the other side, may be those who see God related to us only in forensic justification of those predestined to salvation and in occasional supernatural interventions. Those are certainly not the only options, but they constitute significant alternative interpretations of the Christian faith. The difference between them is spiritually important.

CHAPTER 16

The Three-fold Sense of Scripture: An Evangelical Grammar for Theological Hermeneutics

Alan G. Padgett

It is my pleasure to contribute this chapter to a book in honor of Clark Pinnock, a man from whom I have learned so much over the years. Pinnock has been a friend in Christ, and also a teacher by means of his many theological works. I have long been a fan of his writing; I remember how much I enjoyed and learned from his book *The Scripture Principle*. That book is an excellent defense of the authority of scripture, and of the Christian use of critical historical methods in its interpretation.[1] The present chapter is something of a continuation of that book, especially the last chapter ('The Act of Interpretation'). In particular, it is my exploration of Pinnock's question at the beginning: 'How can readers engage the text so that they can have God speak to them through it?'[2] My question here is slightly different: 'How can the church engage the Bible so that it can function as the Word of God for us today?'

Pinnock is a model of thoughtful, clear and learned evangelical scholarship. He is open-minded in the best sense, gracious and thoughtful, yet constantly drawn to the biblical witness. He is not afraid of new ideas, nor of exploring the height and breadth of gospel truth. This chapter likewise is an exploration: a tentative suggestion about how we might learn to read the Bible as God's Word in the light of contemporary science and critical history. In other words, my proposal is about

---

1   It is characteristic of fundamentalism and other very conservative Christian groups that they reject the use of historical-critical methods in theology. I believe with Pinnock that such methods are useful, when put in their proper place by the gospel. Determining that place is the focus of this chapter.
2   C.H. Pinnock, *The Scripture Principle* (San Francisco: Harper & Row, 1984), p. vi.

Christian theological hermeneutics. There has been a great deal of discussion about a 'canonical' approach to biblical theology, since the publication of B.S. Childs' stimulating work, *Biblical Theology in Crisis*.[3] For this reason, we must be very clear: I am not here writing about the methods of 'Old Testament theology' or other descriptive, historical and/or literary approaches. A clear and important distinction must be made between a faithful and Christian approach to academic biblical studies, and the theological and spiritual interpretation of the Bible by the community of faith.[4] My approach here is from faith to faith, and concerns the fully theological understanding of the Bible for the Christian community, which presumes already faith in Jesus Christ, namely, Christian theological hermeneutics.[5]

Unlike some evangelical or post-liberal theologians, I believe that the historical and academic approach to the Bible is a permanent contribution of the Enlightenment to the Christian faith.[6] We want to appreciate the Bible for what it is, and that means taking seriously the human character of the Bible and its authors. Patient and scholarly work over generations within the academy has provided all of us with a far better understanding of the nature, origin, and background of the various biblical writings. The problem is this: however much we honor the guild of biblical scholarship, however much we have learned over the years thanks to their efforts, the church has very different aims and purposes in reading the Holy Bible. These differing aims and purposes put biblical scholars in conflict with ordinary believers, for difference in purpose produces difference in method.

For example, a pop-artist may approach a can of soup in a very different way than a hungry human being. For the artist, the 'meaning' of the can of soup is cultural and aesthetic (or perhaps, anti-aesthetic or even de-humanizing). Hungry people approach the same can of soup

---

3   Philadelphia: Westminster Press, 1970.

4   In a vast sea of literature, one clear proposal on how the Bible should be used in Christian theology is G. O'Collins and D. Kendall, *The Bible for Theology* (New York: Paulist Press, 1997). For a more developed approach, see Francis Watson, *Text, Church and World* (Edinburgh: T. & T. Clark, 1994), and *Text and Truth* (Edinburgh: T. & T. Clark, 1997). For a collection of essays which discusses the divide between systematic and biblical theology, see Joel B. Green and Max Turner (eds), *Between Two Horizons: Spanning New Testaments Studies and Systematic Theology* (Grand Rapids, MI: Eerdmans, 2000). My concern here is the use of the Bible by the believing community, which would also include the use of the Bible in Christian doctrine.

5   As Robert Wall, 'Reading the Bible from Within our Traditions', in Green and Turner (eds), *Between Two Horizons*, p. 91, correctly notes, 'the most crucial move theological hermeneutics must make is to recover Scripture for its use in Christian worship and formation'.

6   Francis Watson, *Text and Truth*, pp. 33-63, rightly warns against the 'eclipse of history' in the work of some postliberal and/or narrative theologians

with very different goals and purposes. The can of soup has a very different meaning for them. This difference in meaning is a result of different aims and goals for the same thing.

My own study of the sciences has convinced me that not only meaning, but also method, follows the aim and purpose of an academic discipline. As Aristotle once remarked, 'clearly, it is equally foolish to accept probable reasoning from the mathematician and to demand scientific proof from a rhetorician'.[7] That methods mirror aims is the conclusion of several important philosophers of science in the last century. They have helped to over-turn the rationalist dream of an 'exact scientific methodology' which would overcome all ambiguity, be used in every discipline worthy of the name, and present us with a unified system of Nature.[8] The rationalistic dream of there being one and only one 'right' way to read the Bible must be resisted by thoughtful Christians who value the love/knowledge of God above all things. The Christian community, with its goals of worship, discipleship and witness, has very different aims from the academic community of the Bible scholar. Even when exactly the same person participates in these different communities, they will have different goals and methods to follow in each group. The Christian community, as a spiritual fellowship in search of the truth as it is in Jesus (Eph. 4.21) can and will adopt different methods for its purposes in Bible study.

Precisely because it is a spiritual fellowship that seeks the love of God and neighbor, the church will be interested in what we might call a 'spiritual' reading of the scriptures. As far back as there has been a Christian theology, the church has insisted upon some kind of spiritual meaning of the biblical text which goes beyond the literal or historical meaning. Even those faithful theologians who complained against the excesses of allegory, such as Diodore of Tarsus and Martin Luther, used a fuller sense or spiritual interpretation of the text.[9] There are sound theological reasons for this. While I may not go as far as David Steinmetz, who argued for the 'superiority' of pre-critical exegesis, there are serious

---

7   Aristotle, *Nicomachean Ethics* 1.13 (1094B).

8   Particularly important in this regard was the work of Pierre Duhem, *The Aim and Structure of Physical Theory* (New York: Atheneum, 1981 [1906]); N.R. Hanson, *Patterns of Discovery* (Cambridge: Cambridge University Press, 1958); Michael Polanyi, *Personal Knowledge* (Chicago: University of Chicago Press, 1962); and Thomas Kuhn, *The Structure of Scientific Revolutions* (Chicago: University of Chicago Press, 1970). See further A.G. Padgett, *Science and the Study of God* (Grand Rapids, MI: Eerdmans, 2003), where I elaborate upon this basic idea and its importance for the dialogue between theology and science.

9   Diodore and Luther will be discussed and cited later in this chapter.

limitations to the historical-critical method.[10] In his wonderful historical overview of the allegorical interpretation of scripture, Henri de Lubac also provides a kind of *apologia* for the continuation of a spiritual sense today.[11] Surely he is right about this need. But what shape shall such a spiritual reading take? How can we honor the critical insights of historical methods, while at the same time doing justice to the spiritual and theological aims of the church? In this chapter, I will present a three-fold proposal for a Christian theological hermeneutics today, based upon the idea that the Bible presents us with gospel truth, providing a space for our relationship with God. I will suggest an approach that is grounded in the good news about Jesus Christ, and our on-going relationship with him. The three levels of meaning for our evangelical grammar of theological hermeneutics are the conventional, canonical, and contemporary senses.

The main problem with the allegorical methods of old is the lack of control. Basil the Great complained that those who engage in allegorical excess 'believe themselves wiser than the Holy Spirit, and to bring forth their own ideas under a pretext of exegesis'.[12] Centuries later, Martin Luther would also complain about the excesses of allegorical interpretation. Like the other Christian humanists and reformers of the sixteenth century, Luther preferred the literal or historical meaning of the text. The literal meaning gave greater authority to the historical, original text. This was very important to a movement that insisted upon scripture alone as the authority upon which the church must be reformed.

It was excesses of allegory and the need for some kind of limit to imagination in textual interpretation which gave the spiritual sense of scripture a bad name. Even though modern scholars continue to steer clear of allegory, I believe that the evangel itself demands a fuller sense to scripture beyond the ordinary or plain meaning of the text. At the same time, we will still need some kind of control or limit to our theological interpretation, in order to avoid eisegesis. Finding a way between these two problems is a pressing need today.

The gospel itself demands a spiritual reading of the scriptures. The church of Jesus Christ cannot be content merely with an historical-literal reading of the text. Why not? If the claims we make about Jesus at the heart of the gospel are true, then we can no longer approach the Bible in the same old way. Jesus is the Messiah, the Christ. The church proclaims

---

10   D.C. Steinmetz, 'The Superiority of Pre-Critical Exegesis,' *Theology Today* 37 (1980), pp. 27-38; reprinted in Donald McKim (ed.), *A Guide to Contemporary Hermeneutics* (Grand Rapids, MI: Eerdmans, 1986).

11   Henri de Lubac, *Medieval Exegesis* (trans. M. Sebanc and E.M. Macierowski; 2 vols; Grand Rapids, MI: Eerdmans, 1998–2000). See, e.g., I, pp. 234-41.

12   Basil the Great, 'Hexaemeron' homily 9, in P. Schaff and H. Wace (eds), *Nicene and Post-Nicene Fathers*, second series (Peabody, MA: Hendrickson, 1994 [1894]), VIII, p. 102. I owe this quotation to Christopher Hall.

that he is also the Savior of the world, and the Word of God made flesh. If these basic gospel truths are in fact true, then we need to re-interpret the entire scripture of Israel. If Jesus is really Savior, Incarnate Word, and Messiah, then the whole of the Hebrew Bible needs to be read in a new light, in the light of Christ. This is what the apostles themselves did, probably following the practice of their Lord (e.g., Luke 4.16-22).[13]

The facts of the gospel are the basis of the canon of scripture. The Old Testament is the Bible of Jesus and the earliest Christians. The Father of our Lord Jesus Christ is the Holy One of Israel, the God of the Old Testament. While some early Christian heretics, like Marcion, rejected this identity, the identification of the God of Israel with the Father of our Lord Jesus Christ lies at the heart of the claim that Jesus is the Messiah of Israel. Jesus really is the Christ, the Messiah of Israel, and therefore his Father is the God of Israel. At the same time, the books of the New Testament look back to the life and teachings of Jesus, and help us to re-read the Old Testament in the light of the Messiah. These books were accepted by the community of faith as providing authentic witness to their risen Savior. To accept the Bible as a single book, then, is already a statement of faith in Jesus.[14]

It is a clear implication of the gospel that we read the biblical books together, as a unity. If we consider each text in isolation, however, this canonical reading cannot take place. The historical-critical method is rightly committed to reading these texts in their larger cultural, literary and historical contexts. For this reason, the academy *per se* is not committed to the unity of the biblical canon.[15] Rather, academics will study the Bible just like any other ancient book. This must be true even of faithful, believing academics. This issue is not about the individual, but rather about the aims, purposes and methods of the discipline involved. One might say that it has to do with the character of the truth-seeking

---

13 On the historical character of this passage, see I.H. Marshall, *Commentary on Luke* (New International Greek Testament Commentary; Grand Rapids, MI: Eerdmans, 1978), pp. 178-80; John Nolland, *Luke 1–9:20* (WBC, 35A; Dallas, TX: Word, 1989), pp. 192-95.

14 So rightly B.S. Childs, *Biblical Theology of the Old and New Testaments* (Minneapolis: Fortress Press, 1992), p. 80: 'Although the church adopted from the synagogue a concept of scripture as an authoritative collection of sacred writings, its basic stance toward its canon was shaped by its christology. The authority assigned to the apostolic witnesses derived from their unique testimony to the life, death and resurrection of Jesus Christ.'

15 Philip R. Davies, in his recent book *Whose Bible is it Anyway?* (Sheffield: Sheffield Academic Press, 1995), p. 16, goes so far as to proclaim the biblical canon to be 'one of the greatest idols of modern times'—an explicitly anti-Christian remark. Thus, his book is not merely 'non-confessional' as he claims, but actually anti-confessional.

community we are involved with. Both the guild of historical scholarship and the church of Jesus Christ are truth-seeking communities. The truth they seek, however, and the methods they employ are quite distinct.

Because we accept the authority of scripture, the church is committed to the authority of the text. We must let the text speak to us in all its difference, otherness, and historical distance. Only in this way can we respect the authority of the text, and allow it to be used of God to speak afresh in our time. For this and other reasons, Christian theologians have long insisted upon the priority of the historical or literal meaning of the text. I will call this first and primary sense of scripture the 'conventional meaning'. I mean by this what some scholars call the plain meaning of the text, and what others designate as the authorial intention of the text, the historical or literal meaning. These alternative terms have their problems, however.

I prefer 'conventional meaning' to the various alternatives because it is less likely to be confusing. If all we mean by 'authorial intention' is the public character and observable structure of the signs themselves, situated in the community and form-of-life in which they arose and make sense, then this terminology is acceptable.[16] However, many who reject the author's intention as having any importance for hermeneutics understand 'intention' to be an inner, psychological state. As such, intention cannot be recovered by historical and philological research. Because of possible misunderstanding, therefore, I will avoid talking about authorial intention. The terms 'historical sense', while of great antiquity in Christian theology, might suggest that all the biblical texts are history. Of course this is not the case. Likewise the term 'literal' is contrasted with metaphorical, figurative, or poetical literature. Since the Bible contains a great deal of figurative literature, to speak of the literal sense of biblical texts will often be confusing. Finally, 'plain' sense suggests that the alternative is some complex or fancy sense, which is not at all the case. I have therefore decided to use the word 'conventional' to describe this basic sense of the biblical text.

The first sense of scripture is the *conventional sense*. By this term I mean what the classical Christian authors would call the historical sense. In modern terms, this can be understood as the interpretation of an ideal reader familiar with the socio-linguistic conventions of the day, with the language used, and sympathetic to the aims and purposes of the author as they can be found in the text. The conventional meaning is the plain meaning of the text, informed by the original context of utterance/ writing. Conventional meaning does not exclude play and novelty, but

---

16   This is the public sense of 'intention' or 'aim' put forth and defended by (*inter alia*) Ben F. Meyer, *The Aims of Jesus* (London: SCM Press, 1979), and *Critical Realism and the New Testament* (Allison Park, PA: Pickwick, 1989); and by Nicholas Wolterstorff, *Divine Discourse* (Cambridge: Cambridge University Press, 1995).

recognizes that the intelligibility of new language use depends upon recognized, shared and stable linguistic conventions. I emphasize the conventional nature of such reading because the philosophy of Wittgenstein has pointed to the grounds of the meaning of words in their use by a particular linguistic community, and for a particular purpose.[17]

A structuralist approach to meaning, on the other hand, would see linguistic sense arising from a system of signs, or 'code', which a competent speaker of a language follows implicitly and which the linguist makes explicit through scientific investigation. Yet surely such a view puts the cart before the horse. The meaning of words comes not from some abstract systems of 'signs' or 'difference' as some structural and post-structural theorists believe. Structuralist and post-structuralist thinking confuses the abstract system devised by the linguist who studies a language with the power of the 'tools' (words, symbols) themselves. The meanings of words come not from the 'code', but from the actual uses of speakers in particular linguistic communities. To quote from the Marxist Russian philosopher V.N. Volosinov, 'The actual reality of language-speech is not the abstract system of linguistic forms, not the isolated monologic utterance, and not the psychophysiological act of its implementation, but the social event of interaction implemented in an utterance or utterances. Thus, verbal interaction is the basic reality of language.'[18] This is an important conclusion, for the conventional meaning of sentences and texts is recoverable by philological and historical research. Because conventional meaning is a social event, it can be discovered by research, not merely invented by the current reader.

The social, historical and linguistic context of the original text is an important clue to the conventional meaning. Since conventional meaning arises from communities and from use, we must always ask after the use, purpose, or aims of a text. In all the modern emphasis on the power of the reader, I insist that any text has a dimension of 'address' or 'message' which should not be ignored in deciding between rival readings. We cannot retrieve the intention of the author, when that means an inner psychological state. The author is dead, apart from the text. But because meaning is a social event, we can retrieve the message-dimension of a text when we pay attention to the broad social and linguistic context in which the authors and intended readers lived, and out of which their language had meaning.

---

17 See in particular L. Wittgenstein, *Philosophical Investigations* (New York: Macmillan, 1967). This implies that the meaning of terms comes from their *use by speakers of a language*, in and for a particular human, communal activity (what Wittgenstein called a 'language-game').

18 V.N. Volosinov, *Marxism and the Philosophy of Language* (Cambridge, MA: Harvard University Press, 1986), p. 94, italics omitted. I owe this quotation to A.C. Thiselton.

What I am suggesting is that the reader *qua* reader has responsibilities.[19] She is responsible to the text, to herself, and to the community of interpretation to put forth a reading which respects the Otherness of the text and its author. It is wrong to willfully mislead another, and it is just as wrong to willfully misinterpret what my friend says to me. It is wrong to mislead a stranger, or to manipulate my foe. Texts are the remains of friends, foes, or strangers. As such they deserve respect. Since some readings are better than others, the reader owes it to the author, to herself, and to the community of inquiry to put forth as honest a reading as possible. The text itself forms the objective reality from which any and all readings of the text begin, and to which they should return for critical analysis. The author is dead, but the text still has rights because readers have responsibilities and duties toward the text. Critical investigation of the validity or responsibility of any particular reading will necessarily involve a discovery and recovery of the conventional meaning of the text, through careful attention to the text itself and its broader context of utterance.

What is true of texts in general will be especially true for the church in reading and interpreting the holy scriptures. Here we particularly wish to respect the text, its authority and its Otherness. The conventional sense of scripture therefore must be the basis and guide for any further, spiritual sense, as well as the basis for any critique of fuller interpretations. In this insistence, we are in fact following the great doctors of the church, at least in their stated aims if not always in their practice. The priority of the historical is no surprise in an historical religion, whose God is at work in history. The story of God in the Bible is rooted and grounded in history: in exodus, exile, return, incarnation, crucifixion, resurrection. The priority of the original, conventional meaning is not a new idea, nor simply a Reformed notion, but a common teaching of the Christian tradition. As Diodore of Tarsus once wrote, 'history [the literal sense] is not opposed to *theoria* [the spiritual sense]. On the contrary, it proves to be the foundation and basis of the higher senses.'[20] Even Origin could call the historical meaning the 'foundation' for any higher or spiritual sense.[21]

---

19   See Roger Lundin *et al.*, *The Responsibility of Hermeneutics* (Grand Rapids, MI: Eerdmans, 1985).

20   Diodore of Tarsus, 'Prologue', *Commentarii in Psalmos*, I (ed. J.M. Olivier; Corpus Christianorum: Series graeca, 6; Turnhout: Brepols, 1980), p. 7; ET in Karl Froehlich (ed.), *Biblical Interpretation in the Early Church* (Minneapolis: Fortress Press, 1984), p. 85.

21   Origen uses the metaphor 'foundation' for the historical sense in, e.g., discussing Noah's Ark. See Origen, *Hom. Gen.* II.6; *Homelies sur la Genese* (ed. L. Doutreleau; Sources chrétiennes, 7; Paris: Cerf, 1976), pp. 106-108. See also the ET in Origen, *Homilies on Genesis and Exodus* (Fathers of the Church, 71; Washington, DC: Catholic University of America, 1982). See further Karen Jo Torjesen, *Hermeneutical*

Biblical interpretation and application that is Christian may well begin with the conventional sense, but it will also involve a larger, *canonical* sense. As we have just seen, the unity of the books of the Bible in one canon is already a faith statement, grounded in the gospel of Jesus Christ. As T.F. Torrance remarks, for example: 'Since the Scriptures are the result of the inspiration of the Holy Spirit by the will of the Father through Jesus Christ, and since the Word of God who speaks through all the Scriptures became incarnate in Jesus Christ, it is Jesus Christ himself who must constitute the controlling centre in all right interpretation of the Scriptures.'[22] By 'right interpretation', Torrance must mean a right *Christian* reading of the Bible as the Word of God. The canonical sense, then, is christocentric. Jesus as the Living Word constitutes the 'controlling center' of any properly Christian biblical interpretation. Because Jesus is also God Incarnate, this christological framework is finally Trinitarian. When we read the whole Bible together with the whole church, and with Christ as its living center, the result is a Trinitarian canonical sense.[23] Once again, the Holy One of Israel is the Father of our Lord Jesus Christ: this trinitarian identity is central to the gospel. The God of the Old Testament is God the Father, while the Spirit of God and the Word of God become in fully developed Christian thought God the Spirit and God the Son: the blessed Trinity. It was Torrance's teacher and mentor Karl Barth who called attention to the christological and therefore Trinitarian character of divine revelation in recent times.[24] Barth did not invent this idea, however. The christocentric and therefore Trinitarian 'rule of faith' was the framework within which classical Christian theologians of the early period also interpreted the biblical text (e.g., Irenaeus).[25]

Procedure and Theological Method in Origen's Exegesis (Berlin: Walter de Gruyter, 1985), p. 68: 'Origen defines the particular referent of the literal sense differently and very precisely for each book or exegetical genre. The spiritual sense then flows naturally from this definition.'

22   T.F. Torrance, *The Trinitarian Faith* (Edinburgh: T. & T. Clark, 1988), p. 39.

23   See, *inter alia*, R.W.L. Moberly, *The Bible, Theology and Faith* (Cambridge: Cambridge University Press, 2002), pp. 232-37; or R. Wall, 'Reading the Bible from Within our Traditions' and 'Canonical Context and Canonical Conversations', in Green and Turner (eds), *Between Two Horizons*, chs 5 and 9.

24   For an excellent historical introduction to the doctrine of the Trinity, from the Bible to Barth, see R. Olson and C. Hall, *The Trinity* (Grand Rapids, MI: Eerdmans, 2002).

25   See, e.g., Irenaeus, *Against Heresies* 1.10.1, in A. Robertson and J. Donaldson (eds), *The Ante-Nicene Fathers* (Peabody, MA: Hendrickson, 1994 [1885]), I, pp. 330-31. See further James L. Kugel and Rowan A. Greer, *Early Biblical Interpretation* (Philadelphia: Westminster Press, 1986), who discuss Irenaeus on pp. 163-76. They conclude, p. 177, that 'for the early church the Rule of faith supplied the basic hermeneutical principle and framework for interpreting Scripture'.

I am not at all suggesting that we engage in allegory. If the Bible in one verse tells us to hate our enemies, then I am not suggesting that we allegorize the word enemy into meaning our sins, and the like. Let the text speak for itself. However, each particular text will only be authoritative for the church today in conversation with the larger canon. My proposal for a canonical sense concerns the larger significance of entire passages seen within books and Testaments, not allegory. The whole canon, then, provides a larger context of meaning which will shape, adjust and even correct a particular text. As Terry Fretheim puts this point in his Hein/Fry Lectures, the church today should 'seek a unified portrayal of God, but with the understanding that some biblical texts will just not fit; they provide some ongoing over-againstness to that portrayal'.[26] Instead of the typical canon within a canon, we should let each passage speak for itself, even when it is in tension with the overall canonical sense of scripture. This methodology would be very different from the allegorical approach typical of classic Christian theology.

The canonical sense I have in mind is not an allegory, but a larger context of meaning. One might think that Martin Luther, as the father of the Reformation and a critic of allegorical methods used by his Catholic opponents, would stick strictly to the conventional sense alone, and reject any such larger, canonical context. This is not in fact the case, as a careful reading of his work demonstrates. Luther did complain about the excesses of the allegorical method, and especially of Origen's legacy.[27] 'Everywhere we should stick to just the simple, natural meaning of the words, as yielded by the rules of grammar and the habits of speech that God has created among humans.'[28] This is very much what we are calling the conventional sense. His understanding of the clarity and central message of the scriptures, however, was firmly pneumatological and christological. While wishing to start with the simple or plain sense of scripture, he also allowed that the message of the scriptures cannot 'offend against an article of faith'.[29] This is because, for him, Christ is the true meat of the scriptures, and thus the 'simple' sense of the scriptures cannot be understood by those persons who do not have the Holy Spirit and the light of Christ. 'For what solemn truth can the Scriptures still be concealing, now that the seals are broken, the stone

26   T.E. Fretheim and K. Froehlich, *The Bible as Word of God in a Postmodern Age* (Minneapolis: Fortress Press, 1998), p. 125. This book has stimulated my own reflection, particular when read with Pinnock, *Scripture Principle*.
27   See, e.g., M. Luther, *The Bondage of the Will* (trans. J.I. Packer and O.R. Johnston; London: J. Clarke, 1957), p. 192; original text in *D. Martin Luthers Werke* (Weimar: H. Böhlau, 1883–2002), XVIII, p. 701. The *Weimarer Ausgabe* will be cited as *WA* below.
28   Luther, *Bondage*, p. 192 (*WA* XVIII, p. 700).
29   Luther, *Bondage*, p. 192 (*WA* XVIII, p. 700).

rolled away from the door of the tomb, and the greatest of all mysteries brought to light—that Christ, God's Son, became human, that God is Three in One, that Christ suffered for us, and will reign forever?'[30] Luther's grasp of the message and center of scripture is exactly what I am calling the canonical sense, which is christocentric and therefore trinitarian. While Luther might typically be thought of as an opponent of any spiritual sense for scriptural interpretation in the church (and in several places he condemns allegory and a spiritual sense beyond the literal one) in his actual practice he adopted what we are calling a canonical sense for biblical interpretation.[31] For Luther, Jesus Christ, the Living Word, is the key to the scriptures. The light of the gospel of Jesus Christ, therefore, helps to establish the meaning of the biblical text.[32]

So the primacy of the conventional sense does not rule out a larger, canonical sense. To see this larger canonical sense as christocentric and trinitarian is not to impose a rigid dogmatism on the text, but rather to bring each particular passage into conversation with its Testament, and to unify both Testaments around the Living Word, Jesus the Messiah. Since we do give priority to the conventional sense, I am not proposing that we read Jesus or the Trinity back into every verse of the Bible. Remember that we are discussing here a process of interpretation for the church, in faith and under the illumination of the Holy Spirit. It is this ecclesial and evangelical hermeneutic which insists upon a canonical sense, bringing particular texts into conversation with the whole of the canon, with the Living Word, and thus with the Triune God. Confessional interpretation does not have to be restrictive and imposing. If we believe in the truth of the gospel, then confessional interpretation may well be liberating.[33] It is entirely possible that a canonical sense may bring out new insights to be discovered in the conventional sense, or discover important ethical-political dimensions that could be overlooked. Any meaning we propose

---

30   Luther, *Bondage*, p. 71 (*WA* XVIII, p. 607).

31   See further the excellent monograph by Kenneth Hagen, *Luther's Approach to Scripture as Seen in his 'Commentaries' on Galatians 1519–1538* (Tübingen: J.C.B. Mohr, 1993). Among his many insights is the conclusion that, for Luther, a 'commentary' (*enarratio*) was a public narration of gospel faith before God and against the Devil. This is why Luther can claim that his commentary on Galatians 'is not so much a commentary as a testimony of my faith in Christ' (Hagen, *Luther's Approach*, p. 2); and J. Pelikan and H.T. Lehmann (eds), *Luther's Works* (55 vols; St Louis and Philadelphia: Concordia and Fortress Press, 1955–1986), XXVII, p. 159 (herafter *LW*).

32   See, e.g., *LW* I, pp. 223, 281; XXII, p. 157; LII, pp. 171-73.

33   The point is made by Nicholas King, among others. See his 'Society, Academy and Church: Who can Read the Bible?', in D. Kendall and S.T. Davis (eds), *The Convergence of Theology: A Festschrift Honoring Gerald O'Collins* (New York: Paulist Press, 2001), pp. 139-58. See further N. King, *Setting the Gospel Free* (Pietermaritzburg: Cluster Publications, 1995), and *Whispers of Liberation* (New York: Paulist Press, 1998).

to the church as faithful Christian interpreters will be open to revision in light of both the conventional sense of the text and the true heart of scripture, which is Christ.

Consideration of biblical meaning for today brings us to the final sense of scripture: *contemporary*. The contemporary sense is the proposed, imaginative application of the conventional sense of the passage in light of the larger canonical sense. It is the process of applying and appropriating the passage for Christian life and thought today. The Bible has meaning in the church in a larger context of our relationship with God and our lives of Spirit-filled discipleship in the world. Reading the Bible already implies a contemporary application. After all, this is the word of God in human words. All three senses of scripture, then, operate at one and the same time in practice. There is a hermeneutical circle which continues as we move from conventional to canonical to contemporary senses of the text, and then back again. As Gadamer pointed out some years ago, any interpretation is already an implied application.[34] This does not mean, however, that we cannot distinguish between the aims of seeking the conventional meaning of a text, and the aim of seeking a contemporary application. While all three senses come together at once in practice, we can distinguish each sense when we attend to the process of faithful biblical interpretation. When equally sound, faithful, learned, and Spirit-filled Christians disagree about the meaning of the Bible, it will be particularly important to attend to these different senses, and to tease-out the proper meaning in each domain (conventional, canonical, contemporary) along with the criteria of adequacy appropriate for each sense.

As a Christian process of interpretation, we believe the Holy Spirit is at work in all of this. The Spirit inspired the original authors and editors of scripture, as well as the canonical process. The Spirit likewise assists us to grasp the conventional, canonical, and contemporary senses of scripture. But the Holy Spirit is the mother of the church, and has long been active in biblical interpretation. Therefore, the contemporary sense of scripture is best developed in conversation with the history of the interpretation of the text. Of course this can in practice be done only by those with time for serious study. Still, the history of the interpretation of the text ought to guide our application today, just as the history of theology guides our current constructive efforts in systematic theology.

The church has an obligation to preach, teach and live from the Bible. The Bible has been given to us by God as a guide and a word for our time. However we may insist upon the clarity of scripture and simplicity of the gospel, people do misunderstand and abuse the Bible. I believe that this simple three-fold approach to reading the Bible, if taught in con-

---

34   H.G. Gadamer, *Truth and Method* (trans. Joel Weinsheimer and D.G. Marshall; New York: Continuum, 2nd English edn, 1994).

gregations and applied in pulpits, would help Christian people to find the Bible more meaningful for their lives. It can help them to see that we need to read the scriptures in faith, and that not every verse is directly applicable to our lives today. The Bible should be read with the whole of scripture in mind, and especially with Jesus and the gospel in mind. Christian biblical interpretation is guided by the rule of faith, because Christian biblical interpretation speaks from faith to faith.

Perhaps a short example will help clarify my suggestion for a three-fold sense. Remember we are talking here about theological hermeneutics, that is, biblical interpretation in and for Christian faith. I will take as an example a problem text Pinnock also mentions, the editorial summary paragraph at the end of Joshua 10 (vv. 40-43).[35] There our editor claims that 'Joshua defeated the whole land;... he left no one remaining, but utterly destroyed all that breathed as the Lord God of Israel commanded' (Josh. 10.40). First of all, this is a gross exaggeration, if we know anything historically about this period of Hebrew conquest in Canaan. So the text is not historically accurate. Secondly, the text also claims that God commanded Joshua to utterly destroy (*herem*) every living person. But is that consistent with the justice and mercy of God revealed in the whole of scripture? I think not!

First of all, this text demonstrates that historical accuracy is not the basis of our claim that the Bible is true. The inerrancy of scripture—in positive terms the truthfulness and authority of scripture—does not imply that every passage is 100% factually correct in terms of science and history. On the other hand, the shape and character of this narrative would be absurd if there were no conquest at all. Some continuity between biblical claims and historical reality is needed, but not historical inerrancy. Secondly, we need to grasp the conventional meaning of this text in its larger place within the book of Joshua, the Former Prophets, the Old Testament and the whole Bible. Thirdly, in a larger christocentric reading, this text's claim about God's command to utterly destroy every human will need to be modified. That God has the right to take life is not a question. Pinnock is right to see this passage in the larger biblical teaching about the wrath of God. In giving this text a contemporary sense, we will need to place this passage in a larger, eschatological context of judgment against all sin and evil. Even so, in teaching from this passage today we will still question whether God would be so indiscriminate in his judgment. So this text is a good example of doing what Fretheim suggests, namely, allowing some texts to stand in tension against the rest of the canon. As Pinnock suggests in the conclusion of *The Scripture Principle,* biblical inerrancy applies to the whole of scripture,

---

35   Pinnock, *Scripture Principle*, p. 112.

not to its parts; for the whole is greater than the sum of the parts.[36] However, I want to emphasize that we are not judging the Bible in this approach. Rather, we are bringing different and conflicting texts into conversation through a canonical approach with a contemporary meaning. The Bible is correcting itself in this proposal, using Christ as the key to understanding the heart of scripture. This differs from an approach that criticizes the text based upon contemporary human concepts or philosophies.

In this chapter I suggest that the church today should adopt a threefold sense of scripture in our theological interpretation of the Bible. These three senses are the conventional, canonical and contemporary meanings of the biblical text. I have assumed throughout the truth of the central claims of Christian faith, that is, the good news about Jesus Christ. Other readings of the Bible are legitimate and welcome; this one is from faith to faith, in keeping with the overall aim of the church to worship, glorify, and obey the Triune God.

---

36   Pinnock, *Scripture Principle*, pp. 186-96.

CHAPTER 17

Interpreting Scripture for a Theology of Revelation

Kurt Anders Richardson

Disciplinary Domain

The task of theology as a way of knowledge of divine reality in Christ is expositional and testimonial. It seeks to bring to expression objective and subjective truths of Christian faith as embodied in scripture, historically interpreted in the churches and lived out by an individual believer within a particular community of believers and, hopefully, for the sake of the wider ecumenical community of Christians throughout the world. For the theologian, the faithfully privileged text of the scriptures, Old and New Testaments, is a bounded infinite of divine word in human words. These very words, in which the Word has made itself/himself to be captured and stabilized, and yet not captive, is the canonical testimony of the prophets and the apostles. In spite of a great diversity of texts and authors, genres and themes, the Christian churches have adopted them as 'canonical'[1] in a unique sense, as *norma normata* ('norming norm') for all other doctrinal and foundational dimensions of theological exposition and testimony.

In Christian history interpretation is not in the first instance an act of establishing the authority of scripture as much as it is responding to the Holy Spirit working within the church and the believer. As the Word of God in human words it yields not only what it narrates but also comes with its own internal authorization by which believers know its truths and to obey its mandates. The prophecies and apostolic utterances of scripture are themselves the composite of divinely authorized testimony on God's behalf ('speak what I tell you', 'I only speak what I have heard

---

1   Few have explored the full range of theology's use of the word canonicity more than William J. Abraham, *Canon and Criterion in Christian Theology: From the Fathers to Feminism* (Oxford: Clarendon Press, 1998).

from the Father', 'I received this gospel not from man') and of personal testimony on behalf of the prophets and apostles themselves whose lives mediate what Christ the Mediator accomplished and accomplishes on our behalf.[2] What we find is a continuum of knowing and understanding which is reflective of that which the authors of scripture themselves experienced.

As a result of this nexus of factors which surround the taking of scripture as revelation and the ways in which this revelation and its effects radiate out from this unique center, the kind of disciplined thought that is Christian or churchly theology limits conceiving it in comparable or correlative lines. There is a kind of circularity to the interpretive methods of theology that creates its own disciplinary domain.[3] That theology would claim a decisive component of ascertaining all its knowledge in the presence of the same Holy Spirit of God who at various times inspired the scriptures and now, as ever, is required to aid in their interpretation, simply disallows ancillary disciplines within the heart of what theology does in terms of its recourse to the scriptural foundations of its knowledge.

As we shall consider below, although the analytical and critical functions of thinking are present in theology, they do not draw upon external philosophical, literary, political or even religious sources for its practice. By this I mean that for theology to center itself upon a revelation and in so doing also to render an account for this revelation claim creates for itself a special kind of disciplinary activity. Two critical boundaries are present which determine the disciplinary domain of theology. First, God is not the author of our theological texts, and, secondly, the sacredness of scripture is not the product of the theological task. Unless a theologian is prepared to make a new revelation claim for a theological text or believes that theology must instil a sense of the sacred in the scripture-based religion known as Christianity, these boundaries indicate ways in which the theologian is criticized by the special revelation that is otherwise at her or his disposal.

Christological Circularity

Essential to this approach is the reception of the classic understanding of the divinely inspired text, its source in God's gracious revelation to Israel, to the church and to the world. As record of the historic revelations of

---

2   Cf. John R. Levison, *Of Two Minds: Ecstasy and Inspired Interpretation in the New Testament World* (North Richland Hills, TX: Bibal Press, 1999).

3   The struggle to develop rigorous hermeneutical practice and to respect the uniqueness of biblical interpretation is reflected in Petr Pokorny and Jan Roskovec (eds), *Philosophical Hermeneutics and Biblical Exegesis* (Tübingen: Mohr Siebeck, 2002).

God to his prophets and apostles, the scriptures together continue to mediate the knowledge and purpose of this God in the taking of them as a unified whole with divine authority. For Christians, this unity of scripture is manifest in the person and message of Jesus Christ, which is the interpretive or hermeneutical canon of the whole. No passage of the New Testament conveys this quite like the concluding chapter of Luke's Gospel:

but their eyes were kept from recognizing him. (24.16, NRSV)

Then he said to them, 'Oh, how foolish you are, and how slow of heart to believe all that the prophets have declared!' (v. 25)

Then beginning with Moses and all the prophets, he interpreted to them the things about himself in all the scriptures. (v. 27)

When he was at the table with them, he took bread, blessed and broke it, and gave it to them. Then their eyes were opened, and they recognized him; and he vanished from their sight. They said to each other, 'Were not our hearts burning within us while he was talking to us on the road, while he was opening the scriptures to us?' (vv. 30-32).

Then they told what had happened on the road, and how he had been made known to them in the breaking of the bread. (v. 35)

Then he said to them, 'These are my words that I spoke to you while I was still with you—that everything written about me in the law of Moses, the prophets, and the psalms must be fulfilled.' Then he opened their minds to understand the scriptures. (vv. 44-45)

In this passage the matter of interpreting scripture is often overlooked. The resurrection is the first step in their renewal of faith in Jesus and then the interpretation of the scriptures. It is this second dimension to which we attend here.

The problem of understanding traces its way through the passage. The disciples' 'eyes' could 'not recognize' their resurrected Lord. The text will connect eyesight and recognition specifically with knowing him as the resurrected One. But there is another problem, an internal one of understanding. After Jesus criticizes the two disciples on the Emmaus road for their 'foolishness and slowness of heart' to believe 'all that the prophets have declared', he 'interprets' scripture for them. Jesus makes reference here to the entirety of the prophetic witness as centered upon himself. The astonishing comprehensiveness of v. 27 is the presentation of Christ as both the teacher and the object of teaching in terms of the entire corpus of Israelite prophecy beginning with Moses. Essential to this portrayal of Christ as the source of interpretation, according to Luke, is that 'all the scriptures' should from now on be read as testimony 'concerning him'. Messianic exegesis, according to Luke, is a backward glance[4] over the prophetic utterances which preceded the arrival of Jesus. Indeed, throughout Acts, one aspect of Luke's Jewish apologetic will be the irrefutability of Jesus as the promised Messiah (2.31, 36; 3.18; 9.22; 18.5, 28). Jesus' messianic exegesis serves then as the interpretive authority for this claim.

The report[5] of the two disciples who received this instruction accredited his teaching as an 'opening of the scriptures' through their reception of personal instruction from him. Not only are their perceptions no longer dull, but now they have heard him with burning heart. The expression 'opening', in this case of the scriptures, gets transferred to the immediately following passage where Jesus appears to the gathered eleven in order not only to reveal himself as risen but also to instruct them. He 'opened their minds' to the essentials of his teaching: thus, Luke portrays Christ himself as the source of exegesis.[6] Messianic exegesis,[7] in the teaching of Jesus of Nazareth, of the Old Testament begins with himself as its fulfilment. Knowing him, recognition of his resurrection, requires an opening of the eyes; understanding the scriptures requires an 'opening' of the mind.

The message of the life and word of Jesus summed up in the report of his resurrection, along with the sense of the fulfilment of scripture in this life and word, functions as the hermeneutical key to understanding scripture and establishes a criterion of knowledge and authority. The

---

4   Although in the context of the mission of the apostles messianic exegesis makes the universalist claim that the mission of Christ to Israel is to extend to the nations.

5   In anticipation of the problem of belief that Jesus was raised bodily, they testify to recognizing Jesus 'in the breaking of bread', as he will later be recognized for consuming a piece of fish (Lk. 24.41-43).

6   Christological exegesis of the Old Testament by the Gospel writers is explored extensively in Joel Marcus, *The Way of the Lord: Christological Exegesis of the Old Testament in the Gospel of Mark* (Louisville, KY: Westminster/John Knox Press, 1992); John Painter, *The Quest for the Messiah: The History, Literature, and Theology of the Johannine Community* (Nashville, TN: Abingdon, 1993). For a sense of the continuation and modification of intertextual exegesis in early Christian interpretation, cf. Donald Juel, *Messianic Exegesis: Christological Interpretation of the Old Testament in Early Christianity* (Minneapolis: Augsburg Fortress Press, 1994).

7   In contrast to rabbinic practices, cf. Jacob Neusner, *Beyond Catastrophe: The Rabbis' Reading of Isaiah's Vision: Israelite Messiah-Prophecies in Formative Judaism: An Anthology of Pesiqta deRab Kahana for the Seven Sabbaths after the Ninth of Ab* (Atlanta, GA: Scholars Press, 1996); Jacob I. Dienstag, *Eschatology in Maimonidean Thought: Messianism, Resurrection, and the World to Come* (New York: Ktav, 1983); Samson H. Levey, *The Messiah: An Aramaic Interpretation: The Messianic Exegesis of the Targum* (Cincinnati: Hebrew Union College–Jewish Institute of Religion, 1974).

intra-textual nature of this hermeneutic could hardly be more enclosed. Indeed, these features are what have led theologians to speak of the 'self-authentication' and 'perspicuity', or transparency, of scripture. The closest thing to analogous literature is constitutional, charter documents.[8] In this way, theological reasoning manifests a centered circularity as it appropriates knowledge of God 'captured' in the forms of scripture. Several aspects will be considered here in terms of divine reference, divine prerogatives and authorial authority.

The divine reference in scripture comes to us in the form of a *depositum fidei*, that is, the 'deposit of faith' that both author and the communities have canonized and transmitted as the texts of scripture. The 'deposit of faith' that is scripture bears a third degree of reference to revelation (God as primary, inspired author as secondary, text as tertiary). A divinely inspired text is by definition revelatory, but not apart from God's original self-disclosure and the movement of the Holy Spirit within the original author to record the inspired utterances and records.

Nevertheless Primary: Divine Prerogatives

Although scripture mediates the message of the mediators of God's message, this linkage is always taken as an essential justification for receiving it as God's own voice. In one of the most important New Testament texts for pastoral theology, 1 Thessalonians 2.1-13, Paul in v. 13 extols his hearers because

> you received the word of God that you heard from us, you accepted it not as a human word but as what it really is, God's word, which is also at work in you believers. (NRSV)

Earlier in the same chapter, Paul rehearses his apostolic ethic[9] of seeking to please only God in his labors and thereby demonstrates himself to believers to be a reliable agent of the truth of the gospel. What is crucial here is his claim that his hearers had received his words 'not as a human word' but as 'truly God's word'. Their assurance that to do so is correct is based upon their experience as believers where this word is 'at work in you'.

In a profound interconnection of indicators, Paul links his message with the divine message through the effectiveness of his life and the lives

---

8   Cf. David Howlett, *Sealed from Within: Self-authenticating Insular Charters* (Portland, OR: Four Courts Press, 1999).

9   Paul claims before God (1 Thess. 2.5) a chain of virtues for himself—holy, just, blameless—by which both the credibility and the authority of his message are based (1 Thess. 2.10).

of his hearers on account of this very message. The divine word that is at work in them is at work in him in order that he can deliver this same message to them. Paul presupposes that the message, and in this case the text of his letter, contains sufficient indicators for their hearing of God's voice above his own.

Prophetic and Apostolic Authority

One way, and perhaps the best way, of gaining an understanding of how scripture is its own frame of reference to its source is accessing a couple of key texts which link apostolic testimony with prophetic revelation. For our purposes, we will have recourse to a Pauline[10] and then a Petrine passage.

The first is found scattered throughout the opening chapter of the Epistle to the Galatians. Without going into Paul's indication that 'anathema' (1.9) is to be invoked against anyone—including himself— who might come preaching another version of the gospel than that which they originally received, he very clearly refers to the origin of his gospel by revelation.

> For I want you to know, brothers and sisters, that the gospel that was proclaimed by me is not of human origin; for I did not receive it from a human source, nor was I taught it, but I received it through a revelation of Jesus Christ. (Gal. 1.11-12, NRSV)

> But when God, who had set me apart before I was born and called me through his grace, was pleased to reveal his Son to me, so that I might proclaim him among the Gentiles, I did not confer with any human being. (vv. 15-16)

> In what I am writing to you, before God, I do not lie! (v. 20)

Paul begins and ends apophatically. First, his gospel is 'not of human origin', and, secondly, in this written testimony he declares 'I do not lie'. The apophaticism is extended in that he was 'not taught it' and that he 'did not confer' with anybody in his reception of it. Positively, or 'kataphatically', he claims to have received it 'through revelation'. Paul could not be clearer about the origin and essential nature of his message (which we discussed above in the text from 1 Thess. 2.1-13). He regards himself as a bearer if not an agent of revelation—and this latter would not

---

10   Paul's sense of inspiration is explicated well in Allen Rhea Hunt, *The Inspired Body: Paul, the Corinthians, and Divine Inspiration* (Macon, GA: Mercer University Press, 1996).

be too great a stretch to claim for him either. The question then for the reader/hearer at all times is: what does it mean to take a text as revelation? Another crucial text is that found in 2 Peter 1.16-21 (NRSV).

For we did not follow cleverly devised myths when we made known to you the power and coming of our Lord Jesus Christ, but we had been eyewitnesses of his majesty. For he received honor and glory from God the Father when that voice was conveyed to him by the Majestic Glory, saying, 'This is my Son, my Beloved, with whom I am well pleased.' We ourselves heard this voice come from heaven, while we were with him on the holy mountain. So we have the prophetic message more fully confirmed. You will do well to be attentive to this as to a lamp shining in a dark place, until the day dawns and the morning star rises in your hearts. First of all you must understand this, that no prophecy of scripture is a matter of one's own interpretation, because no prophecy ever came by human will, but men and women moved by the Holy Spirit spoke from God.

The apostolic witness begins by claiming that he was an 'eyewitness' of the Lord's 'majesty' (a New Testament *hapax legomenon*), quite literally, 'of divine glory' when the voice of God announced the identity of Jesus to his disciples. Therefore, what is conveyed is not the result of weaving 'cleverly devised myths'. A crucial claim is made between the divine 'voice' and the author's 'making known to you' the truth about Christ and connecting with the past event at which he was present, the Transfiguration—the same 'voice from heaven' which they heard on the 'holy mountain'. Because of this event, the author claims that his hearers have a 'more certain prophetic word'—utilizing a classic theological term linking knowledge and faith in a cognitive experience of assurance and certitude.

Christocentric Circularity

We have quickly considered the above texts because of the weight they carry for their authors relative to their placement within the New Testament canon. When considered together, they render a set of functional claims which have no analogy in other types of literature. Although it is advisable to discern a text's genre or even multiple genres—and certainly scripture has them—genre criticism cannot determine the full functionality of scripture. One ought also to include that although theology may attempt to discern what scripture's philosophical and metaphysical implications are, for example, the nature of 'divine speech acts' mediated by humanly authored texts, correspondence truth, *creation ex nihilo*, foreknowledge, providence, miracle and teleology, among others, these implications are not reflective of the apostolic witness. My argument here, however, is that only by attending to this witness can we determine what New Testament scripture is and how it is to be interpreted and to what ends. Most importantly, New Testament scripture must contain justification for the continuance of scripture beyond that otherwise inviolate text to which it everywhere refers itself. The apostolic witness that is the New Testament signals two characteristics for the continuation of scripture beyond the Old Testament canon: scriptural fulfilment of scripture on account of Jesus Christ, and prophetically authorized testimony to Christ's teaching.

The inter-textual relation between the Testaments delivers the internal arguments for their being joined together—not the one superseding the other.[11] The Old Testament is regarded as anticipating further revelation, banking on messianic hope and exegesis; the New Testament is regarded as the realization of that hope and provides a method by which messianic fulfilment can be assimilated exegetically. In order to justify fully the claim of messianic fulfilment, the apostolic witnesses believe and claim for themselves uniquely authorized divine inspiration as virtual prophets. By using 'virtual prophet' here we pay respect to several qualifiers in the New Testament: Jesus Christ is the last word of God incarnated (Jn 1.14), the final revelation of God through his Son (Heb. 1.1), and the apostles themselves always distinguish themselves from the prophets (e.g., Eph. 4.11) while at the same time regarding their utterances as 'prophetic' (2 Pet. 1.16-21).

And yet because we are only referring to scriptures, as we use them, their arguments for theology become intra-textual and, indeed, only arguments internal to the scriptures could supply the justification for both canonization and exegetical method. At least, we must say, because these arguments are found in scripture and are already operative there, as intrinsic to the revelation itself, we have a completed loop out of which, at times, 'ascends' (*kataphasis*), at other times 'descends' (*apophasis*), and at other time 'extends' the intensity of faith that is the theological knowledge of God.[12] As such we perceive and participate in the *spiral of interpretation* that is the history of Christian thought and proclamation. It is in this way that theology participates in the church's struggle not only to understand but also to obey the word of her Lord in the anticipation of the consummation of all things in him.

The internal referentiality of scripture in its conjoined testamental form, its interpretation and its nature, might give one pause as to its

---

11   Supersessionist theology, i.e., 'replacement' theories that suggest the church has superseded Israel as the people of God, is a bald misreading of such texts as Rom. 9–11.

12   Cf. one of the more fertile expressions of postliberal theology, Daniel W. Hardy, *God's Ways with the World: Thinking and Practicing Christian Faith* (Edinburgh: T. & T. Clark, 1999), who expounds the categories of divine 'intensity' and 'extensity' in quite provocative ways.

external referentiality, that is, as to its effective reference to realities outside itself, particularly historical and metaphysical realities. By the same token, when one inquires after what scripture might mean with respect to the category of 'history' or 'metaphysics' we are on uncertain ground indeed. This is not because one would not justifiably construct a rather 'robust' view of history on scriptural grounds, let alone a weighty metaphysic, but rather that the goal of scripture is not to supply historians, metaphysicians or even linguistic philosophers with a foundation to legitimate their tasks. At most one might say that in a derived, tertiary or inferred way such practitioners might advance foundational theories, but they are, in a sense, 'on their own' in doing so.[13] This said, however, there remains the question of realistic referentiality regardless of one's account of historical and philosophical foundations or how critically one has formulated historical claims for the narratives and events of scripture. Since scripture never presents historical evidence to establish a record of events without also advancing the revelation of God's word in the form of judgments and promises, interpreters have been tortuously divided over the precise nature of the 'historicity' of scripture. The gospel which Paul preached contained scant narration of the life of Jesus and thus one is justified in asking about the historical referentiality of most of the Epistle to the Romans. Certainly, a 'salvation history' runs through the book, but many of its truths refer to the mind of God with historically transcendent truth. Even if we were to shift ground and to construct our account according to metaphysical norms, we are hard pressed to justify or even to admit the claims of scripture based upon its traditional interests. Indeed, it is the limits of historical and metaphysical reasoning vis-à-vis the scriptures that have led many orthodox Christian theologians to renounce metaphysics for the sake of pursuing christocentric, self-authenticating interpretation as foundational to its task.

It turns out, however, that self-authenticating scriptural interpretation is counter-intuitive in many cases. If one is not intent upon the christo-centric circularity of interpretation which one readily comes across in the reading of scripture and the tradition of the churches, foundational metaphysical reasoning comes through the back door in subtler or fragmented forms. One approach is the movement known as 'narrative theology' rooted in late twentieth-century approaches to philosophy and hermeneutics. A defining reason for advancing narrative is the way in which it forces scholars and intellectuals to construct stories of whole selves in the aftermath of extreme specialization where interpretation is

---

13   Such exercises of thought and argument belong to an immense tradition of speculative theology and, indeed, one can hardly avoid speculative inference in theological practice. But the question of systematic inclusion of entirely speculative questions and foundational construction that is not closely reflective of the intention of scripture cannot be said to serve the proper task of theology.

stringently limited to increasingly smaller bits of data and text. Indeed, there is real evidence that self-consciousness is narratival in nature.[14] But one tendency of narrative theology is the separation of narrative meaning from reality referent[15]—it is not necessary for it to function *qua* narrative with a reference. Thus, although we might reject narrative theology for its lack of critical realism, one could be critically realist about the narrative and its integrity to say what it says, to demand of the reader proper attention to authorial intent. Indeed, even if one would say that critical realism demands referentiality if one discerns that the texts demands it, of course the relation cannot be subjected to scientific testing just as no historical fact can be subjected to scientific testing. This does not mean, of course, that historians do not report factually about events, only that they rely upon not experimental data but the greatest number of corroborating witnesses. The narrativity of scripture is one way to hold the text as revelatory since not everyone reads it as such, but, more importantly, not all of its critically realistic referents are historical. When scripture refers to something happening according to divine providence, or announces divine judgment, the reality of either is more than historical. This is because the truth of the matter is contained within the divine life, within the mind of God, and it is simply communicated to be the case with God, whether the world acknowledges, let alone detects, it at all. A truth of the conscience or of the heart would be much the same. Historical criteria for truth have an impressive range of comprehensibility, but they are not all encompassing.

How then are we to take those narratives of scripture where the historical and transcendent dimensions of the text are intertwined and interpenetrate each other? One thing is certain, we cannot immediately treat them as if they are straightforwardly comparable to other types of

---

14   A great deal of constructive engagement of this theme is now present in the literature, much of it quite accessible to theologians. E.g., Gary D. Fireman, Owen J. Flanagan and Ted E. McVay (eds), *Narrative and Consciousness: Literature, Psychology and the Brain* (New York: Oxford University Press, 2003); Adriana Cavarero, *Relating Narratives: Storytelling and Selfhood* (trans. Paul Kottman; New York: Routledge, 2000); Peter Levine, *Living without Philosophy: On Narrative, Rhetoric, and Morality* (Albany, NY: SUNY Press, 1998); Alex Callinicos, *Theories and Narratives: Reflections on the Philosophy of History* (Durham, NC: Duke University Press, 1995); Genevieve Lloyd, *Being in Time: Self-Consciousness, Time and Narrative in Philosophy and Literature* (New York: Routledge, 1993).

15   Cf. Francis Watson, *Text and Truth: Redefining Biblical Theology* (Grand Rapids, MI: Eerdmans, 1997), p. 63 n. 1, where, even though Watson rightly raises the problematic, one wonders about the extent of interpretive, theological practice when he writes: 'As we shall see in connection with the Lucan prologue and the Johannine epilogue, it is precisely the literal meaning of these texts that compels the reader to take seriously their extratextual reference.' Would the historical referent be the terminus of references to truth? What about the transcendent referents?

historical narrative. And yet, even if we were to do so because a robust historical claim is nevertheless present, as theologians, bound to be faithful to the text's intentionality, we must follow the text and not make connections which the text does not lead us to make. We adopt this limitation, not for the sake of ruling out historical or metaphysical or even theological speculation, but because the text gives us no directive to make such a move. And again, we are only justified in this move because scripture is self-referential both in terms of substance and interpretive method.

Thus, as in the case of the birth and resurrection narratives of Jesus, while the faithful reader takes these texts in their full truthfulness and factuality, the referents are wholly embedded in narrative and the unique nature and function of those narratives we know as Gospels. Theologically, instead of proof-texting, apologetically reacting to often uncomprehending scepticism, or even settling for a single narrative or doctrine, one must advance toward scriptural comprehensiveness as much as possible. We are aided in doing so by reference to tradition in the creeds, councils and exemplary theologians of Christian history, as we get a sense of the center and essentials of faithful knowing and action. But scripture in the conjoined Testaments supersedes these, indeed, scripture at times trumps them. In the end, and in the constant act of renewal that should be all theological labor, the question is whether scripture is our 'norming norm' or, as it has been put so aptly in the context of expounding theological realism, whether we are 'conformed to the conforming word'.[16] Of course there is never a moment when this conformity is a finished product, when God through his word does not say to us, 'conform again', and in so doing we are ever reformed by scripture, *semper reformandum.*

---

16   Cf. Andrew Moore, *Realism and Christian Faith: God, Grammar, and Meaning* (Cambridge: Cambridge University Press, 2002), p. 8.

CHAPTER 18

The Pluralist and Inclusivist Appeal to General Revelation as a Basis for Inter-Religious Dialogue: A Systematic Theological Investigation

Archibald J. Spencer

Introduction

The discussion concerning pluralism and inclusivism in recent evangelical theology has tended to take a more positive posture toward general revelation, which assumes that there are certain powers and abilities innate to general revelation as it relates to the universal possession of religious sense (*sensus divinitatis*). Where theorists of religion and theologians do treat 'general revelation' directly, as it relates to their argument, pluralists and inclusivist often fail to give due care and attention to the Reformed critique of general revelation that ought to factor more prominently in the discussion. It is the purpose of this paper to give a proper account of this criticism of the 'religious sense' by bringing it to bear on recent discussions within both pluralist and inclusivist sectors, which are calling for the priority of inter-religious dialogue in theology. This paper is, as such, an exercise in Christian systematic theology, a discipline too often relegated to the periphery in the recent discussions among religious theorists.[1] For that matter, there are theologians of note who are willing to wager all of theology on the

---

1   On an anecdotal note, the subject of this paper came to me in the Spring of 2001 when, with only a few days notice, I was called upon at the beginning of term by McMaster Divinity College to finish teaching two courses for Clark Pinnock who had come down with an illness. One of those courses was his 'Theology and Religious Pluralism', and, though I continued to use his syllabus and to disagree with him on more than one occasion in the class, he remained ever gracious, patient and supportive of this otherwise very junior theologian. Though I continue to disagree with him herein, he has nevertheless played a significant role in helping me formulate my thinking. For all of this I remain a grateful friend.

gambit of inter-religious dialogue. Not too long ago David Tracy wrote: 'As any theologian involved in serious inter-religious dialogue soon learns, her or his earlier theological thoughts on the "other religions" soon become spent. There is no more difficult or more pressing question on the present theological horizon than that of inter-religious dialogue.'[2]

While I agree with the first half of this statement, in that there is little to agree on regarding the comparative substance of the various religions, I disagree with the later half of the statement regarding its priority over all other theological concerns. Yet there are those in evangelicalism today who agree that the issue of inter-religious dialogue is the most pressing theological problem in the present multicultural situation in the West.[3] In reconsidering the Reformed critique of the *sensus divinitatis* I shall give consideration to two declared evangelicals, Clark Pinnock and Gerald McDermott, and one 'former' self-confessed evangelical 'fundamentalist', namely John Hick. Hick is recognized as one of the most prominent exponents of religious pluralism today. For good or ill, he has made pluralism, and therefore all attenuating theories of religion created in response to it, one of the first items on the theological agenda in our times. Thus, we must be prepared to 'give an answer for the faith that lies within us' from that perspective. But let us be clear that while inter-religious dialogue may be one of the most prominent issues in theology today, perhaps, as some think, foisted on theology more by an 'ideology of pluralism' than an actual cultural demand, it is not theology's first and most important subject in terms of the relation between religion and theology. As it relates to the right ordering of the God–human relationship, religion is, in and of itself, a first order topic, just as it always has been, but it is not so in the terms of an 'agreeable' inter-religious dialogue.[4]

---

2   David Tracy, *Dialogue with the Other* (Grand Rapids, MI: Eerdmans, 1990), p. 27.

3   Following Tracy, Clark Pinnock, *A Wideness in God's Mercy: The Finality of Jesus Christ in a World of Religions* (Eugene, OR: Wipf and Stock, 1997), p. 7, affirms: 'I believe this issue is second to none in importance for Christian theology.'

4   For the purposes of this paper I shall focus on three primary works from these three proponents of inter-religious dialogue. Pinnock's views are best represented in his important book called *A Wideness in God's Mercy*, cited above. His position is also presented in his *Flame of Love: A Theology of the Holy Spirit* (Downers Grove, IL: InterVarsity Press, 1996). Gerald McDermott's recent book takes a slightly more conservative, 'quasi inclusivist' approach in his *What Can Evangelicals Learn From World Religions: Jesus, Revelation and Religious Traditions* (Downers Grove, IL: InterVarsity Press, 2000). John Hick's theory of pluralism has been well documented in his many books and regularly commented on in the current scholarly milieu. For our purposes I shall concentrate on his little book entitled *A Christian Theology of Religions: The Rainbow of Faiths* (Louisville, KY: Westminster Press, 1995). I shall

Therefore, in order to establish some critical balance in the present discussion, I intend to bring these three proponents of 'inter-religious dialogue' into contact with the Reformed critique of the *sensus divinitatis* represented in John Calvin and Karl Barth. From them we shall gain some insights as to the adequacy of the appeal to general revelation among these representative proponents of inter-religious dialogue, while not sharing their Reformed view entirely.[5] The goal is not to close off the debate, but to give back to Christian theology its independence as a standpoint in its own right, and not as a culturally driven, epistemologically predetermined, subset of the larger enterprise called 'inter-religious dialogue'. While this may entail a certain posture towards other religions that some will see as dialogue ending, it is nevertheless crucial to Christian theology that it stand in the service of its own constituency first, on this and, for that matter, other central concerns. There is much room in Christian theology for dialogue with, and tolerance of, other religions, but it makes much less of the 'sense of the divine' said to be the common thread of all major religions outside of the Bible than we are led to believe. Let me turn first to Hick, who sets the tone for Pinnock and McDermott in their inclusivist/quasi-inclusivist response to him.

The Pluralist Appeal to the *Sensus Divinitatis*

Hick's pluralist agenda has been well documented in recent scholarship and thus need not be rehearsed here in detail.[6] My purpose is to trace out the argument Hick puts forward in broad terms with a view to outlining precisely how he employs the 'religious sense' in his call for an inter-religious dialogue, which he sees as necessitated by the western pluralist situation.

The first and most critical move that Hick tends to make, in the many places that he has laid out his argument for pluralism, is reductionist in

---

also consult his major treatise *An Interpretation of Religion* (London: Macmillan, 1989).

5   Here I shall rely on Calvin's *Institutes of the Christian Religion* (trans. F.L. Battles; ed. J.T. McNeill; Library of Christian Classics, 20–21; Philadelphia: Westminster Press, 1960). Barth's famous critique of religion can be found in his *Church Dogmatics*, I/2 (trans. and ed. T.F. Torrance and G.W. Bromiley; Edinburgh: T. & T. Clark, 1956).

6   For one of the best treatments of Hick's philosophy of religion, see H. Hewitt, *John Hick's Philosophy of Religion* (London: Macmillan, 1991). Cf also Gavin D'Costa, 'Revelation and Revelations: Beyond a Static Valuation of Other Religions', *Modern Theology* 10.2 (1994), pp. 164-68, and his chapter on the same subject, 'Christ, the Trinity, and Religious Plurality', in G. D'Costa (ed.), *Christian Uniqueness Reconsidered* (New York: Orbis, 1990), pp. 18-30.

nature. That is, he must reduce Christianity to just another of the great religions of the world, whose 'fruits' and 'moral perfections', noticeable in the followers of Christianity, are comparable with other religions. 'The spiritual and moral fruits of these other faiths, although different, are more or less on a par with the fruits of Christianity.'[7] According to Hick, the sum of the comparisons of the great religions in regard to the evil and good they produce does not 'establish the moral superiority of Christian civilization'.[8] Thus Hick concludes:

> We can, I suggest, only come to the negative conclusion that it is not possible to establish the unique moral superiority of any one of the great world faiths. It may be that in the sight of God one of them has in fact been, as an historical reality, superior to the others, but I don't think that from our human point of view we can claim to know this.[9]

Clearly what we know about God must be seen from the standpoint of what we can intuit about him on the basis of rational observation, and not as a result of some 'special' insight or source of knowledge that stands above the sum total of the negative and positive effects we observe in the moral and spiritual lives of religious people. What will establish Christianity as a true religion along with others, or not, will be based on what we observe in the lives of its followers. Since Christian moral pre-eminence cannot be sustained by the available evidence as to any degree better than other religions, it cannot claim special status as a 'transcendently revealed religion'. This means that the claims about the uniqueness of Jesus will also need to be re-assessed in relation to the 'particularity' of Christianity as a revealed religion centered in God's self-revelation in Christ. It is, rather, the *experience of the early disciples* that makes the Christian faith a 'revelation' of sorts. Thus, 'religious faith is this uncompelled interpretive element within all religious experience'.[10] Indeed, the idea that Christianity is a revealed religion with particular status cannot be claimed on the basis of a book that merely contains the shared religious experiences of the followers of Jesus, which can be compared with the religious experiences recorded in the sacred books of other religions. Furthermore, the fact that the divine status of Christ was not established till just before AD 325 is proof enough that such claims are purely human in origin, and not a divinely revealed doctrine as such. Hick concludes: 'I thus see theology as a human

---

7   Hick, *Rainbow of Faiths*, p. 14.
8   Hick, *Rainbow of Faiths*, p. 14.
9   Hick, *Rainbow of Faiths*, p. 15.
10   J. Hick, 'A Pluralist View', in D.L. Okholm and T.R. Phillips (eds), *Four Views on Salvation in a Pluralistic World* (Grand Rapids, MI: Zondervan Publishing, 1995), p. 34.

creation. I do not believe that God reveals propositions to us... I hold that the formulation of theology is a human activity that always, and necessarily, employs the concepts and reflects the cultural assumptions and biases of the theologians in question.'[11]

The appeal to *religious experience* now becomes the touchstone for the unification of all religions under the same religio-critical approach to understanding their significance for humanity in general. This is clearly an appeal to the *religious sense* as a means of grounding the relative value of the major religions, including Christianity. The central shared feature for working out the nature of this universal religious sense is the equally 'universal' desire for salvation. This forms a second crucial aspect of Hick's argument.

It goes without saying that, for Hick, salvation in the 'exclusivist' terms of a necessary knowledge of and faith in the atoning work of Christ is a 'tautology' since the moral fruits (which are of much more importance to Hick as a mark of true religion than spiritual fruits) do not seem to exceed those of other religions. According to Hick, salvation, for Christ, was not about a proper understanding of the atonement, but 'about men's and women's lives' in moral terms.[12] Here he defines the salvation he thinks Jesus is proposing. 'Suppose, then, we define salvation in a very concrete way, as an actual change in human beings, a change which can be identified? when it can be identified by its *moral fruits*.'[13] This being the case, we then find that we are on the same ground as the other religions. 'Each in its different way calls us to transcend the ego point of view, which is the source of all selfishness, greed, exploitation, cruelty, and injustice, and to become re-centered in that ultimate mystery for which we, in our Christian language, use the term God.'[14] All the religions have as their center this moral orientation towards 'the Real' as the fulfilment of our true humanity through self-transcendence. This is the sum total of the *religious sense*. As such the great 'post axial' traditions, including Christianity, 'are directed towards a transformation of human existence from self-centeredness to a re-centering in what in our inadequate human terms we speak of as God, or as Ultimate Reality, or the Transcendent, or the Real'.[15] In this way all religions are centered in the search for 'salvation/liberation'. Given this reality, says Hick, 'it

---

11   Hick, 'A Pluralist View', p. 36.
12   Hick, *A Christian Theology of Religions*, p. 17. Here Hick appeals to 'the parable of the sheep and the goats' (Mt. 25.31-46) as the criterion that Jesus used to establish the reality of salvation. The concern for moral criteria as the defining principle of true religion pervades all of Hick's works. It is very often expressed in Kantian terms.
13   Hick, *A Christian Theology of Religions*, p. 17.
14   Hick, *A Christian Theology of Religions*, p. 17.
15   Hick, *A Christian Theology of Religions*, p. 18.

therefore seems logical for me to conclude that not only Christianity, but also these other world faiths, are human responses to the Ultimate'.[16]

This is the basic substance of the argument for pluralism that Hick trades on in book after book after article. While various nuances are added in subsequent works, usually in response to criticisms, it has remained essentially the same throughout. He does so in relation to the opposing positions, which he calls 'exclusivists', that is, no salvation outside of the knowledge of special revelation in Christ, and 'inclusivists', who argue that salvation can be had only through Christ but who can be met with indirectly, yet ontologically, in other religions. Time does not permit a full exposition of his understanding of these positions here, but suffice it to say that, for Hick, they all express this central desire for salvation. In the end these limiting positions will be revealed as mistaken because 'the great world faiths orient us in this journey, and in so far as they are, as we may say, in soteriological alignment with the Real, to follow their path will relate us rightly to the Real, opening us to what, in different conceptualities, we call divine grace or supernatural enlightenment *that will in turn bare visible fruit in our lives'*.[17]

What are we to make of this appeal to the universal nature of the revelation of the Real through the religious sense, which Hick sees expressed in all the major religions? It would appear that the general consensus of theologians who have studied Hick is that his doctrine of universal revelation is Kantian in nature. One of the most able interpreters of Hick's pluralism, Gavin D'Costa, suggests that 'Kant can be seen as the ambiguous archetype of latter day pluralism' which he understands as 'the term given to those who hold that all religions are revelatory and therefore capable of being means to salvation, and that this salvation is not causally, ontologically, or historically related to Jesus Christ'. Furthermore, he says, 'John Hick is a modern equivalent to Kant, both epistemologically and ethically'.[18] He understands, correctly I think, that Hick's view of revelation is equal to Kant's in that it is universally theocentric rather than exclusively christocentric. 'Hick argues that it was God, and not Christianity or Christ, that counted as normative revelation and it is toward God that the religions were oriented and from whom they gain their salvific efficacy.'[19] Christ is merely a 'mythic' expression, among many others, of this divine self-revelation. When Hick was criticized for being too theocentric by other religionists, to the exclusion of non-theistic religions, his Kantian inclinations became even clearer. In response, Hick 'developed a Kantian-type distinction between a divine

16   Hick, 'A Pluralist View', p. 44.

17   Hick, *A Christian Theology of Religions*, p. 27.

18   Gavin D'Costa, 'Revelation and World Religions', in Paul Avis (ed.), *Divine Revelation* (Grand Rapids, MI: Eerdmans, 1997), pp. 120-21.

19   D'Costa, 'Revelation and World Religions', p. 121.

noumenal reality "that exists independently and outside man's perception of it", which he calls the "eternal One" and the phenomenal world, "which is that world as it appears to our human consciousness", in effect, the various "revelatory" human responses to the Eternal'.[20] This certainly compares with Kant's understanding of God's place as the end point in the metaphysical scheme of his philosophy, as it relates to ethics.[21] But there were deists who could well fit into the same category, notably John Locke. What makes Hick's doctrine of universal revelation purely Kantian is his reduction of all religion to morality.

At the heart of all religions Hick perceives a 'turning away from self-centeredness to Reality-centeredness' that finds its ultimate expression in 'moral fruits'. The 'saints' produced in all religions, that is, those who best exemplify the moral fruits of a given religion, are the only verifiable means for gauging the revelatory value of that religion. As we look to these saints we gain this revelatory perspective from each other in dialogue. Clearly D'Costa is right to suggest that 'while Hick's intentions are noble and serious, his project, like that of Kant's, finally divests all religions of any revelatory power and achieves precisely the opposite of its stated goal', namely, that of inter-religious dialogue.[22] Aside from failing to take the real differences between the world religions seriously, Hick also fails to account for the impossibility of the correspondence between the phenomenon and the perception of the thing-in-itself, which stands today as a core problem of Kant's philosophy, in that it fails to solve the epistemological split between the experience of an object and the absolute knowability of it. This epistemological split denies any real revelatory knowledge as such. As a result, 'Hick is left in the odd position of apparently accepting that all religions are revelatory, but is actually committed to then denying the revelatory claims as made by other religions'.[23] It is *the 'golden rule' of morality* that determines true religion, not authentic, extra-worldly revelation. We are not alone in this assessment of Hick's appeal to the universal religious sense. A number of scholars, evangelical and otherwise, have also pointed this out.[24] As we

---

20   D'Costa, 'Revelation and World Religions', p. 122.

21   I. Kant, *Religion within the Limits of Reason Alone* (New York: Harper and Row, 1992), pp. 145-55. Therein Kant appeals to Mt. 25.35-40, suggesting, p. 150, 'it becomes evident that when the Teacher of the Gospel spoke of rewards in the world to come he wished to make them thereby not an incentive to action but merely (as a soul-elevating representation of the consummation of the divine benevolence and wisdom in the guidance of the human race) an object of the purest respect and of the greatest moral approval when reason reviews human destiny in its entirety'.

22   D'Costa, 'Revelation and World Religions', p. 122.

23   D'Costa, 'Revelation and World Religions', p. 123.

24   See, among others, A.E. McGrath, 'A Particularist View', in Okholm and Phillips (eds), *Four Views of Salvation*, pp. 149-80; H. Netland, *Encountering Religious*

shall see further on, this assessment can potentially be applied to some inclusivists as well.

This reduction of all religion to morality is, furthermore, the primary motivation behind Karl Barth's strident criticism of general revelation, natural theology and/or natural religion. To the degree that his criticism of it annuls this kind of 'agnostic revelation', which, Barth thinks, inevitably flows from the prioritizing of the *sensus divinitatis*, it is instructive for our doctrine of revelation and theology of religions, however overstated. But first we need to briefly note the similarity (not sameness) of the approach to the *sensus divinitatis* in the inclusivism of Clark Pinnock, and the quasi-inclusivist approach of Gerald McDermott, in order to demonstrate that a moderated Reformed critique applies across the board as a caution against an over emphasis on the religious sense.

The Inclusivist Appeal to the *Sensus Divinitatis*

Inclusivist theologians come in many colors. They include the Catholic theologians Karl Rahner, Hans Urs Von Balthasar, Joseph Dinoia, Louis Dupris and Gavin D'Costa, as well as evangelical theologians like Clark Pinnock and Gerald McDermott, to mention a few. While all of these represent a reaction to out-right pluralism as such, they each have their own take on a theology of religions and would seem to 'exclude' one another in various ways. Ultimately, in that sense, even Hick's argument is exclusivist. It is Pinnock and, to a lesser degree, McDermott who have thus far offered the most comprehensive inclusivist theology of religions from an evangelical perspective. For that reason, they deserve our attention here in the current evangelical context. But other inclusivists certainly figure in the debate as well.

Pinnock's inclusivist theology of religions is worked out primarily in his significant book *A Wideness in God's Mercy*, though he comments on his view and summarizes it in other places as well.[25] His approach to other

---

Pluralism (Downers Grove, IL: InterVarsity Press, 2001), pp. 241-43; J.A. Dinoia, *The Diversity of Religions: A Christian Perspective* (Washington, DC: Catholic University of America Press, 1992), *passim*.

25   Besides Pinnock's *A Wideness in God's Mercy*, see also his 'The Finality of Jesus Christ in a World of Religions', in Mark A. Noll and David F. Wells (eds), *Christian Faith and Practice in the Modern World* (Grand Rapids, MI: Eerdmans, 1988), pp. 152-68; 'An Inclusivist View', in Okholm and Phillips (eds), *Four Views of Salvation*, pp. 93-148; *Flame of Love, passim*. Pinnock elaborates his understanding of the pneumatological connection to the 'wideness view' in a recent paper titled, 'Religious Pluralism: A Turn to the Holy Spirit' offered at the annual meeting of the Evangelical Theological Society held in Toronto, 20-22 November 2002. To my knowledge, this has yet to be published. His thesis is essentially that it is the freedom

religions depends on two crucial axioms. The first is Pinnock's proposition that God, as a God of 'unbounded Love', offers *a universal means for salvation*, rather than a restricted means. The means is the redemptive act of God, for the whole world, in Jesus Christ of Nazareth. The second axiom is the uniqueness of this incarnation to the Christian faith. But contrary to the 'restrictivist' approach of Reformed evangelicalism, such a view is completely compatible with a more 'optimistic' view of salvation for the majority of humanity, whether or not they hear the gospel. 'A biblically based Christology does not entail a narrowness of outlook towards other people. The church's confession about Jesus is compatible with an open spirit, with an optimism of salvation... There is no salvation except through Christ, but it is not necessary for everybody to possess a conscious knowledge of Christ in order to benefit from redemption through him.'[26] The tacit reason that Pinnock gives for this unique twist on the evangelical view is that the 'fewness doctrine' of salvation is driving many conscientious evangelicals toward pluralism.[27]

The means whereby God may achieve this wider salvation is through his positive appropriation of some religions, wherein the basic knowledge of God can be ascertained, sufficient to lead the truly pious to a saving knowledge of God, which amounts to an ontological, but not necessarily epistemological, encounter with Christ. Although Pinnock does not endorse every religion as positive, indeed there is much that is evil in many of them, he nevertheless allows for the 'prevenient' work of the Holy Spirit of God in other religions. While we may not be able to identify with certainty which religions are open to this revelation of God, we can say that 'God *may* use religion as a way of gracing people's lives and that it is *one* of God's options for evoking faith and communicating grace'.[28] Thus grace is operative outside of the church and the scriptures, and can be encountered in a salvific way in other religions. Therefore, says Pinnock, evangelicals need to 'buck a strong tradition that refuses to grant any gracious element in general revelation'.[29]

What is of central significance in the availability of salvation in general revelation for Pinnock is its 'noetic impact'. It is more than just the basis upon which we establish human guilt, it is a means whereby humanity can come to a clear and unambiguous knowledge of God. Pinnock bristles at

---

and continuous work of the Holy Spirit in all creation that establishes and undergirds the universal availability of general revelation as prevenient grace. Interestingly it seems to completely submerge the christological aspect of salvation.

26   Pinnock, *A Wideness in God's Mercy*, pp. 74-75.

27   Pinnock, *A Wideness in God's Mercy*, p. 17. Pinnock suggests that the fewness doctrine that sometimes results from a 'restrictivist' soteriology 'invites the pluralist theologies to come into play'.

28   Pinnock, 'An Inclusivist View', p. 100.

29   Pinnock, 'The Finality of Christ', p. 153.

the former suggestion. He writes: 'I am offended by the notion that the God who loves sinners and desires to save them tantalizes them with truth about himself that can only result in their greater condemnation.'[30] Then Pinnock blurs the traditional distinction between general and special revelation with the rhetorical question, 'is there not one author of both general and special revelation?'[31]

In establishing this point Pinnock draws his biblical support from passages like Acts 10.34-35 and 14.17, and then comments on Acts 17.27 as follows:

> People possess truth from God in the context of their own religion and culture... In Paul's speech upon the Aeropagus we hear how God has providentially ordered history 'that they [people in general] should seek God, in the hope that they might feel after him. Yet he is not far from each of us.' (Acts 17:27)[32]

As Christopher Partridge comments: 'quite simply, it is argued that, just as sin is ubiquitous, so is God's love and witness. Hence...Pinnock affirms that non-Christian faiths, "reflect to some degree general revelation and prevenient grace".'[33] Pinnock goes on to suggest, in quite strong and wide-open terms, that, 'because of cosmic or general revelation, anyone can find God anywhere at any time, because he has made himself and his revelation accessible to them. This is the reason we find a degree of truth and goodness in other religions.'[34]

Aside from the theological issues and presuppositions that concern me at this point, Pinnock's reading of the biblical tradition on both the 'universal nature of salvation' and the 'universal availability' of God's self-revelation are problematic on a number of counts, but time does not permit a full engagement of his exegesis here. My concern is to bring his appeal to general revelation into comparison with the pluralist approach so that we can demonstrate the similarity of their appeals to the *universal sense of the divine*, and, therefore, the inclusion of Pinnock in our moderate Reformed critique of general revelation and natural theology.

It would appear to the careful reader of both Pinnock and Hick that while they differ on the important point of christology, they certainly share a very similar understanding of the availability of revelation in other religions. While Pinnock would want to limit its potency in com-

---

30 Pinnock, 'The Finality of Christ', p. 160.
31 Pinnock, 'The Finality of Christ', p. 104.
32 Pinnock, 'The Finality of Christ', p. 158.
33 Christopher Partridge, 'A Hermeneutics of Hopefulness: A Christian Personalist Response to Pinnock's Inclusivism', in Tony Gray and Christopher Sinkinson (eds), *Reconstructing Theology: A Critical Assessment of the Theology of Clark Pinnock* (Carlisle: Paternoster Press, 2000), pp. 184-219.
34 Pinnock, *A Wideness in God's Mercy*, p. 104.

parison to Hick, the end result seems nearly the same; namely the possibility of universal salvation in other religions based on an observation of the piousness of the adherent and their *moral fruits*. Both of them refer to pagan saints as crucial to the argument for prevenient grace in general revelation. Both of them invoke moral uprightness as a means of verifying it, and both affirm the possibility of salvation without hearing the gospel. One recent commentator comes close to suggesting that Pinnock, while he affirms a 'particularist' point of reference in his retention of christology, ostensibly vacates it of any meaning because of his insistence on the 'universal' nature of salvation. There is a tacit admission on Pinnock's part that the Bible is theocentric before it is christocentric, thus placing him in some proximity to Hick. Daniel Strange summarizes what he perceives to be a danger in this approach:

> With regard to upholding both axioms of universality and particularity, I believe Pinnock has failed because the ultimate result of his argument is a subtle universalization of the particular. So while Pinnock still thinks he maintains the finality, particularity and primacy of Christ in soteriology, the real consequence of his thinking is that the incarnation and atonement have been reinterpreted to conform to the universality axiom. This move poses questions concerning the normativity of the incarnation, the necessity and purpose of the atonement, and...the relationship between the work of Christ and the salvation of the unevangelized.[35]

While I agree that Pinnock has done an invaluable service for evangelicals by helping put this question on the theological map within evangelicalism, I must also bring to bare the necessary criticism of the Reformed tradition vis-à-vis natural religion in order to correct the excesses of his appeal to general revelation. It is an appeal that possibly leaves the option of pluralism as open as ever, despite Pinnock's desire to close it off to conscientious evangelicals who cannot abide the 'fewness' doctrine.[36]

---

35   Daniel Strange, 'Presence, Prevenience or Providence? Deciphering the Conundrum of Pinnock's Pneumatalogical Inclusivism', in Gray and Sinkinson (eds), *Reconstructing Theology*, pp. 256-57. See also Strange's extensive treatment of Pinnock in his *The Possibility of Salvation among the Unevangelised: An Analysis of Inclusivism in Recent Evangelical Theology* (Paternoster Biblical and Theological Monographs; Carlisle: Paternoster Press, 2002).

36   See also Netland's critique, *Encountering Religious Pluralism*, pp. 311-23. Hick suggests, in a response to Pinnock, that inclusivism leads further on to pluralism and that Pinnock may not fully understand '*the implications of the reality of saintliness, goodness and piety outside the borders of Christianity*'. That is, in my estimation, Pinnock has not fully accounted for the Kantian nature of his appeal to 'moral fruits' in the lives of other religious 'saints'. J. Hick, 'Response to Clark Pinnock', in Okholm and Phillis (eds), *Four Views of Salvation*, p. 125.

But before we move on to this Reformed critique, I should briefly note a more recent offering from a 'quasi inclusivist' perspective that is a little more cautious in its claims for general revelation, namely Gerald McDermott's *What Can Evangelicals Learn From World Religions?* Yet here too, if I understand the biblical material correctly, is an overly generous assessment of the sense of the divine, but this time through the creation of a third category of revelation. The primary aim of McDermott's approach to an evangelical theology of religions is to ask, and answer affirmatively, the question, 'can evangelicals learn from world religions?' In answering the question McDermott makes certain suggestions about revelation that leave the possibility of God's self-revelation in other religions more open than his conservative sensibilities would like. Granted, he does not go so far as to suggest a saving knowledge of God can be had from these revelations, but he does assert that, just as our forefathers learned from secular philosophy, so 'other traditions *can help us make explicit what is only implicit in our present understanding of Christ'*, as if some things regarding Christ remain hopelessly hidden without the light of other religions.[37] McDermott does not base this idea of 'learning' from other religions on a view of general revelation as traditionally understood. Rather, building on an understanding of revelation gained from the Catholic theologian, Avery Dulles, and the American theologian, Jonathan Edwards, he offers a third option called 'revealed types'.[38] While the various models of revelation offered in Dulles do not 'begin to exhaust God's self-revelation', they do 'begin to open us up to the plethora of meanings for the word, and they suggest that when we ask about revelation in other religions, we must be open to the variety of ways in which that might happen'.[39] Thus, because of the difficulty in defining revelation in terms of modes and interpretations we have, according to McDermott, license to add what he considers a helpful way of attributing a 'type' of revelation to other religions. This is a move that not only complicates the present circumstance, but also leaves much to be desired as a separate mode of revelation.

But at the same time McDermott rightly repudiates any notion that salvation can be had outside of the revelation of God in Christ, in both the noetic and the ontological sense. What McDermott feels is missing in our relationship to other religions, vis-à-vis revelation, is a view of the universal work of the Spirit who uses types to reveal the deeper meanings of various aspects of the Christian faith in other traditions. 'In other

---

37   McDermott, *What Can Evangelicals Learn*, p. 17.

38   McDermott, *What Can Evangelicals Learn*, pp. 61-64. See A. Dulles, *Models of Revelation* (Garden City, NY: Doubleday, 1983). See also his major study, *Jonathan Edwards Confronts the Gods: Christian Theology, Enlightenment Religion, and Non-Christian Faiths* (New York: Oxford University Press, 2000).

39   McDermott, *What Can Evangelicals Learn*, p. 65.

words, Christ is the unique revelation of God, but the Holy Spirit is ever at work, as he was in the history of Israel before Jesus...and some of those insights may come from reflection upon what the Spirit is doing in and with people outside Israel and the Christian church.'[40] The way in which he grounds this approach to revelation is by appealing to Edwards' understanding of the covenant as an inadequate revelation in the Old Testament, but nevertheless a revelation to a degree, and an adequate revelation in the New Testament. Given the difference in the degree of revelation from one to the next, and the fact that they both inform one another, one to a lesser, the other to a greater degree, is it not right to assume that other traditions of faith have a similar relationship to special revelation, even if to a much lesser degree? Indeed, as with Edwards, we may affirm, says McDermott, that typology is 'a system of representation by which God points human beings to spiritual realities'.[41] That is, 'human intuitions can be *typical* of things in the spiritual world'.[42] His point is that this typological approach offers a theological way to conceive of revelation in other religions, which avoids the division and dissension that marks the approach of the past. He then invokes Barth as a regular user of this approach, in a way that not only misses Barth's point in the contexts in which he employs typology, but also completely ignores the anathema that Barth pronounced over the revelation some attribute to other religions, on the basis of a sense or intuition of the divine.[43] Towards the end of his section on 'revealed types', McDermott is so confident that he can affirm 'there is no reason to think that there is not more truth and understanding of Christ and the Biblical revelation yet to be illuminated by the Spirit, and perhaps aided by insights from other religions'.[44]

To be fair to McDermott we cannot really call him an inclusivist in the true sense of the term. But he does share certain presuppositions with Pinnock and Hick that leave him open to the relativity of revelation implicit in Pinnock and explicit in Hick. This is certainly true in terms of his reliance on Pinnock's understanding of 'prevenient grace' available through the agency of the Spirit's universal presence.[45] He also seems to share the same 'optimism of salvation' that undergirds Pinnock's whole

---

40   McDermott, *What Can Evangelicals Learn*, p. 95.

41   McDermott, *What Can Evangelicals Learn*, p. 104.

42   McDermott, *What Can Evangelicals Learn*, p. 105. He uses Eph. 5.28 as an example.

43   McDermott, *What Can Evangelicals Learn*, pp. 108-109.

44   McDermott, *What Can Evangelicals Learn*, p. 118. He goes on to suggest that other religions can be used by the Spirit to induce repentance.

45   McDermott, *What Can Evangelicals Learn*, pp. 93-95. Here he relies on both Pinnock and D'Costa and concludes, p. 95, that 'the doctrine of the Holy Spirit allows us to relate the particularity of Christ to the entire history of humankind'.

approach to the universal availability of salvation. His final appeal to the Cornelius passage, which is key to the inclusivist argument, is cast in almost the same terms as Pinnock. What is absent in his approach is the kind of moral interpretation of salvation and revelation seen in Hick and, to some degree, in Pinnock. In fact, he takes the time to distance himself from this.

In sum, what we have before us, in McDermott's third option and the pluralist/inclusivist appeal to the *sensus divinitatis*, is a generosity of revelation that often appeals to the scriptures for support in a selective way, while avoiding the hard questions of the knowability of this revelation, its lack of efficacy, and its epistemological obtuseness in the direction of relativity at best and agnosticism at worst. There is a tradition of criticism of this approach to the *sensus divinitatis* that, while it also has problems, can nevertheless provide a necessary, if only partial, correction to this over confidence in the *sensus divinitatis*. It is to this tradition, represented by Calvin and Barth, that we can now turn.

The Reformed Critique of the Appeal to the *Sensus Divinitatis*

Calvin's Understanding of the Sensus Divinitatis

I am not suggesting in this paper that Calvin and Barth are in agreement on the issue of the *sensus divintatis*. On the contrary, it is a well established fact that Barth both opposed Calvin in some respects and wanted to read him in a way that was not entirely true to Calvin's position. However, they do share a limiting view of general revelation that has often been shoved aside as 'too restrictivist'. Nevertheless, taken together on the issue of the *sensus divinitatis*, they offer some good reasons for caution in positing a generousness of revelation in other religions. Calvin and Barth disagree as to the function of general revelation, but at the same time share a limiting view for the same reasons.

Calvin's doctrine of general revelation has an objective and subjective side. Subjectively we have a knowledge of God within our rational capacity (*ratio*) known as the *sensus divinitatis*, or *semen religionis* (and/or the *sensus deiti*), which causes us to be religious beings and to agree with one another that some *God* does exist. We sense this either through a general 'religious consciousness', or a sense of 'servile fear of God', or even a 'troubled conscience'. These three modes of revelation, says Calvin, exempt us from any excuse-making at the judgment. The *sensus divinitatis* is a knowledge of God via the negative, subjective side of humanity that has no saving power. The reason is that this knowledge is distorted and made impure by our own sinfulness. Calvin writes:

As experience shows, God has sown a seed of religion in all men. But, scarcely one man in a hundred is met with who cultivated it, and none in whom it ripens—much less shows fruit in season.[46]

Rather than foster this subjective seed of divine knowledge we either: (1) turn away from God and 'flatly deny his existence'; or (2) 'fashion' a God according to our own whim. 'Thus is overthrown that vain defense with which many are want to gloss over with superstition. *For they think that zeal for any religion*, however preposterous, is sufficient.' While this seed of religion is there in humanity and is uncontestable, yet 'by itself it produces only the worst fruits' and not saving knowledge of God.[47]

But there is, according to Calvin, a second source of general revelation. He writes that 'the knowledge of God shines forth in the fashioning of the universe and the continuing government of it'.[48] If the revelation of God, subjectively, leads humanity to obscure it, the revelation of God in creation 'strips us of every excuse'. God discloses himself in the 'whole workmanship of the universe'. Indeed, the human, created in the image of God, is the 'loftiest' of this source of divine self-revelation. This is the substance of God's objective self-revelation. Here we must keep uppermost in our minds the balanced assessment of Calvin's doctrine of revelation offered to us by Edward Dowey. He writes: 'While it is true that a negative sign stands over the whole of revelation in creation in Calvin's theology, we must not allow this sign to erase from our minds the magnitude of the sum thus negated.'[49] Despite our inability and disobedience in regard to receiving general revelation, it is there for us to see. For Calvin, the 'actual guilt of man is the result of actual rejection of an actual revelation that remains clear'.[50] And yet, there is 'a great gulf fixed' for Calvin between the original purposes of revelation in creation and its function. While man was created with the capacity for revelation in both its subjective and objective modes, he is functioning, in fact, 'under the conditions of sin'. 'It no longer achieves its original purpose, but it operates only to involve the whole human race in the same condemnation.'[51] 'Men who are only taught by nature, have no certain, sound or distinct knowledge, but are confined to confused principles, so that they worship an unknown God.'[52] This leads Calvin to an important

---

46   Calvin, *Institutes* 1.1.48.
47   Calvin, *Institutes* 1.1.51.
48   Calvin, *Institutes* 1.1.51.
49   Edward Dowey, *The Knowledge of God in Calvin's Theology* (Grand Rapids, MI: Eerdmans, 1994), p. 73.
50   Dowey, *The Knowledge of God in Calvin's Theology*, p. 73.
51   Calvin, *Institutes* 1.4.1-2.
52   Calvin, *Institutes* 1.5.12.

conclusion vis-à-vis the extent and usefulness of general revelation in both its forms. He writes:

> Vain therefore, is the light afforded us in the formation of the world to illustrate the glory of its author, which though its rays are diffused all around us, is insufficient to conduct us into the right way. Some sparks are kindled, indeed, but they are smothered before they have emitted any great degree of light.[53]

There is no question that Calvin stands at the center of the debate regarding the place of general revelation in religion and theology in the West. He has been read by some theologians as laying the groundwork for a full natural theology (Brunner), and by others as closing off this alternative altogether (Barth). The truth, as usual, is somewhere in the middle. Regardless of one's orientation to Calvin, his argument remains a difficult one to overcome for those who want a generous revelation of God in nature and conscience that leads to saving knowledge on its own merits.

The outcome of this approach hinges on the relationship between the revelation of God as a *sensus divinitatis* and the revelation of God in his works. Contrary to Pinnock and other inclusivists, and pluralists as well, Calvin does not approach his subject with the *intent* to be 'restrictivist' in his denial of the efficacy of general revelation. That is not his goal here. He is merely working out what he sees to be the universal witness to the response to this general revelation, outside of any knowledge of the incarnation, on the basis of scripture.

Calvin understands the relation between the *sense of the divine* and the self-evident works of God in creation as related in a priority of order. Innate knowledge of God is prior to the knowledge of God inferred from creation. Here the sense of the divine is primary, without which we could not infer the knowledge of God from the works. But he understands this *sensus* to be the gift of God implanted in each of us, and not the product of human rationality *per se*. Edward Adams recently wrote that the *sensus divinitatis* in Calvin is 'not simply a gut feeling, intuition, or vague impression, but a cognition, an intellectual consciousness of God the creator'.[54] In Calvin's words it is a 'deep seated conviction that there is a God'.[55] But Calvin feels compelled to take account of the effects of sin in his doctrine of general revelation, a concept not really accounted for adequately in either Pinnock, McDermott or Hick. Calvin argues that the phenomena of religion, idolatry and atheism all point to the corruption of the *sensus divinitas*, while at the same time establishing the existence of

---

53   Calvin, *Institutes* 1.1.51.

54   Edward Adams, 'Calvin's View of the Natural Knowledge of God', *International Journal of Systematic Theology* 3.3 (2001), p. 284. See nn. 11-14.

55   Calvin, *Institutes* 1.3.1.

the *sensus divinitatis*. This is also why Barth refers to human religion as 'unbelief'. This sense of the divine cannot be 'effaced' or 'uprooted' by these phenomena, but neither can it lead to saving knowledge because of sin.[56] Calvin displays a distrust of these phenomena because of his wariness of 'an intellectual works righteousness' in theological investigation, wherein reason threatens to supplant revelation. 'For Calvin, there is no dichotomy of revelation and reason in the sphere of natural theological knowledge. The faculty of human reason has its part to play in the reception of God's communication of himself in nature. It does not operate independently or in a vacuum but is contingent on experience.'[57] But what is clear in Calvin is that the priority of the *sensus divinitatis* is a point of divine revelation and not a natural human knowledge arrived at through some human faculty divided off from the divine. 'Thus, while revelation and reason are viewed as complementary and not antithetical, revelation has priority over reason.'[58] Indeed, Calvin seems to hold that were it not for the fall of Adam, the *sensus divinitatis* could well have established communion between him and God. Calvin is not comparing our 'post-lapsarian' situation with Adam's pre-lapsarian state, 'but our actual situation, with our situation as it might have been had Adam stayed upright. Had history taken a different course, and we were now living in un-fallen conditions, his point seems to be that, natural revelation would alone be sufficient to secure a right standing with God.'[59] Here we must conclude with Dowey that, since sin is the actual course of history we took in Adam, 'the function of natural revelation' in the world in which we live is 'a negative one'. But in the life of the believer it may function as the 'spectacles' through which 'we can see the glory of God, who has become incarnate for us in Christ'.[60]

What Calvin's view does not permit is an understanding of the *sensus divinitatis* outside of the effects of the fall, as with Hick, McDermott and Pinnock. Nor does he permit the reduction of the Christian faith to a set of rationally perceptible moral fruits, as Hick affirms and Pinnock seems to intimate. In short, the debate continues to be that of the priority of reason over revelation, a delicate balance so often forgotten in our desire for inter-religious dialogue. This was a danger that Barth fought to correct throughout his career. While he often overstated his case, it must be remembered that there was a good deal of validity in his argument, especially given his historical situation. There is still something to learn in his trenchant denial of general revelation and natural theology, and therefore in his censure of religion as 'unbelief'. If we take Barth's

---

56   Calvin, *Institutes* 1.3.3; 1.4.4.
57   Adams, 'Calvin's View of the Natural Knowledge of God', p. 290.
58   Adams, 'Calvin's View of the Natural Knowledge of God', p. 290.
59   Adams, 'Calvin's View of the Natural Knowledge of God', p. 291.
60   Dowey, *Knowledge of God in Calvin's Theology*, p. 83.

criticism of the appeal to the *sensus divinitatis* seriously, while not agreeing completely or even mostly disagreeing, we can at least take a more circumspect approach to the subjective aspect of general revelation as it relates to other religions.

Barth's Critique of the Sensus Divinitatis

There is probably no other aspect of Barth's theology that has received more attention and certainly no more criticism than his concept of revelation. However, this body of secondary material must remain largely untouched here, in favor of letting Barth speak for himself. But even here the material is vast and unwieldy. For our purposes we shall focus on the slender section in the *Church Dogmatics* I/2, §17, where Barth offers his most important critique of religion. As will be shown, the reasons for Barth's criticism of the *sensus divinitatis* are much broader than the popular characterization of it in terms of his opposition to the German church and the natural religion of national socialism. Furthermore, to read it solely in terms of his *Nein* to Brunner is equally misleading. Throughout his career as a pastor and theologian, after 1914, Barth is determined to destroy the hegemony of the liberal, 'culture-Protest-antism' that established itself on a basis of natural theology, in which reason and the rational self held sway over God in his self-revelation, witnessed to in the scriptures. This culture-Protestantism had its origins in the natural theology of sixteenth- to eighteenth-century Reformed theology. It was built on the humanistic impulse of the Renaissance, and led to *Neology* and finally to the epistemological agnosticism of Kant, which denied revelation and reduced religion and Christianity to moral-ity. The basic trajectory of his reason for rejecting the revelatory value of other religions can be applied to our three proponents of a generous revelation of God in those religions in various ways. However, it is his careful analysis of the development of the appeal to religious con-sciousness in the European theological tradition that is most important. It is this reason, seen in that historical development, which should give us pause in following Hick, Pinnock and McDermott on the *sensus divinitatis* here, precisely because their approach reflects this tradition, to varying degrees, especially in its terminus in the priority of reason over revelation in Hick's Kantian pluralism. Space does not permit a full exposition of his exhaustive investigation of that tradition, but his conclusions bare directly on the end point of Hick's program, and potentially can be applied to Pinnock and McDermott as well. So I offer it to the latter two as a caution that needs serious consideration in their approach to the *sensus divinitatis*.

Having surveyed the tradition from Aquinas to Buddaeus and Wolleb, wherein the predominant theological method had been a mixture of appeals to general revelation, via the *sensus divinitatis*, and special revelation, Barth concludes that: 'The Christian element [special revelation], and with this the theological reorientation which had threatened since the Renaissance is complete, has now become *a predicate of the natural* and universal human element.'[61] As such, revelation has become merely the historical confirmation of what man can know about himself and therefore about God apart from revelation. The light of nature may in some instances, in terms similar to McDermott and Pinnock, 'show me the true characteristics' of this special revelation. Thus for culture-Protestantism, says Barth:

> No revelation is true, except it conform to the light of nature and increase it... A true revelation must prove itself such in my heart by a divine power and conviction which I can feel...which the light of nature teaches, which therefore leads me on and

---

61   Barth, *Church Dogmatics*, I/2, p. 289. Far from being driven by any political agenda, Barth states the problem of religion in theology clearly in the opening section of §17. I quote it here at length because it is important to recognize it as the driving concern of his whole treatment of religion in this section, indeed, throughout the *Church Dogmatics*, pp. 283-84: 'If we do not wish to deny God's revelation as revelation, we cannot avoid the fact that it can also be regarded from a standpoint from which it may in certain circumstances be denied as God's revelation... The question raised by the fact that God's revelation has also to be regarded as a religion among other religions is basically the plain question whether theology and the Church and faith are able and willing to take themselves or their basis seriously. For there is an extremely good chance that they will not take themselves and their basis seriously. The problem of religion is simply a pointed expression of the problem of man in his encounter and communion with God. It is, therefore, a chance to fall into temptation. Theology and the Church and faith are invited to abandon their theme and object and to become hollow and empty, mere shadows of themselves. On the other hand they have the chance to keep to their proper task, to become really sure in their perception of it, and therefore to protect and strengthen themselves as what they profess to be. In this decision the point at issue cannot be whether God's revelation has also to be regarded as man's religion, and therefore as a religion among other religions... Does it mean that what we think we know of the nature and incidence of religion must serve as a norm and principle by which to explain the revelation of God; or, *vice versa*, does it mean that we have to interpret the Christian religion and all other religions by what we are told by God's revelation? There is an obvious difference between regarding religion as *the* problem of theology and regarding it as *only one problem* in theology... That is the decision which has to be made.' One of the most important questions to be answered in our time is whether we Christians have indeed fallen into this temptation, failed to take our Christian basis seriously and displaced the true object of theology with revelation as religion in general in the interest of a perceived cultural call for 'inter-religious dialogue' understood as pure agreement.

gives me a desire to seek out and challenge such a revelation, and in that way to demonstrate the true religion.[62]

Barth's concern here is to demonstrate the tendency of reason to overtake revelation when, even in the slightest degree, over a period of time, we give increasingly more weight to the universal sense of the divine. While the conservative theologians of the Reformed tradition initially intended to 'find a more or less perfect agreement between the Bible and traditional teaching on the one hand, and on the other the postulates of *religio naturalis*', their efforts actually led to an 'untenable compromise' which issued in the Neologianist reduction of revelation to pure natural religion. 'The Neologians could not convince themselves that all or even most of what had so far been regarded as revelation could be substantiated before the critical authority of reason.'[63] They therefore felt it necessary to submit 'Christian dogma, as well as the Bible, to a very severe criticism on the basis of the *notiones* of *religio naturalis*'.[64] In the parallel philosophical development during this history, this acquiescence issued in the Kantian critique, which for Barth is the final result of this history of accommodation. Barth concludes that the neologians

were followed by Kantian rationalism, which abolished the Neology, reducing *religio naturalis* to an *ethica naturalis*, and ultimately rejecting revelation, except as the actualizing of the powers of moral reason. Then Schleiermacher tried to find in religion as feeling the essence of theology, revelation being a definite impression, which produces a definite feeling and then a definite religion. Then, according to Hegel, and D.F. Strauss, both Christian and natural religion, are only a dispensable prototype of the absolute awareness of philosophy purified by the idea.[65]

What concerned Barth most here is the idea that once Christianity has been reduced to an *ethica naturalis* it can, as well as any other religion, be dispensed with as a mere part of the process on the way to the realization of philosophy as the Idea, the Absolute, or, in Hick's conception, the Real. Clearly this criticism can be applied to Hick, whose pluralism amounts to this complete reduction of all religion to the Real. But we may not, as of yet, say this about Pinnock and certainly not about McDermott. What is important to register is the tendency toward the elevation of reason over revelation that attends an overly generous reading of the *sensus divinitatis*.

---

62   Barth, *Church Dogmatics*, I/2, p. 290.
63   Barth, *Church Dogmatics*, I/2, p. 290.
64   Barth, *Church Dogmatics*, I/2, p. 290.
65   Barth, *Church Dogmatics*, I/2, p. 290.

Conclusion

While I must register my agreement with the vast majority of commentators who criticize Barth for overstating his case here, especially as critiqued by Berkouwer, we must keep in mind that there are also dangers attendant in understating it.[66] It is interesting that precious few who criticize Barth here actually follow closely his careful reading of the tradition at this point. They read him as though his only reason for rejecting natural religion is simply to deny the German church a basis for the natural religion of blood and soil developed to support Nazism.[67] It is a critique of that to be sure. But it is much more than that. It is also the denial of the Protestant-Liberal tradition that allowed for precisely this state of affairs in Germany between 1928–45. But this was something Barth was already clear on after all his theological teachers signed Kaiser Willhelm's declaration of war in 1914. Barth's opposition to the *sensus divinitatis* should be dated from this point just before World War I, and not in the years prior to World War II. It was then, says Barth, that 'all of the Biblical, theological and ethical presuppositions' of his Protestant-Liberal heritage came crashing down.[68] Unfortunately, the narrow, and usually superficial, critique of Barth has blinded us to the value of his critique of the *sensus divinitatis*. We are merely suggesting that this is precisely the problem in recent attempts to offer an evangelical, or any other, theology of religions from a pluralist or inclusivist perspective. In the long run it shares in the concomitant loss of theology's subject, namely God in his self-revelation in Jesus Christ, which Barth (as well as Calvin) correctly sees as the problem of religion in theology. This, and only this, was Barth's reason for characterizing natural religion, and therefore all religiousness, as 'unbelief'. In the current context, it is this loss of theology's true subject that is entailed in the urgent call among theologians of various persuasions to inter-religious dialogue, cast as it is in the pluralism of Hick and the inclusivism of Clark Pinnock. However overstated, Barth's criticism should give us pause for thought in

---

66   See G.C. Berkouwer's excellent treatment of Barth in his *General Revelation: Studies in Dogmatics* (Grand Rapids, MI: Eerdmans, 1955). The whole work amounts to a response to Barth's criticism of the concept of general revelation and natural theology. But we may not read Berkouwer's criticism of Barth as a denial of the validity of Barth's caution as some do. Berkouwer was amply aware of the dangers that Barth highlighted in the appeal to the *sensus divinitatis*. In the end Berkouwer himself takes a position closer to Barth and Calvin than to our protagonists here.

67   The number of scholars who do this is large. In my estimation this puts Barth at a greater advantage in regard to their denials, precisely because he has a greater sense for the development of the tradition.

68   As quoted in E. Busch, *Karl Barth: His Life from Letters and Autobiographic Texts* (Grand Rapids, MI: Eerdmans, 1975), pp. 81-82.

attributing too much to the *sensus divinitatis*. This issue should and must be decided on, as it was for Calvin and Barth, in relation to the one true subject of theology, God, and therefore, decided on *theologically*.

CHAPTER 19

'For all, for all my Saviour Died'

I. Howard Marshall

The most substantial examination of some of the theological issues raised by the work of Clark Pinnock to come from an author in the UK is the detailed critique of his understanding of the scope of salvation by Daniel Strange.[1] Pinnock holds that God's saving purpose is universal in the sense that the offer of salvation is open in principle to all humankind. Strange is concerned primarily with Pinnock's further proposal that the reception of salvation may be a possibility for people who have not heard of Christ.[2] Basically, Strange thinks that Pinnock is directed towards his inclusivism because he is driven by a 'universality axiom consisting of God's universal salvific will, Christ's universal provision in the atonement, universal accessibility to salvation, and the *Heilsoptimismus*'.[3] If this axiom is invalid, the tension that creates Pinnock's inclusivism is eliminated. Therefore, Strange sees it as his task to question the validity of this axiom.

In doing so he upholds the concept of a limited atonement, according to which God's saving purpose was never intended to encompass more than a limited, pre-chosen group of people; Christ died only for the sins

---

1   D. Strange, *The Possibility of Salvation among the Unevangelised: An Analysis of Inclusivism in Recent Evangelical Theology* (Paternoster Biblical and Theological Monographs; Carlisle: Paternoster Press, 2002).

2   To eliminate all possible misunderstanding, I emphasize that the openness of God's offer of salvation to all is not the same thing as the view that God will ultimately save all people, and it does not even imply it, although, of course, it is a necessary presupposition for those who take such a position. Pinnock is not a universalist. Nor is the writer of this paper. See I.H. Marshall, 'The New Testament does *not* teach Universal Salvation', in R. Parry and C. Partridge (eds), *Universal Salvation? The Current Debate* (Carlisle: Paternoster Press, 2003), ch. 4. To avoid confusion in what follows I use Strange's own term 'universality' to refer to the doctrine of provision of salvation for all people in the atonement wrought by Christ.

3   Strange, *Possibility of Salvation*, p. 265.

of this group (the so-called 'elect')[4] and not for all humankind, and his act of penal substitution must be understood as efficacious for those for whom he was a substitute, so that God's purpose cannot be pronounced a failure in respect of anybody for whom Christ died.

Strange recognizes that he is also criticizing the position of evangelicals who would not necessarily share the inclusivist position. He attacks not only the inclusivism of Pinnock but also the doctrine of the universal availability of salvation that is held both by Pinnock and also by many other scholars, evangelists and Christians generally. His critique, therefore, is explicitly directed not just against Pinnock but against all non-Reformed evangelicalism. By this latter term he refers specifically to those who do not accept the kind of theology contained in the Five Points of Dort with their specific reference to limited atonement. It is the universality of salvation which is at issue.[5] In what follows I shall focus on this specific point.[6]

A Hermeneutical Circle

Strange holds that the interpretation of certain key passages of scripture is dependent upon the theological framework that is basic for the interpreter. Early on in the book he claims that the interpretation of such a text as 1 Timothy 2.4 'depends on, and is itself evidence of, whether one holds to the doctrine of unlimited atonement (God desires to save all men) or limited atonement (God desires to save only the elect)'.[7] When he takes up this specific topic in ch. 9, the biblical material is briefly discussed in a single footnote. Here he notes that expressions like 'all men' could refer to 'all without exception' or 'all without distinction',

4   I shall use the term 'pre-chosen' to refer to the hypothetical limited group whom God purposes to save according to the defenders of limited atonement. I do so in order to avoid any possible misuse of the biblical term 'elect' in this sense.

5   Strange, *Possibility of Salvation*, pp. 139-40. Strange's position also includes a commitment to biblical infallibility, and this is said to presuppose a view of divine sovereignty and human freedom that would not be accepted by Pinnock or presumably by non-Reformed evangelicals. It must suffice to say that, however they may explain it, non-Reformed evangelicals are equally committed to the evangelical position on scripture.

6   The essay is thus relevant to the views of a wider group of evangelicals than simply Clark Pinnock. Nevertheless, I hope that its effect may be to win a more sympathetic hearing for a theologian who has publicly stated that a book of mine (I.H. Marshall, *Kept by the Power of God: A Study of Perseverance and Falling Away* [Minneapolis: Bethany Fellowship, 1969]) was one of the influences that led him to question some aspects of the classical Reformed position and attempt to frame a doctrine of God that does better justice to the biblical evidence.

7   Strange, *Possibility of Salvation*, p. 29 n. 83.

and cites D.A. Carson in favour of the view that in Titus 2.11 the grace of God has appeared to all men, whether Jews or Gentiles, slave or free, without distinction (cf. Tit. 2.10), and not necessarily to all without exception. Similarly, passages referring to 'the world' 'do not mean every individual, rather they are referring to the cosmic side of the atonement and the renewal of creation'.[8]

Such a brief dismissal of the biblical evidence is quite inappropriate in an evangelical critique of a theological position.[9] It must be properly examined, or else the critic will fall under the suspicion of ignoring the Bible in the interests of a pre-conceived theological position. Strange's position is that the texts are ambiguous, and the interpretation given of them will depend on the interpreter's theological framework.

It may be, however, that the exegesis is reasonably firmly based and that one side or the other is avoiding the plain meaning and the general purport of scripture.

The issue of principle here is important. There is a general recognition among evangelical Christians that scripture must be interpreted by scripture. Not only is scripture itself the primary context within which individual texts must be understood, but texts are to be understood within the broad theological framework that comes out of scripture as a whole. A hermeneutical circle exists, in which the meaning of the whole is dependent upon the meaning of the parts, and the meaning of the parts is to be ascertained in the light of the whole. Strange's point is that, if texts are ambiguous, then the meaning that is agreeable to what the interpreter takes to be the general theological framework deduced from scripture as a whole is to be preferred. Thus the person who finds that there is a series of texts which compel the Calvinist interpretation that Christ died for a limited number of people will understand ambiguous texts accordingly; texts which appear to support universal atonement must be given an interpretation which is congenial to this theological framework. They are assumed to be 'ambiguous', and the deciding factor in interpretation is the theological framework adopted by the interpreter.

But this is an over-simplification. If there are texts which appear not to fit in to the 'broad theological framework' of scripture, they may be dealt with in different ways. (a) The interpreter may admit that there appears to be no way of reconciling them with the framework as s/he understands it, but since the framework is thought to be absolutely certain, then the problem texts are put on one side and effectively ignored until a fresh interpretation of them can be found. (b) The texts may be given an interpretation which, it is fair to say, would not be

---

8   Strange, *Possibility of Salvation*, p. 279 n. 33.
9   In his defence it must be said that he is entitled to forego the exegesis in a book that is dealing with many other issues, since he can reasonably plead that others have done the groundwork.

thought plausible if one was not trying to fit them into this general scheme of understanding, but is perhaps just remotely possible. (c) The texts may be recognized to be a part of scripture that must contribute to the establishment of the theological framework, and the interpreter may therefore be led to reconsider what the framework really is.[10] (d) The interpreter may be unable to produce a harmonistic reading of the evidence and is forced to admit that there are tensions in scripture which must be allowed to remain; to that extent the interpretation of scripture must remain somewhat open-ended.[11]

Strange fails to ask: (a) Are the texts that are cited in favour of the non-Calvinist view really ambiguous, or might some of them be much more plausibly interpreted otherwise? (b) Are the texts cited in favour of limited atonement (and related theologoumena) unambiguous in what they imply or might it be that they are ambiguous or indeed better interpreted in another way?

The Case for Limited Atonement

For the sake of simplicity I shall focus on the statement of the arguments for limited atonement given by L. Berkhof.[12] His thesis is that 'the atonement not only made eternal salvation possible for the sinner, but actually secured it'. He stresses that the exact point at issue is not whether Christ's work was sufficient for all people, which it is agreed to be, but rather that 'Christ died for the purpose of actually and certainly saving the elect, and the elect only'. He offers the following two-part 'proof'.

First, there are supporting statements.

(a) God's designs are always efficacious and cannot be frustrated. If Christ did die for all and bear their sins, then this would issue in universalism (which for Berkhof is clearly contradicted in scripture).

---

10   There may be cases where there is no clear evidence that a specific writer or document in scripture works within a postulated theological framework based on other scriptural writings. In such a case it is open to question whether it is methodologically correct to assume this framework for this writer. Thus the kind of framework that might be deduced from the Gospel of John might not fit the Synoptic Gospels. In such cases harmony must be sought at a deeper level of understanding.

11   The same strategies arise in relating the actual statements in the Bible to a doctrine of infallibility.

12   L. Berkhof, *Systematic Theology* (Edinburgh: Banner of Truth Trust, 1958), pp 392-99; see also W. Grudem, *Systematic Theology: An Introduction to Biblical Doctrine* (Leicester: IVP, 1994), pp. 594-603; P. Helm, 'The Logic of Limited Atonement', *Scottish Bulletin of Evangelical Theology* 3.2 (Autumn, 1985), pp. 47-54; R. Letham, *The Work of Christ* (Leicester: IVP, 1993), pp. 225-47.

(b) In fact scripture limits those for whom Christ died to 'his sheep', 'his church', 'his people', 'the elect'.

(c) A distinction between the universality of the atonement and the limitation in its application is not possible because the purchase and the actual bestowal of salvation are inseparably connected. Christ's sacrifice and continuing intercession are two aspects of one work. But since his intercession is only for 'those whom thou hast given me' (Jn 17.9), so also is his sacrifice.

(d) Even if salvation is said to be conditional on human repentance and faith, these things are in fact God's own gift and do not depend on the will of people.

Second, the objections to limited atonement can all be refuted:

(a) Christ is said to have died for the world. But the term 'world' does not always include all people.

(b) Similarly, references to Christ dying for all people should not be interpreted in a universal sense. Romans 5.18, 1 Corinthians 15.22, 2 Corinthians 5.14, and Hebrews 2.9-10 refer only to those who are in Christ. Titus 2.11 refers to all classes of people. 1 Timothy 2.4-6, Hebrews 2.9 and 2 Peter 3.9 all refer to the inclusion of both Jews and Gentiles (but not all of each category!).

(c) Some passages are said to imply the loss of those for whom Christ died. However, Romans 14.15 and 1 Corinthians 8.11 speak of a natural result which, however, God will not allow to happen. 2 Peter 2.1 and Hebrews 10.29 are taken to refer to nominal believers.

(d) The counter-argument that a *bona fide* offer of the gospel to those whom God does not intend to save anyway is not possible can be refuted.

God as the Universal Saviour

'Universal statements' are particularly conspicuous in the Pastoral Epistles. These letters form a group[13] and therefore it is fair to claim that together they form the immediate context within which their individual statements must be understood. Let me set out my conclusions based on detailed discussion elsewhere, but taking into account any significant subsequent contributions to the exegesis of the texts.[14] There are three 'universal' passages:[15]

---

13   For the purposes of this article it is immaterial whether they come directly from Paul or are the work of another writer mediating Paul's legacy to a subsequent audience; I shall refer to their author by the name by which he refers to himself, 'Paul'.

14   Here I summarize material previously published: see I.H. Marshall, 'Universal Grace and Atonement in the Pastoral Epistles', in C.H. Pinnock (ed.), *The Grace of God, the Will of Man: A Case for Arminianism* (Grand Rapids, MI: Zondervan, 1989), pp. 51-69, and *The Pastoral Epistles* (Edinburgh: T. & T. Clark, 1999). See now G. Wieland,

This is good, and pleases God our Saviour, who wants *all* people to be saved and to come to a knowledge of the truth. For there is one God and one mediator between God and human beings, Christ Jesus, himself human, who gave himself as a ransom for *all* people. This has now been witnessed to at the proper time. (1 Tim. 2.3-6)

We have put our hope in the living God, who is the Saviour of *all* people, and especially of those who believe. (1 Tim. 4.10)

For the grace of God has appeared that offers salvation to *all* people. (Tit. 2.11)

1. In every case the terms 'save', 'Saviour' and 'salvation' are used in their normal theological sense to refer to spiritual salvation. This is so even in 1 Timothy 4.10, where some scholars have defended the view that God is here the general benefactor of all people in this world and especially so of believers (presumably in that he confers eternal life upon them), and that what we have here is a warning against venerating human beings as gods and saviours.[16] This view can be confidently rejected since it imports a sense of 'saviour' which is unlikely after the clear previous use in 1 Timothy 2.3-6 and indeed throughout the Pastoral Epistles;[17] it also requires that the term be understood very awkwardly in two different senses with the two nouns that are dependent upon it, in a this-worldly non-spiritual sense with the former and in an eschatological spiritual sense with the latter. While a contrast with the use of the title for earthly rulers may be implicit, nothing suggests that here the author is suggesting that the saving activity of his God is of the same kind as theirs.

2. When Paul says that God 'wants' all to be saved (θέλω; 1 Tim. 2.4), this verb cannot be given a weak sense, such that this is merely what God would wish or desire; God here wills or wishes the salvation of all, just as elsewhere in these letters he is said to be the saviour of all.[18]

We may conveniently include here the statement in 2 Peter that God does not want anyone to perish (2 Pet. 3.9). The context is the judgment and destruction of the ungodly, which God does not want anyone to undergo, although it is recognized that some will not repent. According to M. Green, whereas Calvin posits '"a secret decree of God by which the wicked are doomed to their own ruin", the plain meaning is that, al-

---

'The Theology of Salvation in the Pastoral Epistles' (unpublished PhD thesis, University of Aberdeen, 2003).

15   Translations are from TNIV which avoids gender-specific language. I assume that nobody will dispute that both men and women are included in these and other texts.

16   W.D. Mounce, *Pastoral Epistles* (Word Biblical Commentary, 46; Nashville, TN: Nelson, 2000), pp. 256-57, following S.M. Baugh, '"Savior of All People": 1 Tim. 4:10 in Context', *Westminster Journal of Theology* 54 (1992), pp. 331-40.

17   Cf. 1 Tim. 1.1; 2 Tim. 1.10; Tit. 1.3, 4; 2.10, 13; 3.4, 6.

18   So rightly Mounce, *Pastoral Epistles*, pp. 85-86, who recognizes that the Calvinist interpretation cannot be gained here by mistranslation of the verb.

though God wants all men to be saved, and although He has made provision for all to be accepted, some will exercise their God-given free will to exclude God'.[19] R. Bauckham holds that the reference here is to Christians, but that 'the *principle*...can be validly extended...to God's desire that all people should repent'.[20] It is more likely that the writer is applying to his readers a broader principle that God wants all people to repent (cf. Acts 17.30) and this applies in particular to the readers. The alternative is to follow Calvin and postulate a 'secret decree' that cuts across this desire, but this is a highly questionable procedure: how does Calvin, or anybody else, know what God has secretly decreed, and what grounds are there for thinking that he has a secret will that over-rules what he has openly declared?

3. 'All' cannot be scaled down to refer simply to 'many'. I mention this unlikely interpretation because 1 Timothy 2.6 is based on Mark 10.45 where the Son of Man came to give his life as a ransom for 'many', and somebody interested in defending a limited saving purpose by God might be tempted to argue that Mark 10.45 has priority in interpretation. But this latter passage in turn is based on Isaiah 53.11-12, and here it is clear that the use of 'many' is not to make a contrast with 'all' but rather with 'one'; the point is that the action of a single person, the Servant of Yahweh, is effective for a vastly greater number. There are no grounds for thinking that 'all' means less than 'all'. This point is not unimportant, because if 1 Timothy 2.6 is to be understood against this background, then the grounds adduced by some scholars for taking it to mean 'all kinds of' people become all the less persuasive.[21]

4. 'All' cannot be understood to refer (only) to people who have already become believers. This would make nonsense of the texts which are concerned with people who need to believe in order to be saved.

5. The term 'all' is not to be understood as 'all [without exception] of the limited group whom God purposes to save', i.e. 'all the pre-chosen'. Nothing in the immediate contexts suggests such a limitation, and I am not aware of any commentator who has adopted it.

---

19   M. Green, *2 Peter and Jude* (Tyndale New Testament Commentaries; London: Tyndale, 1968), p. 136.

20   R.J. Bauckham, *Jude, 2 Peter* (Word Biblical Commentary, 50; Waco, TX: Word, 1983), p. 314; cf. p. 321. The narrower context is that 'the Lord is patient with you', sc. the readers, and therefore there is a particular warning to any within the congregation who have been misled by the false teachers (2 Pet. 2.1-3; 3.9) and an indication of the Lord's concern lest any of them should perish (2 Pet. 3.11-18). But the wider context includes an extended reference to the scoffers and the ungodly (2 Pet. 3.3-7), and there is no suggestion that they, or anybody else, are excluded from the Lord's concern. I am tempted, therefore, to argue that the text itself is not limited to 'Christians'; but in any case the principle is of broad application.

21   In Rom. 5.12-19 'all' and 'many' alternate without any distinction in reference.

6. The term 'all' is not to be narrowed down to mean 'all kinds of' or (as Strange puts it) 'all without distinction'. On this view the texts are affirming that God's offer of salvation is not confined to Jews (and therefore includes Gentiles as well; 1 Tim. 2.3-6; 4.10) or not confined to free people (and therefore includes slaves; Tit. 2.11). This is the only plausible alternative understanding of the term.[22] The presence of Judaizing tendencies in the false teaching that is being opposed in the Pastoral Epistles may well have led to a stress on the fact that the gospel was for Gentiles, and not simply for Jews; the term 'all' would make this point. Recognition of this fact enables the defender of limited atonement to say that God wants to save people from all nations and classes in society but the text does not, or need not, imply that he wants to save all people within any of these categories.[23]

Paul's intention may be to include this point, but it does not justify the limited interpretation. In 1 Timothy 2.1-7, v. 1 calls for prayer for all people, including those in authority. Now in v. 2 'all in authority' surely means 'all without exception' rather than 'all the different types of people in authority', since no reason can be offered for limiting the prayers to some people in authority and not to others, especially when no criterion is given as to which rulers are or are not to be prayed for. But, if so, v. 1 cannot be limited to prayer for all types of people, especially when there is no criterion for knowing who is included or excluded. Moreover, at this point there is nothing to indicate that there is any special emphasis on Gentiles as well as Jews, although the persons in authority are more likely to be Gentiles. This makes it less than likely that v. 4, which gives the theological backup for the preceding command, is to be taken any less broadly. It would in fact be very odd, if not grotesque, if the statement had to be paraphrased to mean that God wants to save people from all categories but only some of them. Could any first-century reader in Ephesus have tumbled on this interpretation of what Paul really meant? And again in v. 6 it is hard to see any reason for such a translation, even if part of the intention is to ensure that Gentiles are included alongside Jews. Can we really imagine that, if a messenger brought the letter to its destination with instructions to clarify any difficult points (cf. Acts 15.27; Col. 4.7-8), he paused at this point and said, 'But of course you know that God does not want to save every individual person; it's only some Jews and some Gentiles that he wants to

---

22 More precisely, the 'Jews and Gentiles' interpretation is applied in 1 Tim. 2 and the 'free people and slaves' interpretation in Tit. 2.

23 It would be casuistic to argue that, since human individuals are each unique in some kind of way, 'all kinds of people' is ultimately synonymous with 'all people'. Such logic-chopping is inappropriate, but it does indicate that we should beware of rigid distinctions.

save'? It would be rhetorically disastrous to explain that God's grace is limited to 'some people from all categories, but not them all'.

There is the further problem that, if salvation is limited to a preordained group, then there is no point in praying for the non-ordained/reprobate, since nothing can change their fate. True, we do not know who are reprobate and who are in line for salvation, and therefore we don't know whose salvation to pray for, but we are going to have to pray some strange prayers: 'O God, I pray for the salvation of my brother-in-law, if he is one you have chosen for salvation, but if he is not, then I recognize that my prayer is not going to make any difference.' Does anybody, even an upholder of limited atonement, really pray like that?[24] This view is implausible in 1 Timothy 2 because it would carry the implication that in v. 1 prayers are to be offered in general terms for both Jews and Gentiles, but only for some of them, namely those whom God has chosen to save and those rulers who are responsible for curbing persecution of believers.

To gain the 'limited' interpretation of Titus 2.10 it has to be argued that it refers to the different types of people mentioned in the earlier part of the chapter (older people and younger people, both male and female, and slaves), by providing a motivation for the Christian conduct that is expected of all of them. But why should this have needed stress? Did anybody think that any of these groups were possibly not included in God's saving plan? Rather, the point of vv. 11-14 is to indicate how the imperatives regarding Christian conduct are based on the purpose behind God's saving plan and work. There is a use of traditional language in this section, again based ultimately on Mark 10.45, and the universal reference may well have been associated with it.[25]

In 1 Timothy 4.10 there is no reason to think that the Jew/Gentile distinction is within the writer's horizon. There is rather a stress on the universality of God's function as Saviour, which then has to be qualified by recognizing that the condition of faith has to be attached to it. The added phrase is best translated as 'namely, believers' and understood as making it plain that what is potential or available for all, actually becomes a reality for believers. To say that God is the Saviour of (some, namely those whom he has already chosen out of) all kinds of people (e.g. Jews, Arabs, slaves, children), and then to further qualify it by limiting it to believers is not convincing.[26]

---

24   This would suggest that a belief in limited atonement does not in fact affect the evangelistic and prayerful activity of those who in theory hold to it.

25   The verse does not say that God's grace has appeared to all people, but that God's grace that is salvific for all people, has appeared. See, more fully, W.L. Liefeld, *1 and 2 Timothy, Titus* (Grand Rapids, MI: Zondervan, 1999), pp. 337-38.

26   Significantly, Mounce rejects such explanations in favour of the view that 'Saviour' is meant in a non-spiritual sense. See n. 18 above.

The purpose and effect of the phraseology in the Pastoral Epistles is not just to emphasize that Gentiles are included alongside Jews, but to magnify the grace of God who is concerned for all people and not just for some people. On the limited interpretation we have to do one or other of the following. We have to assume that readers would get the meaning 'God wants to save all kinds of people, but of course it must be understood that he doesn't actually want to save everybody. It's not just that there may/will be people who reject salvation, but that he wants to save only some rather than all.' Or we have to assume that this is the secret, unspoken thought of the writer. Such a limitation goes clean against the force of the actual statements and ends up by minimizing the grace of God rather than maximizing it.

But again we have to ask whether there is anything in the broader context that suggests such a limitation. Does anything in the letters imply a purpose that is less than universal, and does it do so in a way that would dispose the readers to take the universal texts in a different sense than the obvious one?

The indications are clear that the writer did not expect everybody to be saved, unless they repented and believed (1 Tim. 1.19-10; 4.1; 5.8; 6.10, 21; 2 Tim. 2.17-19, 25-26; Tit. 1.16). But that does not imply that God does not want everybody to be saved.

There are, however, a couple of references to the 'elect' that might be thought to suggest such a limitation. Elsewhere I have shown that the normal use of this term in the New Testament is to refer to those who have actually become God's people rather than to people who have been chosen beforehand for salvation but have not yet been called and made their response.[27] It is in effect a self-reference by people who know that they now belong to God's chosen people. What of the two references in the Pastoral Epistles?[28]

In Titus 1.1 Paul's apostleship is related to the faith of God's elect. This could refer to the purpose of bringing those who are as yet unsaved to faith, or to the purpose of strengthening the faith of those who already believe, or the whole phrase may mean that Paul's apostleship is exercised in accordance with the faith held by God's people. In view of the uniform usage elsewhere of 'elect' to mean the people of God, i.e. Israel, Mounce agrees that it refers to 'Christians', 'those who have faith'.[29]

---

27   I.H. Marshall, 'Election and Calling to Salvation in 1 and 2 Thessalonians', in R.F. Collins (ed.), *The Thessalonian Correspondence* (Leuven: Leuven University Press, 1990), pp. 259-76.

28   1 Tim. 5.21, with its reference to angels, is irrelevant.

29   Mounce, *Pastoral Epistles*, p. 379. G.W. Knight III, *The Pastoral Epistles* (New International Greek Testament Commentary; Grand Rapids, MI: Eerdmans/Carlisle: Paternoster Press, 1992), pp. 282-83, says that it refers to 'Christians' and then cites W.

In 2 Timothy 2.10 Paul says that he endures everything because of the elect so that they may partake in salvation in Jesus Christ with eternal glory. This could presumably refer to Paul's missionary efforts to ensure that those destined for salvation (but not yet believers) become believers and persevere to entry to God's heavenly kingdom and glory.[30] More probably it refers to his efforts so that those who are now God's people persevere to the end. The immediate context with its promises and warnings in vv. 11-13 strongly favours this interpretation.[31] Since elsewhere in the New Testament the term 'elect' never refers to potential people of God rather than actual people of God, and there is no reason here to take it in any other than its normal sense, we should do so here.

Needless to say, saving is the work of God our Saviour, and therefore we are not surprised by statements to this effect.[32] The proposition that salvation is bestowed by God (cf. Tit. 3.5) is not a matter of dispute; but it is not the same thing as a statement of limited atonement (unless it is insisted that the atonement and conversion are welded together as components of one action of God). The fact that faith and repentance may be thought of as gifts bestowed by God (1 Tim. 1.14) is of course no proof of limited atonement.

There is one reference to the premundane plan of God to save people not according to works but according to his purpose and grace given to us in Christ before eternal ages (2 Tim. 1.9). Here the 'us' are the people who actually form the church, 'us believers'. How we can be said to have received grace before we existed is mysterious. We are to envisage a saving purpose of God that was formed at that point and was so certain to be fulfilled that it could be said to be given at that time. The question that then arises is whether grace was given to specific individuals at that time and only to a limited number. Certainly it would seem that God could be affirming his intention to give grace to 'us', the human race in need of salvation, at that time and then actualizing it at a later date. But does that imply that he gave it only to a limited group and gave it in a way that was bound to lead to the salvation of all of them? This does not follow, unless

---

Bauer, *A Greek–English Lexicon of the New Testament and Other Early Christian Literature* (trans. W.F. Arndt and F.W. Gingrich, 2nd edn rev. and augmented by F.W. Gingrich and F.W. Danker from Bauer's 5th edn [1958]; Chicago: University of Chicago Press, 1979), p. 242: 'those whom God has chosen...and drawn to himself', but seems to take this to include people who have yet to turn to God in faith. The evidence that he cites does not support this latter interpretation.

30   So Knight, *Pastoral Epistles*, p. 399, interpreting in the light of Acts 13.48; 18.9-10.

31   Mounce, *Pastoral Epistles*, pp. 514-15, inclines to the same interpretation.

32   Texts that refer to God's care of those who are saved to keep them from falling away (2 Tim. 2.19) do not imply any limitation of his saving purpose.

one brings in the further axiom that whatever God desires to do he will necessarily accomplish.

Thus there is nothing in the Pastoral Epistles themselves to suggest a theological framework that requires us to understand their teaching in terms of limited atonement. In fact, imposition of this scheme leads to forced and improbable understandings of key texts. But if this is so, may we not have to recognize a different theological framework for the understanding of texts about the atonement?

For Whom did Christ Die?

Statements about Christ dying (or equivalent terms) for certain people or groups of people, mostly employing the preposition *hyper*, are common in the New Testament. The majority of these are stated in terms of those who have been saved and form part of God's people. There is one example of Paul saying that Christ died for him personally (Gal. 2.20); any individual believer is one for whom Christ died (Rom. 14.15). More often it is said that Christ died 'for us' (Rom. 5.8; 2 Cor. 5.21; Gal. 3.13; Eph. 5.2; 1 Thess. 5.10; Tit. 2.14; 1 Jn 3.16; cf. 1 Cor. 15.3 and Gal. 1.4 [our sins]), or for 'all of us' (Rom. 8.32). In a number of places Jesus says that he dies for 'you', meaning his disciples (Lk. 22.19, 20; 1 Cor. 11.24) or a writer may tell his Christian audience that Christ died for them (1 Pet. 2.21; cf. by implication 1 Cor. 1.13).

Other texts state that Christ died for 'the church' (Eph. 5.25) or for 'the sheep' (Jn 10.15) or for the people or nation (Jn 11.50, 51, 52; 18.14; cf. Heb. 2.17). In the latter group of texts there is a *double entendre* in that Caiaphas is thinking of Jesus being put to death for the good of the Jewish people as a whole (to avoid Roman reprisals if there were to be a messianic uprising), whereas John sees in this a prophecy of his death in a salvific manner.

Some texts affirm that Christ died for 'many' (Mk 10.45; 14.24; Mt. 20.28; 26.28; cf. Heb. 2.10; 9.28), but this term is replaced by 'you' in some parallels (Lk. 22.19-20; 1 Cor. 11.24) or by 'all' (1 Tim. 2.6) or by 'us' (Tit. 2.14). The term 'all' also appears in 2 Corinthians 5.14, 15a, 15b, Hebrews 2.9.

Finally, a number of texts emphasize that Christ died for sinners, the ungodly (Rom. 5.6, 8; 1 Pet. 3.18).

What can we draw from these texts? The concept of dying for others (which was well-known in the ancient world[33]) is expressed using language based on Isaiah 53. The words of Jesus at the Last Supper are

---

33   M. Hengel, *The Atonement: The Origins of the Doctrine in the New Testament* (London: SCM Press, 1981), pp. 6-15.

applied to the disciples present ('you'), and this application becomes widespread as preachers and writers addressing Christian believers remind them that Christ died for 'us (all)' or for 'you'.

Jesus came to the existing people of God, the Jews, in order to bring salvation to them. The Jews, despite being the people chosen by God, are sinful and need to have their sins removed (Lk. 2.10; cf. Mt. 1.21). The offer is open to all, even though not all accept it. Therefore, Jesus dies for the people, i.e. the Jewish people as a whole (Jn 11.50-52); but at the same time it is recognized that the scope of his death extends to the world as a whole (Jn 1.29).

Within this context it is natural for Jesus to say that he dies for those who are already his disciples and friends (Jn 15.13-14), but this does not cancel out the sayings where his death is also understood more widely to be for the people or the nation. The imagery of the shepherd must be treated with care. When Jesus picks up the motif of the good shepherd who is willing to die for the welfare of the sheep, the picture is of a shepherd risking his life against a wild animal attacking the sheep who already constitute his flock (Jn 10.12; cf. 1 Sam. 17.34-37). The actuality is rather different in that Jesus dies on account of sin and he receives his life back again. The parabolic material does no more than illustrate the principle of vicarious death. It would be unwise, therefore, to press the parable further and assert that Jesus dies only for his sheep, as if he acquired the flock by dying for them. Of course the sheep are given to him by the Father, but this says nothing about the scope of his death.

To press the language and say that Jesus has prospective sheep, for whom he dies, surely goes beyond the horizon of the imagery. More probably, the thought is primarily of the Jewish people as the flock of God, continuance in which is dependent on coming to Christ; but there are also other sheep not of this fold, for whom presumably he also lays down his life. The saying does not exclude the wider statements of scope found elsewhere in the same Gospel. There is certainly a distinction made between 'my sheep' and his Jewish opponents who are not 'my sheep'. But it would be pressing the metaphor too hard to take from it that there is a boundary already fixed between Jesus' sheep and other sheep, particularly since Jesus is still encouraging people to believe in him (Jn 10.38).

When Jesus is said to have purchased the church by his blood (Acts 20.28) or to have loved the church and given himself for it (Eph. 5.25; here the church is equivalent to 'us' in Eph. 5.2), the metaphor is one of ransoming people (cf. Rev. 5.9-10), and is used confessionally by those who have benefited from what Christ has done. Here the love is for the prospective bride, and it is over-pressing the imagery to say that this means that Christ died only for a limited group of people who are destined to be the bride.

Acts 20.28 is a statement about the importance of caring for 'the church of God' whose value is seen in that he bought it with his own blood. The death of Jesus leads to the redemption of the church, but it is outside the horizon of the metaphor as it is used here to ask whether this implies that God has secretly decided who may enter the church and who is excluded from it.

In Romans 8.32-35 God gave up Jesus 'for us all', who are 'those whom God has chosen', but this is confessional language, spoken by those whom God has admitted to the elect. Again, nothing is said that implies that God has limited the scope of the death of Jesus to this group. In short, these passages suggest that God created a new community by the death of his Son and entry into it gives one a place among those for whom Christ died. The person who is in can confess 'the Son of God loved me and gave himself for me'; the community know that Christ died for our sins.[34]

In 2 Corinthians 5.14-15 Paul states that one died for all, so that those who live might do so no longer for themselves but for the one who died and was raised for them. Supporters of limited atonement urge that 'all' cannot mean 'all without exception' here, since that would imply universalism in that it states that 'all have died'.

We have here the same problem as in Romans 5.18 where 'just as one man's trespass led to condemnation for all, so one man's act of right-eousness leads to justification and life for all' and in 1 Corinthians 15.22 'for as all die in Adam, so all will be made alive in Christ'. In both these texts it is surely the case that the first 'all' refers to all without exception' (cf. Rom. 3.23), and it would be extraordinary if the second 'all' meant anything else.[35] The second parts of both texts refer to the availability of life for all that becomes a reality for them provided that they believe. If so, these texts are about the universal sufficiency of the death of Christ (a doctrine accepted by Berkhof on the basis of other texts). Consequently, we have examples where 'all' does mean 'all without exception' in statements relating to the availability of salvation. The significance of this is that we do not need to take statements about 'all' to refer to 'all apart from those not pre-chosen', and such an interpretation of them is in fact unjustified.

---

34   On the use of 'many' see above. 'Many' is paraphrased as 'all' in 1 Tim. 2.6 and is used interchangeably with 'all' in Rom. 5. It refers to people in general in Isa. 53, and the context does not suggest that it is deliberately chosen to impose a restriction; it is the more appropriate term to use when making the contrast with the one person who dies.

35   If we attempt to interpret these verses in conformity with a doctrine of limited atonement, the thrust of Paul's argument is lost, in that the free gift turns out not to be as great as the trespass. It is understandable how this passage is appealed to by defenders of universalism.

This indicates how we are to take the statements in 2 Corinthians 5:14-15. Since Christ died for all, it follows that all human beings are intended to live for him and not for themselves. Likewise, in 2 Corinthians 5.18-21 Paul is writing about a reconciliation of the world which has become a reality for those ('us') who believe. God truly no longer counts the world's trespasses against it, but this offer of reconciliation becomes a reality only for those who respond to it and do not accept the grace of God in vain.[36]

We are thus encouraged to accept the plain sense of various statements. When Paul says that Christ died for the ungodly (Rom. 5.6, 8), he is no doubt thinking specifically of his readers because he wants to make the point that if Christ died for them while they were still weak, ungodly sinners, he will all the more deliver those who have been justified at the judgment. But there is no reason to qualify the absolute 'the ungodly' by saying that this means only the 'pre-chosen ungodly' who have believed or will believe. Statements that Christ died for 'us' do not carry the logical implication that he died for nobody else.

There are admittedly remarkably few evangelistic statements which state that Christ died for all or for 'you' addressed to those who are not yet saved. But this is readily explained by the fact that most New Testament teaching is addressed to those who are already believers and examples of evangelistic preaching are few. However, when Paul summarizes the gospel that he proclaimed in Corinth as 'Christ died for *our* sins' (1 Cor. 15.3), this is surely a case of the preacher including his unsaved audience with him in an inclusive statement. It most certainly is *not* a statement that he died only for the sins of those who are already believers. Similar statements elsewhere (1 Thess. 5.10) were doubtless part of the kerygma.[37]

It will not do to say that these statements have to do only with the 'sufficiency' or 'availability' (Grudem's term) of the death of Christ, since the language used is exactly the same as in those statements that refer to Christ's death for 'us' as believers. And how can the atonement be sufficient for all if it was limited to some?

---

36   Berkhof, *Systematic Theology*, pp. 396-97, notes Heb. 2.9 and takes 'taste death on behalf of all' to refer only to all who are in Christ (the 'many sons' in v. 10). But there is nothing that requires us to limit 'all' to 'all who will actually be saved', particularly in a letter which talks of the danger of repudiating the salvation offered to the world (Heb. 2.3). To paraphrase the statement as 'taste death for all who are predestined by God for salvation' is to import alien ideas into the text that are not justified by anything in the letter.

37   Space forbids discussion of the problem as to why the vicarious character of Christ's death is not mentioned in the evangelistic speeches in Acts.

The Use of 'World'

We must now take a closer look at the use of 'world'.[38] This motif is especially found in John and 1 John. Jesus came to bring salvation for the world (Jn 1.29; 3.16; 4.42; 6.33, 51; 12.46-47; 1 Jn 2.2; 4.14). The fact that the term does not always include all people does not settle the question of what it means in the crucial texts. It is a flexible term. It can refer to the world or universe in which people live or to the world and its people, with the accent on the latter. It can be used hyperbolically. It signifies primarily the world of human beings rather than inanimate nature.

Strange's comment that 'passages referring to "the world" do not mean every individual, rather they are referring to the cosmic side of the atonement and the renewal of creation'[39] is quite eccentric and incapable of substantiation. John 3.16 is certainly not a statement about the cosmic aspect of the atonement and the renewal of creation. It is about God's love for humankind, and the purpose of his love is specifically stated to be that believers should not perish but have eternal life.[40] There is not a hint here of concern for anything other than the world of human beings. The long tradition that treats this text as an invitation to belief and salvation indicates how it is meant to be understood.

Moreover, the text does not make sense if the real (secret) significance of it is 'God loved the world in such a way that he gave his Son [to die for some of its members] so that whosoever believes may have eternal life'. Such a paraphrase falls down in two respects. (a) It so qualifies the love of God for the world that a statement which appears to be expressing the magnitude of divine love is severely diminished in force. (b) It implies that you can't believe unless you are one of the limited group for whom Christ died.

Nor does the term 'world' itself really mean 'a limited group of people within the world'. Carson rightly points out that God can condemn the sins of people while he still loves them and weeps for all who stand under his condemnation and will not repent. 'He pronounces terrifying condemnation on the grounds of the world's sin, while still loving the world so much that the gift he gave to the world, the gift of his Son, remains the world's only hope.'[41] It is impossible to read this in

---

38   See P. Woodbridge, '"The World" in the Fourth Gospel', in D. Peterson (ed.), *Witness to the World* (Carlisle: Paternoster Press, 1999), pp. 1-31.

39   Strange, *Possibility of Salvation*, p. 279 n. 33.

40   Consequently, it cannot be treated merely as a statement of 'common grace' as opposed to 'saving grace'.

41   D.A. Carson, *The Gospel according to John* (Leicester: Apollos, 1991), pp. 204-205. It is interesting that Carson cannot avoid saying 'so much', even though οὕτως strictly means 'in such a way'.

such a way that the 'gift of his Son' is the hope of only some in the world, a limited number for whose sake Christ came. The death of Christ can hardly be an indication of God's love for the world if that death was not for the world. We also again face the problem of God having an unfulfilled desire which Berkhof is presumably not prepared to allow.[42] Such paraphrases as 'God so loved [some people in] the world that he gave his one and only Son, so that whoever [God has caused to] believe in him shall not perish' are wildly implausible. Jesus came in order to save the world, in order that the world might believe.[43]

The point is confirmed by other references in John which tell us that Christ takes away the sins of the world (Jn 1.29; cf. 6.51), that he is the light of the world and its saviour (8.12; 9.5; 4.42; 1 Jn 4.14), that he came to save the world (12.47), and that he wants his followers to be one so that the world may believe (17.21). The plain sense of such statements is that Jesus offers salvation to anybody who hears the message throughout the world, although he knows well enough that not all will respond positively to his message. It is not possible to limit 'world' to mean 'all without distinction but not all without exception'; the plain sense of the sayings is that salvation is available for all and is offered to all and can be received by those who believe.

1 John 2.2 indicates that Christ died for our sins and the sins of the whole world. Although there has been a distinction in ch. 1 between 'we' and 'you' (1.5), this has disappeared by vv. 6-10 where the readers are included in the preacher's 'we', and this is manifestly the case in 2.1-2. Therefore, it can be ruled out that 'we' are Jewish believers and the 'world' is the pre-chosen among the Gentiles. The added phrase is of enormous importance, because it shows that salvation is not limited to those who have already received it in this letter and that there is no concern for those outside the Christian community. Moreover, it emphasizes that the *whole* world is in view. Commentators rightly recognize that the death of Jesus is 'sufficient to deal with the sins of the whole world, but that his sacrifice does not become effective until people believe in him'.[44] This is the 'natural' meaning of the text and should be adopted unless there is reason to reject it.

---

42   It is impossible for theologians of any school to avoid recognizing that God has unfulfilled desires.

43   The redeemed community naturally speak of the way in which God loves 'us', recognizing that their salvation is due to God's love for them (Rom. 5.8). It is inevitably believers who make confession of God's love and do so in terms of what they personally have experienced. It does not follow, however, that if a person does not belong to 'us' (actually or potentially), then God does not love that person.

44   C.G. Kruse, *The Letters of John* (Leicester: Apollos, 2000), p. 75.

Problems for the Upholders of Universality

The Penalty for Sin is Exacted Twice

Defenders of limited atonement argue that if Christ died for all, and then some people are condemned and suffer the penalty of their sins, this is unfair because it means that the penalty is paid twice for their sins, once by Christ and once by themselves.

The objection is based on the assumption that the bearing of condemnation by Christ is to be understood in the same way as in the case of a human situation; here if a friend of the guilty person bore the penalty due to him (e.g. by paying a fine on his behalf), then it would be unjust for the court to demand that the guilty person should also do so. I am not sure what would happen if the guilty person protested that he was not going to accept the action done on his behalf. Clearly the court would not accept two payments of the fine, but it could respect the guilty person's refusal of the friendly offer. But this aspect of the analogy cannot be pressed with respect to the death of Christ. Here a death takes place which has the potential to deliver all humankind from condemnation, but it does not actually do so unless the sinner is joined by faith to Christ and identified with him. The view then, that the death of Christ is sufficient for all people but does not become effective except for those who accept Christ as their substitute is sound enough. But to say that the death of Jesus is sufficient for all would normally mean that it is a death for all. In the case of the person who rejects Christ, his substitution in respect of them is repudiated.

The Fulfilment of God's Purposes

It is objected that, if Christ died for all, then God's purpose is not carried through because Christ's dying for people and the actual reception of salvation by them are two parts of one, indivisible purpose. But God cannot have purposes that are not fulfilled.

Even on the limited atonement view, however, it is admitted that God must be allowed to have desires that are not fulfilled. The expressions of his regret that people do not trust, love and obey him are clear evidence that his desires are not fulfilled. To get round this, Berkhof has to postulate that what God 'really' wants and purposes is something different and hidden from our view. We have therefore to deal with a God who deceives humanity by saying that he desires the salvation of the wicked but has secretly determined to do nothing about it in the case of some of them by passing over them.

But it is not obvious on Berkhof's premises how it is possible for a perfect God to have unfulfilled desires. For Berkhof's God to have unfulfilled desires is surely a denial of his perfection. Moreover, the line between desires and purposes is a very fine one, and it is dubious whether one can solve the problem by making a distinction between unfulfilled purposes (not possible for God) and unfulfilled desires (possible for God).

The crucial fact is that there is evil in the universe, and there is no way that God can so work it into his purposes and desires that things are entirely as he would have them be. Otherwise, evil would be entirely overcome, or we would have to say that God accepted evil as part of his purpose (which would be extraordinary given the force of his condemnations of it in scripture!).[45] But once it is recognized that God can have desires and purposes which are not fulfilled, then the binding of atonement and actual salvation to one another need no longer be presupposed.[46]

The Inseparability of Atonement and Reception of Salvation

However, we must also question whether there is an inseparable connection between the purchase and the bestowal of salvation. There is no doubt that God provides: (a) the atonement, on the basis of which salvation is possible; and (b) the 'means of grace' through which salvation becomes a reality for the individual. That is not in dispute, and it means that salvation is from start to finish the work of God. But to recognize these two provisions is not the same thing as to say that they are one and the same, and that you cannot have the one without the other.[47] We noted that Berkhof claims to find support for the close link between atonement and the application of its effects in that the sacrificial work of Christ and his intercession are two sides of one and the same work; since the latter is limited to those actually saved, so is the former. He cites John 17.9 where Jesus prays not for the world but for those whom the Father has given to him. However, this overlooks John 17.20, where Jesus says that his prayer is not for them alone but for those who

---

45   Cf. the treatment by D.A. Carson, *Divine Sovereignty and Human Responsibility* (London: Marshall, Morgan and Scott, 1981), pp. 212-14, which recognizes that there is no entirely satisfactory solution.

46   There is also a distinction between the saving purpose of God, that people should be holy, and the actual results. The effects of conversion in terms of ethical life can be very varied in that Christians continue to fall into sin and fail to do good. It would seem that again God has desires or purposes which are not immediately fulfilled.

47   Berkhof, *Systematic Theology*, p. 395, cites Mt. 18.11 (not in modern critical texts); Rom. 5.10; 2 Cor. 5.21; Gal. 1.4; 3.13; Eph. 1.7. Without going into details, I would argue that none of these texts demonstrate that because Christ purchased salvation, it is inevitable that it is accepted and fully realized.

believe in him through their message, and his prayer is that they may be one so that the world may believe that God has sent him. That is surely prayer for the world.[48]

The preaching of the gospel assumes a distinction between what God has done in Christ and the need for people to respond to it, with the recognition that the response may be negative. In 2 Corinthians 5.18-21 God was in Christ reconciling the world to himself, but this is followed by his ambassadors putting an offer before people that they are called upon to accept so that they may in fact be reconciled to God. Nowhere does Paul's language imply that the bearing of sin is purely for those whom he knows will respond positively. We lack any statements that say that Christ died only for some of humankind; here in fact he was reconciling the world to himself, not counting trespasses against 'them', i.e. the people who comprise the 'world'.

Berkhof further argues that 'the atonement secures the fulfilment of the conditions that must be met, in order to obtain salvation'. But the texts he cites do not prove his point.[49] To say that God provides the means of acceptance, namely faith and the gift of the Spirit, does not require that God, having given Christ for the sins of the world, should act to save every individual.

Finally, there is the problem of texts which might suggest that some for whom Christ died may not eventually attain to salvation. The reference in Romans 14.15 to the possible destruction of the brother for whom Christ died is taken by Berkhof to refer to a possibility that God will not allow to happen.[50] Whether that is so or not, Paul was clearly capable of using such language to make his point, and he could not have done so if he believed that Christ's death for somebody infallibly led to their salvation. Berkhof states that 2 Peter 2.1 and Hebrews 10.29 refer to nominal non-elect believers who claimed (falsely) that Christ had bought them. This may be the case, but it is based on the assumption that the pre-chosen cannot fall away and hence is a circular argument.

---

48   In the New Testament prayer and intercession tend to be for believers and are concerned with their perseverance in the Christian life. It seems that the metaphor of intercession is restricted to activity affecting only those already saved. Nevertheless, the powerful language used by Paul with respect to prayer for unsaved Israelites (Rom. 10.1; cf. 9.1-3) shows clearly that prayer was offered for the unsaved.

49   The texts cited (Rom. 2.4; Gal. 3.13-14; Eph. 1.3-4; 2.8; Phil. 1.29; 2 Tim. 3.5-6) do not link God's actions in the bestowal of salvation to the specific act of atonement.

50   Berkhof, *Systematic Theology*, p. 397, appeals to Rom. 14.4 in support of God's protection of the individual concerned; but that text is about the irrelevance of human judgments on other Christians because God will uphold them; it is not about the fact that they may be tempted into sin and destruction. The point is made just as strongly in 1 Cor. 8.11.

The same general point is also developed by Letham who argues that it would be inconsistent for God to provide atonement for all and the means of grace only for some. This, however, is not self-evident. On any understanding of the matter there is a gap between what God wishes to happen and what is achieved. The statements of his love for the world and of his desire that none should perish stand alongside the fact that some do perish. This is parallel to his provision of salvation for all and the fact that it is not received by everybody.

The Slippery Slope to Universalism

Berkhof claims that universality of provision logically leads to universal acceptance of salvation. Christ has removed the guilt of all people, therefore none can be lost. But this is to impute to those who differ from him the same mistake that he makes, namely that anybody for whom Christ dies is infallibly brought to final salvation, and this is simply not true if we recognize that there is a distinction between provision and completion. Here Berkhof is arguing in a circle.

In fact the 'danger of universalism' argument can be applied to both schools of thought and is therefore not an argument that Calvinists can use against Arminians.

For the Arminians there is the puzzle why if God has provided salvation for all, he does not do more to ensure that all receive it. The Arminian reply is to appeal to the mystery of human sin and rebellion which remains an enigma.

For upholders of limited atonement there is the question why God has determined to set the limits so tightly and left out so many people. It is understandable that opponents of limited atonement find that the picture of God that emerges from the notion of a limited atonement is that of a not very attractive God whose decisions border on capriciousness. His character as a God of love has been made secondary to his right to do whatever he pleases. But if he is a God of love, must not that love be characteristic of all that he decides and does?

Justice and Mercy

Here a point should be taken up that is made by various scholars including particularly Helm and Letham. This is the argument that there is a difference in the 'logic' of justice and mercy. 'Justice, by nature, cannot be offset but must be applied by all. On the other hand, mercy is a free gift, unexpected and undeserved, and by its very essence cannot be required as an obligation but instead is exercised sovereignly by whoever dispenses it. We speak of the prerogative of mercy but of the necessity of justice.'[51]

This argument, that God is not under obligation to show mercy to all and is therefore perfectly just in condemning some while showing mercy to others, is frequently used, but it is flawed.

First, justice and mercy cannot be rigidly separated from one another. We expect mercy to be exercised in a just manner. In the human context the prerogative of mercy is generally used when there are over-riding circumstances which justify not exacting a penalty or ameliorating it; thus a pregnant woman might be sentenced to a shorter term of imprisonment than another criminal. Or an amnesty might be announced in the belief that this will be a more effective way of removing large numbers of illegal weapons from circulation than attempting to detect and punish the holders. There may be some contingent degree of unfairness (e.g. for people who failed to meet the deadline for the amnesty), but this does not affect the principle which is that generally the exercise of mercy is done for good cause; the pity shown is justified and not arbitrary. Therefore, the idea that God may arbitrarily exercise mercy to some and not to others must be rejected as unjust. A judge who treats one pregnant woman with mercy but shows none to another one in similar circumstances would not be tolerated.

Second, we must remind ourselves that there are presumably no limits set to the capacity of God's merciful provision. One can understand that in a human situation where there are limited resources (e.g. the availability of supplies of a life-saving drug) arbitrary choices may have to be made as to who receives them and who is denied them. But in the case of God there is surely no limit on his resources, and therefore there is no reason for him to be forced to make an arbitrary distribution of his mercy. If God can show mercy to some, he has the ability to show mercy to all.

Third, the biblical teaching about grace and mercy shows that it is motivated essentially by the need and plight and helplessness of the afflicted (Mt. 9.36; Mk 5.19; 10.47; Lk. 6.35-36; 7.13; 10.33) and sinners (Lk. 15.20; 2 Cor. 8.9; 1 Tim. 1.13; Heb. 2.17-18; cf. Jonah 3.10–4.3). God sees them in danger of perishing and therefore he feels pity for them and acts to save them. The mercy shown by God is not something arbitrary that arises purely from his own inscrutable purposes; on the contrary, it is aroused by his recognition of the need of helpless sinners. It is this that explains the gracious action of God in giving his Son as Saviour and creating the church to be the ambassador of salvation and reconciliation (cf. Eph. 2.1-10).

---

51   Letham, *Work of Christ*, p. 238.

But here we face the objection that according to Paul the mercy of God is selective in its application. Appeal is made to Romans 9.6-24 where it appears that God's mercy is shown to some and not to others. Paul's overall point here is that God's promises do not fail simply because the chosen people have failed to follow the Messiah. However, his primary point is to emphasize that mercy is God's prerogative and is not his response to human works (Rom. 9.11-12, 16); consequently, it cannot be claimed as of right or as something deserved by anybody but remains the act of God in his freedom (Rom. 9.15). This is illustrated by the choice of Jacob to be the father of the chosen people rather than his brother Esau; it did not depend on anything done by either to deserve favour from God. By the end of the section Paul is declaring that God's purpose in the light of Christ is to 'have mercy on them all' (Rom. 11.32), where the thought is primarily of both Jews and Gentiles, both of which as groups had been disobedient and fallen under judgment; the earlier distinctions between Isaac and Ishmael and between Jacob and Esau are overcome in the fulfilment of God's purposes. If Paul is working here with a distinction between the Jews, who were chosen as God's people, and the Gentiles, who were not chosen, he is saying that this is no longer a barrier to Gentiles receiving the mercy of God; and if there is a hardening in part of Israel at the present time, it is not permanent. Consequently, Paul's argument from past history that people cannot claim mercy on the basis of their works does not entail that his mercy is now selective and arbitrary. In fact the opposite is true; if the choice of Israel were in any sense to be seen as the arbitrary exclusion of the Gentiles, the redemption in Christ for Jews *and* Gentiles ends that completely. He anticipates a remarkable incoming of Gentiles and Jews to salvation.

To be sure, this does not solve all our problems. It does not explain why the gospel has not reached and does not reach all people, as if God was unable or unwilling to evangelize the world, despite his commanding the disciples to go into all the world and make disciples of all nations; if it be objected that this does not refer to every individual person but only to nations, the point still stands that many nations have never heard the gospel.

It is impossible to produce a theodicy that answers all our questions. Letham himself has to invoke this point when he tries to explain the relation between the particularity and the universality of the atonement. This means that we cannot dismiss either the limited atonement or universality understandings on the grounds that either of them leaves us with questions. Rather, the purpose of this article is to insist that we must do justice to the teaching of scripture and not produce a doctrine of God which is out of harmony with scriptural teaching. The doctrine of limited atonement does not do justice to the biblical teaching; it requires a forced, unnatural reading of the texts. The doctrine of universality treats the texts in a better way, even though it does not solve all the problems.

Preaching to the Reprobate

Finally, there is the argument put forward by upholders of limited atonement that this doctrine is not incompatible with the *bona fide* preaching of the gospel to those who have no hope of being saved because Christ did not die for them. Berkhof argues in defence of it:

(a) The gospel offer is simply a promise of salvation to those who believe without revealing the secret will of God.

(b) Any offer is conditional on faith and repentance wrought by the Holy Spirit.

(c) The offer of salvation does not say that Christ has made atonement for all and God intends to save each one. It simply says that the atonement is sufficient for all people, describes the nature of the faith and repentance that are required, and promises that those who come with true repentance and faith will be saved.

(d) The preacher's task is not to harmonize God's secret will and his declarative will, but simply to preach the gospel indiscriminately.

(e) God may properly call the non-elect to do something that he delights in.

(f) The preaching of the gospel serves to remove every vestige of excuse from sinners whose sin then culminates in refusing to accept it.

These arguments are fallacious. The defender of limited atonement says that the death was only for the pre-chosen (and so not really for 'the world') but it could have sufficed for a larger number, whereas the defender of unlimited atonement says that the death was on behalf of all but becomes effective in deliverance from condemnation only for those who accept it. The defenders of limited atonement need to have a death which is sufficient for all so that those who reject Christ have really rejected something that was available to them. But once that is admitted, their view begins to look like playing with words. The latter interpretation has the clear advantage that it takes the texts in a straightforward manner.

But to say that the atonement is sufficient for all people but has not been made for all is meaningless. How can the atonement be sufficient for people for whom it has not been made? This is sheer unconvincing casuistry. Further, it contradicts Berkhof's own principle that the atonement and the application of salvation are two indissoluble parts of one purpose of God. For on his premises how can this God produce an atonement that is sufficient for all people without also providing gifts of effectual calling which are sufficient for all people?[52] Nor is it just for God to call the non-chosen to do what they cannot by definition do. So long as God has refused to extend to them the same grace as he does to the pre-chosen, they have the excuse that he has asked them to do what is impossible for them (since by definition they cannot repent unless God enables them).

The fact that Berkhof is reduced to such specious, unconvincing arguments shows up only too clearly the flaws in his basic position.

Conclusion

I have argued that the New Testament clearly teaches that the death of Christ was not limited in its scope, and that the texts that positively affirm this should be taken in their plain sense rather than having a forced sense imposed upon them in the interests of a dogmatic framework. It is the framework that requires revision rather than the clear teaching of scripture. The New Testament does not teach that the death of Christ is limited in its scope to those pre-chosen for salvation. It follows that the attempt to undermine this part of the foundation of Clark Pinnock's theological explorations is not successful, and the issues that he raises cannot be so easily avoided or regarded as improper. At the same time, it is the case that one of the Five Points of Dort is shown to fail exegetically, and we should be content to recognize that there are some issues about salvation which are not to be solved by appeal to a secret decree of God that goes against his expressed love for the world and desire that none should perish but rather by a recognition that the mystery of evil is beyond our comprehension.[53]

52   This is an *argumentum ad hominem*, but a justifiable one, since the point is to show that Berkhof's position is self-contradictory on its own premises.

53   I am grateful to Kent Brower for his comments on this article.

CHAPTER 20

Is Conversion an Act of Violence? A Public Response to a Common Public Question

John G. Stackhouse, Jr.

What comes to mind when we think of conversion down through history?

• The apostles being threatened and then flogged or stoned by Jewish authorities for refusing to recant their beliefs.
• Early Christians being compelled by imperial Rome to burn incense to the genius of Caesar or be condemned to the arena.
• Residents of North Africa and the Levant being forced by Muslim armies to convert, accept second-class status (if Christians or Jews), leave, or be killed.
• Medieval Saxons being forced to profess Christianity at the point of Charlemagne's sword.
• European Jews being impelled by Christians to worship Jesus of Nazareth as God under threat of the Inquisition.
• Aboriginal children being torn from their tribal cultures and placed in Canadian residential schools to learn the English language, the Christian religion, and western civilization—whether they wanted to or not.
• Citizens of present-day Iran being compelled by roving bands of fanatical clerics to practice strict conformity to their peculiar brand of Islam.
• Taxi drivers in western India wearing necklaces with large crucifixes as they hope to be left alone in the conflicts between Hindus and Muslims.

These images, among many others, might come to mind when we hear the word 'conversion'. They certainly come to the minds of many of our contemporaries. Any of us might well acknowledge the joy expressed by acquaintances, and perhaps family members and friends, when they adopt a new religion. Still, we must pause when we hear again the cries that echo down the corridors of history from those who faced conversion as only a threat: as a denial of who they were and as a demand to conform to someone else's ideology.

Today, in Canada, the United States, Australia, New Zealand, and elsewhere—that is, in any society committed to the ideal of *multiculturalism*—interaction between people of different opinions with the slightest hint of pressure, let alone coercion, can raise hackles. Each recent generation has its own way of putting the philosophy of staying out of each other's way and letting each other be: 'Live and let live'; 'do your own thing'; 'whatever works for you'; or most economically, 'whatever'.

In the light of this conviction, then, the notion of 'conversion' seems both out of place and out of time, a throwback to the bad old days of military, political, economic and ideological imperialism. So for Christians who try to honour both the Great Commission to make disciples of their neighbours and the Great Commandment to love their neighbours as themselves, the question arises: Is conversion in fact an act of violence, or is it an act of love?

I

To falsely profess a religion in order to gain advantage is not true conversion according to any religion I know of. The Jews in late medieval Spain who were oppressed by the Inquisition did not, therefore, truly convert: How could the threat of persecution cause them to sincerely embrace Jesus as Lord? They instead went through motions that would preserve—underground, as it were—their lives, their families and their actual faith.

The Saxons, a few centuries earlier, finally capitulated to Charlemagne's religious and political campaign of subjection and assimilation. But their tribal religion did not disappear. Instead, their folkways continued to guide their daily life. Christianity was simply a veneer pounded down on top of these traditions by Charlemagne's hammer. Thus scholars have examined medieval Christianity in Europe and found it remarkably isomorphic with the previous tribal religions. Indeed, many have argued that the European population at large was not truly converted to Christianity—not even exposed to a basic presentation of the gospel—until Catholics and Protestants swept back and forth across it during the Reformation, seeking to win support *by persuasion* for their distinctive versions of Christianity.

Islam, one of the three great missionary religions (Buddhism and Christianity being the others), enthusiastically promotes the rule of Islamic law throughout the world, even by the exertion of political force as necessary. But the Qur'an explicitly forbids the idea of coerced *conversion* (2:256). Christians and Jews can maintain their religions, albeit in a seriously-compromised, second-class status of *'dhimmitude'*.

All others face a more dreadful choice: they must convert, leave, or die. But they *can* leave, according to the Qur'an. A person's decision about God is preserved in the privacy of the heart.

(I am leaving entirely aside, for the purposes of this discussion, the theological and epistemological questions of just how someone decides on one religion or another. I have, in fact, discussed them several times elsewhere. Thus I am using 'conversion' and 'proselytizing' more or less synonymously here. For the record, I believe that Christians can and should proselytize, but only God himself actually converts someone to authentic faith. But in this essay I want to argue 'publicly', so I am not deploying such peculiarly Christian concepts in my argument.)

We conclude, then, that those Jews, Muslims, Christians, Hindus, and Buddhists who have forced others to comply, not merely with their particular political regimes, but with the spiritual and liturgical dimensions of these traditions, have in fact contravened the express teaching of their own religions in doing so. True conversion—the true changing of the self from one religious identity or state to another—cannot result merely from outside pressure, but requires the authentic consent of the individual. The sacred precinct of the individual heart must not be violated by the zealous missionary. Genuine conversion indeed *cannot* ever result from an act of violence, and therefore *must* not be pursued as such.

II

Still, in our multi-cultural setting—that is, not only a situation in which there exist multiple cultures, but also a situation governed by the conviction that *it is good* for multiple cultures to coexist peaceably and without the dominance of one over another—in this multi-cultural setting, conversion is yet often seen as an act of violence. Indeed, in our hyper-sensitive era, the very act of trying to persuade someone that her religion or philosophy or outlook is in some ways deficient compared with your own can be denounced as a presumptuous and injurious act. Thus some people would respond to any act of proselytizing as they would to an act of physical violation: 'You are invading my space and must therefore be both labeled and repelled as an *invader* and *oppressor*.'

Let's step back a moment, then, and consider *why* someone would *try* to convert someone else—that is, to persuade someone else about anything at all—and see if we might judge any such act of attempted persuasion as legitimate.

Suppose we are attending a lecture at a public university. Here, we assume, is an epitome of our society's most civil discourse. The distinguished speaker is halfway through his peroration on, say, 'Multiculturalism: Why Can't We All Just Get Along?' At this very moment, a stranger bursts into our peaceful room and shouts, 'Get out! There's been a bomb threat!' Since we free-spirited and independent-minded university types are not about to be bullied by someone we don't even know, we each properly respond, 'Who are *you* to construe reality for me—and then presume to tell me how to behave in the light of that construal?'

Now, let us consider that this response of ours is not necessarily inappropriate. Perhaps the alarmist is a well-known prankster or mental patient and someone else in the room identifies him as such, thus instantly defusing the situation. We are right not to mindlessly follow just anyone who cries, 'Wolf!' But if this messenger instead is actually a person of intelligence, good will, and compassion, he will naturally be rather impatient with any resistance to his message. 'Look, folks, the fire trucks and bomb squad are on their way. Please, get out of here now!'

Suppose that we do not know, in fact, that this person is telling us an untruth. Yet suppose we persist in our autonomous dubiety: 'Actually', we reply, 'it's awfully rude of you to impose your view of reality on us, and then imperiously tell us what to do. You're acting oppressively, and you must stop.' Does this response of ours make sense? Is the interrupting person in fact committing an act of violence by trying to persuade us to change our minds about our safety, and we are right to resist him?

Let's take a trickier case. Mr Jones, say, is an alcoholic. His family loves him and has tried to persuade him to quit drinking so much. Finally, they follow the advice of an addiction counselor and intervene in a directly confrontational way. Mr Jones is now, quite against his will, faced with the consequences of his actions by the people who love him most in the world. He is also faced with a decision he would prefer to avoid. Is this intervention an act of violence, or an act of love?

A third instance. My father retired a few years ago from the practice of medicine, a practice that in his case involved a good deal of cancer surgery. Every week, sometimes every day for many days in a row, he would have to sit across from someone who felt perfectly healthy and tell her that she was, in his opinion, dangerously mistaken about the state of her own body. She was instead, in his judgment, desperately sick and in need of a drastic change both in her outlook and her behaviour. He was trying, in short, to convert her from seeing the world as a healthy person to seeing the world as a cancer patient. And, like many who try to convert others, he frequently met with resistance, denial, and even anger. Was his persistent attempt to convince such people of the superiority of his views an act of violence, or an act of love?

Here is a more general case. Consider the last election in your city or country. Were the candidates and their publicists acting properly when they sought to convince the electorate of the virtues of their parties over the alternatives? Was their attempt—or any sincere attempt—to persuade the public that their way of looking at politics, and acting in politics, was superior to another an act of violence, or an act of love?

Students at colleges and universities are constantly encountering a certain class of people who—let's put it bluntly—think that they know better. Worse, these people spend much of each day telling those students what they should think instead of what they currently do think. Often, these strange people go further to tell these students how to act over against how students might prefer to act. In sum, they try to convert students into a new culture: the culture of academia. These overbearing, self-satisfied pundits are called 'professors', and the amazing and wonderful thing is that students actually pay them considerable sums of money and time to be told by them what to think and what to do! So is teaching—at its best, now, and not in its truly abusive instances—inherently an act of violence, or an act of love?

I hope that it is clear from these examples that we must conclude either that all of the above are truly oppressive and inappropriate, and thus all attempts to persuade truly are condemned, or that at least some forms of persuasion are legitimate and, indeed, to be welcomed as an act by which one person or group serves the interests of another.

Even if the proselytizer turns out to be mistaken, furthermore, the very act of engaging another with an alternative point of view can prove beneficial to both parties involved. (The modern university is dedicated to this kind of serious exchange, however much various factions and ideologies seem determined to compromise it in the name of one or another form of dogmatic righteousness.) Indeed, even if the exchange seems fruitless, we might still credit the proselytizer at least with the commendable motive of genuine concern to benefit his neighbour with what he thinks are better ideas—however useless we may finally judge his proffered viewpoint actually to be.

To condemn *a priori* instead the free and even passionate exchange of concerns—to rule out the give-and-take of conversation partners earnestly trying to convince the other of the superiority of this or that idea while also paying respect to the other's views—is to condemn the university project. And it finally is to rule out the essence of a liberal democratic society.

So perhaps we can agree that *some* attempts to persuade *some* people of *some* things are *some*times legitimate, and even beneficial. Let us turn to the particular question, then, of religious conversion. Why would, and perhaps should, someone try to convert someone else religiously?

III

A religion fundamentally is a map to the cosmos and particularly a map to the properly-lived life. Most religions teach that their particular map is the best map, and perhaps the only reliable map, there is. But even devotees of religions that are not so exclusivist understandably want to share what they have found with others, particularly those closest to them. Such would be the case also with the increasingly common 'home-made' religions in which individuals construct a way of life from whatever resources that they find valuable. Indeed, such people also understandably and evidently feel a moral obligation to offer what they have found to be good to those they love. For in any form of religion, of course, life-and-death issues literally are at stake: What is the nature of the best possible *life*, and what is the best possible response to the inevitability of *death*?

To be sure, throughout history people have sought to convert others from decidedly ulterior motives. Some have wanted to assert personal or ethnic superiority. Others have wanted to exercise control—whether over individuals in their families or whole nations in their empires—in the name of religion. Still others have wanted merely to acquire religious merit for themselves by proselytizing without concern for the other person's true welfare. The history of conversion reeks of disreputable agendas.

All I want to assert here, though, is that there is a *prima facie* case to be made for the integrity of the proselytizing impulse. One can offer what one has found to be a life-changing blessing as a gift to another without thereby necessarily committing an act of unkindness, much less violence. And however much you or I might be repelled by the idea of someone trying to convert him or her, we must recognize that those who *have* been converted under the influence of others' testimony and advocacy have been grateful.

There are other grounds, however, upon which we might reject the very idea of proselytizing. Some of these have to do with convictions regarding the nature of religions or of religious claims to knowledge.

In the former instance, that of the nature of religions themselves, some of us might reject attempts at conversion in the name of religious pluralism: the conviction that all religions lead to the same goal and therefore there is no actual need to switch from one religion to another.

I don't have space here to consider the question of religious pluralism in the depth that this question deserves. For our present purpose, however, perhaps the following observation is sufficient: namely, that to say that 'all religions basically say the same thing and all achieve the same purpose' is itself a very particular and hotly debated proposition about the nature of religion. It is a proposition, furthermore, at least implicitly denied by the vast majority of the world's religious population—which is the vast majority of the world. Such a proposition does deserve careful and respectful consideration. But it is not at all self-evident and indeed is, from the point of view of most human beings, extremely dubious. It cannot serve, therefore, as a universal ground for the repudiation of proselytization, but is itself merely a particular point of view to which many, many people would need to be converted in order for it to rule our common life.

In the latter instance, that of the nature of religious knowledge, some of us might reject attempts at conversion in the name of epistemological skepticism. 'All of these religions make such diverse and often divergent claims about the impossibly complicated subjects of human nature, the divine, the cosmos, and so on', one might argue. 'Who can possibly claim to know what lies beyond the grave, or up in heaven, or at the heart of the universe, or within the soul?' Indeed, in the light of the postmodern critiques of knowledge, we all ought to be on our guard against any metanarratives, suspicious of any claim to have the 'whole story' that explains all the others.

As several wits have suggested, however, we do well not to allow a proper hermeneutic of suspicion to degrade into a hermeneutic of paranoia. Simply because we can't know everything, or even any particular thing with absolute certainty, does not necessarily leave us adrift in a tossing sea of subjectivism. There are clues to the meaning of things, and religions purport to offer some of the most important clues for our consideration.

In this regard, we should observe that no major religion has asked its followers to exercise 'blind faith'. Each offers what it thinks is sufficient warrant—not totally convincing and infallible proof, but sufficient warrant—to believe its claims with complete commitment. The inquirer properly weighs up those claims and the proffered evidence for them, considers carefully what criteria are appropriate in such cases, and makes up his or her mind as best he or she can. Such critical scrutiny should be welcomed by any religion worthy of human allegiance.

Only the cynic despairs of such investigation. And such cynicism always then faces its own troubles in formulating a livable ethic for both individual and community life. (How do you teach your children right from wrong in a consistently cynical way?)

Moreover, most of us are not outright cynics in most other areas of life: We do think that, even if we can never be absolutely certain about this biological theory, or that political philosophy, or this romantic relationship, or that religious commitment, we can still make responsible choices and thereby live a life better than if we just chose options at random. We also think that those choices are best made when we are properly informed of other people's wisdom. And that is what religion is finally about: deciding upon the right sort of life as seen in the very long term.

A quite different sort of resistance to conversion, however, is common in our society these days. When faced with someone intent on converting us, many of us naturally respond, 'Who are you to tell me what to think and how to live?' We might even resort to colloquialisms of violence: 'I hate it when people try to shove their beliefs down my throat and impose their morality on me.'

So let us reiterate that anyone who does attempt to coerce belief in this or that religion and to impose a particular religion's ideology or morality on someone else is wrong according to both the principles of the major religions themselves and the principles of a liberal democracy. But we cannot move immediately from this extreme case to generalize that everyone who offers to someone else a point of view or a way of life that she has found advantageous, even transformative, is thereby guilty of an act of arrogance, much less of violence. Isn't it instead to your advantage and mine, isn't it literally in our considered self-interest, to at least occasionally reflect upon our lives and upon whether the messages of others might improve them? Would we all be better off, really, if everyone kept to themselves the insights and experiences that make their lives most worth living?

In sum, I submit that while egregious violence has been done in the name of religious conversion, genuine conversion is always a free, uncoerced experience. I submit also that the major religions of the world, including the most missionary ones, agree with this principle. I submit furthermore that it is in the interest of each one of us, and of our communities, for everyone to freely offer and critically receive each other's messages about what is most real and valuable to know and practice in life. Therefore we must not allow any one ideology—whether secularist, or Christian, or anything else—to silence such conversations under its domination. Indeed, I submit finally that to curtail such exchanges is fatal to the flourishing of a free society.

CHAPTER 21

Being Open to God's Sacramental Work: A Study in Baptism

Anthony R. Cross

The question of baptism, and the related and broader discussion of Christian initiation, is experiencing something of a revival of interest.[1] Of particular importance is that this is occurring across confessional boundaries, the theological spectrum and the various theological disciplines—biblical, historical, liturgical and ecumenical studies, historical and systematic theology—each, often, informing the others. This renewed interest is also evident among Baptists[2] and evangelicals,[3] two traditions with whom Clark Pinnock is identifed, and with which I also identify myself. For the present purpose it is the evangelical perspective that

---

1   For an overview, see Stanley E. Porter and Anthony R. Cross, 'Introduction: Baptism in Recent Debate', in Stanley E. Porter and Anthony R. Cross (eds), *Baptism, the New Testament and the Church: Studies in Honour of R.E.O. White* (Journal for the Study of the New Testament Supplement Series, 171; Sheffield: Sheffield Academic Press, 1999), pp. 33-39; and Stanley E. Porter and Anthony R. Cross, 'Introduction: Baptism—An Ongoing Debate', in Stanley E. Porter and Anthony R. Cross (eds), *Dimensions of Baptism: Biblical and Theological Studies* (Journal for the Study of the New Testament Supplement Series, 234; Sheffield: Sheffield Academic Press, 2002), pp. 1-6. (I am grateful to Rev. Dr Brian Haymes for his most helpful suggestions in the preparation of this essay.)

2   See, e.g., Anthony R. Cross, *Baptism and the Baptists: Theology and Practice in Twentieth-Century Britain* (Studies in Baptist History and Thought, 3; Carlisle: Paternoster Press, 2000); James Leo Garrett, Jr., 'Baptists Concerning Baptism: Review and Preview', *Southwestern Journal of Theology* 43.2 (2001), pp. 52-67; and Stanley K. Fowler, *More Than a Symbol: The British Baptist Recovery of Baptismal Sacramentalism* (Studies in Baptist History and Thought, 2; Carlisle: Paternoster Press, 2002).

3   E.g., many of the contributions to the two volumes mentioned in n. 1 are either Baptist or evangelical, and often both.

predominates,[4] though the Baptist perspective will often be examined, not least because it is one of the most predominantly evangelical of the mainline traditions.

While Pinnock has not written extensively on baptism his contribution is nevertheless, I believe, an important and timely one in at least three overlapping areas: he stresses the importance of the role of the Holy Spirit in baptism, the sacramental nature of baptism, and God's use of material means to mediate his gracious working in people's lives.

The Holy Spirit's Role in Baptism

The work of the Spirit has recently been taken up by Clark Pinnock who, rejecting any dualism between matter and spirit, notes that today we tend to 'perceive Spirit as something ghostly, intangible, impalpable, numinous, lacking concreteness. There is resistance to linking the Spirit to the material' with the result that many 'shy away from physical manifestations of the divine presence and expect intangible, not real-life effects of the Spirit'.[5] Along with a growing number of scholars, Pinnock is seeking to address these issues with a view to recovering a genuinely biblical sacramental theology of baptism.

Pinnock agrees with Calvin that the Spirit is the key to the effectiveness of the sacraments: 'The sacraments duly perform their office only when accompanied by the Spirit...whose energy alone penetrates the hearts, stirs up the affections, and procurs access for the sacraments into our souls.'[6] But the divine work in the sacraments needs to be engaged by the human response. To this end, he concurs with Vatican II that faith is also

---

4   I am using the term 'evangelical' in the sense defined by D.W. Bebbington, *Evangelicalism in Modern Britain: A History from the 1730s to the 1980s* (London: Unwin Hyman, 1989), pp. 2-17, as those characterized historically by the four-fold emphasis of conversionism, activism, biblicism and crucicentrism. As such I see no problems with acknowledging Clark Pinnock as an evangelical, not least in the light of his recent writings.

5   Clark H. Pinnock, *Flame of Love: A Theology of the Holy Spirit* (Downers Grove, IL: InterVarsity Press, 1996), p. 119. See the whole of his discussion 'Spirit and Church', pp. 113-47.

6   John Calvin, *Institutes of the Christian Religion* (trans. Henry Beveridge; 2 vols; London: James Clarke, 1949 [1559]), 4.14.9, a passage cited by Pinnock in *Flame of Love*, p. 123, and 'The Physical Side of Being Spiritual: God's Sacramental Presence', in Anthony R. Cross and Philip E. Thompson (eds), *Baptist Sacramentalism* (Studies in Baptist History and Thought, 5; Carlisle: Paternoster Press, 2003), p. 19. For an overview of Calvin's baptismal theology, see Anthony R. Cross, 'Baptism in the Theology of John Calvin and Karl Barth', in Carl R. Trueman and Neil B. MacDonald (eds), *Karl Barth, Reformed Theology and the Bible* [provisional title] (Carlisle: Paternoster Press, forthcoming 2004).

required: 'In order that the sacred liturgy may produce its full effect, it is necessary that the faithful come to it with proper dispositions..., that they cooperate with divine grace lest they receive it in vain.' The 'pastors of souls', therefore, must ensure more than just the 'valid and licit' observance of the sacraments, but also that 'the faithful take part knowingly, actively, and fruitfully'.[7] This two-fold emphasis of the divine and human is fundamental to a biblical sacramentalism which avoids the connotations of mechanical efficacy, *ex opere operato*, on the one hand and, on the other, seeing baptism as nothing more than a confession of a faith already received. That baptism is understood as both a divine and human action is shown in key biblical passages.[8] In answer to the crowd's question as to what they should do, Peter instructs them to repent and be baptized and that they will receive the gift of the Spirit (Acts 2.38), while in Colossians 2.12 we see that in baptism we are buried and raised with Christ through faith in the power of God. We will examine the human side in the next section, but must begin with the divine dimension which revolves around the work of the Spirit in baptism.

In accord with what is clearly stated in the New Testament (e.g., Acts 2.38, 1 Cor. 12.13 and Tit. 3.5), Pinnock asserts that '[b]aptism is the moment when the Spirit is imparted... [It is] an expression of the obedience of faith and the moment when God gives the Spirit',[9] and in so doing agrees with the increasing body of scholarly opinion that recog-

---

7   *Constitution of the Sacred Liturgy* ch. 1 para. 11, in W.M. Abbott (ed.), *The Documents of Vatican II* (London: Geoffrey Chapman, 1966), p. 143, a passage cited by Pinnock in *Flame of Love*, p. 123, and 'Physical Side of Being Spiritual', p. 19.

8   Cf. H. Wheeler Robinson, *The Life and Faith of the Baptists* (London: Kingsgate Press, 2nd edn, 1946), p. 147: 'there is needed a new and clear teaching of the doctrine of the Holy Spirit, as against the rationalism that rejects all mystery, and the externalism which materializes mystery into manageable forms. The true emphasis is that of the New Testament—on personal faith as the human condition of divine activity, which is the truth supremely expressed in believer's baptism.' On Robinson's baptismal theology, see Anthony R. Cross, 'The Pneumatological Key to H. Wheeler Robinson's Baptismal Sacramentalism', in Cross and Thompson (eds), *Baptist Sacramentalism*, pp. 151-76; and Fowler, *More Than a Symbol*, pp. 89-97.

9   Pinnock, *Flame of Love*, p. 124. On the basis of Acts 10.44-48, he concedes that the Spirit may be manifested before baptism, though 'water remains the sign of the Spirit's coming'. However, I want to argue that the exact order in which the various elements in conversion occur become less significant when we take into account that 'becoming a Christian' (a more neutral phrase than 'conversion-baptism' or 'conversion-initiation') is a process and the order in which the various elements occur, or are manifested, is less important than has often been assumed. On this see, e.g., Cross, '"One Baptism" (Ephesians 4.5): A Challenge to the Church', in Porter and Cross (eds), *Baptism*, pp. 176-77.

nizes that New Testament baptism is conversion-baptism,[10] more commonly termed conversion-initiation.[11] He recognizes that the norm is that '[t]he Spirit is normally given with water in response to faith' and it is this which 'makes baptism a sacrament and means of grace. Proper initiation is water baptism coupled with Spirit baptism.'[12]

It is at this point that Pinnock notes that his own tradition, the Baptists, and we should add other churches too,[13] seldom link Spirit- and water-baptism in this way, but rather interpret water-baptism in terms only of a human response.[14] The most systematic and sustained argument for this comes in the mature thinking of Karl Barth, who understands Spirit-baptism as entirely the work of God, which is a person's salvation, while water-baptism is the believer's first step of faithful obedience,[15] the latter being dependent on the former.[16] Fundamental to Barth's separation of

---

10   George R. Beasley-Murray, 'βαπτίζω', in Colin Brown (ed.), *The New International Dictionary of New Testament Theology. Volume 1: A-F* (Exeter: Paternoster Press, 1975), p. 146: 'Baptism is conversion-baptism.' See also his *Baptism Today and Tomorrow* (London: Macmillan, 1966), pp. 37-38, where he regards it as 'axiomatic that conversion and baptism are inseparable, if not indistinguishable. In the primitive apostolic Church baptism was "conversion-baptism".'

11   This term was coined by James D.G. Dunn, *Baptism in the Holy Spirit: A Re-examination of the New Testament Teaching on the Gift of the Spirit in Relation to Pentecostalism Today* (London: SCM Press, 1970), e.g., pp. 3-7. For a detailed list of scholars who accept this, see Cross, '"One Baptism"', pp. 173-76, esp. nn. 4-8.

12   Pinnock, *Flame of Love*, p. 124.

13   John E. Colwell, *Living the Christian Story* (Edinburgh: T. & T. Clark, 2001), p. 156, observes that 'Since the Reformation (though anticipated in previous centuries), partly perhaps in reaction to the extremes of sacerdotalism, partly also perhaps in response to rationalistic reductionism, the significance of baptism and the Lord's Supper as truly divine events have been undermined'. He then, pp. 156-57, comments that baptism regarded as merely an outward witness to personal faith is 'all too common in present-day Baptist churches', and that the Zwinglian denial of the real presence in the Lord's Supper 'dissolves the sacrament into a *merely* human event' (italics his) and that this 'is similarly all too common, *and that not just among Baptist churches*' (italics added).

14   For examples of this, see Anthony R. Cross, 'Dispelling the Myth of English Baptist Baptismal Sacramentalism', *Baptist Quarterly* 38.8 (2000), pp. 367-69, and *Baptism and the Baptists*, pp. 10-14, 98-102 and *passim*; and Fowler, *More Than a Symbol*, pp. 1-4, 174-78 and *passim*. This anti-sacramentalism is increasingly being challenged by a growing and significant number of Baptists; see the works just cited.

15   Karl Barth, *Church Dogmatics* IV/4. *The Christian Life (Fragment)* (Edinburgh: T. & T. Clark, 1960), p. 2. On the shift evident in this final volume of the *Church Dogmatics* from his earlier sacramental to an anti-sacramental position, see Herbert Hartwell, 'Karl Barth on Baptism', *Scottish Journal of Theology* 22.1 (1969), pp. 10-29. See also the detailed discussions of Barth's theology of baptism in Fowler, *More Than a Symbol*, pp. 178-95, and Cross, 'Baptism in Calvin and Barth'.

16   Barth, *Church Dogmatics* IV/4, p. 158.

the two is his belief that no action can be at the same time both divine *and* human,[17] but this has been rightly criticized on both theological and exegetical grounds. John Colwell asks: 'how can any theology that reflects upon the Incarnation question the integrity of a human act on the grounds that it is, at the same time, a divine act?' He states: 'If Jesus Christ is truly God and, simultaneously, truly human, this categorical division of human action from divine action is not just unnecessary, it is erroneous.'[18] Pinnock concurs when he asserts that 'baptism in water and baptism in Spirit coincide. The spiritual and the physical flow together.'[19] Stanley K. Fowler demonstrates that Barth's attempts to ground this baptismal dichotomy exegetically only succeeds in showing that there is 'a *possible* exegetical basis for a non-sacramental view of baptism'[20] and he then offers detailed alternative exegetical and theological arguments for a sacramental interpretation of baptism.[21] Fowler also shows that at a key place in his argument—his list of proof texts for sacramentalism—Barth omits two passages (Acts 2.38 and 1 Cor. 12.13)[22] which would have seriously undermined his argument.

We must return briefly to the interpretation of 1 Corinthians 12.13 because James Dunn has put forward a strong exegetical argument that there is no reference here to water-baptism but only to Spirit-baptism.[23] Dunn argues that 'baptize in' is usually followed by the element in which the baptism occurs (e.g. 1 Cor. 10.2), but while this is possible, Everett Ferguson believes that this is unlikely because every other use of 'baptized' in 1 Corinthians is with reference to water-baptism (1.13-17; 10.2; 15.29) and so he believes 'in one Spirit' is to be understood instrumentally. Paul, therefore, means that '"by means of the one Spirit" a person is baptized into the one body'. This is the way 'in one Spirit' is

17 Barth, *Church Dogmatics* IV/4, p. 106.
18 Colwell, *Living*, pp. 150-51.
19 Pinnock, *Flame of Love*, p. 87.
20 Fowler, *More Than a Symbol*, p. 193, italics his.
21 Fowler, *More Than a Symbol*, pp. 156-247.
22 Fowler, *More Than a Symbol*, p. 180. Colwell, *Living*, p. 151, states that Barth's 'consequent attempt to eliminate every element of divine action from the New Testament references to baptism reeks of special pleading', a point which is, to my mind, demonstrated by Stanley E. Porter, 'Baptism in Acts: The Sacramental Dimension', in Cross and Thompson (eds), *Baptist Sacramentalism*, pp. 117-28. See also Colwell, *Living*, pp. 152-53. Cross, 'Baptism in Calvin and Barth', argues that in claiming to have demonstrated that the New Testament distinguishes between Spirit- and water-baptism, Barth only demonstrates what he first presupposes.
23 Dunn, *Baptism and the Holy Spirit*, pp. 127-31. Another leading proponent of this view is Gordon D. Fee, *The First Epistle to the Corinthians* (New International Commentary on the New Testament; Grand Rapids, MI: Eerdmans, 1987), pp. 604-606, and *God's Empowering Presence: The Holy Spirit in the Letters of Paul* (Peabody, MA: Hendrickson, 1994), pp. 176, 180 and 854.

used in 1 Corinthians 12.9 and in 6.11 in which the use of the aorist tense indicates that the same event is in view. Ferguson concludes: 'The Spirit is the agent of the effects of baptism.'[24]

The role of the Spirit in baptism is clearly key to a sacramental understanding of baptism,[25] but for it to be a biblical sacramentalism it must be balanced with the human dimension of baptism. To this we now turn.

The Sacramental Nature of Baptism

As the title of this chapter suggests there is something in Pinnock's and others' explorations in openness theology which I believe can deepen and enrich our understanding of baptism. While not an openness theologian myself but a historian of Christian thought, I find the emphasis of openness theology on the genuine and free interaction of God and humanity as an important dimension of baptism which has been too often overlooked. So, for example, Pinnock writes: '[The openness model] places the emphasis upon the genuine interactions that take place between God and human beings: how we respond to God's initiatives and how he responds to our responses.'[26] Later, Pinnock agrees with fellow openness theologian, John Sanders, that one of the four major points of the openness model is that 'God has sovereignly decided to make some of his actions contingent on our requests and actions'.[27] As is self-evident, baptism is, at the very least, a Christian act ordained by Christ (Mt. 28.19), but also, on one reading of 1 Peter 3.21, a prayer

---

24   Everett Ferguson, *The Church of Christ: A Biblical Ecclesiology for Today* (Grand Rapids, MI: Eerdmans, 1996), pp. 192-93. Importantly, on p. 193 n. 45, Ferguson states that Dunn, and others, are 'guilty of an ahistorical reading of the New Testament without reference to the practices and literature of the church in the early centuries. Only a few Gnostics...tried to dehydrate the New Testament references to baptism.' This observation is also made, along with pointing out inconsistencies in the arguments of Dunn and Fee in particular, by Anthony R. Cross, 'Spirit- and Water-Baptism in 1 Corinthians 12.13', in Porter and Cross (eds), *Dimensions of Baptism*, pp. 120-48.

25   Cf. Ernest A. Payne and Stephen F. Winward, *Orders and Prayers for Church Worship: A Manual for Ministers* (London: Carey Kingsgate Press, 1960), p. xiii: 'Only by the activity of the Holy Spirit can both word and sacrament become means of grace... Effective sacraments, like effective preaching, depend on the activity of "the Lord and giver of life".'

26   Clark H. Pinnock, *Most Moved Mover: A Theology of God's Openness* (Carlisle: Paternoster Press, 2001), p. 4.

27   Pinnock, *Most Moved Mover*, p. 5, cross referencing to John Sanders, *The God Who Risks: A Theology of Providence* (Downers Grove, IL: InterVarsity Press, 1998), p. 282.

(ἐπερωτάω) to God.[28] But even someone such as George Beasley-Murray, who prefers the translation of 'a pledge to God', recognizes that in this passage 'baptism is...defined as God acting for man talking to him— whether the latter is addressing him in prayer or in faith's confession'.[29] He believes that 'the conception of baptism as a vehicle of surrender in faith and obedience to God is inseparable from the thought of prayer in the act of baptism, and the definition so understood would suit the context'.[30] Any objections to seeing baptism as in some sense a prayer are, to my mind, dispelled by Ananias' words to Saul: 'And now why do you delay? Get up, be baptized, and have your sins washed away, *calling on his name*' (Acts 22.16).[31] What is 'calling on his name' if it is not prayer? Another scholar to see baptism in this way is John Colwell. In the course of his rejection of Barth's dualism of Spirit- and water-baptism he maintains that baptism is more than '*merely* a human action', for it is a genuine means of grace because the 'baptism with the Holy Spirit...is mediated through the proclamation of the Church and through the form of prayer that is water baptism'.[32]

But there are many who will object to such an argument on the grounds that it acribes too much to baptism. Many will raise the question mentioned by Ramsey Michaels: 'How is it, then, that baptism "saves"?' Michaels supplies the answer: 'Probably in much the same sense in which Jesus says on several occasions in the Gospels, "Your faith has saved you"' (cf. Mt. 9.22 and par.; Mk 10.52 and par.; Lk. 7.50; 17.19; cf. Js 2.14). He then notes that a 'purist might properly insist that only God "saves"', to which he responds that 'salvation can be associated either with the divine initiative or the human response'.[33] It is the recognition of this which I believe opens the way for evangelicals to recognize the sacramental nature of baptism as the sovereign action of God, a position which can be demonstated from the teaching of the New Testament.

---

28   On the interpretation of ἐπερωτάω here as either a 'prayer' or, more likely, a 'pledge', see, e.g., G.T.D. Angel, 'ἐρωτάω', in Colin Brown (ed.), *The New International Dictionary of New Testament Theology. Vol. 2: G-Pre* (Exeter: Paternoster Press, 1976), pp. 879-81, esp. pp. 880-81; and Peter H. Davids, *The First Epistle of Peter* (New International Commentary on the New Testament; Grand Rapids, MI: Eerdmans, 1990), pp. 144-45.

29   G.R. Beasley-Murray, 'The Authority and Justification for Believers' Baptism', *Review and Expositor* 77.1 (1980), p. 65.

30   G.R. Beasley-Murray, *Baptism in the New Testament* (Exeter: Paternoster Press, 1972 [1962]), p. 261.

31   Throughout I have used the NRSV.

32   Colwell, *Living*, p. 153, italics his.

33   J. Ramsey Michaels, *1 Peter* (Word Biblical Commentary, 49; Waco, TX: Word Books, 1988), p. 217.

Scripture is clear: salvation is of God (cf. Jn 3.16; Eph. 2.8). But the dominant view since the fifth century has been that of the Augustinian-Calvinist tradition that God predestines those whom he will save by granting faith to them. While this view has been challenged, not least by the Arminian tradition, it is the Reformed view that has continued to predominate both explicitly but also implicitly, for many forms of evangelicalism are deeply influenced by the Reformed tradition without realizing it. But as the title of this volume reminds us, each generation has a duty before God to re-examine its understanding of scripture, to test everything, even the traditions to which it owes so much. It is not just individual believers and the church that is to be *semper reformandum*, 'ever subject to reform', but theology too. Many years ago Rudolf Bultmann reminded us of the importance of presuppositions and that presuppositionless exegesis is not possible,[34] yet we continue to read scripture with the spectacles of our own traditions. While the existence of presuppositions does not invalidate those traditions they should make us aware of the possible pitfalls of not being conscious of them as we study scripture, and also help us to appreciate new perspectives which challenge our often deeply engrained views, thereby enabling us to study afresh God's written word. For example, the majority view within the Baptist tradition, to which both Pinnock and I belong, often states dogmatically that baptism is not a sacrament and that Baptists have always been anti-sacramental. However, this is simply not true of Baptist history, for many early Baptists were sacramentalists and there has been a continuous tradition of Baptist sacramentalists, even if at times in the minority, since their beginings in the early seventeenth century.[35] Openness theology, with its emphasis on both what God graciously does and people's free response to him, encourages us to look afresh at what the New Testament says about becoming a Christian and baptism's role in that process.

34   Rudolf Bultmann, 'Is Exegesis without Presuppositions Possible?', in S.M. Ogden (ed.), *New Testament and Mythology and Other Basic Writings* (London: SCM Press, 1984), pp. 145-53.
35   See Cross, 'Dispelling the Myth', pp. 367-91; Fowler, *More Than a Symbol*, pp. 10-88; and Philip E. Thompson, 'A New Question in Baptist History: Seeking a Catholic Spirit among Early Baptists', *Pro Ecclesia* 8.1 (1999), pp. 66-68, 71-72, and 'Practicing the Freedom of God: Formation in Early Baptist Life', in David M. Hammond (ed.), *Theology and Lived Christianity* (The Annual Publication of the College Theological Society, 45; Mystic, CT: Twenty-Third Publications, 2000), pp. 126-31. Stephen Holmes, *Tradition and Renewal in Baptist Life* (The Whitley Lecture 2003; Oxford: Whitley Publications, 2003), pp. 25-35, also notes this early sacramentalism and argues that '[i]ts disappearance...was a real and genuine loss from our Baptist life'. He maintains that 'there was no good reason to discard the old Baptist tradition of teaching a real work of God in the sacraments' and that this tradition 'slipped from view through a combination of erroneous theology, factionalism and improper accom-modation to the prevailing moods of the culture'.

Evangelicals agree that people are saved by grace through faith (e.g. Jn 3.16; Rom. 5.1; Gal. 3.36; Eph. 2.8) and that faith comes from hearing God's word (Rom. 10.14, 17). But a common misunderstanding of such a key text as Ephesians 2.8 is that in the same way that salvation is God's gift to humanity so also is faith.[36] But this is not how καὶ τοῦτο οὐκ ἐκ ὑμῶν, θεοῦ τὸ δῶρον should be understood. Andrew Lincoln observes that the parallelism between vv. 8b and 9 ('this is not your own doing; it is the gift of God' and 'not the results of works...') indicates that both refer to v. 8a's 'by grace you have been saved through faith' and 'thus to the whole process of salvation it describes, which of course includes faith as its means'.[37] Everett Ferguson expresses this well when he brings together this passage with the biblical teaching that faith comes by the hearing of the word, a word that is associated in Hebrews 1.3 with God's power, which is identified with the gospel in Romans 1.16 and the word of the cross in 1 Corinthians 1.18 (see also Rom. 10.14, 17 and Js 1.21). Ferguson then writes: 'Since faith comes from hearing the word, there is a sense in which one might say that faith is given by God.' He notes Ephesians 2.8-9 and the misunderstanding we have just noted, then continues:

Nevertheless, faith is not human generated. An individual does not produce faith in him/herself or in another person. Only the word that sets forth the mighty, loving, salvific action of God can do this. God's loving action has always, throughout biblical history, launched faith. *Faith is not faith in faith, but faith in God's action* (Heb. 11:6). Since God supplies the content of faith and the means by which it is created, he is the one who gives faith. He may, furthermore, give the influences that make for receptivity and so prepare for faith (Acts 16:14). On the other hand, God does not directly create the response. He does not give faith to some and withold it from others. Since the word that produces faith is God's word, God is the ultimate source of faith. The preached word produces faith.

---

36   E.g. G.B. Caird, *Paul's Letters from Prison* (Oxford: Oxford University Press, 1976), p. 53.

37   Andrew T. Lincoln, *Ephesians* (Word Biblical Commentary, 42; Dallas, TX: Word, 1990), pp. 111-12. (In passing it is worth noting that an increasing number of biblical scholars and theologians recognize that becoming a Christian is a process. This has implications for the correction of the widespread evangelical tradition which has seen conversion more in punctiliar terms [see Cross, '"One Baptism"', pp. 176-77], and addresses many Christians who have come to faith [often within Christian families] whose conversion has been gradual, to the point that many cannot actually pinpoint when it was that they became a Christian.) See also F.F. Bruce, *The Epistles to the Colossians, to Philemon, and to the Ephesians* (New International Commentary on the New Testament; Grand Rapids, MI: Eerdmans, 1984), pp. 289-90.

Hence Ferguson's belief that '[t]he consistent order of conversion is summarized in Acts 18:8, "Many of the Corinthians who heard Paul became believers and were baptized"'.[38]

A major key to interpreting baptism sacramentally is highlighted in the many writings on baptism by George Beasley-Murray and his demonstration that baptism in the New Testament is to be understood as nothing less than faith-baptism.[39] While it is not possible to go into all that Beasley-Murray says,[40] it is worth noting what he says on two key baptismal passages—Galatians 3.26-27 and 1 Peter 3.21.

Galatians 3.26-27 is of foundational importance because it signifies the fundamental element of baptism as relating to union with Christ: 'for in Christ Jesus you are all children of God *through faith*. As many of you *as were baptized* into Christ have clothed yourselves with Christ.' Baptism here is said to mean 'putting on' Christ as one puts on a garment, and in Christ we share sonship with God through faith. 'Self-evidently', he comments, 'one cannot be in Christ without sharing his sonship; which suggests that it is faith which receives Christ in baptism; accordingly it is the man exercising faith who is the object of the divine work in baptism'.[41] More simply: 'in Paul's view the experience of baptism and that of faith are one.'[42]

Therefore, 'if faith is to be taken seriously, so is baptism' and he rejects the tendency of many exegetes to 'either exalt baptism at the expense of faith or faith at the expense of baptism'. This leads to the conclusion that

---

38   Ferguson, *Church of Christ*, pp. 163-64, quotations from p. 164, italics added.

39   Pinnock, *Flame of Love*, p. 81, agrees: 'By faith and baptism we enter the human situation by virtue of solidarity with the One by whom it was accomplished by God.' Also R.E.O. White, *The Biblical Doctrine of Initiation* (London: Hodder & Stoughton, 1960), p. 226: 'We may speak of Paul's sacramentalism, provided we remember that to his mind efficacy belongs not to the ceremony of baptism as such but to the action of God, by the Spirit, within the soul of the convert who at this time and in this way is making his response to the grace offered him in the gospel. *There is no dualism here between faith and baptism simply because for Paul baptism is always, and only, faith-baptism*: given that, Paul is emphatically a sacramentalist', italics added. Later, p. 275, White extends this to the other New Testament writers: 'for each New Testament school, amid all the fuller development of its sacramental implications, baptism remains emphatically confessional, *a faith-sacrament* rightly shared only with those who thereby respond in belief and surrender to the Christian evangel', italics added.

40   For a detailed study, see Anthony R. Cross, 'Faith-Baptism: The Key to an Evangelical Baptismal Sacramentalism' (The Second Dr G.R. Beasley-Murray Memorial Lecture, 4 May 2003), forthcoming in the *Journal of European Baptist Studies*.

41   Beasley-Murray, 'Authority and Justification', p. 64.

42   G.R. Beasley-Murray, 'Faith in the New Testament: A Baptist Perspective', *American Baptist Quaterly* 1.2 (December, 1982), p. 141.

Baptism is the baptism of faith and grace, so that in it faith receives what grace gives. Above all grace gives Christ, for Christ is the fullness of grace; faith therefore receives Christ in baptism. If Paul were pressed to define the relationship of the two statements in vv. 26-27, I cannot see how he could preserve the force of both sentences apart from affirming that baptism is the moment of faith in which the adoption is realized—in the dual sense of effected by God and grasped by man— which is the same as saying that in baptism faith receives Christ in whom the adoption is effected. The significance of baptism is the objective facts to which it witnesses, the historic event of redemption and the present gift that it makes possible, embraced through faith in that God who acted and yet acts. Through such an alliance of faith and baptism, Christianity is prevented from evaporating into an ethereal subjectivism on the one hand and from hardening into a fossilized objectivism on the other. The two aspects of Apostolic Christianity are preserved in *faith-baptism*.[43]

This final phrase is worth emphasizing. Verse 27 is especially important 'as illustrating that the essential significance of faith-baptism is its setting the believer in Christ and that in Christ full salvation is his'.[44]

1 Peter 3.21 states 'baptism...now saves you—not as a removal of dirt from the body, but as an appeal to God for a good conscience, through the resurrection of Jesus Christ'. Here the essential feature of baptism is not the washing of the body but the spiritual transaction in which the baptized makes their appeal to God in faith and prayer and experiences the power of the risen Lord to save.[45] Beasley-Murray concludes:

Surely we are not interpreting amiss in believing that once more we have the representation of baptism as the supreme occasion when God, through the Mediator Christ, deals with a man who comes to Him through Christ on the basis of his redemptive acts. It is a meeting of God and man in the Christ of the cross and resurrection; it is *faith* assenting to God's grace and receiving that grace embodied in Christ. This is more important than Noah and the Flood and the disobedient spirits, but all together combine to magnify the greatness of the grace revealed in the suffering and exalted Lord who meets us in the Christian βάπτισμα.[46]

Beasley-Murray concludes that 'The inextricable link between Baptism and faith is observable not only in baptismal statements but in a comparison of these with the apostolic teaching about faith'. In short, 'the New Testament writers associate the full range of salvation on the one hand with baptism and on the other hand with faith'.[47]

Beasley-Murray notes that when the New Testament's baptismal passages are closely examined 'an extraordinary duality appears in the

---

43   Beasley-Murray, *Baptism*, p. 151, italics added.
44   Beasley-Murray, *Baptism Today and Tomorrow*, pp. 46-47.
45   Beasley-Murray, 'Authority and Justification', p. 65.
46   Beasley-Murray, *Baptism*, p. 262, italics added.
47   Beasley-Murray, 'Authority and Justification', p. 65.

means whereby God imparts his saving grace'.[48] What emerges is that the full range of salvation is promised to faith, but also to baptism. Forgiveness is promised to faith in Romans 4.5-7 and 1 John 1.9, but to baptism in Acts 2.38 and 22.16. In Romans 3–5 and Galatians 2–3 justification is by faith alone, for example, Romans 3.28, but in 1 Corinthians 6.11 it is assigned to baptism. In Ephesians 3.17 union with Christ is through faith, while in Galatians 3.27 it is rooted in baptism. In Galatians 2.20 being crucified with Christ is by faith alone, but in Romans 6.2-11 it occurs in baptism. Sharing in Christ's death and resurrection is by faith in Romans 8.12-13, but in Romans 6.2-11 and Colossians 2.12 it is in baptism. In John 1.12 sonship is promised to faith, but in Galatians 3.26-27 it is related to faith and baptism. In Galatians 3.2-5 and 14 the Spirit is given to faith, but in Acts 2.38 and 1 Corinthians 12.13 to baptism. Entry into the church is by faith in Acts 5.14 and Galatians 3.6-7, but in baptism according to Galatians 3.27 and 1 Corinthians 12.13. Regeneration and life are granted to faith in John 3.14-16 and 20.31, but to baptism in Titus 3.5 and John 3.5. The kingdom and eternal life are promised to faith in Mark 10.15 and John 3.14-16, yet in 1 Corinthians 6.9-11 it is given to those who have abandoned the sins that exclude from it, for they have been washed clean in baptism, something also seen in Acts 22.16. Finally, salvation is given to faith in Romans 1.16 and John 3.16, but to baptism in 1 Peter 3.21.[49]

---

48   George R. Beasley-Murray, 'Baptism in the New Testament', *Foundations* 3 (1960), p. 28.

49   Diagrammatically this looks as follows:

Gift of God	Faith	Baptism
Forgiveness	Rom. 4.5-7; 1 Jn 1.9	Acts 2.38; 22.16
Justification	Rom. 3–5 (e.g. 3.28); Gal. 2–3	1 Cor. 6.11
Union with Christ	Eph. 3.17	Gal. 3.27
Being crucified with Christ	Gal. 2.20	Rom. 6.2-11
Death and Resurrection	Rom. 8.12-13	Rom. 6.2-11; Col. 2.12
Sonship	Jn 1.12	Gal. 3.26-27
Holy Spirit	Gal. 3.2-5 and 14	Acts 2.38; 1 Cor. 12.13
Entry into the church	Acts 5.14; Gal. 3.6-7	Gal. 3.27; 1 Cor. 12.13
Regeneration and Life	Jn 3.14-16; 20.31	Tit. 3.5; Jn 3.5
The kingdom and eternal life	Mk 10.15; Jn 3.14-16	1 Cor. 6.9-11
Salvation	Rom. 1.16; Jn 3.16	1 Pet. 3.21

This table is taken from Cross, 'Faith Baptism', p. 18, and its contents are based on Beasley-Murray's *Baptism Today and Tomorrow*, pp. 27-37; 'Authority and Justification', pp. 65-66; and 'Baptism in the New Testament', p. 28. Cf. also Ferguson, *Church of Christ*, pp. 180-95, where he discusses the many key ideas involved in conversion which are associated with baptism.

From this it is clear, therefore, that God's gift to baptism and faith is one, namely, salvation in Christ.

> There is no question of his giving one part in baptism and another to faith, whether in that order or in the reverse. He gives *all* in baptism and *all* to faith... God's gracious giving to faith belongs to the context of baptism, even as God's gracious giving in baptism is to faith. Faith has no merit to claim such gifts and baptism has no power to produce them. It is all of God, who brings a man to faith and to baptism and has been pleased so to order his giving.

This New Testament theology of baptism is based on the axiom that baptism is administered to converts. 'It is regarded as equally axiomatic that conversion and baptism are inseparable, if not indistinguishable' because '[i]n the primitive apostolic Church baptism was conversion-baptism'.[50] This can all be summarized as follows: 'If God gives his gracious gifts to faith *and* baptism, he gives them in association, *i.e.* he gives them to faith *in* baptism, or (which amounts to the same thing) to baptism *in faith*.'[51] In the New Testament baptism was never conceived of apart from the faith that turns to God for salvation and any interpretation of baptism that diminishes 'the crucial significance of faith is unfaithful to the apostolic gospel'.[52]

Such an understanding of baptism precludes any notion that the efficacy of baptism is automatic (*ex opere operato*) precisely because it is faith-baptism. Such idea is explicitly ruled out by Colossians 2.12: 'you were buried with [Christ] in baptism...[and]...raised with him *through faith in the power of God*.' Similarly, 1 Peter 3.21 rules out any magical dimension to baptism for 'baptism...now saves you...*through the resurrection of Jesus Christ*'. Ferguson puts it succinctly: 'Baptism is an act of faith, not a work in the sense of Romans 4.'[53] It is no more a work than faith is. Ferguson continues: 'One cannot define work in such a way as to include baptism and exclude faith. There is a sense in which faith itself is a work: "They said to him, 'What must we do to perform the works of God?' Jesus answered them, 'This is the work of God, that you believe in him whom he has sent'" (John 6:28-29).'[54] The New Testament is clear that God requires an outward and physical response from those who respond to his word. God's promise of salvation, 'the gift of God', has to be received and it is received in an outward act which

---

50 Beasley-Murray, *Today and Tomorrow*, p. 37; cf. pp. 93, 135.

51 Beasley-Murray, 'Baptism in the New Testament', p. 28. Also, *Today and Tomorrow*, p. 127: 'the New Testament utterances about baptism take it as axiomatic that faith is not merely an accompaniment of baptism but an inherent element of it.'

52 Beasley-Murray, 'Baptism in the New Testament', p. 29.

53 Ferguson, *Church of Christ*, p. 169.

54 Ferguson, *Church of Christ*, p. 170.

is an expression of faith. The crowd's question, 'What should we do?' was answered by Peter's instruction, 'Repent, *and be baptized* every one of you in the name of Jesus Christ so that your sins may be forgiven; and you will receive the gift of the Holy Spirit' (Acts 2.37-38), while Paul tells us that 'As many of you *as were baptized* into Christ *have clothed yourselves* with Christ' (Gal. 3.27).

Our conclusion, then, has been well-expressed by Graham Watts:

> Christian baptism must be viewed fully as a human action which is grounded in and only properly constituted by God's action. It is perfectly possible to regard such human action as free yet, at the same time, as an expression of the true freedom granted by God's action in the Spirit. If baptism is the supreme place where the hidden work of God is celebrated openly, then we see in the public act of human promise a response which is only made possible by the Spirit drawing us into participation in the divine life; we are drawn into the open future of God's activity in the world through the Spirit's liberating action. This does not imply any sense in which God's action is manipulated by our human action; that would deny the theology of the Spirit... To speak of baptism as this sort of act is to describe the manner of our response as promise and pledge, a 'yes' which is grounded in God's prior 'yes' to us in Christ and made possible by the gracious activity of the Spirit.[55]

Material Means as Media of God's Grace

Another objection to the kind of sacramental understanding of baptism outlined here is that God does not need to use water as a means of grace, rather all that is needed is a spiritial encounter between God and humanity. But this has led to a form of evangelical gnosticism where all that is important is what a person believes while any outward, physical dimension is regarded as irrelevant.[56] But the importance of the outward

55 Graham Watts, 'Baptism and the Hiddenness of God', in Porter and Cross (eds), *Dimensions of Baptism*, pp. 276-77. Cf. Emil Brunner, *The Divine–Human Encounter* (London: SCM Press, 1944), p. 128, and the enlarged and revised version, *Truth as Encounter* (London: SCM Press, 1964), p. 181: 'In baptism it is God, first and sovereign, who acts, who forgives sin, who cleanses man and regenerates him. But man too acts in baptism. He allows this cleansing of himself to take place, he lets himself be drawn into the death of Christ, he confesses his faith and his attachment to Christ. Baptism is not merely a gift to man, but also an active receiving and confession on the part of man. Indeed, Baptism, precisely as this free confession of man, is the stipulation for the individual's joining the Church. Baptism is not only an act of grace, but just as much an act of confession stemming from the act of grace.'

56 Cf. Curtis W. Freeman, '"To Feed Upon by Faith": Nourishment from the Lord's Table', in Cross and Thompson (eds), *Baptist Sacramentalism*, pp. 203-204, who observes that 'Free Church faith and practice affirms that God can be present...almost

and physical expression of a person's faith is shown in the fact that God has ordained it: Jesus commanded his followers to make disciples by means of 'baptizing and teaching them' (Mt. 28.19), while Peter informed the hearers on the day of Pentecost that the response needed to the gospel included both inward disposition and outward expression: 'Repent and be baptized...' (Acts 2.38).

For Calvin, whose understanding of baptism (and the eucharist) is deeply sacramental,[57] the sacraments are secondary to the word from which they derive their significance.[58] But more than that they are an accommodation by God to the human inability to discern spiritual things by using 'earthly elements to lead us to himself'. So much is this so that 'a sacrament consists of the word and the sign', their purpose being to strengthen the believer's faith in God's promises. God nourishes the faith of believers by means of the sacraments 'whose only office is to make his promises visible to our eye...to be pledges of his promises'.[59]

As we have noted, the major influence on evangelicalism has been the Reformed tradition, but it is interesting to note that in their non-sacramentalism—and often anti-sacramentalism, as seen, for example, in many Baptist groups—evangelicals owe more to Zwinglianism than to the Calvinist tradition.[60] In so doing they have broken with what Pinnock describes as 'the remarkable and ancient consensus that baptism and the Lord's Supper were means of grace and works of God... [Zwingli] did not believe that God was at work in these rituals to bestow benefits of the

anywhere...except on the communion table'. Of the four heterodox factors Freeman identifies as informing this position, the second 'is a *latent Gnosticism* that sharply distinguishes between spiritual and material and is thus skeptical of identifying the divine presence with anything in the physical (or biological) world often accompanied by an *incipient Marcionism* that separates the spheres of creation and redemption'. Cf. also Elizabeth Newman, 'The Lord's Supper: Might Baptists Accept a Theory of Real Presence?', in Cross and Thompson (eds), *Baptist Sacramentalism*, p. 218: 'To relate to Jesus as a Spirit who communes with our inner spiritual selves is more gnostic than it is Christian. Such gnosticism is especially apparent in the conviction that creation and therefore the church are not *necessary* for salvation.' See also pp. 223-27.

57   See Calvin *Institutes*, 4.14.

58   I am happy to agree with Calvin that the sacraments are secondary so long as this is understood in the sense that grace precedes faith, but I would resist any notion that their being secondary diminishes their importance (cf. 1 Pet. 3.21) and makes their observance unnecessary (as with the Quakers and Salvation Army) or optional (as in the case of too many Baptists who have members who have never been baptized, either as infants or believers, and see no reason to be baptized).

59   Calvin, *Institutes* 4.14.3, 4.14.4 and 4.14.12 respectively. See Ronald S. Wallace, *Calvin's Doctrine of the Word and Sacrament* (Edinburgh: Oliver and Boyd, 1953), e.g., pp. 138-41, 159.

60   Barth, *Church Dogmatics* IV/4, pp. 128-30, also identifies himself as a neo-Zwinglian which is, of course, consistent with his Spirit- and water-baptism dichotomy.

work of Christ on the faithful' and in so doing dispensed with 'the historic understanding' of the sacraments. Such practices were only given for the sake of the congregation, for example as a public testimony, but they have no effect upon the recipients. Zwingli, therefore, 'separated grace from the sacraments and warned against confusing matter and spirit. In effect, he introduced a metaphysical dualism into our understanding of the ordinances and rejected fifteen hundred years of Christian thinking on the subject.'[61] It is this spirit–matter dualism which is so reminiscent of Gnosticism and it is widespread in evangelicalism.

As far as generalizations are ever true, evangelicalism has tended to major on the authority of scripture, their soteriology has focused on the doctrine of the atonement and the necessity of personal conversion,[62] the necessity of evangelism[63] and the need for personal holiness.[64] Yet there are other important doctrines which evangelicalism needs to integrate within its thought. These include pneumatology (revived within various movements since the Evangelical Revival, but especially by Pente-

61   Pinnock, 'Physical Side of Being Spiritual', p. 9. For a detailed discussion of and references to Zwingli's views, see Jack W. Cottrell, 'Baptism according to the Reformed Tradition', in David W. Fletcher (ed.), *Baptism and the Remission of Sins: An Historical Perspective* (Joplin, MO: College Press, 1990), pp. 65-68; and Huldrych Zwingli, 'Of Baptism', in *Zwingli and Bullinger* (ed. G.W. Bromiley; Library of Christian Classics, 24; Philadelphia: Westminister Press, 1953). I also wonder the extent to which Zwingli's iconoclasm has also infiltrated evangelical thinking and underscored any non- and anti-sacramental attitudes. Cf. Pinnock's comment, *Flame of Love*, p. 121, that '[i]conoclasm has impoverished the life of the church and often reduced worship to a cognitive affair', a statement which reflects his openness to the many positive dimensions of the charismatic movement.

62   Which, it should be noted, ties in with ecclesiology, that the church is made up of the elect, or, in the Free Churches/believers church tradition, that it is made up of those who profess personal faith in Christ. I would also want to add the doctrine of justification by grace through faith as implicit in this emphasis.

63   These four emphases are identified as characteristic of evangelicalism by, for example, D.W. Bebbington, 'Evangelicalism', in Alister E. McGrath (ed.), *The Blackwell Encyclopedia of Modern Christian Thought* (Oxford: Blackwell, 1993), p. 183.

64   Harriet A. Harris, 'Evangelical Theology', in Trevor Hart (ed.), *The Dictionary of Historical Theology* (Carlisle: Paternoster Press, 2000), p. 198, adds this latter emphasis to those already mentioned by Bebbington. Significantly for our discussion, Harris opposes evangelicalism's emphasis on 'prioritizing the experience of becoming a Christian and knowing Jesus as one's personal saviour' and 'sanctification through holy living' over against 'the sacraments' and 'Christ's presence in the sacraments' respectively. Later, p. 199, Harris states: 'The sacraments may not feature in an evangelical account of Christian faith' though 'Baptism and Holy Communion are sometimes called "ordinances"...rather than "sacraments", or a means of grace by which Christ pledges his presence', though she does recognize that there are 'sacramental churches' within the evangelical tradition.

costalism and the charismatic movement, and coming to greater
prominence in the last few decades of the twentieth century), creation and
the incarnation to name but three. We have already discussed the
pneumatological dimension, but Pinnock notes that little room for God's
presence and activity is allowed by modernity where '[w]hat is "real" is
what can be scientifically established'. It looks for physical causation but
disregards God's action; it is materialistic, exalting sceptical reason, and
discounts revelation and tradition. When this outlook influences religion,
he notes, it becomes 'powerless in both its sacramental and charismatic
dimensions', and 'does not expect God to be present or to move in
power'. A further factor is that modern people 'tend to perceive Spirit as
intangible, impalpable, numinous, lacking in reality and concreteness'
and this leads many to deny that the Spirit is linked to such material
actions as the sacraments: 'It is as though the Spirit were a "holy ghost"
which never deals with the material, never creates real effects, never
manifests itself and never transforms concrete situations. We struggle here
against a matter/spirit dualism.'[65] But a deeper appreciation of the
doctrine of creation and the word of God both challenges and transforms
this. We should not lose sight of the fact that the first creation is the work
of the Spirit of God (Gen. 1.2), that the Spirit continues to be active in
the world,[66] and that the new creation is also the work of that same Spirit
(Jn 3.5 and Tit. 3.5).[67] We should value the physical universe in which
God has placed us, which he has not only placed into our stewardship but
uses as the locus of divine–human encounters. According to the clear
teaching of the New Testament, in baptism we receive the gift of the Holy
Spirit (Acts 2.38) and forgiveness of sin (Acts 2.38, 22.16), and are
united with Christ in his death and resurrection (Rom. 6.3-8; Col. 2.12).
In short, God uses this baptism in water as the place where grace meets
faith.[68]

---

65   Pinnock, 'Physical Side of Being Spiritual', p. 10.

66   Pinnock, *Flame of Love*, pp. 122-23: 'The physical and the spiritual are not
antithetical but cooperative and synergistic. The Spirit is passed from one person to
another, from Moses to Joshua, from Elijah to Elisha. God comes to us and deals with us
through material signs.' See also pp. 55 and 63.

67   Pinnock, *Flame of Love*, p. 50: 'Spirit is involved in implementing both
creation and new creation'; and 'Physical Side of Being Spiritual', p. 18: 'Both in
creation and new creation, the material serves as a vehicle of the spiritual. Grace operates
through the medium of the material and temporal.'

68   E.g. Martin Luther understood baptism 'as the "trysting place" or the *porta Dei*
appointed by God for his encounters with mankind', so Jonathan D. Trigg, *Baptism in
the Theology of Martin Luther* (Leiden: Brill, 2001 [1994]), p. 59. See the whole
discussion of this, pp. 13-60. Cf. also Beasley-Murray, *Baptism*, p. 305, who uses this
phrase (though there is nothing to indicate that he was indebted to Luther for it): 'It
behoves us...to make much of baptism. It is given as the trysting place of the sinner with
his Saviour; he who has met Him there will not despise it.'

Another scholar to see this is Paul Fiddes, who recognizes that sacraments are 'pieces of earthly stuff that are meeting places' with God. They are 'outward and visible signs of an inward and spiritual grace', and as such there is no need to think of grace as 'a kind of substance or divine fluid, but as God's gracious coming and dwelling with us. They are signs which enable us to participate in the drama of death and resurrection which is happening in the heart of God'. Fiddes' aim is to enable us to see 'that the world is a sacrament in the sense of being a place of encounter with God'.[69] Elsewhere, Fiddes contends that '[u]sing an element of His creation, water, God offers an opportunity in baptism for a gracious encounter that is rich in experience and associations' and he explores this by examining five motifs associated in scripture with water: birth, cleansing, conflict, refreshment and journey: 'The five water motifs...indicate some of the range of experiences through which God enters into relationship with us in life—experiences of new beginning, cleansing, conflict, crossing boundaries, and refreshment of spirit. These experiences that come from living in God's creation are "focused" in the event of baptism.'[70]

This high view of creation, however, receives its ultimate support in the doctrine of the incarnation.[71] Pinnock, for example, links the Spirit,

---

69   Paul S. Fiddes, *Participating in God: A Pastoral Doctrine of the Trinity* (London: Darton, Longman and Todd, 2000), pp. 281 and 292 respectively. See also his 'Baptism and Creation', in Paul S. Fiddes (ed.), *Reflections on the Water: Understanding God and the World through the Baptism of Believers* (Regent's Study Guides, 4; Oxford: Regent's Park College/Macon, GA: Smyth & Helwys, 1996), p. 47 (which has been revised in Fiddes' *Tracks and Traces: Baptist Identity in Church and Theology* [Studies in Baptist History and Thought, 13; Carlisle: Paternoster Press, 2003], pp. 107-108), where he writes similarly and takes the discussion a little further: 'the sacraments are pieces of matter that God takes and uses as special places of encounter with Himself; grace transforms nature, and grace is nothing less than God's gracious coming to us and to His world... In the sacraments God's action in creation and redemption thus fuses into a particular focus.'

70   Fiddes, 'Baptism and Creation', p. 61/*Tracks and Traces*, p. 120. It is worth noting that another Baptist scholar, H. Wheeler Robinson, also explored the issues we are examining here, though he did so in terms of the objective–subjective and internal–external dimensions of baptism. For a detailed discussion, see Cross, 'Pneumatological Key', pp. 161-62, 165 and 171-72.

71   Barth, however, argues the opposite to the point being made here—from the incarnation to Christ being the only sacrament. See the two editors of *Church Dogmatics* IV/4, G.W. Bromiley and T.F. Torrance, 'Editors' Preface', p. v, who explain that for Barth 'only in the incarnation of the Son of God in the man Jesus is there a real sacramental unity between God and man'. Baptism and the Lord's Supper are human responses to Christ and, therefore, 'not themselves sacraments since they are not recurrent actualisations of the incarnation or means through which supernatural power is infused into believers'. (This was true for Barth in later life, not for the earlier Barth. See

creation and incarnation when he comments that 'the Spirit is not a ghost
but the giver of life, shaper of the material of creation and the power of
the resurrection. He implemented the coming of the Son in flesh and
bone, anointed him in body, mind and spirit, brought about many
concrete changes in life, and will bring about a new creation.'[72] If God
did not value the material and physical world then it makes little sense for
him to have sent his only Son not just into the world but into it as a
human in order to save humanity.[73]

Further, we must not overlook the fact that people need tangible
evidence of unseen things. Perhaps the simplest example is love. Love
can be present and even put into words, both spoken and written, but it
needs to be expressed and mediated by actions: a kiss, a touch, a hug,
some flowers, a gift, a ring—all these are means by which love is not just
shown but mediated. Since this is how we are made as people, should
there be any wonder that God has taken such into account and ordained
material media to minister his grace to humanity? Calvin's comments are
very much to the point:

> in corporeal things we are to see spiritual, just as if they were actually exhibited to
> our eye, since the Lord has been pleased to represent them by such figures; not that
> such graces are included and bound in the sacrament, so as to be conferred by its
> efficacy, but only that by this badge the Lord declares to us that he is pleased to

---

John E. Colwell, 'Baptism, Conscience and the Resurrection: A Reappraisal of 1 Peter
3.21', in Porter and Cross [eds], *Baptism*, e.g., p. 226, who describes as a 'quite
remarkable reversal' Barth's concern, which is evident throughout the whole of the
Church Dogmatics, that affirms 'the human and the divine in their connectedness and
non-contradiction'. Colwell, n. 58, shows that in *Church Dogmatics* IV/2, pp. 54-55,
Barth had been happy to speak of 'the one sacrament of the incarnation of Christ as the
basis for the "concurrence" of "a divine and human, an outward and inward, a visible and
invisible operation and reception of grace in the 'sacramental' actions of baptism and the
Lord's Supper"'.) A different conclusion, however, is offered by Edward Schillebeeckx,
Christ the Sacrament of the Encounter with God (London: Sheed and Ward, 1963), who
argues from the incarnation as 'the primordial sacrament', p. 15, to the church as a
sacrament of encounter and the sacraments as ordinarily understood by the term, pp. 43-
44.

72   Pinnock, 'Physical Side of Being Spiritual', p. 10. See also pp. 12-13. In *Flame
of Love*, p. 50, Pinnock comments that the Nicene Creed's 'Lord and giver of life' 'calls
on us to think of Spirit as active in the world and history, especially in its development
and consummation. The universe in its entirety is the field of its operations, which are so
fundamental for Christology, ecclesiology, salvation and more.' In *Most Moved Mover*,
p. 34, Pinnock succinctly states: 'The fact is that God loves to draw near to us through
nature, theophany and incarnation.'

73   We should note that Paul's discussion in 1 Cor. 15 includes a resurrection body
and also not lose sight of the witness of the book of Revelation that God's plan of
salvation includes 'a new heaven and a new earth' (Rev. 21.1).

bestow all these things upon us. Nor does he merely feed our eyes with bare show; he leads us to the actual object, and effectually performs what he figures.[74]

Concluding Issues

Two final matters need to be discussed: the definition of the term sacrament and, following on from this, the number of sacraments.

To this point we have effectively defined 'sacrament' in terms of a divine–human encounter, but more than this is needed.[75] Some objections to the use of the term founder on the fact that there is no agreed definition of what the term means.[76] For instance, the patristic scholar J.N.D. Kelly notes that in the fourth and fifth centuries 'the conception of sacrament was still elastic'[77] and this is still the case. The best known definition is probably that of the Augustinian-Calvinist tradition of 'a visible sign of a sacred thing, or a visible form of an invisible grace'.[78]

But while there have been a range of meanings attributed to it down through the centuries it was not until the nineteenth century that this term, and the theology attached to it, became widely derided and rejected by Baptists and many evangelicals[79] because of its use by the Oxford Movement and the connotations of magical efficacy.[80] However, neither the abuse of the term[81] nor its loose employment,[82] should prevent its

---

74   Calvin, *Institutes* 4.15.14.

75   Throughout this discussion I am aware that I move quite freely between defining sacraments in general and baptism as a sacrament. Given the constraints of space, this is intentional.

76   The range of definitions is discussed, e.g., by Bernard Leeming, *Principles of Sacramental Theology* (London: Longmans/Westminster, MD: Newman Press, 2nd edn, 1960), *passim*.

77   J.N.D. Kelly, *Early Christian Doctrines* (London: A. & C. Black, 5th edn, 1977), p. 423.

78   Calvin, *Institutes*, 4.14.1.

79   Ferguson, *Church of Christ*, p. 186, notes that Protestants have focused on the sign aspect, so that God's forgiveness is either given to an already existing faith (as in believer's baptism) or to a future faith (as in infant baptism). He adds: 'Against these ideas, the New Testament teaches that baptism has real value but draws that value only from the command of God and from an active faith.'

80   On baptism in the Oxford Movement, see David M. Thompson, 'Baptism, Church and Society in Britain since 1800' (unpublished Hulsean Lectures for 1983–84, 1984), pp. 18-35; and Baptist reactions to it, Cross, *Baptism*, pp. 10-17, 26-29.

81   So Pinnock, *Flame of Love*, p. 129.

82   So George R. Beasley-Murray, 'The Sacraments', *The Fraternal* 70 (October, 1948), p. 3.

use—nor necessarily should the fact that is not a biblical term,[83] for neither is 'trinity'—rather it calls for a more careful and biblical definition. 'Sacrament' is a term which requires meaning and this meaning, I believe, must be drawn from the New Testament. This is what, for example, George Beasley-Murray does. While he is aware of the various definitions of the term he allows the New Testament teaching of baptism to give meaning to it as a sacrament.[84] This said, Beasley-Murray does approve of two definitions: *sacramentum*, because he finds it to be in accord with 1 Peter 3.21[85] and 'means of grace'. By 'means of grace' he means more than is usually meant, for '[i]n the Church of the Apostles...the whole height and depth of grace is bound up with the experience of baptism. For to the New Testament writers baptism was nothing less than *"the climax of God's dealing with the penitent seeker and of the convert's return to God."*'[86] As I have tried to argue here, a sacrament is, therefore, 'the Word of God in action' which 'must be responded to in the act of participating'.[87] Sacraments are, quite simply, means of grace.[88] Beasley-Murray tacitly rejects any suggestions of the magical efficacy of the sacraments because 'their effectiveness derives from the nature of God, his promises in the Gospel, the work of Christ, the mysterious working of the Holy Spirit, *and the answering of faith of the believer.* Grace is the love of God in action. A means of grace is therefore any channel through which the love of God reaches and enriches the human heart.'[89] Pinnock concurs: sacraments 'are God-given and embodied means of grace... [They] are events in which the Spirit comes and we respond.'[90] Another Baptist theologian, Christopher Ellis, also focuses on this in his defintion of 'sacrament', which, he maintains, 'suggests the power of symbols to link us to the depths of

---

83   Note the hesitation of Ferguson, *Church of Christ*, pp. 255-56.

84   See Cross, 'Faith-Baptism', p. 7.

85   George R. Beasley-Murray, *Worship and the Sacraments* (The Second Holdsworth-Grigg Memorial Lecture; Melbourne: Whitley College, The Baptist College of Victoria, 1970), n.p. (but p. 6): 'the convert is enrolled in the army of the Lord, and baptism makes his pledge of obedience to God'.

86   George R. Beasley-Murray, 'Baptism Controversy—"The Spirit is There"', *Baptist Times* 10 December 1959, p. 8, italics his.

87   George R. Beasley-Murray, 'Baptism and the Sacramental View', *Baptist Times* 11 February 1960, p. 9.

88   Pinnock, 'Physical Side of Being Spiritual', p. 19, remarks that 'Christians have almost always seen sacraments as a means of grace. They have seen them not merely as acts of human obedience but as events where God moves.'

89   Beasley-Murray, *Worship and the Sacraments*, p. 9, italics added.

90   Pinnock, *Flame of Love*, p. 129.

reality, and points us to the use by God of material means to mediate His saving action'.[91]

Beasley-Murray believes that baptism and the Lord's Supper are 'pre-eminent among the means of grace',[92] though they are not the only means. While Protestants have traditionally rejected the seven sacraments of the Roman Catholic Church reducing their number to two, the definition being advanced here of a means of grace opens the door to accepting many more media of God's grace. Pinnock agrees with the defintion advanced here when he states: 'Sacraments are media that transmit the grace of God to bodily creatures, and thank God, there are many of them.'[93] For example, the contributors to *Baptist Sacramentalism* explore the sacramental dimension of not just baptism and the Lord's Supper, but also ordination, ministry and preaching, while Pinnock adds to this list the church, singing, prayer, praise, thanksgiving, greeting, fellowship, teaching, instruction, loving acts, the holy kiss, footwashing, the weekly meeting, the laying on of hands and church leaders.[94] He believes that 'God uses every manner of communication, every symbol and sign, to build a friendship with his creatures. This is why there are so many means of grace, so many ways of being touched by God and be brought into closer contact.'[95] He concludes that there is, therefore, no limit to the number of sacraments.[96] But it must not be forgotten that what makes a sacrament is not simply the divine action but also the human response of faith. This Pinnock underscores when he declares: 'The sacraments do not work automatically but derive their effectiveness from the Spirit in relation to faith.'[97] Colwell adds that

---

91   Christopher Ellis, 'Baptism and the Sacramental Freedom of God', in Fiddes (ed.), *Reflections on the Water*, p. 36.

92   Beasley-Murray, *Worship and the Sacraments*, p. 9, citing a Baptist World Alliance Executive Committee report on the doctrine of the church in 1950. I cannot disagree with this, for they have been recognized as such throughout the history of the church precisely because they were ordained by Christ (cf. Mt. 28.19 and 1 Cor. 11.23).

93   Pinnock, *Flame of Love*, p. 122. Cf. p. 120: 'Sacraments exist simply because we are bodily creatures inhabiting a material world. There is in theory no limit to the number of them. Created reality is richly imbued with sacramental possibilities. The world reflects God's glory; therefore anything can mediate the sacred, where there are eyes to see and ears to hear', i.e., where there is faith.

94   Pinnock, 'Physical Side of Being Spiritual', pp. 13, 14 and 17. See the whole of his discussion, pp. 11-17.

95   Pinnock, 'Physical Side of Being Spiritual', pp. 8-9. Cf. *Flame of Love*, p. 62: 'practically anything in the created order can be sacramental of God's presence'.

96   Pinnock, 'Physical Side of Being Spiritual', p. 18.

97   Pinnock, *Flame of Love*, p. 127. Cf. Brunner, *Truth as Encounter*, p. 182/*Divine–Human Encounter*, p. 129: 'To be sure, faith does not produce the sacrament; but the sacrament is not accomplished, it is no true sacrament, without faith.'

'through faith [baptism] is a means of an authentically divine action, or, to express the matter in more traditional terms, it is a means of grace'.[98] The answer to those who would object to this broadening of the sacraments to include whatever God chooses to act as means of his grace is two-fold. First, there is no reason why 'sacrament' should not be used in this way for it is a term whose meaning depends upon the definition given to it by those who use it. When understood as means of grace, I cannot see how anyone could object to seeing the '[c]reated reality [as] richly imbued with sacramental possibilities'.[99] And, secondly, recognition of the sovereign freedom of God opens up 'a rich and exciting series of affirmations about baptism while at the same time avoiding some of the historic dangers of sacramental theology. To say, "God is here" is good. To say, "God is here but not only here" is better. To say, "God is here, therefore we can meet Him here and be equipped to meet Him elsewhere" is best of all.' Moreover, Ellis continues: 'The freedom of God means that He is free to work through the means of grace that He has given to His church. But this freedom also declares that He need not only work through such means.'[100]

Pinnock brings the three issues we have discussed conveniently together and it is fitting, in a study in his honour, to allow him the final word:

> As bodily creatures, we need bodily expressions such as baptism and Eucharist to make inward grace visible and tangible. Worship is rich when it makes use of material media. Without them it can be thin, abstract, notional. Symbols help believers apprehend the invisible things of God and serve as channels of grace. God acts in the sacraments in the context of the response of faith. They are neither magical actions nor mere symbols of human response. In the sacraments God offers grace that is effective when people receive it. The sacraments do not work automatically but derive their effectiveness from the presence of the Spirit in relation to faith.[101]

---

98 Colwell, *Living*, p. 153.
99 Pinnock, *Flame of Love*, p. 120.
100 Ellis, 'Baptism', p. 41. See the important study by Philip E. Thompson, 'Toward Baptist Ecclesiology in Pneumatological Perspective' (PhD thesis, Emory University, 1995) [forthcoming as *The Freedom of God: Towards Baptist Theology in Pneumatological Perspective* (Studies in Baptist History and Thought; Carlisle: Paternoster Press, 2005)], who argues that the theological genius of the early Baptists was their distinctive emphasis on the freedom of God, a freedom from all bounds and to use whatever means he chooses.
101 Pinnock, *Flame of Love*, p. 127. Cf. 'Physical Side of Being Spiritual', p. 19.

CHAPTER 22

Celebrating Eternity: Christian Worship as a Foretaste of Participation in the Triune God

Stanley J. Grenz

The character of worship is always decided by the worshipper's conception of God and...relation to God: that is to say, whatever its ritual expression may be, it always has a theological basis. *Evelyn Underhill*[1]

But the hour is coming, and is now here, when the true worshipers will worship the Father in spirit and truth, for the Father seeks such as these to worship him. (John 4.23)

After this I looked, and there was a great multitude that no one could count, from every nation, from all tribes and peoples and languages, standing before the throne and before the Lamb, robed in white, with palm branches in their hands. They cried out in a loud voice, saying, 'Salvation belongs to our God who is seated on the throne, and to the Lamb!' And all the angels stood around the throne and around the elders and the four living creatures, and they fell on their faces before the throne and worshiped God, singing, 'Amen! Blessing and glory and wisdom and thanksgiving and honor and power and might be to our God forever and ever! Amen.' (Revelation 7.9-12 NRSV)

In the eyes of many contemporary theologians, the greatest contribution the twentieth-century discussion has made to their discipline has been the renaissance of trinitarian theology. In the opinion of many contemporary practitioners, the greatest need of the church at the turn of the twenty-first century is for a thorough-going renewal of worship. Despite the continual clamor for, and even the halting steps toward renewal that have been evident over the last several years, Ralph Martin's judgment rings as true today as it did in 1982, when he declared: '"Renewal of worship" is

---

1   Evelyn Underhill, *Worship* (New York: Harper and Brothers, 1957 [1936]), p. 60.

indeed a noble slogan, but the results that have accrued after two or three decades of serious study, suggestive adaptations, and revised liturgies have been meagre.'[2]

Martin was not content to bemoan the situation, however. He also pinpointed a crucial cause of the malaise: 'One reason for this scantiness lies in a failure to construct a systematic theology of worship.'[3] He is surely correct in suggesting that worship renewal must be undergirded by, and flow out of, a solid worship theology. Yet his implied prescription requires augmentation. The systematic theology of worship that can serve as a foundation for renewal does not arise *sui generis*, but must be rooted in something deeper. More specifically, a truly helpful theology of worship requires a profound understanding and particular application of the Christian teaching regarding the triunity of God. Only then can the church's practice of worship be grounded in its proper theological basis.

Although trinitarian theology and a renewal of Christian worship may at first glance appear to be disparate, they are not only closely connected but also integrally related. In the patristic era, the teaching about God as triune to a large degree arose out of the practices of the community. Today's situation calls for a reversal of this direction. The recent renaissance of theological interest in the doctrine of the Trinity not only *can* but also *must* provide a needed resource for the renewal of contemporary church practice in general and for renewal in the worshiping life of the people of God in particular.

Taking a cue from what is increasingly emerging as a consensus among theologians, in what follows I offer a sketch of the manner in which I believe communal Christian worship arises out of, is intimately linked to, and therefore ought to reflect the trinitarian dynamic. To this end, I begin by reviewing the central themes of what has become in many Protestant circles the 'classic' theology of worship. I then expand the classic view by drawing insights from the patristic concept of salvation as *theosis*. Finally, I offer a broad synopsis of the implications of our eschatological participation in the triune life for a trinitarian-theological understanding of worship.

Extolling God: The 'Classic' Theology of Worship

Writing in 1936, Evelyn Underhill began her widely-read treatment of the topic by declaring, 'Worship, in all its grades and kinds, is the response of the creature to the Eternal'.[4] In saying this, she sounded a note that finds

---

2   Ralph P. Martin, *The Worship of God: Some Theological, Pastoral, and Practical Reflections* (Grand Rapids, MI: Eerdmans, 1982), pp. 1-2.
3   Martin, *Worship of God*, p. 2.
4   Underhill, *Worship*, p. 3.

echo in many descriptions of the phenomenon. Thus, in her entry in the *HarperCollins Bible Dictionary*, Susan Rattray defines worship as 'the attitude and acts of reverence to a deity'.[5] Wayne Grudem sounds a similar note when he declares, 'Worship is the activity of glorifying God in his presence with our voices and hearts'.[6] In his essay on the topic in the *Evangelical Dictionary of Theology*, R.G. Rayburn echos these sentiments: 'to worship God is to ascribe to him the worth of which he is worthy'.[7] And in his paradigmatic definition of worship, Ralph Martin reflects the same idea, while adding a connection to the conduct of the worshiper: 'Worship is the dramatic celebration of God in his supreme worth in such a manner that his "worthiness" becomes the norm and inspiration of human living.'[8]

Descriptions of worship such as these are, of course, helpful. As many scholars have pointed out, 'worship' basically means attributing worth or honor to one who is worthy.[9] Yet, as important as the focus on the divine worthiness is, left by itself it cannot take us to the heart of Christian worship. For this reason, most recent theologies of worship delve deeper into the topic, generally augmenting the basic definition with two additional themes.

First, in their descriptions of Christian worship, theologians often enrich the general conception by delineating exactly what about God is worthy of adoration. God is to be worshiped, they declare, because of who God is. Thus, the nineteenth-century Baptist scholar, Alvah Hovey, asserts, 'By worship we mean the homage of the soul paid to God in view of his attributes and prerogatives'.[10] More recently, Everett Harrison defines worship in a similar manner, as 'the lifting up of the redeemed spirit toward God in contemplation of his holy perfection'.[11] In addition to extolling God because of the divine perfections, theologians routinely

---

5   Susan Rattray, 'Worship', in Paul J. Achtemeier (ed.), *HarperCollins Bible Dictionary* (San Francisco: HarperCollins, 2nd edn, 1996), p. 1222.

6   Wayne Grudem, *Systematic Theology: An Introduction to Biblical Doctrine* (Grand Rapids, MI: Zondervan, 1994), p. 1003.

7   R.G. Rayburn, 'Worship in the Church', in Walter A. Elwell (ed.), *Evangelical Dictionary of Theology* (Grand Rapids, MI: Baker, 2nd edn, 2001), p. 1300.

8   Martin, *Worship of God*, p. 4.

9   See, for example, Alan Richardson, 'Worship', in Alan Richardson and John Bowden (eds), *Westminster Dictionary of Theology* (Philadelphia: Westminster Press, 1983), p. 605. See also the typical dictionary definition of worship: 'To pay divine honors to; to reverence with supreme respect and veneration; to perform religious service to; to adore; to idolize', *New Websters Dictionary of the English Language* (n.p.: Delair, 1971), p. 1148.

10   Alvah Hovey, *Manual of Christian Theology* (New York: Silver, Burkett, and Company, rev. edn, 1900), p. 332.

11   E.F. Harrison, 'Worship', in Elwell (ed.), *Evangelical Dictionary of Theology*, p. 1300.

suggest that worship is evoked by what God does. Like many of his colleagues, Dale Moody brings the two together. After asserting that 'Worship is devotion to that which is of supreme worth',[12] he adds, 'the most basic thing in Christian worship seems to be gathering together to celebrate the acts of God in creation and redemption'.[13]

Such declarations are in keeping with the spirit of scriptural texts that direct the focus of worship to the divine being, together with the divine action in creation and redemption. Repeatedly the biblical texts enjoin us to attribute worth to the God who is the Holy One. The Psalmist typifies the writers of scripture: 'Ascribe to the LORD the glory of his name; worship the LORD in holy splendor' (Ps. 29.2 NRSV; see also 96.8; 1 Chron. 16.29). When we follow this admonition, we not only join the ancient Hebrew community and the church of all ages, but we also unite our voices with the angelic hosts, who continually proclaim, 'Holy, holy, holy, the Lord God the Almighty, who was and is and is to come' (Rev. 4.8 NRSV; see also Isa. 6.3). The scripture texts also speak about worshiping God because of the divine action in creating the universe. Repeatedly the biblical writers declare that as Creator, God is worthy of awe and praise (e.g., Ps. 29.3-10). For example, in his vision of the heavenly court, John observed the twenty-four elders (who symbolize the whole people of God) declare, 'You are worthy, our Lord and God, to receive glory and honor and power, for you created all things, and by your will they existed and were created' (Rev. 4.11 NRSV).

Above all, however, the biblical writers direct worship toward the God who acts savingly on behalf of creatures. The Old Testament prophets continually admonished Israel to worship the God who had graciously entered into covenant with them (1 Chron. 16.15) and as a result had done great wonders (v. 12), especially in rescuing them from their enemies. According to the New Testament, the focal point of God's saving work is Jesus. For this reason, as we gather to commemorate the foundational events of our redemption, we extol the One who in Christ delivered us from bondage to sin, the One who 'so loved the world that he gave his only Son, so that everyone who believes in him may not perish but may have eternal life' (Jn 3.16 NRSV).

In addition to delineating why God is worthy of worship, theological treatises often connect worship to a second theme, namely, God's intention for creatures. For example, Hughes Oliphant Old begins his study of Reformed worship by declaring, 'We worship God because God created us to worship him'.[14] Geoffrey Wainwright echos the point: 'As

---

12   Dale Moody, *The Word of Truth: A Summary of Christian Doctrine Based on Biblical Revelation* (Grand Rapids, MI: Eerdmans, 1981), p. 473.

13   Moody, *Word of Truth*, p. 474.

14   Hughes Oliphant Old, *Worship: Reformed according to Scripture* (Louisville, KY: Westminster John Knox, rev. edn, 2002), p. 1.

creator and redeemer, God calls for worship on the part of human-kind.'[15] Grudem, in turn, takes the matter a step further, seeing worship as an aspect of our human vocation. In his estimation, worship is 'a *direct* expression of our ultimate purpose for living', which, citing biblical texts such as Ephesians 1.12 (but also reminiscent of the Westminster Cate-chism), he describes as 'to glorify God and fully to enjoy him forever'.[16] Rather than limiting the concept to humans, Underhill extends the worshiping vocation to encompass all creation: 'There is a sense in which we may think of the whole life of the Universe, seen and unseen, conscious and unconscious, as an act of worship, glorifying its Origin, Sustainer, and End.'[17]

This theme can also claim scriptural warrant. The biblical authors repeatedly announce that the fundamental purpose of all creation is to glorify God. Thus, the Psalmist indicates that extolling God's glory is the divinely-given task of nature: 'The heavens are telling the glory of God; and the firmament proclaims his handiwork' (Ps. 19.1 NRSV). As God's special creation and the recipients of God's special concern, humans are especially called to praise their Creator, and this, according to the Psalmist, is not a drudgery: 'How good it is to sing praises to our God; for he is gracious, and a song of praise is fitting' (Psa. 147.1 NRSV). Furthermore, Christians have been purchased by Christ so that they might exist for the sake of God's glory. Paul asserts that God predestined us to be adopted into the divine family and included us 'in Christ', so that we might live 'to the praise of [God's] glorious grace that he freely be-stowed on us in the Beloved' (Eph. 1.6 NRSV; cf. 1.11-14). In fact, the apostle is convinced that the joyous task of praising God will not end with the passing of life as we now know it. Rather, throughout eternity we will continue to bring glory to God by being those through whom God is able to show the incomparable riches of the divine grace (Eph. 2.6-7).

The commonly-voiced theme of extolling God is helpful in providing a theological context for understanding worship. Yet, even when en-hanced by the themes suggested in the preceding paragraphs, this perspective does not encapsulate fully the foundational motif of Christian worship. Although it points in the right direction, the widely-articulated 'classic' Protestant view cannot provide an adequate basis for a worship theology that is able to foster a truly effectual renewal of worship in Christ's church.

---

15   Geoffrey Wainwright, 'Worship', in Bruce M. Metzger and Michael D. Coogan (eds), *Oxford Companion to the Bible* (New York: Oxford University Press, 1993), p. 819.

16   Grudem, *Systematic Theology*, p. 1004.

17   Underhill, *Worship*, p. 3.

Participating in God: The Foundation of a Trinitarian Theology of Worship

Worship does involve extolling God, of course. Nevertheless, the classic conception of worship must be expanded. Christian worship, I would suggest, entails glorifying the God disclosed in the biblical narrative who, in accordance with the divine eternal intention, glorifies us in Christ by the indwelling presence of the Spirit who brings us to participate in the divine life. As the trinitarian structure of this description indicates, a truly helpful theology of worship must be trinitarian. Indeed, the ultimate theological basis for worship lies in the eternal trinitarian dynamic and, by extension, in God's intention that we participate in that dynamic, which constitutes the *telos* of our existence and the final goal of the divine work of salvation. Allow me to explicate this idea.

The contemporary rediscovery of trinitarian theology has brought a renewed interest in the concept of participation in the divine life. For example, Anglican theologian Peter Adam writes, 'We should not regard the call to imitate Christ as being anything less than trinitarian: for the Son has been sent by the Father, and is empowered by the Spirit. The example of Christ is an insight into the Trinity, and the imitation of Christ is a participation in the life of the Trinity.'[18] Similarly, James Torrance asserts, 'By sharing in Jesus' life of communion with the Father in the Spirit, we are given to participate in the Son's eternal communion with the Father',[19] and hence in the trinitarian life of God.[20]

This contemporary focus is surely correct. The doctrine of the Trinity was birthed in the patristic era out of an intense interest on the part of church leaders to maintain the biblical *kerygma*, the gospel of God's saving action in Christ. During the heated controversies of the day, Athanasius declared unequivocally that unless the Son and the Spirit are fully divine, we are not truly saved through their work. Hence, if Jesus is not fully God incarnate, he argued, we cannot receive divine life in him.[21] And if the Spirit who enters our hearts as believers is not fully divine, we do not become sharers of the divine nature through the Spirit's

18   Peter Adam, 'The Trinity and Human Community', in Timothy Bradshaw (ed.), *Grace and Truth in the Secular Age* (Grand Rapids, MI: Eerdmans, 1998), p. 61.

19   James B. Torrance, 'The Doctrine of the Trinity in Our Contemporary Situation', in Alasdair I.C. Heron (ed.), *The Forgotten Trinity* (London: British Council of Churches/Council of Churches for Britain and Ireland, Inter-Church House, 1989), p. 7.

20   Torrance, 'Doctrine of the Trinity', p. 15.

21   Athanasius, *De Incarnatione* 54, in Henry Bettenson (ed.), *The Early Christian Fathers* (London: Oxford University Press, 1969), p. 293; Athanasius, *Contra Arianos* 2.70, in *Early Christian Fathers*, p. 293. See also J.N.D. Kelly, *Early Christian Doctrines* (San Francisco: Harper and Row, rev. edn, 1978), p. 243.

presence.[22] In both of these arguments, Athanasius appealed to a particular understanding of the nature and goal of God's saving activity. Like other Greek fathers, he viewed salvation as participation in the divine nature, life or glory. This perspective, which is often denoted 'deification' (*theosis*), has been deemed by many theologians throughout church history to be simply the outworking of the general New Testament idea of the nature of salvation. Nevertheless, it finds its most direct biblical basis in Peter's declaration:

His divine power has given us everything needed for life and godliness, through the knowledge of him who called us by his own glory and goodness. Thus he has given us, through these things, his precious and very great promises, so that through them you may escape from the corruption that is in the world because of lust, and may become participants of the divine nature. (2 Pet.1.3-4 NRSV)

Theosis, or the idea of participation in the divine life, found its classical articulation in the Greek fathers, for whom it provided the soteriological basis for an innovative anthropology. The patristic thinkers were not content with the philosophical principle that the human person is a microcosm of the universe. Rather, they claimed that the true greatness of humankind lies in being a 'deified animal'[23] or a created existence 'which has received the command to become a god',[24] to cite the descriptions offered by Gregory of Nazianzus. The eighth-century theologian, John of Damascus, reiterated this crucial idea, when he declared regarding the human person, 'here, that is, in the present life, his life is ordered as an animal's, but elsewhere, that is, in the age to come, he is changed and—to complete the mystery—becomes deified by merely inclining himself towards God; becoming deified, in the way of participating in the divine glory and not in that of a change into the divine being.'[25]

---

22   Athanasius, *Epistle as Serapionem* 1.24, in Bettenson (ed.), *Early Christian Fathers*, p. 296.

23   Gregory of Nazianzus, *Oration* 45 [*The Second Oration on Easter*], 7, in Philip Schaff and Henry Wace (eds), *Nicene and Post-Nicene Fathers*, second series (Peabody, MA: Hendrickson, 1994 [1893]), VII, p. 425. See also *Oration* 38 [*On the Theophany, or Birthday of Christ*], 11, in Schaff and Wace (eds), *Nicene and Post-Nicene Fathers*, second series, VII, p. 348.

24   For a citation of this quotation from Gregory of Nazianzus, *Funeral Oration on Basil the Great*, see Panayiotis Nellas, *Deification in Christ: Orthodox Perspectives on the Nature of the Human Person* (trans. Normal Russell; Crestwood, NY: St Vladimir's Seminary Press, 1987), p. 30.

25   John of Damascus, *Exposition of the Orthodox Faith* 2.12, in Philip Schaff and Henry Wace (eds), *Nicene and Post-Nicene Fathers*, second series (Peabody, MA: Hendrickson, 1995 [1898]), IX, p. 31.

As the final phrase in this statement indicates, the Greek fathers did not view deification as eradicating the distinction between the human and the divine. On the contrary, they introduced *theosis* as a safeguard against the soteriological dangers inherent in certain christological heresies of the day, such as Eutychianism (or Monophysitism), which, they believed, led to a conception of salvation that viewed it as absorption into God.[26] Furthermore, the quotation from John of Damascus indicates that according to the Greek fathers, Christ's saving work entails not merely rescuing fallen humankind from sin, but also effecting eschatological deification. Citing John's spiritual predecessor, Maximus the Confessor, contemporary Orthodox theologian Panayiotas Nellas writes:

> The Lord redeemed man from slavery to sin, death and devil, but He also put into effect the work which had not been effected by Adam. He united him with God, granting him true 'being' in God and raising him to a new creation. Christ accomplishes the salvation of man not only in a negative way, liberating him from the consequences of original sin, but also in a positive way, completing his iconic, prelapsarian 'being'. His relationship with man is not only that of a healer. The salvation of man is something much wider than redemption; it coincides with deification.[27]

Above all, however, the quotation from John of Damascus suggests that in the estimation of the patristic thinkers, deification is closely connected to our being placed 'in Christ'. The link between deification and our status as those who are in Christ lends a trinitarian cast to the concept of *theosis*. It leads to an understanding of deification as involving a trinitarian dynamic.

The New Testament repeatedly suggests that participation in Christ means sharing in his filial relationship with the one he called 'Father'. This is evident, for example, in Jesus' invitation to his disciples to address God as 'Our Father in heaven' (Mt. 6.9 NRSV). It is reiterated in the resurrected Christ's instruction to Mary Magdalene to tell his 'brothers', 'I am ascending to my Father and your Father, to my God and your God' (Jn 20.17 NRSV). The idea surfaces as well in Paul's declaration, found twice in his epistles, that through Christ believers approach God as 'Abba' (Gal. 4.6; cf. Rom. 8.15), thereby indicating that Jesus' followers have the privilege of sharing in the relationship with God that he himself enjoyed. For Paul, this great prerogative, which he equates with our status as those who are 'in Christ', is connected to the role of the Spirit in believers' lives. The liberty of addressing God as 'Abba' is the direct result of the presence of the indwelling Spirit, whom the apostle identifies as 'the Spirit of [God's] Son'. The Spirit, who leads those who are 'in

---

26   Nellas, *Deification in Christ*, pp. 39-40.
27   Nellas, *Deification in Christ*, p. 39.

Christ' to address God as 'Abba', constitutes them as 'heirs of God and joint heirs with Christ' (Rom. 8.17 NRSV).

By opening a window into the eternal basis for God's action in human salvation in what is often termed his 'high priestly prayer', Jesus adds an important further aspect: 'Father, I desire that those also, whom you have given me, may be with me where I am, to see my glory, which you have given me because you loved me before the foundation of the world' (Jn 17.24 NRSV). Our Lord's petition indicates that the dynamic within the triune life involves the glorification endemic to a reciprocal sharing of love. The Father eternally lavishes unbounded love upon the Son and thereby glorifies the Son. The Son, in turn, reciprocates the love received from the Father and in this manner glorifies the Father eternally, just as Jesus brought glory to his heavenly Father through the completion of his earthly mission (Jn 17.4).

Taken together, these New Testament declarations indicate that by incorporating believers into Christ, the Spirit gathers them into the dynamic of the divine life. Yet the Spirit does so in a particular manner. The Spirit places us specifically and solely 'in the Son'. Through the Spirit, believers are 'in Christ', and as those who are in the Son, they share in the eternal relationship that the Son enjoys with the Father. Because participants in this new community are co-heirs with Christ, the Father bestows upon them what he eternally lavishes on the Son, namely, the glorious divine love who is the Holy Spirit. And as those who are in Christ, they participate in the Son's eternal act of glorifying the Father.

The concept of salvation as *theosis*—sharing in the divine life by being 'in Christ' by the Spirit—that arises out of the New Testament provides the basis for a fuller understanding of the nature of the church as a whole and the character of Christian worship in particular. More specifically, it leads to a worship theology that weaves together in the tapestry of the church's mandate to be a worshiping people threads from the doctrine of the Trinity and from the biblical vision of the eschatological consummation, understood as the point at which God's *telos*—i.e., our deification—is fully actualized.

Anticipating Eternity: The Worshiping Church as the Foretaste of *Theosis*

Theologians routinely appeal to Jesus' words to the Samaritan woman, which I quoted at the beginning of this essay, for a dominical basis for the worship mandate that we, as his church, have received. Moreover, many commentators see in the phrase 'in spirit and truth' a reference to a particular quality of Christian worship. Writing in the monumental hallmark of turn-of-the-twentieth century homiletical exegesis, the *Pulpit*

Commentary, H.R. Reynolds articulated in the language of the day what remains a widely-held view: 'The worship in spirit is worship contrasted with all mere carnal concomitants, all mere shadows of the good things to come, all mere ritual, all specialties of place, or time, or sacrament, or order... *And in truth*; i.e. as dealing with reality, the adequate and veracious expression of genuine desires and veritable emotions.'[28]

Reading the phrase as connoting a contrast between genuine worship and the focus on place and ritual indicative of the Samaritan cult ought not to obscure the cryptic trinitarian overtones of the presence in this text of the designations Father, Spirit and Truth. This choice of words suggests that Christian worship of the Father must not only be spiritual, as opposed to ritualistic, not only truthful, in contrast to insincere. It must also occur in the one who truly is Spirit and the one who alone is Truth. Viewed in this light, Jesus' statement not only suggests the *fact* that we are mandated to worship, it also suggests that worship is trinitarian in *character*. Worship that would genuinely be 'in spirit and truth' (i.e., 'spiritual and sincere') must be 'in Spirit and Truth'. Hence genuine worship is trinitarian worship.

In suggesting this perspective, Jesus' statement opens the way for a trinitarian conception of worship, to an understanding of Christian worship that arises out of our awareness of, and commitment to, the biblical God, whom we have come to know as triune. The concept of *theosis* provides insight into how a theology of worship can be rooted in trinitarian soil. As the community of Christ, our worship arises ultimately out of our eschatological participation in the Son's relationship to the Father by the Spirit. That is, it emerges from the consummation of the divine work of salvation understood as deification.

The doctrine of *theosis* declares that at the eschatological consummation the Spirit will gather the participants in the new community (together with all creation) fully and completely into the Son, who as the *logos* is the one in whom all things 'hold togther' or find their interconnectedness (Col. 1.17). At the heart of our eschatological participation in the Son is our participation in his response to the Father, which provides the basis for perfect worship. In the eschatological consummation, we will be numbered among the countless multitudes of saints that John the seer saw standing before the throne and positioned at the head of the great chorus of praise that included the angelic hosts as well as the four living creatures, who, in the opinion of many commentators, represent all creation. This great gathering—or, perhaps better stated, 'in-gathering'—is the work of the Spirit, who, in placing us in the Son, molds us, together with all creation, into one great chorus of praise

---

28   H.R. Reynolds, *The Gospel according to St John*, in H.D.M. Spence and Joseph Exell (eds), *Pulpit Commentary* (2 vols; New York: Funk and Wagnalls, n.d.), I, p. 169.

to the Father after the pattern of the Son.[29] Thus, as those who are in Christ by the Spirit, we share in the Son's eternal glorification of the Father. Insofar as the eschatological fulfilment entails a dynamic of glorification involving the three members of the Trinity and hence our participation in the intra-trinitarian life, we might say that 'trinitarian worship' will mark all eternity. The new creation will be characterized by the unceasing worship directed toward the Father on the part of those who, by virtue of the incorporating work of the Spirit, are 'in' the Son.

Yet Christian worship does not arise simply out of the worship that we will offer in all eternity as those who are in Christ. Rather, it derives from the reciprocal character of the divine dynamic into which we are placed by the Spirit. Indeed, our salvation is not a one-directional reality. In eternity, believers not only participate in the Son's act of eternal response to the Father. They are also co-recipients with the Son of the eternal treasures that the Father lavishes on them as those who are 'in Christ'. By being drawn into the dynamic of the triune life, believers participate in the eternal *reciprocal* glorification that characterizes the relationship between the Father and the Son. Consequently, being placed by the Spirit into the eschatological worshipping community in Christ comprises our glorification as well, for as the Spirit leads those who are 'in Christ' to glorify the Father through the Son, the Father glorifies us in the Son.[30] In this way, our perfect worship of the Father as those who are in the Son by the Spirit constitutes the fulfilment of God's eternal design for our existence. In this manner, it becomes our glorification as well.

'Deification', therefore, is an eschatological reality, as is the perfect worship endemic to it. Nevertheless, as Jesus' declaration to the Samaritan woman, 'But the hour is coming, and is now here' (Jn 4.23 NRSV), indicates, the New Testament writers also view this participation as proleptically present—present in an anticipatory manner—in the here-and-now. Furthermore, they declare that the focus of this proleptic reality is the church, the community of those whom the Spirit calls together so that they might gather around the name of Jesus and belong to the family of God as children of Jesus'—and their—heavenly Father. At the heart of the vocation or divine calling of this community is the mandate to be the foretaste in the present of the eschatological fulness that constitutes our eternal *telos* or destiny, a mandate that includes worship.

Its orientation toward the future as the perspective from which to engage in the practice of worship in the present sets Christian worship

---

29   Wolfhart Pannenberg, 'Constructive and Critical Functions of Christian Eschatology', *Harvard Theological Review* 77 (1984), pp. 135-36.

30   This idea is present even in certain conservative Calvinist theologians. E.g., Anthony A. Hoekema, *Created in God's Image* (Grand Rapids, MI: Eerdmans, 1986), p. 92, states in a matter-of-fact manner, 'Since Christ and his people are one, his people will also share in his glorification'.

apart from the conception found in many other religious traditions. Most of the ancient religions posit a golden past, a mythic origin *in illo tempore*, to cite Mircea Eliade's characterization, to which they return in worship. In his classic study, *Cosmos and History: The Myth of the Eternal Return*, Eliade explains that 'these ceremonies...suspend the flow of profane time, of duration, and project the celebrant into a mythical time, *in illo tempore*'.[31] Among the Hebrews, however, a quite different perspective on time arose, namely, the awareness of history as the flow of time, climaxing in the end of time. Eliade notes that in contrast to that of other ancient religious traditions, the Hebrew perspective led to a focus on the future as the point that would regenerate time, that is, would restore its original purity and integrity. 'Thus', he writes, '*in illo tempore* is situated not only at the beginning of time but also at its end'. And the 'victory over the forces of darkness and chaos no longer occurs regularly every year but is projected into a future and Messianic *illud tempus*'.[32]

The shift toward a historical and profoundly eschatological perspective regarding time, in turn, generated a corresponding shift in the understanding of worship. Christian worship retains a cyclical dimension, which is especially evident in the church calendar year. Yet at a deeper level it is always and by its very nature forward-looking. In worship, Christians are not primarily hankering after a golden age in an ever-receding, primordial past. Nor are liturgical acts believed to be the means by which worshippers either participate in an idyllic realm at the beginning of time or regenerate time in accordance with a supposedly lost paradise. Rather, in worship Christians anticipate a glorious future that is already dawning on the horizon and that exercises a transforming effect on life in the present.

If worship characterizes eternity—if all creation is glorified by means of being caught up in an eternal act of worship—then worship is no mere temporal dimension of life. Worship is not enjoined on the Christian community as one of the many various tasks that we share in the here-and-now. Worship is not simply one aspect of the manifold duties that we are commanded to do, while we wait for the dawning of eternity. Instead, worship is integrally connected to our journeying into the future. This perspective repeatedly finds its way into treatises on the topic of Christian worship. To cite one example, in his study *Worship as Praise and Empowerment*, David Newman declares: 'Worship celebrates the future God has in store for the world as present even before that future is fully

---

31   Mircea Eliade, *Cosmos and History: The Myth of the Eternal Return* (trans. Willard R. Trask; New York: Harper and Row, 1959), p. 76. See also pp. 30-31, 58, 72, 83, 95.

32   Eliade, *Cosmos and History*, p. 106.

actualized.'[33] John Burkhart, in turn, concurs: 'As Christians assemble they *rehearse* life lived within the unitive purposes of God. In coming together, being gathered and gathering, they not only acknowledge but also enact a vision of reality. The have been concerned, given the privilege and function, gift and task, to be pioneers in what God wills for the world.'[34] And Don Saliers appropriately entitled his important treatise *Worship as Theology: Foretaste of Glory Divine*. Indeed, Saliers is surely correct when he connects Christian worship practices with the future: 'Every song, every prayer, every act of washing, eating, and drinking together, is eschatological—that is, God intends it to point toward completion in the fullness of time.'[35]

Not only does worship *look* to the future, however, worship *participates* in the future. Worship, therefore, is an eternal act. To engage in worship in the here-and-now is to participate in an anticipatory and celebratory manner in the eternal future toward which true Christian worship casts our gaze. For this reason, the church gathered for worship is the ultimate prolepsis of our eschatological participation in the eternal dynamic of the triune God.

This brings us back to the quotations with which these reflections began. Because theological vision does determine the character of worship, as Underhill rightly noted, Christian worship is connected to a particular theological vision that goes beyond the focus explicated in what has become the classic Protestant understanding. Ultimately, we do not worship merely because God commands it or even because God deserves it. Rather, as Jesus indicated in the great trinitarian declaration lying at the heart of his conversation with the Samaritan woman, we worship the Father because the Spirit places us 'in Christ' who is the Truth. Moreover, the vision of Revelation 7 reminds us that the Spirit's goal is nothing short of joining our voices with those of a great company consisting of redeemed humankind, the angelic hosts and even all creation. In this manner, the Spirit brings us to take our place within the drama of the ages as those who participate by grace in the eternal intra-trinitarian movement of the triune God. And this eschatological reality is ours to celebrate—even if only proleptically, imperfectly and partially— in the here-and-now. For as those who in the brokenness of the present experience a joyous foretaste of our eschatological participation in the triune life in the great act of worship, we are through that act forthrightly bearing witness to what is ultimately real.

---

33   David R. Newman, *Worship as Praise and Empowerment* (New York: Pilgrim, 1988), p. 6.

34   John E. Burkhart, *Worship* (Philadelphia: Westminster Press, 1982), p. 50.

35   Don E. Saliers, *Worship as Theology: Foretaste of Glory Divine* (Nashville, TN: Abingdon, 1994), pp. 210-11.

When Christian worship flows out of a keen sense of our eternal future within the divine life in the new creation, it becomes much more than merely our obedience to dominical command. Instead, it comes to entail a joyful celebration of, and even an anticipatory participation in, a worship dynamic that will continue throughout eternity. In short, it becomes a celebration of eternity. No wonder Karl Barth exclaimed, 'Christian worship is the most momentous, the most urgent, the most glorious action that can take place in human life'.[36]

---

36   As cited in J.J. von Allmen, *Worship: Its Theology and Practice* (trans. Harold Knight and W. Fletcher Fleet; New York: Oxford University Press, 1965), p. 13.

A Select Bibliography of the Writings of Clark H. Pinnock

Authored Books and Monographs

Set Forth Your Case: Studies in Christian Apologetics (Nutley, NJ: Craig Press, 1967 [reprinted by Chicago: Moody Press, 1971]).

A Defense of Biblical Infallibility (Philadelphia: Presbyterian and Reformed Publishing, 1967).

A New Reformation: A Challenge to Southern Baptists (Tigerville, SC: Jewel Books, 1968).

Evangelism and Truth (Tigerville, SC: Jewel Books, 1969).

Biblical Revelation: The Foundation of Christian Theology (Chicago: Moody Press, 1971 [reprinted with Foreword by J.I. Packer, Phillipsburg, NJ: Presbyterian & Reformed, 1985]).

Truth on Fire: The Message of Galatians (Grand Rapids, MI: Baker Book House, 1972).

Live Now, Brother (Chicago: Moody Press, 1972 [reprinted as *Are There Any Answers?* (Minneapolis, MN: Bethany, 1976)]).

Reason Enough: A Case for Christian Faith (Downers Grove, IL: InterVarsity Press, 1980 [reprinted as *A Case for Faith* (Minneapolis, MN: Bethany, 1985)]).

The Scripture Principle (New York: Harper & Row, 1984).

The Untapped Power of Sheer Christianity (Burlington, ON: Welch, 1985).

Three Keys to Spiritual Renewal: A Challenge to the Church (Minneapolis, MN: Bethany Fellowship, 1985 [published in Canada as *The Untapped Power of Sheer Christianity* (Burlington, ON: Welch, 1985]).

Theological Crossfire: An Evangelical/Liberal Dialogue, with Delwin Brown (Grand Rapids, MI: Zondervan, 1990).

Tracking the Maze: Finding our Way through Modern Theology from an Evangelical Perspective (New York: Harper & Row, 1990).

A Wildeness in God's Mercy: The Finality of Jesus Christ in a World of Religions (Grand Rapids, MI: Zondervan, 1992).

The Openness of God: A Biblical Challenge to the Traditional Understanding of God, with Richard Rice, John Sanders, William Hasker and David Basinger (Downers Grove, IL: InterVarsity Press, 1994).

Unbounded Love: A Good News Theology for the 21st Century, with Robert C. Brow (Downers Grove, IL: InterVarsity Press, 1994).

Flame of Love: A Theology of the Holy Spirit (Downer Grove, IL: InterVarsity Press, 1996).

Most Moved Mover: A Theology of God's Openness (Carlisle: Paternoster Press, 2001).

Edited Books

Toward a Theology of the Future, with David F. Wells (Carol Stream, IL: Creation House, 1971).

Grace Unlimited (Minneapolis, MN: Bethany Publishing House, 1975).

The Grace of God, The Will of Man: The Case for Arminianism (Grand Rapids, MI: Zondervan, 1989 [reprinted by Minneapolis, MN: Bethany House, 1995]).

Searching for an Adequate God: A Dialogue Between Process and Free Will Theists, with John B. Cobb, Jr (Grand Rapids, MI: Eerdmans, 2000).

Chapters in Books

'On the Third Day', in Carl F. H. Henry (ed.), *Jesus of Nazareth: Saviour and Lord* (Grand Rapids, MI: Eerdmans, 1966), pp. 145-55.

'The Inspiration of the New Testament', in Merrill C. Tenney (ed.), *The Bible: The Living Word of Revelation* (Grand Rapids, MI: Zondervan, 1968), pp. 141-61.

'A Theological Evaluation and Critique', in Luther B. Dyer (ed.), *Tongues* (Jefferson City, MO: Le Roi, 1971), pp. 128-41.

'Prospects for Systematic Theology', in Clark H. Pinnock and David F. Wells (ed.), *Toward a Theology for the Future* (Carol Streams, IL: Creation House, 1971), pp. 93-124.

'The Philosophy of Christian Evidence', in E.R. Geehan (ed.), *Jerusalem and Athens: Critical Discussions on the Theology and Apologetics of Cornelius Van Til* (n.p.: Presbyterian and Reformed, 1971), pp. 420-27.

'The Secular Prophets and the Christian Faith', in Carl F.H. Henry (ed.), *Quest for Reality: Chrisitanity and the Counter Culture* (Downers Grove, IL: InterVarsity Press, 1973), pp. 133-35.

'Limited Inerrancy: A Critical Appraisal and Constructive Alternative', in John Warwick Montgomery (ed.), *God's Inerrant Word: An International Symposium on the Trustworthiness of Scripture* (Minneapolis, MN: Bethany Fellowship, 1974), pp. 143-58.

'The Inspiration of Scripture and the Authority of Jesus Christ', in John Warwick Montgomery (ed.), *God's Inerrant Word: An International Symposium on the Trustworthiness of Scripture* (Minneapolis, MN: Bethany Fellowship, 1974), pp. 201-18.

'Introduction', in Clark H. Pinnock (ed.), *Grace Unlimited* (Minneapolis, MN: Bethany Publishing House, 1975), pp. 11-20.

'Responsible Freedom and the Flow of Biblical History', in Clark H. Pinnock (ed.), *Grace Unlimited* (Minneapolis, MN: Bethany Publishing House, 1975), pp. 95-109.

'The New Pentecostalism: Reflections of an Evangelical Observer', in Russell P. Spittler (ed.), *Perspectives on the New Pentecostalism* (Grand Rapids, MI: Baker Book House, 1976), pp. 182-92.

'Three Views of the Bible in Contemporary Theology', in Jack B. Rogers (ed.), *Biblical Authority* (Waco, TX: Word Books, 1977), pp. 47-73.

'Biblical Authority, Past and Present, in the Believers' Church Tradition', in Jarold K. Zeman, Walter Klaasen and John D. Rempel (eds), *The Believers' Church in Canada: Addresses and Papers from the Study Conference in Winnipeg, May 15–18, 1978* (Waterloo, ON: The Baptist Federation of Canada and Mennonite Central Committee (Canada), 1979), pp. 75-86.

'The Need for a Scriptural, and Therefore a Neo-Classical Theism', in Kenneth S. Kantzer and Stanley N. Gundry (eds), *Perspectives on Evangelical Theology: Papers from the Thirtieth Annual Meeting of the Evangelical Theological Society* (Grand Rapids, MI: Baker Book House, 1979), pp. 37-42.

'The Modernist Impulse at McMaster University, 1887–1927', in Jarold Knox Zeman (ed.), *Baptists in Canada: A Search for Identity amidst Diversity* (Burlington, ON: Welch, 1980), pp. 193-207.

'A Pilgrimage in Political Theology: A Personal Witness', in Ronald Nash (ed.), *Liberation Theology* (Milford, MI: Mott Media, 1984), pp. 101-20.

'How I Use the Bible in Doing Theology', in Robert K. Johnston (ed.), *The Use of the Bible in Theology/Evangelical Options* (Atlanta, GA: John Knox Press, 1985), pp. 13-34.

'Assessing Barth for Apologetics', in Donald K. McKim (ed.), *How Karl Barth Changed My Mind* (Grand Rapids, MI: Eerdmans, 1986), pp. 49-51.

'Biblical Authority and the Issues in Question', in Alvera Mickelsen (ed.), *Women, Authority, and the Bible* (Downers Grove, IL: InterVarsity Press, 1986), pp. 51-58.

'Eschatological Hopes in the Protestant Tradition', in Frederick E. Greenspahn (ed.), *The Human Condition in Jewish and Christian Traditions* (Hoboken, NJ: Ktav, 1986), pp. 235-55.

'God Limits His Knowledge', in D. Basinger and R. Basinger (eds), *Predestination and Free Will: Four Views of Divine Sovereignty and Human Freedom by John Feinberg, Norman Geisler, Bruce Reichenbach, and Clark Pinnock* (Downers Grove, IL: InterVarsity Press, 1986), pp. 141-62.

'Our Audience: Atheist or Alienated?', in M. Branson and C. Padilla (eds), *Conflict and Context: Hermeneutics in the Americas* (Grand Rapids, MI: Eerdmans, 1986), pp. 37-49.

'Schaeffer on Modern Theology', in Ronald W. Ruegsegger (ed.), *Reflections on Francis Schaeffer* (Grand Rapids, MI: Zondervan, 1986), pp. 173-93.

'Between Classical and Process Theism', in Ronald H. Nash (ed.), *Process Theology* (Grand Rapids, MI: Baker Book House, 1987), pp. 309-27.

'Parameters of Biblical Inerrancy', in *The Proceedings of the Conference on Biblical Inerrancy 1987* (Nashville, TN: Broadman Press, 1987), pp. 95-101.

'What Is Biblical Inerrancy?', in *The Proceedings of the Conference on Biblical Inerrancy 1987* (Nashville, TN: Broadman Press, 1987), pp. 73-80.

'Peril with Promise', in James H. Olthuis *et al.* (eds), *A Hermeneutics of Ultimacy: Peril or Promise?* (Lanham, MD: University Press of America, 1987), pp. 53-69.

'A Critical Response to A. James Reimer's Mennonite Theological Self-Understanding', in Calvin Wall Redekop (ed.), *Mennonite Identity: Historical and Contemporary Perspectives* (Lanham, MD: University Press of America, 1988), pp. 63-67.

'Apologetics', in Sinclair B. Ferguson, David Wright and J.I. Packer (eds), *New Dictionary of Theology* (Downers Grove, IL: InterVarsity Press, 1988), pp. 36-37.

'Revelation', in Sinclair B. Ferguson, David Wright and J.I. Packer (eds), *New Dictionary of Theology* (Downers Grove, IL: InterVarsity Press, 1988), pp. 585-87.

'Baptists and the "Latter Rain": A Contemporary Challenge and Hope for Tomorrow', in Jarold K. Zeman (ed.), *Costly Vision: The Baptist Pilgrimage in Canada* (Burlington, ON: Welch, 1988), pp. 255-72.

'Christology at the Reformation', in Joseph D. Ban (ed.), *The Christological Foundation for Contemporary Theological Education* (Macon, GA: Mercer University Press, 1988), pp. 121-36.

'The Finality of Jesus Christ in a World of Religions', in Mark A. Noll and David F. Wells (eds), *Christian Faith and Practice in the Modern World: Theology from an Evangelical Point of View* (Grand Rapids, MI: Eerdmans, 1988), pp. 152-68.

'The Pursuit of Utopia', in Marvin Olasky (ed.), *Freedom, Justice, and Hope: Toward a Strategy for the Poor and the Oppressed* (Westchester, IL: Crossway Books, 1988), pp. 65-83.

'Time', in Geoffrey W. Bromiley (ed.), *The International Standard Bible Encyclopedia* (Grand Rapids, MI: Eerdmans, 1979–88), IV, pp. 852-53.

'From Augustine to Arminius: A Pilgrimage in Theology', in Clark H. Pinnock (ed.), *The Grace of God, the Will of Man: A Case for Arminianism* (Grand Rapids, MI: Zondervan, 1989), pp. 15-30.

'Introduction', in Clark H. Pinnock (ed.), *The Grace of God, the Will of Man: A Case for Arminianism* (Grand Rapids, MI: Zondervan, 1989), pp. ix-xiv.

'Bernard Ramm: Postfundamentalist Coming to Terms with Modernity', in Stanley Grenz (ed.), *Perspectives on Theology in the Contemporary*

World: Essays in Honor of Bernard Ramm (Mercer, GA: Mercer University Press, 1990), pp. 15-26.

'Defining American Fundamentalism: A Response', in Norman J. Cohen (ed.), *The Fundamentalist Phenomenon: A View from Within, A Response from Without* (Grand Rapids, MI: Eerdmans, 1990), pp. 38-55.

'Acts 4:12: No Other Name Under Heaven', in William V. Crockett and James G. Sigountos (eds), *Through No Fault of Their Own* (Grand Rapids, MI: Baker, 1991).

'The Changing Face of Evangelical Theology', in R. Albert Mohler (ed.), *The Changing of the Evangelical Mind* (Nashville, TN: Broadman Press, 1992).

'The Conditional View', in William V. Crockett (ed.), *Four Views of Hell* (Grand Rapids, MI: Zondervan, 1992), pp. 135-66.

'Evangelism and Other Living Faiths', in Harold D. Hunter and Peter D. Hocken (eds), *All Together in One Place* (Sheffield: Sheffield Academic Press, 1993), pp. 208-14.

'Holy Spirit as a Distinct Person in the Godhead', in Mark W. Wilson (ed.), *Spirit and Renewal* (Sheffield: Sheffield Academic Press, 1994), pp. 34-41.

'Systematic Theology', in Clark Pinnock, Richard Rice, John Sanders, William Hasker and David Basinger, *The Openness of God: A Biblical Challenge to the Traditional Understanding of God* (Downers Grove, IL: InterVarsity Press, 1994), pp. 101-25.

'An Inclusivist View', in Dennis Okholm and Timothy Phillips (eds), *More Than One Way? Four Views on Salvation in a Pluralistic World* (Grand Rapids, MI: Zondervan, 1995), pp. 95-123.

'The Great Jubilee', in Michael Bauman (ed.), *God and Man: Perspectives on Christianity in the 20th Century* (Hillsdale, MI: Hillsdale College Press, 1995), pp. 91-102.

'Evangelical Theology in Progress', in Roger Badham (ed.), *Introduction to Christian Theology* (Louisville, KY: Westminster John Knox Press, 1998).

'New Dimensions in Theological Method', in David S. Dockery (ed.), *New Dimensions in Evangelical Thought: Essays in Honor of Millard J. Erickson* (Downers Grove, IL: InterVarsity Press, 1998), pp. 197-208.

'The Holy Spirit in the Theology of Donald G. Bloesch', in Elmer M. Colyer (ed.), *Evangelical Theology in Transition: Theologians in Dialogue with Donald Bloesch* (Downers Grove, IL: InterVarsity Press, 1999), pp. 119-35.

'Clark Pinnock's Response to Part 1', 'Clark Pinnock's Response to Part 2' and 'Clark Pinnock's Response to Part 3', in Tony Gray and Christopher Sinkinson (eds), *Reconstructing Theology: A Critical Assessment of the Theology of Clark Pinnock* (Carlisle: Paternoster Press, 2000), pp. 81-87, 147-52, 259-65.

'Toward a More Inclusive Eschatology', in David W. Baker (ed.), *Looking into the Future: Evangelical Studies in Eschatology* (Grand Rapids, MI: Baker, 2001).

'The Physical Side of Being Spiritual: God's Sacramental Presence', in Anthony R. Cross and Philip E. Thompson (eds), *Baptist Sacramentalism* (Carlisle: Paternoster Press, 2003), pp. 8-20.

Articles in Journals and Periodicals

'In Defense of the Resurrection', *Christianity Today* (1965), pp. 6-8.

'The Structure of Pauline Eschatology', *Evangelical Quarterly* 37 (1965), pp. 9-20.

'Southern Baptists and the Bible', *Christianity Today* (1966), pp. 30-31.

'Our Source of Authority: The Bible', *Bibliotheca Sacra* 124 (1967), pp. 150-56.

'Tombstone That Trembled', *Christianity Today* (1968), pp. 6-11.

'Toward a Rational Apologetic Based upon History', *Journal of the Evangelical Theological Society* 11 (1968), pp. 147-51.

'A Long Night's Journey into Day', *HIS* (1970), pp. 17-18, 23.

'Cultural Apologetics: An Evangelical Standpoint', *Bibliotheca Sacra* 127 (1970), pp. 58-63.

'The Harrowing of Heaven', *Christianity Today* (19 June 1970), pp. 7-8.

'The Secular Wasteland', *HIS* (1970), pp. 26-28.

'A Truce Proposal for the Tongues Controversy', with Grant R. Osborne, *Christianity Today* (8 October 1971), pp. 6-9.

'Theology and Myth: An Evangelical Response to Demythologizing', *Bibliotheca Sacra* 128 (1971), pp. 215-26.

'For Those Who Don't Despair', *HIS* (1972), pp. 1-3.

'The Living God and the Secular Experience', *Bibliotheca Sacra* 129 (1972), pp. 316-20.

'In Response to Dr. Daniel Fuller', *Journal of the Evangelical Theological Society* 16 (1973), pp. 67-72, 333-35.

'The New Pentecostalism: Reflections by a Well-Wisher', *Christianity Today* (14 September 1973), pp. 6-10.

'The Problem of God', *Journal of the Evangelical Theological Society* 16 (1973), pp. 11-16.

'An Interview with Clark Pinnock', *HIS* 1 (1974), pp. 4-7.

'Baptists and Biblical Authority', *Journal of the Evangelical Theological Society* 17 (1974), pp. 193-205.

'Credo', *Post American* (1974), p. 20.

'Faith and Reason', *Bibliotheca Sacra* 131 (1974), pp. 303-10.

'How Trustworthy? Review of Scripture, Tradition, and Infallibility, by Dewey M. Beegle', *Christianity Today* (1974), pp. 37-38.

'The Acts Connection', *Post American* (1974), pp. 24-25.

'The Beginnings of a "Theology for Public Discipleship"', *TSF News* (1974), pp. 2-8.

'The Coming of Christ', *Post American* (1974), pp. 5-8.

'The Moral Argument for Christian Theism', *Bibliotheca Sacra* 131 (1974), pp. 114-19.

'A Selective Bibliography for the Study of Christian Theology', *TSF News* (1975), pp. 3-12.

'Charismatic Renewal for the Radical Church', *Post American* (1975), pp. 16-21.

'Theology of Public Discipleship', *Post American* (1975), pp. 16-19.

'A Call for the Liberation of North American Christians', *Sojourners* (September, 1976), pp. 23-25.

'Acrimonious Debate on Inerrancy', *Eternity* (1976), pp. 40-41.

'Evangelical Theology of Human Liberation', *Sojourners* (1976), pp. 30-36.

'Inspiration and Authority: A Truce Proposal', *The Other Side* (1976), pp. 61-65.

'Liberation Theology: The Grains, the Gaps', *Christianity Today* (16 January 1976), pp. 13-15.

'No-Nonsense Theology: Pinnock Reviews Pannenberg', *Christianity Today* (1976), pp. 14-16 (part 2 of 'Pannenberg's Theology: Reasonable Happenings in History').

'Pannenberg's Theology: Reasonable Happenings in History', *Christianity Today* (1976), pp. 19-22.

'Why Is Jesus the Only Way?', *Eternity* (1976), pp. 13-15, 32.

'Reasons for Faith (a 7-part series)', *HIS* (October, 1976), pp. 16-18, (November, 1976), pp. 20-22, (December, 1976), pp. 20-22, (January, 1977), pp. 8-9, (February, 1977), pp. 26-29, (March, 1977), pp. 20-22, (April, 1977), pp. 12-15.

'Fruits Worthy of Repentance: The True Weight of Biblical Authority', *Sojourners* (1977), p. 29.

'Karl Barth and Christian Apologetics', *Themelios* (1977), pp. 66-71.

'Langdon Gilkey: A Guide to His Theology', *TSF Notes and Reviews* (1977), pp. 15-16.

'Schaefferism as a World View: A Probing Perspective on How Should We Then Live?', *Sojourners* (1977), pp. 32-35.

'Second Mile Lifestyle: A Short Manual for Resurrection People', *Sojourners* (1977), pp. 31-32.

'Evangelicals and Inerrancy: The Current Debate', *Theology Today* 35.1 (April, 1978), pp. 65-69.

'Fails to Grasp Ontological Basis for Problem', *Journal of the American Scientific Affiliation* 30 (1978), pp. 158-59.

'Joyful Partisan of the Kingdom: A Reflection on Karl Barth', *Sojourners* (1978), p. 26.

'Triangles and Tangents', *Sojourners* (1978), p. 32.

'An Evangelical Theology: Conservative and Contemporary', *Christianity Today* (5 January 1979), pp. 23-29.

'ICBI Statement', *TSF News and Reviews* (1979), pp. 7-8.

'The Incredible Resurrection: A Mandate for Faith', *Christianity Today* (1979), pp. 12-17.

'The Ongoing Struggle over Biblical Inerrancy', *Journal of the American Scientific Affiliation* 31 (1979), pp. 69-74.

'Alive in the Spirit', *The Canadian Baptist* (1980), pp. 5-7.

'An Evangelical Observes a WCC Assembly', *TSF Bulletin* (1980), pp. 7-8.

'Baptists and Confessions of Faith', *The Canadian Baptist* (1980), pp. 4-7.

'Chalcedon: A Creed to Touch off Christmas', *Christianity Today* (1980), pp. 24-27.

'Following Jesus', *The Canadian Baptist* (1980), pp. 12-13.

'Loving the Truth', *The Canadian Baptist* (1980), pp. 4-5.

'The Inspiration and Interpretation of the Bible', *TSF Bulletin* (1980), pp. 4-6.

'The Study of Theology: A Guide for Evangelicals', *TSF News and Reviews* (1980), pp. 1-5.

'"...This Treasure in Earthern Vessels": The Inspiration and Interpretation of the Bible', *Sojourners* (1980), pp. 16-19.

'A Response to Rev A. Koivisto', *Journal of the Evangelical Theological Society* 24 (1981), pp. 153-55.

'Can Evangelicals Face the Intellectual Challenge?', *The Canadian Baptist* (1981), pp. 25-26.

'Can the Unevangelized Be Saved?', *The Canadian Baptist* (1981), pp. 5-9.

'Making Theology Relevant', *Christianity Today* (1981), pp. 48-49.

'Opening the Church to the Charismatic Dimension', *Christianity Today* (12 June 1981), p. 16.

'Response by Clark Pinnock (to Nicholas Wolterstorff, "Is Reason Enough? A Review Essay")', *The Reformed Journal* (1981), pp. 25-26.

'Sagan's Humanist Metaphysic: Fantasy, Not Fact', *Christianity Today* (1981), pp. 98-99.

'Critical Conservatism', *Christianity Today* (1982), p. 66.

'Hermeneutics: A Neglected Area', *TSF Bulletin* (1982), pp. 3-5.

'How I Use Tradition in Doing Theology', *TSF Bulletin* (1982), pp. 2-5.

'Liberals Knock the Center out of Theological Education', *Christianity Today* (1982), pp. 32-33.

'Mainline Theological Education: A Loss of Focus', *TSF Bulletin* (1982), p. 15.

'New Thinking about Biblical Inspiration', *The Canadian Baptist* (1982), pp. 22-23.

'The Theology of the SBC', *Eternity* (1982), p. 19.

'The Vision We Need to Recover (Guest Editorial)', *The Canadian Baptist* (1982), p. 3.

'Tradition Can Keep Theologians on Track: It Safeguards Against Liberalism on the One Side and Roman Catholicism on the Other', *Christianity Today* (1982), pp. 24-27.

'I Was a Teenage Fundamentalist', *The Wittenburg Door* (December 1982–January 1983), p. 18.

'Having Ascension Eyes', *The Canadian Baptist* (1983), pp. 15-16.

'Theology's Struggle Today', *The Canadian Baptist* (1983), pp. 15-16.

'A Political Pilgrimage', *Eternity* (1984), pp. 26-29.

'Building the Bridge from Academic Theology to Christian Mission', *Themelios* 9 (1984), pp. 3-6.

'Interview with Clark H. Pinnock', *Faith and Thought* (1984), p. 56.

'Reflections on Liberation Theology', *The Canadian Baptist* (1984), pp. 8, 56.

'"A Revolutionary Promise". Review of Power Evangelism, by John Wimber and Kevin Springer', *Christianity Today* (1986), p. 19.

'Catholic, Protestant, and Anabaptist: Principles of Biblical Interpretation in Selected Communities', *Brethren in Christ, History and Life* 9 (December, 1986), pp. 264-75.

'Relfections on the Scripture Principle', *TSF Bulletin* (1986), pp. 8-11.

'A Comment on "Is There Anything Which God Does Not Do?"', *Christian Scholar's Review* 16 (1987), pp. 392-93.

'Boarding a Moving Train', *The Canadian Baptist* (1987), pp. 12-14.

'Fire, Then Nothing', *Christianity Today* (1987), pp. 40-42.

'God's Megatrends', *The Canadian Baptist* (1987), pp. 10-12.

'"Liberation Theology's Curious Contradiction". Review of *Will It Liberate? Questions about Liberation Theology*, by Michael Novak', *Christianity Today* (1987), pp. 54, 56.

'Pursuit of Utopia, Betrayal of the Poor', *Crux* (1987), pp. 5-14.

'Spring Rains are Coming', *The Canadian Baptist* (1987), pp. 6-7.

'Who are the Evangelicals in Canada?', *Ecumenism* (1987), pp. 4-5.

'Rice's Reign of God: A SDA Theology for the Masses', *Spectrum* (1988), pp. 56-58.

'Battle over the Bible', *Equipping the Saints* (1989), pp. 15-18.

'Climbing out of a Swamp: The Evangelical Struggle to Understand the Creation Texts', *Interpretation* 43.2 (1989), pp. 143-55.

'Responses to Delwin Brown', *Christian Scholar's Review* 19 (1989), pp. 73-78.

'The Destruction of the Finally Impenitent', *Criswell Theological Review* 4.2 (1990), pp. 243-59.

'Toward an Evangelical Theology of Religions', *Journal of the Evangelical Theological Society* 33.3 (1990), pp. 359-68.

'The Arminian Option', *Christianity Today* (19 February 1990), p. 15.

'Desert Storm...A Just War?', *The Canadian Baptist* (March, 1991), pp. 17-18, 20.

'Doing Theology in the Context of the University', *Prolegomena* 2.2 (1991), pp. 5-9.

'Salvation by Resurrection', *Ex Auditu* 9 (1993), pp. 1-12.

'The Role of the Spirit in Interpretation', *Journal of the Evangelical Theological Society* 36.4 (1993), pp. 491-97.

'The Work of the Holy Spirit in Hermeneutics', *Journal of Pentecostal Theology* 2 (1993), pp. 3-23.

'Assessing the Apologetics of C.S. Lewis', *Canadian C.S. Lewis Journal* (May 1995).

'God's Sovereignty in Today's World', *Theology Today* 53.1 (April, 1996), pp. 15-21.

'Review of Gordon Fee, *God's Empowering Presence: The Holy Spirit in the Letters of Paul* (Hendrickson, 1994)', *Pneuma* 18.2 (Fall, 1996), pp. 230-34.

'Role of the Spirit in Creation, Role of the Spirit in Redemption', *Asbury Theological Journal* 52 (1997), pp. 47-62.

'Does Christian Unity Require Some Form of Papal Primacy?', *Journal of Ecumenical Studies* 35.3–4 (1998), pp. 380-82.

'Evangelical Theologians Facing the Future: Ancient and Future Paradigms', *Wesleyan Theological Journal* 33.2 (1998), pp. 7-28.

'Biblical Texts—Past and Future Meanings', *Wesleyan Theological Journal* 34.2 (Fall, 1999), pp. 136-51, and *Journal of the Evangelical Theological Society* 43 (2000), pp. 71-81.

'Response to Daniel Strange and Amos Yong', *Evangelical Quarterly* 71.4 (October, 1999), pp. 349-57.

'Divine Relationality: A Pentecostal Contribution to the Doctrine of God', *Journal of Pentecostal Theology* 16 (2000), pp. 3-26.

'God as Most Moved Mover: A Theology of the Openness of God', *Worship Leader* 9 (November/December, 2000), pp. 32-39.

'God's Fair Beauty—The Social Trinity', *Spirit and Church* 4.1 (2002).

'There Is Room for Us: A Reply to Bruce Ware', *Journal of the Evangelical Theological Society* 45 (2002), pp. 213-19.

Index of Names